Contents

Contributors: Lindsey Bennett, Tom Saleh, Iain Bailey, Amy Coombs, Adam Coombs, John Owen, Gary Lipton, Simon Leonard, Andy Shaw, John and June Berry, Jon Howard. **Brochure Design:** GLD Design.

The Offers

All restaurants provide **one** of the following discounts, please check the listings for full offer details.

The 2 for I offer. Comes in three sizes.

 With this offer, you purchase one main course and a second main course will be provided for free. This free dish will always be the cheaper of the two. This offer is only valid on main courses.

 With this offer you purchase a main course and either a starter or dessert. The cheapest main course and the cheapest starter or dessert (depending on your choice) will be free.

 The 2 for I on 3 courses grants diners a free starter, main course and dessert with the purchase of a starter, main course and dessert. Which one is free? The cheapest of each course, of course!

How many people?
ONE dining card will get you **ONE** free meal per party.

Restaurants will often allow a **maximum of two** cards per party, so the purchase of two meals will result in a further two being given to you for free.

The percentage offer. Comes in two sizes.

 25% off your complete food **and** drinks bill.

50%OFF FOOD There is a 50% offer at some restaurants. The discount applies to the total food bill only. Drinks are not included in this offer.

How many people?
Only one dining card per party is required. Some restaurants may limit the number of people the discount applies to and this is indicated on the table icon as shown.

Any number of people may dine, but the discount will only apply up to this maximum.

You cannot use multiple cards to increase the allowed party size.

Which offer is best?
All of the offers are great! But if you want to maximise your savings, you could choose a restaurant according to the size of your party. Couples fit neatly into the 2 for I offer and larger parties usually see better savings with the 25% and 50% offers.

Remember the offer applies to the à la carte menu only.

THE OFFERS

HOW TO USE
YOUR GOURMET SOCIETY DINING CARD

Choose
a participating restaurant from within these pages, or from our website **www.gourmetsociety.co.uk**. The website will highlight all the great new restaurants who have joined the Gourmet Society since publishing this guide.

Check
out the Gourmet Society offer. The offer applies to the à la carte menu. Either **2 for 1 meals** or **25% off** the total food and drink bill. Make sure the offer is available on the day and time you want it. The inside cover has explanations of all the icons used.

Call
the restaurant to book your table and inform them you will be using your Gourmet Society card (or cards if in a larger party wishes to use more than one card).

Arrive and Dine
at your chosen venue and dine off the à la carte menu. Present your Gourmet Society membership card when requesting the bill.

Save
Enjoying your saving and spread the word about the Gourmet Society to friends and family

General Conditions
CHECK THE INDIVIDUAL RESTAURANT'S OFFER DETAILS PRIOR TO BOOKING.

AVAILABILITY OF OFFER
Some restaurants may restrict use of the Gourmet Society Dining Card to certain days and times throughout the week. **This is clearly identified on the offer details for each restaurant in this directory.** Many restaurants may also have a different policy for some or all of the following; Bank Holidays, Valentine's Day, New Year's Eve, Mothers/Fathers Day, Chinese New Year, Diwali, Ramadan and over the Christmas period and its build up etc.
Always call ahead when planning to use the Gourmet Society card on Bank Holidays and other special event days to check the availability of the Gourmet Society offer.

REPEAT OFFERS
Although the majority of our restaurants accept members again and again, some restaurants may limit the number of times you can take advantage of the Gourmet Society card. They do this by inserting their code numbers onto the back of your membership card. To check code numbers visit www.gourmetsociety.co.uk/numbers.

SET MENUS AND SPECIAL OFFERS
The Gourmet Society offer is available when dining from the normal à la carte menu and cannot typically be used in conjunction with set menus or other special offers.

Remember the offer applies to discount off the à la carte menu only.

3

Welcome

to the biggest Gourmet Society annual guide we have ever produced. We take enormous pride in featuring every one of the great restaurants, bistros, gastro pubs, cafes and bars offering members delicious food at appetising discounts for yet another year.

Gourmet Society scouts have discovered some great new restaurants to join us this year; we now boast over 4,000 venues (1,000 more than last year) including more independent Michelin, AA and Good Food Guide recommendations as well as local establishments with outstanding local reputations and awards. As ever, quality of food and service is the primary benchmark. This extends to our increasing number of regional and national chains; here, consistency of the above is essential.

"Over the last year, our members saved in excess of £100 million in our partner restaurants"

We believe this guide is now easier to use and bursting with helpful information that will save you hundreds of pounds on food and drink. We have membership tips throughout, even more features on the fabulous national brands we work in partnership with and, new for this year, a short and highly informative description of every establishment. Whilst this is all as delightfully filling as a three course meal (at 2 for 1 prices), we also recommend you visit our new look website www.gourmetsociety.co.uk for the latest money saving offers and member reviews.

Gourmet Society is the biggest and best dining club; the card is simple to use. And the accumulated benefits for members now extend well beyond the culinary, into hotels, retail, leisure and charitable giving; in a campaign - which will be continuing this year, we raised over £10,000 for local schools.

So we thank you, the members for all of this. The more you use your card, the more easily we can enrol increasing numbers of venues and partners into our mission.

Great food, at great prices.

TOP TEN TIPS
for using your Gourmet Society Card

1 Always follow the guidelines and conditions for using your card. **If it doesn't say otherwise, the offer only applies to the à la carte menu.**

2 Always check the Gourmet Society listings for a restaurant before visiting. Check the offer and any conditions on it, such as when you can use the offer. This directory and the website are the only places to do this.

3 The Gourmet Society is based on an agreement between restaurants and diners. Remember that your patronage affects the reputation of the society as whole and our ability to recruit more top-notch restaurants.

4 As soon as you start using your Gourmet Society card, you start saving money. Use it only once a month and you'll save on average a whopping £300 a year.

5 We know that like ourselves, Gourmet Society members live to eat. So enjoy yourself whilst using the card and don't hold back from ordering an extra pudding, coffees or even a delicious cocktail to kick start your evening. After all, as a member you're already saving serious money.

6 Every week new restaurants join the Gourmet Society. A quick inspection of our website will tell you who they are, where they are and which money saving offer you can dine off **www.gourmetsociety.co.uk**

7 Another way to make sure you know about all the newest restaurants as well as competitions, foodie events and everything else Gourmet, is to sign up to our email newsletter.

8 If you have any problems using your Gourmet Society card, let us know straight away. The best method is to email our customer services team on **info@gourmetsociety.co.uk**

9 Always call restaurants to book ahead on bank holidays and other special event days, such as during the Christmas period and its build up, Easter weekend, Mothers Day, Fathers Day, Ramadan, Diwali and Chinese New Year (for example).

10 Recommend a friend – great food at great prices just cannot be kept to yourself and in addition you'll receive a free gift from us for your troubles.

more Gourmet Society

Below are just a handful of the useful, interesting and brilliant organisations who have fantastic money saving offers for Gourmet Society members.

Get a little more out of your membership by logging onto the members area of our website **www.gourmetsociety.co.uk** to access the full menu of discounts.

BBC GoodFood show | **Great Ticket Prices**

241 HOTEL CLUB

MASSIVE DISCOUNTS AT ODDBINS
in store and at Oddbins direct

ticketmaster SAVE up to 50%

on selected music, theatre and sports events when you book with Ticketmaster.

As a Gourmet Society member you can enjoy fantastic discounts off selected tickets when you book through our dedicated members' page.

NICKY CLARKE | **UP TO 50% OFF** your first hairstyling appointment

"I like them: they've got good taste, a generous nature and voracious appetites . . . and they're good tippers!" Bristol restaurateur

Sound familiar? Of course it does, that's because they're talking about you – a Gourmet Society member.

When you use your GS card, you personally are identified as a member; so not only are you claiming great discounts, you're representing the Gourmet Society itself.

The Gourmet Society is a co-operative aiming to enhance the dining experience of all members and helping to recognise the UK and Ireland's best restaurants.

Therefore we encourage you, when using your card , to book restaurants in advance quoting your membership of the Gourmet Society, do order a drink from the menu and acknowledge the staff with friendliness (and, we humbly suggest, a tip of 10-12% of the sum the bill would have been, without your membership discount).

These three small things improve the experience for all. It's that simple.

"It takes many good deeds to build a good reputation, and only one bad one to lose it" Benjamin Franklin

It was true then and it's just as true now. Help us keep our good reputation.

As we go up and down the country searching for new restaurants to join the Gourmet Society, our reputation precedes us. And that reputation is built, as for every club or society, on the actions of all members.

It is imperative that we all work together to ensure that our reputation is maintained and enhanced. With this in mind always remember that you are a Gourmet Society member and your actions will influence how restaurants view all of us.

The reputation of The Gourmet Society is based on not just the members, but our restaurant recommendations. Therefore we need to know if a restaurant doesn't cut the mustard any longer. We like to give the benefit of the doubt and we'd ask you to do the same. Please remember everyone can have an 'off night'. Sometimes glitches happen; the restaurant changes hands or there's been a misunderstanding. However, if we don't know about a problem we can't investigate it and resolve it.

GS *in focus*

Some of our finer details, explained...

Why do we ask you to book in advance?

Booking tables works. Restaurants will know in advance to apply your discount to the bill. They can easily see numbers of visiting GS members – demonstrating the benefits to their business and encouraging them to remain with the Society.

For these reasons we ask you to book ahead when using your card whenever you see the ☎ symbol displayed. You should always book ahead for bank holidays and special event days such as Fathers/Mothers Day, Valentines Day, the Christmas period, Easter, etc. There's no icon to indicate that you should do this for an individual restaurant as it applies to ALL partner restaurants.

If you don't book a table in advance mentioning the GS card, the restaurant may refuse to honour the offer.

Why do restaurants have different offers?

We're proud to offer you a massive range of restaurants so you can use your card for different culinary adventures and occasions.

Similarly our restaurants find their dining experience most suited to different discounts. Mezzes and tapas, for example, work well with a 25% discount off the à la carte menu.

But either way, for every occasion, using your Gourmet Society card guarantees you will save a significant amount of money, on average, £25.

À la carte dining.

Gourmet Society offers apply to all dishes on a restaurants' full à la carte menu. With à la carte dining, diners can create their own meals by choosing individually priced dishes from the menu. This is opposed to set menus where choice is restricted and the price is fixed across two, three or more courses.

Although many of our restaurants also offer set menus and some, table d'hôte (again a limited range of foods at a set price) the Gourmet Society discount is invariably applied to the à la carte dining options.

We would rather restaurants offer this, so that our members can sample the best of dining out and the full range of a kitchens' gastronomic experience as opposed to a limited selection offered in set menus.

Why isn't the GS card accepted every day of the week at some restaurants?

You will find that many of our partner restaurants are happy to accept the Gourmet Society card every day of the week, but understandably some limit use of the GS card during their busiest periods.

As we've said before, members consistently say that they prefer to have a greater number and range of restaurants to sample at a discounted price, at least some of the time, over a smaller choice of restaurants in the first place.

And if a restaurant is busy . . . then that's a good sign we think! And we're very happy to welcome a bustling establishment as a Gourmet Society partner restaurant.

GS ONLINE
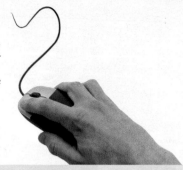
www.gourmetsociety.co.uk

A great way to search for restaurants, read and contribute reviews and discover the many other benefits of membership.

We've improved our website, making it easier to use and packed full of benefits for members.

Log in to members area to begin restaurant search.

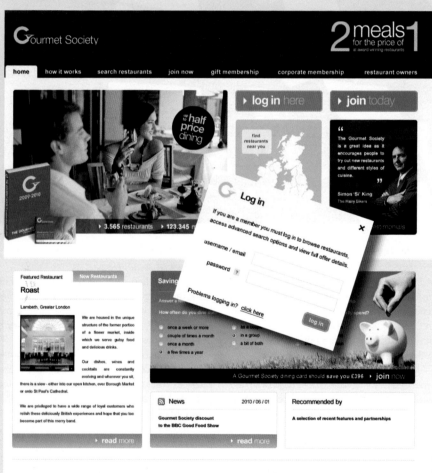

The website now displays more information about the restaurants in your search area for quicker, easier comparison and selection.

Find all the information about a restaurant on one page: Gourmet Society promotion offered, address, member reviews and more.

Write your own review and rate the restaurants you've visited. Help other members find the right restaurant for different occasions.

Stay online and check out the other benefits of GS membership. Read the news, book hotels, claim discounts with many other organisations and discover the latest restaurants to join the Gourmet Society.

Sign up to our e-newsletter for regular updates, new restaurants and other great offers.

www.gourmetsociety.co.uk

JOHN O'GROATS

↓

LANDS END

– The Gourmet Way –

Gourmet Society members June and John Berry, left their home in Derbyshire last Autumn to embark on an incredible and memorable journey from John O'Groats to Lands End via the East Coast. This is a quick account of their voyage . . . and a model of how to use your GS card for a culinary tour all of your own.

“ It started with John's desire to do something special to celebrate being 70, something demanding to show that even if life does not begin at 70, it need not end there. It was quite a simple idea. We would use public transport exclusively to get to one end of the country, travel the length of the country and then get home. Our most important consideration was that this would be a holiday, not an endurance test. It was an opportunity to see a lot of places we had not seen before and visit friends we had not seen for some time. Whilst it might prove quite challenging, it was being done for the fun of it rather than for its achievement.

Having booked B&Bs, we assumed that our meals each day would consist of a large breakfast, a snack for lunch and an evening meal. We could have left the choice of restaurants to be decided each evening. After all, this would allow us to determine what sort of meal we felt like eating. But then we considered the 'lottery factor', and instead decided to use the review sites on the internet to find possible recommendations which were relatively close to the places where we were staying.

And then we remembered the Gourmet Society. It is UK wide. Now we were faced by the prospect of eating out on as many as 24 occasions. We decided to join.

We used the Gourmet Society website, in conjunction with others, to choose and book the restaurants we would visit. In selecting, we deliberately chose a varied and potentially exciting range of foods – Scottish, Italian, French, Belgian, Indian, Chinese, Thai, Greek, Turkish etc. And we set a budget for the total cost of food per day at £15 each. We were well within our budget for food and saved over £120 using the Gourmet Society card.

THE JOURNEY.

We took 24 days during which we travelled 2700 miles using 79 buses and trains – as well as visiting 48 places we had never been to before, meeting 6 groups of friends and going to 5 theatres.

We have never had a better holiday, where every day was an experience and where every day seemed to last a satisfyingly long time.

EXPERIENCES.

It was 'the holiday of a lifetime'. We have been fortunate to visit many far-off places and see many remarkable things. How have we gone for 70 years without seeing so many great places on our own island? We learnt so much on our travels of our history, from Highland Clearances and Culloden Moor to castles and cathedrals to fishing decline and naval battles.

And the restaurants? A stunning selection, we recommend all of them. In Bradleys (Kings Lynn) we had the most memorable meal, combining outstanding food and service. And, without the GS card, how else would we have found the wonderful Schoolhouse Restaurant in John O'Groats?

The physical concerns we had beforehand (would backs and bodies cope with sitting for so long, carrying rucksacks every day, and lying in a new bed every night) did not materialise. The mental concerns (would watching the time every day be stressful and would the journeys become boring) never happened.

We had a good idea, we developed a good plan, we spent a lot of time preparing the details and we left sufficient flexibility to create each day anew.

REFLECTIONS.

And now we are home, how do we look back on it? The fact that it took nearly two weeks to get to a pattern of life at home indicates that we found a new routine whilst we were away. And the fact that, two days after returning, we started to think about the next tour says it all. So here's to the 'other half' – from Lands End to John O'Groats via the west coast and north coast. But to make it a bit different we hope to use boats to island hop the west coast of Scotland and postal buses in the north of Scotland.

Our only worry is that this type of trip might catch on with other golden oldies. And our first choice B&Bs and restaurants will be booked up by them. *"*

June and John used their Gourmet Society Card at the following restaurants from this year's directory:

Ash, Inverness (pg 301)

The Schoolhouse, John O'Groats (pg 300)

Dogma, Lincoln (pg 241)

Bradleys, Kings Lynn (pg 191)

Café Belge, Canterbury (pg 95),

Sense, Weymouth (pg 64)

The Duke of Cornwall, Plymouth (pg 60)

The Bay, Penzance (pg 57)

With sincere thanks to June and John Berry for sharing their account.

Beer
for all occasions Jon Howard, CAMRA

Outside of the beer world, it's a little known fact that there are now over 750 breweries operating across the UK, brewing more than 2,500 different varieties of real ale.

There are now more breweries dotted around the country than any time since the end of the Second World War, so, what better moment to learn more about the myriad of tastes and aromas present in real ale?

In recent years, brewers have reiterated the notion that wine and food matching is outdated, and in fact beer, which can be hoppy, spicy, fruity, creamy, chocolatey or malty and much, much more, is the perfect choice for any dining occasion.

A typical few courses with beer might take on the following appearance. An aperitif to liven the palate could be a sharp, hoppy bitter to get the tongue tingling. Moving onto starters, for any rich paté, a similarly rich, malty ale is a perfect partner. For more delicate dishes such as smoked salmon, a genuine pilsner has all the floral, citrus notes for a delightful accompaniment. For main courses, look no further than a robust Northern bitter for dark meats, the lemon notes of a classic wheat beer for poultry, or the ginger and lemongrass infusions of those beers which provide the perfect sidekick to spicy dishes.

For dessert, why not make the beer the dessert itself? One of my all time favourite beers is the Trappist Rochefort 10, brewed by monks in Belgium. It's the ultimate finisher to any great meal.

CAMRA campaigns for real ale, real pubs and consumer rights, and is an independent, voluntary organisation with over 115,000 members.
www.camra.org.uk

HOTELS *at*
great prices
for our members.

Members of the Gourmet Society can enjoy up to 70% off the rack rate at great hotels across the UK and Europe. From boutique to designer, cosy to corporate and 5* or budget choices, maximise your membership at **www.gourmetsociety.co.uk/hotels**

No matter what your accommodation preferences, when you use our hotel search facility you enjoy 24 hour booking, no booking fees and telephone support 24/7.

See where your hotel search takes you. **www.gourmetsociety.co.uk/hotels**

Recommend
a Friend

Share the pleasures and benefits of Gourmet Society membership with a friend. When they join, both of you will receive a little something from us.

Make sure your friend quotes your Gourmet Society membership number when they join and we will send you a complimentary bottle of wine; to say 'thank you'.

We will give your friend a special concessionary rate on membership; to say 'thanks for joining the country's best dining club'.

To recommend a friend visit our website at **www.gourmetsociety.co.uk/join** and use your membership number as the promotional code on the 'join now' page.

Or call the Customer Services Team on **0845 257 4477**
(calls are charged at a local rate from a BT landline).

You can also complete the form at the back of this guide and send to us in the post

In order to receive complimentary bottle of wine, your friend must become a member of the Gourmet Society and quote your membership number at the time of joining. This offer is not valid in conjunction with any other promotional joining offer. We reserve the right to substitute wine for a gift of similar value.

Corporate *Membership*

Do you own or manage a business, or work for a company that could benefit from corporate membership of the Gourmet Society?

Corporate membership offers great opportunities to business of all sizes from SMEs to blue-chip companies.

Excellent discounted corporate rates are available on all orders of over ten memberships.

"Our most popular employee benefit for the third year running!!"

A unique addition to your employee benefits or rewards scheme.

A fantastic sales promotion tool. Offer Gourmet Society memberships as an incentive to potential clients.

Reduced entertaining expenses. Use your Gourmet Society discount card for great discounts when entertaining guests.

Email: corporate@thegourmetsociety.co.uk or call **0845 257 4477**
(calls are charged at a local rate from a BT landline).

YOU DINE ^AND_THEY LEARN

HOW CHEFS-TO-BE GAIN THEIR SKILLS

Of the great restaurants participating in the Gourmet Society, we maintain a special enthusiasm for the college establishments and the charity-owned restaurant joining us this year as part of our impetus to support young people and those starting out in the industry.

Training colleges are places where young people (and sometimes adult learners) practice their cooking in bona-fide restaurants whilst studying for nationally recognised qualifications. Each time members of the public visit, these ambitious and dedicated trainees can practice and hone their considerable skills, all the while overseen by professionals with years of industry experience.

For their hospitality and cooking students, colleges will generally have a restaurant on-site or affiliated so that students can acquire work-based experience. College restaurants offer fine dining, à la carte menus, and often theme nights, so that trainees try their hand at world cuisines. College restaurants are usually licensed and matching and serving wines is an important part of students' learning. There's no skimming on décor, service and ambience either. Restaurants may or may not be situated on college campuses, but either way they are

CYGNETS

venues where the finest attention to detail is maintained and dining experience is important, from the glassware to the maitre d's welcome to the atmosphere created through the furnishings and music.

> 'The professional development of our learners' culinary skills is our main priority and their dedication to be at the top of their field shines through in every dish that they prepare.'
>
> Marion Danby,
> Curriculum Manager, Hospitality & Catering
> Accrington & Rossendale College (Traders Brasserie)

Indeed the only notable difference between college-based restaurants and any other may be opening hours; we would always recommend phoning ahead to ensure an opportunity to be among the first to sample the cooking and service of some Britain's next top chefs.

There are other kitchens where chefs in training can access much needed exposure in the demanding working environment of a busy restaurant.

TRADERS BRASSERIE

The owners of the popular Greenhouse Brassiere believe in 'growing talent' and are committed to offering would be entrants to the workforce their first job in a commercial restaurant. They employ apprentices and students from the adjacent college of further education and helpfully arrange shifts around study. A 'Gourmet Society Members Dinner' was held in the summer and chefs and front of house staff received a standing ovation.

'One of the best meals I have had for a long time. Quality of service was good too. Loved this place and what a wonderful ethos. - good food, good works. I will be back.

This comment from the visitor's book neatly encapsulates what we try to do in, the Hoxton Apprentice. Training long-term unemployed is important but if the food we serve and the service or ambience do not come up to standard, people will not return. And I am glad to say this is not the case. The young chefs we train are enthusiastic about their profession - and they graduate after an intensive 8 months training to work in prestigious places such as Buckingham Palace and the flagship Hilton at Tower Bridge.'

Patricia Haikin

Managing Director, Training for Life (Hoxton Brasserie)

The Hoxton Apprentice is a charity-owned restaurant which offers a route to a vocation for the long term unemployed (minimum 6 months); this includes younger adults who may have experienced life problems including homelessness, nor gained formal qualifications, let alone employment, before. The rigorous apprenticeship programme, with the onus on maintaining the fine standards of the restaurant, is an excellent way for apprentices to learn not only vocational but life skills too.

Several of the training restaurants joining us this year have won local if not national awards -

ROUGE

competing against restaurateurs who have been in business for many years and adding to the number of award-winning restaurants available to GS members.

Chef in Waiting boasts World Skills UK medal winners, whilst Rouge restaurant is a former winner of the Best Modern European Restaurant (London Regional Food & Drink Awards 2009). The Academy won gold medals galore at the Welsh and Wessex Salon Culinaire competitions earlier in 2010.

With the promise of excellent and affordable food, unremitting attention to detail, the chance to invest in the future of people starting out in professional life and now the attraction of the Gourmet Society's dining promotion, could there be any more compelling reasons to sample a training restaurant this year?

CAFÉ ROUGE

RESTAURANT   BAR   CAFÉ

Café Rouge is the UK's premier French restaurant brand with an all-day offer of classic French dishes and wines. The first restaurant opened in 1989 and over the years Café Rouge has developed an iconic status.

Today it is now the most recognised and successful French restaurant brand in the UK.

Open all day, Café Rouge serves breakfast, lunch and dinner as well as catering for those who are popping in for a passing snack, a bottle of wine or a moment to themselves with a cappuccino and the paper.

The dinner menu offers some favourite French classics with onion soup, mussels and chicken liver parfait all on offer.

Gourmands can then progress with Toulouse sausages and mash, corn-fed chicken with Roquefort and cream sauce, or boeuf bourguignon and French beans. Nonetheless, steaks are what Café Rouge are most proud of, offering some really interesting French cuts such as the Bavette marinated in rosemary and garlic, manifesting a true Gallic experience.

The Menu pour les Enfants gives children plenty to choose from with all dishes analysed by an independent nutritionist to ensure they are well balanced. All dishes come with a choice of vegetable or salad as well as fruit for dessert, to ensure they get their 'five a day'.

The 100+ Café Rouge establishments across the country are located conveniently, allowing Gourmet Society members many chances to take advantage of this excellent dining promotion.

THE LIVING ROOM

The national Living Room brand is now synonymous with great food and drink, excellent service and stylish surroundings. Their thirteen neighbourhood restaurant-and-bars demonstrate a mature attitude to dining and socialising, offering wonderful menus of food and drink.

The Living Room remains a popular destination thanks to the imagination and creativity applied to every aspect of the guest's experience, from the development of menus right through to the music played. However at its heart the core offering is always presented: great food and drinks prepared simply and served impeccably.

Living Room venues are cool, airy piano bars and restaurants in earthy tones that aim to provide quality without exclusivity and high levels of service without high prices. The chic, standalone restaurant in each venue offers a choice of wholesome dishes from an extensive à la carte menu.

Culinary influences are eclectic, yet the

focus remains on two broad types of cuisine. A selection of 'home comforts' honour that long-loved gastro pub flavour: dishes to satisfy an honest appetite for wholesome, hearty cooking, served always with a 'Living Room' twist.

The second style suits those with more varied tastes: an elegant European/global fusion interspersed with fine British classics. These dishes are set to make an impression, yet the theory behind them is simple: fresh ingredients expertly infused with flavours known, loved and trusted.

Drinks menus are extensive and eclectic. Over 80 cocktails are offered and bar staff will happily help you create your own blend. The wines – contemporary, classic, world-class – are chosen to match the menus, with changing monthly guest wines to accompany the seasonal flavours

Minimum of 3 courses per person including main course must be purchased

PREZZO

Our partnership with Prezzo, the authentic Italian restaurant, enters another year, continuing to offer members the chance to claim two for one on main meals.

Prezzo offers great quality Italian food and uses the finest seasonal products, many of which are imported direct from Italy.

The restaurants are particularly stylish with their contemporary design. Some may be situated in historic listed buildings or those of local interest, while others occupy the most modern of urban developments. The differing designs all add to the special experience you will receive at Prezzo. What's more, there are more than 120 restaurants nationwide stretching from Falmouth in Cornwall to Edinburgh in Scotland, so your nearest branch is never too far away.

The menu pleases all with some comforting Italian food amongst a tempting variety of dishes. Try the al forno baked pasta specialties such as the pollo mariano with its seasoned chicken, spicy Italian sausage, roasted peppers and fusilli in a tomato sauce, or opt for a traditional lasagne with a garlic, tomato and basil bruschetta. In many of the branches you can witness the chefs in their open kitchens hand stretching the dough to create one of their freshly baked pizzas, cooked to perfection in traditional stone ovens.

For something different try classic Italian rice dishes such as the risotto Mediterraneo, made with crayfish in a creamy saffron sauce or for a lighter dish, sample the oak-roasted fillet of salmon salad. Prezzo have a wide range of vegetarian dishes as well as children's portions for many of the meals – perfect for dining out with the whole family.

2FOR1
MAIN COURSE

&U FRI SAT DEC

Harry Ramsden's

World Famous Fish & Chips

Established in 1928, Harry Ramsden's is as much of an institution as fish & chips themselves. Originating in a wooden hut, Harry Ramsden served traditional fish & chips which soon became a roaring success.

Today, Harry Ramsden's continue to serve great tasting fish & chips. Fish is hand-battered to produce a light, fluffy yet crisp batter and the golden chips are hand cut from British Maris Piper potatoes. Enjoy with tartar sauce, mushy peas, curry sauce or simply with a lemon wedge. Delicious!

With restaurants across the country, from Glasgow & Gateshead to Bournemouth & Blackpool, Harry Ramsden's venues provide the ideal atmosphere to accompany this all time classic dish.

Treat yourself to some traditional comfort food or relive the holiday experience with the unmistakeable taste of the seaside; make Harry Ramsden's your first choice for fish & chips.

Gourmet Society members are welcomed in Harry Ramsden's restaurants across the UK.

Please check availability on bank holidays. Not available during August or in takeaways

The best of
BRITISH PUBS

Best of British pubs are a collection of some of the best traditional pubs Britain has to offer. The collection is proud to offer venues ranging from charming, character-filled local taverns to quaint country dining pubs. There are also a few gems tucked away in some of the UK's top tourist destinations.

Families, friends and the solo visitor receive a true landlord's welcome, in a cosy home-from-home environment that is the heart of every great British pub.

Each of the pubs is different, with a character all of their own that celebrates their history and local community.

Landlords are rightly proud of the high standard of the produce served to guests, from the tempting food menus to the wide range of drinks. Next time you are looking for a leisurely Sunday roast, Cask Marque accredited real ales, fantastic wines from around the world or simply don't want to do the washing up, then visit a Best of British pub and allow yourself be looked after.

From Ben Nevis to the South Coast, the Best of British pubs sign is a guarantee of the type of public house experience only to be found on these shores.

2FOR1
2 COURSES

xU **SKY** **☎**

2 courses must be ordered. Not available on Bank holidays. Must call ahead to check offer is available during the Christmas period and its build up.

29

Dragon Pubs

Take everything good about a British local pub – great beer and wine, classic food dishes, that home from home feel, and combine it with the most fantastic authentic Thai restaurant.

This is the experience which awaits a visitor to the eclectic collection of Dragon pubs based around London, Nottingham, Leeds and Manchester. These friendly pubs offer a place to chat and unwind in elegant and comfortable surroundings and are open all day with a menu offering traditional British dishes plus a selection of Thai classics.

In the evening the stunning, Thai influenced,

contemporary restaurants open for a relaxed yet premium Thai dining experience.

Explore everything that South East Asian cooking has to offer, from weeping tigers to colourful curries with an array of exciting and amazing flavours in between. Truly authentic cuisine, all freshly created by the team of Thai chefs.

Diners can choose between four banquets, specially created to provide a true taste of the Orient, with a little something for everyone.

Alternatively the main menu offers delights such as pla takrai (steamed sea bass with lemongrass and ginger), the ever popular kaeng dang (Bangkok's famous Thai red curry) or one of the chargrilled specialities, presented sizzling to the table.

The fantastic Dragon pubs now welcome Gourmet Society members with a great dining promotion.

25%OFF TOTAL

Must call ahead to check offer is available on bank holidays, during the Christmas period and its build up.

DRAGON PUB

GREAT BRITISH CARVERY

Everyone loves the humble carvery, but for a while it felt like it had been rather neglected. So, after much thought and hard work, the concept was given a radical roasting resulting in the birth of the Great British Carvery.

This selection of delightful, very individual pubs are dotted throughout the UK from Devon to Glasgow and bring you all the tradition you would expect from a carvery, combined with everything else you wouldn't.

With stunning restaurant areas, a feature carvery and warm and friendly table service, the Great British Carvery pubs are the perfect place for enjoying a lunchtime or evening meal with friends or family, whatever the size of your party and whatever the occasion.

Always offered, is the choice of dining from either the premium carvery serving the very best British Farm Assured produce or an extensive main menu. This comes fresh from the kitchen and offers good old traditional delights, a selection of favourites with a modern twist as well as some more contemporary seasonal creations.

There is also a huge choice of delicious home-made starters and desserts with something for everyone, so you will not be leaving hungry!

The wine list offers a broad choice from 10 countries worldwide, giving you the chance to experiment whilst enjoying a premium glass of wine.

Kids are not forgotten either, they get to choose from mini versions of some the British favourites as well as - of course - the carvery.

The bar areas, being friendly and informal, mean you can sit and relax before or after your meal with a pint of cask ale or a fairtrade coffee.

With outside dining and gardens, a seasonal menu and extra cold beers you are invited to enjoy some fabulous food in stunning surroundings all year round.

Great British Carvery restaurants welcome Gourmet Society members this year with a great promotion.

2FOR1
MAIN COURSE

£U ☎ **$₩**

Must call ahead to check offer is available on Bank Holidays, during Christmas period and its build up.

LOCH FYNE
RESTAURANTS

Loch Fyne Restaurants are all about great food and great flavours. The superb seafood dishes are simply prepared with a focus on high-quality, fresh ingredients and choices to suit all tastes and appetites.

The business originated at Loch Fyne on the west coast of Scotland where its founders started out by selling fresh oysters from a small road-side shack. Times moved on and this original Oyster Bar became increasingly successful, spawning a group of more than 40 restaurants across the UK – all taking their core produce of shellfish and smoked fish direct from the shores and smokehouse at Loch Fyne.

Nowadays, fresh fish and shellfish are delivered daily at dawn into the restaurants ready to feature in the hot dishes and varied selection of cold dishes and platters. This freshness is tangible when you watch Loch Fyne's chefs creating shellfish platters at the restaurant's marble counters – a mouth-watering spectacle.

All the produce served at Loch Fyne is sustainably sourced and the restaurant group has been a pioneer in supporting UK-based, small day-fishing boats rather than harmful deep-sea trawlers. There's something for everyone on the menu – not just seafood

lovers. The à la carte menu starters include pan-fried squid with balsamic dressing, lobster bisque and a melt-in-the-mouth wild mushroom, spinach and goats cheese tart.

Mains include a 'From the Loch' selection featuring oysters, mussels and stunning seafood platters. If shellfish isn't your thing then tuck into salmon with shiitake mushrooms, ginger and bok choi; whole sea bass with rosemary and herbs or a simple but delicious smoked fish pie. Specials appear on the chalkboards every day based on fresh catch and seasonal produce.

Meat lovers will be delighted to see fabulous Scottish-reared produce on the menu including the highly-acclaimed Glen Fyne steak; tender, juicy and well-deserving of its great reputation.

Many of the restaurants are in listed buildings and Loch Fyne's architects have gained a reputation for sensitively and beautifully restoring historic properties. The venues are warm and inviting with rich wooden floors and stunning artwork depicting the Scottish origins and provenance of the produce.

Plenty of the restaurants are open all day, from breakfast and brunch (try the world-famous kippers or smoked salmon and scrambled egg) right through to dinner. Whatever time of day you drop in, be it for a light snack or full à la carte feast, you are assured of a friendly welcome and relaxed dining experience.

LOCH FYNE

Coal Grill + Bar is known for fresh food and sensible prices. The quality of the product, coupled with competitive pricing and value driven menus, has been the key to Coal's success.

Established in 2007, Coal Grill + Bar has grown into a vibrant chain of national restaurants offering a comfortable modern atmosphere combined with a fantastic selection of food.

All of the menus in Coal are developed by Group Executive Chef, Antonio Dias, who is originally from Coimbra, Portugal. Antonio mixes his Mediterranean roots with his passion for cooking to produce the range of delicious items available on the menu. He regularly develops and enhances the dishes on offer in order to bring Coal customers seasonal products and diversity.

Coal's trademark dish is the 'flame-grilled firesticks': skewers of prime meat and fish served on a hot skillet with fire-roasted sweet peppers, courgettes, mushroom and red onion ratatouille, complimented by a selection of dips and the choice of rice, dauphinoise potatoes or thick-cut chips.

This year Gourmet Society members can enjoy a great dining promotion at the delightful Coal Grill + Bar restaurants sites including the original Wimbledon branch through to the recently opened restaurants in Exeter and Guildford.

Not in conjunction with any other offer or on the prix-fixé menu

GRAND UNION

The Grand Union Group is an independent chain of bar-grill venues and a pub-restaurant within London and the Home Counties.

The GU's relaxed venues, where eating, drinking and music go hand in hand all promise a certain quality, yet nonetheless each retain their independent feel.

GU prides itself on providing a relaxed atmosphere in beautifully designed spaces, with furniture sourced from reclamation yards, vintage shops and auction houses around London. This creates a contemporary, yet vintage feel and a homely environment to relax and enjoy food and drink in the company of friends, family and colleagues.

By day the Grand Union is the perfect place to relax on comfy leather sofas while enjoying freshly prepared food, notably quality burgers and hand-cut chips. As the sun goes down the Bar-Grill venues transform into an ideal environment for post-work food and drinks while listening to funk, soul and indie, while on Friday and Saturday nights they are the place to celebrate the weekend with live DJs and late licences until 3:30am.

To drink, there is an extensive range of fine wines and champagnes, premium draught beers and exceptional cocktails, all expertly mixed by some of the best mixologists in the business.

Visit the wonderfully individual Grand Union venues and benefit from their great offer to Gourmet Society members

2FOR1
MAIN COURSE

GU FRI SAT DEC ☎

Not available Sunday lunch.

Auberge
bar & restaurant

Popular dishes include the Gigonette d'Agneau, braised lamb shank served with champ potato, French beans and a light rosemary jus, and the ever popular Moules Marinière served in the cooking pot with a side of French fries.

Frequently changing specials will entice you on repeat visits, whilst the classics hit the spot every time.

Auberge has over a decade of experience serving classic French dishes within unique restaurants with attentive service. Using the tastiest market fare with a hearty dash of French inspiration and style, food is freshly prepared on site.

Dine à la carte over a long and intimate dinner, enjoy a glass of wine or two in the relaxing surroundings, or take your pick from the express menu which offers the roll call of French favourites and is perfect for a quick work lunch or pre-theatre meal.

The Auberge restaurants are each unique in style but consistent in quality and purpose. Wine, dine, relax and unwind, there is an Auberge to suit every occasion and every person.

2FOR1
MAIN COURSE

xU ☎

Azzurro

ITALIAN BAR · KITCHEN

The menu offers all the Italian classics, some contemporary suggestions and a great drinks menu, all created with a fresh approach and dedication to flavour. The wine list is excellently sourced with a choice to suit every budget and occasion.

Welcoming you for an after-work drink, a lunch 'rapido' or a delicious evening meal, Azzurro promises delicious dining, great service and tempting chef's specials to consider anew on each visit.

2FOR1
MAIN COURSE

xU ☎

MIS○

with sumptuous flavour and smell – a real delight. This type of cooking ensures the maximum nutritional value of food and thus enhances mind, body and soul.

2FOR1
MAIN COURSE

xU

With prominent London and South East locations, the rapidly expanding Miso Noodle Bars are testament to their own success. The food on offer is healthy, tasty, fun and affordable and appeals to every age group, which may explain why the Miso Noodle Bars are always buzzing.

When you place your order the authentic Soho-trained chefs toss all the fresh ingredients into a wok and stir-fry to taste. The fresh noodles arrive steaming and sizzling at amazing speed

OLD ORLEANS

LET THE GOOD TIMES ROLL

Old Orleans salutes the heritage of Louisiana. Chefs find culinary inspiration in the blending of cuisines from the American South, Creole and Cajun cultures that make the food of the region so special. The atmosphere and service is relaxed and genuine, reminiscent of New Orleans.

Old Orleans is perfect for any occasion, from big parties to quiet evenings with friends. The menu features classic Louisiana and Cajun dishes such as the signature Jambalaya, freshly prepared daily to the chef's own recipe. There's also a whole heap of American favourites

with a Deep South twist, from the hot and spicy 'Voodoo Burger' to the delicious Cajun-blackened catfish.

Famous cocktails are inspired by the rich heritage of New Orleans. Try the signature 'Howard's Way' cocktail, created by Old Orleans' very own mixologist. It's a premium mojito with a twist, using 7-year-old Havana rum, fresh mint and brown sugar, balanced with sweet strawberry and raspberry flavours. Also recommended is the 'Streetcar Named Desire', a potent blend of Courvoisier, Cointreau,

Enjoy a little Southern spirit and the Gourmet Society dining promotion at Old Orleans across the UK.

lemon juice and apricot jam. And if you prefer something more traditional, the extensive drinks menu is full of old favourites too. From icy cold American beers, to a wide range of carefully selected wines from around the world, to the fiery Crabbie's Alcoholic Ginger Beer, there's something for everyone!

Old Orleans really do pride themselves on Southern hospitality and rightly so, enjoying giving customers a little something extra. With generous portions, regular menu sampling and friendly service that goes the extra mile, staff do their best to deliver the best possible experience for every customer that walks through the door.

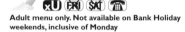

2FOR1
MAIN COURSE

Adult menu only. Not available on Bank Holiday weekends, inclusive of Monday

$\mathcal{H}an\partial$ PICKED
HOTELS

BUILT FOR PLEASURE

Hand Picked Hotels ... fanatical about great food and wine.
Great dining and fine wines define the Hand Picked Hotels experience.

The award-winning Hand Picked Hotels collection, created by former City lawyer Julia Hands MBE, are luxurious country house hotels renowned for exquisite food, fine wines and excellent service in stylish, architecturally stunning surroundings.

There are 18 hotels, seven with spas, located across the UK. Each has an individual identity: the gentle relaxation of the Wood Hall Hotel, Wetherby; the luxury of Nuffield Priory, Surrey; and the stately history of New Hall Hotel and Spa, Birmingham, England's oldest inhabited moated manor house.

Hand Picked Hotels focuses on the quality of service and cuisines; all 18 hotels have achieved AA rosette status, 15 have two and Norton House Hotel & Spa in Edinburgh has won three. Five hotels have achieved red star status, being recognised as amongst the AA's top 200 hotels in the UK & Ireland.

Great dining and fine wines define the Hand Picked Hotels experience and, where possible, produce is sourced from local farmers, often producing small yields to a very high standard for the very best quality and flavour.

Julia also takes a personal interest in excellent wine and is the mastermind behind the development of a truly remarkable collection of Hand Picked wines from around the world, including high-quality British wines.

Hand Picked Hotels invite their talented chefs to continue to re-invent the British dining experience, and their guests to simply indulge.

The Hand Picked Hotels across the country each offer a bespoke promotion to members at their amazing, regularly award-winning restaurants.

Del'Aziz is a group of elegant restaurants, bars and boutique bakeries in one. Open from breakfast to dinner, delighting guests with an array of offerings from coffee to cocktails, and charcuterie to cous cous.

Designed to mimic a colourful Middle Eastern bazaar, Del'Aziz is a one-stop shop for gourmets, bon viveurs, and lovers of good food and beautiful objects and is fast becoming a truly versatile treasure trove of culinary delights. Embracing the Eastern tradition of sociable eating, each Del'Aziz boasts huge sharing tables and a lively atmosphere with a steady stream of foodies at all hours of the day.

Showcasing the very best of Eastern Mediterranean and North African cuisines, the menu offers modern adaptations of traditional recipes from Morocco and Lebanon through to Greece and Turkey. Dishes dance with the intense and exotic flavours from this region and sparkle with fruity, sharp or sweet overtones.

The mouth-watering à la carte menu features a plethora of mezzes including marinated kasaar with pine nuts; florines stuffed with feta and herbs; grilled Merguez sausages and delicious kebabs such as the Persian chicken marinated in saffron and tiger prawn with chilli and lime. All offer exceptional value for money.

Typical mains include the flavoursome Moroccan lamb fillet kebab with cumin; a selection of tagines such as chicken with preserved lemon and olives or lamb with prunes and almonds, as well as seven hour braised lamb shank with parsnip purée.

The bakery is both a visual treat and a cake lovers' heaven with beautiful displays groaning under the weight of fresh-baked breads, cakes and pastries; perfect for dessert or to accompany a morning or afternoon coffee.

Each of the five Del'Aziz are located in bustling spots around London and when you spot one be sure to enjoy the Gourmet Society promotion.

2FOR1
MAIN COURSE

handmade burger Co

The handmade burger Co. offers a variety of more than 40 delicious burgers, handmade and pressed in each restaurant every single day.

The beef burgers are prepared from traditionally reared 100% prime Scotch beef, mixed together with a selection of fresh ingredients and seasoned, before being flame-grilled to order to create the best tasting burgers. With more than 20 fresh chicken, lamb, fish and vegetarian burgers, along with a fantastic selection for children, handmade burger Co. has something for everyone on their menu. In fact they have the biggest variety of burgers in the UK.

It's not just the burgers that are made by hand. The potatoes are peeled, cut and double fried in every restaurant every day to give you fresh chips that will rival the home-made ones your mum used to make. As for the freshly made coleslaw, smokey flame-grilled vegetables and fabulous onion rings, we recommend getting an order of each and sharing so that you can try every yummy one!

Those wishing to customise their burgers, or with any specific dietary requirements, should know that they are well catered for, as all the food is made freshly to the customer's order.

The award-winning teams at handmade burger Co. look forward to welcoming you in their restaurants located across the country.

hotels that dare to be different

Malmaison dares to be different at every level and this philosophy is echoed in its food and drink.

Indeed guests regularly find some of the region's most delectable food secrets served on their plates, such is the commitment of individual chefs to consistently source local specialities to add to the winning Mal menu.

The compelling combination of divinely tasty cuisine and the chance to take a trip around the world's finest wines is carried off to perfection

There are hotels and there are Mals. Choose these stunning boutique hotels across the UK, for a perfect, stylish city break.

Eating out? Imagine divinely tasty, beautifully presented cuisine prepared with incredible local ingredients and served with passion.

and has ensured consistently high praise. Eight of the group sport an AA rosette and Edinburgh and London have each achieved two AA rosettes for their respective brasseries.

All the Mal bars have lashings of attitude, and have been designed with an eye to the hip, trendy and chic. They are a super-cool venue in which to sip delicious signature cocktails or try a great glass of vino from the eclectic wine list.

Overnight guests will enjoy large rooms decorated in super-slinky style. The bold colours and rich designs create a sense of drama, and are furnished with a focus on serious comfort. All rooms have great beds for sleepy heads, power showers, CD players with libraries, satellite TV, wines of the world and naughty nibbles. Other luxuries include, take home toiletries and 'vroom' room service for breakfast, dinner or midnight munchies.

Great Food. Great Wine. Simply Dare to be Different.

From the converted church of Malmaison Glasgow to the world-renowned award winning transformation of Oxford Prison, the Mal team pride themselves on reinventing unique spaces. With daringly different hotels in the UK and more in the pipeline catering for the business of pleasure and the pleasure of business, it looks like passion is well and truly here to stay.

That's Mal Life.

Gourmet Society members can enjoy fabulous dining offers at eleven Malmaison brassieres.

Check the individual hotels for details.

Malmaison, Oxford Prison

Hotel du Vin & Bistro

I think. Therefore I du Vin.

Think quintessential British style. Elegant and unpretentious. Combine this with great spirit, wit, an unquestionable devotion to wine, and you have captured the essence of Hotel du Vin.

Picture sensitively converted spaces, like a Georgian townhouse, a brewery, or a hospital, eclectically furnished in a timeless manner. Imagine a trademark bistro, serving simple classics, an outstanding cellar. Egyptian linen and monsoon showers for your room. A glorious Laroche tasting room for the wine-lover, a cigar shack in its gardens, and inspiring original art in its halls.

With nationally acclaimed bistros, Hotel Du Vin promises an exceptional dining experience time and time again. Many of the Hotel du Vin bistros have been awarded at least one AA rosette, Harrogate, Henley upon Thames, Winchester and Edinburgh all have a well-deserved two rosettes. Absolute validation that Hotel du Vin's philosophy, to serve good food, produced from the finest and freshest local produce, cooked simply and priced sensibly, is achieved.

Each bistro has an extensive and eclectic wine list, including an impressive array of by the glass bottles and a small selection of good value wines to complement the dishes. On hand is a Master Sommelier who will help you match your wine with a course from the menu.

No matter where you find yourself, the nearest Hotel du Vin will be synonymous with style and hospitality.

The answer is simple. Think du Vin.

Gourmet Society members can enjoy different offers at the Hotel du Vin bistros. **Check the individual hotel listings for details.**

Di Maggio's

'Our family serving your family'
Independent family orientated pizzerias.

Located in the Strathclyde region, Di Maggio's offers the finest Italian cuisine in their local neighbourhood pizzerias. The essence of the Italian family is absolutely paramount to the workings of every Di Maggio's. Although each has its own character according to its locale, they all provide the same exacting standards of good, freshly cooked food and first-rate service.

Di Maggio's have a great reputation that has been built over generations and thus it should come as no surprise that they have been lauded as 'Scotland's best Italian.'

Try a different pizza at each of the seven Di Maggio's offering GS members a great discount.

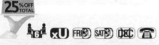

BROOK HOTELS

Brook Hotels is a collection of unique, historical 4 star and 3 star hotels at great locations across the UK all within close range of leisure and tourist attractions. Popular with locals and guests alike, all the hotels boast superb restaurants, perhaps even two, for different dining moods.

Your destination Brook Hotel may be an elegant manor house set in extensive grounds, inviting you to a round of golf before a delicious à la carte meal. Or you may choose a modern, city centre hotel for a refreshing lunch between a busy day of culture and shopping.

Brook Hotels is committed to realising their guest's needs and achieve these by developing and providing innovative, daring and excellent hospitality served by devoted, committed, highly trained, vibrant people, striving always for high levels of service.

For the first time Gourmet Society members can enjoy a great dining promotion at all of the spectacular Brook Hotel restaurants across the country.

25% OFF TOTAL xU ☎

The food on offer and the dining experience is unique to each of the hotels. Diners enjoy the popular British and European cuisine at the convivial No 5 Bistro, Royal Oak Hotel in Sevenoaks. The menu at the Tewkesbury Park Hotel in Gloucestershire is replete with local ingredients, whilst the prestigious restaurant at the George Hotel in Huddersfield is one of the finest dining rooms in the region.

South West

Nowhere has the renaissance in English cuisine been felt more than the South West. With local chefs looking not only to preserve tradition but also experiment, this region is quickly becoming a cornerstone of the gourmet map, underpinned by a cornucopia of great seafood, quality cheeses, cider (cyder) and, of course, the Cornish pasty whose delights head up an important industry all of its own.

The UK is enjoying a revival of cheese-making and the South West thanks to its wet climate and thriving dairy industry is poised to fly the flag for Britain. Delicacies like Cornish Yarg have become internationally known amongst cheese connoisseurs and are prized for their taste. Of course to describe West Country cheeses and not mention Stinking Bishop is a crime against cuisine and this quirkily named cheese is the match in taste (and smell) of any French import. Clotted cream is also a regional export and is a crucial part of a Devonshire cream tea, that evergreen delicious indulgence .

Although you cannot be further than seventy miles from the coast in the UK the best places for seafood are right on it, gazing at the sparkling seas. The South West is no exception. Old dishes like Stargazy Pie, so named because the heads of the fish poke skywards out of the pie-crust sit comfortably with less traditional dishes on many a coastal menu.

When such a wealth of ingredients is combined with the passionate zeal of the chefs in this region to challenge the stereotype of English cuisine, diners are able like never before to ride the waves of great cooking.

We have also included the outstanding restaurants in the Channel Islands, in this region.

Avon

AHMED'S CURRY CAFE
Indian
1E Chandos Road, Bristol, BS6 6PG
0117 946 6466
Authentic food, expertly prepared to bring forward the exotic flavours and textures of fine Indian cooking. Renowned for their special haandi dishes, which are the essence of home-cooked Indian food.

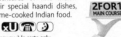

Must order min 2 courses pp.not takeaway, à la carte only.

AHMED'S MASALA CAFE
Indian
2 Jacob Wells Road, Hotwells, Bristol, BS8 1EA
0117 930 4194
A cosy curry café; relaxed and unpretentious. Great food, perfect for a pop-in nosh, takeaway or home delivery.

Not valid for takeaway orders.

ANTIX
English and Continental
44 Park Street, Bristol, BS1 5JG
0117 925 1139
Fresh tiger prawns and Greek halloumi salads, delicious pasta dishes and fantastic home-made burgers all occupying the menu. The quality of the food guarantees the restaurant an excellent reputation.

AQUA ITALIA
Italian
Welsh Back, Bristol, BS1 4RR
0117 915 6060
A venue serving healthy, tasty and beautifully presented Italian cuisine all day, to be enjoyed with Italian cocktails, aperitivos, grappas, fine espresso coffees and an extensive Italian wine list.

AQUA ITALIAN RESTAURANT
Italian
153 Whiteladies Road, Bristol, BS8 2RF
0117 973 3314
A venue serving healthy, tasty and beautifully presented Italian cuisine all day, to be enjoyed with Italian cocktails, aperitivos, grappas, fine espresso coffees and an extensive Italian wine list.

AQUA RESTAURANT
Italian
88 Walcott Street, Bath, BA1 5BD
01225 471 371
Based in a beautiful former church house, this restaurant is perfect for lunch and dinner; the best of Italian cuisine is on the menu, creating a genuinely authentic feel combined with delicious food.

ASSILAH BISTRO
Moroccan
194 Wells Road, Totterdown, Bristol, BS4 2AX
07816 202 827
With 30 years experience at hand, this family-run restaurant specialises in home-made Moroccan cuisine. Boasting a menu of traditional dishes at moderate prices, diners can simply sit back and enjoy.

BRISTOL BRIDGE RESTAURANT
Turkish
45-47 Baldwin Street, Bristol, BS1 1RA
0117 922 1333
A haven of a restaurant that offers Turkish and Mediterranean food to be enjoyed in authentically adorned surroundings. Be met by welcoming smiles and served by amiable staff.

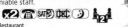

Formerly Bosphorus Restaurant

CADBURY HOUSE HOTEL
British
Frost Hill, Bristol, BS49 5AD
01934 834 343
An ideal place to dine for any occasion, be it an intimate dinner for two or a large family celebration. Award-winning chefs use their passion for good food to produce fine dishes for all to enjoy.

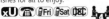

CAFÉ ROUGE
French
15 Milsom Street, Bath, BA1 1DE
01225 462 368
An attractive restaurant, a boulevard café or a Parisian-style wine bar; however you see Café Rouge, consistently excellent classic French dishes are always guaranteed.

CAFÉ ROUGE
French
85 Park Street, Bristol, BS1 5PJ
0117 929 2571
An attractive restaurant, a boulevard café or a Parisian-style wine bar; however you see Café Rouge, consistently excellent classic French dishes are always guaranteed.

CAFÉ ROUGE
French
Unit R4, The Mall, Bristol, BS10 7TG
0117 950 8730
An attractive restaurant, a boulevard café or a Parisian-style wine bar; however you see Café Rouge, consistently excellent classic French dishes are always guaranteed.

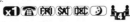

CAFÉ ROUGE
French
Cabot Circus, Bristol, BS1 3BD
0117 954 4808
An attractive restaurant, a boulevard café or a Parisian-style wine bar; however you see Café Rouge, consistently excellent classic French dishes are always guaranteed.

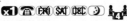

CARRIAGES RESTAURANT
European
Alveston, Thornbury, Bristol, BS35 2LA
01454 415 050
Award-winning restaurant offering both formal and informal dining experiences. Immerse yourself in the relaxed setting of the conservatory as you enjoy drinks and canapés and browse the scintillating menu.

CASSIA
Indian
79 Gloucester Road, Bristol, BS34 5JQ
0117 969 0907
Imaginatively created recipes are used in this terrific Indian restaurant. Unique flavours characterise each dish.

Gourmet Society discount applies to the à la carte menu

CHEUNG KONG
Oriental

2B North View, Westbury Park, Bristol, BS6 7QB
0117 973 5165

Authentic recipes from different Chinese regions with a contemporary setting and warm atmosphere. Specialises in Cantonese and Pekingese dishes.

COAL GRILL + BAR
Mediterranean

Cabot Circus, Glass House, Bristol, BS1 3BD
0117 954 4624

Combined with great service and a stylish ambience, this grill and bar produces delectable food and captivating cocktails. Dishes to suit all tastes are created with passion and flair.

Not to be used with any other offer or the Prix Fixé menu

CURRY HOUSE
Indian

393 Bath Road, Brislington, Bristol, BS4 3EQ
0117 977 9090

This award-winning restaurant offers a varied menu, from Indian classics to specials such as quail and kangaroo. The modern and comfortable décor help build a relaxing atmosphere with a fine wine list.

DELMONICO
International

217A Gloucester Road, Bristol, BS7 8NN
0117 944 5673

Offering regularly changing menus that are based on locally sourced produce. Guests love the extensive array of food on offer, from classic Anglo-French cuisine to Asian and Italian influenced dishes.

DOLCE VITA
Italian

76 Victoria Street, Bristol, BS1 6DF
0117 922 6688

Dolce Vita blends a relaxed atmosphere and the style of 1960s Italian cinema with an exciting and delicious selection of pizzas, pasta dishes, salads and steaks. A great venue for evening dining.

EASTERN SPICE
Indian

269 Two Mile Hill Road, Kingswood, Bristol, BS15 1AX
0117 935 2335

With a large base of regular diners it is clear this venue delivers quality food every time. Dishes are well-prepared and presented, and full of authentic flavour and spice, especially the chef's specials.

EL PUERTO
Spanish

57 Prince Street, Bristol, BS1 4QH
0117 925 6014

Vibrant Spanish tapas, freshly prepared, pan-flash cooked food, served in a bright and informal atmosphere with cosmopolitan flare. A venue not to be missed.

FISHERS SEAFOOD RESTAURANT
Seafood

35 Princess Victoria Street, Clifton, Bristol, BS8 4BX
0117 974 7044

Having established itself in Oxford, this maritime seafood restaurant provides a quirky, welcoming ambience for its fresh, unfussy, distinctly flavoured dishes.

GANESHA AUTHENTIC INDIAN CUISINE
Indian

54-56 Bedminster Parade, Bedminster, BS3 4HS
0117 953 3990

This Bristol-based Indian restaurant prides itself on the imaginativeness of its menu, moving away from curry house staples with piquant, authentically Indian recipes.

GEORGE INN
British

High Street, Norton St Philip, Bath, BA2 7LH
01373 834 224

A relaxed inn that places its emphasis on good food and drink, and on a hospitable welcome for all, whether it be for a drink, a coffee, a bite for lunch, a languid dinner or a more prolonged stay.

Offer excludes Sunday lunch and Christmas menus

HOMEWOOD PARK HOTEL
British

Abbey Lane, Hinton Charterhouse, Bath, BA2 7TB
01225 723 731

Taste double AA rosette-rated English cuisine at this graceful country house hotel. The technique, flair and imagination which goes into each dish is self-evident in both taste and presentation.

Booking is essential.

HOPHOUSE
British

16 Kings Road, Clifton, Bristol, BS8 4AB
0117 923 7390

A vibrant pub situated in a lovely, lively area of Bristol. Take advantage of an excellent array of quality food and fine beers, with enough choice to cater for every guest.

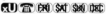

Offer excludes Sunday lunch and Christmas menus

HOTEL DU VIN
European

Sugar House, Narrow Lewins, Mead, Bristol, BS1 2NU
0117 925 5577

The finest, freshest local produce, simple European recipes, a stunning choice of wines; these are the elements of the trademark Hotel du Vin bistro. A magnificently restored Bristol venue. 1 AA Rosette.

JAMUNA INDIAN CUISINE
Indian

9-10 High Street, Bath, BA1 5AQ
01225 464 631

A classic combination of knowledge, tradition and unique experience. Guests are offered sophisticated fine dining with effortlessly charming staff, discreet service and tantalising food.

KASHMIR
Indian

15 High Street, Easton, Bristol, BS5 6DL
0117 952 0004

A popular eatery serving classic and regional dishes from the foothills of the Himalayas. Curries are divided into spice levels for both the initiated and newcomers, and all can expect a real Indian feast.

KRISHNA'S INN
Indian

4 Byron Place, Triangle, South Clifton, Bristol, BS8 1JT
0117 927 6864

Owned by the largest South Indian restaurant chain in England, here you can expect high quality cuisine prepared by incredibly experienced chefs. A menu so wonderful it has fans lining up at the door.

SOUTH WEST

LA FLAMENCA RESTAURANT
Spanish

12A North Parade, Bath, BA2 4AL
01225 463 626
Enjoy fine Spanish tapas and other classic dishes in an authentic environment, which plays host to a warm and hospitable atmosphere. Dine in the restaurant or at the tapas bar for a lighter meal.

LIME RESTAURANT @ HOMEWOOD PARK
English and Continental

Abbey Lane, Hinton Charterhouse, Bath, BA2 7TB
01225 723 731
Two AA Rosettes in recognition of the technique, flair and imagination of the dishes. Head Chef Daniel Moon, designs the menus, taking great pride in everything he creates and serves for guests. Sublime.

LOCH FYNE
Seafood

24 Milsom Street, Bath, BA1 1DG
01225 750 120
From the roadside oyster bar that once was, Loch Fyne restaurants now successfully inject energy and passion into great food and wonderful flavours, whilst ensuring their seafood is sustainably sourced.

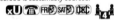

LOCH FYNE
Seafood

The Granary, 51 Queen Charlotte St, Bristol, BS1 4HQ
0117 930 7160
From the roadside oyster bar that once was, Loch Fyne restaurants now successfully inject energy and passion into great food and wonderful flavours, whilst ensuring their seafood is sustainably sourced.

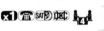

MARCO'S RISTORANTE LTD
Italian

59 Baldwin Street, Bristol, BS1 1QZ
0117 926 4869
With a menu that combines clear, fresh-to-the-palate flavours and fulsome, rich meats and sauces, this welcoming, cosy restaurant is a hidden gem in the centre of Bristol.

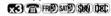

MARHABA BISTRO
Moroccan

611 Fishponds Road, Fishponds, Bristol, BS16 6AA
0117 965 0752
Specialised Moroccan cuisine with heavy influence from the Mediterranean. Authentic ingredients are used to create truly superb dishes offering a unique experience for an enjoyable and special evening.

MERCURE BRIGSTOW HOTEL
European

Ellipse Restaurant, 4 Welsh Back, Bristol, BS1 4SP
0117 929 1030
One of the premier places to dine out on the popular Welsh Back, renowned for a stylish atmosphere with an ever-changing menu that reflects the seasons. Only the finest, freshly cooked food is served.

MEZZALUNA RESTAURANT
Italian

7A Kingsmead Square, Bath, BA1 2AB
01225 466 688
Imaginative flavours to accompany smooth, tasty home-made pasta in this centrally located Italian restaurant with a great sense of hospitality; the restaurant takes especial pride in its silky panna cotta.

MUMTAZ RESTAURANT
Indian

7 St Mary Street, Bristol, BS35 2AB
01454 411 764
If classic and flavoursome is what you're looking for then this popular Indian restaurant is for you. Exceptional service, good quality food and a warm atmosphere underpins its popularity.

MUMTAZ RESTAURANT
Indian

61 High Street, West-On-Trym, Bristol, BS9 3ED
0117 950 3084
Skilled chefs cook traditional recipes to perfection, producing classic dishes that are bursting with aromatic flavours and smack of authenticity. A critically acclaimed fine Indian dining experience.

MUSET
English and Continental

16 Clifton Road, Bristol, BS8 1AF
0117 973 2920
The welcoming atmosphere paves the way to a splendid night enjoying fine English and Continental dishes in a stylish setting. The walls are decoratively lined with the artwork of local artists.

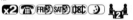

NO 5 RESTAURANT
French

5 Argyle Street, Bath, BA2 4BA
01225 444 499
One of Bath's most popular independent restaurants. Passionately committed to producing traditional values of French cuisine, freshness and tastiness are never absent.

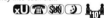

NO.4 RESTAURANT & BAR, RODNEY HOTEL
Classic French/ English

4 Rodney Place, Clifton, Bristol, BS8 4HY
0117 973 5422
Resembling a cosy Georgian property, the modern art displays provide the otherwise classically traditional interior with a modern vibrant feel. British and French flavours find their way into each dish.

OAKWOOD AT THE PARK
British

The Park Hotel & Golf Resort, Wick, BS30 5RN
0117 937 1800
In this beautiful, striking Jacobean manor house, the Head Chef uses a wood-stone oven to make fabulous, trademark dishes. The home-made breads and decadent desserts are an especial delight.

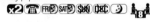

OH CALCUTTA
Indian

216 Cheltenham Road, Bristol, BS6 5QU
0117 924 0458
Fresh ingredients and loving preparation makes the food here extremely tasty. A local favourite, the high-quality food and exceptional service make this an extremely popular Indian restaurant.

ONE FISH TWO FISH
Seafood

10 North Parade, Bath, BA2 4AL
01225 330 236
Exquisite seafood finely cooked and prepared. Closely resembling the cellars of a beautiful French château, this evocative restaurant has a restful ambience that ensures a sublime dining experience.

54

Sign up to our newsletter for latest restaurants, offers and more

ORCHID RESTAURANT
Oriental
81 Whiteladies Road, Bristol, BS8 2NT
0117 973 2198
A true taste of the Orient in the South West. Head to the restaurant's noodle bar where dishes from Singapore will set your night alight, while the à la carte menu offers many delicious delights.

RIVER GRILLE
British
The Bristol Hotel, Prince Street, Bristol, BS1 4QF
0117 923 0333
A light, airy quayside restaurant within a luxurious hotel, delivering wholesome hand crafted dishes using the finest ingredients such as fresh fish, juicy steak, and divine West Country cheeses.

PLANET PIZZA
Pizza
83 Whiteladies Road, Clifton, Bristol, BS7 8BG
0117 907 7112
Planet Pizza is a vibrant restaurant serving out-of-this-world pizzas and heavenly salads, all in a contemporary and friendly setting.

ROMA TRATTORIA
Spanish
91 Regent Street, Kingswood, Bristol, BS15 8LJ
0117 961 9311
A strikingly classy interior and a vibrant bar scene make this a wonderful place to enjoy excellent food. Dishes are imaginatively infused with a Latin zest making each and every choice a great one.

PLANET PIZZA
Pizza
187 Gloucester Road, Bishopston, Bristol, BS7 8BG
0117 944 4717
Planet Pizza is a vibrant restaurant serving out-of-this-world pizzas and heavenly salads, all in a contemporary and friendly setting.

RUSTIC VINE
European
157-159 St Michael's Hill, Bristol, BS2 8DB
0117 973 5937
A consistent and cosy Bristol haunt that spends its days as a quietly buzzy café, and its nights as a candlelit, comely restaurant. From hours spent over a coffee to a hearty pie dinner, it duly delivers.

RACKS BAR AND KITCHEN
English and Continental
St. Paul's Road, Clifton, Bristol, BS8 1LX
0117 974 1626
In a building bursting with character, this is the perfect place to eat, drink and be merry. Diners can sample the tasty English and continental dishes whilst enjoying the fine selection of beverages.

SANDS RESTAURANT
Lebanese
95 Queens Road, Clifton, Bristol, BS8 1LW
0117 973 9734
Allow the tempting aromas to excite you as you step into this stylish oasis of a restaurant. You'll be more than satisfied by the tasty recipes and the very best ingredients that go into each dish.

RED LION
British
Bath Road, Woolverton, Bath, BA2 7QS
01373 830 350
A traditional pub delivering flavoursome, home-cooked food and delicious local beers all day long. Enjoy food and drink in the wonderful garden area in summer, or by roaring log fires in the winter.

Offer excludes Sunday lunch and Christmas menus

SEVERNSHED
Mediterranean
The Grove, Bristol, BS1 4RB
0117 925 1212
A lovely, harbour-side restaurant coupled with a buzzing atmosphere, highly regarded in the area. Simply fantastic food and service, offering diners a delicious, varying menu.

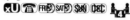

REDWOOD HOTEL & COUNTRY CLUB
British
Beggar Bush Lane, Failand, Bristol, BS8 3TG
01275 393 901
Visit this lovely Brook Hotel and enjoy a fine dining experience with a modern twist. Try gourmet dishes in a relaxed atmosphere, or indulge in a little intimacy in one of the elegant private dining rooms.

SPICE OF INDIA
Indian
13 Small Street, Bristol, BS1 1DE
0117 929 9222
Incredible value for money can be found at this brilliant Indian restaurant. Unusual yet tasty dishes such as curried salmon with home-made chutney have guaranteed this restaurant an admirable reputation.

RICE & THINGS JAMAICAN RESTAURANT
Caribbean
120 Cheltenham Road, Bristol, BS6 5RW
0117 9244832 / 07890 627749
Offering an array of dishes prepared and cooked in the traditional Jamaican way, this restaurant brings together people from across the city, encouraging them to celebrate all things Caribbean.

STRADA
Italian
Beau Nash House, Sawclose, Bath, BA1 1EU
01225 337 753
Modern and stylish Italian restaurant that is nevertheless rooted in the homely traditional flavours of its cuisine; aiming at authenticity, Strada sources its produce carefully and cooks them classically.

RENATOS NUMERO UNO
Italian
203 Whiteladies Road, Bristol, BS8 2XT
0117 974 4484
A restaurant that consistently offers exquisite Italian food and charmingly attentive service. Everything from the pasta sauces to the pizza doughs are freshly made on the premises.

THAI EDGE BRISTOL
Thai
Unit 4 Broad Quay, South Block, Bristol, BS1 4DA
0117 927 6088
Every dish combines a unique array of herbs, roots and spices such as galangal and krachai to create a subtle blend of flavours. The authentic Thai cuisine will have you coming back for more.

SOUTH WEST

55

THE BAY BAR AND KITCHEN
European
4-6 North Street, Bedminster, Bristol, BS3 1HT
0117 953 1446
Try this warm, contemporary restaurant in Bristol for thoroughgoing British and modern European food, from Angus to lamb shank, brie tart to Greek salad.

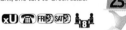

THE BURGER JOINT
American
32 Cotham Hill, Bristol, BS6 6LA
0117 3290 887
A contemporary restaurant that has its sights set on changing the perception of burgers as mere fast food. Here, you'll get finely cooked burgers of all stripes, with a range of flavour combinations.

THE FOOD HUT
European
Golden Acres, 35 Clevedon Road, Tickenham, BS21 6RA
01275 853 050
Known for its exciting and adventurous menus, the Food Hut Café experiments with many different genres and styles, offering light lunches, snacks, and drinks from fresh weekly menus.

After first visit, discount applies only to food.

THE GARDENERS ARMS
British
35 Silver Street, Cheddar, BS27 3LE
01934 742 235
Retaining many features of the original building built circa 1560, The Gardener's Arms delivers quality traditional British cuisine, including melt-in-the-mouth pies and snug, warming soups.

THE LIVING ROOM
British
Harbourside, 11 Canon's Way, Bristol, BS1 5LF
0117 925 3993
Step into The Living Room and you can count on the savvy, distinctive neighbourhood vibe that plays home to eclectically drawn, supremely tasty cuisine. Ease back in the limpid light of this Bristol haunt.

Must purchase min. of 3 courses per person, inc. main.

THE OLIVE TREE
British
The Queensberry Hotel, 4 Russel Street, Bath, BA1 2QF
01225 447 928
This double AA Rosette-winning restaurant serves wonderful modern British cuisine in a friendly ambience. Experienced Head Chef Paul Burrows draws on an eclectic range of influences in his superb dishes.

THE RUMMER HOTEL
Modern British
All Saints Lane, Bristol, BS1 1JH
0117 929 0111
Whatever you fancy to eat, head here for a choice of hot and cold dishes for breakfast through to supper. Emphasis is placed on the hearty seasonal British fare with a little continental panache thrown in.

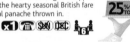

THE STAR AND DOVE
British
78 - 78 St Lukes Road, Bristol, BS3 4RY
0117 300 3712
Simple but stylish, this pub restaurant serves imaginative and accomplished contemporary British cuisine; warm and rich dishes marked by their clarity of flavour and clean, elegant presentation.

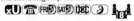

TILLEYS BISTRO
French / European
3 North Parade Passage, Bath, BA1 1NX
01225 484 200
A popular, bijou little bistro that serves up warm and rich cuisine, specialising in French dishes. Try the bitoke roquefort for a delicious, if a little decadent, combination of flavours and textures.

YAK YETI YAK
Nepalese
12 Pierrepont Street, Bath, BA1 1LA
01225 442 299
Experience the rich culinary history of Nepal as this restaurant takes you back centuries with its delicious blend of flavours. The Nepalese chefs focus on the meaning of authentic, natural food.

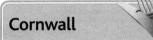
Cornwall

BARCLAY HOUSE
Fine Dining
St. Martins Rd, Looe, PL13 1LP
01503 262 929
Magnificent river views are the perfect counterpart to the delightful Cornish coastal cuisine. Highlights are Looe Day-Boat fish matched with Camel Valley wines from nearby Bodmin. Awarded 1 AA Rosette.

BOTTREAUX RESTAURANT
British
Camelford Road, Boscastle, PL35 0BG
01840 250 231
A spacious, airy restaurant that provides an atmospheric setting for a memorable evening. Although specialising in succulent steaks and sauces, many other dishes are equally superb.

FISTRAL BLU
Locally Sourced
Fistral Beach, Headland Road, Newquay, TR7 1HY
01637 879 444
A serene, surf vibe in this beachfront restaurant; the bright dining room catches gorgeous sunsets, while the food is wholesome, broad-ranging and well-conceived.

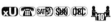
Excludes August.

FOWEY HALL HOTEL - HANSONS
Fine Dining
Hanson Drive, Fowey, PL23 1ET
01726 833 866
Fowey Hall is an experience to enjoy. Hanson's fine dining restaurant holds the 2 coveted AA Rosettes and is an opportunity to relax and unwind over high-quality local produce cooked to perfection.

Booking is essential.

INDIAN OCEAN
Indian
Fore Street, Bosney Road, Tintagel, PL34 0DB
01840 779 000
Experience delightful delicacies and mouth-watering cuisine in an enchanting atmosphere. Using recipes that come directly from India, the chefs prepare and present truly original and delicious Indian food.

Visit the website regularly to discover the latest restaurants joining the GS

LAMP LIGHTER RESTAURANT
British

Fore Street, Probus, Truro, TR2 4JL
01726 882 453
Taking the finest produce from both land and sea, the kitchen makes extensive use of the freshest ingredients available to ensure every dish is delicious. The restaurant has gained two AA Rosettes.

MANOR HOUSE INN
Modern British

Rilla Mill, Callington, Cornwall, PL17 7NT
01579 362 354
An enchanting rural inn that features some of the best Cornish produce and delivers exquisite modern British cuisine. Indulge in Michelin-rated food whilst sampling the hand-picked selection of fine wines.

MORRELLS BISTRO
British

Higher Market Street, East Looe, PL13 1BW
01503 263 604
A cosy bistro that focuses on putting a fresh twist on classic British dishes. Imaginative combinations of flavours and generous helpings combine with a warm ambience for an excellent meal.

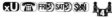

PAUL AINSWORTH AT NO 6
British

6 Middle Street, Padstow, PL28 8AP
01841 532 093
Quality dining where customer experience and value for money is the key feature. Delicious British cuisine served by diligent staff in a beautifully converted Georgian town house. Awarded 2 AA Rosettes.

During Summer Season (June-Oct.) also open Sundays.

PREZZO
Italian

The Old Post Office, The Moor, Falmouth, TR11 3QA
01326 314 564
With a character all of its own, Prezzo oozes contemporary style and enduring charm. Signature pastas, stone-baked pizzas and classic Italian dishes promise a perfect dining choice for the whole family.

ROCK ISLAND BISTRO
Mediterranean

Alexandra Road, Porth, TR7 3NB
01637 877 271
A delightful family-run restaurant catering for all palates and appetites. The beautiful riverside location provides a tranquil and relaxing environment in which you can enjoy fabulous food and fine wines.

TAVISTOCK ARMS HOTEL
International

Fore Street, Gunnislake, PL18 9BN
01822 832 217
Take refuge in a picturesque Cornish village and allow this charming restaurant to provide an intriguingly tasty menu and a ranging drinks selection. A warm welcome and pleasurable visit guaranteed.

THE BAY RESTAURANT
European

Britons Hill, Penzance, TR18 3AE
01736 366 890
Enjoy magnificent views across Mount's Bay as you indulge in divine European cuisine. The knowledgeable waiting staff will help you choose from the many regional and modern dishes. 2 AA Rosettes.

THE CHAINLOCKER & SHIPWRIGHTS
Modern British

Quay Street, Falmouth, TR11 3HH
01326 311 085
Outstandingly fresh seafood is the base ingredient at this pub restaurant, part of the Best of British group. On the seafront, the tang of the sea-air gives an edge to the fish and your pint of local cask.

THE CORMORANT RESTAURANT
European

Golant, Fowey, Cornwall, PL23 1LL
01726 833 426
Immerse yourself in the scenery and peruse the fine à la carte menu that makes use of the best Cornish fish, meat, cheese and other produce. Also offers a large variety of choice wines.

THE JOURNEYMAN
Multi-Cuisine

Mellingey Mill, Mellingey, St Issey, PL27 7QU
01841 540 604
Choose from over 50 dishes that have been specially selected from the world's finest cuisines. Long summer nights and cosy winter evenings can enjoyably be spent here, whatever your party size.

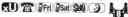

Devon

ANGEL OF WITHERIDGE
European

The Square, Witheridge, EX16 8AE
01884 860 429
An award-winning restaurant situated in the heart of Devon. The mouth-watering European cuisine ensures its popularity.

ASIA CHIC
Thai

East Quay House, Plymouth, PL4 0HX
01752 263 758
A concept simply described as exotic Asian cuisine, Chinese dim sum, wok and Japanese sushi are all served tapas-style, to be shared and enjoyed in a stylish setting. Refined and unforgettable dining.

BALTI KING
Indian

5 Ticklemore Street, Totnes, TQ9 5EJ
01803 868 095
A terrific Indian restaurant perfect for a quiet evening out. Alternatively, take your delicious dishes home with you and take delight in familiar comforts as you enjoy your feast.

BED RESTAURANT
Mediterranean

42 Bretonside, Plymouth, PL4 0AU
01752 252 555
Take a trip to Bed, only not in the way you know it. Vibrant Mediterranean and French cuisine is served in generous portions, to be enjoyed in the restaurant's chilled ambience.

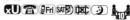

SOUTH WEST

BIANCO'S RISTORANTE *Italian*
38 Torwood Street, Torquay, TQ1 1EB
01803 293 430
Enjoyment of fine Italian cuisine and wines is of utmost importance here. The proprietor Mauro gives a warm welcome to all; those celebrating a special occasion are in excellent hands.

July and August excluded.

BICKLEIGH MILL BISTRO *British*
Bickleigh Mill, Bickleigh, Tiverton, EX16 8RG
01884 855 419
A rural shopping, eating and recreation destination is found within an 18th century working water mill. The homely bistro caters for shoppers looking to refuel through to intimate diners.

BISTRO 67 *British*
67 Fore Street, Totnes, TQ9 5NJ
01803 862 604
Hearty meals and epic desserts. An inviting atmosphere can be enjoyed as soon as the warm welcome greets you at the door. Bistro-style dishes are tenderly prepared by a highly experienced chef.

BISTRO ONE *Bistro*
68 Ebrington Street, Plymouth, PL4 9AQ
01752 313 315
This hidden gem in one of Plymouth's memorable districts is sure to guarantee a good time, delivering dishes that surprise and delight, all locally sourced to ensure the best of flavours.

BLACKBERRIES *British*
19 Fore Street, Bampton, Tiverton, EX16 9ND
01398 331 842
Part of the distinct attractiveness of the local area, this family-run establishment not only looks exceptional, but also offers fantastic food and personal service that will guarantee maximum enjoyment.

BLACK HORSE INN *British*
Old Honiton Road, Sowton, Exeter, EX5 2AN
01392 366 649
A pub-restaurant that has re-opened following a comprehensive, fantastic refurbishment, The Black Horse offers an extensive range of beers, fresh and fabulous food and fine wines in a relaxed atmosphere.

Offer not avail Sunday lunch or on Christmas menus.

CAFÉ ASIA *Pan Asian*
46 The High Street, Totnes, TQ9 5SQ
01803 868 803
Café Asia proudly captures new Asian tastes that provide the well-travelled diner with culinary delights from the Far East. Those new to Asian cuisine will be blown away by exotic treats.

CAFÉ ROUGE *French*
24 Bedford Street, Princesshay, Exeter, EX1 1GJ
01392 251 042
An attractive restaurant, a boulevard café or a Parisian-style wine bar; however you see Café Rouge, consistently excellent classic French dishes are always guaranteed.

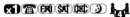

CAFÉ ROUGE *French*
11 Whimple St, St Andrews Close, Plymouth, PL1 2DH
01752 665 522
An attractive restaurant, a boulevard café or a Parisian-style wine bar; however you see Café Rouge, consistently excellent classic French dishes are always guaranteed.

CAFECINO PLUS *Bistro*
25 Mill Street, Bideford, EX39 2JW
01237 473 007
The quality of West Country meats and produce can be tasted in the superb home-cooked food offered in this swell restaurant. Allow the smooth sounds of jazz to ease you into a food lover's paradise.

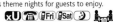

CHURCHILLS RESTAURANT *British*
The Elfordleigh Hotel, Colebrook, Plympton, PL7 5EB
01752 336 428
Leave the world behind as you indulge in a well-deserved break. Try your hand at golf, go for a swim or treat yourself to a facial in the Hotel spa. The restaurant holds theme nights for guests to enjoy.

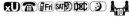

CILANTRO *Indian*
75 Torquay Road, Paignton, TQ3 2SE
01803 664 626
This tasteful and stylish restaurant offers a delicate and contemporary take on Indian cuisine. The friendly staff and fine food deliver a pleasurable experience that is hard to beat.

CINNAMONS *Authentic Indian*
10 South Street, Axminster, EX13 5AD
01297 631 175
Warm and down-to-earth Indian restaurant in Axminster which successfully brings together dishes from different parts of the subcontinent. They've an especial line in creamy, rich Makhani and Xakuti dishes.

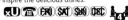

COAL GRILL + BAR *Mediterranean*
18 Bedford Street, Exeter, EX1 1GJ
01392 420 070
This restaurant is known for fresh, delectable food and captivating cocktails. Executive Chef Antonio Dias has combined his Mediterranean roots and passion for cooking to inspire the delicious dishes.

Not to be used with any other offer or the Prix Fixé menu

ELEPHANT RESTAURANT *Contemporary*
3-4 Beacon Terrace, Torquay, TQ1 2BH
01803 200 044
Michelin-starred gourmet dining from exceptional, acclaimed Head Chef Simon Hulstone; a sublime seafront restaurant amongst the burgeoning culinary scene of the English Riviera.

FISH ON THE HARBOUR *British*
1 Riverside Road, Lynmouth, EX35 6EX
01598 753 600
Bright and airy space in this beautiful seaside location for classic, fresh, delicious fish and chips as well as neat, sophisticated seafood dishes.

When booking restaurants always mention your GS membership

FRENCHS COSMOPOLITAN BISTRO
European
Combe House, Fore Street, Chulmleigh, EX18 7BR
01769 580 023
Wholesome, full-bodied French-style bistro food in this warm, friendly and accommodating Devon restaurant.

HARRY RAMSDEN'S
British
Junction 30 Sandygate Roundabout, Exeter, EX2 7HF
01392 446 559
Feast on the classic combo of fish and chips, cooked to perfection by this great British institution. The food can always be relied upon here, so relax and enjoy a true taste of the seaside.

Not available during August or in takeaway.

HARRY'S GRILL BAR
European
6 Northernhay Place, Bailey Street, Exeter, EX4 3QJ
01392 438 545
Delivering their own brand of dining, this bar-grill offers a host of great-tasting food, including delicious home-made ice creams, breads and beautifully cooked, well-presented classic dishes.

ELLIOT'S @ HOLIDAY INN PLYMOUTH
International
Armada Way, Plymouth, PL1 2HJ
01752 639 900
Gaze out over Plymouth Sound from 11th-floor Elliot's Restaurant, where a breakfast buffet of sausage and eggs and a delicious dinner menu is served. Snacks are served in the bar next door.

Only one card can be used per table.

ILFRACOMBE
Indian
13-14 High Street, Ilfracombe, EX34 9DF
01271 866 453
A unique and modern dining venue where chefs demonstrate the ability to craft and serve an exquisite array of Bangladeshi and Indian cuisine. Experience fine Eastern food in a sophisticated atmosphere.

INN @ THE GROSVENOR
British
Belgrave Road, Torquay, TQ2 5HG
01803 294 373
Bringing guests comfort and warmth in a friendly atmosphere, this venue delivers traditional food made from fresh West Country produce, to be complemented by a selection of real ale and fine wine.

KITLEY HOUSE HOTEL & RESTAURANT
Fine Dining
Kitley House, Plymouth, PL8 2NW
01752 881 555
In acres of lovely countryside, this stately restaurant does a fine line in everything from cream teas to saddle of lamb, with its attention to local produce thoughtfully prepared and presented.

LA ROSETTA
Italian
High Street, Newton Poppleford, EX10 0DW
01395 568 136
A fine Italian restaurant housing a kitchen driven by passion for food and a team of staff committed to its diners. Dishes are impressively prepared and cooked in a traditionally authentic Italian way.

MIAHS INDIAN RESTAURANT
Indian
12 Victoria Parade, Torquay, TQ1 2BB
01803 292 851
First-class Indian food and service. The menu is a joy to behold, yielding traditional and modern dishes all cooked to perfection by top chefs. Excellent food with an ambience that adds to the experience.

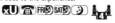

NUTWELL LODGE HOTEL
Carvery
Exmouth Road, Exeter, EX8 5AJ
01392 873 279
Enjoy the best of British food at this Great British Carvery venue. An inviting pub that once belonged to Sir Francis Drake, dining here will undoubtedly leave you feeling like a conquering hero.

Call beforehand for special event days.

OLD ORLEANS
American
Barbican Leisure Park, Coxside, Plymouth, PL4 0LG
01752 256 470
An extraordinarily accurate taste of the Deep South can be found in this unique restaurant. The kitchen deals in classic Louisiana and Cajun recipes such as jambalaya and gumbo to create an exciting menu.

Not available on Bank Holiday weekends. Adult menu only.

ON THE STEPS
British
Church Steps, Lynton, EX35 6HY
01598 753 614
An outstanding restaurant serving fine British cuisine such as steak with horseradish cream, halibut with chorizo and tomato sauce, and crème brûlée. Each and every dish tastes as good as it sounds.

POOPDECK RESTAURANT
Seafood
14 The Quay, Brixham, TQ5 8AW
01803 858 681
A little quayside restaurant whose speciality, naturally, is seafood, offering sublimely fresh fish, superbly cooked to bring out the subtle texture and flavours of each variety.

POPPLEFORDS
British
Exeter Road, Newton Poppleford, EX10 0DE
01395 568 672
A great local restaurant serving fantastic British dishes for all to enjoy. Guests can happily while away an evening in a relaxed environment.

PREZZO
Italian
202 High Street, Exeter, EX4 3EB
01392 477 739
With a character all of its own, Prezzo oozes contemporary style and enduring charm. Signature pastas, stone-baked pizzas and classic Italian dishes promise a perfect dining choice for the whole family.

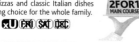

PREZZO
Italian
38-39 The Strand, Exmouth, EX8 1AH
01395 269 409
With a character all of its own, Prezzo oozes contemporary style and enduring charm. Signature pastas, stone-baked pizzas and classic Italian dishes promise a perfect dining choice for the whole family.

SOUTH WEST

59

PREZZO
Italian

96 High Street, Barnstaple, EX31 1HS
01271 376 310
With a character all of its own, Prezzo oozes contemporary style and enduring charm. Signature pastas, stone-baked pizzas and classic Italian dishes promise a perfect dining choice for the whole family.

PREZZO
Italian

1 Vaughan Parade, Torquay, TQ2 5EG
01803 389 525
With a character all of its own, Prezzo oozes contemporary style and enduring charm. Signature pastas, stone-baked pizzas and classic Italian dishes promise a perfect dining choice for the whole family.

ROCCO Y LOLA
Spanish

East Quay House, Sutton Harbour, Plymouth, PL4 0HX
01752 224 711
Allow this irresistible Spanish tapas to transport you to the ultra stylish dining bars of northern Spain. Local produce is interwoven with scrumptious Spanish staples such as chorizo and Serrano ham.

SAFFRON
Indian

104 Queen Street, Newton Abbot, TQ12 2EU
01626 363 963
With its great food and friendly, inviting atmosphere, this restaurant is extremely popular and enjoys an admirably varied clientèle. Successfully caters for meat lovers and vegetarians alike.

SAILS RESTAURANT
International

22 South Embankment, Dartmouth, TQ6 9BB
01803 839 281
A tranquil haven offering the most delectable of dishes. Local fish is used to create divine and delicious meals, whilst an enticing wine list provides a suitable beverage whatever the chosen dish.

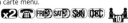

SAMPSONS FARM RESTAURANT
Fine Dining

Sampsons Restaurant, Newton Abbot, TQ12 3PP
01626 354 913
Experience spectacularly wonderful Devon food in the most charming of places. Relax by the log fires as you indulge in pre-dinner canapés or eat from the ever-popular à la carte menu.

STEPS BISTRO
European

1A Fleet Street, Torquay, TQ1 1BX
01803 200 770
Friendly, good vibrations kind of a bistro that serves fresh fish from local waters, mouth watering entrées and delicious home made desserts, not to mention some silky sauces and gorgeous, juicy burgers.

THAI IN THE PARK
Thai

32 Commercial Road, Plymouth, PL4 0LE
01752 205 010
The Thai chefs here successfully create some superbly delicious, authentic cuisine. If you love Thai food, in all its freshness, colour and eclecticism, then this is the perfect choice.

THE BABA INDIAN RESTAURANT
Indian

17 Bretonside, Plymouth, PL4 0BB
01752 250 677
There is something very homely about this Indian restaurant; you can count on being well treated and well fed, with their plethora of classic curry dishes cooked swiftly, freshly and to superb effect.

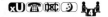

THE COACHMANS REST
European

London House, Broadclyst, Exeter, EX5 3ET
01392 461 472
At the heart of a National Trust village with a menu that changes to reflect the seasons, bringing with it fresh produce. Superb home-made food served in a pleasant atmosphere.

THE COURTYARD RESTAURANT
Modern European

South Street, Woolacombe, EX34 7BB
01271 871 187
Highly skilled and experienced chef Noel Corston sources top-quality produce to craft elegant dishes and present diners with uncluttered flavours. A relaxed and serenely stylish atmosphere tops things off.

THE DUKE OF CORNWALL HOTEL
European

Millbay Road, Plymouth, PL1 3LG
01752 275 850
Elegant, extravagant, and famous for its grand design; the food, influenced by West Country produce, has a clear emphasis on quality and freshness. All to be enjoyed in the warm and inviting atmosphere.

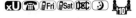

THE FISH MARKET
Saefood

Pinnacle Quay North, Sutton Harbour, Plymouth, PL4 0BN
01752 665325
The delicious menus here are written daily based on the morning's catch and served, fresh, that same day. If not fish, choose from a selection of succulent local meat, chicken and vegetarian dishes.

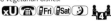

THE GALLEY RESTAURANT
Fish and Seafood

41 Fore Street, Topsham, Exeter, EX3 0HU
01392 876 078
This venue brings a contemporary twist and unique style to their seafood dishes, which are exotic, healthy, and touched with elegance. The restaurant is run by celebrity Master Chef Paul Da Costa Greaves.

THE GANDHI
Indian

4a Parkside Road, Paignton, TQ4 6AE
01803 551 166
Smart and serious but very convivial Indian restaurant in Paignton that looks to distinguish itself in the quality of its ingredients and preparation. Enjoy a delicious meal in, or partake of the takeaway.

THE GEORGE INN
Fresh Fish/Pub Classics

Main Street, Blackawton, Totnes, TQ9 7BG
01803 712 342
Tucked away in a lovely little Devon village, you'll enjoy a warm welcome at The George. For locals and visitors alike, this is your first port of call for a superbly ranging menu of fulsome, tasty food.

Enjoy massive leisure and retail savings with more Gourmet Society

THE LAMB INN
Longdown, Exeter, EX6 7SR
01392 811 711
European

A tantalising selection of food that will satisfy every appetite. The ever-changing menu draws always on fresh produce; their home-made soups, pâtés and salads are top notch.

THE NESS
Ness Drive, Shaldon, Teignmouth, TQ14 0HP
01626 873 480
European

The temptingly fresh aromas of morning coffee initiate the start of the day at this elegant Georgian pub. After having your daily kick-start, indulge in a casual lunch as you take in the unmissable views.

THE ROYAL OAK INN
Station Road, South Brent, TQ10 9BE
0136 472 133
Modern European

The small peaceful Dartmoor village of South Brent is home to this award-winning local inn, where terrific ales and restaurant-quality food at pub prices can be found. Great cooking by talented chefs.

Closed Mondays.

THE SEA TROUT INN
Staverton, Totnes, TQ9 6PA
01803 762 274
Modern British

Top-notch modern British cuisine in this classically homely Devon inn. Beautifully set, in an area that supplies the vast majority of the restaurant's fresh produce, you'll be tickled by its cosy charm.

THE SEVEN STARS
13 Mill Street, Kingsbridge, TQ7 1ED
01548 852 331
Contemporary

Firm and versatile modern British cuisine; interesting chef's specials as well as some tasty traditional favourites. Flaky, creamy fish pie or a zingy fajita, you'll be well oriented with the Seven Stars.

THE SOUK
Pinnacle Quay, Sutton Harbour, Plymouth, PL4 0BJ
01752 221 111
Moroccan

A tiny piece of Morocco is recreated in this intimate eatery. A glorious kaleidoscope of marketplace tastes and colours influence the eastern-flavoured tapas-style servings.

THE STEAK HOUSE
Searock Apts, Wilder Road, Ilfracombe, EX34 9AR
01271 879 394
Fine Dining

Thorough, juicy and rambunctiously flavoured steaks constitute the base; neat little starters and intriguing global touches can be enjoyed in this pretty little restaurant near the harbour in Ilfracombe.

THE VINE
Radway Place, Sidmouth, EX10 8TL
01395 519 494
Fine Dining

The use of West Country free range produce makes every dish as deliciously heavenly as each other. Even the most demanding palate will be far from disappointed at this marvellous restaurant.

ZUCCA
Discovery Wharf, Sutton Harbour, Plymouth, PL4 0RB
01752 224 225
Italian

Spend your afternoon lunching or enjoy an al fresco dinner as you watch the gently swaying masts in Plymouth marina. Otherwise, step in from the cold and enjoy their marvellous Italian-based food.

Dorset

AVON CAUSEWAY HOTEL
Avon Causeway, Hurn, Christchurch, BH23 6AS
01202 482 714
British

This beautiful, traditional, four-star hotel is home to a restaurant serves a wholesome, broad array of classic pub grub. Settle back and enjoy a Cask Marque-credited Wadworth ale to wash it all down.

Offer excludes Sunday lunch and Christmas menus

BALTI ISLAND
191 Chiswell, Portland, DT5 1AP
01305 822 822
Indian

A great local restaurant providing tasty Indian cuisine to a regular crowd of customers. Guests will be greeted with a warm welcome and served with a smile.

BANGKOK PALACE
313 Charminster Road, Bournemouth, BH8 9QP
01202 528 882
Thai

A little piece of Thailand on the south coast boasting probably the most extensive vegetarian Thai menu available anywhere. Care is taken to present authentic, healthy food with spices customised to taste.

CAESAR'S BISTRO
15 Dunyeats Road, Broadstone, BH18 8AA
01202 694 343
British

With an impressive array of awards and an enviable reputation, this restaurant offers a nicely varied menu and delicious daily specials. Al fresco dining can be enjoyed in the wonderful outside courtyard.

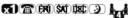

CAFÉ ROUGE
67-71a Seamoor Rd, Bournemouth, BH4 9AE
01202 757 472
French

An attractive restaurant, a boulevard café or a Parisian-style wine bar; however you see Café Rouge, consistently excellent classic French dishes are always guaranteed.

CHILLIES
10 Queen Street, Weymouth, DT4 7HZ
01305 766 602
Indian

Warmly recommended by local diners, Chillies in Weymouth serves up delectable Indian dishes, not only fixed on the old favourites but with some more expansive and intriguing alternatives.

61

CIAO
Italian

144 Old Christchurch Road, Bournemouth, BH1 1NL
01202 555 657
This restaurant offers a variety of Italian and Mediterranean cuisine in a modern and stylish setting. With fresh, seasonal ingredients imported from Italy they offer a great menu and daily specials.

CLIFFHANGER CAFE
British

Waterford Road, Highcliffe, Christchurch, BH23 5JA
01425 278 058
Delicious food and outstanding views are guaranteed to take your breath away. Enjoy breakfast, lunch or an evening meal with the intimate company of another or a large celebratory party.

CORIANDER RESTAURANT
Mexican

22 Richmond Hill, Bournemouth, BH2 6EJ
01202 552 202
With a vibrant and fun atmosphere, Coriander offers a light siesta menu and traditional Mexican meals. Its unique décor with cacti, sombreros and traditional woven blankets offer an authentic experience.

COYOTE UGLY
European

The Waterfront Complex, Bournemouth, BH2 5AA
08700 111 960
Part of Jongleurs comedy clubs, Coyote Ugly offers a mouth-watering selection of platters, gourmet burgers and pizzas complemented by some of the best comedy around for a fantastic time.

CROWN HOTEL
European

8 West Street, Blandford Forum, DT11 7AJ
01258 456 626
Gastronomic menu in a classic, elegant English coaching house: try a silken Stargazy Pie or the tender roast monkfish, washed down with one of their deep, golden cask ales.

CYGNETS RESTAURANT
Classic British/ French

Weymouth College, Cranford Ave, Weymouth, DT4 7LQ
01305 208 979
Support the talented chefs of the future at this terrific on-site restaurant. Wonderful dishes are prepared by chefs-in-training, guaranteeing guests a first-class dining experience.

DYLAN'S
British

Courtyard Craft Centre, Huntick Rd, Poole, BH16 6BA
01202 631 030
All day breakfasts, home-made lunches and the finest cream teas too good to feel guilty about can all be enjoyed in this family-run restaurant. Ideally located in the Courtyard Centre.

FRAMPTON ARMS
British

Hurst Road, Moreton, Dorchester, DT2 8BB
01305 852 253
Hardy Country is the perfect home for this traditional family-run inn which sits across from the old railway station in Moreton village. It serves creative, well-conceived menus in a welcoming atmosphere.

HARRY RAMSDEN'S
British

Undercliffe Drive, East Beach, Bournemouth, BH1 2EZ
01202 295 818
World famous fish and chips from a British institution. Enjoy classic seaside food: from crisp batter to golden chips, nobody does it quite like Harry Ramsden's.

Not available during August or in takeaway.

HIGHCLIFF GRILL
Mediterranean

Marriott, 105 St Michaels Rd, West Cliff, B'mouth, BH2 5DU
01202 200 800
1 AA Rosette testifies to the quality of this Dorset hotel restaurant where the fresh breath of sea air and expansive views complement the accomplished, clear flavours of their dishes.

HOTEL DU VIN
European

Thames Street, the Quay, Poole, BH15 1JN
01202 785 570
The finest, freshest local produce, simple European recipes, a stunning choice of wines; these are the elements of the trademark Hotel du Vin bistro. A fine eatery with 1 AA Rosette.

INDIAN OCEAN
Indian

4 West Cliffe Road, Bournemouth, BH2 5EY
01202 311 222
A premier destination for authentic Indian cuisine prepared by expert chefs, providing diners with a variety of tastes and aromas from across India. Both classics and specialities will delight your palate.

LA BRASSERIE
Italian

73/75 Commercial Road, Lower Parkstone, Poole, BH14 0JB
01202 734 009
An informal, comfortable and spacious restaurant and bar offering mouth-watering Italian and Mediterranean dishes. Guests can expect genuine home-cooked food made from the finest Italian ingredients.

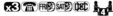

LA GONDOLA RESTAURANT
Italian

9-10 Lansdowne House, Christchurch Rd, BH1 3JP
01202 558 079
Bearing his extensive experience and masterful expertise, owner Luca arrived at La Gondola to provide diners with the most phenomenal Italian dining experience and cuisine.

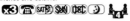

LA STALLA
Italian

270A Wallisdown Road, Bournemouth, BH10 4HZ
07703 055 175
La Stalla provides an amiable atmosphere that offers exquisite cuisine in a home away from home. Whilst a warm ambience will completely relax you, the food will have you jumping for joy.

LA TRATTORIA
Italian

10-12 High Street, Swanage, BH19 2NT
01929 423 784
An array of Italian treats bursting with flavour are on offer at this intimately small evening restaurant. Local crab and lobster make tremendous dishes for the avid seafood fan.

Recommend a friend to the Gourmet Society and receive a free gift.

LEE ORIENTAL RESTAURANT — *Chinese*
34 High West Street, Dorchester, DT1 1UP
01305 756 088
Enjoy traditional Chinese and Oriental cuisine. An extensive array of dishes, from classics to specialities, all filled with their own unique mouth-watering flavours and fragrant aromas.

 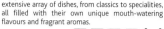

LITTLE INDIA RESTAURANT — *Indian*
244 Old Christchurch Road, Bournemouth, BH1 1PF
01202 317 117
An Indian restaurant that delivers quality-made dishes and attentive service. The menu is filled with classics and adventurous spice-laden options for the more daring guest.

LOCH FYNE — *Seafood*
Sea Witch Hotel, 47 Haven Rd, Canford Cliffs, Poole, BH13 7LH
01202 609 000
From the roadside oyster bar that once was, Loch Fyne restaurants now successfully inject energy and passion into great food and wonderful flavours, whilst ensuring their seafood is sustainably sourced.

 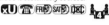

MAGNUMS — *Modern British*
20 Post Office Road, Bournemouth, BH1 1BA
01202 558 399
That little bit of luxury for breakfast, lunch and dinner, or just a well-deserved drink. Outstanding service in a stylish setting with a tasty menu full of British and American classics.

MA'S PIZZA & PASTA — *Italian*
87 High Street, Poole, BH15 1AH
01202 678 600
Tucked away in Poole, Ma's is a coffee shop restaurant that feels like a cosy retreat, and offers an excellent range of italianate dishes, full and mellow flavours, and superbly decadent desserts.

MONKBERRY'S — *European*
36-40 Poole Hill, Soho Quarter, Bournemouth, BH2 5PS
01202 291 533
A classic bar and brasserie with a stylish modern twist, a real neighbourhood joint. A place to meet your friends for a snack, a long lunch, a cosy dinner or just a drink at the bar.

OCEAN BAY RESTAURANT — *British*
2 Ulwell Road, Swanage, BH19 1LH
01929 422 222
Situated in the picturesque town of Swanage, this fabulously modern restaurant offers wonderful views to be enjoyed while you savour the fantastic food - whether you arrive by land or by sea.

OLD GRANARY — *European*
The Quay, Wareham, BH20 4LP
01929 552 010
A talented team of chefs now operate under the roof of this old grain store. An indulgent menu offers traditional dishes and adventurous Mediterranean cuisine.

OLIVE BRANCH — *European*
East Borough, Wimborne, BH21 1PF
01202 884 686
Once believed to be the home of an infamous 19th century smuggler, this traditional pub serves wholesome, flavourful food and offers a range of fabulous wines to suit all tastes and pockets.

PACIFIC 23 — *International*
75 Mudeford, Mudeford, Christchurch, BH23 3NJ
01202 485 105
An attractive menu offering traditional pub food and tasty Thai cuisine. This popular bar offers both set and à la carte menus which present dishes such as spicy king prawns or delicious duck.

PIZZA STEAK HOUSE — *Italian*
2 Drakes Way, Broad Street, DT7 3QP
01297 444 788
An outstanding choice of heavenly pizzas and local steaks of the finest quality, as well as other delectable Mediterranean dishes. The emphasis is on quality food at a sensible price.

Not available during August.

PREZZO — *Italian*
56 St Thomas Street, Weymouth, DT4 8EQ
01305 787 600
With a character all of its own, Prezzo oozes contemporary style and enduring charm. Signature pastas, stone-baked pizzas and classic Italian dishes promise a perfect dining choice for the whole family.

DETAILED DESCRIPTIONS AVAILABLE ON
www.gourmetsociety.co.uk

PREZZO — *Italian*
Purbeck House, 5 West Borough, Wimborne, BH2 1LT
01202 881 119
With a character all of its own, Prezzo oozes contemporary style and enduring charm. Signature pastas, stone-baked pizzas and classic Italian dishes promise a perfect dining choice for the whole family.

PREZZO — *Italian*
Judge Jeffreys, 6 High West St, Dorchester DT1 1UJ
01305 259 678
With a character all of its own, Prezzo oozes contemporary style and enduring charm. Signature pastas, stone-baked pizzas and classic Italian dishes promise a perfect dining choice for the whole family.

PREZZO — *Italian*
43 East Street, Blandford Forum, DT11 7DX
01258 489 625
With a character all of its own, Prezzo oozes contemporary style and enduring charm. Signature pastas, stone-baked pizzas and classic Italian dishes promise a perfect dining choice for the whole family.

PREZZO — *Italian*
3 Bridge Street, Christchurch, BH23 1DY
01202 496 100
With a character all of its own, Prezzo oozes contemporary style and enduring charm. Signature pastas, stone-baked pizzas and classic Italian dishes promise a perfect dining choice for the whole family.

2FOR1 MAIN COURSE

PREZZO — *Italian*
58 Westover Road, Bournemouth, BH1 2BZ
01202 556 399
With a character all of its own, Prezzo oozes contemporary style and enduring charm. Signature pastas, stone-baked pizzas and classic Italian dishes promise a perfect dining choice for the whole family.

2FOR1 MAIN COURSE

QUATTRO GATTI — *Italian*
11 East Street, Blandford Forum, DT11 7DU
01258 451 955
Quattro Gatti serves authentic, mouth-watering Italian cuisine just as you would find it in the heart of Italy. Truly exquisite dishes, the superb flavours drawn out with the use of fine produce.

2FOR1 MAIN COURSE

RAJPOOT RESTAURANT — *Indian*
43 High West Street, Dorchester, DT1 1UT
01305 257 492
Exclusive and exciting Indian restaurant in Dorchester, looking to move a degree beyond the classic British Indian dining scene. Its cool, calm atmosphere hosts some scintillating, imaginative dishes.

25% OFF TOTAL

SAMBUCA RESTAURANT — *Italian*
324 Wimborne Road, Winton, BH9 2HH
01202 515 105
Secret family recipes and tasty unique dishes are cooked up in the kitchen at this exquisite Italian restaurant. Allow the sumptuous dishes to tantalise your taste buds and leave you more than satisfied.

25% OFF TOTAL
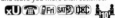

SENSE — *European*
46 St Mary Street, Weymouth, DT4 8PU
01305 777 222
Offers fantastic European dishes in a warm and friendly atmosphere. The carefully selected wines, the deliciously satisfying food and the accommodating staff make every experience here a special occasion.

25% OFF TOTAL

SPYGLASS INN — *Carvery*
Bowleaze Coveway, Overcombe, DT3 6PN
01305 833 141
A fine member of the Great British Carvery group offering the best of British food. A great team of staff provide warm welcomes in this pleasant pub that boasts marvellous views of the Channel.

2FOR1 MAIN COURSE

Call beforehand for special event days.

ST PETER'S FINGER — *British*
Dorchester Road, Lytchett Minster, Poole, BH16 6JE
01202 622 275
Unique by name, this inn delivers scrumptious food, award-winning beers, and unbeatable hospitality to every one of its guests. All ingredients are regionally sourced, even their delicious ice cream.

25% OFF TOTAL

STATUE HOUSE — *Spanish*
109 St Mary Street, Weymouth, DT4 8PB
01305 830 456
Delicious, authentic Spanish tapas with an emphasis on healthy, home-cooked food. They offer a great selection of classic Spanish dishes that all can be enjoyed in one sitting, as well as chef's specials.

25% OFF TOTAL

THE ANGEL INN — *British*
Ringwood Road, Longham, Wimborne, BH22 9AP
01202 873 778
A classically English pub serving fine cask ales and freshly cooked food at affordable prices. The owners focus on the maintenance of the traditional village pub by providing a warm homely atmosphere.

25% OFF TOTAL

THE BALTI HOUSE — *Indian*
865 Christchurch Road, Bournemouth, BH7 6AT
01202 422 634
Creative and thoughtful full-flavoured balti dishes in this traditional, unpretentious and friendly Indian restaurant situated in the heart of Boscombe.

2FOR1 MAIN COURSE

THE BRASSERIE — *French*
9 West Street, Wareham, BH20 4JS
01929 556 061
A sophisticated high street eatery offering guests sumptuous menus throughout the day. The perfect venue for a cup of fresh ground coffee, all the way through to intimate fine dining.

25% OFF TOTAL

OSCARS RESTAURANT — *British*
De Vere Royal Bath Hotel, Bath Rd, Bournemouth, BH1 2EW
01202 555555
The Royal Bath is a grand Victorian hotel with panoramic views out over the Channel. Named for Mr. Wilde, a regular visitor to the Royal, Oscars is a place that stands for consistency and quality.

NEW
2FOR1 MAIN COURSE

Ask for other Gourmet Society member offers

THE EYE OF THE TIGER — *Indian*
207 Old Christchurch Road, Bournemouth, BH1 1JZ
01202 780 900
Established venue that offers a range of gourmet Indian and Bangladeshi dishes, its speciality being the 'Tiger Special'. Large capacity, and renowned for once cooking the biggest curry in the world.

2FOR1 MAIN COURSE

THE FOX INN — *British*
Ansty, Dorchester, DT2 7PN
01258 880 328
A traditional and relaxing atmosphere complements the imaginative menu. Fine, fresh, local produce is used to create all the dishes, and the restaurant is versatile to cater for individual dietary needs.

2FOR1 2COURSES

THE GREYHOUND INN — *British*
The Square, Corfe Castle, Wareham, BH20 5EZ
01929 480 205
Shipped straight from the bay, the vast range of seafood on offer here is guaranteed to be fresh, locally sourced, and deliciously flavoursome. Exquisite afternoon Dorset cream teas can also be enjoyed.

25% OFF TOTAL

Discounted hotel rates for GS members on our website

THE RISING SUN GASTRO PUB
British
1 Dear Hay Lane, Poole, BH15 1NZ
01202 771 246
A light modern pub that draws on continental influences, whilst also retaining a traditionally friendly atmosphere. Classic pub meals as well as more adventurous dishes are all on offer.

THE SPICE CENTRE
Indian
37-38 High West Street, Dorchester, DT1 1UP
01305 267 450
Great Indian cuisine is served at The Spice Centre, where dishes of all spice levels are on offer. Friendly staff are happy to cater to your every need.

THE SPRINGHEAD
European
Sutton Road, Sutton Poyntz, Weymouth, DT3 6LW
01305 832 117
Beautifully and intimately tucked away beneath the chalk downs, this village pub provides the warmest of welcomes. The freshest of food can be enjoyed all year round, from light bites to hearty meals.

VIA VENETO
Italian
Salterns Harbourside Hotel, 38 Salterns Way, Poole, BH14 8JR
01202 707 321
The panoramic sea views that accompany the outstanding contemporary Italian cuisine will leave you wanting to come back here over and over again. Perfect for that special occasion.

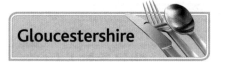

Gloucestershire

CAFÉ ROUGE
French
31 - 41 The Promenade, Cheltenham, GL50 1NW
01242 529 989
An attractive restaurant, a boulevard café or a Parisian-style wine bar; however you see Café Rouge, consistently excellent classic French dishes are always guaranteed.

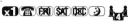

COLESBOURNE INN
British
Colesbourne, Cheltenham, GL53 9NP
01242 870 376
Fine real ales, long drinks, wines by the glass as well as extensive wine list, the Colesbourne Inn has lots to tempt you. You can count on something good, whether it be a light bite or a fantastic feast.

Offer excludes Sunday Lunch and Christmas menus

COTSWOLD SPICE
Bangladeshi/ Indian
A429 Fosse Way, Rowborough, GL56 9RE
01608 661 920
Presenting the cutting edge in fine dining in the area, this restaurant has a modern style that retains a traditional ethic, with highly experienced chefs creating various Indian fusion and classic dishes.

D-FLY BAR AND RESTAURANT
Thai/British
Clarence Street, Cheltenham, GL50 3NX
01242 246 060
Combine business with pleasure in this inviting yet discreet bar and restaurant, perfect for business meetings and lunches. Alternatively, pop in for a coffee with friends for that well-deserved break.

GRILLE RESTAURANT
Turkish
49 Winchcombe Street, Cheltenham, GL52 2NE
01242 771 444
A lively restaurant serving traditional dishes from this delicious cuisine. Let the warmth of the open fire envelop you and relax into the great food, drink, service and décor.

HASSAN'S
Indian
37 Bath Road, Cheltenham, GL53 7HG
01242 226 229
A venue satisfying the need of the more sophisticated diner, being awarded several prestigious industry accolades for quality of food and service. Modern dining with a certain sense of exclusivity.

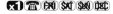

HOTEL DU VIN
European
Parabola Road, Cheltenham, GL50 3AQ
01242 588 450
The finest fresh local produce, simple European recipes, a stunning choice of wines; these are the trademark of a fine Hotel du Vin bistro. This venue boasts a cigar shack for the aficionado. 1 AA Rosette.

MY GREAT GRANDFATHERS
Contemporary
84 Church Street, Tewkesbury, GL20 5RX
01684 292 687
A modern restaurant set against the historical backdrop of the medieval town of Tewkesbury. Here you'll find British food with a delightful exotic twist. The Thai-style lobster fish cakes are heavenly.

NOEL ARMS HOTEL
Thai/British
High Street, Chipping Campden, GL55 6AT
01386 840 317
Whatever your appetite, the wonderfully varied menu will cater for you. A promising array of dishes are on offer which are all cooked with flair and imagination by a talented kitchen.

RESTAURANT AT THE HOTEL
British
38 Evesham Road, Cheltenham, GL52 2AH
01242 518 898
The location will set you on your way towards a good and lovely mood; that's even before you dip into the cool waters of the fine-dining menu, with its vivid, clean and accomplished recipes.

À la carte menu only

PREZZO
Italian
46 Southgate Street, Gloucester, GL1 2DR
01452 414 022
With a character all of its own, Prezzo oozes contemporary style and engaging charm. Signature pastas, stone-baked pizzas and classic Italian dishes promise a perfect dining choice for the whole family.

PREZZO
Italian

1 The Brewery, Henrietta St, Cheltenham, GL50 4FA
01242 227 703
With a character all of its own, Prezzo oozes contemporary style and enduring charm. Signature pastas, stone-baked pizzas and classic Italian dishes promise a perfect dining choice for the whole family.

2FOR1
MAIN COURSE

PREZZO
Italian

99-101 The Promenade, Cheltenham, GL50 1NW
01242 524 437
With a character all of its own, Prezzo oozes contemporary style and enduring charm. Signature pastas, stone-baked pizzas and classic Italian dishes promise a perfect dining choice for the whole family.

2FOR1
MAIN COURSE

SOPHIE'S RESTAURANT
French

The Priory, 20 High Street, Stroud, GL6 9BN
01453 885 188
A popular family-run French restaurant serving simple, traditional cuisine that is high-quality, well-cooked, and affordable. Food accompanied by a carefully selected 100% French wine list.

2FOR1
2 COURSES

Only open lunchtimes and Saturday evenings.

SPICE LODGE
Thai/Indian

Montpellier Drive, Cheltenham, GL50 1TY
01242 226 300
Premier pan-Asian cuisine provides an exciting taste of the Orient. In a majestic setting chefs craft delicious, traditional food to delight and satisfy diners, providing a unique and luxurious experience.

2FOR1
MAIN COURSE

TATYAN'S
Chinese

27 Castle Street, Cirencester, GL7 1QD
01285 653 529
A select menu offering dishes with an emphasis on sumptuous taste and fresh, healthy ingredients. Authentic Chinese food, fine French wines and attentive service in pleasant surroundings.

25%OFF
TOTAL

TEWKESBURY PARK HOTEL
Modern British

Lincoln Green Lane, Tewkesbury, GL20 7DN
01684 295 405
Experience a variety of traditional English and classic European dishes, created with skill and passion from locally sourced produce, all within the restaurant of this fine Brook hotel.

25%OFF
TOTAL

THE COTSWOLDS 88 HOTEL
European

88 Room, Kemps Lane, Painswick, GL6 6YB
01452 813 688
Hotel-based restaurant with a bold amalgam of historic and hip; you'll enjoy the stunning views across the Cotswolds as you luxuriate in a finely cooked, well-realised, delicious meal.

2FOR1
MAIN COURSE

THE GARDENERS ARMS
British

Beckford Road, Alderton, GL20 8NL
01242 620 257
A friendly, family-run country pub and restaurant situated in a peaceful village. They serve home-cooked food that includes seasonal produce and local game bird. A popular meeting place in the area.

25%OFF
TOTAL

THE GREYHOUND
Modern Pub

Ashton Road, Siddington, Cirencester, GL7 6HR
01285 653 573
Home-cooked food, exciting specials, including market fish dishes, a wide range of real ales and choice of fine wines makes The Greyhound an excellent venue for warmth and hospitality. Family friendly.

25%OFF
TOTAL

Offer excludes Sunday lunch and Christmas menus.

THE HOLLOW BOTTOM
British

Guiting Power, Cheltenham, GL54 5UX
01451 850 392
Al fresco eating in the summer, cosy dining in the winter. Traditional British food served all day offering a relaxed atmosphere and fully stocked bar.

25%OFF
TOTAL

Offer not valid on champagne.

THE KINGS ARMS HOTEL
British

Market Square, Stow on the Wold, GL54 1AF
01451 830 364
With its award-winning Head Chef (Young Chef of the Future 2003) and its atmospheric setting, this versatile inn delights; try a stirling French onion soup with Welsh rarebit, or the quirky pheasant curry.

25%OFF
TOTAL

THE MALT HOUSE
Seafood/ Fine Dining/ Vegetarian

22 Marybrook Street, Berkeley, GL13 9BA
01453 511 177
Boasting a comfortable interior, tasteful furnishings and intimate, relaxing surroundings, this family hotel and restaurant offers delicious food and a great place to stay in the heart of the Cotswolds.

2FOR1
MAIN COURSE

THE QUEEN'S HOTEL
British

The Napier Restaurant, Cheltenham, GL50 1NN
08704 008 107
Overlooking the Montpelier Gardens, the restaurant may ooze glamour and style but the ambience is friendly and relaxed. The local cheeseboard – presented by a knowledgeable waiter – is highly recommended.

25%OFF
TOTAL

THE WYNDHAM ARMS
Modern British

The Cross, Clearwell, Coleford, GL16 8JT
01594 833 666
A hotel that is flush with rustic charm and sits among beautiful countryside surroundings. With a team of great chefs in the kitchen, the restaurant here makes the best of Gloucestershire's fine produce.

2FOR1
MAIN COURSE

THE YEW TREE
British

The Yew Tree, Cliffords Mesne, GL18 1JS
01531 820 719
A characterful old building plays host to this classic pub-restaurant whose menu takes the hearty classics and adds a contemporary inflection to each. Try out this glorious Gloucestershire outpost.

2FOR1
MAIN COURSE

WESLEY HOUSE RESTAURANT
European

High Street, Winchcombe, Cheltenham, GL54 5LJ
01242 602 366
An extremely popular restaurant; a treat whether for a light lunch or a romantic meal for two. Enjoy the open fire in the winter and the marvellous views from the Atrium in the summer. 2 AA Rosettes.

2FOR1
MAIN COURSE

Gourmet Society discount applies to the à la carte menu

Somerset

ALLERFORD INN
British

Norton Fitzwarren, Taunton, TA4 1AL
0182 346 1119

With an award-winning chef specialising in fresh fish, seafood and prime local cuts of meat seven days a week, diners are in for a real treat. Excellent service and atmosphere complement the quality food.

2FOR1 MAIN COURSE

ANTON'S BISTROT
British

The Crown at Wells, Market Place, Wells, BA5 2RP
01749 673 457

Overlooked by the magnificent Wells cathedral, this is an ideal place to rest, dine and drink after touring the surrounding attractions. Superb food served all day long.

25%OFF TOTAL

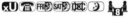

FLAVOURS
European

59 High Street, Wellington, TA21 8QY
01823 662 006

With a real emphasis on experimentation, Flavours produces intriguing, surprising and delicious combinations in its dishes.

25%OFF TOTAL

GEORGE HOTEL
British

Market Place, Frome, BA11 1AF
01373 462 584

A relaxed and friendly Frome hotel which offers delicious home-cooked food, fine wine and some great beers. Welcoming and hospitable, you're sure to enjoy a languid drink and a sumptuous dinner.

25%OFF TOTAL

Offer excludes Sunday lunch and Christmas menus

LOTUS FLOWER THAI
Thai

89/91 Station Road, Taunton, TA1 1PB
01823 324 411

Top-notch Thai cuisine that takes seriously the traditional value of balance in its recipes. The restaurant places emphasis on fresh, vibrant flavours for a range of different tastes.

25%OFF TOTAL

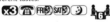

MILLERS AT THE ANCHOR
British

Porlock Weir, Porlock, Minehead, TA24 8PB
01643 862 753

Chef Andrew Clark brings a wealth of high-level experience as well as his enthusiasm; the fine dining on offer here is all about quality of produce, prepared simply and superbly.

2FOR1 MAIN COURSE

MULBERRYS
European

9 Union Street, Yeovil, BA20 1PQ
01935 434 188

Sample the outstanding quality of local meats available in this exceptional bistro. Specialising in grills and steaks, the kitchen proudly balances tasty and delicious food with healthy ingredients.

25%OFF TOTAL

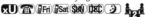

PREZZO
Italian

30 Cornhill, Bridgwater, TA6 3BY
01278 433 600

With a character all of its own, Prezzo oozes contemporary style and enduring charm. Signature pastas, stone-baked pizzas and classic Italian dishes promise a perfect dining choice for the whole family.

2FOR1 MAIN COURSE

PREZZO
Italian

25 Fore Street, Taunton, TA1 1JW
01823 339 233

With a character all of its own, Prezzo oozes contemporary style and enduring charm. Signature pastas, stone-baked pizzas and classic Italian dishes promise a perfect dining choice for the whole family.

2FOR1 MAIN COURSE

PREZZO
Italian

Old Sarum House, 49 Princes Street, Yeovil, BA20 1EG
01935 426 381

With a character all of its own, Prezzo oozes contemporary style and enduring charm. Signature pastas, stone-baked pizzas and classic Italian dishes promise a perfect dining choice for the whole family.

2FOR1 MAIN COURSE

RING O BELLS
Modern Pub

High St, Ashcott, TA7 9PZ
01458 210 232

A welcoming 18th century "free house" pub which has been family run for over 25 years. The quality of the home-cooked food as well as ales from local micro-breweries, has brought regional acclaim.

25%OFF TOTAL

SIGNATURE VICEROY
Authentic Indian

98 Middle Street, Yeovil, BA20 1NE
01935 426 210

Yeovil's Signature Viceroy warms the heart with its healthy portions of dazzlingly flavoured Indian dishes. It's accommodating and friendly, with a low-key thrum about it, and promises a good, tasty meal.

2FOR1 MAIN COURSE

THE BLACKBROOK TAVERN
Carvery

Ilminster Rd, Taunton, TA3 5LU
01823 443 121

One of the many Great British Carveries that offers the much loved classic dish with a modern twist. This 18th century tavern is a wonderfully pleasant venue to while an afternoon.

2FOR1 MAIN COURSE

Call beforehand for special event days.

THE FOUNTAIN INN & BOXER'S RESTAURANT
Bistro

1 St. Thomas Street, Wells, BA5 2UU
01749 672 317

The award-winning Fountain Inn & Boxer's Restaurant has a well-deserved reputation for superb quality food and an excellent choice of wine. Based on fine local produce, this home-cooked cuisine is a treat.

25%OFF TOTAL

THE FULL MOON AT RUDGE
British

Lower Rudge, Frome, BA11 2QF
01373 830 936

Classic pub-restaurant fare is to be found in this pretty coaching inn near Frome. Its food is sourced locally, in a good spirit of community it is cooked freshly and with skill, and is supremely hearty.

2FOR1 MAIN COURSE

SOUTH WEST

67

THE MILL AT RODE
British

Rode, Frome, BA11 6AG
01373 831 100
Whilst maintaining the external character and charm of its industrial past, this charismatic restaurant renders a more modern feel inside. Renowned for its great food and relaxed atmosphere.

THE PHEASANT INN
Italian

Wells Road, Worth, BA5 1LQ
01749 672 355
Allow the popular sublime cheesy black truffle sauce and fresh pasta tantalise your taste-buds and melt your heart. Tuscany stew is another firm favourite and challenges even the best English hotpot.

VICEROY INDIAN RESTAURANT
Indian

100 Middle Street, Yeovil, BA20 1NE
01935 421 758
Yeovil's Viceroy Indian Restaurant has a welcoming ambience, with something of a buzz about the place. They've an especial line in creamy, rich Makhani and Xakuti dishes.

2FOR1 MAIN COURSE

WINE & SAUSAGE
British

Corner House Hotel, Park Lane, Taunton, TA1 4DQ
01823 422 333
Following the success of the first Wine and Sausage, this Taunton restaurant follows suit with its unfussy but magnificent food, underpinned by a thorough investment in quality regional produce.

2FOR1 MAIN COURSE

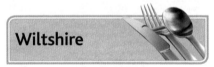

Wiltshire

CHISELDON HOUSE RESTAURANT
European

New Road, Chiseldon, Swindon, SN4 0NE
01793 741 010
Create happy memories of those special occasions in this splendidly opulent restaurant at Chiseldon House Hotel. Allow the intimate candlelight create a warm ambience around you as you enjoy your meal.

25%OFF TOTAL

FAT FOWL
European

Silver Street, Bradford on Avon, BA15 1JX
01225 863 111
Inviting restaurant with a ranging menu; specialises in vibrant tapas and fulsome mains. Also stages great live music.

25%OFF TOTAL

GASTROBISTRO
European

The Pheasant Inn, 19 Salt Lane, Salisbury, SP1 1DT
01722 414 926
Eclectic bistro-style cuisine, with fulsome, slow-cooked French classics like bouillabaisse and cassoulet, along with unfussy, succulent and seasoned burgers.

2FOR1 MAIN COURSE

Fri and Sat eve, offer applies between 6-8pm on orders of 2/3 courses, à la carte.

GEORGE INN
British

Sandy Lane, Chippenham, SN15 2PX
01380 850 403
The traditional frontage of this country pub near Chippenham draws you in; their ever-changing seasonal menu, featuring daily deliveries of fresh fish and locally reared meat, promises a beautiful dinner.

Offer excludes Sunday lunch and Christmas menus

HINTON GRANGE
British

Hinton Grange Hotel, Dyrham, Hinton, SN14 8HG
0117 937 2916
A wonderful, unique restaurant perfect for intimate and romantic dining. The cuisine and wine cellar are superb; dishes are served in front of a roaring fire, while everything on their menu is home-made.

HOX BRASSERIE
Indian

155 Fisherton Street, Salisbury, SP2 7RP
01722 341 600
A restaurant with a focus on South Indian food. The spices used in their dishes are traditional and authentic, and can truly be described as real, quality Indian food in a modern, contemporary environment.

2FOR1 MAIN COURSE

RECOMMEND A FRIEND

see page 18

LALBAGH INDIAN RESTAURANT
Indian

171 Rodbourne Road, Swindon, SN2 2AY
01793 535 511
Having reached the final of the National Curry Chef competition, the chef at Lalbagh is proud of the restaurant's status as a success, serving outstanding quality food.

25%OFF TOTAL

LAMBTONS RESTAURANT
British

The Bear Hotel, Market Place, Devizes, SN10 1HS
01380 722 444
A delicately decorated restaurant, where beautiful angelic dusky pinks and fresh whites are set against the classicism of dark leather and silver dining ware. Exquisite food prepared by talented chefs.

25%OFF TOTAL

LANSDOWNE ARMS
British

Derry Hill, Calne, SN11 9NS
01249 812 422
Built in 1843 this pub has outstanding views of the Avon Valley, so take a break from countryside walking and indulge in traditional British fare, washing it down with Wadworths and seasonal guest ales.

25%OFF TOTAL

Offer excludes Sunday lunch and Christmas menus

LANSDOWNE STRAND HOTEL
European

The Strand, Calne, SN11 0EH
01249 812 488
A glorious place to eat, drink and be merry. This 16th century hotel offers luxurious en-suite rooms as well as two bars and a bistro. Enticing open fires provide a warm welcome to guests and visitors.

25%OFF TOTAL

Sign up to our newsletter for latest restaurants, offers and more

MADISON HOTEL
Modern European

Oxford Road, Stratton Street, Margaret, Swindon, SN3 4TL
01793 831 333
A bright, modern restaurant from the Brook hotel group that offers diners comfort and style. The menu features classic European dishes such as smoked duck salad and pan-fried snapper. Lighter options are available for lunch.

PREZZO
Italian

52 High Street, Salisbury, SP1 2PF
01722 341 333
With a character all of its own, Prezzo oozes contemporary style and enduring charm. Signature pastas, stone-baked pizzas and classic Italian dishes promise a perfect meal.

PURPLE MANGO
Indian

1 Victoria Road, Swindon, SN1 3AJ
01793 526 161
A fusion of traditional and modern India finds its way into the cuisine and the décor at Purple Mango. The Head Chef heads a kitchen full of talent, where passion goes into creating every dish.

RAFU'S
Indian

22 High Street, Shrivenham, Swindon, SN6 8AA
01793 780 300
Delicately prepared and spiced food served within an intimate setting. Helpful staff guide diners through an accommodating menu that covers all tastes and preferences, including vegetarian options.

RAFU'S
Indian

29/30 High Street, Highworth, Swindon, SN6 7AQ
01793 765 320
Delicately spiced and prepared food served within an intimate setting. Helpful staff guide diners through an accommodating menu that covers all tastes and preferences, including vegetarian options.

GALLERY AT STANTON MANOR
European

Stanton Saint Quintin, Chippenham, SN14 6DQ
01666 837 552
Classic British cuisine overflowing with flavour, created by stunning seasonal produce and with flair worthy of their AA Rosette. Coupled with a beautiful backdrop, this makes for a fine dining experience.

THE CROWN INN, CHOLDERTON
British

Cholderton, Salisbury, SP4 0LR
01980 629 247
This delightful village pub was beautifully refurbished in 2006, has a picture-postcard thatched roof, and serves a top range of full-flavoured British fare and tasty bar snacks to go with your silky pint.

THE CROWN INN, ALVEDISTON
Traditional English Fare

Alvediston, Salisbury, SP5 5JY
01722 780 335
Appealingly selective menu shows this restaurant's keen investment in its dishes. The steak and kidney pudding is rich and sumptuous; the chef's fish pie warming and tender with a personal touch.

THE GEORGE AND DRAGON
British

High Street, Rowde, Devizes, SN10 2PN
01380 723 053
This award-winning restaurant specialises in seafood which is delivered daily, with the full menu boasting locally sourced meat and game dishes. Awards include 2 AA Rosettes and a Michelin recommendation.

THE SWAN
British

1 Church Street, Bradford on Avon, BA15 1LN
01225 868 686
A wonderful family-friendly pub situated in a beautiful listed building. Children can enjoy smaller portions of the freshly cooked dishes which are all made with the finest local ingredients.

ZEN
Chinese

109-111 Cricklade Road, Gorse Hill, Swindon,SN2 1AB
01793 486 223
Smart, up-to-date Chinese restaurant that serves up reams of well-seasoned, quality dishes. Lively and welcoming with a very attentive staff team, it is a great place to enjoy a good Chinese meal.

Guernsey/Jersey

L'HORIZON HOTEL (BRASSERIE & THE GRILL)
British

La Route de la Baie, St Brelade, Jersey, JE3 8EF
01534 743 101
Overlooking the beautiful bay in St. Brelade, this Hand Picked Hotels venue boasts The Grill, specialising in fresh, delicious local seafood, and a genial brasserie for tasty, informal eating. 2 AA Rosettes.

MENU BRASSERIE
Indian/Thai/ Chinese/ Traditional

Mallard Complex, Le Villiaze Rd, Guernsey, GY8 0HG
01481 264324
Menu Brasserie is the only restaurant on the wonderful Island of Guernsey offering top quality Chinese, Indian and pizzas all under one roof.

NEW

DETAILED DESCRIPTIONS AVAILABLE ON

www.gourmetsociety.co.uk

THE GARDEN @ ST. MARGARET'S LODGE
French

Forest Road, St Martin, Guernsey, GY4 6UE
01481 235 757
A wonderful retreat at the end of the day, this hotel-based restaurant offers a brilliant range of options. Making use of fresh local seafood and produce, its dishes keep the flavours clear and clean.

SOUTH WEST

South East

Such a large region as the South East has many flavours, from the coasts of Sussex and Hampshire to the chalk downs of Surrey and wide countryside of Berkshire and Buckinghamshire. This massive diversity in topography allows this region to benefit from some of the most varied produce in the UK. Delicious lobster and crab found in Selsey Bill, sparkling wines of Surrey, the renowned hops in Kent and Hampshire honey, produced by the hardest working bees in the country. Classic puddings, such as Eton Mess, famously concocted at Eton College is an example of a local dish which showcases very simply the high standard of the local produce it contains.

Yet authentic dishes from across the world can also be sampled within these borders; there is a long history of foreign influences in the region which heads back over the centuries. From across the Channel, the North Seas and more latterly the Commonwealth, people have settled bringing their cuisines and crops with them. The Home Counties' current dining out scene benefits hugely from this legacy and the ongoing cosmopolitan influence exerted by the capital. This creates a colossal collection of great restaurants offering a plethora of dining styles and flavours to savour.

This year we are considering all areas inside the M25 to be part of Greater London. Diners in the South East should also check the Greater London section so they do not miss out on any great restaurants.

Bedfordshire

LA CAMPANA
Italian

The Bell, Dunstable Road, Dunstable, LU6 2QG
01582 872 460
An excellent restaurant situated in idyllic countryside. The Sicilian-trained chef cooks up divinely tasty rustic Italian dishes full of intense rich flavours.

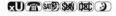

CHEZ JEROME
French

26 Church Street, Dunstable, LU5 4RU
01582 603 310
Award-winning chef serves contemporary French cuisine in this renowned restaurant. The staff combine culinary skill with a passion for European cuisine to create a magical blend of exciting menus.

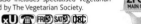

LUMPINI THAI RESTAURANT
Thai

105 High Street South, Dunstable, LU6 3SQ
01582 601 788
This traditional Thai restaurant offers fast, sumptuous lunches at a great price, as well as a vibrant, ranging menu for a relaxed dinner. To be enjoyed, with a welcoming atmosphere and excellent service.

COCONUT GARDEN
Thai

212 High Street North, Dunstable, LU6 1AU
01582 472 688
Indulge in the fragrant and exotic flavours of South-east Asian food. Delight in a traditional menu of favourites that also includes specialised vegetarian dishes recognised by The Vegetarian Society.

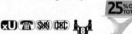

PEKING PALACE
Chinese

9 St Johns Street, Bedford, MK42 0AH
01234 272 727
Specialising in Peking and Cantonese cuisine, the food here is bursting with flavour after being created with the finest ingredients. Many dishes to choose from, with 100 appetising selections available.

EARL'S RESTAURANT
European

119 Dunstable Street, Ampthill, MK45 2NG
01525 404 024
Warm, homely bistro-style restaurant serving well-crafted dishes that combine flavours imaginatively.

Offer not available Wednesday eve.

RIOBELLO
Italian

6 St Mary's Street, Bedford, MK42 0PS
01234 364 430
Simply authentic Italian cuisine served in a beautiful location, combined with impeccable service and fine choice wines. Sample a true taste of Italy at the Riobello.

THE PLOUGH
British

Woodside Road, Woodside, Luton, LU1 4LU
01582 720 923
The Plough is a good, friendly pub. the menu is broad and offers a good range of very tasty, hearty pub classics. It's a family-friendly place, with a great garden and some quality ales on tap.

NEW

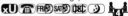

STAR AND GARTER
British

14/16 High Street, Silsoe, MK45 4DR
01525 860 250
In a gorgeous location, packed with history, this pub-restaurant serves seasoned and savoury home-cooked specialities, to be washed down with a fine pint of something starry-eyed.

FAJITAS MEXICAN RESTAURANT
Mexican

4 The Kings Arms Yard, Ampthill, MK45 2PJ
01525 404 303
Fine Mexican cuisine and drinks are served in the rather surprising yet wonderfully preserved home of a former workhouse. The interior is replete with original features that create intimate dining spaces.

THE BARNS HOTEL
European

Cardington Road, Bedford, MK44 3SA
01234 270 044
A sleek and stylish restaurant in this characterful hotel near Cannock Chase plays host to some modern classic dishes, cooked freshly to order. Kick back and enjoy the ranging menu.

FIGARO RESTAURANT
Italian

67 Commercial Road, Bedford, MK40 1QS
01234 211 411
A warm and welcoming ambience comes as standard at this traditional family-run restaurant. Offers a menu and specials selection to tempt everyone's taste buds, with choice wines to complement each dish.

THE BELL BEDFORD
British

2 Bedford Road, Marston Moretain, MK43 0ND
01234 768 310
Classic and homely local pub that serves real ales that will provide an accompaniment to the hale and hearty English fare served up by the kitchens; great meals of beef, you'll eat like wolves.

HARPURS
British

46 Tavistock Street, Bedford, MK40 2RD
01234 347 877
Let your taste buds run wild with freshly prepared foods, and enjoy a specially selected wine list in an atmosphere perfect for relaxation. Varied menus to cater for all tastes and budgets.

THE COCK INN
Carvery

26 High Street, Leighton Buzzard, LU7 0NR
01296 688 214
One of the many Great British Carveries that offers the well-loved classic with a modern twist. Enjoy the best of British food in this charming country inn situated in the most picturesque of villages.

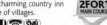

Call beforehand for special event days.

Gourmet Society discount applies to the à la carte menu

THE CROWN
British
2 High Street, Henlow, SG16 6BS
01462 812 433
A picturesque pub full of character with a hospitable and timeless atmosphere. Superb service delivering straightforward food produced using high-quality ingredients.

THE FANCOTT
British
Near Toddington, Luton, LU5 6HT
01525 872 366
A warm welcome awaits as diners enjoy great food in this traditional family pub. Food is available all day every day, with tasty grill options and unmissable fish dishes included on this hearty menu.

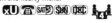

THE KNIFE AND CLEAVER
European
The Grove, Houghton Conquest, MK45 3LA
01234 740 387
A roaring log fire in winter and a wonderful garden ideal for summer evenings can be enjoyed in this warm welcoming pub. The Knife and Cleaver is a cracking English inn.

THE OLD SWAN
Modern British
58 High Street, Cheddington, LU7 0RQ
01296 668 226
A beauty of a higgeldy-piggeldy thatched pub whose home-cooked, eclectic recipes take in a number of different regional cuisines but all come up trumps with fresh, thorough and delicious flavours.

THE PARK
British
98 Kimbolton Road, Bedford, MK40 2PF
01234 409 305
Sample traditional favourites with a unique twist and pizzas from the stone-fired oven in surroundings expertly designed with harmony and comfort in mind. A striking restaurant serving great food.

THE RED LION
Contemporary
22 Market Square, Toddington, Dunstable, LU5 6BS
01525 872 524
Welcoming, unfussy and no-nonsense kind of a pub in this little market town; you'll enjoy a good range of guest ales, a warm and cosy ambience and a great line in down-home fresh food without fripperies.

RIVER ROOM AT THE BEDFORD SWAN
Modern British
The Embankment, Bedford, MK40 1RW
01234 346 565
This 18th century hotel is truly fabulous. Occupying a formidable location with spectacular views, this is a superb place to dine, drink, celebrate and stay.

THE WYVERN
British
Eaton Green Road, Luton, LU2 9HB
01582 480 090
Broad-based delicious eating in this sleekly contemporary pub-restaurant in Luton. From lustrous scampi to magnanimous duck salad, you'll enjoy a Wyvern that's more Paradiso than Inferno.

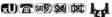

TOFF'S INDIAN LOUNGE
Indian
41 Wellington Street, Luton, LU1 2QH
01582 729 526
Step into the world of Toff's, where the fusion of both Bangladesh and India are incorporated into its Bengali cuisine. Here you will be amazed by the diversity and quality of the many different dishes.

TONG SAM
Oriental
84 High Street North, Dunstable, LU6 1LH
01582 666 880
A fantastic family-run establishment where the authenticity of the food proves to be more than satisfying. Experience delicious and flavoursome dishes from a variety of Asian countries.

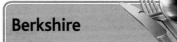

Berkshire

ACQUA
Modern British
Crowne Plaza Hotel, Richfield Ave, Reading, RG1 8BD
0118 925 9988
Dining at this double AA Rosette-winning hotel equates to a mix of contemporary elegance and stunning views across the River Thames. With a menu created to cater for all tastes, you're sure to remember it.

BEIJING RESTAURANT
Chinese
103 Old Wokingham Road, Crowthorne, RG45 6LH
01344 778 802
An enjoyable evening is guaranteed at this marvellous Chinese restaurant. Szechuan and Peking dishes make up a comprehensive à la carte menu, which offers over 170 dishes.

RECOMMEND A FRIEND
see page 18

BEL AND THE DRAGON
Modern European
Blakes Lock, Gas Works Road, Reading, RG1 3DH
0118 951 5790
A beautiful renovation blends classic architecture with modern décor, while the pub-restaurant delivers hearty but contemporary pub food. The wine list and tranquil riverside views only add to its appeal.

BEL AND THE DRAGON
British
Thames Street, Windsor, SL4 1PQ
01753 866 056
Situated in an ancient 11th century alehouse, the pub holds all the splendour and charm expected from such a location. The warm intimacy of the interior draws guests from far and wide.

SOUTH EAST

73

BEL AND THE DRAGON
British

High Street, Cookham, SL6 9SQ
01628 521 263
Toast your toes by the huge log fire in the winter or enjoy the charm of the enchanting garden during those warmer months. Deliciously fresh food to be enjoyed whatever the weather.

BENGAL REEF
Indian

8-11a The Walk, Reading, RG1 2HG
0118 956 8811
With a renowned attitude to modern Indian cuisine, usual suspects and lesser known classics collide as chefs create a treat for your palate, delivering diners a choice of many eclectic dishes.

BINA TANDOORI
Indian

21 Prospect Street, Caversham, Reading, RG4 8JB
0118 946 2116
An effective combination of good food and great service, this modern restaurant has many fans and offers a mix of both traditional Indian specialities and Anglicised dishes.

BROAD STREET TAVERN
English / Gastropub

29 Broad Street, Wokingham, RG40 1AU
0118 977 3706
This tavern is a local institution that sets itself at the heart of the community. Chilled, friendly and social, it serves an array of moreish pub classics that you can wash down with some fine cask ale.

CAFÉ ROUGE
French

Unit R16, The Oracle Centre, Reading RG1 2AG
0118 957 5223
An attractive restaurant, a boulevard café or a Parisian-style wine bar; however you see Café Rouge, consistently excellent classic French dishes are always guaranteed.

CAFÉ ROUGE
French

30 Market Place, Wokingham, RG40 1AP
0118 979 9128
An attractive restaurant, a boulevard café or a Parisian-style wine bar; however you see Café Rouge, consistently excellent classic French dishes are always guaranteed.

CAFÉ ROUGE
French

31-32 Royal Station Pde, Thames St, Windsor SL4 1PJ
01753 831 100
An attractive restaurant, a boulevard café or a Parisian-style wine bar; however you see Café Rouge, consistently excellent classic French dishes are always guaranteed.

CARNARVON ARMS
British

Winchester Road, Whitway, Newbury, RG20 9LE
01635 278 222
Sample quality food at good prices prepared by highly experienced chef Rob Clayton. Grasping a firm hold on the traditional country inn style, the kitchen offers simple yet sensational pub classic dishes.

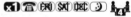

CROWN AND GARTER
British

Inkpen Common, Inkpen, Hungerford, RG17 9QR
01488 668 325
The experienced Head Chef creates exquisite classic dishes using the best local produce. They aim to provide a gastronomic experience with a traditional country inn décor and atmosphere.

EDEN BAR & RESTAURANT
Fine Dining

Wexham Park Lane, George Green, Slough, SL3 6AP
01753 896 400
AA Rosette-winning hotel-based restaurant with a stylish, contemporary feel. Freshly flavoured starters and robust, earthy mains characterise the menu.

GLO READING
Pan Asian

62-63 St Mary's Butts, Reading, RG1 2LG
0118 959 9025
Contemporary, casual eating. A place for guests to relax in style with good food and great company. With a delicious pan-Asian cuisine on offer, guests can unwind with their appetites truly satisfied.

CERISE @ THE FORBURY
Fine Dining

The Forbury Hotel, 26 The Forbury, Reading, RG1 3EJ
01189 527770
Cerise is a stylish brasserie - low-key, offbeat and contemporary. The menu is seasonal and accomplished, with a focus on modern British cuisine, with influences from around the world.

IVORY LOUNGE
Spanish

Unit 2, Grenfell Island, Maidenhead, SL6 1DY
01628 784 652
Passionate about providing every customer with the very best service, the staff offer an affable service whilst the kitchen creates dishes to die for. Evocatively atmospheric.

IVORY LOUNGE
European

Unit 5, Oracle Centre, Reading, RG1 2AG
01189 566 832
Whether it be a lazy lunch, a relaxing dinner, or a cheeky drink, this venue has it all. As day turns to night the candles are lit, the music increases, and this is truly a bar with style.

Excludes tapas.

KHUKURI
Nepalese

82 London Street, Reading, RG1 4SJ
0118 951 1881
Experience faithful versions of Nepalese and Thai classics that are fresh, healthy and delectable. A family-run restaurant that has offered authentic dishes of the highest quality since 1990.

LA BETTOLA
Italian

Old Bath Road, Colnbrook, Slough, SL3 0NZ
01753 681 600
Loved by its regulars, Raimondo Cagnino's restaurant sets its stall out to provide classic hospitality and the highest quality traditional Italian food. In the summer, it offers relaxed outdoor dining.

Sign up to our newsletter for latest restaurants, offers and more

LOCH FYNE
Seafood
The Maltings, Bear Wharf, Fobney St, Reading, RG1 6BT
01189 185 850
From the roadside oyster bar that once was, Loch Fyne restaurants now successfully inject energy and passion into great food and wonderful flavours, whilst ensuring their seafood is sustainably sourced.

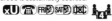

LOCH FYNE
Seafood
Plough, London Road, Wokingham, RG40 1RD
01189 123 260
From the roadside oyster bar that once was, Loch Fyne restaurants now successfully inject energy and passion into great food and wonderful flavours, whilst ensuring their seafood is sustainably sourced.

LOCH FYNE
Seafood
The Crispin, Windsor Road, Winkfield, Windsor, SL4 2DE
01344 894 760
From the roadside oyster bar that once was, Loch Fyne restaurants now successfully inject energy and passion into great food and wonderful flavours, whilst ensuring their seafood is sustainably sourced.

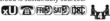

LSQ2 BAR AND BRASSERIE
European
220 South Oak Way, Reading, RG2 6UP
0118 987 3702
Twice recognised by the Michelin Guide, this urbane brasserie occupies a languid setting near to Reading and combines unfussy, flavourful dishes with a bright, inviting ambience and excellent service.

MALMAISON
European
18-20 Station Road, Reading, RG1 1JX
0118 956 2300
Relax in inimitable Malmaison style and savour deliciously contemporary brasserie dishes, whilst enjoying the marvellous surroundings of this newly refurbished, richly historical building. 1 AA Rosette.

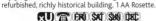

NELSONS DINER
American
Kingsclere Station, Newbury Rd, Kingsclere, RG20 4TA
01635 298 193
Experience the reality of an All-American-style diner in this wonderfully fun-filled restaurant. Dine alongside classic cars and Fifties-style memorabilia as you feast on burgers and thick-shakes.

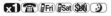

OCEAN VILLAGE
Indian
117 Bridge Road, Maidenhead, SL6 8NA
01628 638 129
Both local curry lovers and guests from further afield have professed admiration for the fantastic Indian cuisine on offer at this popular Maidenhead restaurant.

OLD ORLEANS
American
Unit 5, The Oracle Centre, Reading, RG1 2AG
0118 951 2678
An extraordinarily accurate taste of the Deep South can be found in this unique restaurant. The kitchen deals in classic Louisiana and Cajun recipes such as jambalaya and gumbo to create an exciting menu.

Not available on Bank Holiday weekends. Adult menu only.

PEACOCK FARM
British
Peacock Lane, Bracknell, RG12 8SS
0134 442 3481
A traditional, rustic open-plan interior where original beams and wood burners create a warm and welcoming environment. Wonderful home-made food features highly on the restaurant's list of attributes.

PREZZO
Italian
10-12 King Street, Reading, RG1 2HF
0118 959 6092
With a character all of its own, Prezzo oozes contemporary style and enduring charm. Signature pastas, stone-baked pizzas and classic Italian dishes promise a perfect dining choice for the whole family.

PREZZO
Italian
58 Cheap Street, Newbury, RG14 5DH
01635 31957
With a character all of its own, Prezzo oozes contemporary style and enduring charm. Signature pastas, stone-baked pizzas and classic Italian dishes promise a perfect dining choice for the whole family.

PREZZO
Italian
31 Broad Street, Wokingham, RG40 1AU
0118 978 5139
With a character all of its own, Prezzo oozes contemporary style and enduring charm. Signature pastas, stone-baked pizzas and classic Italian dishes promise a perfect dining choice for the whole family.

PREZZO
Italian
3 The Plaza, Denmark Street, Wokingham, RG40 2LD
0118 989 2090
With a character all of its own, Prezzo oozes contemporary style and enduring charm. Signature pastas, stone-baked pizzas and classic Italian dishes promise a perfect dining choice for the whole family.

QUEEN'S ARMS HOTEL
British
Newbury Road, Lambourn, RG17 7ET
01488 648 757
A beautiful country inn where staple dishes include beer-battered fish and rare-breed gammon steak. Enjoy delectable traditional snacks as well as meals, all home-made and locally sourced.

READING MOAT HOUSE
International
BW, Mill Lane, Sindlesham, Wokingham, RG41 5DF
0118 949 9988
By the banks of the Loddon, this hotel restaurant is modern and comfortable and offers a diverse range of breakfast, lunch and dinner options, inspired by modern international cuisines, for all the family.

Only one card can be used per table.

FRANCESCO'S MAIDENHEAD
Italian
73-75 King St, Maidenhead, SL6 1DU
01628 777815
In a restaurant where even the pizza dough is made at least twice a day, it's no surprise that the food is amazing. Enjoy delicious dishes in a style in keeping with the Italian way of life.
NEW

SOUTH EAST

75

FRANCESCO'S WINDSOR
Italian

53 Peascod Street, Windsor, SL4 1DE
01753 863773
In a restaurant where even the pizza dough is made at least twice a day, it's no surprise that the food is amazing. Enjoy delicious dishes in a style in keeping with the Italian way of life.

THE FIVE HORSESHOES
Modern British

Maidensgrove, Henley-on-Thames, RG9 6EX
01491 641 282
16th Century pub with brass, wrought iron, beams, burning fires, fine ales and excellent wines. Head chef Duncan Welgemoed is passionate about preparing high quality, traditional food with local produce.

SASSO
Italian

10-12 George St, Kingsclere, Newbury, RG20 5NQ
01635 297 446
A lovely local Italian restaurant offering a carefully fashioned menu. Succulent meat, fresh fish and creamy pasta dishes.

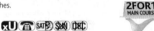

THE HARE RESTAURANT AND BAR
European

Ermin Street, Lambourn, Woodlands St Mary, RG17 7SD
01488 71 386
In an area of outstanding beauty, delivering fine dining with a tempting choice of traditional and contemporary cuisine. Carefully selected ingredients are used to create stunning dishes. 2 AA Rosettes.

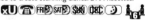

SHAHI
Indian/Nepalese

8 Wildriding Square, Bracknell, RG12 7SJ
01344 409 933
A wide range of flavoursome dishes are available in this wonderfully atmospheric Indian restaurant. Opt for your favourite Indian and Nepalese meal or try something exciting and new from the menu.

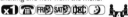

THE LONG WALK BRASSERIE
British

46 Kings Road, Windsor, SL4 2AG
01753 863 916
Adhering strictly to its philosophy which insists on fresh, seasonal dishes in an inviting atmosphere, this restaurant is always pleasing. A fine, exclusive wine will add the finishing touch to your meal.

SILSILA TANDOORI
Indian

100 Royal Avenue, Calcot, Reading, RG31 4UT
0118 941 7551
Lovely, well-established Indian restaurant with a real emphasis on the freshness of its ingredients and the depth of its flavours. Friendly, convivial and homely atmosphere for an enjoyable curry.

THE OLD BOOT INN
European

Stanford Dingley, Reading, RG7 6LT
0118 974 4292
A charmingly charismatic restaurant that boasts a deliciously tasty menu. Try the moules marinières for a scrumptious starter and the duck breast with cranberry sauce for a delectable main meal.

STANDARD TANDOORI
Indian/Nepalese

141-145 Caversham Rd, Reading, RG1 8AU
0118 959 0093
An attractive blend of Nepalese and Indian dishes occupy an extensive menu. The chefs make full use of the finest ingredients, and proudly grind their own herbs and spices to create unique flavours.

THE OLIVE TREE
British

BW West Grange, Bath Rd, Cox's Lane, Migham, RG7 5UP
01635 273 074
Allow the tranquil ambience to envelop you as you dine in a beautifully charismatic restaurant overlooking an enclosed courtyard. Dishes demonstrate their own modern interpretation of European cuisine.

THAI RIVER GARDEN AND GRILL
Thai

8-9 Church Street, Windsor, SL4 1PE
01753 832 757
Arm yourself with your own alcohol to accompany the famous Weeping Tiger steak or the popular Larb chicken salad. The cobble-stoned terrace and blackboard menus create a warm vibe.

THE PERSEVERANCE PUBLIC HOUSE
Locally Sourced

2 High Street, Wraysbury, TW19 5DB
01784 482 375
A charming example of traditional English hospitality. With a powerful combination of real ales, good food and a friendly welcome, this Wraysbury favourite can guarantee a pleasant evening out.

THE BLACK BOY
British

Shinfield Road, Reading, RG2 9BP
01189 883 116
Classic, fulsome English pub fare is served in this newly renovated, smart and accommodating traditional inn. Enjoy a hearty dinner from its full-flavoured menu, or a lighter meal earlier in the day.

THE SWAN INN
European

Newtown, Newbury, RG20 9BH
01753 862 069
When done right, there are few things to match a good pub meal; the Swan Inn does it perfectly. Succulent meats and beautifully fresh vegetables, a ranging menu and array of ales, it's a place to savour.

THE DUKE OF CONNAUGHT
British

165 Arthur Road, Windsor, SL4 1RZ
01753 840 748
Beautifully restored Victorian pub offering a contemporary and pleasant environment to dine throughout the seasons. High standards in food and service delivered with a great wine list and real ales.

THE VINEYARD AT STOCKCROSS
Fine Dining

Stockcross, Newbury, RG20 8JU
01635 528 770
A tantalising menu will alert your senses to innovative and exciting dishes that make the best use of fresh local produce. Experience a journey through appealing flavours and tastes. Awarded 4 AA Rosettes.

Visit the website regularly to discover the latest restaurants joining the GS

WATERLOO HOTEL
Traditional English Fare
Duke's Ride, Crowthorne, Bracknell, RG45 6DW
01344 467 900
Dine in style at the in-house Grove Brasserie at this Brook hotel, where you can enjoy a selection of contemporary dishes prepared using fresh local ingredients in a light and elegant dining room.

CAFÉ ROUGE
French
25-27 Station Road, Gerrards Cross, SL9 8ES
01753 880 601
An attractive restaurant, a boulevard café or a Parisian-style wine bar; however you see Café Rouge, consistently excellent classic French dishes are always guaranteed.

WINDSOR TERRACE
Thai
9 Thames Street, Windsor, SL4 1PL
01753 851 410
Enjoy lazy mid-morning breakfasts, post-sightseeing coffee and cake or an intimate evening meal at this relaxed family-friendly restaurant. The Thai menu offers a whole range of delights.

CALCUTTA BRASSERIE
Indian
7 St Pauls Court, Stony Stratford, MK11 1LJ
01908 566 577
By its use of a myriad of delectable tastes and flavours, this Indian brasserie reveals a culture that boasts a spectacular array of rich ingredients, spices and cooking styles.

CHEF IN WAITING (Milton Keynes College)
English and Continental
Bletchley Campus, Sherwood Drive, Milton Keynes, MK3 6DR
01908 637 373
Support the talented chefs of the future at this terrific on-site restaurant. Wonderful dishes are prepared by chefs-in-training, guaranteeing guests a first-class dining experience.

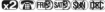

Buckinghamshire

ANNIE BAILEYS
British
Chesham Road, Great Missenden, HP16 0QT
01494 865 625
Enjoy a relaxing meal in the most comfortable surroundings. Sup a beer by the fire in winter or in summer months bask with a wine in hand in the beautiful, secluded courtyard. 1 AA Rosette.

EAT THAI
Thai
14 Easton Street, High Wycombe, HP11 1NT
01494 532 888
Authentic food originating from the royal kitchens of Thailand and served to the Thai Royal family and high ranking aristocrats for decades. Enjoy fragrant and aromatic flavours with every quality dish.

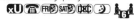

BLUE ORCHID
Thai
The Square, Aspley Guise, MK17 8DF
01908 282 877
Thai furnishings and exotic foliage enhance the character and atmosphere of this delightful restaurant. Inside the listed 19th century building you'll find a place of luxurious intimacy.

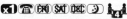

Minimum party spend of £20 pp.

FOUR PILLARS TANDOORI
Indian
60 High Street, Olney, MK46 4BE
01234 714 083
Flavoured with the finest herbs and spices, dishes on offer here are carefully prepared with fresh produce, and are influenced and adapted from all over the vast Indian subcontinent.

CAFÉ ROUGE
French
30 Mortimer Square, The Hub, Milton Keynes, MK9 2FB
01908 241 709
An attractive restaurant, a boulevard café or a Parisian-style wine bar; however you see Café Rouge, consistently excellent classic French dishes are always guaranteed.

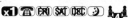

FOX & PHEASANT
Carvery
Gerrards Cross Road, Slough, SL2 4EZ
01753 662 047
One of the many Great British Carvery pubs that offers the best of British food with a stylishly modern twist. This likeable establishment is irresistibly attractive to both locals and visitors from afar.

Call beforehand for special event days.

FUSIONS RESTAURANT
Fine Dining
145 West Wycombe Road, High Wycombe, HP12 3AB
01494 430 378
Imaginative, lively combinations of flavours in this AA Rosette-recognised restaurant. Fine dining with a thoroughgoing attention to fresh, seasonal and high-quality produce.

DETAILED DESCRIPTIONS AVAILABLE ON
www.gourmetsociety.co.uk

CAFÉ ROUGE
French
Queens Court, Milton Keynes, MK9 3ES
01908 605 282
An attractive restaurant, a boulevard café or a Parisian-style wine bar; however you see Café Rouge, consistently excellent classic French dishes are always guaranteed.

GRAYS RESTAURANT
French
Grove Road, Burnham, SL1 8DP
01628 600 150
Located within an original Georgian mansion, elegant surroundings are combined with contemporary cuisine. Sit back, enjoy the ambience and the mouth-watering food freshly prepared by talented chefs.

SOUTH EAST

77

SOUTH EAST

KARDAMOM LOUNGE *Indian*
34 High Street, Stony Stratford, BMK11 1AF
01908 567 538
A fantastic place to enjoy truly authentic Bangladeshi and Indian cuisine served in a welcoming environment. The menu is a diverse mix of authentic and regional dishes with a major focus on quality.

LA COLLINA @ THE GEORGE INN *Italian*
Watling St, Little Brickhill, MK17 9NB
01525 261 298
Here at the Inn the staff are consistently striving to deliver high quality food with exceptional service. Guests will relish the delicious dishes that are fresh and made to order.

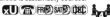

LOCH FYNE *Seafood*
The White Horse, 70 London End, Oxford Rd, HP9 2JD
01494 679 960
From the roadside oyster bar that once was, Loch Fyne restaurants now successfully inject energy and passion into great food and wonderful flavours, whilst ensuring their seafood is sustainably sourced.

LOCH FYNE *Seafood*
19 Market Place, Woburn, MK17 9PZ
01525 290 877
From the roadside oyster bar that once was, Loch Fyne restaurants now successfully inject energy and passion into great food and wonderful flavours, whilst ensuring their seafood is sustainably sourced.

LOCH FYNE *Seafood*
3 Chelsea House, Holkam Walk, Milton Keynes, MK9 2FS
01908 546 570
From the roadside oyster bar that once was, Loch Fyne restaurants now successfully inject energy and passion into great food and wonderful flavours, whilst ensuring their seafood is sustainably sourced.

MELA RESTAURANT *Indian*
103 London Road, Aston Clinton, HP22 5LD
01296 630110
Unique Indian restaurant offering delightful authentic cuisine. The staff value good service and are dedicated to ensuring all guests feel entirely at home. The Bengal fish curry is not to be missed.

ORTEGA MILTON KEYNES *Spanish*
Unit N1, Theatre District, Milton Keynes, MK9 3PU
01908 674 322
A vibrant tapas bar that captures the magical liveliness of a bustling Spanish city. Accompany your array of dishes or sizzling grill with freshly made Sangria or a premium Spanish beer.

PASSAGE TO INDIA *Indian*
10-11 Cotteridge Close, Stony Stratford, MK11 1BY
01908 567 610
With a chef who has won a prestigious local award for his cooking, this restaurant consistently offers wonderfully tasty Indian cuisine. Customers will enjoy restaurant-quality takeaway food.

PREZZO *Italian*
39/41 Buckingham Street, Aylesbury, HP20 2NQ
01296 339 437
With a character all of its own, Prezzo oozes contemporary style and enduring charm. Signature pastas, stone-baked pizzas and classic Italian dishes promise a perfect dining choice for the whole family.

PREZZO *Italian*
3 Whielden Street, Amersham, HP7 0HT
01494 727 228
With a character all of its own, Prezzo oozes contemporary style and enduring charm. Signature pastas, stone-baked pizzas and classic Italian dishes promise a perfect dining choice for the whole family.

PREZZO *Italian*
36 High Street, Buckingham, MK18 1NU
01280 823 844
With a character all of its own, Prezzo oozes contemporary style and enduring charm. Signature pastas, stone-baked pizzas and classic Italian dishes promise a perfect dining choice for the whole family.

RAJDHANI *Indian*
706 Midsummer Boulevard, Milton Keynes, MK9 3NT
01908 392 299
Enjoy luxury banquet menus, deluxe buffets and chef specialities at this wonderful Indian restaurant. Ideally located in the cosmopolitan hub of Milton Keynes, this is a great place to dine.

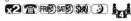

ROYAL EMPEROR CHINESE *Chinese*
79 Victoria Road, Bletchley, Milton Keynes, MK2 2NZ
01908 370 733
Sizzling Mandarin-style fillet of steak and steamed jumbo king prawns are just two of the chef's specialities at this restaurant. Peking and Cantonese dishes are available for dining in or taking away.

ROYAL THAI RESTAURANT *Thai*
32 High Street, Stony Stratford, MK11 1AF
01908 565 338
Using traditional recipes many generations old, the kitchen at this traditional Thai restaurant insists upon providing tasty and devilishly tempting dishes. Try the popular gang mussamun for a real treat.

SHIRAZ *Persian*
702 Midsummer Boulevard, Milton Keynes, MK9 3NT
01908 394 600
Take a voyage of discovery through some of the world's most celebrated dishes, as chefs prepare mouth-watering dishes infused with a delicate blend of herbs and spices to produce truly flavourful food.

Offer only on the à la carte menu.

THAI ON THE RIVER *Thai*
10 Lakeside, Watermead, Aylesbury, HP19 0FU
01296 433 123
Award-winning Thai restaurant where the warm atmosphere is inviting and the beautifully prepared dishes are plentiful. The à la carte menu provides an endless supply of first-class appetisers.

78

When booking restaurants always mention your GS membership

THAI THAI RESTAURANT
Thai

Heart in Hand, Cores End Road, Bourne End, SL8 5HH
01628 523 331
Vividly contemporary but thoroughly authentic Thai cuisine; Thai Thai's kitchen shows great skill at drawing the out eclectic, vibrant flavours and colours in these beautifully presented dishes.

THE BLACK HORSE
English / Gastropub

1 Bedford Street, Woburn, MK17 9QB
01525 290 210
In the pretty village of Woburn sits The Black Horse. Enter the 18th century building to find a cosy bar and a smart restaurant waiting for you, whilst the courtyard garden is well worth discovering.

2FOR1 MAIN COURSE

Must order two courses pp.

THE CORIANDER
Indian

Metro Court, Amersham, HP6 5AZ
01494 726 370
Stylish and sophisticated Indian restaurant with a focus on superb service and a specialisation in the richness and piquancy of North Indian and Bangladeshi cuisine.

2FOR1 MAIN COURSE

THE CROOKED BILLET
British

2 Westbrook End, Newton Longville, MK17 0DF
01908 373 936
A nationally recognised gastro-pub, with praise and awards aplenty for their food and wine. Quality food prepared by experienced staff; a prime example of excellent dining. Awarded 1 AA Rosette.

25% OFF TOTAL

THE FIVE ARROWS HOTEL
European

High Street, Waddesdon, HP18 0JE
01296 651 727
This versatile restaurant caters for a range of occasions but maintains its thoughtful, imaginative style and technical accomplishment throughout. You'll enjoy a relaxed ambience and great range of dishes.

2FOR1 MAIN COURSE

THE KING AND QUEEN
Seafood

17 South Street, Wendover, HP22 6EF
01296 623 272
A local pub serving an extensive menu of good, hearty food. With an outdoor seating area, guests can enjoy real ales in the open air when the sun shines.

25% OFF TOTAL

THE TWO BREWERS
34 High Street, Olney, MK46 4BB
01234 711 393 *British*

2FOR1 MAIN COURSE

© beergenie.co.uk

The Two Brewers in Olney benefits from the old adage that great things come in twos. Although revitalised with a recent refurbishment, it retains the character of a traditional public house and boasts a cosy fire for the winter months. Likewise, the menu suggests an enjoyable, gastro-pub experience will be had, but at the same time promises great value prices.

This is also a family-friendly and business-friendly pub. The garden, landscaped in recent months, boasts a children's play area, alongside - but a world away

from - plenty of tranquil seating areas. For business folk, the convenience of both the Two Brewer's excellent location and wi-fi make it an ideal meeting point to talk business and enjoy the menu.

The menu offers traditional favourites, each home cooked with fresh, locally sourced ingredients, such as the meat which hails from Olney's traditional butcher, located nearby. As befits a pub which welcomes families with open arms, children are also well catered for.

SOUTH EAST

79

THE LIVING ROOM
British

401 Witan Gate, Milton Keynes, MK9 2BQ
01908 827 299

Step into The Living Room and you can count on the savvy, distinctive neighbourhood vibe that plays home to eclectically drawn, supremely tasty cuisine. Take a smooth moment in this Milton Keynes venue.

Must purchase min. 3 courses pp inc. main course.

THE OLD SWAN
Modern British

58 High Street, Cheddington, LU7 0RQ
01296 668 226

A beauty of a higgeldy-piggeldy thatched pub whose home-cooked, eclectic recipes take in a number of different regional cuisines but all come up trumps with fresh, thorough and delicious flavours.

THE RED LION BRADENHAM
British

Bradenham Wood Lane, Bradenham, HP14 4HF
01494 562 212

Situated in an unspoilt historical village, the pub offers enjoyable food under a friendly and hospitable landlord, well-kept ales and tasty food. Head there on a Sunday for a spot of jazz to end the week.

THE SWAN
English / Gastropub

2 Wavendon Road, Salford, MK17 8BD
01908 281 008

Fans of traditional pub-grub will love the delightful menus on offer at The Swan. Aberdeen steaks, juicy sausages and pan-fried fish appear on the list of firm favourites with guests.

THE SWAN AT IVER
Italian

2 High Street, Iver, SL0 9NG
01753 655 776

Fine dining in the à la carte restaurant offers the very best of English and Italian dishes. The welcoming pub also serves delightful food.

DETAILED DESCRIPTIONS AVAILABLE ON

www.gourmetsociety.co.uk

THE TREE AT CADMORE END
International

Marlow Road, Stokenchurch, High Wycombe, HP14 3PF
01494 881 183

This gastro-pub takes pride in its exquisite quality of food and the charming ambience it exudes. Placing emphasis on comfort, the interior décor is captivating and ensures a winning experience.

FRANCESCO'S MARLOW
Italian

13 Spittal Street, Marlow, SL7 3HJ
01628 473532

NEW

In a restaurant where even the pizza dough is made at least twice a day, it's no surprise that the food is amazing. Enjoy delicious dishes in a style in keeping with the Italian way of life.

SAPORI
Italian

2-3 Leighton Street, Woburn, MK17 9PJ
1525290033

NEW

With a focus on food from the Puglia region of southern Italy, the menu features a wide variety of dishes ranging from much loved favourites to more unusual regional specialities.

THE WOBURN BRASSERIE
British

13 Bedford Street, Woburn, Milton Keynes, MK17 9QB
01525 290 260

Receive a warm welcome whether it be for a leisurely lunch, an evening meal, or simply a relaxing drink. Become accustomed with the diverse choice of local, fresh produce used to craft each delicious dish.

THE WOBURN FORT
Indian

33 High Street, Woburn Sands, MK17 8RB
01908 282 002

Unafraid to try out new and exciting ventures when it comes to food, guests enjoy the innovative ways in which the chefs often use fruit to enhance the flavours of their dishes. A fabulous place to dine.

East Sussex

ABERDEEN STEAK HOUSE
British

27 Preston Street, Brighton, BN1 2HP
01273 326 892

If you like a steak, then this is a great choice. High-quality cuts, great sides, all at reasonable prices. Attentive and friendly staff ensure diners have a memorable experience.

AL DUOMO
Italian

7 Pavilion Buildings, Brighton, BN1 1EE
01273 326 741

Sure to suit all tastes and pockets, this Italian restaurant boasts a menu of huge variety from fresh pizzas to tempting desserts, all representing good value for money. Perfect for all occasions.

ALROUCHE RESTAURANT
Lebanese

44 Preston Street, Brighton, BN1 2HP
01273 734 810

A cosy and friendly family-run restaurant that showcase the qualities of Lebanese cuisine. Choose from an array of well-prepared dishes that offer diners a host of divine flavours.

ARGANIA RESTAURANT
Moroccan

118-120 St Georges Road, Brighton, BN2 1EA
01273 682 200

Evocative Moroccan restaurant which serves the gamut of superb, warming flavours that characterise the country's cuisine; accomplished dishes and an atmospheric ambience make this a treat.

ARISTOCRATS SIZZLING RESTAURANT — *Filipino*
54 Preston Street, Brighton, BN1 2HE
01273 748 388
A lively establishment, perfect for dining with family and friends. The menu offers a delightful assortment of mouth-watering dishes, and is accompanied by a fine selection of wines and beers.

CAFÉ BELGE — *French*
45 The Marina, Bexhill-On-Sea, TN40 1BQ
01424 731 513
A restaurant that serves great quality Belgian food, full of interesting mixtures like the beautiful sea bass ragout, and clear, classic flavours such as the perennially delicious moules frites.

BENGAL BRASSERIE — *Indian*
66 London Road, Bexhill-On-Sea, TN39 3LE
01424 736 007
A variety of Indian dishes are on offer at Bengal Brasserie. Curry lovers will be impressed by the wide-ranging menu.

CAFÉ ROUGE — *French*
24 Prince Albert St, Brighton, BN1 1HF
01273 774 422
An attractive restaurant, a boulevard café or a Parisian-style wine bar; however you see Café Rouge, consistently excellent classic French dishes are always guaranteed.

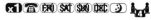

BIRDCAGE WALK — *European*
300 Ditchling Road, Brighton, BN1 6JG
01273 561 757
The Head Chef offers guests magnificent modern European cuisine that is perfect for any occasion. By insisting on the use of seasonal and local produce, the chef guarantees all diners the freshest food.

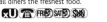

CAFÉ ROUGE — *French*
The Waterfront, Brighton Marina, Brighton, BN2 5WA
01273 622 423
An attractive restaurant, a boulevard café or a Parisian-style wine bar; however you see Café Rouge, consistently excellent classic French dishes are always guaranteed.

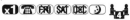

BLANCH HOUSE — *British*
17 Atlingworth Street, Brighton, BN2 1PL
01273 603 504
A perfect backdrop to enjoy classic brasserie-style cuisine with a truly delectable seasonal menu, where all involved are dedicated to food, service and wines without any pretensions.

CHAMBERS BISTRO — *Bistro*
Old Town Hall, High St., Shoreham-by-sea, BN43 5DD
01273 446 677
Seasonal and refreshing contemporary bistro-style food at this little restaurant in the old Town Hall of picturesque Shoreham-by-sea. Simple dishes, cooked beautifully to bring out the best in the produce.

BLENIO BISTRO — *European*
87 Dyke Road, Brighton, BN1 3JE
01273 220 220
Catch the scent of fresh rosemary and thyme and savour delectable, rustic dishes based on the best natural ingredients. A welcoming, stylish bistro serving flavoursome food from breakfast till dinner.

COMPTON LOUNGE — *British*
12 Grand Parade, Compton St, Eastbourne, BN21 4EJ
01323 731 662
Renowned Head Chef Peter has experience working in some of the top European restaurants, and chefs here use the finest ingredients and their unique knowledge to create exciting and seasonal dishes.

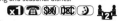

BRASSERIE FISH AND GRILL — *Seafood*
3a Waterfront, Brighton Marina, Brighton, BN2 5WA
01273 698 989
Fine fish dishes are on offer in this wonderful seafood restaurant. Enjoy the relaxing ambience as you take in the views of the nautical world of Brighton marina.

DEVOUR — *Modern British*
1 East Beach Street, Hastings, TN34 3AR
01424 440 052
A modern European restaurant and private diners lounge offering fabulously tasty food at wonderfully affordable prices. Enthusiasm for good food overflows in the kitchen and can be tasted in every dish.

BUXTED PARK HOTEL — *British*
The Dining Room Restaurant, Buxted, Uckfield, TN22 4AY
08450 727 412
Enjoy your favourite classic British dish with a modern twist, or indulge in one of the chef's many creations at this Hand Picked Hotels group restaurant that will delight and excite you. 2 AA Rosettes.

DUE SOUTH — *British*
139 Kings Road Arches, Brighton, BN1 2FN
01273 821 218
Head Chef Michael Bremner is passionately committed to creating sophisticated food with uncompromising integrity. A monthly changing menu reflects the seasonal produce used in the kitchen. 1 AA Rosette.

CAFÉ BELGE — *Belgian*
64a High Street, Battle, TN33 0AG
01424 772 344
A restaurant that serves great quality Belgian food, full of interesting mixtures like the beautiful sea bass ragout, and clear classic flavours such as the perennially delicious moules frites.

EAST STREET — *Steakhouse*
70 East Street, Brighton, BN1 1HQ
01273 726 006
Fans fond of succulent steaks unite at this popular, ideally located restaurant. A carefully selected wine list offers guests an easy route to choosing the perfect accompaniment to their meal.

ESTIA
Greek
3 Hampton Place, Brighton, BN1 3DA
01273 777 399
Modern, stylish restaurant that serves mellow, fragrant Greek Cypriot cuisine in a warm, welcoming ambience.

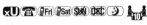

FLACKLEY ASH HOTEL
European
Peasmarsh, Rye, TN31 6YH
01797 230 651
This Michelin-recommended restaurant focuses on traditional English recipes and Mediterranean twists. Customers can enjoy full, natural, flavoursome dishes in a serene, stately location.

FLAMENCO TAPAS RESTAURANT
Spanish
8 Cornfield Terrace, Eastbourne, BN21 4NN
01323 641 444
Eclectic and vibrant tapas dishes in this well-set, highly regarded Spanish restaurant in Eastbourne.

THE GOURMET FISH & CHIP CO
British
18 The Waterfront, Brighton Marina Village, BN2 5WA
01273 670701
Gourmet Fish and Chip Co. have given traditional fish and chips a makeover and taken what is recognised as the UK's No.1 celebrated food into the 21st Century. An essential pit stop on any Brighton visit.

GRAZE RESTAURANT
Modern British
42 Western Road, Hove, BN3 2FD
01273 823 707
A lavish interior gives a modern edge as the Head Chef combines fresh and intense flavours to create seasonally based menus using locally sourced, organic and free-range produce. Awarded 2 AA Rosettes.

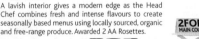
Must order minimum 2 courses

GURKHA CHEF NEPALESE CUISINE
Nepalese
20 Grand Parade, St. Leonards-On-Sea, TN37 6DN
01424 444 440
Indulge in unique Nepalese cuisine filled with delicious, authentic flavours that combine an array of traditional herbs and spices. A large selection of regional dishes offer a real taste of Nepal.

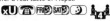

HANGLETON MANOR
British
Hangleton Valley Drive, Hove, BN3 8AN
01273 413 266
In the oldest secular building surviving in Brighton and Hove this restaurant delivers real food by talented chefs. A classic yet inspiring menu with dishes including the renowned Tanglefoot ale pie.

HARRIS RESTAURANT
Spanish
58 High Street, Hastings, TN34 3EN
01424 437 221
Look no further for a well-established venue offering the finest selection of authentic Spanish tapas. Well-priced food, all freshly prepared to the highest culinary standards.

HARRY RAMSDEN'S
British
258-262 Terminus Road, Eastbourne, BN21 3DE
01323 417 454
The classic fish and chips combo, perfected. Britain's best loved 'chippy', renowned for their famous seaside food, serving guests quality dishes time and time again.

Not available during August or in takeaway.

HARRY RAMSDEN'S
Traditional English Fare
1-4 Marine Parade, Brighton, BN2 1PA
01273 690 691
For the finest fish and chips, this national treasure never fails to deliver. Harry Ramsden's is a well-established British institution, that guarantees a true taste of the seaside.

Not available during August or in takeaway.

HOTEL DU VIN
European
Ship Street, Brighton, BN1 1AD
01273 718 588
The finest, fresh local produce, simple European recipes, a stunning choice of wines; these are the elements of the trademark Hotel du Vin bistro. Situated in the heart of the famous 'Lanes'. 1 AA Rosette.

IL BISTRO
Mediterranean
6/7a Market Street, Brighton, BN1 1HH
01273 324 584
A genuine Mediterranean experience where the Head Chef utilises his experiences in the kitchen. Set in a beautiful 18th century cottage, this restaurant boasts a delicious menu and excellent service.

IN VINO VERITAS
European
103 North Road, Brighton, BN1 1YW
01273 622 522
This restaurant is all about good food and wine without the expensive price tag. Diners can enjoy tapas-sized continental food and a glass of wine from the vast Old and New world selection.

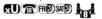

INDIAN SUMMER
Indian
69 East Street, Brighton, BN1 1HG
01273 711 001
Popular, authentic Indian restaurant with all the staple favourites along with some stand-out specialities; try the classic East Indian chingri malai, or one of the richly spiced vegan options. A hot spot.

JALI
Indian
The Chatsworth Hotel, Hastings, TN34 1JG
01424 457 300
An AA Rosette restaurant serving only the finest dishes made from authentic ingredients, inspired by India's grand culinary traditions. A memorable experience setting the new standard for Indian cuisine.

LA FOURCHETTE
French
104 -105 Western Rd, Brighton, BN1 2AA
01273 722 556
With tastes and inspirations from France, Executive Chef Stéphane Frelon's menu demonstrates a bold use of flavour giving an unexpected taste to classic French brasserie fare.

Recommend a friend to the Gourmet Society and receive a free gift.

MORE BAR AND RESTAURANT — *Mediterranean*
98 Trafalgar Street, Brighton, BN1 4ER
01273 693 377
A vibrant family friendly bar and restaurant offering something for everyone, with award-winning Mediterranean cuisine that is created using superb locally sourced produce.

 2FOR1 MAIN COURSE

NEW STEINE BISTRO — *French*
10& 11 New Steine, Brighton, BN2 1PB
01273 681 546
Award-winning hotel restaurant offering the most delicious continental fare from breakfast to dinner. Guests will love the extensive breakfast buffet which will ensure you get the most out of your day.

 2FOR1 MAIN COURSE

NORTHERN LIGHTS — *Scandinavian*
6 Little East Street, Brighton, BN1 1HT
01273 747 096
Classic Scandinavian dishes and drinks are available in this quaint fisherman's cottage close to the seafront. Try sautéed reindeer or one of the many flavoured vodkas for a real experience.

 2FOR1 MAIN COURSE

OKINAMI — *Japanese*
6 New Road, Brighton, BN1 1UF
01273 773 777
Contemporary minimalist design delightfully contrasts the Regency period features of this restaurant. Guests are guaranteed to enjoy the authentic Japanese cuisine that the kitchen has to offer.

 2FOR1 MAIN COURSE

PABLO'S — *Italian*
36 Ship Street, Brighton, BN1 1AB
01273 208 123
Warm welcomes and charming smiles can be expected from the cheerful staff at this fantastic Italian restaurant. The spaghetti alla puttanesca is deliciously spicy.

 25%OFF TOTAL

PICCOLO RESTAURANT — *Italian*
56 Ship Street, Brighton, BN1 1AF
01273 380 380
Simple and authentic, this Italian restaurant delivers delicately flavoured food combined with competitive prices, attentive service, and a friendly and lively atmosphere.

 25%OFF TOTAL

PREZZO — *Italian*
Unit 6, The Waterfront, Brighton BN2 5WA
01273 680 582
With a character all of its own, Prezzo oozes contemporary style and enduring charm. Signature pastas, stone-baked pizzas and classic Italian dishes promise a perfect dining choice for the whole family.

 2FOR1 MAIN COURSE

PREZZO — *Italian*
Terminus Building, Upperton Rd, Eastbourne BN21 1BA
01323 722 667
With a character all of its own, Prezzo oozes contemporary style and enduring charm. Signature pastas, stone-baked pizzas and classic Italian dishes promise a perfect dining choice for the whole family.

2FOR1 MAIN COURSE

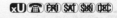

PUB DU VIN
7 Ship Street, Brighton, BN1 1AD
01273 718 588 *European*

2FOR1 MAIN COURSE

So what is Pub du Vin?

Some would presume it is a 'pub of wine'. Not so my learned friends. Imagine a traditional British pub from the award-winning Hotel du Vin brand. Imagine, local legendary ales served in traditional pewter tankards accompanied with homemade warm signature pies, the best traditions of an old British pub.

The Brighton Pub du Vin is the first of this young, growing bran and also features 11 deluxe bedrooms.

Welcome to your new local.

PREZZO
Italian

173 High Street, Lewes, BN7 1YE
01273 472 179
With a character all of its own, Prezzo oozes contemporary style and enduring charm. Signature pastas, stone-baked pizzas and classic Italian dishes promise a perfect dining choice for the whole family.

PREZZO
Italian

The Old School House, High St, Hailsham, BN27 1AR
01323 442010
With a character all of its own, Prezzo oozes contemporary style and enduring charm. Signature pastas, stone-baked pizzas and classic Italian dishes promise a perfect dining choice for the whole family.

RASA BRIGHTON
Indian

2-3 Little East Street, Brighton, BN1 1HT
01273 771 661
Inspired by the authentic home cooking of beautiful, spice-rich Kerala, this restaurant's passion is food prepared always with devotion, love, and the finest ingredients. Experience the essence of India.

RIDDLE & FINNS
Seafood

12b Meeting House Lane, Brighton, BN1 1HB
01273 323 008
Exquisite seafood is served in stylish surroundings. Scrumptious aromas create irresistible temptations, which can be given in to with any one of the dishes on the menu.

RIDGWAYS
British

42-44 Meads Street, Meads, Eastbourne, BN20 7RG
01323 726 805
Sample the delights of this traditional, high-quality restaurant that specialises in beautifully crafted English cuisine. They offer a diverse, good-value menu with a continental element.

RIVER SPICE
Indian

17 Preston Street, Brighton, BN1 2HN
01273 739 183
A stunning contemporary interior awaits you at this marvellous Indian restaurant. The kitchen hosts a talented team of chefs who place all of their energy and passion into creating the most divine dishes.

RIVERSIDE BRASSERIE
Brasserie

Riverside, Cliffe Bridge, Lewes, BN7 2AD
01273 472 247
This most delightful of venues offers a riverside view that will guarantee you leave feeling calm, relaxed and refreshed. Peruse the menu or enjoy a steaming hot cappuccino with a heavenly pastry.

SAM'S OF BRIGHTON
British

1 Paston Place, Brighton, BN2 1HA
01273 676 222
For great quality food and a desirable relaxed atmosphere, this bistro-style restaurant never fails to deliver. Located between the pier and the marina, this is a wonderful place to dine.

À la carte menu only - does not apply to set lunch.

SEVEN DIALS RESTAURANT
British

1 Buckingham Place, Seven Dials, Brighton, BN1 3TD
01273 885 555
Impressive family-owned restaurant serving wonderful award-winning European cuisine. Led by a highly experienced Head Chef, the kitchen aims to provide the ultimate fine dining experience.

À la carte menu only - does not apply to set lunch.

SILLETTS COTTAGE RESTAURANT
British

Church Farm, Selmeston, BN26 6TZ
01323 811 343
A beautifully well preserved listed farmhouse where that perfect dining experience at a real country restaurant can be found. Charming and relaxed, guests can enjoy the pretty garden or the crackling fire.

SKYBAR AND RESTAURANT
Contemporary

54 Meeting House, Brighton, BN1 1HB
01273 207 040
A place to enjoy excellent drinks and food, in comfortable and inviting surroundings. Serving modern cuisine where popular dishes include mouth-watering, creamy linguine with chicken and wild mushrooms.

SOFIA'S BRIGHTON
Italian

24 Ship St, Brighton, BN1 1AD
01273 321 233
Taking the Greek word for 'wisdom' as its name, Sofia's is definitely a wise choice for a splendid evening out. Classic, authentically cooked Italian dishes are served by amiable staff.

ST CLEMENT'S LIMITED
British

3 Mercatoria, St. Leonards-On-Sea, TN38 0EB
01424 200 355
A Michelin Bib Gourmand winner serving seasonal produce in a tranquil atmosphere. The surrounding areas are rich in produce and this is reflected by the divine flavours evident in each and every dish.

WATERSIDE SEAFOOD RESTAURANT
Seafood

11-12 Royal Parade, Eastbourne, BN22 7AR
01323 646566
Set fair on Eastbourne's Royal Parade, the Waterside is a boutique hotel and restaurant that's light, bright and welcoming in feel. The flavours are clear and the restaurant holds an AA Rosette.

TERRE À TERRE
Vegetarian

71 East Street, Brighton, Brighton, BN1 1HQ
01273 729 051
Dining at Terre à Terre is a culinary experience like no other, with intense flavours, sublime textures and a daring combination of ingredients. Truly fine vegetarian food. Awarded 2 AA Rosettes.

THE APOSTROPHE
English and Continental

The Shelleys, 135-136 High Street, Lewes, BN7 1XS
01273 472 361
Stylish and sophisticated hotel-restaurant serving an array of smartly conceived dishes bursting with fresh and clear flavours, like the rainbow trout with spring onion potato cake and saffron cream sauce.

Discounted hotel rates for GS members on our website

THE GALLERY RESTAURANT
Traditional English

28 East Street, Brighton, BN1 1HL
01273 773 327

A large heated terrace overlooking the vibrant seafront is just one of the many highlights of this restaurant. Elegant, stylish surroundings create an idyllic haven to enjoy seasonal British cuisine.

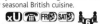

THE GREENHOUSE
European

10 Station Street, Eastbourne, BN21 4RG
01323 738 228

Delivers great food and drink, and excellent service, in stylish and pleasing surroundings. The customer's requirements are first on the agenda here, with all visitors being exceptionally looked after.

THE HOPE INN
British

West Pier, Newhaven, BN9 9DN
01273 515 389

Home-cooked pub grub with an emphasis on locally sourced fish. Visitors can enjoy food whilst experiencing the stunning views over the estuary and harbour where the pub is situated. A warm welcome for all.

THE LAUGHING FISH
Fresh Fish/Pub Classics

Isfield, Uckfield, TN22 5XB
01825 750 349

Pop in for a well-deserved drink after a hard day at work, or enjoy a three course meal with friends and family at this well-maintained pub. Guests love the hearty home-made food and phenomenal service.

THE MEADOW
British

64 Western Road, Hove, BN3 2JQ
01273 721 182

Awarded 2 AA Rosettes for its quality food, and popular for an atmosphere full of conviviality. A menu that places British cuisine at its forefront, with notes of classic French and Italian influence.

THE MERRIE HARRIERS
British

Cowbeech, Herstmonceux, BN27 4JQ
01323 833 108

Both setting and food offer a quintessentially English experience at this delightful village inn. New British classics appear on the extensive menu, whilst lighter bites to eat can be enjoyed at the bar.

THE OCEANA RESTAURANT
British

The Cooden Beach Hotel, Cooden Sea Road, TN39 4TT
01424 842 281

Stunning sea views, traditional English fare and attentive silver service all make this beach restaurant incredibly attractive. Sunday lunch is a firm favourite with regular guests.

THE OLD SHIP INN
British

Uckfield Road, Ringmer, BN8 5RP
01273 814 223

Classic country inn with a welcoming atmosphere that's a pleasure to enjoy. Changing regularly, their menu can see you pass from the juicy twang of steak Diane to the zip of fruit pavlova.

THE PILOT PUB
British

89 Meads Street, Meads, Eastbourne, BN20 7RW
01323 723 440

Hearty meals to be enjoyed after a warm welcome greets you at the door. Local produce is used to create the most scrumptious British dishes, whilst weekly specials are available alongside the regular menu.

THE REGENCY RESTAURANT
Fish and Seafood

131 Kings Road, Brighton, BN1 2HH
01273 325 014

Supremely charismatic and highly regarded seafront restaurant where the fish is of fabulous quality, simply cooked and deliciously so. The price, too, is right: something as fresh as the sea air.

THE SHIMLA PALACE
Indian

9111 Seaside, Eastbourne, BN22 7NB
01323 410 339

Enjoy a warm welcome and a meal that's warmer still. Take your pick from the great range of full-flavoured classic curries and a selection of inviting signature dish.

THE STAR INN
English and Continental

The Star Inn, Normans Bay, Pevensey, B24 6QG
01323 762 648

Both adults and children are well catered for at this delightful family-friendly pub. The extensive menu and the Mediterranean buffet are extremely popular, whilst the carvery offers a Sunday treat.

THE STAR, ALFRISTON
British

High St, Alfriston, BN26 5TA
01323 870 495

This charming Tudor hotel may not offer the safe lodgings once given to pilgrims, but it will offer exquisite AA Rosette-worthy food and affable service. Everything is made on the premises, even the bread.

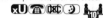

THE WHITE HORSE
British

Silverhill, Hurst Green, TN19 7PU
01580 860 235

A former Georgian farmhouse, this building has been dramatically transformed into a restaurant and bar which oozes its own full-bodied character. The Head Chef's experience shines through every dish.

TIN DRUM HOVE
Modern British

10 Victoria Grove, Second Avenue, Hove, BN3 2LJ
01273 747 755

Lively and lovely brasserie-style café bar-restaurant that's as good for a coffee and a calm glance at the paper as it is for a smart, fresh and beautifully cooked evening meal.

TIN DRUM KEMPTOWN
Modern British

43 St James Street, Brighton, BN2 1RG
01273 624 777

Lively and lovely brasserie-style café bar-restaurant that's as good for a coffee and a calm glance at the paper as it is for a smart, fresh and beautifully cooked evening meal.

SOUTH EAST

TIN DRUM SEVEN DIALS
Modern British

95-97 Dyke Road, Brighton, BN1 3JE
01273 777 575
Lively and lovely brasserie-style café bar-restaurant that's as good for a coffee and a calm glance at the paper as it is for a smart, fresh and beautifully cooked evening meal.

V-BAR
British

Pelham Yard, High Street, Seaford, BN25 1PQ
01323 492 574
Great little bar tucked away in Seaford where you can count on a simple, unfussy drink and bite to eat; a welcoming and friendly local spot.

2FOR1 MAIN COURSE

VBITES
Vegan

Hove Lagoon, Kingsway, Hove, BN3 4LX
01273 933 757
Bright, enthusiastic and committed vegan restaurant in Hove Lagoon owned by Heather Mills; with a great range of dishes whose vibrant flavours will both surprise and delight you.

Closed for winter

WARUNG TUJUH
Indonesian

7 Pool Valley, Brighton, BN1 1NJ
01273 720 784
This Indonesian restaurant in Brighton gains rave reviews for its intriguing, thoroughly tasty dishes and for its excellent service. Their signature, slow-cooked beef in coconut milk and spices, hits home.

2FOR1 MAIN COURSE

 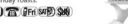

YE OLDE PUMPHOUSE
British

64 George Street, Hastings, TN34 3EE
01424 422 016
From a daytime moment of calm to a buzzy part of a night out, Ye Olde Pump House puts together an array of classic English dishes with an especial line in hearty, wholesome Sunday roasts.

2FOR1 MAIN COURSE

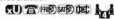

ZAFFERELLI
Italian

31-32 New Road, Brighton, BN1 1UG
01273 206 662
Don't think twice: this warmly atmospheric Italian restaurant in the heart of Brighton stands out for its fresh, flavoursome dishes with a lot of down-home, genial and authentic character.

25%OFF TOTAL

Hampshire/ Isle of Wight

AUDLEYS WOOD HOTEL
European

The Gallery, Alton Rd, Basingstoke, RG25 2JY
01256 817 555
Distinctive, delectable food is served in the grand surroundings of this magnificent country house. Boasting two AA Rosettes, this Hand Picked Hotels group dining venue is ideal for that special occasion.

25%OFF TOTAL

AVIATOR BRASSERIE
European

Farnborough Road, Farnborough, GU14 6EL
01252 555 895
Following in the hotel concept from Malmaison's creators, this venue is sleek, sophisticated and sexy. The dishes here are simple with a twist of indulgence, mirroring the stunning interior.

25%OFF TOTAL

AZZURRO PORTSMOUTH
Italian

Upper Level, Gunwharf Quays, Portsmouth, PO1 3TA
02392 832 111
Occupying a stunning seafront location, this is an ideal place to enjoy contemporary Italian dishes in the fine dining room. When the sun prevails, Azzurro is a perfect spot for al fresco eating.

2FOR1 MAIN COURSE

BAMBOOS
Asian Fusion

85-87 Queensway, Southampton, SO14 3HU
02380 331 337
Offers appetisingly fresh Chinese and Japanese dishes that are fantastic value for money. Vegetarians are extremely well catered for.

2FOR1 MAIN COURSE

BANKS BAR BISTRO
British

The Old Granary, Bank St, Bishops Waltham, SO32 1AE
01489 896 352
Michelin star-trained chefs bring to the kitchen their extensive experience to create exquisite dishes for lunch and evening meals. The menu focuses on modern British dishes with a continental twist.

25%OFF TOTAL

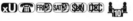

BARTONS MILL
British

Bartons Lane, Old Basing, Basingstoke, RG24 8AE
01256 331 153
A country pub haven set within a conservation area near to the historical Basing house ruins. Enjoy delicious home-made food and Wadworth ales by the calming waters of the River Loddon.

25%OFF TOTAL

Offer excludes Sunday lunch and Christmas menus

BASMATI INDIAN RESTAURANT
Indian

10A Centre Way, Locks Heath, Southampton, SO31 6DX
01489 575 556
The combination of fine, fresh ingredients with traditional herbs and spices is the secret to these flavoursome recipes. This award-winning establishment offers a wide variety of dishes for you to enjoy.

2FOR1 MAIN COURSE

BENGAL BRASSERIE
Indian

7 Bedford Place, Southampton, SO15 2DB
02380 230 988
A great local restaurant serving terrific Indian cuisine. Friendly staff are happy to cater to your every need.

2FOR1 MAIN COURSE

BRITANNIA THAI
Thai

1 High Street, Milford On Sea, Lymington, SO41 0QF
01590 642 226
A most exquisite dining experience for any guest as expert chefs immaculately execute and present a wide selection of authentic dishes in a stylish venue, offering fantastic value for money.

2FOR1 2 COURSES

Gourmet Society discount applies to the à la carte menu

BUON GUSTO
Italian

1 Commercial Road, Southampton, SO15 1GF
02380 331 543
This classic, authentic Italian restaurant serves hearty, wholesome and traditional dishes in a superb location, whether as part of your night at the theatre, or simply for an intimate meal.

CAFÉ ROUGE
French

Gunwharf Quays, Portsmouth, PO1 3FA
02392 754 849
An attractive restaurant, a boulevard café or a Parisian-style wine bar; however you see Café Rouge, consistently excellent classic French dishes are always guaranteed.

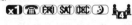

CAFÉ ROUGE
French

20A Winchester Street, Basingstoke, RG21 7DZ
01256 334 556
An attractive restaurant, a boulevard café or a Parisian-style wine bar; however you see Café Rouge, consistently excellent classic French dishes are always guaranteed.

CHOWDHURY'S CURRY LOUNGE
Indian

206 Shirley Rd, Southampton, SO15 3FH
02380 338 833
A large number of loyal diners as well as new guests are accommodated at this impressive Indian restaurant. The adventurous curry fan will love the wide range of unusual, less well-known dishes.

COAL GRILL + BAR
Mediterranean

Festival Place, Basingstoke, RG21 7BB
01256 358 898
Executive Chef Antonio Dias has created a range of tantalising dishes that are both fresh and delectable, regularly changing to bring diners seasonal products and diversity.

Not to be used with any other offer or the Prix Fixé menu

DHAKA INDIAN CUISINE
Bangladeshi/ Indian

11 Onslow Road, Southampton, SO14 0JD
02380 336 662
Sometimes there is nothing better than a simple curry, created and served by passionate staff in a welcoming environment.

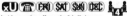

EL SABIO TAPAS
Spanish

60 Eastgate Street, Winchester, SO23 8DZ
01962 820 233
Effervescent, vivid and classic Spanish tapas at this family-run restaurant by the riverside in Winchester.

GOURMET PIZZA
Pizza

21 The Square, Winchester, SO23 9EX
01962 842 553
Nestled among local boutiques, this family-friendly venue offers a hearty and creative menu filled with heavenly pizzas and other classic options, served in a rustic dining room to an unpretentious crowd.

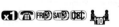

Must mention GS on arrival. No use with any other offers.

GURKHA CHAUTARI
Nepalese

18 Station Road, Liphook, GU30 7DR
01428 729 355
Take shelter on the trails of Nepal and sample the culinary delights on offer. An authentic atmosphere serving the finest, most delicious Nepalese cuisine.

HOBBITS RESTAURANT BAR
European

6B High Street, Hythe, Southampton, SO45 6AH
02380 848 524
A totally unique venue that delivers simple, fresh food every single day of the week. A great atmosphere is coupled with friendly staff who endeavour to ensure every guest is relaxed and content.

HOTEL DU VIN
European

Southgate Street, Winchester, SO23 9EF
01962 841 414
The finest, fresh local produce, simple European recipes, and stunning choice of wines; the trademark Hotel du Vin bistro. The original Hotel Du Vin wrought in Georgian splendour. Winner of 2 AA rosettes.

HUDSON'S
Caribbean

44 St Mary Street, St Mary's, Southampton, SO14 1NR
02380 232 332
Superb Caribbean food, cooked from scratch using the freshest, quality ingredients for a truly authentic Caribbean dining experience. Home delivery service is now available and large parties are welcome.

JASPER'S RESTAURANT
British

54 Station Road, Hayling Island, PO11 0EL
02392 463 226
Flair and imagination ignite the many dishes on offer in this fabulous restaurant. With a bar, à la carte and Sunday lunch menus, it is no surprise that this venue has a strong, loyal following.

RELENTLESS STEAK AND LOBSTER HOUSE
Seafood/ Fine Dining/ Vegetarian
NEW

85 Elm Grove, Southsea, Portsmouth, PO5 1JF
02392 822888
A Portsmouth restaurant with a descriptive name, a warm ambience and a great range of tasty, no-nonsense dishes, from a hearty surf 'n' turf to some neat crab cakes.

LA KING INN
Chinese

42 Osborne Road, Southsea, Portsmouth, PO5 3LT
02392 755 722
A great local restaurant serving authentic Chinese and Malaysian cuisine. Affable staff provide warm welcomes and efficient service.

LA MARGHERITA
Italian

1 Town Quay, Southampton, SO14 2AQ
02380 333 390
Combining terrific Italian cuisine with superb entertainment, this wonderfully popular restaurant offers great service and wonderful hospitality. A perfect venue to dine, drink and dance the night away.

www.gourmetsociety.co.uk

JSW

20 Dragon Street, Petersfield, GU31 4JJ

01730 262 030   *British*

JSW stands for Jake Saul Watkins, chef proprietor, serving exceptional food in stylish yet simple surroundings. The 17th century former coaching inn has all the prerequisites of this era: old beams, a well, a cellar (stocked with over 700 wines) and three tunnels to other buildings in the ancient town, including one to a past nunnery.

Jake's cooking style is based around the belief that cooking is a craft. He allows the ingredients to speak for themselves. With a focus on seasonal British food, fish is sourced from the nearby Solent, lamb, beef and pork from Cumbria and vegetables and soft fruit are sourced locally. 'Technically brilliant', according to one guide, his food is beautifully presented. This is cooking by someone with a passion for his work, while sensible pricing, lack of service charge and a policy of never turning tables, demonstrate Jake's wish to share his culinary prowess.

JSW has been awarded a Michelin star and three AA Rosettes, amongst other accolades.

LA ORIENT
Chinese

138 West Street, Fareham, PO16 0EL

01329 234 682

Offers a menu bursting with the finest Eastern dishes. Staff are incredibly helpful and are committed to ensuring every guest has a happy dining experience that exceeds satisfaction.

LANDINGS
Modern European

Falcon Hotel, 68 Farnborough Road, Farnborough, GU14 6TH

01252 545 378

If you are in need of an exquisite place for that all-important romantic meal, than look no further. A stunningly lit dining room offers the most elegant ambience.

LANES OF LYMINGTON
British

Ashley Lane, Lymington, SO41 3RH

01590 672 777

Discover this charming haven of a restaurant, located inside an architecturally stunning 19th century building. A simply elegant interior offers guests a calm and serene environment to enjoy.

LOCH FYNE
Seafood

Gunwharf Quays, Portsmouth, PO1 3BF

02392 778 060

From the roadside oyster bar that once was, Loch Fyne restaurants now successfully inject energy and passion into great food and wonderful flavours, whilst ensuring their seafood is sustainably sourced.

LOCH FYNE
Seafood

18 Jewry Street, Winchester, SO23 8RZ

01962 872 930

From the roadside oyster bar that once was, Loch Fyne restaurants now successfully inject energy and passion into great food and wonderful flavours, whilst ensuring their seafood is sustainably sourced.

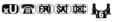

LUPA ITALIAN RESTAURANT
Italian

123-124 High Street, Southampton, SO14 2AA

02380 331 849

With a lively and contemporary continental ambience, Lupa serves classical, richly flavoured Italian dishes, including a broad and inviting array of pizzas.

MAHARAJA
Indian

55 High Street, Shanklin, Isle of Wight, PO37 6JJ

01983 867 083

Having honed his experience in acclaimed kitchens across the UK, Fozizur Rahman now leads the team at this restaurant in Shanklin, producing vibrant, rich and tasty Indian dishes in a cheerful atmosphere.

MANZIL TANDOORI
Indian

54 Onslow Road, Southampton, SO14 0JN

02380 227 423

A treasured curry house that is extremely popular with the local community. Reasonably priced Indian cuisine is available until late, making it the perfect place to dine either before or after a night out.

Sign up to our newsletter for latest restaurants, offers and more

MAYFLOWER
Chinese
1 May Place, Basingstoke, RG21 7NX
01256 328 989
This accommodating restaurant, perfectly sited in Basingstoke, provides a broad-based menu of dishes from the different regions and culinary traditions in China; fragrant, seasoned and delicious Chinese.

OLD DELHI EATERY
Indian
1 Oxford Street, Southampton, SO14 3DJ
02380 233 433
Award-winning restaurant that has earned itself an enviable reputation for providing marvellously tasty cuisine. Offers excitingly unusual creations such as their famous chocolate and chilli dish.

MOJA RESTAURANT
Indian
2 Holly Close, Locks Heath, Southampton, SO31 7BW
01489 571 999
A classic, traditional menu that allows diners to experience exotic Indian flavours at a venue that prides itself on a welcoming, friendly atmosphere, and the care and attention paid to guests.

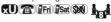

OLIVE TREE
Mediterranean
29 Oxford Street, Southampton, SO14 3DJ
02380 343 333
Locals are well acquainted with the delights of this fine Mediterranean restaurant, while newcomers rapidly become familiar with its excellence. Fresh fish and succulent meats are cooked to perfection.

MOWCHAK TANDOORI
Indian
270 Havant Road, Portsmouth, PO6 1PA
02392 375 007
Add a touch of spice to your life with the award-winning Mowchak Tandoori restaurant which provides exquisite, stylish Indian food, modern surroundings and warm, friendly staff.

PLUMMERS BISTRO AND CAFE
British
35 High Street, Ringwood, BH24 1AD
01425 474 563
A delightful bistro situated in a pleasant historic market town, with a focus on simple, high-quality food. Caters for all needs, day and night, with snacks, meals, and even traditional tea and cakes.

MOZZARELLA JOES
Italian
Clarence Esplanade, Southsea, Portsmouth, PO5 3AE
02392 295 004
Insists upon great food and superb service in a fresh and contemporary atmosphere. Offering fabulous stone-baked pizzas and enormous gourmet burgers cooked in a lively open-plan kitchen.

PREZZO
Italian
27 Market Place, Ringwood, BH24 1AN
01425 471 200
With a character all of its own, Prezzo oozes contemporary style and enduring charm. Signature pastas, stone-baked pizzas and classic Italian dishes promise a perfect dining choice for the whole family.

MR SO CHINESE RESTAURANT
Chinese
3 Jewry Street, Winchester, SO23 8RZ
01962 861 234
Providing dishes from different provinces of China, this authentic restaurant maintains its popular reputation for offering meals to suit every taste. The crackling pork is superbly tasty.

PREZZO
Italian
1-2 Market Square, Alton, GU34 1HD
01420 85580
With a character all of its own, Prezzo oozes contemporary style and enduring charm. Signature pastas, stone-baked pizzas and classic Italian dishes promise a perfect dining choice for the whole family.

NASHAA
Indian
51 Leigh Road, Eastleigh, SO50 9DF
02380 651 861
A fabulous subcontinental cuisine restaurant with a full open-view kitchen where you can see the skilled chefs at work, preparing mouth-watering traditional and modern Indian dishes.

PREZZO
Italian
43 The Boardwalk, Port Solent, Portsmouth, PO6 4TP
02392 387 951
With a character all of its own, Prezzo oozes contemporary style and enduring charm. Signature pastas, stone-baked pizzas and classic Italian dishes promise a perfect dining choice for the whole family.

NV RESTAURANT AND LOUNGE
British
129 High Street, Southampton, SO14 2PB
02380 332 255
A luxuriously grand restaurant that will impress every new arrival. Situated in a stunning listed building, the kitchen serves up lunch and à la carte menus that feature divine and delicious meals.

PREZZO
Italian
25 Oxford Street, Southampton, SO14 3DJ
02380 226 181
With a character all of its own, Prezzo oozes contemporary style and enduring charm. Signature pastas, stone-baked pizzas and classic Italian dishes promise a perfect dining choice for the whole family.

ODDBALLS WINE BAR & RESTAURANT
International
12 Clarendon Road, Southsea, Portsmouth, PO5 2EE
07793 110 453
An impressive, eclectic menu drawing on global influences, providing a refreshing variety of imaginative and creative dishes. Successfully caters for parties large or small, lively or intimate.

PREZZO
Italian
16 Jewry Street, Winchester, SO23 8BB
01962 864 256
With a character all of its own, Prezzo oozes contemporary style and enduring charm. Signature pastas, stone-baked pizzas and classic Italian dishes promise a perfect dining choice for the whole family.

PREZZO *Italian*
55 High Street, Lymington, SO41 9AH
01590 677 910
With a character all of its own, Prezzo oozes contemporary style and enduring charm. Signature pastas, stone-baked pizzas and classic Italian dishes promise a perfect dining choice for the whole family.

PREZZO *Italian*
The Old Pump House, 20 High St, Lyndhurst, SO43 7BD
02380 282 680
With a character all of its own, Prezzo oozes contemporary style and enduring charm. Signature pastas, stone-baked pizzas and classic Italian dishes promise a perfect dining choice for the whole family.

PREZZO *Italian*
Unit L1A, Swan Leisure Centre, Eastleigh, SO50 5SF
02380 610 772
With a character all of its own, Prezzo oozes contemporary style and enduring charm. Signature pastas, stone-baked pizzas and classic Italian dishes promise a perfect dining choice for the whole family.

PREZZO *Italian*
21 Palmerston Street, Romsey, SO51 8GF
01794 517 353
With a character all of its own, Prezzo oozes contemporary style and enduring charm. Signature pastas, stone-baked pizzas and classic Italian dishes promise a perfect dining choice for the whole family.

RAJDHANI *Indian*
21 Bevois Valley Road, Southampton, SO14 0JP
02380 231 002
Excellent food until 3am, 7 days a week. Renowned for distinctive flavourings and tender meat, the whole menu is prepared and cooked to perfection, served by friendly staff in a contemporary atmosphere.

REGGINA'S ITALIAN RESTAURANT *Italian*
15 High Street, Botley, Southampton, SO30 2EA
01489 782 068
In the picturesque village of Botley, with quiet elegance, enjoy a menu of creative cuisine to delight your palate and fix your appetite, with a wide selection of excellent wines to complement every dish.

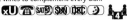

RHINEFIELD HOUSE HOTEL *Fine Dining*
Rhinefield House, Rhinefield Rd, Brockenhurst, SO42 7QB
0845 072 7516
The blend of fine dining and a special atmosphere at this Hand Picked Hotels restaurant has two AA rosettes testifying to its exceptional quality. Settle in for sophisticated, nuanced British recipes.

SAFFRON RESTAURANT *Indian*
1-3 Kingston Road, Portsmouth, PO1 5RX
02392 779 797
Expect a substantial and refined menu populated by good quality, eclectic Indian dishes at this restaurant in Portsmouth. Service is both friendly and knowledgeable; you can count on a top-notch curry.

BAR RISA *English/Gastro pub*
Boulevard Bdgs, Gunwharf Quays, Portsmouth, PO1 3TW
02392 298563
Whether you want to enjoy a generous serving of traditional fish and chips or tuck into the outstanding hunters chicken then this is the place to be, set in the lush backdrop of the famous Gunwharf Quays.

SARA'S THAI CUISINE *Thai*
273 Portswood Road, Southampton, SO17 2LD
02380 676 063
This intimate restaurant comes well recommended for its reasonable prices and glorious Thai food. Their vegetarian, stir-fried and Thai grilled dishes are all scrumptiously good.

SEASHELL RESTAURANT & GRILL *Seafood/ Fine Dining/ Vegetarian*
Appley Beach, Ryde, Isle of Wight, PO33 1ND
01983 811 212
Outstandingly delicious dishes can be expected at this appealing restaurant. Cooked with accomplishment and verve, the gourmet food can be enjoyed whilst taking in unrivalled views of the Solent.

TAP'S *European*
William Street, Northam, Southampton, SO14 5QL
02380 228 621
Based on a historical site, this nautical-themed restaurant offers a full and varied Mediterranean menu using only the finest produce available. Tasty and wholesome food in a pleasant, friendly setting.

THE VINE *Traditional English*
West Side, Waterlooville, PO7 4RW
02392 632419
The Vine in Waterlooville delivers everything you could want in a traditional English pub. With great food and warm service, this charming hostelry is a local favourite.

THE BRASSERIE AT LANGSTONE *Modern British*
Langstone Hotel, Northney Rd, Hayling Isl., PO11 0NQ
02392 465 011
Sleek and sophisticated dishes populate the menu of this modern, cool and relaxing hotel restaurant. Recognised with an AA Rosette for its food; occupies a serene, calming location.

THE BUSH INN *British*
Ovington, Alresford, SO24 0RE
01962 732 764
Ensconced in beautiful Hampshire countryside, this pub restaurant is an inviting place for that languid drink or dinner. The menu is fresh and accomplished, serving thoroughly tasty gastro-pub fare.

Offer excludes Sunday lunch and Christmas menu

THE FLYING BULL INN *English/Gastro pub*
London Road, Rake, GU33 7JB
01730 892 285
Enjoy affordable quality and comfort at this wonderful inn situated in a peaceful village. Attentive staff ensure a superb experience while providing well presented, home-made food cooked to perfection.

Visit the website regularly to discover the latest restaurants joining the GS

THE HIGH CORNER INN
British

Linwood, Ringwood, BH24 3QY
01425 473 973
This beautiful country inn is ensconced in the New Forest and serves as a calming, welcoming retreat. A great place to take a room and explore the local area, it also serves fabulous, classic British fare.

Offer excludes Sunday lunch and Christmas menu

THE KEEPERS ARMS
British

Terwick Lane, Trotton, Petersfield, GU31 5ER
01730 813 724
Comfortably nestled on the hillside above the river Rother, the welcoming character of this country pub exceeds expectations. Real ales, simple meals and more elegant dishes are all available.

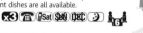

THE NEW TAJ MAHAL
Indian

54 Kingston Road, North End, Portsmouth, PO2 7PA
02392 661 021
A welcome commingling of the opulent old with the bang up to date at the New Taj Mahal. Enjoy the breadth of their menu and the depth of their flavours with rich spice, silky sauce and piquant marinades.

THE NURSE'S COTTAGE
Fine Dining

Station Road, Sway, Lymington, SO41 6BA
01590 683 402
A haven for tourists wanting comfort and cosiness. The owners are passionate about first-rate service and are proud of the restaurant's award-winning cuisine.

THE OLD HOUSE HOTEL
British

The Square, Wickham, PO17 5JG
01329 833 049
Recipient of two AA Rosettes, the kitchen focuses on combining classic British cuisine with contemporary influences. Guests enjoy the local Hampshire fare as the owners promote regional food and drink.

Offer excludes Sunday set menu

THE RED LION
International

High Street, Oakhanger, Bordon, GU35 9JQ
01420 472 232
Built in 1550, this is a typically traditional country pub with real open fires and fresh home-made dishes. Internationally inspired food ensures its local reputation and popularity for exquisite meals.

Sundays, offer lunchtime only.

THE THREE LIONS
European

Stuckton, Fordingbridge, SP6 2HF
01425 652 489
Situated in the lush haven of the New Forest National Park, The Three Lions is a wonderful place to sample local produce and feast on exquisitely prepared dishes. The 150 bin wine list is an added treat.

THE TROOPER INN
British

Alton Road, Froxfield, Petersfield, GU32 1BD
01730 827 293
This beautiful pub is high up in Hampshire; steal a march and enjoy its location while you take your choice of classic pub fare or something more eclectic. Exceptionally welcoming and accomplished inn.

THE WELLINGTON ARMS
European

Stratfield Turgis, Hook, RG27 0AS
01256 882 214
In the exceptionally elegant, charming Wellington Arms Hotel, you can enjoy quality, refined food that won't leave you thinking of the proverbial boot, but rather the fabled beef.

THE WESTGATE HOTEL
British

2 Romsey Road, Winchester, SO23 8TP
01962 820 222
In bright and refined dining rooms, you can enjoy one of the best steaks in town: thick and rich and aged for flavour. Add to that the fresh, seasonal flavours and you're in for a treat.

THREE HORSESHOES
British

Bighton, Arlesford, SO24 9RE
01962 732 859
A venue bursting with charming character, showcasing a staunchly British menu prepared to perfection. This pub brings back memories of a sadly missed tradition of English hospitality.

TIGER TIGER
British

Gunwharf Quays, Portsmouth, PO1 3TP
02392 882 244
Dine and drink in Portsmouth's most famous bar, restaurant and club. With its six individual and unique areas, Tiger Tiger will suit you whatever the atmosphere you're after.

TOSCAS ITALIAN RESTAURANT
Italian

44 Commercial Road, Southampton, SO15 1GD
02380 572 844
The variety of choice, from tasty pizzas and pasta dishes to a full à la carte menu, make this restaurant an excellent option. The dramatic setting makes it a perfect choice for theatregoers.

TRUFFLES FRANÇAIS
French

67 Castle Road, Southsea, Portsmouth, PO5 3AY
02392 730 796
No need for a Gallic shrug with respect to this terrific restaurant in Southsea: you'll not be diffident after trying the tournedos of venison and wild boar, or any other of the French classics here.

WATERS EDGE@MERCURY YACHT HARBOUR
European

Satchell Ln, Hamble, Southampton, SO30 4HQ
02380 457 220
A restaurant set on the famous river Hamble where the dazzling variety of wildlife meets with the bustle of the yachting fraternity. Here dining and drinking can be enjoyed any time of the day or evening.

WESTOVER HALL
European

Parklane, Milford on Sea, Lymington, SO41 0PT
01590 643 044
Westover Hall envelops you with its magical and individual style, with sea views and dishes formulated superbly from award-winning ingredients. Its excellence is grounded in clever use of local produce.

www.gourmetsociety.co.uk

WHITE HORSE INN
Indian

South Hill, Droxford, SO32 3PB
01489 877 490
Down-to-earth village pub that serves a tasty array of Indian food along with some pub classics. Enjoy the easy feel and the accommodating atmosphere.

WHITE SWAN
Carvery

Mansbridge Road, Southhampton, SO18 3HW
02380 473 322
A member of the Great British Carvery group which offers the well-loved classic feast with a modern twist. Situated in a picturesque, semi-rural location, this pub has a charmingly pleasant nature.

Call beforehand on special event days.

YENZ
Chinese

Lyndhurst Road, Brockenhurst, SO42 7RL
01590 622 005
A conveniently located gem serving great Chinese and Cantonese cuisine. The tastefully decorated restaurant as well as the function room means that this restaurant is suitable for all party sizes.

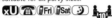

Hertfordshire

ALBAN TANDOORI
Indian

145 Victoria Street, St Albans, AL1 3TA
01727 862 111
Family-run Indian restaurant with a modern and comfortable atmosphere. The aim is to make all guests' dining experience a pleasurable one, where food is prepared with passion and served with care.

ASIA
Pan Asian

2 Beaconsfield Road, St Albans, AL1 3RD
01727 800 002
This restaurant boasts a precisely crafted interior and innovative dishes, along with carefully selected wines. Through passion, Asia has created some enviable dishes with a reputation to prove it.

BORDERS @ HOLIDAY INN
International

London Road, Markyate, AL3 8HH
01582 449 988
A Holiday Inn idyllically located in a peaceful location surrounded by countryside. Wake up to a hot buffet breakfast or enjoy a beautiful evening meal in the brasserie-style restaurant.

1 card per table.

CAFÉ ROUGE
French

29 Holywell Hill, St Albans, AL1 1HD
01727 832 777
An attractive restaurant, a boulevard café or a Parisian-style wine bar; however you see Café Rouge, consistently excellent classic French dishes are always guaranteed.

CAFÉ ROUGE
French

296-298 High Street, Berkhamsted, HP4 1AH
01442 878 141
An attractive restaurant, a boulevard café or a Parisian-style wine bar; however you see Café Rouge, consistently excellent classic French dishes are always guaranteed.

CAFÉ ROUGE
French

3 Parliament Square, Hertford, SG14 1EX
01992 535 363
An attractive restaurant, a boulevard café or a Parisian-style wine bar; however you see Café Rouge, consistently excellent classic French dishes are always guaranteed.

CAFÉ ROUGE
French

11 High Street, Hitchin, SG5 1BH
01462 432 962
An attractive restaurant, a boulevard café or a Parisian-style wine bar; however you see Café Rouge, consistently excellent classic French dishes are always guaranteed.

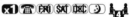

CIBO DIVINO
Italian

4-5 Waddington Road, St Albans, AL3 5EX
1727899189
A proper ristorante, with real verve and colour in the cooking and an array of traditional Italian recipes that you won't find on every menu. A restaurant of high regard.

CINTA GARDEN RESTAURANT
Chinese

8 The Colonnade, Verulam Road, St Albans, AL3 4DD
01727 837 606
Oriental cuisine carefully chosen to create a varied and exciting menu with a choice of fine wines. This well-laid-out restaurant offers diners a night of entertainment in the centre of St. Albans.

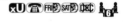

COCHIN CUISINE
Indian

61 High Street, Hemel Hempstead, HP1 3AF
01442 233 777
Master chefs from Kerala produce their unique, naturally healthy cuisine with fresh and aromatic spices. The restaurant blends taste and tradition to create an unforgettable experience.

DARCY'S RESTAURANT
European

2 Hatfield Road, St Albans, AL1 3RP
01727 730 777
Independent restaurant in picturesque St Albans. Drawing imaginatively on culinary influences from Asia, Australia and Europe, Darcy's puts together stylish and contemporary dishes in a warm ambience.

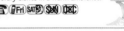

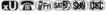

DE JA VU
Indian

19 High Street, Cheshunt, EN8 0BX
01992 636 325
De Ja Vu brings the best of exotic Indian cuisine to the beating heart of Hertfordshire. Flawless service and a laid-back vibe have made it a firm favourite with the locals.

No GS offer on special days/entertainment nights. Call ahead.

When booking restaurants always mention your GS membership

DESTINATIONS @ HOLIDAY INN
International
St Georges Way, Stevenage, SG1 1HS
01438 722 727
Dine at Destinations and you won't be disappointed. An ideal venue for private dining events, the restaurant offers a differently themed menu every night of the week. Sumptuous exotic dishes guaranteed.

DOUGHTY'S
British
87 Bancroft, Hitchin, SG5 1NQ
01462 456 363
Set in a beautifully restored building in the heart of Hitchin's vibrant town centre, Doughty's offers the finest seasonal produce, prepared simply to delight the most discerning of tastes.

DOWN HALL HOTEL (IBBETSONS)
British
Matching Road, Hatfield Heath, CM22 7AS
01279 731 441
An elegant Hand Picked Hotels restaurant situated in a leading country house hotel, offering a fine dining menu that reflects British traditions in timeless surroundings. Awarded 2 AA Rosettes.

DOWN HALL HOTEL (THE GRILL)
European
Matching Road, Hatfield Heath, CM22 7AS
01279 731 441
Informal dining throughout the day at this Hand Picked Hotels restaurant, with a stunning interior and abundance of natural light. Delivers a contemporary British menu that changes seasonally.

MOKOKO
English/ Chinese/Thai
26 Verulam Road, St Albans, AL3 4DE
01727 852287
A cool, sophisticated cocktail, champagne and wine bar in the heart of St Albans, Mokoko adds to the great ambience and laid-back vibe an excellent "finger dinners" menu.

NEW

FREDDIE'S
European
52 Adelaide Street, St Albans, AL3 5BG
01727 811 889
Bright, smart and contemporary European-style restaurant that serves an eclectic array of beautifully realised and presented dishes in a cosy, welcoming atmosphere.

GREAT HALLINGBURY MANOR
European
Tilekiln Green, Great Hallingbury, Bishops Stortford, CM22 7TJ
01279 506 475
Prepare to delight your taste buds with a unique country dining experience that's also excellent value for money. Attractive and exquisitely prepared food; the culmination of many years experience.

HANBURY MANOR HOTEL
French
Zodiac & Oakes, Cambridge Road, Ware, SG12 0SD
01920 487 722
Situated within a majestic Marriot hotel, boasting high-quality services and facilities, the Zodiac restaurant and Oakes Grill delivers blissful, 2 AA Rosette fine dining with many contemporary offerings.

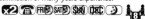

HARPENDEN HOUSE HOTEL
British
18 Southdown Road, Harpenden, AL5 1PE
01582 449 955
A new outpost of the exceptional team from the Vineyard at Stockcross, this exceptional hotel-based restaurant is unfussy in manner and deliciously precise in execution.

JADE GARDEN
Oriental
16 Spencer Street, St Albans, AL3 5EG
01727 856 077
A popular restaurant within the city allowing guests to indulge in predominately Cantonese-style cooking enhanced by the tasteful décor. A wonderful selection of dishes offers something new every time.

LE MOULIN
European
3 Mill Walk, Wheathampstead, St Albans, AL4 8DT
01582 831 988
Bijou little restaurant with attached patisserie offering beautifully cooked French and modern European cuisine, from delicate tapas dishes to a full-bodied cassoulet.

LE RENDEZ-VOUS
French
64 High Street, Ware, SG12 9DA
01920 461 021
Welcoming, charismatic restaurant with an emphasis on beautifully cooked combinations of fresh local ingredients, all with a healthy French influence. Take a look at their imaginative, bubbly specials.

LE SPICE MERCHANT
Indian
14 High Steet, Ware, SG12 9BX
01920 468 383
Light and lively Indian food in this coaching inn, with a real attention to freshness. The menu is encompassing and the setting open and inviting.

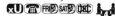

LOCH FYNE
Seafood
5/5b Verulam Road, St Albans, AL3 4DA
01727 799 050
From the roadside oyster bar that once was, Loch Fyne restaurants now successfully inject energy and passion into great food and wonderful flavours, whilst ensuring their seafood is sustainably sourced.

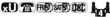

LOCH FYNE
Seafood
130 Fore Street, Hertford, SG14 1AJ
01992 585 440
From the roadside oyster bar that once was, Loch Fyne restaurants now successfully inject energy and passion into great food and wonderful flavours, whilst ensuring their seafood is sustainably sourced.

MARTINS POND
Modern British
The Green, Potten End, Berkhamsted, HP4 2QQ
01442 864 318
Set in a picturesque, historical village, Martins Pond serves a tasty array of classic British food; try the cleanly flavoured potted ham with celeriac remoulade, and the thoroughgoing, hearty pork belly.

MEDUSA BAR RESTAURANT
Mediterranean

1 Queensway, Stevenage, SG1 1DA
01438 360 500
Sleek, modern ambience in this restaurant whose emphasis is on an array of Mediterranean flavours along with classic grill fare: from meaty, tart souvlaki to a variety of steak cuts with the trimmings.

MUHINUR TANDOORI HOUSE
Indian

1 Green Yard, Waltham Abbey, EN9 1RD
01992 766 333
Deliciously tasty Indian cuisine will have you wanting to return here over and over again. Classic curries sit side by side with more unusual dishes, whilst the lower oil levels make much healthier dishes.

OSCAR'S PIZZA COMPANY
Italian

21 High Street, Kings Langley, WD4 8AB
01923 263 800
Sicilian family-owned restaurant offering consistently high-quality food at affordable prices. A well-respected, popular venue that offers perfect pasta dishes and delicious pizzas.

OUTSIDE IN
Locally Sourced

Beales Hotel, Comet Way, Hatfield, AL10 9NG
01707 288 500
A bright environment in which you can enjoy beautifully prepared food. The dishes available have been specifically designed so that accompaniments enhance the intense flavours of the main ingredient.

PREZZO
Italian

15 Leyton Road, Harpenden, AL5 2HX
01582 469 007
With a character all of its own, Prezzo oozes contemporary style and enduring charm. Signature pastas, stone-baked pizzas and classic Italian dishes promise a perfect dining choice for the whole family.

PREZZO
Italian

Unit 9, Stevenage Leisure Park, Stevenage, SG1 2UA
01438 355 591
With a character all of its own, Prezzo oozes contemporary style and enduring charm. Signature pastas, stone-baked pizzas and classic Italian dishes promise a perfect dining choice for the whole family.

PREZZO
Italian

128 High Street, Old Town, Stevenage, SG1 3DB
01438 361 576
With a character all of its own, Prezzo oozes contemporary style and enduring charm. Signature pastas, stone-baked pizzas and classic Italian dishes promise a perfect dining choice for the whole family.

PREZZO
Italian

Unit 4, 15 Bancroft, Hitchin, SG5 1JQ
01462 453 366
With a character all of its own, Prezzo oozes contemporary style and enduring charm. Signature pastas, stone-baked pizzas and classic Italian dishes promise a perfect dining choice for the whole family.

SAVANNA RESTAURANT
British

The Blacklion, 198 Fishpool St, St Albans, AL3 4SB
01727 891 040
Located in a traditional English inn which maintains its 18th century character, this restaurant provides the most enjoyable retreat for both business and leisure guests seeking fine dining.

SINATRA'S RISTORANTE ITALIANO
Italian

75 Waterhouse Street, Hemel Hempstead, HP1 1ED
01442 240 030
Cool and collected Italian restaurant in Hemel Hempstead whose menu is ranging, authentic and full of the zip, heart and mellowness you want from an Italian meal.

TEMPLE BAR & RESTAURANT
Indian/Bangladeshi

1-4 Tudor Square, West Street, Ware, SG12 9XF
01920 484 675
Plush and cosy Indian restaurant where you'll enjoy an excellent meal in comfortable, atmospheric surroundings; try their wholesome, tasty fusion-style cuisine, with all the traditional favourites to boot.

THAI ON THE HILL
Thai

30 Holywell Hill, St Albans, AL1 1BZ
01727 832 841
A refreshingly vibrant dining scene where you will find fabulously authentic Thai cuisine at excellent prices. Specialities such as the red tilapia fillet steamed with Chinese leaf are well worth trying.

THE CABINET
Contemporary

High Street, Reed, Royston, SG8 8AH
01763 848 366
An acclaimed and renowned inn offering real quality in an informal setting. The menu is eclectic, drawing on a number of different national cuisines but always featuring superb, carefully sourced produce.

PONSBOURNE PARK

Newgate Street Village, Hertford, SG13 8RF
01707 876191
Ponsbourne Park's restaurant is smart and elegant in style, complementing the fine surroundings. The menu plays on this very English location with some excellent takes on local meat and game.

NEW

THE LEMON TREE
British

14-16 Water Lane, Bishops Stortford, CM23 2LB
01279 757 788
Dine in the most pleasurable surroundings at The Lemon Tree. Situated within a well-preserved 16th century building, the modern British-themed menu offers exquisite dishes for lunch and dinner.

THE PANTRY
British

4 Harding Parade, Harpenden, AL5 4SW
01582 765 544
At this newly refurbished Harpenden restaurant you'll find modern British cuisine prepared with classic inflections, firmly fixed on its local suppliers and a real sense of place.

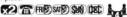

94

Enjoy massive leisure and retail savings with more Gourmet Society

THE PAVILION
Indian
38 High Street, Markyate, AL3 8PB
01582 841 843
Bright and vital Indian restaurant in Markyate with a strong sense of unity and commitment in purpose. The restaurant puts together warm and richly spiced recipes in a thoroughly accommodating ambience.

THE PLOUGH AND HARROW
British
88 Southdown, Harpenden, AL5 1PR
01582 715 844
Atmospheric and lively local pub with live music, quiz, and a genial, appealing relationship with its regulars. Enjoy a hearty and classic pub meal as part of a great night.

THE THREE HORSESHOES
Traditional English
74 High Street, Hinxworth, Baldock, SG7 5HQ
01462 742 280
From classic, fluffy breaded mushrooms to the superbly savoury twang of their ham, eggs and chips, this pub-restaurant is a warm and lovely place to eat, in a charismatic old thatched building.

THE WHITE LION INN
English Gastropub
Startops End, Marsworth, Tring, HP23 4LJ
01442 822 325
Discreetly located by the side of the canal, this delightful inn is completely fitting for its picturesque surroundings and serves superbly savoury gastro-pub dishes with British and French influences.

RECOMMEND A FRIEND
see page 18

THREE HORSESHOES
English and Continental
Three Horseshoes, East Common, Harpenden, AL5 1AW
01582 713 953
The perfect destination to enjoy a good, hearty meal, with its fabulous gardens and cosy interior. All dishes are freshly prepared and are altered with the seasons. Enjoy with ales and wine by the glass.

YOUNG PRETENDER
Carvery
Hempstead Road, Kings Langley, WD4 8BR
01923 263 150
One of the many Great British Carveries on offer for Gourmet Society members. Enjoy the best of British in this handsome pub that successfully offers great food and good service.

Call beforehand for special event days.

ZEUS HOTEL AND RESTAURANT
Greek
20 High Street, Baldock, SG7 6AX
01462 893 620
Located in the heart of one of Hertfordshire's oldest towns sits this wonderful hotel and restaurant, where a talented team of kitchen staff provide exquisite tasting Greek cuisine.

Kent

ALEXANDRA RISTORANTE ITALIANO
Italian
70 Harbour Parade, Ramsgate, CT11 8LP
01843 590 595
An authentic Ramsgate restaurant offering diners a wide choice of authentic Italian pizza, pasta, meat, fish and vegetarian specialities, all exceptionally prepared and creatively produced.

ANTONIAS
Italian
160 High Street, Tonbridge, TN9 1BB
01732 368 877
An unforgettable dining experience awaits you at Antonias. Tempting aromas lead to tantalizing tastes at this modern and comfortable Italian restaurant.

ATRIUM RESTAURANT
Contemporary
86 High Street, Rochester, ME7 1NA
01634 847 776
A modern venue run by a former army veteran who once cooked for the Queen, serving a unique fusion of British and Mediterranean cuisine. Service is great while the breadth of the wine list is unparalleled.

BEST WESTERN DONNINGTON MANOR
European
London Road, Dunton Green, Sevenoaks, TN13 2TD
01732 462 681
Step back in time and enjoy a meal in the unrivalled, intimate ambience of the Chartwell restaurant. Wholesome British dishes prepared to the highest standards using great, fresh produce.

BLUE RAYS RESTAURANT
Malaysian
186a High Street, Rochester, ME1 1EY
01634 813 888
A unique restaurant offering delicious dishes guaranteed to awaken your senses. Offers Malaysian food which captures an impressive variety of tastes and spices.

BRANDS HATCH PLACE HOTEL & SPA
British
The Dining Room, Brands Hatch Rd, Fawkham, DA3 8NQ
0845 072 7395
Traditional favourites meet new creations at this Hand Picked Hotels group establishment. Find exceptionally satisfying dishes that make use of quality local produce. Awarded 2 AA Rosettes.

CAFÉ BELGE
French
89 St Dunstans, Canterbury, CT2 8AD
01227 768 222
Beautifully located within a 15th century hall, the restaurant has magnificent vaulted ceilings that add to the evocative atmosphere that is created by the historic beauty of the building.

SOUTH EAST

95

CAFÉ BELGE
French
High Street, West Malling, ME19 6QH
01732 843 247
A food lover's paradise, where mouth-watering cuisine can be enjoyed in a great environment. Situated inside a 15th century hall, the restaurant boasts stained glass panels and fine decorative ironwork.

CAFÉ ROUGE
French
Unit 3 & 5, Longmarket, Canterbury, CT1 2JS
01227 784 984
An attractive restaurant, a boulevard café or a Parisian-style wine bar; however you see Café Rouge, consistently excellent classic French dishes are always guaranteed.

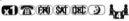

CAFÉ ROUGE
French
Bligh's Meadow, Pembroke Road, Sevenoaks, TN13 1AS
01732 450 395
An attractive restaurant, a boulevard café or a Parisian-style wine bar; however you see Café Rouge, consistently excellent classic French dishes are always guaranteed.

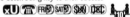

CAFÉ ROUGE
French
43 High Street, Tenterden, TN30 6BJ
01580 763 029
An attractive restaurant, a boulevard café or a Parisian-style wine bar; however you see Café Rouge, consistently excellent classic French dishes are always guaranteed.

CANTINA
Mexican
61 Dover Street, Canterbury, CT1 3HD
01227 450 288
With its own unique Californian style this restaurant offers up funky, bright décor and an uncompromising attitude towards cooking popular, quality food, with attention to detail being key to their success

CHILSTON PARK HOTEL
British
Culpeper Restaurant, Sandway, Lenham, ME17 2BE
08450 727 426
Whether you arrive with a firm favourite dish in mind, or you fancy being a little more adventurous, the chef aims to please all at this Hand Picked Hotels group venue. Awarded 2 AA Rosettes.

CHINA PALACE
Chinese
35 Maidstone Road, Rochester, ME1 1RL
01634 401 777
Colourful and vibrant plates of brilliant, bright Chinese food. A welcoming and accommodating restaurant with the bonus of a superb resident pianist who plays at the weekend.

CHOPSTICKS RESTAURANT
Chinese
Island Road, Hersden, CT3 4EY
01227 719 719
Great little characterful Chinese restaurant on the Cowley Road. Serves an array of colour-filled, spicy dishes. A selection of menus are also on offer, ideal for business lunches or an evening meal.

COCO DINER
Indian
330 High Street, Chatham, ME4 4NR
01634 842 489
The emphasis here is on healthy food by using less oil, sugar and artificial additives, and more herbs and spices. Gourmet flavours of South India are recreated with a wealth of knowledge.

CROWN POINT INN
Carvery
Seal Hollow Road, Sevenoaks, TN15 0HB
01732 810 669
One of the many Great British Carveries that takes a modern twist on the well loved classic feast. Allow the friendly staff to treat you like a king in this comfortably furnished pub.

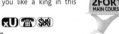

Call beforehand on special event days.

DON GIOVANNI
Italian
18 Bouverie Road West, Folkestone, CT20 2SZ
01303 850 962
A long-established restaurant delivering authentic Italian cuisine, with a vast menu offering dishes that will appeal to all diners. Also boasts a wine list that will please all palates and wallets.

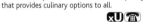

FISHERMANS WHARF
Contemporary
The Quay, Sandwich, CT13 9RU
01304 613 636
With its perfect waterfront location, flower-filled courtyard and unique atmosphere, this is a perfect venue to sample their succulent contemporary menu that provides culinary options to all.

FLAMING HENRY'S
British
62/63 High Street, Maidstone, ME14 1SR
01622 669 333
Exuberant Tudor-themed restaurant that serves abundant helpings of succulent meat, fish and vegetables with all the big, hale heartiness of Henry VIII's court.

FOOD FOR THOUGHT
European
19 The Green, Westerham, TN16 1AX
01959 569 888
Diverse food from around the world is on the menu here, with everything cooked fresh and changing with the seasons. Perfect venue throughout the day offering guests extensive choice.

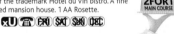

HOTEL DU VIN
European
Crescent Road, Tunbridge Wells, TN1 2LY
01892 526 455
The finest, freshest local produce, simple European recipes, a stunning choice of wines; these are the elements of the trademark Hotel du Vin bistro. A fine grade II listed mansion house. 1 AA Rosette.

KALARED BAR AND RESTAURANT
Chinese
83 Bank Street, Maidstone, ME14 1SD
01622 686 683
Quench your thirst and feed your appetite in this stylish bar and restaurant. Luxurious settings provide guests with the perfect backdrop to their dining experience. Oriental set feasts are available.

Recommend a friend to the Gourmet Society and receive a free gift.

KING CHARLES HOTEL
British

King Charles Hotel, Brompton Rd, Gillingham, ME7 5QT
01634 830 303

A beautiful hotel houses this wonderful restaurant that serves English and International dishes. Both guests and non-residents can enjoy the extensive à la carte menu created by highly imaginative chefs.

LE RESTAURANT FABRICE
French

London Road, Teynham, Sittingbourne, ME9 9PS
01795 521 330

An award-winning restaurant serving plush, classical French cuisine. Gourmet dishes and an accommodating, luxurious setting.

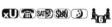

LIME TREE ON THE SQUARE
British

8-10 The Square, Lenham, ME17 2PQ
01622 859 509

A perfectly balanced blend of modern vibrancy and traditional surroundings, this restaurant is a wonderful place to dine. Creatively mastered European cuisine is complemented by a worldwide wine list.

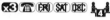

LOCH FYNE
Seafood

63-65 High Street, Sevenoaks, TN13 1JY
01732 467 140

From the roadside oyster bar that once was, Loch Fyne restaurants now successfully inject energy and passion into great food and wonderful flavours, whilst ensuring their seafood is sustainably sourced.

MARLOWES
English and Continental

55 St Peter Street, Canterbury, CT1 2BE
01227 462 194

Enjoy English and continental cuisine in a laid-back atmosphere, whilst sampling one of the many stocked beverages. Eat inside, or out front when the sun permits, at this simple yet satisfying venue.

MEXXA MEXXA
Mexican

40 Earl Street, Maidstone, ME14 1PS
01622 662 020

A wide range of favourite and the less well-known dishes are on offer in this efficient and friendly Mexican restaurant. The paella and patata con carne come highly recommended.

MONTROSE RESTAURANT
Modern European

35 Queens Rd, Tunbridge Wells, TN4 0RX
01892 513 161

Montrose restaurant is named after the famous French vineyard Château Montrose, founded by a group of food and wine professionals, offering a truly unique boutique dining experience.

MOOLI NEPALESE CUISINE
Indian/ Nepalese

57-59 Calverley Road, Tunbridge Wells, TN1 2UY
01892 545 499

With a reputation established from their acclaimed Oxted restaurant, the award-winning Mooli team have brought their expertise in the delicate flavours of Nepalese cuisine to this new location in Kent.

MORTON'S FORK
British

42 Station Road, Minster, CT12 4BZ
01843 823 000

With its classic wooden beams, this restaurant is packed with character in which to enjoy its fulsome dishes, from the classic, hearty mixed grill to the vibrant duck in vodka and black cherry sauce.

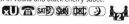

PALIO
Italian

84-86 Grosvenor Road, Tunbridge Wells, TN1 2AS
01892 515 558

Superb wines accompany the second-to-none Italian dishes that are on offer. Highly experienced staff provide a friendly and attentive service, making this an ideal venue whatever the occasion.

PAPERMAKERS ARMS
British

The Street, Plaxtol, Sevenoaks, TN15 0QJ
01732 810 407

A wonderful local village pub that offers everything from home-made meals to well kept ales. Friendly staff ensure every guest is made to feel welcome. The fish and chips is a firm favourite.

PATOGH
Persian

2 Effingham Street, Ramsgate, CT11 9AT
01843 852 631

Patogh is Persian for a place to relax and unwind and that is exactly what you will find at this stylish Ramsgate favourite. Delicious Persian food will entice you in. A must-visit restaurant.

POCO LOCO
Spanish

58 High Street, Chatham, ME4 4DS
01634 844 198

Prepare your palate for a taste extravaganza as you enter the culture of Mexico and experience the food on offer. A zingy menu formed with traditional dishes that offer diners an explosion of flavour.

PREZZO
Italian

29 High Street, Canterbury, CT1 2AZ
01227 379 571

With a character all of its own, Prezzo oozes contemporary style and enduring charm. Signature pastas, stone-baked pizzas and classic Italian dishes promise a perfect dining choice for the whole family.

PREZZO
Italian

16 Albion Street, Broadstairs, CT10 1LU
01843 871 188

With a character all of its own, Prezzo oozes contemporary style and enduring charm. Signature pastas, stone-baked pizzas and classic Italian dishes promise a perfect dining choice for the whole family.

PREZZO
Italian

1-3 High Street, Whitstable, CT5 1AP
01227 276 508

With a character all of its own, Prezzo oozes contemporary style and enduring charm. Signature pastas, stone-baked pizzas and classic Italian dishes promise a perfect dining choice for the whole family.

PREZZO
Italian

45 Earl Street, Maidstone, E14 1PD
01622 677 499
With a character all of its own, Prezzo oozes contemporary style and enduring charm. Signature pastas, stone-baked pizzas and classic Italian dishes promise a perfect dining choice for the whole family.

PREZZO
Italian

84 Mount Pleasant Road, Tunbridge Wells, TN1 1RT
01892 547 558
With a character all of its own, Prezzo oozes contemporary style and enduring charm. Signature pastas, stone-baked pizzas and classic Italian dishes promise a perfect dining choice for the whole family.

PREZZO
Italian

52 High Street, Tenterden, TN30 6AU
01580 764 769
With a character all of its own, Prezzo oozes contemporary style and enduring charm. Signature pastas, stone-baked pizzas and classic Italian dishes promise a perfect dining choice for the whole family.

**DETAILED DESCRIPTIONS
AVAILABLE ON**

www.gourmetsociety.co.uk

THE BULL HOTEL
English/Gastro pub

The Bull Hotel, Bull Lane, Sevenoaks, TN15 7RF
01732 789800
The Bull Hotel is a smart, bright, colourful place to visit. The menu is imaginative and well-conceived, from the subtly sharp celeriac and apple soup to the pheasant leg confit.

NEW

RIGGINGS
Seafood

6 East Street, Herne Bay, CT6 5HN
01227 361 880
A family-run continental restaurant specialising in fresh local fish straight from the water, complemented with 32 different varieties of wine from all over the globe.

À la carte menu only.

SAMPHIRE AT HAM
British

Hay Hill, Ham, Sandwich, CT14 0ED
01304 617 362
Delightful cuisine is proudly presented as being 'Kentish with a twist' at this charmingly charismatic restaurant. Every hint of creativity and thought can be tasted in all dishes.

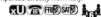

STRADA
Italian

10-11 Sun Street, Canterbury, CT1 2HX
01227 472 089
A dedicated menu offering traditional Italian dishes in a stylish and contemporary setting. The chefs use only the finest ingredients such as Parma ham and buffalo mozzarella imported directly from Italy.

SURIN
Thai

30 Harbour Street, Ramsgate, CT11 9QD
01843 592 001
Chef-proprietor Miss Damarong counts the Thai Royal family amongst her patrons; regularly praised in the press, join her for excellent Thai, Cambodian and Laotian cuisine.

TABLA, BAR & INDIAN RESTAURANT
Indian

Best Western, West Parade, Hythe, CT21 6DT
01303 268 263
A contemporary lounge, bar and Indian restaurant offer guests a wonderful place to drink and dine. Spectacular views of the English Channel can be taken in as you savour a taste of India.

TACOS LOCOS
Mexican

29 Lower Stone Street, Maidstone, ME15 6LH
01622 759 555
The ultimate Mexican party venue. Experience huge variety with a menu boasting over 70 succulent dishes and tapas, as well as an extensive cocktail menu, not forgetting their famous Margaritas.

THE AMBRETTE
Fine Dining

44 King Street, Margate, CT9 1QE
01843 231 504
Stunning fine dining Indian restaurant with a clipped, eclectic menu of artful and delicious dishes by chef Dev Biswal. With exceptionally seasoned, crafted cuisine, The Ambrette is a special experience.

Formerly The Indian Princess.

THE BARN RESTAURANT
British

507 Lower Rainham Road, Rainham, ME8 7TN
01364 361 363
This family-run restaurant takes delight in exceeding customer expectations. Inspired traditionally English meals are balanced by modern presentation, bringing old dishes into the 21st century.

THE COASTGUARD
British

The Bay, St Margaret's Bay, Dover, CT15 6DY
01304 851 012
Right on the seafront, The Coastguard is beautifully situated and has a keen sense of place. Its food is simple but rich in story and tradition; fresh local fish in a relaxed, convivial ambience.

THE COURTYARD
British

Brogdale Farm, Brogdale Road, Faversham, ME13 8XZ
01795 530 013
You'll find yourself the beneficiary of a full-throated breakfast or a delightful, fulsome lunch at this charming little eatery in Kent. Its beautiful location is reflected in the fresh and tasty dishes.

Open lunches & Friday and Saturday eve.

THE CUBAN CANTERBURY
Cuban

41 High Street, Canterbury, CT1 2RY
0333 240 2000
A revolutionary eating and drinking experience with an atmosphere emanating Latin flair. Authentic dishes inspired by the taste of a culture, complemented by a bar featuring classic cocktails.

Discounted hotel rates for GS members on our website

THE DOG INN AT WINGHAM
Fine Dining
Canterbury Road, Wingham, CT3 1BB
01227 720 339
A picturesque inn with an enviable reputation for their excellence and variety, as dishes benefit from the freshest local produce available. Highly regarded for the depth and range of their wine cellar.

THE DUCK INN
British
Pett Bottom, CT4 5PB
01227 830 354
Supremely picturesque, a favourite haunt of James Bond author Ian Fleming and mentioned in You Only Live Twice, The Duck Inn takes its name from the low doorway, and serves thoroughly tasty English fare.

THE FOX AND HOUNDS
European
Toys Hill, Westerham, TN16 1QG
01732 750 328
In an area of outstanding beauty, a superb menu offers fresh local produce and wonderful fish dishes prepared by an excellent chef. A good selection of wine, lager, and ales accompanies the food here.

THE GEORGE AND DRAGON
Modern Pub
The Street, Ightham, Sevenoaks, TN15 9HH
01732 882 440
With a weight of history and folklore behind it, this food-led Kentish inn offers a gorgeous, warm ambience to go with the unfussy, delightfully prepared, good and honest fare.

THE MARQUIS AT ALKHAM
English and Continental
Alkham Valley Road, Alkham, CT15 7DF
01304 873 410
Great flavour is everything at The Marquis. Seasonally inspired menus make use of locally sourced ingredients, whilst every dish is elegant in appearance and delicious in taste.

THE ROYAL OAK HOTEL
European
High Street, Sevenoaks, TN13 1HY
01732 451 109
The No 5 Bistro in a fine Brook hotel is a popular choice locally and for visitors; well known for its excellent food, wine and service, delivered in a highly stylish and airy dining room.

THE SANDGATE HOTEL
European
8-9 Wellington Terrace, Folkestone, CT20 3DY
01303 220 444
Sophisticated and accommodating hotel-restaurant focusing on the quality of its produce to concoct superbly savoury, supremely cooked dishes. Draws on classic recipes and adds contemporary nuance.

THE ST. JAMES RESTAURANT
British
3a Broad Street, Ramsgate, CT11 8NQ
07511 018 764
With home-made soups, pâtés and ice cream, sumptuous main meals and exceptional sandwiches, this restaurant in Ramsgate is calm, relaxed and appealingly low-key.

THE WIFE OF BATH
European
4 Upper Bridge Street, Ashford, TN25 5AF
01233 812 232
With a character not quite so frank as Chaucer's famous figure, this restaurant is full of smooth charisma and admirable gentility. Pop in for lunch, settle down for a superb dinner or stay for the night.

TOPES RESTAURANT
European
60 High Street, Rochester, ME1 1JY
01634 845 270
Experience modern-style dishes within the grand setting of this 15th, 16th and 17th century location. Take in the history of this venue and feast on modern European cuisine. Awarded 2 AA Rosettes.

RECOMMEND A FRIEND

see page 18

TRIPLE J'S
African
10 High Street, Gillingham, ME7 1BB
01634 577 786
Down-home African Caribbean cuisine on the High Street in Gillingham, from the warm tang of a good goat curry to rice and peas with little or no nonsense about it. You'll not feel a jerk at Triple J's.

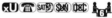

TUDOR PARK HOTEL
British
Conical Grill, Ashford Road, Bearsted, ME14 4NQ
01622 734 334
Maintaining simplicity at the core, the rustic menu at the Tudor Park is careful not to overcomplicate its dishes, and service is friendly and efficient. Only the very best seasonal produce is used.

VAUDREYS
European
Rings Hill, Hildenborough, Tonbridge, TN11 8LX
01732 832 944
A thoroughly fresh feel to this open, airy restaurant that has menus to suit all sorts of times and occasions. It serves high quality, well-seasoned dishes that are full of flavour, all at a good price.

ZARIN
Indian/ Bangladeshi
31 Bank Street, Ashford, TN23 1DQ
01233 620 511
In dazzling, contemporary style this Indian and Bangladeshi restaurant pulls together eclectic subcontinental flavours, ancient and modern; dig into its highly regarded dishes for a thoroughly tasty meal.

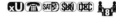

ZEST
British
4 Manor Row, High Street, Tenterden, TN30 6HP
01580 766 696
Making good use of the produce from 'The Garden of England', Zest places a slight twist on tasty English classics. Be sure to try the scrumptious home-made desserts and the classic French wines.

Oxfordshire

SOUTH EAST

CAFÉ ROUGE
French

Marriott's Close, Woodford Way, Oxford, OX28 6GW
01993 775 014
An attractive restaurant, a boulevard café or a Parisian-style wine bar; however you see Café Rouge, consistently excellent classic French dishes are always guaranteed.

ANTICO RESTAURANT
Italian

49-51 Market Place, Henley-on-Thames, RG9 2AA
01491 573 060
A beautiful blend of modern and traditional Italian cuisine occupies the menu. The escalope of veal in white wine with Parma ham and sage is superb, and can be complemented by one of the many fine wines.

CAFÉ ROUGE
French

37 Hart Street, Henley-on-Thames, RG9 2AR
01491 411 733
An attractive restaurant, a boulevard café or a Parisian-style wine bar; however you see Café Rouge, consistently excellent classic French dishes are always guaranteed.

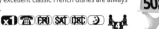

AVANTI
Italian

85 High Street, Wallingford, OX10 0BW
01491 835 500
Fresh Italian cuisine created with pride, offering a vast menu with an emphasis on fish and seafood. This venue caters for all, not least with the temptation of its indulgent home-made desserts.

CHERRY TREE
British

33 High Street, Steventon, Abingdon, OX13 6RZ
01235 831 222
This oak-beamed, low, cosy inn is a past master in the arts of a quiet drink, a homely and hearty meal, and a friendly, accommodating welcome. Settle back and enjoy a classic pub dinner.

Offer excludes Sunday lunch and Christmas menus

BIRD IN HAND
English and Continental

Whiteoak Green, Hailey, Witney, OX29 9XP
01993 868 321
A classic country inn in the heart of the Cotswolds. Rich in charm and charisma, the inn offers mouth-watering food that will satisfy every appetite. Enjoy magnificent views on the outdoor patio.

CHOPSTICKS RESTAURANT
Chinese

126 Broadway, Didcot, OX11 8AB
01235 813 333
Great little characterful Chinese restaurant in Didcot. Serves an array of colour-filled, spicy dishes; a selection of menus are also on offer, ideal for business lunches or a relaxed evening meal

BOMBAY RESTAURANT
Indian

82 Walton Street, Oxford, OX2 6EA
01865 511 188
A great choice of dishes are offer in this successful Indian restaurant, where the 'BYO' policy proves extremely popular. Try the chicken shashlik to be guaranteed a fabulous dining experience.

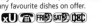

CHOPSTICKS RESTAURANT
Chinese

244 Cowley Road, Oxford, OX4 1UH
01865 725 688
A great little characterful Chinese restaurant. Serves an array of colour-filled, spicy dishes; a selection of menus are also on offer, ideal for business lunches or a relaxed evening meal.

BRANCA
Italian

111 Walton Street, Oxford, OX2 6AJ
01865 556 111
Impressive service provides exquisite tasting food in this informal Italian restaurant. Regular diners enjoy the complementary focaccia bread, before feasting on one of the many favourite dishes on offer.

CINNAMONS
Indian

81 High Street, Wheatley, Oxford, OX33 1XP
01865 876 688
Great local Indian restaurant that is locally popular for its range of classic dishes and for its genial, buzzy atmosphere. Enjoy the freshness and vibrancy of the flavours on offer.

BROTHERTONS BRASSERIE
Contemporary

1 High Street, Woodstock, OX20 1TE
01993 811 114
Deeply burnished timber and glowing gaslight create a heart-warming environment in which guests can enjoy delicious dishes. The wild boar casserole and the chargrilled swordfish are both great choices.

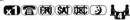

CLANFIELD TAVERN
British

Bampton Road, Clanfield, Bampton, OX18 2RG
01367 810 223
Combining a traditional pub with oak beams and flagstone floors with a contemporary conservatory, this venue offers a choice of home-made classics and more elaborate dishes that are well regarded locally.

CAFÉ ROUGE
French

11 Little Clarendon St, Oxford, OX1 2HP
01865 310 194
An attractive restaurant, a boulevard café or a Parisian-style wine bar; however you see Café Rouge, consistently excellent classic French dishes are always guaranteed.

COCKADOO
Oriental

Nuneham Courtenay, OX44 9NX
01865 341 030
Taste the very best of East Asian cuisine with service and a setting fit for royalty. The highest standards are maintained throughout yet this remains a relaxing and convivial place to dine.

100

Gourmet Society discount applies to the à la carte menu

CORI
Italian

53 High Street, Banbury, OX16 5JJ
01295 263 664

A warm and welcoming family-run Italian restaurant, whose traditional and authentic food includes freshly made pizzas. A culinary treat in the centre of Banbury, where all occasions are catered for.

2FOR1 MAIN COURSE

FALLOWFIELDS COUNTRY HOUSE
Modern British

Faringdon Road, Kingston Bagpuize, OX13 5BH
01865 820 416

A paean to peace, calm and an exceptional quality of simple cooking using fresh, locally sourced produce, including a great deal that is grown on their own grounds; all enjoyed in a light and open space.

2FOR1 MAIN COURSE

DIL RAJ RESTAURANT
Indian

6 Ock Street, Abingdon, OX14 5AW
01235 524 722

A renowned establishment boasting a repertoire of fine food, delivering unfaltering perfection with every taste. Experience a world of culinary delights with authentic and heated Indian flavours.

25%OFF TOTAL

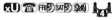

FISHERS SEAFOOD RESTAURANT
Seafood

36/37 St Clements, Oxford, OX4 1AB
01865 243 003

This acclaimed and popular flagship restaurant serves lucid, unfussy and well-seasoned seafood dishes in an open, informal atmosphere.

25%OFF TOTAL

DOOR 74
British

74 Cowley Road, Oxford, OX4 1JB
01865 203 374

Dedicated to serving the finest contemporary British cuisine all day long, using seasonal and locally sourced ingredients. Beautiful presentation of each dish sets Door 74 apart.

25%OFF TOTAL

Offer not available after 5pm on Thursday

GALLERY RESTAURANT
English and Continental

Crown & Thistle Hotel, 18 Bridge St, Abingdon, OX14 3HS
01235 522 556

Refurbished 17th century inn offering a range of quality British and continental dishes, that also caters for different dietary requirements. Ideal for larger private events including weddings and parties.

25%OFF TOTAL

EDEN BAR AND GRILL
British

Spread Eagle Hotel, 16-17 Cornmarket, Thame, OX9 2BW
01844 213 661

Haute cuisine inflected in a contemporary British style at this charismatic inn in Thame. Accomplished, sophisticated flavours, along with a down-home 'comfort cooking' section of the menu.

25%OFF TOTAL

HOTEL DU VIN
European

New Street, Henley-on-Thames, RG9 2BP
01491 848 400

The finest, freshest local produce, simple European recipes, a stunning choice of wines; these are the elements of the trademark Hotel du Vin bistro. Housed in a converted riverside brewery. 2 AA Rosettes.

2FOR1 MAIN COURSE

ELAICHI
Bangladeshi/Indian

9 Millbrook Square, Grove, Wantage, OX12 7JZ
01235 772 010

Holding a great reputation, this establishment delivers affordable Bangladeshi cuisine that showcases an array of flavours and spices to satisfy every individual taste. A high standard of food and service.

2FOR1 MAIN COURSE

HI-LO JAMAICAN EATING HOUSE
Caribbean

68-70 Cowley Road, Oxford, OX4 1JB
01865 725 984

A popular venue that appeals to all ages, delivering traditional Jamaican home cooking that includes jerk pork and Caribbean sea fish. Live music offers an authentic and entertaining night.

25%OFF TOTAL

THE RESTAURANT AT WITNEY LAKES RESORT
Contemporary

Witney Lakes Resort, Downs Road, Witney, OX29 0SY
01993 893012

A beautiful lakeside setting on the edge of the Cotswolds, where all food is freshly prepared by a team of skilled Chefs; from their own recipe chutneys and home-baked breads to elaborate main dishes.

NEW

25%OFF TOTAL

HIMALAYAN TANDOORI
Nepalese

16 Reading Road, Henley-on-Thames, RG9 1AG
01491 410 939

Enjoy fine traditional Indian and Nepalese cuisine superbly crafted and delivered by exemplary staff in a great atmosphere. A varied choice of vegetarian dishes ensures all tastes are catered for.

2FOR1 MAIN COURSE

FABIOS RISTORANTE ITALIANO
Italian

4-5 North Bar Street, Banbury, OX16 0TB
01295 250 507

Rich, full flavours of traditional, homely Italian cuisine in this cosy, warm and friendly family-run restaurant in Banbury.

25%OFF TOTAL

INDIAN DREAM
Indian

32-34 Wantage Road, Didcot, OX11 0BT
01235 817 711

Prepared and served following the traditions of India, the food here is simple, authentic, and provides a real taste of India's excellent culinary culture. An ideal venue for any occasion, even a takeaway.

2FOR1 2COURSES

FALKLAND ARMS AT CHIPPING NORTON
English Gastropub

Great Tew, Chipping Norton, OX7 4DB
01608 683 653

A traditional local pub that thrives on those well-established values of hospitality and sociability. It also serves some delicious pub food. Grab a moment's serenity, a bite to eat and a leisurely drink.

25%OFF TOTAL

Offer excludes Sunday lunch and Christmas menus. Residents only.

JEE SAHEB RESTAURANT
Indian

15 North Parade Avenue, Oxford, OX2 6LX
01865 513 773

Classic Asian cuisine from across the subcontinent. An array of traditional and creative dishes from Bangladesh, India and Pakistan that have been beautifully crafted from fresh, quality produce.

2FOR1 MAIN COURSE

LA TASCA
Spanish

5 Oxford Castle, Oxford, OX1 1AY
01865 246 464
La Tasca is all about terrific tapas. The 30 plus dishes that are on offer are perfect for sharing with friends and loved ones. Sip on a glass of the ever-popular sangria in wonderfully warm surroundings.

Tapas menu only

LOCH FYNE
Seafood

55 Walton Street, Oxford, OX2 6AE
01865 292 510
From the roadside oyster bar that once was, Loch Fyne restaurants now successfully inject energy and passion into great food and wonderful flavours, whilst ensuring their seafood is sustainably sourced.

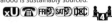

LOCH FYNE
Seafood

20 Market Street, Henley-on-Thames, RG9 2AH
01491 845 780
From the roadside oyster bar that once was, Loch Fyne restaurants now successfully inject energy and passion into great food and wonderful flavours, whilst ensuring their seafood is sustainably sourced.

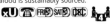

MALMAISON
Modern British

3 Oxford Castle, New Road, Oxford, OX1 1AY
01865 268 400
Guests will want to lock themselves up and throw away the key in this magnificent 'Mal', impeccably transformed from a prison. The brasserie features mouth-watering food and fantastic wine. 1 AA Rosette.

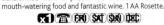

MAXWELL'S
American

36 Queen Street, Oxford, OX1 1ER
01865 242 192
A well-established late night bar and grill. The winning formula of top-quality service and a famous burger menu satisfies every guest, whilst the stylishly chic interior provides a relaxing ambience.

MEMORIES OF BENGAL
Indian

12 Wallingford Road, Cholsey, Wallingford, OX10 9LQ
01491 652 399
Be tempted by an unrivalled range of authentic and imaginative fusion dishes, delicately crafted to reveal the true tastes and aromas of a culture with an exemplary culinary history.

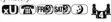

MEM-SAAB
Indian

1 Horse Fair, Banbury, OX16 0AA
01295 264 365
With its unique combination of traditional values and contemporary sophistication, this restaurant offers the authentic taste of the East in a fine dining atmosphere.

MILL BROOK ROOM
British

Mill House Hotel, Kingham, Chipping Norton, OX7 6UH
01608 658 188
With two AA Rosettes, Head Chef Matt Dare's clean, fresh flavours populate this restaurant's à la carte menus. The superb quality of cuisine is complemented by the restaurant's calm, luxurious setting.

PORTABELLO
Modern British

7 South Parade, Summertown, Oxford, OX2 7JL
01865 559 653
Cooked with imagination and flair, the food is fresh and flavourful, whilst the service is markedly efficient. Unwind in a calm atmosphere with the pick of some delicious dishes and watch the world go by.

PREZZO
Italian

2 Oxford Castle, Oxford, OX1 1AY
01865 791 748
With a character all of its own, Prezzo oozes contemporary style and enduring charm. Signature pastas, stone-baked pizzas and classic Italian dishes promise a perfect dining choice for the whole family.

PREZZO
Italian

12A Buttermarket, Thame, OX9 3DX
01844 218 542
With a character all of its own, Prezzo oozes contemporary style and enduring charm. Signature pastas, stone-baked pizzas and classic Italian dishes promise a perfect dining choice for the whole family.

RESTAURANT 1649
British

Wroxton House Hotel, Wroxton, Banbury, OX15 6QB
01295 730 777
Expertly prepared food offering a personal interpretation of classic British dishes and an imaginative use of fresh local produce. Includes a select wine list emphasising quality and value.

RJ @ 21
Mediterranean

21 Cowley Road, Oxford, OX4 1HP
01865 201 120
A stylish, fun and relaxed taste of the Mediterranean. Inspired by the cafés and restaurants of Barcelona, the menus are updated regularly to represent the best in seasonal, fresh, simply cooked food.

ROCOCO BRASSERIE
Mediterranean

11 The Square, West Way Centre, Botley, OX2 9LH
01865 792 696
A stylish, laid-back restaurant where classic Mediterranean cooking is served up by friendly and welcoming staff. The fabulously vast menu includes everything from crêpes and salads to decadent desserts.

SAN CARLO
Italian

36-37 Parsons Street, Banbury, OX16 5NA
01295 703 073
Traditional Italian home-made food that will have you coming back time and time again. Scrumptious stone-baked pizzas and tasty salads as well as pastas from all regions of Italy.

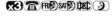

SAN SICARIO
Italian

28 High Street, Wallingford, OX10 0BU
01491 834 078
A highly popular Italian restaurant where traditional culinary methods are used to ensure authentic tastes and flavours are locked into every dish. The fabulous menu represents all regions of Italy.

Sign up to our newsletter for latest restaurants, offers and more

SHANGHAI 30'S
Chinese
82 St Aldates, Oxford, OX1 1RA
01865 242 230
Provides a menu that focuses on both classic and contemporary dishes. Cuisine from Shangai and the surrounding areas is met by better-known food from Szechuan and Canton.

SPICE LOUNGE
Indian
193 Banbury Road, Summertown, Oxford, OX2 7AR
01865 510 072
Chefs produce stunningly delicious dishes with an emphasis on organic and creative food. Traditional recipes are used providing customers with a diverse, unusual menu while focusing on healthy eating.

SPIRES RESTAURANT
British
Linton Lodge, 11-13 Linton Road, Oxford, OX2 6UJ
01865 553 461
Contemporary and accomplished dining in this hotel-based restaurant in Oxford. Modern and open styling with a wide-ranging menu to match.

TASTE OF INDIA
Indian
34 The Green, Oxford, OX33 1RP
01865 874 800
A convivial and informal Indian restaurant and takeaway. Enjoy their curry and spices in the comfortable dining area or public bar.

THAI SHIRE CUISINE
Thai
Chipping Norton, Chipping Norton, OX7 5AL
01608 645 888
Lovely accommodating Thai restaurant which has also opened its ambit to Chinese and Malaysian-style dishes, and has a wide-ranging menu that you can enjoy for a relaxed, peaceable meal.

Not for set menu. À la carte only.

THE BEETLE AND WEDGE
International
Ferry Lane, Moulsford, OX10 9JF
01491 651 381
Enjoy the tranquillity and peace of the riverside setting as you dine in this beautiful old beamed Boathouse. Watch your meal come together as it is grilled on a magnificent open charcoal fire.

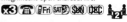

THE BIG BANG
British
124 Walton Street, Jericho, Oxford, OX2 6AH
01865 511 441
With a responsible approach to sourcing as its watch-word, The Big Bang is a must-eat for those serious about food ethics; also for those who simply love a stupendous cooked breakfast or bangers & mash.

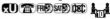

THE BOWLING GREEN STEAKHOUSE HOTEL
British
The Bowling Green, Overthorpe Rd, Banbury, OX17 2XA
01295 263 465
Has a reputation for the finest steaks in the area, from succulent rump to tasty t-bone, using locally reared beef. The menu also boasts the best of traditional fare, with some international favourites.

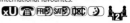

THE DASHWOOD
British
South Green, Heyford Road, Oxford, OX5 3HJ
01869 352 707
Award-winning chef Emma Berriman creates a truly unique blend of textures and tastes using fresh seasonal and local ingredients. Suitable for all occasions, providing a pleasant, informal environment.

THE DUCK ON THE POND
English and Continental
Main Street, South Newington, OX15 4JE
01295 721 166
This wonderfully located pub and restaurant has been lovingly maintained. The original features enhance the interior cosiness, and offer a perfect backdrop to a fabulous dining experience.

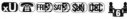

THE GRIFFIN INN
European
9 Culworth Rd, Chipping Warden, Banbury, OX17 1LB
01295 660 311
Allow yourself to be engrossed by the tremendous atmosphere that awaits you in this commendable bistro pub. The attractiveness of its location is transferred to the interior décor and the outstanding meal.

THE INN AT EMMINGTON
British
Sydenham Road, Chinnor, OX39 4LD
01844 351 367
A classic countryside inn dedicated to providing good food in a friendly atmosphere. Well-prepared, locally sourced produce complemented by fine real ales, beers, and wines. A great venue all year round.

THE LIVING ROOM
British
1 Oxford Castle, New Road, Oxford, OX1 1AY
01865 260 210
Step into The Living Room and you can count on the savvy, distinctive neighbourhood vibe that plays home to eclectically drawn, supremely tasty cuisine. Ease down in this hip Oxford locale.

Must purchase min. 3 courses per person inc. main course.

THE MIRABAI RESTAURANT
Indian/ Bangladeshi
70 London Road, Headington, Oxford, OX3 7PD
01865 762 255
A wide selection of both Bangladeshi and Indian dishes are on offer in this popular tandoori restaurant. Its many regular diners testifies to its excellence.

THE NUT TREE INN
British

Main Street, Murcott, Kidlington, Oxford, OX5 2RE
01865 331 253
This Michelin-starred, 2 AA Rosette venue is part of the local community, alongside being an extraordinary fine dining spot. Its quality brooks no debate; the food speaks for itself.

THE OLD RED LION
Caribbean

40 High Street, Tetsworth, Thame, OX9 7AS
01844 281 274
Radiating a magic and welcoming character, the lively atmosphere is just one of the pub's appealing factors. The patio area is perfect for summer barbecues and spit roasts.

THE PARLOUR RESTAURANT
Traditional English

Common Leys Farm, Waterperry Common, OX33 1LQ
01865 351 266
Sure-footed traditional English cuisine in this charming and exceptionally homely village restaurant. In serene, still and stunning surrounds, savour a sumptuous dinner of great richness in flavour.

THE PARTRIDGE
Classic British/ French

32 St Mary's Street, Wallingford, OX10 0ET
01491 825 005
Offers superb modern British cuisine and rustic French fare. Before your meal, enjoy a drink in the open garden just moments from the river's edge. Awarded 1 AA Rosette.

THE TREE, ANNORA INTERNATIONAL
International

63 Church Way, Iffley Village, Oxford, OX4 4EY
01865 775 974
The restaurant is proud to present a menu bursting full of exciting and interesting flavours. Try exceedingly tasty, quirky English dishes as well as divine, authentic Indian and Thai cuisine.

THE VINES
International

Burford Road, Black Bourton, Bampton, OX18 2PF
01993 843 559
Warm and inviting hotel restaurant in the Cotswolds, where you'll enjoy excellent quality inn-style food in a special design interior. It's something more than meets the eye.

THE WHITE HART HOTEL
European

26 High Street, Dorchester on Thames, OX10 7HN
01865 340 074
An AA Rosette-awarded restaurant in a gorgeous old coaching inn. Plush and cosy inside, its menus are all about simplicity and subtlety, with light sauces and little variations making all the difference.

TRIGGER POND
British

Bicester Road, Bucknell, Bicester, OX27 7NE
01869 252 817
A delightful country inn on the outskirts of Bicester, in a lovely rural location. Enjoy excellent service and a menu filled with delicious home-made food and an abundance of real ales.

Offer excludes Sunday lunch and Christmas menus

VERDE PIZZERIA
Italian

212-214 Cowley Road, Oxford, OX3 1UQ
01865 246 222
Doing exactly what its name promises, this cracking pizzeria offers a terrific array of choices, from salads to exciting pizzas. Amiable staff and an inviting atmosphere are added bonuses.

VICTORIA ARMS
British

Mill Lane, Old Marston, Oxford, OX3 0PZ
01865 241 382
A picturesque pub priding themselves on a perfect pint and a perfect view. Dine on classic, hearty pub food and settle back and enjoy a Cask Marque-credited Wadworth ale to wash it all down.

Offer excludes Sunday lunch and Christmas menus

WALLINGFORD TANDOORI
Indian

4 High Street, Wallingford, OX10 0BJ
01491 836 249
Distinctive Indian cuisine with a characteristic lightness (little oil and no artificial colourings) conceived by the restaurant's new head chef who brings his experience from a 5* Indian hotel group.

XI'AN RESTAURANT
Chinese

197 Banbury Road, Summertown, Oxford, OX2 7AR
01865 554 239
The perfect place to try something new, with pleasure to be found at Xi'an. Allow the blend of different tastes to produce a great sense of delight in the palate. An endless choice of beverages available.

Surrey

39 PRIME
Steakhouse

39 Church Street, Reigate, RH2 0AD
01737 237 977
39 Prime invites you to enjoy the finest steaks and a mouth-watering choice of the best and most tender cuts of beef from around the world.

ASIANA RESTAURANT
Indian

114 Hermitage Road, St Johns, Woking, GU21 8TT
01483 488 122
Experience true Indian spice and fragrance, with every dish being of sublime quality. Whether an intimate meal or a family gathering, this venue offers a unique Indian fine dining experience.

AUBERGE
French

274 High St, Guildford, GU1 3JL
01483 506 202
A grand glass entrance opens onto two contemporary-styled floors. Auberge adopt a simple approach, using fresh ingredients combined with a little French inspiration to serve classic dishes for all.

Visit the website regularly to discover the latest restaurants joining the GS

AUBERGE
French

1st Flr., Peacocks Centre, Woking, GU21 6GD
01483 764 080

Auberge adopt a simple approach, using fresh ingredients combined with a little French inspiration, serving classic dishes for you to enjoy. This Woking venue is ideal to start an evening's entertainment.

BEIJING RESTAURANT
Chinese

95-99 High Street, Horsell, Woking, GU21 4SY
01483 768 788

Offers authentic Chinese food in an amiable atmosphere, making it an ideal place to dine whatever your party size. Irresistibly tasty dishes are available for all to enjoy.

BEL AND THE DRAGON
British

Bridge Street, Godalming, GU7 3DU
01483 527 333

A beautiful blend of the old and new. Modern décor is met by the maintenance of the characteristic charm of the building's original features. A majestic place to eat, drink and relax.

BEST WESTERN GATWICK MOAT HOUSE
International

Gatwick, Horley, RH6 0AB
0871 226 1931

Situated close to Gatwick, this hotel restaurant is modern and comfortable and offers a diverse range of breakfast, lunch and dinner options, inspired by modern international cuisines, for all the family.

Only one card can be used per table.

BRASSERIE RHONE
French

134 High Street, Woking, GU22 9JN
01483 750 610

Drawing on influences from the cooking style of the Rhône valley, the kitchen successfully achieves a Provençal cuisine making great use of rustic ingredients such as tomatoes, aubergines and herbs.

CAFÉ ROUGE
French

8-9 Chapel St, Guildford, GU1 3UH
01483 451 221

An attractive restaurant, a boulevard café or a Parisian-style wine bar; however you see Café Rouge, consistently excellent classic French dishes are always guaranteed.

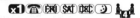

CAFÉ ROUGE
French

Town Hall Buildings, 4-5 The Borough, Farnham, GU9 7ND
01252 733 688

An attractive restaurant, a boulevard café or a Parisian-style wine bar; however you see Café Rouge, consistently excellent classic French dishes are always guaranteed.

CAFÉ ROUGE
French

1 Church Street, Reigate, RH2 0AA
01737 223 700

An attractive restaurant, a boulevard café or a Parisian-style wine bar; however you see Café Rouge, consistently excellent classic French dishes are always guaranteed.

CAFÉ ROUGE
French

170-172 High Street, Dorking, RH4 1BG
01306 743 400

An attractive restaurant, a boulevard café or a Parisian-style wine bar; however you see Café Rouge, consistently excellent classic French dishes are always guaranteed.

THE LOCK
English and Continental

Runnymede-on-Thames Hotel, Windsor Rd, Egham, TW20 0AG
01784 436171

Fabulously situated, overlooking the Thames but you're just as likely to have your attention monopolised by the restaurant's warm tones and textures. The eclectic menu takes in a range of different styles.

NEW

CHINA TOWN RESTAURANT
Chinese

369 London Road, Camberley, GU15 3HQ
01276 66422

Burgeoning young Chinese restaurant in Camberley that serves a great variety of dishes covering the whole range of classics with verve and flavour.

COAL GRILL + BAR
Mediterranean

244/246 High Street, Guildford, GU1 3JF
01483 449 625

This restaurant is known for fresh, delectable food and captivating cocktails. The quality of the dishes, coupled with great service and a stylish ambience, has been the key to their popularity.

Not to be used with any other offer or the Prix Fixé menu

DORKING BRASSERIE
Indian

Highland Cottage, Junction Road, Dorking, RH4 3HB
01306 742 448

This renowned Indian restaurant has a reputation for one of the best curries in Surrey. Their traditional menu and diverse daily specials promise a delicious, exciting, healthy experience for every diner.

FLAVOUR OF GOA
Indian

3 Frimley Road, Camberley, GU15 3EN
01276 671 555

Passionate and contemporary Indian restaurant serving a proper range of dishes at good value for money.

FOUR SEASONS
European

14-22 High Street, Chobham, GU24 8AA
01276 857 238

Family-run restaurant in a charming and curious historical building which serves classic and sophisticated cuisine; warm and fulsome flavours prepared and combined with great skill.

GATTON MANOR HOTEL
European

Standon Lane, Ockley, Dorking, RH5 5PQ
01306 627 555

In a serene, green and stately location, Gatton Manor Hotel is a superb retreat, and in its restaurant you can enjoy warming, wholesome, well-conceived menus that change every month.

SOUTH EAST

GULAAB INDIAN CUISINE
Indian

1 Brighton Road, Redhill, RH1 6PW
01737 769 009

A fabulous restaurant offering great food. Although the menu accommodates the finest Indian dishes, cooked to perfection, the lamb pasanda and butter chicken are particularly notable.

GURKHA DURBAR
Nepalese

30 Headley Road, Grayshott, GU26 6LD
01428 605 855

Dine on cuisine that exhibits delicate, simple flavours and a touch of spice. Cooking combines fine Chinese and Indian cuisine with an approach that relies on skilfully blending ingredients.

JAIPUR RESTAURANT
Indian

49 Chertsey Road, Woking, GU21 5AJ
01483 772 626

The subtle tastes and flavours of this restaurant's cuisine differs from many others. Drawing influences from all five regions of India, a menu of culinary delights has been crafted to satisfy all palates.

KAPADOKYA
Turkish

2 Crossways Road, Grayshott, GU26 6HJ
01428 607 088

Feast on authentic and delectable Turkish cuisine in a warm and friendly setting, where staff are attentive and help diners choose a fine meal from the exceptional menu and wine list.

KAR LING KWONG RESTAURANT
Chinese

47-50 East Street, Farnham, GU9 7SW
01252 714 854

Wonderful, authentic cuisine is created by a talented chef and served by knowledgeable staff. All dishes deliver fragrant aromas and delicious flavours, the hallmark of the best Hong Kong cooking.

LA BARBE RESTAURANT
French

71 Bell Street, Reigate, RH2 7AN
01737 241 966

Well deserving of its loyal, appreciative following, this truly French restaurant offers delectable, classical and provincial cuisine. Wonderful French and New World wines are also on offer.

LA LANTERNA
Italian

73 Bell Street, Reigate, RH2 7AN
01737 245 113

Whether you require a perfect venue for an intimate evening out, or a relaxed setting for an important business lunch, La Lanterna can cater for you. Outstanding Italian dishes that are irresistibly tasty.

LA LUNA
Italian

10 Wharf Street, Godalming, GU7 1NN
01483 414 155

Classic flavours of Italy are a priority in this charming Italian restaurant. Fish dishes are especially superb, with the scallops in dry Martini being particularly popular. Awarded 2 AA Rosettes.

LA PIAZZA
Italian

2 The Parade, Frimley, GU16 7HY
01276 64484

Appealing Italian cuisine is offered in an admirably relaxed atmosphere. Try the gamberi rossi or the prosciutto crudo before hitting the outstandingly tasty main dishes.

LOCH FYNE
Seafood

Centenary Hall, Chapel Street, Guildford, GU1 3UH
01483 230 550

From the roadside oyster bar that once was, Loch Fyne restaurants now successfully inject energy and passion into great food and wonderful flavours, whilst ensuring their seafood is sustainably sourced.

LOCH FYNE
Seafood

3 Downing Street, Farnham, GU9 7NX
01252 748 030

From the roadside oyster bar that once was, Loch Fyne restaurants now successfully inject energy and passion into great food and wonderful flavours, whilst ensuring their seafood is sustainably sourced.

LOCH FYNE
Seafood

5-6 High Street, Egham, TW20 9EA
01784 414 890

From the roadside oyster bar that once was, Loch Fyne restaurants now successfully inject energy and passion into great food and wonderful flavours, whilst ensuring their seafood is sustainably sourced.

M.BRASSERIE
Brasserie

36-40 London Road, Guildford, GU1 2AE
01483 303 030

A truly memorable gastronomic experience awaits you in this treasured venue. Traditional and contemporary cuisine makes the most of the fresh, local produce that the area has to offer.

Offer available on Fri. & Sat. for seatings until 7pm.

NAMASTE NEPALESE & INDIAN
Indian

21 High Street, Woking, GU21 6BW
01483 773 311

Exciting Nepalese and Indian dishes award this restaurant an enviable reputation. Locally renowned for providing one of the the very best curries in the area.

NEW DIWAN-E-KHAS
Indian/ Bangladeshi

413 London Road, Camberley, GU15 3HZ
01276 23500

Offers fine Indian cuisine, suitable for both meat lovers and vegetarians. Exciting, creative meals sit alongside the traditional favourites to be found on their excellent, eclectic menus.

NUTFIELD PRIORY HOTEL (CLOISTERS)
Fine Dining

Nutfield Rd, Nutfield, Redhill, RH1 4EL
08450 727 485

Whether you fancy a four course gourmet meal or are craving for a simple snack, the kitchen can cater for you, with a range of dining options on offer at this Hand Picked Hotels restaurant. 2 AA Rosettes.

The offer excludes Sunday lunch.

When booking restaurants always mention your GS membership

OISI JAPANESE RESTAURANT
Japanese

41 Old Woking Road, West Byfleet, KT14 6LG
01932 350 962
A dedicated following of diners serves as testimony to the excellence of this restaurant and what it has to offer. Originally aiming to fill a gap in the market, its Japanese cuisine has done the trick.

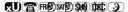

OLIVETTO
Italian

124 High Street, Guildford, GU1 3HQ
01483 563 277
Genial staff with affable smiles serve traditional Italian cuisine. The kitchen makes use of favourite recipes that accompanied the chefs from their homeland. Children are happily catered for.

OLIVO RISTORANTE ITALIANO
Italian

53 Quarry Street, Guildford, GU1 3UA
01483 303 535
A delightful haven of understated sophistication. Guests enjoy authentic cuisine cooked by talented Italian chefs who insist on using the freshest ingredients. Passion for food can be tasted in every dish.

PREZZO
Italian

11 The Atrium, Park Street, Camberley, GU15 3GP
01276 23945
With a character all of its own, Prezzo oozes contemporary style and enduring charm. Signature pastas, stone-baked pizzas and classic Italian dishes promise a perfect dining choice for the whole family.

PREZZO
Italian

8 Queen Street, Godalming, GU7 1BD
01483 428 746
With a character all of its own, Prezzo oozes contemporary style and enduring charm. Signature pastas, stone-baked pizzas and classic Italian dishes promise a perfect dining choice for the whole family.

PREZZO
Italian

7 The Borough, Farnham, GU9 7NA
01252 737 849
With a character all of its own, Prezzo oozes contemporary style and enduring charm. Signature pastas, stone-baked pizzas and classic Italian dishes promise a perfect dining choice for the whole family.

PREZZO
Italian

21-25 Church Street, Leatherhead, KT22 8DN
01372 379 625
With a character all of its own, Prezzo oozes contemporary style and enduring charm. Signature pastas, stone-baked pizzas and classic Italian dishes promise a perfect dining choice for the whole family.

PREZZO
Italian

33 London Road, Redhill, RH1 1NJ
01737 779 927
With a character all of its own, Prezzo oozes contemporary style and enduring charm. Signature pastas, stone-baked pizzas and classic Italian dishes promise a perfect dining choice for the whole family.

PRIDE OF THE VALLEY
British

Tilford Road, Churt, Farnham, GU10 2LH
01428 605 799
A luxurious and stylish environment where chefs use fresh produce to craft a menu filled with high-quality food, and diners can choose select wines direct from the wall. Reasonable prices guaranteed.

QUAYS
Carvery

Coleford Bridge Road, Mytchett, Camberly, GU16 6DS
01252 372 656
One of the many Great British Carveries that Gourmet Society members can enjoy. Feast on the British classic dish in the beautiful lakeside location, which has quickly become a hotspot.

Call beforehand on special event days.

RED CHILLI
Indian

Horsham Road, Mid-Holmwood, Dorking, RH5 4EH
01306 644 816
Immaculately presented, the food served here is simple and delicious, offering diners a taste of Indian culture. Authentic cooking, fresh ingredients and wonderful spices mould each dish to perfection.

RED LION INN
British

The Green, Shamley Green, Guildford, GU5 0UB
01483 892 202
With a view of the village and beautiful cricket green, enjoy hearty, traditional dishes throughout the year, combining with a variety of lagers and choice wines to ensure a memorable visit.

RED ROSE
Indian

87 High Street, Egham, TW20 9HF
01784 434 303
Expertly crafted Bangladeshi and Indian cuisine, with a myriad of dishes on offer that represent the variety of tastes and cultures found across the Indian subcontinent.

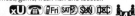

ROYAL OAK INN
European

Caterfield Lane, Staffhurst Wood, Oxted, RH8 0RR
01883 722 207
Capturing the very essence of classic English and European dishes, the menu at this award-winning restaurant provides a superb selection of locally sourced meat, game, fresh fish and lobster.

SON OF SOMBRERO
Mexican

52A Chertsey Street, Guildford, GU1 4HD
01483 453 434
A highly popular restaurant where tantalising food is plentiful, with a quality of service to match. A great venue with lively, authentic surroundings.

TASTE OF SPICE
Indian

26 Brighton Road, Salfords, Redhill, RH1 5BX
01293 773 995
Warm and accommodating local Indian restaurant in Salfords where you can enjoy any of the classic Indian dishes along with some chef's specialities that are always worth a try.

THE ANCIENT RAJ
Indian
9 The Parade, Frimley, GU16 7HY
01276 21503
Carefully selected spices are traditionally blended to add the most wonderful flavours to every dish. Generous portions are served by courteous staff in a relaxed environment.

THE HARE AND HOUNDS
Traditional English
Bletchingly Road, Godstone, RH9 8LN
1883742296
A pretty Surrey pub with a contented atmosphere that accompanies a good range of wine and beers with a selection of simple and satisfying, freshly made pub food. Check out the specialities.

THE GURKHA NEPALESE RESTAURANT
Nepalese
140 Frimley Road, Camberley, GU15 2QN
01276 684 919
Authentic and richly spiced Nepalese specialities punctuate the menu of this Indian restaurant. Enjoy its ambience and the warm homeliness of its dishes.

THE HAMPSHIRE ARMS
British
Pankridge Street, Crondall, Farnham, GU10 5QU
01252 850 418
Serving a plenitude of hearty but extremely well crafted pub-style dishes, this inn-restaurant can be relied upon for its commitment to local produce and to a warm, convivial English pub welcome.

THE MULBERRY TANDOORI
Indian
Station Hill, Farnham, GU9 9AD
01252 716 724
Enjoy the exotic tastes of India in the comfort of your own home or in the lively and vibrant atmosphere of one of Farnham's most popular bars and restaurants.

THE GALLERY RESTAURANT
International
Denbies Wine Estate, London Road, Dorking, RH5 6AA
01306 734 661
Situated on the top floor of England's largest vineyard, Denbies Wine Estate, The Gallery Restaurant is one of the most unique venues in Surrey with 360° panoramic views of the vineyard.

THE PARROT
British
Forest Green, Dorking, RH5 5RZ
01306 621 339
Quirky and eclectic contemporary restaurant in an invitingly classic setting. Enjoy a look at the vegetable garden which serves the restaurant for its produce, before savouring one of their hearty meals.

THE ROSE VALLEY
Indian
50 Chertsey Street, Guildford, GU1 4HD
01483 572 572
A well-respected restaurant serving only the finest Indian-Bangladeshi cuisine. Occupying an enviable position as a restaurant of the highest quality, the helpful staff further its excellence.

THE SPOTTED COW
European
Bourne Grove, Lower Bourne, Farnham, GU10 3QT
01252 726 541
Be enchanted as you discover the magical location of this idyllic country pub. The surrounding grounds are perfect for families with children and dogs. Inside, you will be met by great food and fine wines.

THE STAR INN
British
Wynh Hill, Hook Heath, Woking, GU22 0EU
01483 889 111
Fabulous traditional pub grub at a good price; from a bluff and unfussy Guinness, steak and cheddar pie to a silken mushroom stroganoff, or even a down-home weekend roast dinner.

VILLAGE BRASSERIE
Indian
10 West Street, Reigate, RH2 9BS
01737 217 445
French name, Indian cuisine; this restaurant combines the best of both worlds in its commitment to breezy, easygoing enjoyment and fresh, accessible flavours.

WATERMARK RESTAURANT
British
Bacon Lane, Churt, Farnham, GU10 2QD
01252 795 161
The Watermark Restaurant's menu is wide-ranging, accomplished, and strongly individual - the kind that makes it hard for you to rule things out. The restaurant space is charming, refined and welcoming.

West Sussex

ALEXANDER HOUSE HOTEL
European
Alexanders Restaurant, East St, Crawley, RH10 4QD
01342 714 914
Dine in this two AA Rosette restaurant based in a luxury spa hotel that delivers the very best in hospitality. A passion for food and the stunning location result in a quintessential dining experience.

BADGERS
European
Coultershaw Bridge, Petworth, GU28 0JF
01798 342 651
One of the best pubs in the area. A truly charming venue known for high quality, hearty food matched by diligent service, providing assistance to choose that perfect wine or beer.

BASMATI INDIAN RESTAURANT
Indian British
Swan House Cellars, Petworth, GU28 0AH
01798 343 414
This cool cellar serves some of the hottest curries in town. The menu features a blend of old and new, with traditional Indian cuisine sitting comfortably next to some British inventions.

Enjoy massive leisure and retail savings with more Gourmet Society

CAFÉ ROUGE
French

30 Southgate, Chichester, PO19 1DP
01243 781 751
An attractive restaurant, a boulevard café or a Parisian-style wine bar; however you see Café Rouge, consistently excellent classic French dishes are always guaranteed.

 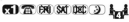

CAFÉ ROUGE
French

33 The Broadway, Haywards Heath, RH16 3AS
01444 440 888
An attractive restaurant, a boulevard café or a Parisian-style wine bar; however you see Café Rouge, consistently excellent classic French dishes are always guaranteed.

 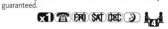

CASSONS RESTAURANT
Fine Dining

Arundel Road, Tangmere, Chichester, PO18 0DU
01243 773 294
Enjoy fine dining in relaxed surroundings. This charismatic restaurant is a charming asset to the area, with its impeccable food and outstanding service.

CHEQUERS HOTEL & RESTAURANT
International

Church Place, Pulborough, RH20 1AD
01798 872 486
A fabulous hotel and restaurant boasting stunning views of the Arun Valley. The famous Black Rock Grill makes use of volcanic granite stone for healthier cooking and a unique culinary experience.

CLAUDE'S CREPERIE
French - Crepes

15 Bedford Row, Worthing, BN11 3DR
01903 201 300
This family-run restaurant specialises in savoury and sweet crepes but also offers salads and omelettes. They serve a wide choice of ciders, wines and unusual French beers for a unique experience.

CUZINI
Sri Lankan

22 The Boulevard, Crawley, RH10 1XP
01293 533 350
A mouth-watering menu that reflects the variety of influences upon Sri Lankan cuisine. The kitchen aromas, the taste of the food and the attractive furnishings will all completely invigorate your senses.

DRAGON
Chinese

125 Sea Lane, Rustington, Littlehampton, BN16 2SG
01903 773 354
Set sail on your voyage in this delightful South Coast restaurant. Cantonese, Peking and Szechuan dishes can be accompanied by one of the many fine wines from the extensive drinks menu.

FILIPPO'S
Italian

5A Park Place, Horsham, RH12 1DF
01403 271 125
A family-run restaurant delivering a wonderful range of authentic Italian and Sicilian cuisine, from mouth-watering steaks and sauces to traditional pizzas and lasagne, all freshly cooked to order.

 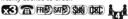

FROGSHOLE FARM
Modern British

Maidenbower Drive, Maidenbower, RH10 7QF
01293 885 081
Newly rebuilt but based on the legacy of its 16th-century forebear, this nook of a pub-restaurant, part of the Best of British group, serves great British fare with an enviable local reputation.

GARDENERS ARMS
British

Selsfield Road, Ardingly, RH17 6TJ
01444 892 328
Found in a rural location, this venue serves traditional pub food, satisfying diners with real hearty meals. A listed building with some original features also offers a beer garden and patio area.

HAMILTON ARMS NAVA THAI
Thai

School Lane, Stedham, GU29 0NZ
01730 812 555
A traditional country pub combined with a Thai restaurant. Indulge in an extensive range of succulent and authentic dishes served by Thai staff in traditional Thai dress.

HAPPY MEETING RESTAURANT
Chinese

76 The Boulevard, Crawley, RH10 1XH
01293 518 118
A locally renowned contemporary restaurant boasting a gigantic menu of traditional dishes and westernised offerings. Offering food at tremendously good value, this restaurant deserves its reputation.

JAMDANI
Indian

9 Jengers Mead, Billingshurst, RH14 9PB
01403 780 380
Indian cuisine made the authentic way, with the freshest local ingredients and traditional herbs and spices. Now available for takeaway, so enjoy classic flavourful dishes in the comfort of your own home.

JIDAPHAS THAI CAFE AND RESTAURANT
Thai

3 Bath Place, Worthing, BN11 3BA
01903 232 424
Outstanding, tasty Thai food that offers diners great value for money. Renowned for diligent service and quality of food, delivering extensive buffet lunches and sumptuous evening meals.

 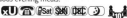

MEGHDOOT'S MYSTIQUE MASALA
Indian

East Street, Petworth, GU28 0AB
01798 343 217
Meghdoots offers the gamut of tasty Indian dishes. Its driving force, Sanjay, brings his experience from restaurants in India and the UK; he and wife Mili also run demonstrations of Indian cooking.

MONTAGUES TEX MEX
Tex-Mex

187 Montague Street, Worthing, BN11 3DA
01903 208 080
Friendly, helpful staff delivering delicious food that has been cooked to order. Montagues Tex Mex offers a vast drinks menu, which accommodates legendary margaritas.

SOUTH EAST

109

NIZAM INDIAN RESTAURANT
Indian

139 South Road, Haywards Heath, RH16 4LY
01444 457 527
A wonderful menu accommodating outstandingly tasty dishes can be found at this excellent Indian restaurant. A light and contemporary environment makes this an idyllic place to relax and enjoy great food.

OLD FORGE RESTAURANT
British

6 Church Street, Storrington, RH20 4LA
01903 743 402
Having succeeded with their restaurant, owners Cathy and Clive Roberts expanded their business with a delicatessen and wine cellar. An à la carte menu sits alongside a table d'hôte option.

PICCOLO'S
Italian

24 West Street, Horsham, RH12 1PB
01403 263 281
Warm welcomes are offered to old and new customers at this quietly tucked-away restaurant. Italian cuisine is traditionally prepared and served by efficient staff.

PREZZO
Italian

61 South Street, Chichester, PO19 1EE
01243 536 951
With a character all of its own, Prezzo oozes contemporary style and enduring charm. Signature pastas, stone-baked pizzas and classic Italian dishes promise a perfect dining choice for the whole family.

PREZZO
Italian

60 High Street, Crawley, RH10 1BT
01293 512 459
With a character all of its own, Prezzo oozes contemporary style and enduring charm. Signature pastas, stone-baked pizzas and classic Italian dishes promise a perfect dining choice for the whole family.

PREZZO
Italian

46 Carfax, Horsham, RH12 1EQ
01403 230 245
With a character all of its own, Prezzo oozes contemporary style and enduring charm. Signature pastas, stone-baked pizzas and classic Italian dishes promise a perfect dining choice for the whole family.

PREZZO
Italian

60 The Broadway, Haywards Heath, RH16 3AR
01444 451 001
With a character all of its own, Prezzo oozes contemporary style and enduring charm. Signature pastas, stone-baked pizzas and classic Italian dishes promise a perfect dining choice for the whole family.

PREZZO
Italian

Ground Floor, West Street, Midhurst, GU29 9NQ
01730 817 040
With a character all of its own, Prezzo oozes contemporary style and enduring charm. Signature pastas, stone-baked pizzas and classic Italian dishes promise a perfect dining choice for the whole family.

PREZZO
Italian

13 High Street, East Grinstead, RH19 3AF
01342 300 211
With a character all of its own, Prezzo oozes contemporary style and enduring charm. Signature pastas, stone-baked pizzas and classic Italian dishes promise a perfect dining choice for the whole family.

RESTAURANTE ANDALUCIA
Spanish

60 Ferring Street, Worthing, BN12 5JP
01903 502 605
A family-run business specialising in tasty tapas and perfect paella. Stylishly Spanish, this wonderful restaurant has a lively atmosphere to match the vibrancy of the food.

SAFFRON LOUNGE
Indian

5 Grand Parade, High Street, Crawley, RH10 1BU
01293 529 946
Authentic Indian food in a modern retro setting. Enjoy a relaxing evening sampling the à la carte menu with dishes from across the diverse culinary regions of India.

SHANGHAI COTTAGE
Chinese

Market Square, Petworth, GU28 0AH
01798 343 949
A wonderful restaurant offering tasty Chinese cuisine for lunch and dinner. Enjoy an evening out with great food and good company, or opt for the takeaway option and feast in the comfort of your own home.

SILK ROAD RESTAURANT
Turkish

8-10 Arcade Road, Littlehampton, BN17 5AP
01903 722 055
Guests who dine here will fall in love with the Mediterranean delights and attention to detail. Enjoy magnificently tasty cuisine served on your own unique antique plate. Weekly live entertainment.

TAKANZO
Pan Asian

19 Swan Corner, Pulborough, RH20 1RJ
01798 874 141
A vibrant blend of oriental cuisines can be enjoyed in this relaxing and comfortable restaurant and bar. Chinese, Malaysian, Thai and Japanese dishes feature highly on the eclectic menu.

THE 3 AMIGOS @ THE VINYARD LODGE
Tex-Mex

42 High Street, Hurstpierpoint, BN6 9RG
01273 835 000
Promoting fantasies of Mexican paradise, authenticity is the key at this restaurant, with stand-out dishes including Maryland crab cakes, chilli con carne, three bean chilli & Mississippi mud pie.

THE BEACH HOUSE
British

77 Rookwood Road, West Wittering, PO20 8LT
01243 513981
A New England style café and restaurant located in a coastal Area of Outstanding Natural Beauty. Outstanding British cuisine can be enjoyed outdoors, on the heated veranda on bright days.

Enjoy massive leisure and retail savings with more Gourmet Society

THE BOARS HEAD TAVERN
British
The Boars Head, Worthing Rd, Horsham, RH13 0AD
01403 254 353
A wonderfully cosy local pub where the atmosphere is reminiscent of the traditional English dining room. Dine in the fully heated al fresco conservatory as you gaze over miles of beautiful countryside.

THE COUNTRYMAN INN
Locally Sourced
Countryman Lane, Shipley, RH13 8PZ
01403 741 383
A traditional rural hostelry with fantastic open country views, a cosy bar and a superb award-winning à la carte restaurant. Fresh, quality food served in a warm and welcoming atmosphere.

THE CROWN INN
British
Worthing Road, Dial Post, Horsham, RH13 8NH
01403 710 902
Fabulous food-led pub with an imaginative, accomplished chef-patron. The pub has a great sense of heritage and personality about it; enjoy, for example, the musky and creamy Sussex Smokie, a Crown jewel.

THE CURRY INN
Indian
58 Commercial Square, Haywards Heath, RH16 1EA
01444 415 141
Smart, bright and popular Indian restaurant in Haywards Heath; mouthwateringly piquant and rich curry dishes with a freshness in their flavours.

THE DINING ROOM
British
31 North Street, Chichester, PO19 1LY
01243 537 352
A well-established restaurant offering a tranquil and stylish setting for diners to enjoy whatever the occasion. Charming interior, superb food, and detailed wine list resulting in a lovely venue.

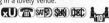

THE FORESTERS ARMS
British
The Street, Graffham, GU28 0QA
01798 867 202
Accomplished, richly flavourful dishes at this country pub on the cusp of the South Downs. The 'credit-crunch' menus are excitingly ranging; you can count on quality, tasty fare throughout the seasons.

THE GEORGE INN
British
Brittens Lane, Eartham, PO18 0LT
01243 814 340
Records show that The George has been serving the public since 1840 and its guests can drink and dine in a historically rich environment. Traditional English food to be enjoyed in complete comfort.

THE HORNBROOK
British
Brighton Road, Horsham, RH13 6QA
01403 252 638
Good old-fashioned English pub that is nevertheless bang up to date in its quality of service and welcome. Serves hearty British pub fare, which you can enjoy in the company of a great real ale.

THE MARQUIS OF GRANBY
Traditional English
1 West Street, Sompting, BN15 0AP
01903 231 102
A delightful pub that combines luxury and comfort, providing the perfect dining experience. Home-cooked bar snacks and meals can be enjoyed by the crackling fire or al fresco during the warmer months.

THE MUSE
Modern European
2-8 Castle Mews, Tarrant Street, Arundel, BN18 9DG
01903 883 477
A small and intimate restaurant neatly nestled on Castle Mews hill. Delectable Mediterranean cuisine can be enjoyed in quaint surroundings, either inside or al fresco during the warmer months.

THE NOAH'S ARK
British
The Green, Urgashall, GU28 9ET
01428 707 346
Leave your worries at the door and relax by the inglenook fire as you soak up the warm atmosphere and indulge in traditional British food with a contemporary twist.

DETAILED DESCRIPTIONS AVAILABLE ON
www.gourmetsociety.co.uk

THE PARSONAGE
British
6-10 High Street, Tarring, Worthing, BN14 7NN
01903 820 140
Fantastically rich and vibrant plates of searingly good produce with a real feel of the home-cooked meal about them. The calves liver is spectacular, the duck with calvados sauce superb.

THE WHEATSHEAF
British
Wool Lane, Midhurst, GU29 9BX
01730 813 450
Generous portions and simple, top-notch pub grub at this inn; whether a classic fish supper or brash, juicy gammon steak, along with its excellent array of beers, you're in for a good time.

THE WHEATSHEAF
British
Ellens Green, Rudgwick, Horsham, RH12 3AS
01403 822 155
The live jazz performances make this a splendid place to spend your evening drinking and dining. The inglenook fire and comfy leather sofas enhance the warm and charming nature of this traditional inn.

WOODIES WINE BAR AND BRASSERIE
English and Continental
10-13 St Pancras, Chichester, PO19 7SJ
01243 779 895
From an ever-varying menu and in deeply lit, relaxing and ambient surroundings, enjoy the imaginative and stylish combinations of contemporary flavours at this chic Chichester brasserie.

| | |

Greater London

London needs no introduction as a hub for cosmopolitanism, and its food cultures remain true to that form. For a sense of London's distinctive, eclectic culinary scene we might begin with the old markets by the Thames: at Borough and at Billingsgate, London has long received traders of produce from around the world; if distribution habits have changed, the spirit of receptivity hasn't. The diversity of cultures and cuisines in London testifies to this old and ongoing co-relation between food and free trade.

London's restaurants are symbiotic with these vibrant centres of produce: from down-to-earth pie and mash to pie-in-the-sky haute cuisine, you'll find in our listings an array of places to eat drawing on flavours, techniques and recipes from more or less every culture under the sun. What's more, whether you're grabbing a curry on Brick Lane, trying out an old Venetian recipe in Soho or a Lebanese five-spice lamb in Piccadilly, you'll be enjoying a local speciality.

This year all restaurants inside the M25 are listed in the Greater London region and arranged into geographic zones. Do be sure to browse East Anglia and the South East regions too, for restaurants near the boundaries.

There is the new inclusion of a map of Central London. Restaurants within this area have a grid reference which refers to this map and are ordered from the centre of the map outwards. Furthermore, on the map, the page numbers of the restaurants listed in smaller areas are shown so you can choose an area and find restaurants easily. Alternatively to search for the approximate location of a particular restaurant in this 'central' zone, we have included an alphabetical index of restaurants and grid reference.

Another new feature is the inclusion of the closest rail or tube station to the most of the restaurants here, which should also help you to get your bearings!

St.Johns Wood

St John's Wood

Maida Vale

MAIDA VALE

Warwick Ave

Primrose Hill

p. 144

REGENT'S PARK

p. 128

Mornington Crescent

p. 144

Somers Town

EUSTON STATION

Euston Square

Warren Street

p. 129

Regents Park

Great Portland Street

Goodge Street

Fitzrovia

p. 135

p. 136

MARYLEBONE STATION

Baker Street

Lisson Grove

Edgware Road

PADDINGTON

Royal Oak

PADDINGTON STATION

Paddington

Bayswater

Lancaster Gate

p. 136

p. 136

p. 136

Marble Arch

p. 127

MARYLEBONE

Bond Street

Oxford Circus

Tottenham Court Rd

p. 119

SOHO

Leic Squ

Bayswater

HYDE PARK

p. 132
GARDENS

MAYFAIR

p. 126

Hyde Park Corner

Green Park

Piccadilly Circus

St James's

p. 124

GREEN PARK

ST.JAMES' PARK

Knightsbridge

KENSINGTON

Knightsbridge

p. 132

p. 133

p. 132

St.James Park

WESTMINSTER

VICTORIA STATION

p. 132

Gloucester Road

South Kensington

South Kensington

Sloane Square

Belgravia

Pimlico

Pimlico

p. 134

p. 134
CHELSEA

Duke of York

Brompton

CHELSEA BRIDGE

p. 144

1   2   3   4

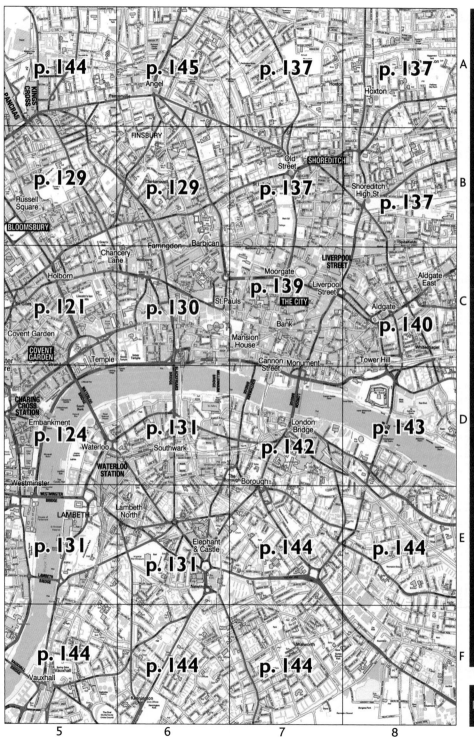

p. 144
p. 145
p. 137
p. 137
A

KINGS CROSS
PANCRAS
Angel
Pentonville
Hoxton
Hoxton

FINSBURY

p. 129
p. 129
Old Street
SHOREDITCH
Shoreditch High St
p. 137
B

Russell Square
Clerkenwell
p. 137

BLOOMSBURY

Farringdon
Barbican
Spitalfields

Chancery Lane
Holborn
Moorgate
LIVERPOOL STREET
Aldgate East

Holborn
p. 139
Liverpool Street
C

St Giles
Lincoln's Inn
p. 121
p. 130
St.Pauls
THE CITY
Aldgate

Covent Garden
Bank
p. 140

COVENT GARDEN
Temple
Inner Temple
Mansion House
Whitechapel

ter re
Cannon Street
Monument
Tower Hill

CHARING CROSS STATION
BLACKFRIARS BRIDGE
MILLENNIUM BRIDGE
SOUTHWARK BRIDGE
LONDON BRIDGE
D

Embankment
South Bank
p. 131
London Bridge
p. 143

p. 124
Waterloo
Southwark
p. 142

WATERLOO STATION
Tate Borough
Borough

Westminster

WESTMINSTER BRIDGE
Lambeth North

LAMBETH
p. 131
Elephant & Castle
p. 144
p. 144
E

p. 131
LAMBETH BRIDGE
p. 131
Newington

Walworth

p. 144
VAUXHALL BRIDGE
Vauxhall
p. 144
p. 144
F

Kennington

5
6
7
8

GREATER LONDON

GREATER LONDON RESTAURANT INDEX

RESTAURANT NAME	GRID Ref	RESTAURANT NAME	GRID Ref
ESCA	C7	Lena	B7
Fakhreldine	C3	Levant	C3
Fine Burger Co.	A6	Levanza	B8
Fire and Spice	C3	Little Hanoi	B8
Fishworks Marylebone	C3	Locale County Hall	E5
Fishworks Piccadilly	D4	Londinium	D7
Francos	D4	Los Locos	C5
Frankie's Criterion	E2	Lovage	D8
Fratelli Grill	E1	Luc's Brasserie	C7
Fuego	D7	LVPO Bar	C4
Galileo's Restaurant	D4	Made In Italy	F2
Gandhi's Restaurant	C5	Madsen Restaurant	F1
Gay Hussar	C4	Maida Restaurant	B8
Gaylord Restaurant	C3	Maison Touareg	C4
Gem Bar	C4	Malmaison	B6
Getti Jermyn Street	D4	Marco Pierre White Steak & Alehouse	C8
Getti Marylebone	B2	Marechiaro	F2
Gourmet Pizza	D6	Masala Brick Lane	C8
Gow's Restaurant & Oyster Bar	C7	Massala Hut	B4
Grace	D4	Massis Lebanese Grill & Bar	C1
Grand Union Islington	A6	Maxwell's Bar and Grill	C5
Grand Union Kennington	E6	Mediterranean Cafe	C4
Greig's Grill & Restaurant	D3	Mediterraneo	A5
Haandi	E2	Melati	C4
Hampshire Bar & Restaurant	D4	Memories of India	E1
Haozhan	C4	Mews of Mayfair	C3
Hemingway's	C8	Mezza Express	A3
Henry's Cafe Bar Covent Garden	C5	Mint Leaf Lounge	C7
Henry's Cafe Bar Piccadilly	D4	Mint Leaf Restaurant	D4
Henry's Cafe Bar Blomfield St	C7	Miso Hoxton	B7
Hoxton Apprentice	B7	Miso Islington	A6
Idlewild	B1	Miss Q's	E1
Il Giardino	F2	Monza Restaurant	E2
Imli	C4	Moti Mahal	C5
Incognico	C5	Mumtaz London	B2
Indigo South Bank	D6	Mura Restaurant	C2
Indigo Chelsea	F2	mybar at myhotel Chelsea	F2
Jakobs Cafe & Deli	F2	Navajo Joe	C5
Jamies	C8	Norfolk Arms	B5
Jerusalem	C4	Nueva Costa Dorada	C4
Jetlag Restaurant & Bar	B4	Nuocmam	C3
Jewel Bar Piccadilly	D4	Off the Hook @ The Paxtons Head	E2
Jewel Lounge Covent Garden	D5	On Anon	D4
Josephine's Restaurant	C4	Opal Bar & Restaurant	D5
JuJu	F2	Original Tagines	C3
Juno	B8	Ortega Leadenhall	C7
Karavas	A4	Özer Restaurant	C4
Kasturi	C8	Pakenham Arms	B5
Kazan City	C8	Palm Court Brasserie	C5
Kazan Victoria	E4	Palms of Goa	B4
Kenza	C8	Papadoms	C8
Kings Road Steakhouse & Grill	F2	Parveen Tandoori	A6
Kumo	E2	Pasha	A6
Kym's	E4	Pattersons Restaurant	C4
La Locanda	D4	Phi Brasserie	C2
La Luna	F7	Pier 1 Haymarket	D4
La Pizzeria	F2	Piya Piya	B7
Langtrys Restaurant	E3	Pizza On The Park	E2
Lati Ri	B8	PJ's Bar and Grill	F2
Laya'Lina	E2	Planet Hollywood	D4
Le Bouchon Breton	C8	Preem and Prithi	B8
Le Saint Julien	C6	Preem Restaurant	B8
Leicester Sq Bar & Restaurant	C4	PrezzoTheatreland	C5

www.gourmetsociety.co.uk

RESTAURANT NAME	GRID Ref	RESTAURANT NAME	GRID Ref
Prezzo Charing Cross	D5	The Atrium	E5
Prezzo Haymarket	D4	The Bathhouse	C7
Prezzo Mayfair	D3	The Borough Bar & Dining	D7
Prezzo Marble Arch (North side)	C3	The Brickhouse	B8
Prezzo Marble Arch (South side)	C3	The Chancery	C6
Prezzo Euston	B4	The Chesterfield Mayfair	D3
Prezzo Victoria	E4	The Collection	E2
Prohibition	D8	The Contented Vine	F4
Queen's Head & Artichoke	B3	The Coriander	F5
Raffaello	D6	The Cuban Bar	C7
Ragam	B4	The Delhi Brasserie Soho	C4
Rasa Maricham	A5	The Delhi Brasserie Kensington	E2
Rasa W1	C3	The Dover Street Restaurant & Bar	D4
Red Chilli	C8	The Drunken Monkey	B8
Reema Balti House	B8	The Empress	C8
Regina Margherita	A6	The Famous Curry Bazaar	B8
Renaissance	A6	The Fish Restaurant	D7
Rhodes W1 Brasserie & Bar	C3	The Fox	B7
Ristorante Biagio	D4	The Globe	B8
Roast	D7	The Grill - Flemings Hotel	D3
Rodon Live	A5	The Hour Glass	E2
Ruby Blue	D4	The India Restaurant	C7
Ryath Indian Tandoori	C2	The Junction Restaurant	B4
Sajna Grill Restaurant	C8	The Landseer British Kitchen	C4
Salsa!	C4	The Langley	C5
Salvador and Amanda	C5	The Light Bar and Restaurant	B8
Santa Lucia	F1	The Livery	C7
Satori Robata	E2	The Living Room	D4
Shampan	B8	The Longacre	C5
Sheba Restaurant	B8	The Loop Bar	C3
Sheraz Bangla Lounge	C8	The Maharani	A4
Shezan	E2	The Monsoon	C8
Shikara	C3	The Poet	C8
Silk	C4	The Punch Tavern	C6
Silka	D7	The Samuel Pepys	B6
Sitaaray	C5	The Talbot Belgravia	E3
Smithfield Bar and Grill	C6	The Terrace In The Fields	C5
Smithy's	A5	The Thames Indian Cuisine	D5
Smollensky's on The Strand	D5	The Va Bene	C4
So Restaurant	D4	The Wall	C7
Sofra Covent Garden	C5	The Warwick	D4
Sofra Mayfair	D3	Tibits	D4
Spicy World Balti House	E4	Tiger Tiger	D4
Stanza	C4	Tower Tandoori	E7
Strand Carvery	C5	Trishna	C3
Stringray Globe Cafe	A8	Vecchio Parioli	B6
Sway	C5	Verve	C5
Swithins Restaurant	C7	Via Condotti	C4
Tamarai	C5	Vine	C5
Tamesis Dock (Boat)	F5	Volupte	C6
Tandoori Nights	C5	Wheelers of St. James's	D4
Tandoori Raj	C5	Wine Wharf	D8
Taormina Restaurant	C1	Wodka	E1
Taste of India Aldgate	C8	Woodlands Marylebone	C3
Taste Of India Covent Garden	C5	Woodlands Restaurant Leicester Square	D4
Ten Tables	E1	Yard	B7
Tentazioni Restaurant	D8	Zayna	C3
Terrace Restaurant	D4	Zebrano	C4
Terranostra	C6	Zebrano Ganton St	C4
Thai Thai East	B7	Zeen - Flavour of India	B4
Thai Tiger	C8	Zen Garden	B6
		Zia Teresa	E2
		Zonzo Restaurant	C2

Sign up to our newsletter for latest restaurants, offers and more

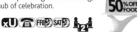

Central London

AMUSE BOUCHE SOHO
British

Poland Street, W1F 8QQ
Map: C4   Nearest Station: Oxford Circus
020 7287 1661
A sleek and intimate venue boasting an exceptional champagne and cocktail list as well as an inventive, modern bar menu. The canapés are great for sharing, and the bar itself is a hub of celebration.

ARTISAN AT THE WESTBURY
European

Westbury Hotel, Bond Street, W1S 2YF
Map: C4   Nearest Station: Oxford Circus
020 8382 5450
Executive Chef Andrew Jones, a Roux scholar and one of the great talents of world cooking, showcases innovative cuisine in visually warm and quietly sensual surroundings. Awarded 2 AA Rosettes.

BACK TO BASICS
Seafood

21a Foley Street, W1W 6DS
Map: C4   Nearest Station: Goodge Street
020 7436 2181
A unique seafood restaurant that epitomises freshness. 'Today's Catch' is precisely that, offering guests 15 varieties of seafood dish as well as many complementing international wines.

BAR DU MARCHE
French

19 Berwick Street, W1F 0PX
Map: C4   Nearest Station: Piccadilly Circus
020 7734 4606
Live life the French way without moving from the city streets of London. Delicious French dishes are complemented by clean-tasting wines which can be enjoyed in a warm and welcoming atmosphere.

Not available on Thursday Evening

CAFÉ ROUGE
French

264 Tottenham Court Road, W1T 7RH
Map: C4   Nearest Station: Tottenham Court Road
020 7631 3075
An attractive restaurant, a boulevard café or a Parisian-style wine bar; however you see Café Rouge, consistently excellent classic French dishes are always guaranteed.

CAFÉ ROUGE
French

43 Charing Cross Road, WCH2 0AP
Map: C4   Nearest Station: Leicester Square
020 7434 2635
An attractive restaurant, a boulevard café or a Parisian-style wine bar; however you see Café Rouge, consistently excellent classic French dishes are always guaranteed.

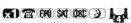

BAR SOHO
International

23-25 Old Compton Street, Soho, W1D 5JL
Map: C4   Nearest Station: Tottenham Court Road
020 7439 0439
Swinging in the sixties and booming today, the bricks and mortar of Bar Soho have no doubt seen it all. Here's betting the carnival atmosphere will sweep you up until long after the last tube leaves.

CARNABY
European

19 Great Marlborough Street, W1F 7HL
Map: C4   Nearest Station: Oxford Circus
020 7297 5568
Uncluttered and pared-down contemporary styling that is reflected in the restaurant's thoroughly unfussy menu of smooth, appealingly flavourful dishes.

Must purchase min 2 courses.

C'EST ICI BRASSERIE
Mediterranean

11 Kingly Street, W1B 5PW
Map: C4   Nearest Station: Oxford Circus
020 7439 1199
An established venue for great events and enjoyable live music, this restaurant has a magnificent menu offering fresh seafood, meats and vegetarian dishes. The charcoal grill ensures exceptional tastes.

DENISE'S RESTAURANT
European

79 Southampton Row, WC1B 4ET
Map: C4   Nearest Station: Russell Square
020 7436 1562
Whether you are hungry for a scrumptious lunch, or require an evening meal in a reliable restaurant, Denise's never fails to please. Healthy fresh dishes are prepared to perfection.

ELENA'S L'ETOILE
French

30 Charlotte Street, W1T 2NG
Map: C4   Nearest Station: Goodge Street
020 7636 7189
Well-balanced, charismatic bistro that serves superbly realised, thoroughgoing French cuisine; a relaxed and appealing touch of nostalgia in its styling and its dishes.

GAY HUSSAR
Hungarian

2 Greek Street, W1D 4NB
Map: C4   Nearest Station: Tottenham Court Road
020 7439 4788
For over 50 years this venue has served exquisite Hungarian cuisine, from national specialities to the finest Hungarian wines. The unique décor is on par with the food, and the service is impeccable.

GEM BAR
English/Gastro pub

10 Beak St, W1F 9RA
Map: C4   Nearest Station: Piccadilly Circus
020 7437 0239
A stylish and trendy bar in Soho serving guests an eclectic mix of drinks as well as a fine offering of international dishes such as mouth-watering tapas. Happy hour is not to be missed.

HAOZHAN
Chinese
8 Gerrard Street, W1D 5PJ
Map: C4   Nearest Station: Leicester Square
020 7434 3838
Exquisite Chinese fusion food brimming with great warmth and charm. Truly exemplary food served with great care and attention, providing diners with a modern oriental dining experience.

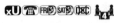

IMLI
Indian
167-169 Wardour Street, W1F 8WR
Map: C4   Nearest Station: Oxford Circus
020 7287 4243
A casual but sophisticated dining experience, with innovative cooking that is accessible and affordable, with a design that fuses the simple elegance of modernity with the richness of Indian tradition.

JERUSALEM
European
33-34 Rathbone Place, W1T 1JN
Map: C4   Nearest Station: Goodge Street
020 7255 1120
A delightful haven of quietly cultured sophistication. This stylishly simple eatery offers a mouth-watering menu of wholesome, hearty and reasonably priced food.

JOSEPHINE'S RESTAURANT
Filipino
4 Charlotte Street, W1T 2LP
Map: C4   Nearest Station: Goodge Street
020 7580 6551
Highly experienced chefs serve delicious Filipino cuisine in an inviting and friendly atmosphere. Guests can taste the talent that can be found in the kitchen as they enjoy tasty authentic meals.

LEICESTER SQ BAR & RESTAURANT
Modern British
Radisson Edwardian, 3-6 St Martins Street, WC2H 7HL
Map: C4   Nearest Station: Leicester Square
0207 451 0114
A restaurant specialising in beautifully cooked, seasoned seafood dishes in an airy, limpid and stylish space.

LVPO BAR
European
50 Dean Street, W1D 5BQ
Map: C4   Nearest Station: Leicester Square
020 7317 9260
A warm evocative atmosphere, a spacious setting and a laid-back crowd can be expected from this popular city bar. Unique LVPO creations can be found amongst a menu of classic cocktails.

MAISON TOUAREG
Lebanese
23-24 Greek Street, W1D 4DZ
Map: C4   Nearest Station: Tottenham Court Road
020 7334 7006
A Moroccan Lebanese kitchen. Enter a haven of Moroccan food, furnishings and atmosphere. Home-cooked dishes are perfect to share whilst the tranquil environment will transport you away from day-to-day life.

MEDITERRANEAN CAFE
Mediterranean
18 Berwick Street, W1F 0PX
Map: C4   Nearest Station: Piccadilly Circus
020 7437 0560
A Soho favourite, the Mediterranean Café and its menu take you on a grand tour of the tastes and style of the Med. Dishes have been selected from Italy, Greece and Turkey for all their unique flavours.

MELATI
Malaysian
21 Great Windmill Street, W1D 7LB
Map: C4   Nearest Station: Piccadilly Circus
020 7437 2745
Popular and well-regarded locally, Melati serves the fragrant and fulsome traditional cuisines of Indonesia and Malaysia, from a wide-ranging, inviting menu.

NUEVA COSTA DORADA
Spanish
47-55 Hanway Street, W1T 1UX
Map: C4   Nearest Station: Tottenham Court Road
020 7631 5117
Whether you are a party of one or a hundred, this delightful tapas restaurant and bar can cater for you. After indulging in traditional Spanish cuisine, here you can dance the rest of the night away.

ÖZER RESTAURANT
Middle East
5 Langham Place, London, W1B 3DG
Map: C4   Nearest Station: Oxford Circus
020 7323 0505
Özer is a sumptuous, atmospheric restaurant that draws on the vast culinary influences of the Ottoman Empire. Chefs combine interesting ingredients, serving unique dishes with a light, modern touch.

PATTERSONS RESTAURANT
Modern British
4 Mill Street, W1S 2AX
Map: C4   Nearest Station: Oxford Circus
020 7499 1308
Understated, confident and treasured by its discerning West End clientèle, a family-run restaurant that distinguishes itself with assured service, a lengthy wine list and highly enjoyable classical food.

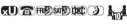

SALSA!
Tex-Mex
96 Charing Cross Road, WC2H 0JG
Map: C4   Nearest Station: Tottenham Court Road
020 7379 3277
Sizzling lamb steaks marinated in garlic and paprika, king prawns with hot Spanish guindilla peppers and superbly tasty fajitas can all be found at this colourfully cultural venue.

SILK
Pan Asian
19-21 Great Marlborough Street, W1F 7HL
Map: C4   Nearest Station: Oxford Circus
020 7297 5538
A Michelin-recommended, Hilton hotel-based restaurant whose imaginative Asian-fusion cuisine jostles for your attention with the magnificent vaulted glass ceiling of its former courthouse setting.

Gourmet Society discount applies to the à la carte menu

STANZA
British

1st Floor, 93 - 107 Shaftesbury Ave, W1D 5DY
Map: C4   Nearest Station: Leicester Square
020 7494 3020
A lively atmosphere that houses great modern British food, with signature dishes such as the mouth-watering smoked haddock risotto. With cocktails also on the menu, this is a venue that has it all.

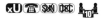

THE DELHI BRASSERIE
Indian

44 Frith Street, W1D 4SB
Map: C4   Nearest Station: Tottenham Court Road
020 7437 8261
Serving diners with a broad range of North Indian cuisine in the most fashionable part of London's trendy Soho. Well established with food of exceptionally high quality.

THE LANDSEER BRITISH KITCHEN
British

The Bloomsbury, 16-22 Great Russell St, WC1B 3NN
Map: C4   Nearest Station: Tottenham Court Road
020 7347 1222
An architecturally stunning neo-Georgian building houses this charming hotel. Explore the myriad of local treasures before taking a well-earned break in the exceptional restaurant and bar.

THE VA BENE
Italian

46 Brewer Street, W1F 9TF
Map: C4   Nearest Station: Piccadilly Circus
020 7437 8516
In the warmly lit dining room of this ristorante, sample the ambience and vivid Italian food that make this such a popular neighbourhood spot; warm, mellow, colourful and authentic flavours.

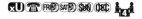

VIA CONDOTTI
Italian

23 Conduit Street, W1S 2XS
Map: C4   Nearest Station: Oxford Circus
020 7493 7050
Here find delightful signature dishes of incredible standard and quality. Cuisine created by a Head Chef who uses his outstanding talent in the kitchen to reaffirm his love of his country. 1 AA Rosette.

ZEBRANO
Modern European

18 Greek St, W1D 4DS
Map: C4   Nearest Station: Tottenham Court Road
020 7287 5267
The place where a fun-filled time is always on the table. The Zebrano chefs have it covered, whether you want a casual lunch or a celebration with friends. The cocktails are sure to satisfy all.

ZEBRANO GANTON ST
Modern European

14-16 Ganton St, W1F 7BT
Map: C4   Nearest Station: Oxford Circus
020 7287 5267
The place where a fun-filled time is always on the table. The Zebrano chefs have it covered, whether you want a casual lunch or a celebration with friends. The cocktails are sure to satisfy all.

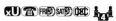

BACCO RESTAURANT & WINE BAR
Italian

25-26 Red Lion Street, WC1R 4PS
Map: C5   Nearest Station: Holborn
020 7242 7900
The perfect place for after work catch-ups and pre-theatre dinners with al fresco dining in summer. Quality Italian food to be enjoyed with a glass from the carefully selected regional Italian wine list.

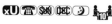

BHATTI INDIAN CUISINE
Indian/Punjabi

37 Great Queen Street, WC2B 5AA
Map: C5   Nearest Station: Holborn
020 7831 0817
Snack on an Indian appetizer or simply savour a delicious main meal. Whether you like your food nice and spicy or meek and mild, the many dishes on offer provide something for everyone.

BLOOMSBURY ST BAR & RESTAURANT
International

9-13 Bloomsbury Street, WC1B 3QD
Map: C5   Nearest Station: Tottenham Court Road
020 8817 0944
Cool and intimate, this bar and restaurant is an ideal place to start the day with a scrumptious breakfast, or end it with a chilled out dinner. The chef has an admirable sense of flavour and taste.

BOULEVARD BRASSERIE
French

40 Wellington Street, WC2E 7BD
Map: C5   Nearest Station: Covent Garden
020 7240 2992
Classically simple French brasserie dishes are served in this popular eatery. Hearty beef bourguignon and succulent steaks are delightful choices, whilst the wine list offers an accompaniment for any dish.

CAFÉ DES AMIS
European

11-14 Hanover Place, WC2E 9JP
Map: C5   Nearest Station: Covent Garden
020 7379 3444
A Covent Garden classic. Modern European cuisine is subjected to a divine French twist, which ensures every dish locks in delicious flavours. Enjoy a tasty cheese platter in the champagne bar.

CAFE MODE
Mediterranean

57-59 Endell Street, WC2H 9AJ
Map: C5   Nearest Station: Covent Garden
020 7240 8085
Perfectly situated for the theatres, this welcoming little red restaurant is bright and cheerful inside and serves a mean array of flavour-filled, herby Italian dishes and juicy grill-time specialities.

CAFE PASTA
Italian

2-4 Garrick Street, WC2E 9BH
Map: C5   Nearest Station: Covent Garden
020 7497 2779
A well-established Italian restaurant, offering traditional cuisine in comfortable surroundings. A comprehensive hand-picked wine list offers a perfect accompaniment for every dish.

CAFE PASTA
Italian

184 Shaftesbury Avenue, WC2H 8JB
Map: C5   Nearest Station: Tottenham Court Road
020 7379 0198
A charming and friendly restaurant on Shaftesbury Avenue. Watch the world go by as you enjoy a frothy cappuccino, or indulge in traditional Italian dishes in a cosy, candlelit setting.

 2FOR1 MAIN COURSE

INCOGNICO
French / Italian

117 Shaftesbury Avenue, WC2H 8AD
Map: C5   Nearest Station: Tottenham Court Road
020 7836 8866
Award-winning Chef Francesco Zanchetta's array of French and Italian dishes will delight your palate whilst the list of cocktails and after-dinner drinks will dazzle and satisfy your soul.

 2FOR1 3COURSES

CAFÉ ROUGE
French

77 Kingsway, WC2B 6SR
Map: C5   Nearest Station: Holborn
020 7430 1416
An attractive restaurant, a boulevard café or a Parisian-style wine bar; however you see Café Rouge, consistently excellent classic French dishes are always guaranteed.

 50%OFF FOOD

LOS LOCOS
Mexican

24 Russell Street, WC2B 5HF
Map: C5   Nearest Station: Covent Garden
020 7379 0220
A brilliantly lively place for tasty, thoroughbred Tex-Mex food; the spicy signature dishes and hearty, home-made accompaniments are an especial pleasure.

 2FOR1 3COURSES

CAFÉ ROUGE
French

34 Wellington Street, WC2E 7BD
Map: C5   Nearest Station: Covent Garden
020 7836 0998
An attractive restaurant, a boulevard café or a Parisian-style wine bar; however you see Café Rouge, consistently excellent classic French dishes are always guaranteed.

 50%OFF FOOD

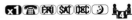

MAXWELL'S BAR AND GRILL
American

8 James Street, WC2E 8BH
Map: C5   Nearest Station: Covent Garden
020 7836 0303
The vibrant atmosphere at Maxwell's is a great setting for the hearty, classic American food it serves. Come here for its major helpings of a wide range of freshly cooked, fulsome grill dishes.

 25%OFF TOTAL

CREATION BAR AND RESTAURANT
Modern British

97 Great Russell Street, WC1B 3BL
Map: C5   Nearest Station: Holborn
020 7666 2068
Perfectly placed to the nearby theatres, Creation is partly about performance - with the kitchen on show behind a glass divide - and mostly about plates packed with succulent, seasoned flavours.

 25%OFF TOTAL

MOTI MAHAL
Indian

45 Great Queen Street, WC2B 5AA
Map: C5   Nearest Station: Holborn
020 7240 9329
Situated in Covent Garden, this acclaimed restaurant takes inspiration from the ever-evolving culinary texture of rural India, mixing a mastery of the classic recipes with fresh and imaginative flavours.

 2FOR1 MAIN COURSE

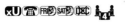

DIAL BAR AND RESTAURANT
Modern British

20 Monmouth Street, WC2 9HD
Map: C5   Nearest Station: Covent Garden
020 7845 8607
Located in the centre of fashionable Covent Garden and serving contemporary British cuisine, Dial is rapidly becoming one of London's most popular venues.

25%OFF TOTAL

NAVAJO JOE
South West American

34 King Street, WC2E 8JD
Map: C5   Nearest Station: Covent Garden
020 7240 4008
On the cusp of Covent Garden's famous piazza, experience a blend of Pacific Rim and South West American flavour. Renowned for its extensive range of tequilas, rum, and other world favourites.

 25%OFF TOTAL

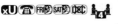

GANDHI'S RESTAURANT
Indian

35 Grays Inn Road, WC1X 8PG
Map: C5   Nearest Station: Chancery Lane
020 7831 6208
This restaurant has a unique friendly ambience that closely mirrors the warm hospitable nature of Indian culture. Every dish is infused with the finest ingredients, herbs and spices.

25%OFF TOTAL

PALM COURT BRASSERIE
European

39 King Street, WC2E 8JS
Map: C5   Nearest Station: Covent Garden
020 7240 2939
Classic 1920s art décor creates an elegant time capsule and an oasis of sophisticated calm. This intimate Parisian-style brasserie offers a menu that captures the essence of classic European cuisine.

 25%OFF TOTAL

HENRY'S CAFE BAR
European

5 Henrietta Street, WC2E 8PS
Map: C5   Nearest Station: Covent Garden
020 7379 1871
An oasis for every type of person with a delicious, well-prepared menu; ideal for lunch, dinner or a light snack. Henrys also boasts an extensive wine and champagne list and array of cocktails to die for.

 25%OFF TOTAL

PREZZO
Italian

116 St Martins Lane, WC2N 4BF
Map: C5   Nearest Station: Leicester Square
020 7240 0352
With a character all of its own, Prezzo oozes contemporary style and enduring charm. Signature pastas, stone-baked pizzas and classic Italian dishes promise a perfect dining choice for the whole family.

2FOR1 MAIN COURSE

Visit the website regularly to discover the latest restaurants joining the GS

SALVADOR AND AMANDA
Spanish
8 Great Newport Street, WC2H 7JA
Map: C5   Nearest Station: Leicester Square
020 7240 1551
Spanish passion is aplenty in this extraordinarily outstanding restaurant. A menu that boasts an eclectic variety of Spanish dishes such as prawns seared in garlic and mouth-watering paella.

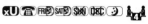

SITAARAY
Indian
167 Drury Lane, WC2B 5PG
Map: C5   Nearest Station: Holborn
020 7269 6422
A glamorous atmosphere that captures the essence of Indian cinema and cuisine. Diners are treated to a unique experience combining the genres and moods of Hindi cinema, yet the real star is the food.

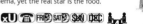

SOFRA
Middle East
73 Tavistock Steet, WC2E 7PB
Map: C5   Nearest Station: Covent Garden
020 7240 3773
Sofra promises high-quality recipes with an accent on healthy options, choice and uncompromising tastes. Order a feast of mezzes or savour a succulent tagine, and experience Turkish dining redefined.

2FOR1 MAIN COURSE

STRAND CARVERY
British
Strand Palace Hotel, Exeter Street, WC2R 0JJ
Map: C5   Nearest Station: Covent Garden
020 7497 4158
In the heart of London's theatre-land, this carvery restaurant serves big and bold, succulent roast dinners; the Shakespearean injunction for 'great meals of beef and iron and steel' chimes beautifully.

25%OFF TOTAL

SWAY
Mediterranean
61-65 Queen Street, WC2B 5BZ
Map: C5   Nearest Station: Holborn
020 7404 6114
From home comforts to sophisticated, rustic Mediterranean platters, there's something for all in this contemporary, stylish eatery, complete with premium draught beers and a range of cocktails and wines.

50%OFF FOOD

TAMARAI
Pan Asian
167 Drury Lane, WC2B 5PG
Map: C5   Nearest Station: Holborn
020 7831 9399
Asian flavours derived from the whole of Asia's culinary lexicon. A highly experienced Head Chef produces fine dishes full of fragrance and flavour, offering a true taste of Eastern culture.

2FOR1 MAIN COURSE

TANDOORI NIGHTS
Indian
35 Great Queen St, WC2B 5AA
Map: C5   Nearest Station: Holborn
020 7831 2558
This venue offer diners a splendid range of curries and Tandoori specialities prepared by master chefs . A rendezvous for all who enjoy the exotic, spicy and healthy dishes of the Indian subcontinent.

25%OFF TOTAL

TANDOORI RAJ
Indian
65 Red Lion Street, WC1R 4NA
Map: C5   Nearest Station: Holborn
020 7405 8072
Warm and well-thought-out Indian restaurant in Holborn, where dishes are classic, exceptionally well flavoured and concocted with care; the place is atmospheric, well-located and very accommodating.

TASTE OF INDIA
Indian
25 Catherine Street, WC2B 5JS
Map: C5   Nearest Station: Covent Garden
020 7836 2538
A strong range of quality Indian food in this central restaurant, close to Covent Garden market, in an inviting, welcoming interior.

25%OFF TOTAL

THE LANGLEY
International
5 Langley Street, WC2H 9JA
Map: C5   Nearest Station: Covent Garden
020 7836 5005
Nestled amongst the popular streets of Covent Garden, the retro-cool atmosphere will guarantee you a great time. The mouth-watering cocktail menu includes tasty classics with perfect signature dishes.

25%OFF TOTAL

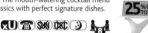

THE LONGACRE
English and Continental
1-3 Long Acre, WC2E 9LH
Map: C5   Nearest Station: Leicester Square
020 7520 6920
An ideally located restaurant accommodating a superb menu, fully complemented by the outstanding wine list. Full-bodied New World wonders will round off any dish from the menu.

2FOR1 MAIN COURSE

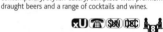

THE TERRACE IN THE FIELDS
Modern British
Lincoln's Inn Fields, WC2A 3LJ
Map: C5   Nearest Station: Holborn
020 7430 1234
With a mission to demystify Caribbean produce, chef Patrick Williams integrates ingredients from the around the islands into British cooking. Discover exciting new textures and invigorating flavours.

50%OFF FOOD

VERVE
European
1 Upper St Martin's Lane, WC2H 9NY
Map: C5   Nearest Station: Leicester Square
020 7395 1200
Dining and partying go hand in hand at Verve. Providing a tremendous all-day menu, a chandelier-strewn bar and basement club, Verve is perfect from lunch until late.

50%OFF FOOD

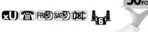

VINE
Italian
48 Grays Inn Rd, WC1X 8LT
Map: C5   Nearest Station: Chancery Lane
020 7404 6230
A low-key, smooth and stylish little joint on Grays Inn Road that does a fine line in broad-based, cosmopolitan city cooking; a place that is accessible but does not shirk on quality.

2FOR1 3 COURSES

GREATER LONDON

123

AZZURRO
Italian

Arch 145, Sutton Walk, SE1 7ND
Map: D5   Nearest Station: Waterloo
020 7620 1300

A spectacular Italian restaurant and bar perfectly located close to many of London's attractions. With a delicious cocktails and an inviting dance floor. Azzurro reflects the essence of Italian culture.

BELOWZERO RESTAURANT & LOUNGE
European

31-33 Heddon Street, W1B 4BN
Map: D4   Nearest Station: Piccadilly Circus
020 7478 8910

A venue that embodies its title. Boasting a unique bar made out of ice, here you are guaranteed a great time, so good you'll be wishing you could freeze the moment. Snacks and meals are available.

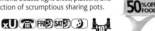

JEWEL LOUNGE COVENT GARDEN
International

29-30 Maiden Lane, WC2E 7JS
Map: D5   Nearest Station: Charing Cross
020 7845 9980

Make a night of it with dining combined with delicious cocktails and an inviting dance floor. The mouth-watering menu boasts light bites, platters, and an extensive selection of scrumptious sharing pots.

BENIHANA
Japanese

37 Sackville Street, W1S 3DQ
Map: D4   Nearest Station: Oxford Circus
020 7494 2525

The third restaurant of the chain, Benihana was one of the first to bring teppanyaki style dining to London. Guests will enjoy their own private theatre as the chefs cook on a teppan right in front of you.

OPAL BAR & RESTAURANT
European

Hungerford House, Victoria Embankment, WC2N 6PA
Map: D5   Nearest Station: Embankment
020 7389 9933

Tasty tapas treats are on offer for you to enjoy in this ideally located venue. Natural light floods this riverside restaurant, enhancing the amiable, relaxed atmosphere.

CHOR BIZARRE
Indian

16 Albemarle Street, W1S 4HW
Map: D4   Nearest Station: Green Park
020 7629 9802

The inspiring collection of Indian furnishings and the large number of regular Indian diners offer a testimony to the authenticity of this restaurant and the smart, sassy and spicy food it serves.

Lunch Mon-Sat. Offer also for dinner Sun/Mon only. Not available on Thursday Evening

PREZZO
Italian

31/32 Northumberland Ave, WC2N 5BW
Map: D5   Nearest Station: Charing Cross
020 7930 4288

With a character all of its own, Prezzo oozes contemporary style and enduring charm. Signature pastas, stone-baked pizzas and classic Italian dishes promise a perfect dining choice for the whole family.

DOLADA
Italian

Arcade House, 13 Albemarle St, W1S 4HJ
Map: D4   Nearest Station: Oxford Circus
020 7409 1011

The Dolada restaurant run by the De Pra family is famed for its classy yet effortless atmosphere and its moreish cuisine. The exquisite five course tasting menu is a must for those who love fine food.

SMOLLENSKY'S ON THE STRAND
International

105 The Strand, WC2R 0AA
Map: D5   Nearest Station: Temple
020 7497 2101

One of the great names in grill restaurants and has been at the forefront of the London bar and restaurant scene for over 20 years. Simply fantastic food, superb service and great value for money.

FISHWORKS
Seafood

7-9 Swallow Street, W1B 4DE
Map: D4   Nearest Station: Piccadilly Circus
020 7734 5813

A sleek seafood restaurant with its own fish counter where you can buy fresh from a full cohort; vivid, classic dishes populate the menu and the restaurant is serenely ensconced just away from Piccadilly.

THE THAMES INDIAN CUISINE
Indian/ Bangladeshi

79 Waterloo Road, SE1 8UD
Map: D5   Nearest Station: Waterloo
020 7928 3856

A locally renowned restaurant mixing well-known favourites with rarer delicacies from the subcontinent. Diners may wish to break away from their habitual curry choice to try something unusual.

FRANCOS
Italian

61 Jermyn Street, SW1Y 6LX
Map: D4   Nearest Station: Piccadilly Circus
020 7499 2211

Locally renowned, long-standing Italian and Mediterranean restaurant by St James's; Franco's serves warming, balanced and wholesome dishes from its à la carte menu, along with ever-changing daily specials.

AL DUCA
Italian

4-5 Duke of York Street, SW1Y 6LA
Map: D4   Nearest Station: Piccadilly Circus
020 7839 3090

This Michelin Bib Gourmand winner delivers the best elements from one of the most acclaimed gastronomic regions of the world, with a wide range of delicious classic and modern-style dishes. 1 AA Rosette.

GALILEO'S RESTAURANT
Italian

71 Haymarket, SW1Y 4RW
Map: D4   Nearest Station: Piccadilly Circus
020 7839 3939

A clear-minded restaurant that serves distinctively Tuscan cuisine; its full but uncluttered dishes accentuate the clean, foundational flavours of Mediterranean herbs and olive oil.

When booking restaurants always mention your GS membership

GETTI JERMYN STREET
Italian
16-17 Jermyn Street, SW1Y 6LT
Map: D4   Nearest Station: Piccadilly Circus
020 7734 7334
With a great deal of verve, in a cool, bright ambience, Getti dispatches dishes with the earthy, full flavours of Italian cuisine from across its distinctive regional specialisations.

GRACE
English/Gastro pub
42-44 Great Windmill Street, W1D 7NB
Map: D4   Nearest Station: Piccadilly Circus
020 7479 4422
Grace is the hottest new venue in the capital to sip and be seen, where the affordable modern British menu boasts all the classics and the drinks list is extensive. Sleek and sexy.

HAMPSHIRE BAR & RESTAURANT
Modern European
Leicester Square, WC2H 7LH
Map: D4   Nearest Station: Leicester Square
020 7839 9399
A luxurious bar and restaurant with a menu reflecting a fusion of British and Mediterranean influences, served in a contemporary environment. One of the best-known places for a smart West End breakfast.

HENRY'S CAFE BAR
European
80 Piccadilly, W1J 8HX
Map: D4   Nearest Station: Green Park
020 7491 2544
An oasis for every type of person with a delicious, well-prepared menu; ideal for lunch, dinner or a light snack. Henrys also boasts an extensive wine and champagne list and array of cocktails to die for.

JEWEL BAR PICCADILLY
Spanish
4-6 Glasshouse Street, W1B 5DQ
Map: D4   Nearest Station: Piccadilly Circus
020 7478 0780
A chic, luxurious bar and club in the heart of the West End renowned for being celebrity haunt. Encompasses superb design, exquisite sharing platters and excellent service, all with an air of exclusivity.

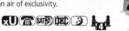

LA LOCANDA
Italian
35 Heddon Street, W1B 4BR
Map: D4   Nearest Station: Piccadilly Circus
020 7734 6689
One of the area's best kept secrets. Veal escalope with mozzarella and Parma ham, baked mushrooms with spinach and parmesan and tagliatelle are just some of the restaurant's specialities.

MINT LEAF RESTAURANT
Indian
Suffolk Place, Haymarket, SW1Y 4HX
Map: D4   Nearest Station: Piccadilly Circus
020 7930 9020
An outstanding menu tenderly prepared by the kitchen's talented Head Chef at this traditional Indian restaurant. The stylish, sophisticated interior is only one of the highlights. 1 AA Rosette.

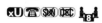

PIER 1
Oriental
66 Haymarket, SW1Y 4RF
Map: D4   Nearest Station: Piccadilly Circus
020 7930 4800
A quality fish and chips experience. Finest cuts of line-caught fish are freshly prepared and filleted by experienced fishmongers. Classic, great tasting food.

ON ANON
British
London Pavilion, Piccadilly Circus, W1V 9LA
Map: D4   Nearest Station: Piccadilly Circus
020 7287 8008
Get in the mix and enjoy the party with great food, drinks, and of course music. A popular and thriving club that also offers delicious food and a range of cocktails to start the night off perfectly.

PLANET HOLLYWOOD
American
57-60 Haymarket, SW1Y 4QX
Map: D4   Nearest Station: Piccadilly Circus
020 7287 1000
Experience the glamour of Hollywood with a large cocktail bar and extravagantly themed rooms filled with mega-star memorabilia. Freshly prepared, quality American food delivering a taste of the States.

PREZZO
Italian
Kinghouse, 8 Haymarket, SW1Y 4BP
Map: D4   Nearest Station: Piccadilly Circus
020 7839 1129
With a character all of its own, Prezzo oozes contemporary style and enduring charm. Signature pastas, stone-baked pizzas and classic Italian dishes promise a perfect dining choice for the whole family.

RISTORANTE BIAGIO
Italian
189 Piccadilly, W1J 9ES
Map: D4   Nearest Station: Piccadilly Circus
020 7434 1921
Enjoy freshly made breads, pastas and catch of the day cooked to northern Italy recipes in a venue inspired by Philippe Starck and the style of 1950s Italy. Leave room for the pastries prepared on-site.

RUBY BLUE
European
1 Leicester Place, WC2H 7BP
Map: D4   Nearest Station: Leicester Square
020 7287 8050
With delicious food in the restaurant, an extensive selection of drinks at the bar and a vibrant nightclub, Ruby Blue really does have everything going for it. Live pianists play as you dine.

SO RESTAURANT
Japanese
3-4 Warwick Street, W1B 5LS
Map: D4   Nearest Station: Piccadilly Circus
020 7292 0767
Sophisticated Japanese cuisine infused with unique European flavours. Select dishes are prepared on a customised grill and cooked over volcanic rocks imported from Mt. Fuji. Awarded 2 AA Rosettes.

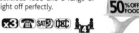

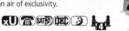

125

www.gourmetsociety.co.uk

TERRACE RESTAURANT
International

21 Piccadilly, W1J 0BH
Map: D4   Nearest Station: Green Park
020 7851 3085

A wonderful place to take a break from the hustle and bustle of the city without removing yourself from it. The soothing, relaxed ambience provides a great contrast to the activity of London Piccadilly.

THE DOVER STREET RESTAURANT & BAR
Mediterranean

8-10 Dover Street, W1S 4LQ
Map: D4   Nearest Station: Green Park
020 7629 9813

Award-winning for its superb live entertainment, guests can be guaranteed a great evening out at this popular restaurant and bar. Enjoy Mediterranean cuisine in an extremely fashionable location.

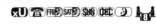

THE LIVING ROOM
British

3-9 Heddon Street, W1B 4BE
Map: D4   Nearest Station: Piccadilly Circus
020 7292 0570

Step into The Living Room and you can count on the savvy, distinctive neighbourhood vibe that plays home to eclectically drawn, supremely tasty cuisine. Kick back in this stylish venue off Regent Street.

Must purchase min 3 courses/person inc main.

THE WARWICK
International

1-3 Warwick Street, W1B 5LR
Map: D4   Nearest Station: Piccadilly Circus
020 7734 4409

The extensive selection of beers and wines will undoubtedly provide a perfect companion for your mouth-watering meal. Come and feed your appetite after that hard day of strolling and shopping.

TIBITS
Vegetarian

12-14 Heddon Street, W1B 4DA
Map: D4   Nearest Station: Piccadilly Circus
020 7758 4110

A menu that suitably reflects the seasons and uses fresh, locally sourced produce, meeting your needs all day long. Arrive expecting only the very best for both your taste buds and a healthy lifestyle.

Can also redeem a '4 for 2' with one card.

TIGER TIGER
International

29 The Haymarket, SW1Y 4SP
Map: D4   Nearest Station: Piccadilly Circus
020 7930 1885

Tiger Tiger provides relaxed dining, chilled out drinking, and all night partying. Located in the west end, the famous restaurant offers an admirable menu that can be enjoyed in style and comfort.

WHEELERS OF ST. JAMES'S
Fish and Seafood

72-73 St James Street, SW1A 1PH
Map: D4   Nearest Station: Green Park
020 7408 1440

A revival of the world's oldest and finest fish restaurant in a distinguished location. With its traditional exterior and its glamorous interior, this is an extremely popular fine dining destination.

WOODLANDS
South Indian Vegetarian

37 Panton Street, SW1Y 4EA
Map: D4   Nearest Station: Piccadilly Circus
020 7839 7258

South Indian vegetarian cuisine at its very best. The award-winning kitchen accommodates chefs with at least 15 years of experience from other Woodlands restaurants.

BABBLE
Mediterranean

Lansdowne House, 59 Berkeley Square, W1 6ER
Map: D3   Nearest Station: Green Park
020 7758 8255

Dine on light dishes and sharing plates being lounging to the laid back sounds of funky tunes in the opulent surroundings of Babble's club.

BENARES
Indian British

12A Berkeley Square, W1J 6BS
Map: D3   Nearest Station: Green Park
020 7629 8886

Michelin-starred and double AA Rosette restaurant serving phenomenal Indian cuisine with subtle spices and authentic flavours. Admire the menu which is based on ingredients from all over India.

Not available on Bank Holidays.

GREIG'S GRILL & RESTAURANT
British

26-28 Bruton Place, W1J 6NG
Map: D3   Nearest Station: Bond Street
020 7629 5613

Established in the 1950s by Alistair Greig, serving some of the best steaks in London. Half a century later the steaks are still cooked on a coal grill; the restaurant also offers great British classics.

RECOMMEND A FRIEND

see page 18

PREZZO
Italian

17 Hertford Street, W1J 7RS
Map: D3   Nearest Station: Hyde Park Corner
020 7499 4690

With a character all of its own, Prezzo oozes contemporary style and enduring charm. Signature pastas, stone-baked pizzas and classic Italian dishes promise a perfect dining choice for the whole family.

SOFRA
Turkish

18 Shepherd Street, W1J 7JG
Map: D3   Nearest Station: Green Park
020 7493 3320

Sofra promises high-quality recipes with an accent on healthy options, choice and uncompromising tastes. Order a feast of mezzes or savour a succulent tagine and experience Turkish dining, redefined.

Gourmet Society discount applies to the à la carte menu

THE CHESTERFIELD MAYFAIR
British

35 Charles Street, W1J 5EB
Map: D3   Nearest Station: Green Park
020 7514 5706
An integral part of the Chesterfield Hotel, the luxurious Butlers Restaurant offers a carefully selected array of dishes that provide satisfaction for all palates and appetites.

THE GRILL - FLEMINGS HOTEL
Modern European

Fleimngs Hotel, Half Moon Street, W1J 7BH
Map: D3   Nearest Station: Green Park
020 7499 0000
The glamorous and opulent new restaurant at one of London's oldest established luxury hotels, Flemings. Strong on British produce, Flemings is a culinary destination with excellent service and rave reviews

Offer applies to two courses from the set menus.

108 MARYLEBONE LANE
Modern British

108 Marylebone Lane, W1U 2QE
Map: C3   Nearest Station: Bond Street
020 7969 3900
A fine addition to Marylebone's culinary scene. Their food philosophy is simple, using only the best ingredients to create simple, classic dishes, sourcing from local supplier when possible.

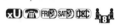

ASCOTS BAR & RESTAURANT
Modern British

350 Oxford Street, W1N 0BY
Map: C3   Nearest Station: Bond Street
020 7629 7474
A retreat from the surrounding hubbub, this luxuriously appointed bar and restaurant is a recent recipient of an AA Rosette. The chef's simple approach to combining ingredients shines throughout the menu.

AUBERGE
French

6-8 St Christopher's Place, W1U 1ND
Map: C3   Nearest Station: Bond Street
020 7486 5557
Auberge adopt a simple approach, using fresh ingredients combined with some French inspiration, serving classic dishes for all to enjoy. Perfect after a long, hard day on London's illustrious streets.

CAFÉ ROUGE
French

46-48 James St, W1U 1HA
Map: C3   Nearest Station: Bond Street
020 7487 4847
An attractive restaurant, a boulevard café or a Parisian-style wine bar; however you see Café Rouge, consistently excellent classic French dishes are always guaranteed.

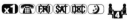

CHUTNEY AND LAGER
Indian

43-51 Gt Titchfield St, W1W 7PQ
Map: C3   Nearest Station: Oxford Circus
020 7636 8009
This fashionable and friendly lounge bar offers delicious food, great wine and excellent beer. This restaurant aims to provide stylish, quality dining with exceptional service from their friendly staff.

DEVILLE
British

Mandeville Place, W1U 2BE
Map: C3   Nearest Station: Bond Street
020 7935 5599
Delicious modern British cuisine served in a decadently decorated restaurant. Indulge in a flavoursome main dish, but don't forget to leave room for the phenomenal home-made ice cream. 1 AA Rosette.

FAKHRELDINE
Lebanese

85 Piccadilly, Green Park, W1 7NB
Map: C3   Nearest Station: Bond Street
020 7493 3424
Upholding their thirty year reputation, this restaurant epitomises quality Middle Eastern cuisine, presenting a fusion of authentic Lebanese tradition and the glamour of London life.

FIRE AND SPICE
International

4 Bryanston Street, W1H 7BY
Map: C3   Nearest Station: Marble Arch
020 7487 0678
Nestled away near Marble Arch, this restaurant serves full-bodied grill food with delicious, piquant marinades in a cool, cosy setting.

FISHWORKS
Seafood

89 Marylebone High Street, W1U 4QW
Map: C3   Nearest Station: Baker Street
020 7935 9796
A sleek seafood restaurant with its own fish counter where you can buy fresh from a full cohort; vivid, classic dishes populate the menu and the restaurant is serenely ensconced just off Oxford Street.

GAYLORD RESTAURANT
Indian

79-81 Mortimer Street, W1W 7SJ
Map: C3   Nearest Station: Oxford Circus
020 7580 3615
With a particular specialisation in tandoori recipes, this North Indian restaurant covers the gamut of classic dishes, adding distinctive flavours into the mix.

LEVANT
Lebanese

Jason Court, 76 Wigmore Street, W1U 1BQ
Map: C3   Nearest Station: Bond Street
020 7224 1111
Enter the sensuously exotic Levant and dine in a stunningly authentic dining room of traditional décor and Arabic music. The extensive menu showcases eclectic Lebanese cuisine at its finest. 1 AA Rosette.

MEWS OF MAYFAIR
European

10-11 Lancashire Court, W1S 1EY
Map: C3   Nearest Station: Bond Street
020 7518 9395
Cool, calm and quirky restaurant ensconced off New Bond Street; the food is eclectic, accomplished and full of flavour. Awarded 1 AA Rosette.

NUOCMAM
Japanese

35 Great Portland Street, W1W 8QQ
Map: C3   Nearest Station: Oxford Circus
020 7631 2080

Rejecting commercial cooking methods in favour of those traditionally passed down, this unique restaurant provides an admirably innovative fusion of Japanese and Vietnamese cuisine.

THE LOOP BAR
English and Continental

19 Dering Street, W1S 1AH
Map: C3   Nearest Station: Oxford Circus
020 7493 1003

If you are looking for all the comforts of home-made food but desire the ease of having it made for you, head to The Loop Bar and indulge in one of the irresistible dishes from the well-mastered menu.

ORIGINAL TAGINES
Moroccan

7a Dorset Street, W1U 6QN
Map: C3   Nearest Station: Baker Street
020 7935 1545

A restaurant boasting all the qualities of a good, friendly local. Sample the culinary delights of Morocco in a contemporary venue that delivers a truly authentic, well-executed menu.

TRISHNA
Indian

15-17 Blandford Street, W1U 3DG
Map: C3   Nearest Station: Bond Street
020 7935 5624

Dine in the very heart of Marylebone village. With its innovative twists on South West Indian cuisine, this restaurant is today regarded as one of London's greatest Indian restaurants. 2 AA Rosettes.

PREZZO
Italian

7-9 Great Cumberland Street, W1H 7LU
Map: C3   Nearest Station: Marble Arch
020 7723 7172

With a character all of its own, Prezzo oozes contemporary style and enduring charm. Signature pastas, stone-baked pizzas and classic Italian dishes promise a perfect dining choice for the whole family.

WOODLANDS
South Indian Vegetarian

77 Marylebone Lane, W1U 2PS
Map: C3   Nearest Station: Bond Street
020 7486 3862

South Indian vegetarian cuisine at its very best. The award-winning kitchen accommodates chefs with at least 15 years of experience from other Woodlands restaurants.

PREZZO
Italian

15 North Audley Street, W1K 6WZ
Map: C3   Nearest Station: Bond Street
020 7493 4990

With a character all of its own, Prezzo oozes contemporary style and enduring charm. Signature pastas, stone-baked pizzas and classic Italian dishes promise a perfect dining choice for the whole family.

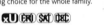

ZAYNA
Indian

25 New Quebec Street, W1H 7SF
Map: C3   Nearest Station: Marble Arch
020 7723 2229

Highly regarded restaurant serving North Indian and Pakistani food as its speciality. The restaurant gives great attention to detail; its dishes stand out for their vibrancy and rich distinct flavours.

RASA W1
Indian

6 Dering Street, W1S 1AD
Map: C3   Nearest Station: Bond Street
020 7629 1346

Inspired by the authentic home cooking of beautiful, spice-rich Kerala, this restaurant's passion is food prepared always with devotion, love, and the finest ingredients. Experience the essence of India.

BASE BRASSERIE
Mediterranean

195 Baker Street, NW1 6UY
Map: B3   Nearest Station: Baker Street
020 7486 7000

Base Brasserie has been established for 7 years and serves delicious Mediterranean cuisine. Food is sourced from local markets, and the specials board changes daily to offer the freshest dishes.

RHODES W1 BRASSERIE & BAR
British

Great Cumberland Place, W1H 7DL
Map: C3   Nearest Station: Marble Arch
020 7616 5930

Dip into this trendy hotel brasserie for a quick lunch or fulfilling dinner. With an exceptional menu from celebrity chef Gary Rhodes, the food here is crafted with skill and verve. 1 AA Rosette.

CINNAMON SPICE
Indian

12-14 Glentworth Street, NW1 5PG
Map: B3   Nearest Station: Baker Street
020 7935 0212

A delicate blend of contrasting flavours makes the most exquisite tasting dishes in this wonderful Indian restaurant. Curry fans will fall head over heels for the lamb moslini or the cinnamon chicken.

SHIKARA
Indian

65 Great Titchfield Street, W1W 7PS
Map: C3   Nearest Station: Goodge Street
020 7636 6555

Creating an intoxicating blend of old and new, this wonderful Indian restaurant is proud of its well-balanced menu which combines traditional favourites with unique creations.

QUEEN'S HEAD & ARTICHOKE
Modern European

30-32 Albany St, NW1 4EA
Map: B3   Nearest Station: Great Portland Street
020 7916 6206

One of London's best gastro pubs, serving delightful modern English food as well as a delicious tapas menu. Excellent service and an extensive beverages selection.

Enjoy massive leisure and retail savings with more Gourmet Society

AMARETTO
Italian
116 Tottenham Court Road, W1T 5AJ
Map: B4   Nearest Station: Warren Street
020 7387 6234
For a delicious authentic taste of Italy without leaving the country, head to this informal modern Italian restaurant. The specialities include the succulent black tiger prawns, which really are a treat.

ARCHIPELAGO
European
110 Whifield street, W1T 5ED
Map: B4   Nearest Station: Warren Street
020 7383 3346
A sensual dining experience as an indulgence of tantalising global dishes awaits you, featuring hallmark exotic dishes such as crocodile and kangaroo. London's culinary portal to world cuisine.

ASTON BAR & RESTAURANT
Modern British
130 Tottenham Court Road, W1P 9HP
Map: B4   Nearest Station: Warren Street
020 7387 7394
A luxury bar and restaurant that serves fine contemporary British cuisine, which draws together classic cooking techniques and simple, fresh local ingredients. Enjoy a drink or meal in comfort and style.

JETLAG RESTAURANT & BAR
International
125 Cleveland Street, W1T 6QB
Map: B4   Nearest Station: Great Portland Street
020 3370 5838
From the unique cocktails and premium beers to the delicious food, Jetlag exudes quality and freshness. Perfect for those looking for first-class luxury without the first-class price tag.

MASSALA HUT
Indian
161-163 Drummond St, NW1 2PB
Map: B4   Nearest Station: Euston Square
020 7387 6699
Comfortably set back from the harry around Euston, this recently refurbished Indian restaurant is a great place to retreat for a quality curry from its ranging menu.

PALMS OF GOA
Indian
160 New Cavendish Street, W1W 6YR
Map: B4   Nearest Station: Goodge Street
020 7580 6125
Courtesy of its Portuguese heritage, Goan cuisine combines Indian and European influences to create its deliciousness. This restaurant is famous for its pumpkin curry and tasty dishes such as lamb xacutti.

PREZZO
Italian
161 Euston Road, NW1 2BD
Map: B4   Nearest Station: Mornington Crescent
020 7387 5587
With a character all of its own, Prezzo oozes contemporary style and enduring charm. Signature pastas, stone-baked pizzas and classic Italian dishes promise a perfect dining choice for the whole family.

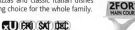

RAGAM
Indian
57 Cleveland Street, W1T 4JN
Map: B4   Nearest Station: Goodge Street
020 7636 9098
Renowned reputation for producing a pure and proven South Indian cuisine whilst demonstrating variety on their cheerful menu. A light, healthy, and delicious dining experience.

THE JUNCTION RESTAURANT
European
Holiday Inn, Carburton Street, W1W 5EE
Map: B4   Nearest Station: Great Portland Street
020 7874 9011
The Junction is a stylish establishment built with both the individual traveler and families in mind. With a menu comprised of many old favourites and great service, this London eatery is set to impress.

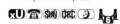

ZEEN - FLAVOUR OF INDIA
Indian
130 Drummond Street, NW1 2PA
Map: B4   Nearest Station: Euston Square
020 7387 0606
Classic dishes are served amongst the many great new recipes that Zeen provides for the more cosmopolitan palate. The chefs' passion for food can be tasted in the deliciously authentic dishes they cook up.

CHUTNEY RAJ
Indian
137 Grays Inn Road, WC1X 8TU
Map: B5   Nearest Station: Chancery Lane
020 7831 1149
Bangladeshi fish dishes appear strongly on the menu at this terrific central London restaurant. With specific ingredients being flown in fresh from the East, vivid tastiness is guaranteed in every dish.

NORFOLK ARMS
Modern European
28 Leigh Street, WC1H 9EP
Map: B5   Nearest Station: Kings Cross St Pancras
020 7388 3937
Combining traditional English food with a Spanish serving style. Tapas dishes can be ordered at the bar, allowing you to experience all the comforts of England in an enjoyable European way.

PAKENHAM ARMS
British
1 Pakenham Street, WC1X 0LA
Map: B5   Nearest Station: Kings Cross St Pancras
020 7837 6933
Passionate about making every guest feel happy and comfortable, the warm environment found here creates a 'home from home' atmosphere. Reasonably priced food and real ales make this a local firm favourite.

ANEXO BAR AND RESTAURANT
Spanish
61 Turnmill Street, EC1M 5NP
Map: B6   Nearest Station: Farringdon
020 7250 3401
Fresh Spanish-style tapas dishes and yummy bar snacks are available at this enjoyable bar and restaurant. Mediterranean inspired à la carte dishes are ideal for any dining occasion.

GREATER LONDON

CAFE SAFFRON
Indian
17b Aylesbury Street, EC1R 0DR
Map: B6 Nearest Station: Farringdon
020 7253 4300
Unusual dishes from Goa, Chennai and Bangladesh feature on the menu as well as the more well-known curry dishes at this popular Indian restaurant. Try the fiery chicken xacutti for a real treat.

CAFÉ VN
Vietnamese
144 Clerkenwell Road, EC1R 5DP
Map: B6 Nearest Station: Farringdon
020 7278 4123
An authentic Vietnamese café, bar and restaurant specialising in traditional pho, bun and salads. Enjoy a tasty dish from the divine menu or sample gourmet coffee direct from Vietnam.

CLERKENWELL HOUSE
Turkish
23-27 Hatton Wall, EC1N 8JJ
Map: B6 Nearest Station: Farringdon
020 7404 1113
This fresh and funky venue's décor reflects the vibrancy of the local area thanks to the support of local artists. Their freshly prepared mezze dishes offer variety and flavour for the delighted diner.

DARBUCKA
Lebanese
182 St John Street, EC1V 4JZ
Map: B6 Nearest Station: Farringdon
020 7490 8295
Named after the drum used in Middle Eastern music, Darbucka offers a wide range of entertainment in an Arabic setting. Syrian and Lebanese dishes dominate the menu.

RECOMMEND A FRIEND
see page 18

MALMAISON
European
18-21 Charterhouse Square, EC1M 6AH
Map: B6 Nearest Station: Barbican
020 7012 3700
Divinely tasty, beautifully presented cuisine prepared with incredible local ingredients, served with professionalism and passion. A beautifully chic brasserie with a lively atmosphere. 2 AA Rosettes.

THE LIGHT BAR AND RESTAURANT
International
233 Shoreditch High Street, E1 6PJ
Map: B8 Nearest Station: Shoreditch High Street
020 7247 8989
Head Chef Mark Caplin and his capable team have created a tempting menu of classic dishes which sit comfortably alongside the wide array of wines, beers and cocktails.

NEW

130

THE SAMUEL PEPYS
European
Stew Lane, EC1V 0BY
Map: B6 Nearest Station: Farringdon
020 7489 1871
On the fabulously monikered Stew Lane, tucked away across from South Bank, you can enjoy rich and classic English flavours - like a beauty of a herby Cumberland - along with broader cosmopolitan flavours.

VECCHIO PARIOLI
Italian
129 Aldersgate Street, EC1A 4JQ
Map: B6 Nearest Station: Barbican
020 7253 3240
Smart, classic feel to this on-the-corner Italian joint right by Barbican. Cool and calm atmosphere, flexible with their menu, and a trattoria vibe between the whitewashed walls and the colourful plates.

ZEN GARDEN
Chinese
88 Leather Lane, EC1N 7TT
Map: B6 Nearest Station: Farringdon
020 7242 6128
Zen Garden's eclectic menu contains some real treats of unique and distinctive flavours; it has a good array of dishes that are skillfully and attentively produced and packed with full, rich tastes.

CAFÉ ROUGE
French
5 Condor House, St Paul's Churchyard, EC4M 8AY
Map: C6 Nearest Station: St. Paul's
020 7489 7812
An attractive restaurant, a boulevard café or a Parisian-style wine bar; however you see Café Rouge, consistently excellent classic French dishes are always guaranteed.

CHARTERHOUSE BAR
English/Gastro pub
38 Charterhouse Street, EC1M 6JH
Map: C6 Nearest Station: Barbican
020 7608 0858
A stylish place to party as well as eat. From lunchtime into the evening, guests can enjoy great quality food and a fabulous choice of beverages. Allow the fun-filled atmosphere ease away the day.

LE SAINT JULIEN
French
62-63 Long Lane, EC1A 9EJ
Map: C6 Nearest Station: Barbican
020 7796 4550
Charming brasserie with all the trimmings, that serves elegant, distinctive and authentic French cuisine.

MORE RESTAURANTS ONLINE
www.gourmetsociety.co.uk

Sign up to our newsletter for latest restaurants, offers and more

SMITHFIELD BAR AND GRILL
Steakhouse/ Seafood

2-3 West Smithfield, EC1A 9JX
Map: C6   Nearest Station: Barbican
020 7246 0900
Open early to late, providing a high-quality dining experience with a menu including first-class steaks and grilled ostrich. Offers a large drink selection from wine to cocktails, and exceptional service.

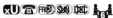

Not offered lunch Thurs/Fri Kobe steaks and lobster dishes excluded.

TERRANOSTRA
Italian

27 Old Bailey, EC4M 7HS
Map: C6   Nearest Station: City Thameslink
020 3203 0077
The most discerning diners enjoy the scrumptious Sardinian food on offer at this city restaurant. The splendid combination of great food and friendly service has had customers flocking to its door.

THE CHANCERY
Modern European

9 Cursitor Street, EC4A 1LL
Map: C6   Nearest Station: Chancery Lane
020 7831 4000
An elegant little restaurant serving exceptional, sophisticated flavours by its talented and experienced chef-patrons. Fine dining in a cosy, personable environment off Chancery Lane. 2 AA Rosettes.

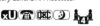

THE PUNCH TAVERN
British

99 Fleet Street, EC4Y 1DE
Map: C6   Nearest Station: City Thameslink
020 7353 6658
Situated in an architecturally beautiful building steeped in history, the kitchen ensures fresh produce is used in all of its home-made cooking. A popular venue for parties and corporate functions.

VOLUPTE
European

7-9 Norwich Street, EC4A 1EJ
Map: C6   Nearest Station: Chancery Lane
020 7831 1622
Prepare to enter a complete world of pleasure and exquisite delight. Volupte offers everything from old movie clips to accompany your cocktail, to all day afternoon tea to complete your day out.

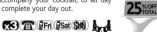

AUBERGE
French

1 Sandell St, SE1 8UH
Map: D6   Nearest Station: Waterloo
020 7633 0610
Auberge adopt a simple approach, using fresh ingredients combined with some French inspiration, serving classic dishes for all to enjoy. A rustic venue that promises to charm guests the moment they enter.

BALTIC
European

74 Blackfriars Road, SE1 8HA
Map: D6   Nearest Station: Southwark
020 7928 1111
Baltic's cuisine is full of the strong flavours and robustness of great country cooking from the east of Europe. The menu changes monthly reflecting the seasonal influences, whilst the décor is exemplary.

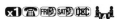

DEL'AZIZ
Mediterranean

Blue Fin Building, 5 Canvey Street, SE1 9AN
Map: D6   Nearest Station: Southwark
020 7633 0033
From sun up to sun down, Del'Aziz offers a truly versatile treasure trove of food delights. A vibrant Eastern Mediterranean deli and restaurant that is beautifully located, ideal for al fresco dining.

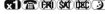
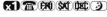

GOURMET PIZZA
Pizza

Gabriel's Wharf, SE1 9PP
Map: D6   Nearest Station: Southwark
020 7928 3188
Popular with pizza lovers and people watchers alike, this buzzy city restaurant offers pizzas heaped with colour in spacious and comfortable surroundings. A special menu offers alternative treats.

Must mention GS on arrival. Not in conj. with other offers.

INDIGO
Bangladeshi/ Indian

56 Stamford Street, South Bank, SE1 9LX
Map: D6   Nearest Station: Southwark
020 7593 0009
A contemporary environment for you to relax and enjoy superb Indian and Bangladeshi cuisine. Choose a great meal from a selection of classic curries and other dishes, as well as starters and naan breads.

RAFFAELLO
Italian

202-206 Union St, SW1 0LH
Map: D6   Nearest Station: Victoria
020 7261 0209
The real spirit of Italy is available right here, where a stylish interior, meticulous cooking and choice wines are on offer. Dedicated staff ensure a complete experience.

GRAND UNION
American

111 Kennington Road, SE11 6SF
Map: E6   Nearest Station: Elephant &Castle
020 7582 6685
With a classically stylish ambience and a buzzing music scene of an evening, this restaurant dispatches heartening, full plates of thoroughgoing, wide-ranging bar and grill fare.

Not available Sunday lunch.

LOCALE COUNTY HALL
Italian

3b Belvedere Road, SE1 7GP
Map: E5   Nearest Station: Lambeth North
020 7401 6734
Cool and collected Italian restaurant with all the classic dishes and flavours; hearty and flavourful pasta and risotto, and a line in beautifully seasoned meat and fish with smart accompaniments.

131

THE ATRIUM
British

4 Millbank, W1P 3JA
Map: E5   Nearest Station: St James's Park
020 7233 0032

This Westminster restaurant prides itself on its excellent location, the superb quality of light in its vast and roomy dining area, and its roll call of illustrious diners past and present.

BALLS BROTHERS
British

50-52 Buckingham Palace Road, SW1W 0RN
Map: E4   Nearest Station: Victoria
020 7828 4111

Famous throughout the capital, Balls Brothers has a reputation for excellence, maintaining a high service standard along with delicious, flavoursome food and a vast selection of simply divine wine.

KAZAN VICTORIA
Turkish

93-94 Wilton Road, SW1V 1DW
Map: E4   Nearest Station: Victoria
020 7233 7100

Experience food with all five senses at this extraordinarily ambitious Turkish restaurant. Offering an authentic experience by surrounding guests with Ottoman relics and antique textiles.

KYM'S
Chinese

70-71 Wilton Road, SW1V 1DE
Map: E4   Nearest Station: Victoria
020 7828 8931

In the heart of the city, enjoy scrumptious Chinese cuisine in a relaxing environment where friendly service is never absent. Guests will be more than satisfied with their dining experience.

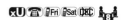

PREZZO
Italian

4 Victoria Buildings, 22 Terminus Place, SW1V 1JR
Map: E4   Nearest Station: Victoria
020 7233 9099

With a character all of its own, Prezzo oozes contemporary style and enduring charm. Signature pastas, stone-baked pizzas and classic Italian dishes promise a perfect dining choice for the whole family.

SPICY WORLD BALTI HOUSE
Indian

76 Wilton Road, SW1V 1DE
Map: E4   Nearest Station: Victoria
020 7630 9951

A culmination of popular dishes, rich with succulent flavours and spices, have been created through years of experimentation to bring out the incomparable taste of India in every mouthful.

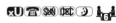

BUMBLES
British

16 Buckingham Palace Road, SW1W 0QP
Map: E3   Nearest Station: Victoria
020 7828 2903

Contemporary influences and local sourcing are married together in this fabulous restaurant in the heart of London; try signature dishes including Miller's pork and feta salad with a tomato sorbet.

CAFÉ ROUGE
French

Victoria Place Ctr., Buckingham Palace Rd, SW1W 9SJ
Map: E3   Nearest Station: Victoria
020 7931 9300

An attractive restaurant, a boulevard café or a Parisian-style wine bar; however you see Café Rouge, consistently excellent classic French dishes are always guaranteed.

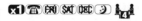

DA SCALZO
Italian

2 Eccleston Place, SW1W 9NE
Map: E3   Nearest Station: Victoria
020 7730 5498

Combining contemporary art with exceptional cuisine is the ethos of this restaurant, run by two brothers with an infectious passion for art and food. The listed building venue adds to the charm.

LANGTRYS RESTAURANT
British

21 Pont Street, SW1X 9SG
Map: E3   Nearest Station: Knightsbridge
020 7201 6619

Whilst maintaining all the magnificence of the building's historic grandeur, the restaurant has been subtly modernised to suit the contemporary diner. A wonderful, languidly charming place to dine.

THE TALBOT BELGRAVIA
British

1-3 Little Chester Street, SW1X 7AL
Map: E3   Nearest Station: Victoria
020 7235 1639

Soak up the atmosphere all year round in this cheerful, lively venue. During those warmer months, enjoy the large beer garden as you sample the traditional fare and enjoy the unique surroundings.

CURRY PLACE
Indian

36 Queensway, W2 3RX
Map: D1   Nearest Station: Queensway
020 7243 8992

The luxurious décor and delightful aromas offer a warm welcome to this Indian-inspired venue. They infuse passion and experience into every dish to create a gourmet experience that won't be forgotten.

68-86 RESTAURANT
Modern British

68-86 Cromwell Street, SW7 5BT
Map: E1   Nearest Station: Gloucester Road
020 7666 1891

Sample the delights of the best of British food fused with influences from the Pacific Rim, whilst enjoying a heavenly cocktail at the specially commissioned contemporary glass bar.

AS GREEK AS IT GETS
Greek

233 Earl's Court Road, SW5 9AH
Map: E1   Nearest Station: Earl's Court
020 7244 7777

A truly authentic Greek experience. Perfect for lunch or dinner boasting a delectable menu filled with Greek flavours and specialities, most definitely to be enjoyed with classic wine or some feisty ouzo.

Recommend a friend to the Gourmet Society and receive a free gift.

AUBREY
European

109-113 Queens Gate, SW7 5LR
Map: E1   Nearest Station: South Kensington
020 7589 6300
Memorable surroundings to enjoy food at breakfast, lunch, dinner, choosing from the restaurant's eclectic menu, which blends fresh British fare with flavours from around the world.

AWANA MALAYSIAN RESTAURANT
Malaysian

85 Sloane Avenue, SW3 3DX
Map: E2   Nearest Station: South Kensington
020 7584 8880
Awaken to the world of Malaysian cuisine, some of Asia's most exciting food. Adapting rich culinary history this venue creates flavoursome dishes using innovative modern interpretations. 1 AA Rosette.

FRATELLI GRILL
British

147 Cromwell Road, SW5 0TH
Map: E1   Nearest Station: Earl's Court
020 7341 6205
Wholesome, flavourful classic staples cooked in the Fratelli Grill's open kitchen are served in the airy and stylish dining room. Recommended that you leave room for the lavish dessert menu.

CAFÉ ROUGE
French

27-31 Basil Street, SW3 1BB
Map: E2   Nearest Station: Knightsbridge
020 7584 2345
An attractive restaurant, a boulevard café or a Parisian-style wine bar; however you see Café Rouge, consistently excellent classic French dishes are always guaranteed.

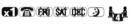

MEMORIES OF INDIA
Indian

18 Gloucester Road, SW7 4RB
Map: E1   Nearest Station: Gloucester Road
020 7589 6450
Memories of India serves a range of classic, flavourful curries in unfussy, smart surroundings.

FRANKIE'S CRITERION
Italian

3 Yeoman's Row, SW3 2AL
Map: E2   Nearest Station: Knightsbridge
020 7590 9999
Flagship restaurant of the Marco Pierre White-Frankie Dettori axis, the vibrant American styling of Frankie's Criterion is home to a range of tasty and rich Italian fare.

MISS Q'S
American

180-184 Earls Court Road, SW5 9QG
Map: E1   Nearest Station: Earl's Court
020 7370 5358
Experience this intoxicating diner and saloon in Earl's Court, London. Fixing itself on the great American standards, Miss Q's is all about full plates of tasty food, a classic bar, and a superb ambience.

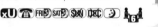

HAANDI
Indian

7 Cheval Place, SW7 1EW
Map: E2   Nearest Station: South Kensington
020 7823 7373
A restaurant specialising in North Indian cuisine, producing fine food cooked to order in an open plan kitchen, allowing you to view the expert chefs at work. An exemplary venue where quality is paramount.

 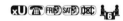

BODEANS BBQ
American

4 Fulham Broadway Chambers, Fulham, London, SW6 1EP
Map: Off Map   Nearest Station: Fulham Broadway
0207 610 0440
Bodeans is the brainchild of Andre Blais who set out in 2002 to bring the taste and the style of classic Kansas City barbecue to London. A fresh twist on Americana that makes for a great place to relax.

(NEW)

KUMO
Japanese

11 Beauchamp Place, SW3 1NQ
Map: E2   Nearest Station: Knightsbridge
020 7225 0944
Adhering to the glitz and glamour of its location, this stylish Japanese-inspired sushi bar is an ideal place to drink, dine and dance. Evocative and attractive surroundings to enjoy a classic cocktail.

TEN TABLES
European

61 Gloucester Road, SW7 4PE
Map: E1   Nearest Station: Gloucester Road
020 7584 8100
An ideally located restaurant in perfect walking distance of all major local attractions. Sample a warm home-made soup or take delight in the popular lamb shanks and succulent steaks.

LAYA'LINA
Lebanese

2-3 Beauchamp Place, SW3 1NG
Map: E2   Nearest Station: Knightsbridge
020 7581 4296
Reflecting the glamour and sophistication of its location, this attractive restaurant and bar is stylish yet intimate enough to relax in. Relish delightful cocktails and mouth-watering Lebanese canapés.

WODKA
Polish

12 St Albans Grove, W8 5PN
Map: E1   Nearest Station: High Street Kensington
020 7937 6513
This bright space plays host to an array of warm, surprising and imaginative takes on Polish and Eastern European food, from a tart and vibrant Chlodnik to a warming Golabki. Add the eponymous to taste.

 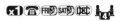

MONZA RESTAURANT
Italian

6 Yeoman's Row, SW3 2AH
Map: E2   Nearest Station: South Kensington
020 7591 0210
Tucked away in Knightsbridge, Monza is known for its rich Milanese dishes, along with the full range of flavourful and hearty Italian recipes. The restaurant has a homely feel for a cosy dining experience.

133

GREATER LONDON

OFF THE HOOK @ THE PAXTONS HEAD *European*
153 Knightsbridge, SW1X 7PA
Map: E2   Nearest Station: Knightsbridge
020 7589 6627
A traditional English pub and restaurant presenting an instant interest to all who are keen to sample a slice of English gastronomic heritage. The food is fresh, uncomplicated, and reasonably priced.

PIZZA ON THE PARK *Pizza*
11 Knightsbridge, SW1X 7LY
Map: E2   Nearest Station: Hyde Park Corner
020 7235 7825
Enjoy pizzas with a perfect crispy base, topped with the freshest ingredients, or other dishes such as the prime scotch entrecôte steak that satisfy even the biggest of appetites.

Must mention GS on arrival. Not in conj. with other offers.

SATORI ROBATA *Japanese*
28-30 Knightsbridge, SW1X 7JN
Map: E2   Nearest Station: Knightsbridge
020 7235 1943
Japanese cuisine is more than simply sushi, and this restaurant puts that fact on full display with its vibrant and tongue-tingling flavours off of the robata grill. Stylish, sultry interior.

SHEZAN *Indian/Punjabi*
16-22 Cheval Place, SW7 1ES
Map: E2   Nearest Station: Knightsbridge
020 7584 9316
In the heart of London's prestigious Knightsbridge sits a wonderful restaurant serving fabulous Indian cuisine. This well-established venue hosts live classical music in a relaxed atmosphere.

THE COLLECTION *Pan Asian*
264 Brompton Road, SW3 2AS
Map: E2   Nearest Station: South Kensington
020 7225 1212
Unique and tantalizing Pan-Asian cuisine. The Mezzanine Restaurant, drenched in natural light by day and kissed by candle light at night, is a perfect setting for a sophisticated dining experience.

THE DELHI BRASSERIE *Indian*
134 Cromwell Road, SW7 9HA
Map: E2   Nearest Station: South Kensington
020 7370 7617
A fabulous Indian restaurant in the heart of Kensington. Guests will love the exotic spiciness of the dishes available. For a more unusual dining experience, try the quails marinated in yoghurt.

THE HOUR GLASS *British*
279 - 283 Brompton Road, SW3 2DY
Map: E2   Nearest Station: South Kensington
020 7581 2840
Down-to-earth, delicious dishes at this traditional-style pub in SW3. Open fires will warm you against the cold, whilst the outside seating is a sun-trap in summer. Enjoy locally sourced classics.

ZIA TERESA *Italian*
6 Hans Road, SW3 1RX
Map: E2   Nearest Station: Knightsbridge
020 7589 7634
Rated by The Independent as 'Best Neighbourhood Restaurant', this charming haunt just off the Brompton Road in Knightsbridge hits the spot with its fresh, seasonal, beautifully presented Italian dishes.

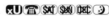
Offer not applicable on Bank Holidays.

COUSCOUS DARNA RESTAURANT *Moroccan*
91 Old Brompton Road, SW7 3LD
Map: F1   Nearest Station: South Kensington
020 7584 2919
The distinctive aromas, colours and textures of Morocco are brought out to their full extent in this restaurant that sets its stall on an authentic, dusky Maghrib experience.

Booking is essential.

DALL'ARTISTA *Italian*
243 Old Brompton Road, SW5 9HP
Map: F1   Nearest Station: Earl's Court
020 7373 1659
Guests at this wonderful local restaurant are always delighted with the genuine Italian experience it offers. An honest and authentic taste of Italy can be enjoyed by all the family.

MADSEN RESTAURANT *Scandinavian*
20 Old Brompton Road, SW7 3DL
Map: F1   Nearest Station: South Kensington
020 7225 2772
Serves Scandinavian cuisine in a characteristically limpid, uncluttered style. Fresh, clear flavours characterise the region, and are reflected in the space and the service. Awarded 1 AA Rosette.

Sunday open for lunch only, 12-4pm

SANTA LUCIA *Italian*
2 Hollywood Road, SW10 9HY
Map: F1   Nearest Station: Fulham Broadway
020 7352 8484
Intimately tucked away in a cosy residential street, the food at this local Italian restaurant will win over your taste buds and satisfy your stomach.

BENIHANA *Japanese*
77 King's Road, SW3 4NX
Map: F2   Nearest Station: Sloane Square
020 7376 7799
The second restaurant of the chain, Benihana was one of the first to bring teppanyaki style dining to London. Guests will enjoy their own private theatre as the chefs cook on a teppan right in front of you

BLUEBIRD RESTAURANT *British*
350 King's Road, SW3 5UU
Map: F2   Nearest Station: South Kensington
020 7559 1000
Combining sophisticated graphic design with warm, rich colours and subtle lighting, this restaurant is the perfect place for contemporary cocktails or that modern British intimate dinner.

Gourmet Society discount applies to the à la carte menu

BASIL & MINT BAR AND RESTAURANT
Indian

238-240 Munster Road, Fulham, SW6 6BA
Map: Off Map   Nearest Station: Parsons Green
020 7381 8150
Basil and Mint may seem an unusual combination, yet at this Fulham restaurant the choice of rarely combined herbs is a reflection of a successfully executed fusion.

LA PIZZERIA
Italian

125 Sydney Street, SW3 6NR
Map: F2   Nearest Station: Sloane Square
020 7823 3878
Take delight in authentic Italian tastes as this restaurant cooks pizza to perfection in their traditional wood-fired oven. When the sun prevails the garden area makes for fine al fresco dining.

ELISTANO
Italian

25-27 Elystan Street, SW3 3NT
Map: F2   Nearest Station: South Kensington
020 7584 5248
Popular, accommodating neighbourhood Italian restaurant that serves full-bodied, stylishly contemporary Italian food.

MADE IN ITALY
Italian

257 Kings Road, SW3 5EL
Map: F2   Nearest Station: Sloane Square
020 7352 1880
The first in the group of 'Made in Italy' restaurants. Famous for its authentic Neapolitan food and genuine Italian ambience, the rustic interior ensures all guests have a memorable dining experience.

IL GIARDINO
Italian

119 Sydney Street, SW3 6NR
Map: F2   Nearest Station: Sloane Square
020 7352 2718
Sumptuous Italian cuisine and wine, combined with a simple, stylish décor, make this venue the perfect setting for business or pleasure. Sit inside or out and enjoy quality food and good company.

MARECHIARO
Italian

257 Kings Road, SW3 5EZ
Map: F2   Nearest Station: Sloane Square
020 7351 2417
On the Kings Road in Chelsea, Marechiaro offers the smoky, sensuous aromas of classic Neapolitan cooking, with a strong sense of place, authenticity, and hospitality.

INDIGO
Indian

153 Fulham Road, SW3 6SN
Map: F2   Nearest Station: South Kensington
020 7589 7749
A simple, unique and exceptional venue offering dishes prepared using organic produce infused with traditional herbs and spices to create a menu full of fragrant and exotic dishes.

MYBAR AT MYHOTEL CHELSEA
International

35 Ixworth Place, SW3 3QX
Map: F2   Nearest Station: South Kensington
020 7225 7535
Cool and contemporary, the restaurant at this stunning boutique hotel has an unmissable vibrancy to it. Its memorable atmosphere plays host to buffet breakfasts, light lunches and late night dinners.

JAKOBS CAFE & DELI
Middle East

84 Fulham Road, SW3 6HR
Map: F2   Nearest Station: South Kensington
020 7998 3797
A friendly establishment showcasing quality Middle Eastern food and classical food dishes. Everything is freshly prepared and cooked beautifully, delivering delicious tastes at a most reasonable price.

PJ'S BAR AND GRILL
Modern European

52 Fulham Road, SW3 6HH
Map: F2   Nearest Station: South Kensington
020 7581 0025
A perennial favourite, this attractive Bar and Grill offers good quality food and a fantastic place to relax. The famous PJ's brunch will quickly become a weekend tradition.

Sundays only available after 6pm

JUJU
Thai

316-318 King's Road, SW3 5UH
Map: F2   Nearest Station: South Kensington
020 7351 5998
A stunningly sleek, acclaimed addition to London's bar scene, JuJu is renowned for its mixology, but can also be relied upon for some outstandingly tasty, Far East-influenced sharing platters.

AKASH TANDOORI
Indian

500a Edgeware Road, W2 1EJ
Map: B1   Nearest Station: Edgware Road (Bakerloo)
020 7706 1788
Real home-made Indian food, prepared and presented in the true Indian way, including a great selection of appetising starters, delicious curries and fresh poppadoms, all delivering great value for money.

KINGS ROAD STEAKHOUSE & GRILL
Steakhouse

386 Kings Road, SW3 5UZ
Map: F2   Nearest Station: South Kensington
020 7351 9997
Succulent juicy steaks will have your mouth watering and your taste buds tingling at this traditional steakhouse. Timeless English dishes are also available in this popular vibrant restaurant.

CAFÉ ROUGE
French

30 Clifton Road, W9 1ST
Map: B1   Nearest Station: Warwick Avenue
020 7286 2266
An attractive restaurant, a boulevard café or a Parisian-style wine bar; however you see Café Rouge, consistently excellent classic French dishes are always guaranteed.

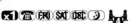

IDLEWILD
Modern British

55 Shirland Road, W9 2JD
Map: B1   Nearest Station: Warwick Avenue
020 7266 9198
An unusual deluxe pub complete with a sophisticated dining area. Revel in wonderfully simple food that follows the rules of seasonality and tradition, delivered in a beautifully luxurious venue.

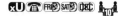

50% OFF FOOD

GETTI MARYLEBONE
Italian

42 Marylebone High Street, W1U 5HD
Map: B2   Nearest Station: Baker Street
020 7486 3753
With a great deal of verve, in a cool, bright ambience, Getti dispatches dishes with the earthy, full flavours of Italian cuisine from across its distinctive regional specialisations.

2FOR1 MAIN COURSE

MUMTAZ LONDON
Indian

4-10 Park Road, NW1 4SH
Map: B2   Nearest Station: Baker Street
020 7723 0549
Conveniently located restaurant serving a superbly delicious array of authentic North Indian cuisine. Named after the Queen Mumtaz Mahal, the restaurant prides itself on its warm Moghal style ambience.

25% OFF TOTAL

ARIANA RESTAURANT
Middle East

108 Bourne Terrace, W2 5TH
Map: C1   Nearest Station: Royal Oak
020 7266 9200
An excellent Iranian/Afghan restaurant with authentic décor and a warm, friendly atmosphere. Fine Persian cuisine at great prices, complemented by traditional live music.

2FOR1 3 COURSES

BEL CANTO
French

Corus Hotel Hyde Park, 1 Lancaster Gate, W2 3LG
Map: C1   Nearest Station: Lancaster Gate
020 7262 1678
A theatrical dining experience, where your waiters are opera singers and their performance and service perform a rondo, conjuring up an unforgettable night of music and food.

25% OFF TOTAL

CAFÉ ROUGE
French

Whiteleys Centre, Queensway, W2 4SB
Map: C1   Nearest Station: Bayswater
020 7221 1509
An attractive restaurant, a boulevard café or a Parisian-style wine bar; however you see Café Rouge, consistently excellent classic French dishes are always guaranteed.

50% OFF FOOD

CHERRY JAM
International

58 Porchester Road, W2 6ET
Map: C1   Nearest Station: Royal Oak
020 7727 9950
With zingy tapas and tongue-tingling Thai bites, cherryjam is all about the vim and verve of the venue.

50% OFF FOOD

MASSIS LEBANESE GRILL & BAR
Lebanese

9 Sheldon Square, W2 6HY
Map: C1   Nearest Station: Paddington
020 7286 8000
This cosy, welcoming Lebanese restaurant is ensconced just off Oxford Street and offers all the mix of mellowness and zest that characterises Lebanese cuisine.

2FOR1 MAIN COURSE

Must mention GS on arrival. Not in conj. with other offers.

TAORMINA RESTAURANT
Italian

19 Craven Terrace, W2 3QH
Map: C1   Nearest Station: Lancaster Gate
020 7262 2090
A family-run restaurant where chefs create a stunning range of mouth-watering, traditional Italian dishes. Warm, friendly and stylish décor creates an air of authenticity for all diners.

50% OFF FOOD

CONNOISSEURS INDIAN TANDOORI
Indian

8 Norfolk Place, W2 1QL
Map: C2   Nearest Station: Paddington
020 7402 3299
A two-storey restaurant that offers a relaxed space in which to dine. Bright Bangladeshi paintings add a vibrancy to the venue, making it a lovely place to enjoy Indian cuisine.

25% OFF TOTAL

DELIMA MALAYSIAN RESTAURANT
Chinese/ Malaysian/Thai

36 Southwick Street, W2 1JQ
Map: C2   Nearest Station: Paddington
0207 262 0050
A dining experience you won't want to miss. Serving deliciously tasty Malaysian food in a relaxed atmosphere. The à la carte and dessert menus are highly recommended.

25% OFF TOTAL

MURA RESTAURANT
Japanese

10 Seymour Place, W1H 7ND
Map: C2   Nearest Station: Marble Arch
020 7723 1001
A treasured restaurant in the heart of Portman village, the Japanese dishes on offer here are second to none. Sushi, sashimi and mura classics are all expertly cooked by a team of talented chefs.

50% OFF FOOD

RECOMMEND A FRIEND
see page 18

PHI BRASSERIE
English and Continental

Hotel Indigo, 16 London Street, W2 1HL
Map: C2   Nearest Station: Paddington
020 7706 4444
Experience superior tastes at the Phi Brasserie where there is a love of fresh, locally sourced produce, ensuring every single dish is crafted perfectly, breakfast, lunch, and dinner.

2FOR1 3 COURSES

Discounted hotel rates for GS members on our website

RYATH INDIAN TANDOORI
Indian
32 Norfolk Place, W2 1QH
Map: C2   Nearest Station: Paddington
020 7723 8954
Clean plates are always the outcome of every diner's experience at this popular Indian restaurant. Generous portions of freshly made Indian halal dishes are presented with impeccable service.

ZONZO RESTAURANT
Italian
342 Edgware Road, W2 1EA
Map: C2   Nearest Station: Edgware Road (Bakerloo)
020 7723 9777
A unique combination of extraordinary Italian cuisine, beautiful décor and affordable prices. Renowned as a friendly, local eatery providing quality Italian food firmly rooted in tradition.

BACCHUS PUB AND KITCHEN
Modern British
177 Hoxton Street, N1 6PJ
Map: A7   Nearest Station: Hoxton
020 7613 0477
Escape the hustle and bustle of daily life and revive yourself with good, honest, and simple cooking. The perfect place to relax and unwind with cool interior, great music, good beers, and hearty food.

STRINGRAY GLOBE CAFE
Italian
109 Columbia Road, E2 7RL
Map: A8   Nearest Station: Hoxton
020 7613 1141
A quality pizzeria serving delicious food at affordable prices, with many tempting specials on the menu. Also offers a large selection of beers, spirits and cocktails, as well as fresh organic juices.

BLUU
Modern British
1 Hoxton Square, N1 6NU
Map: B7   Nearest Station: Old Street
020 7613 2797
Bluu is an atmospheric restaurant and bar that is as fashionable as its location. The restaurant offers a wide choice of tasty snacks and treats as well as a modern European menu for a larger appetite.

HOXTON APPRENTICE
European
16 Hoxton Square, N1 6NT
Map: B7   Nearest Station: Hoxton
020 7749 2828
Support the talented chefs of the future at this Michelin-recommended restaurant. Wonderful dishes are prepared by chefs in training, guaranteeing guests a first-class dining experience.

LENA
Italian
66 Great Eastern Street, EC2A 3JT
Map: B7   Nearest Station: Old Street
020 7739 5714
Specialising in the earthy, full flavours of southern Italian cuisine, Lena is run with a keen investment in traditional hospitality, in a light, vibrant Shoreditch space.

MISO
Oriental
45-47 Hoxton Square, N1 6PB
Map: B7   Nearest Station: Old Street
020 7613 5621
Testament to its own success, Miso offers stir-fried noodles that arrive steaming, sizzling and sumptuous. A vibrant buzz and happy customers can always be found in this successful eatery.

PIYA PIYA
Pan Asian
1 Oliver's Yard, City Road, EC1Y 1HQ
Map: B7   Nearest Station: Old Street
0845 475 1971
Exotic Pan-Asian cuisine is served in a fashionably elegant dining space whilst diners enjoy a range of drinks including expertly mixed cocktails, offered full use of the intimately sensual lounge area.

THAI THAI EAST
Thai
110 Old Street, EC1V 9BD
Map: B7   Nearest Station: Old Street
020 7490 5230
Stay healthy whilst being blown away by the excellent culinary skill that goes into each dish. Here, you will be guaranteed a highly enjoyable dining experience in an elegantly decorated restaurant.

THE FOX
European
28 Paul Street, EC2A 4LB
Map: B7   Nearest Station: Old Street
020 7729 5708
Simple straightforward cooking offered from the bar, an à la carte menu in the restaurant, and highly personal service in the private dining area. Focus is on quality ingredients and relaxed atmosphere.

YARD
Pizza
140 Tabernacle Street, EC2A 4SD
Map: B7   Nearest Station: Old Street
020 7336 7758
A trendy pizza joint located in a converted fire station. An extremely popular restaurant renowned for its yard-length pizzas and the shredded duck or Parma ham toppings.

Must mention GS on arrival. Not in conj. with other offers.

ALADIN
Indian
132 Brick Lane, E1 5DD
Map: B8   Nearest Station: Bethnal Green (LU)
020 7247 8210
Traditionally a meeting place for the settling community of Brick Lane, where residents could enjoy home-spun Bangladeshi cuisine; that fine Indian cooking is still available here today.

CINNAMON BRICK LANE
Indian
134 Brick Lane, E1 6RL
Map: B8   Nearest Station: Aldgate East
020 7377 5526
The contemporary cuisine is characterised by its delicate blend of herbs and spices, fused to create rich and unique dishes. The staff take great care to provide an enjoyable and modern experience.

GREATER LONDON

137

CITY SPICE
Indian
138 Brick Lane, E1 6RU
Map: B8   Nearest Station: Shoreditch High Street
020 7247 1012
This Bangladeshi-inspired restaurant combines traditional dishes and décor to create an authentic experience. The relaxed atmosphere and friendly service provide a memorable night out.

CURRY AND TANDOORI
Indian
118 Brick Lane, E1 6RU
Map: B8   Nearest Station: Shoreditch High Street
020 7247 3713
With most of their dishes oven-cooked and oil kept to a minimum, this Balti house offers fresh and original curries. The kind, knowledgeable staff are always on hand to guide you and even offer lessons.

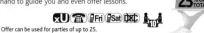
Offer can be used for parties of up to 25.

JUNO
International
134-135 Shoreditch High Street, E1 6JE
Map: B8   Nearest Station: Shoreditch High Street
020 7729 2660
An internationally inspired menu combining elements of modern European and North African cuisine. Enjoy a cocktail or cold beer as you lounge in the intimate basement or try your luck on arcade classics.

LATI RI
International
Rivington Place, Rivington Street, EC2A 3BE
Map: B8   Nearest Station: Shoreditch High Street
020 7739 5909
Conscientiously dedicated to bringing a regularly changing contemporary menu for guests to enjoy. Offers a wide selection of cured meats and cheeses, to be enjoyed with speciality bread and pastries.

LEVANZA
Indian
50-52 Hanbury Street, E1 5JL
Map: B8   Nearest Station: Shoreditch High Street
020 7539 9200
Warm and welcoming mixture of tastes from India and Lebanon in a cosy, lounge-worthy Arabic-style interior.

LITTLE HANOI
Vietnamese
147 Curtain Road, EC2A 3QE
Map: B8   Nearest Station: Old Street
020 7729 6868
Little Vietnamese restaurant tucked away off the main drag on Curtain Road in Shoreditch. Serves a dizzying but hugely inviting range of dishes, rich, salty and spiced. A down-to-earth classic.

MAIDA RESTAURANT
Indian
148 Bethnal Green Road, E2 6DG
Map: B8   Nearest Station: Shoreditch High Street
020 7739 2645
A modern Indian restaurant, Maida combines traditional Indian dishes with Indo-Chinese fusion flavours. Swift and attentive service caps the tasty, filling but fresh dining at the restaurant.

PREEM AND PRITHI
Indian
124 Brick Lane, E1 6RL
Map: B8   Nearest Station: Aldgate East
020 7377 5252
The secret is in the cooking, providing diners with enhanced flavours and unquestionable quality of taste. All vegetables are organic, and attentive staff are happy to advise the indecisive guest.

Offer can be used for parties of up to 25.

PREEM RESTAURANT
Indian
120 Brick Lane, E1 6RL
Map: B8   Nearest Station: Aldgate East
020 7247 0397
The secret is in the cooking, providing diners with enhanced flavours and unquestionable quality of taste. All vegetables are organic, and attentive staff are happy to advise the curious guest.

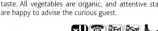
Offer can be used for parties of up to 25.

REEMA BALTI HOUSE
Indian/ Bangladeshi
48 Hanbury Street, E1 5JL
Map: B8   Nearest Station: Aldgate East
020 7655 4544
Reema is one of the longest serving and most popular Indian Restaurants in London's famous Brick Lane. A tribute perhaps, to their belief in the importance of a comfortable environment for guests to appreciate the wonders served up by the kitchen

SHAMPAN
Indian
79 Brick Lane, E1 6QL
Map: B8   Nearest Station: Shoreditch High Street
020 7375 0475
Captures the very essence of Bangladeshi culture and tradition through its delicious dishes, cooked to perfection. Perfectly located to bring out the special character and flavour of the subcontinent.

SHEBA RESTAURANT
Indian/ Bangladeshi
136 Brick Lane, E1 6RU
Map: B8   Nearest Station: Shoreditch High Street
020 7247 7824
Passionate about attending to customer's needs, desires and appetites, the staff at Sheba are welcoming, attentive and efficient. Both regular and new guests enjoy the fine Indian cuisine on offer.

THE BRICKHOUSE
Modern European
152c Brick Lane, E1 6RU
Map: B8   Nearest Station: Shoreditch High Street
020 7247 0005
Vibrant and sassy venue on Brick Lane where the verve of their live entertainments in no way overshadows the superb quality of the food on offer, produced by acclaimed and talented chef Matt Reuter.

THE DRUNKEN MONKEY
Chinese
222 Shoreditch High Street, E1 6PJ
Map: B8   Nearest Station: Shoreditch High Street
020 7392 9606
An early pioneer of the drinking and dim sum trend in London, serving potent cocktails and a tantalising selection of delicious Chinese food. This innovative bar is firmly the king of the swingers.

Sign up to our newsletter for latest restaurants, offers and more

THE FAMOUS CURRY BAZAAR
Indian/ Bangladeshi
77 Brick Lane, E1 6QL
Map: B8   Nearest Station: Shoreditch High Street
020 7375 1986
Large selection of Indian dishes providing succulent flavours at reasonable prices. Using only traditional ingredients, dishes are prepared by experienced chefs and an exceptional menu caters for all.

THE GLOBE
European
100 Shoreditch High Street, E1 6JQ
Map: B8   Nearest Station: Shoreditch High Street
020 7613 9816
Breathtaking views of the city are more than enough to ensure you a wonderful dining experience at this top-floor restaurant. Delicious breakfasts, lunches and evening meals are equally superb.

1901 AT THE ANDAZ HOTEL
British
40 Liverpool Street, EC2M 7QN
Map: C7   Nearest Station: Liverpool Street
020 7618 7000
Introducing an entirely fresh and dynamic approach to fine dining, with sumptuous dishes created using the most diverse home-grown produce, cooked simply and delivered with style.

ABACUS
International
24 Cornhill, EC3V 3ND
Map: C7   Nearest Station: Bank
020 7337 6767
Drink, dance, dine and recline all under one roof. Enjoy nibbles complemented by an enormous drinks selection, or indulge in the internationally inspired menu, topped up by chef's specials.

AGENDA
English and Continental
Minster Court, 3 Mincing Lane, EC3R 7AA
Map: C7   Nearest Station: Fenchurch Street
020 7929 8399
Stylishly designed, perfect for post-work relaxation or a pre-party chat with the addition of delicious food. Entertain your palate with a dish off the enticing menu combined with a choice of beverages

AMBER
English and Continental
City Point, 1 Ropemaker Street, EC2Y 9AW
Map: C7   Nearest Station: Moorgate
020 7382 1691
A fresh and funky party destination in the heart of the city, great for quick lunches, after work drinks, partying the night away or a fabulous VIP experience in a private booth.

BALLS BROTHERS
British
Minster Court, Mincing Lane, EC3R 7PP
Map: C7   Nearest Station: Fenchurch Street
020 7283 2838
Famous throughout the capital, Balls Brothers has a reputation for excellence, delivering classic British cuisine with a modern twist, served in a beautiful contemporary bar with an array of wine on offer.

BALLS BROTHERS
British
5-6 Carey Lane, EC2V 8AE
Map: C7   Nearest Station: St. Paul
020 7600 2720
Famous throughout the capital, Balls Brothers has a reputation for excellence, bringing together fine food with wines that have been selected from many of the world's top growers.

BALLS BROTHERS
British
52 Lime Street, EC3M 7BS
Map: C7   Nearest Station: Fenchurch Street
020 7283 0841
Famous throughout the capital, Balls Brothers has a reputation for excellence, proving a popular spot for lunch and dinner, serving excellent, predominantly British food with a huge selection of wine.

BARCELONA TAPAS BAR
Spanish
13 Well Court, EC4M 9DN
Map: C7   Nearest Station: Mansion House
020 7329 5111
An expanding family business offering delicious Spanish food in an authentic atmosphere. The restaurant's main feature is the large mosaic lizard that has come to be a symbol of the Barcelona chain.

CATCH AT THE ANDAZ HOTEL
Seafood
40 Liverpool Street, EC2M 7QN
Map: C7   Nearest Station: Liverpool Street
020 7618 7200
A shrine to the sea, the stunning stained glass windows and wood paneled walls create an exceptional atmosphere in which sensational seafood dishes can be thoroughly enjoyed.

EASTWAY AT THE ANDAZ HOTEL
Brasserie
40 Liverpool Street, EC2M 7QN
Map: C7   Nearest Station: Liverpool Street
020 7618 7400
Eclectic, full-bodied food at this New York-style brasserie. Distinctive grill dishes and signature cocktails top things off in a stylish and lively atmosphere.

ESCA
European
Accountants Hall, 1 Moorgate Place, EC2R 6EA
Map: C7   Nearest Station: Moorgate
020 7920 8625
Traditional Italian cuisine with a modern twist served in comfortable surroundings. Offering delicious lunches and a superb à la carte menu. An extensive choice of food for all tastes and palates.

Open Mon-Fri, 12-3.30pm.

GOW'S RESTAURANT & OYSTER BAR
Seafood
81 Old Broad Street, EC2M 1PR
Map: C7   Nearest Station: Liverpool Street
020 7920 9645
Classic, long-established restaurant whose speciality is fresh, flavourful seafood of exceptional quality. Ideal for oyster lovers and for those who like to watch the world go by.

GREATER LONDON

HENRY'S CAFE BAR
European
4 London Walls, Blomfield Street, EC2M 5NT
Map: C7   Nearest Station: Liverpool Street
020 7614 0075
In the heart of the City, Henrys successfully combines a busy restaurant with a relaxing bar environment. Exemplary service with quality food and drink will make every visit very memorable.

THE INDIA RESTAURANT
Indian
21 College Hill, Cannon St, EC4R 2RP
Map: C7   Nearest Station: Cannon Street
020 7248 5855
Dine in the snug and cosy underground space of The India. Whitewashed vaulted ceilings and comfy leather chairs provide a wonderful intimate dining space. Try the thali which offers small dishes of heaven.

LUC'S BRASSERIE
French
17-22 Leadenhall Market, EC3V 1LR
Map: C7   Nearest Station: Monument
020 7621 0666
The handsome dining room of this Parisian-style brasserie goes with its classical, appetising French dishes for an uncluttered, refined meal in the centre of London.

THE LIVERY
English and Continental
130 Wood Street, EC2V 6DL
Map: C7   Nearest Station: St. Paul
020 7600 9624
Weaving together the finest ingredients to deliver tasty dishes. Here, you can fully rely on the magic that takes place in the kitchen to satisfy your appetite. Fantastic wines complete every meal.

MINT LEAF LOUNGE
Indian
12 Angel Court, EC2R 4HB
Map: C7   Nearest Station: Barbican
020 7600 0992
This supremely stylish venue serves mouth-watering classic Indian dishes with a contemporary edge; it is also known as a top location for vibrant cocktails and socialising.

Not available on Thursday Evening

THE WALL
British
45 Old Broad Street, EC2N 1HU
Map: C7   Nearest Station: Liverpool Street
020 7588 4845
Transferring you to a Parisian-style location, The Wall has fabulous terraces and lavish interiors which make a fabulous dining experience. Good pub food at affordable prices with a wine list to match.

ORTEGA
Spanish
26-27 Leadenhall Market, EC3V 1LR
Map: C7   Nearest Station: Monument
020 7623 1818
A vibrant tapas bar that captures the magical liveliness of a bustling Spanish city. Accompany your array of dishes or sizzling grill with freshly made Sangria or a premium Spanish beer.

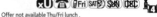

Offer not available Thu/Fri lunch .

ADDENDUM RESTAURANT
European
Apex London Hotel, 1 Seething Lane, EC3N 4AX
Map: C8   Nearest Station: Tower Hill
020 7977 9500
A restaurant with understated, modern décor and a menu that seduces an ever-increasing crowd of gastronomic disciples due to the chef's passion and extensive experience. A glamorous, gourmet venue.

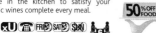

SWITHINS RESTAURANT
Seafood
21 St Swithins Lane, EC4N 8AD
Map: C7   Nearest Station: Bank
020 7623 6853
One of London's finest seafood restaurants specialising in fish and crustaceans. Situated in an elegant dining room, diners can enjoy divine food with complementing fine wines and vintage champagnes.

AUBERGE
French
56 Mark Lane, EC3R 7NE
Map: C8   Nearest Station: Fenchurch Street
020 7480 6789
Auberge adopt a simple approach, using fresh ingredients combined with some French inspiration, serving classic dishes for all to enjoy, with an impressive bar area recalling the grandeur of 1920's Paris.

THE BATHHOUSE
British
7-8 Bishopsgate Churchyard, EC2M 3TJ
Map: C7   Nearest Station: Liverpool Street
020 7920 9207
Embark on a journey through time as you step into this 19th century restaurant and bar. The poignant undercurrents of a Victorian London encourage a decadent return to the past.

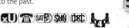

BARCELONA TAPAS BAR
Spanish
15 St Botolph Street, EC3A 7DT
Map: C8   Nearest Station: Aldgate
020 7377 5111
An expanding family business offering delicious Spanish food in an authentic atmosphere. Barcelona boasts a bright, colourful interior and hosts a vibrant display of original flamenco costumes.

THE CUBAN BAR
Cuban
1 Ropemaker Street, EC2Y 9AW
Map: C7   Nearest Station: Moorgate
020 7256 2202
Stylish bar with lots of vitality where you can enjoy bright, zingy Cuban tapas and grill-style mains with fruity, spicy marinades. Worth topping off with a sparkling Habanero cocktail.

BENGAL CUISINE
Indian
12 Brick Lane, E1 6RF
Map: C8   Nearest Station: Aldgate East
020 7377 8405
The colourful history and culture of the Bengal region is fully reflected in its diverse cuisine. Enjoy the delights of Bengali food lovingly and authentically cooked by award-winning chef Mrs. Kazi.

140

Visit the website regularly to discover the latest restaurants joining the GS

BRICK LANE CLIPPER
Indian

104 Brick Lane, E1 6RL
Map: C8   Nearest Station: Aldgate East
020 7377 0022
Complete your experience of the city by heading to the curry capital of London. This fabulous Brick Lane restaurant offers contemporary Indian cuisine in elegant surroundings.

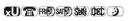

BUNDU KHAN
Indian

43 Commercial Street, E1 6BD
Map: C8   Nearest Station: Aldgate East
020 7375 2595
A great environment to eat, relax, and host a special event in. The superb menu offers an outstanding array of dishes and specialities which are completely unique to the restaurant.

CAFÉ NAZ
Indian/ Bangladeshi

46-48 Brick Lane, E1 6RF
Map: C8   Nearest Station: Aldgate East
020 7247 0234
A well-loved restaurant offering outstanding food and affable service. Both tourist and local curry lovers enjoy the reasonably priced Indian cuisine on offer in this contemporary setting.

CAFÉ SPICE NAMASTÉ
Indian

16 Prescot Street, E1 8AZ
Map: C8   Nearest Station: Aldgate East
020 7488 9242
An elaborate menu demonstrates the kitchen's passion for a redefined Indian cuisine, incorporating influences from across Asia. Expect unusual meats and unique spice fusions. Awarded 1 AA Rosette.

CHILLIES
Indian

76 Brick Lane, E1 6RL
Map: C8   Nearest Station: Aldgate East
020 7247 7539
Freshly prepared dishes can be tailored to every palette, whether you enjoy your curry exceptionally spicy or gentle and mild. Speciality, seafood and vegetarian dishes are available.

CLIFTON RESTAURANT
Indian

1 Whitechapel Rd, E1 6TY
Map: C8   Nearest Station: Aldgate East
020 7377 5533
The Bangladeshi, Pakistani and Indian-inspired menu promotes the unique cuisine of South Asia. Natural and organic spices are used in the creation of healthy dishes. Watch chefs in the open-plan kitchen.

HEMINGWAY'S
European

19 Bevis Marks, EC3A 7JB
Map: C8   Nearest Station: Aldgate
020 7220 7170
A privately owned independent wine bar, restaurant and function room where high quality food is made from fine seasonal ingredients. Simply great food and wine, offering excellent value.

JAMIES
British

155 Bishops Gate, EC2A 2AA
Map: C8   Nearest Station: Old Street
020 7256 7279
Wine bar & restaurant with a reputation for delivering quality and value. This venue offers a unique environment for casual dining. Unfussy food and an eclectic mix of wine, champagne, and cocktails.

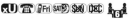

KASTURI
Indian

57 Aldgate High Street, EC3N 1AL
Map: C8   Nearest Station: Aldgate
020 7480 7402
Focusing on the special qualities of Pakhtoon cuisine, Kasturi aims to preserve the glorious heritage of Indian subcontinental cuisine by retaining its authentic nature.

KAZAN CITY
Turkish

4 Houndsditch, EC3A 7DB
Map: C8   Nearest Station: Aldgate
020 7626 2222
Focuses on the luxuriousness of Ottoman culture and cuisine. Offers clientèle a rich menu of authentic enticing flavours, making use of the owners familial cooking tradition and recipes.

KENZA
Moroccan/ Lebanese

10 Devonshire Square, EC2M 4YP
Map: C8   Nearest Station: Liverpool Street
020 7929 5533
Meaning 'treasure' in Arabic, Kenza is an ode to refinement and luxury. Be charmed by Middle Eastern hospitality as you relax and relish the richness of authentic, home-style Moroccan and Lebanese dishes.

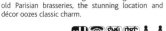

LE BOUCHON BRETON
French

8 Horners Square, E1 6EW
Map: C8   Nearest Station: Aldgate East
0800 0191 704
Enjoy the champagne and shellfish at this impressive French restaurant. Drawing on the magnificence of old Parisian brasseries, the stunning location and décor oozes classic charm.

MARCO PIERRE WHITE STEAK & ALEHOUSE
British

East India House, Middlesex Street, E1 7JF
Map: C8   Nearest Station: Liverpool Street
020 7247 5050
The name needs no introduction; this open, airy steakhouse combines the full cohort of cuts, perfectly cooked and stylishly accompanied, with an array of melting, savoury English classics. 2 AA Rosettes.

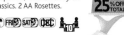

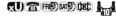

MASALA BRICK LANE
Indian

88 Brick Lane, E1 6RL
Map: C8   Nearest Station: Aldgate East
020 7539 9448
A cool and contemporary interior with a neutral décor allows diners to relax and unwind as they enjoy the authentic Indian cuisine on offer. The roop chanda is delicious and highly recommended.

GREATER LONDON

141

www.gourmetsociety.co.uk

PAPADOMS
Indian/Bangladeshi

94 Brick Lane, E1 6RL
Map: C8   Nearest Station: Aldgate East
020 7377 9123

Boasting an award-winning curry chef, it is not surprising that this restaurant is reputable for its exceedingly tasty food. Fine ingredients and exotic spices come together to create irresistible flavour.

THE MONSOON
Bangladeshi

78 Brick Lane, E1 6RL
Map: C8   Nearest Station: Aldgate East
020 7375 1345

Channeling their energy into the traditional culinary art of Bangladeshi cooking, the chefs at The Monsoon produce divine dishes, making use of wonderful fragrant spices and fresh ingredients.

RED CHILLI
Indian

137 Leman Street, E1 8EY
Map: C8   Nearest Station: Aldgate East
020 7481 3300

Traditional Indian cuisine transported to London with vivacious staff and clientèle, as well as modern, sleek interior. The menu boasts Indian favourites, popular monthly menus and various specialities.

THE POET
International

82 Middlesex Street, E1 7EX
Map: C8   Nearest Station: Aldgate East
020 7422 0000

A spacious bar in a convenient location. Find fabulous food and a tempting selection of drinks on offer from lunch through to the evening. Pool tables and quiz nights provide excellent entertainment.

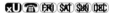

SAJNA GRILL RESTAURANT
Indian/Bangladeshi

30 Osborn Street, E1 6TD
Map: C8   Nearest Station: Aldgate East
020 7392 2100

Characterised by its wonderful variety of tasty foods, varying in spice and texture. Impeccable Indian and Bangladeshi cuisine provides a decadent taste of the very best Eastern dishes.

ABBEY RESTAURANT
International

30-33 Minories, Aldgate, EC3N 1DD
Map: C8   Nearest Station: Aldgate
020 7488 1918

Abbey Restaurant in the pulsing City of London is a refuge from the sombre offices all around. Everything is freshly made from the best ingredients the chefs can lay their mitts on.

NEW

SHERAZ BANGLA LOUNGE
Bangladeshi/Indian

13 Brick Lane, E1 6PU
Map: C8   Nearest Station: Aldgate East
020 7247 5755

One of the very first Indian restaurants in the area. Proud to be a founding part of the East End's rich heritage, the kitchen focuses its energy on customer preferences and informed choices.

APPLEBEE'S FISH CAFE
Fish and Seafood

5 Stoney Street, Borough Market, SE1 9AA
Map: D7   Nearest Station: London Bridge
020 7407 5777

Both café and fishmonger, the daily changing menu offers the best of the previous days' catch, simple, seasonal and delicious. Any fish may be bought directly from the fish counter and cooked to order.

TASTE OF INDIA
Indian

76 Aldgate High Street, EC3N 1BD
Map: C8   Nearest Station: Aldgate
020 7481 4010

Step aside from busy Aldgate High Street for a well-conceived classic Indian meal in this bright, accommodating restaurant. It's tandoori specialities are well worth checking out.

AZZURRO
French

31 Cottons Centre, Tooley Street, SE1 2QJ
Map: D7   Nearest Station: London Bridge
020 7407 5267

An ideal place to enjoy contemporary Italian dishes, colourful and cooked to perfection.

THAI TIGER
Thai

96 Brick Lane, E1 6RL
Map: C8   Nearest Station: Aldgate East
020 7247 0733

A welcome splash of Thai eclecticism on the already vibrant Brick Lane. Here, in the restaurant's well-conceived dining space, you can enjoy uncluttered flavours and presentation with a touch of panache.

BALLS BROTHERS
British

2 St Mary at Hill, EC3R 8EE
Map: D7   Nearest Station: Monument
020 7626 0321

Famous throughout the capital, Balls Brothers has a reputation for excellence, and this venue is tucked away from the hustle and bustle of the city. Options for all with bar and à la carte menus.

THE EMPRESS
Indian

141 Leman Street, E1 8EY
Map: C8   Nearest Station: Aldgate East
020 7265 0745

Previous winners at the British Curry Awards, this family-run restaurant prides itself in delivering exceptional food. Astonishingly diverse flavours offered to diners alongside a great wine list.

BAVARIAN BEERHOUSE
German

190 City Road, EC1V 2QH
Map: D7   Nearest Station: Old Street
0844 330 2005

For excellent food, outstanding service and great German beer, head to the Bavarian Beerhouse. Hearty Bavarian meals can be enjoyed in the rustic beer-cellar environment which attracts regular guests.

When booking restaurants always mention your GS membership

CAFÉ ROUGE
French

Hays Galleria, Tooley Street, SE1 2HD
Map: D7   Nearest Station: London Bridge
020 7378 0097
An attractive restaurant, a boulevard café or a Parisian-style wine bar; however you see Café Rouge, consistently excellent classic French dishes are always guaranteed.

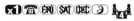

CHAMPOR-CHAMPOR
Asian Fusion

62-64 Weston Street, SE1 3QJ
Map: D7   Nearest Station: London Bridge
020 7403 4600
Be seated at a uniquely decorated table, where select dishes are created and served in their own unique way. Tribal artefacts and statues rub shoulders with stylish modern art pieces. 1 AA Rosette.

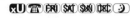

FUEGO
Spanish

1A Pudding Lane, EC3R 8AB
Map: D7   Nearest Station: Monument
020 7929 3366
Vital, warming Spanish food in a bright, welcoming space on Pudding Lane. Fuego has a friendly, cosmopolitan buzz with a good sense of fun, tradition and wholesome cooking.

LONDINIUM
British

8-18 London Bridge Street, SE1 9SG
Map: D7   Nearest Station: London Bridge
020 7855 2225
Roman history mixed with contemporary design, delivering patrons an astonishing selection of delectable dishes, complemented by relaxing music and a welcoming ambience. A recipe for an enjoyable evening.

ROAST
British

The Floral Hall, Borough Market, Stoney St, SE1 1TL
Map: D7   Nearest Station: London Bridge
0845 0347 300
With a view from every seat, be it the open kitchen or the beauty of St Paul's Cathedral. Serves gutsy food and delicious drinks. Awarded 1 AA Rosette. NB 2 cards & max of 2 comp meals/party.

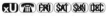

Only available Weds, Thurs & tel bookings only.

SILKA
Indian

6-8 Southwark St, Borough Market, SE1 1TL
Map: D7   Nearest Station: London Bridge
020 7378 6161
Enter this relaxing haven of a restaurant, where the calm and soothing atmosphere provides a perfect antidote to the hustle and bustle of the city. Eclectic Indian dishes make for a divine menu.

THE BOROUGH BAR & DINING
English and Continental

10-18 London Bridge Street, SE1 9SG
Map: D7   Nearest Station: London Bridge
020 7407 6962
A comfortable bar and restaurant with its own unique character. Enjoy a snack at the bar or a meal in the raised dining area, taking advantage of the English and continental cuisine and the nightly music.

THE FISH RESTAURANT
Seafood

Hays Galleria, Counter Street, SE1 2HD
Map: D7   Nearest Station: London Bridge
020 7407 4301
Vital restaurant near to London Bridge station with a fine line in excellent fish and seafood having been delivered daily; enjoy the range and calm versatility of their menu.

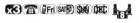

BENGAL CLIPPER
Indian

1-12 Cardamon Building, Shad Thames, SE1 2YR
Map: D8   Nearest Station: London Bridge
020 7357 9001
Traditional, flavoursome dishes are created by chefs who draw their inspiration from across the subcontinent. The Sunday buffet is a great way to sample many dishes, such as the creamy murgh sagrana.

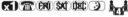

CAFE ROUGE
French

Quayside Road, St Katherine's Docks, E1W 1AA
Map: D8   Nearest Station: Tower Hill
020 7702 0195
An attractive restaurant, a boulevard café or a Parisian-style wine bar; however you see Café Rouge, consistently excellent classic French dishes are always guaranteed.

LOVAGE
Indian

13 Queen Elizabeth Street, SE1 2JE
Map: D8   Nearest Station: London Bridge
020 7403 8886
Lovage's sumptuous dishes derive from a range of Indian culinary traditions; try the piquant and intense Goan seafood dishes for a speciality. The restaurant's sleek décor add to the sense of occasion.

WINE WHARF
European

Stoney Street, SE1 9AD
Map: D8   Nearest Station: London Bridge
020 7940 8335
One of those hard-to-find wine bars whose staff know their stuff, this retreat from the hustle of Borough Market also serves some fabulous dishes with fresh, simple and clear flavours. A little gem.

PROHIBITION
British

Unit 1 Tower Bridge House, E1W 1AA
Map: D8   Nearest Station: Tower Hill
020 7702 4210
Banished are inferior food and cheap beer; here it's all about the best drinks, the tastiest dishes, and the coolest tunes. Drink cocktails and enjoy scrumptious food with quality in-house entertainment.

Must purchase minimum of 2 courses/person inc. main.

TENTAZIONI RESTAURANT
Italian

2 Mill Street, SE1 2BD
Map: D8   Nearest Station: Bermondsey
020 7237 1100
This warm, familial Italian restaurant boasts a signature menu with an array of strong, colourful dishes that bring out all the deep and rich flavours that characterise authentic Italian cuisine.

TOWER TANDOORI
Indian

74-76 Tower Bridge Road, SE1 4TP
Map: E7   Nearest Station: Borough
020 7237 2247

Inspired by the cool shady courtyards of Indian palaces, the interior of this wonderful Indian restaurant is truly divine. Current trends in Indian cuisine are reflected on the extensive menu.

DEL'AZIZ
Mediterranean

11 Bermondsey Square, SE1 3UN
Map: E8   Nearest Station: Borough
020 7407 2991

From sun up to sun down, Del'Aziz offers a truly versatile treasure trove of food delights. Discreetly nestled in one of London's hippest districts, the restaurant is ever popular for its exotic cuisine.

LA LUNA
Italian

380 Walworth Road, SE17 2NG
Map: F7   Nearest Station: Kennington
020 7277 1991

Made famous for their fresh, traditional stone oven-baked pizzas, this award-winning restaurant also boasts a menu that features other classic Italian dishes. Truly authentic and delicious cuisine.

Offer only on reduced à la carte menu

THE CONTENTED VINE
European

17 Sussex Street, SW1V 4RR
Map: F4   Nearest Station: Pimlico
020 7834 0044

Restaurant, wine bar and brasserie in Pimlico with a fresh and vivid ambience and a line in high-quality produce for clean, clear contemporary flavours. Enjoy the glass-fronted open kitchen.

Essential to book in advance.

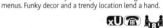

ALFIES BAR & KITCHEN
Modern European

Bermondsey Square Hotel, Tower Bridge Road, SE1 3UN
Map: E7   Nearest Station: London Bridge
0207 378 24 56

NEW

Head Chef Mike is pioneering an outstanding contribution to European cuisine taking all the innovations of recent years to present stunning seasonal menus. Funky decor and a trendy location lend a hand.

TAMESIS DOCK (BOAT)
International

Albert Embankment, SE1 7TP
Map: F5   Nearest Station: Vauxhall
020 7582 1066

Guests will love the Tamesis' converted Dutch barge on the banks of the Thames, just down from the Houses of Parliament. Be luminous with your cocktail and with wholesome, hearty food at a fabulous price.

THE CORIANDER
Indian/ Bangladeshi

332 Kennington Lane, SE11 5HY
Map: F5   Nearest Station: Vauxhall
020 7582 9569

Stylish and sophisticated Indian restaurant with a focus on superb service and a specialisation in the richness and piquancy of North Indian and Bangladeshi cuisine.

BRASSERIE TOULOUSE LAUTREC
French

140 Newington Butts, SE11 4RN
Map: F6   Nearest Station: Elephant & Castle
020 7582 6800

Named after the painter of the Moulin Rouge, this classic French brasserie offers a winning combination of good food and great wine. The confit of duck completely steals the show.

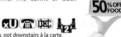

Offer for the upstairs wine bar menu, not downstairs à la carte.

MEZZA EXPRESS
Lebanese

47 Parkway, NW1 7PN
Map: A3   Nearest Station: Camden Town
020 7267 7111

Dine-in and takeaway options are both highly popular at this fantastic Lebanese restaurant. The hot and cold mezze selection is phenomenal, whilst the vast main menu offers delicious chargrilled dishes.

ANDY'S TAVERNA
Greek

81-81A Bayham Street, NW1 0AG
Map: A4   Nearest Station: Camden Town
020 7485 9718

Feel at home in this fantastic taverna that offers good food and wine to go with great company. The friendly relaxed atmosphere has maintained its fantastic reputation and regular clientèle.

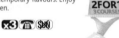

ELIXIR BAR
Mediterranean

162 Eversholt Street, NW1 1BL
Map: A4   Nearest Station: Mornington Crescent
020 7383 0925

A versatile entertainment venue that serves excellent, fresh food; home-baked bread and tasty, eclectic Mediterranean and Middle Eastern dishes.

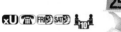

KARAVAS
Greek

87-88 Plender Street, NW1 0JN
Map: A4   Nearest Station: Camden Town
020 7388 4121

The centrality of its location is not this restaurant's only outstanding attribute. The fresh and tasty Greek cuisine on offer also guarantees guests a great evening out.

THE MAHARANI
Indian

109a Camden High Street, NW1 7JN
Map: A4   Nearest Station: Mornington Crescent
020 7387 6551

Indulge in a menu that successfully fuses traditional and contemporary dishes, all made from the freshest ingredients and finest spices. Taste the care and attention that goes into every single meal.

MEDITERRANEO
Italian

112 Kings Cross Road, WC1X 9DS
Map: A5   Nearest Station: Kings Cross St Pancras
020 7837 5108

Focusing on the clear, straightforward flavourfulness of traditional Italian cooking, this trattoria places emphasis on quality cooking, a personal touch in its service, and a homely Italian setting.

Gourmet Society discount applies to the à la carte menu

RASA MARICHAM
Indian

Holiday Inn, 1 Kings Cross Rd, WC1X 9HX
Map: A5   Nearest Station: Kings Cross St Pancras
020 7833 9787
Inspired by the authentic home cooking of beautiful, spice-rich Kerala, this restaurant's passion is food prepared always with devotion, love, and the finest ingredients. Experience the essence of India.

RODON LIVE
Greek

7 Pratt Street, NW1 0AE
Map: A5   Nearest Station: Camden Town
020 7267 8088
Treat your friends and family to an exceptionally special dining experience at this wonderful Greek restaurant. A fun and lively venue that offers traditional cuisine as well as fantastic entertainment.

SMITHY'S
European

The Stables, 15 Leeke Street, WC1X 9HY
Map: A5   Nearest Station: Kings Cross St Pancras
020 7278 5949
Holds an enviable reputation for fine food, choice wines, and attentive staff. A modern European menu that offers diners great variety coupled with exquisite flavours, with dishes made to high standards.

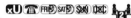

ANAM BAR
English and Continental

3a Chapel Market, N1 9EZ
Map: A6   Nearest Station: Angel
020 7278 1001
A funky cocktail bar mixing a blend of soulful uplifting dance music with an exquisite selection of premium spirit-based cocktails, plus freshly cooked dishes. The life and soul of the party.

BOMBAY LOUNGE
Indian

3 Penton Street, N1 9PT
Map: A6   Nearest Station: Angel
07771 720 793
A taste of India can be found in this attractive restaurant. The kitchen overflows with enthusiasm from the chefs, who work hard to bring diners an enjoyable meal and an unforgettable experience.

DI MONFORTE
Italian

70-72 Liverpool Road, N1 0QH
Map: A6   Nearest Station: Angel
020 7226 1475
A perfect dining venue, encompassing the true authenticity of an Italian restaurant whilst also offering a blend of sophistication and ambience for intimate dining. Fine ingredients imported from Italy.

EMNI
Indian

353 Upper Street, N1 0PD
Map: A6   Nearest Station: Angel
020 7226 1166
This well-received, neatly tucked-away Indian restaurant serves a great range of smartly conceived contemporary Indian cuisine in a stylish, airy space.

FINE BURGER CO.
American

330 Upper Street, N1 2XQ
Map: A6   Nearest Station: Angel
020 7359 3026
This classic burger kitchen sets its stall on fresh, high quality ingredients. Try the quirky milkshakes and crisp, flavourful onion rings.

GRAND UNION
American

153 Upper Street, Islington, N1 1RA
Map: A6   Nearest Station: Angel
020 7226 3303
With a classically stylish, calmly welcoming ambience on Upper Street this restaurant dispatches hearteningly full plates of wholesome, wide-ranging bar and grill fare.

Not available Sunday lunch.

MISO
Oriental

67 Upper Street, N1 0NY
Map: A6   Nearest Station: Angel
020 7226 2212
Vibrant and buzzy, this popular eatery offers tasty food and a fun environment. Testament to its own success, Miso offers stir-fried noodles that arrive steaming, sizzling and sumptuous.

PARVEEN TANDOORI
Indian

6 Theberton Street, N1 0QX
Map: A6   Nearest Station: Angel
020 7354 5993
The oldest Indian restaurant in Islington enjoys an excellent reputation amongst locals for their mouth-watering cuisine, prepared on site since 1977.

PASHA
Turkish

301 Upper Street, N1 2TU
Map: A6   Nearest Station: Angel
020 7226 1454
Deliciously tasty Turkish delights to be discovered in a fashionable location. Traditional influences are married with modern tastes, bringing Turkish cuisine with a difference.

REGINA MARGHERITA
Italian

57-58 Upper Street, N1 0NY
Map: A6   Nearest Station: Angel
020 7704 8882
Another Made in Italy group restaurant where you can expect a true Italian dining experience. Simply authentic, with every dish on the exceptional menu prepared and presented as it truly should be.

RENAISSANCE
Italian

316 St. John Street, EC1V 4NT
Map: A6   Nearest Station: Angel
020 7713 0409
A sleek, stylish restaurant whose contemporary European menu draws most heavily on fresh-flavoured Italian cuisine. A hip little place to dip into after work, over lunch or for a languid weekend afternoon.

145

North West

BASE BISTRO
European

71 Hampstead High Street, Hampstead, NW3 1QP
Nearest Station: Hampstead
020 7431 2224
Well-established bistro, enviably located in a beautiful listed building. Dishes to tantalise your taste buds include the wonderful prawn risotto and the popular grilled asparagus.

BLUE CHECK RESTAURANT
European

144-146 High Street, Bushey, WD23 3D2
Nearest Station: Bushey
020 8421 8811
This bright and brassy big restaurant in Bushey serves full-flavoured, high-quality dishes in its accommodating and lively atmosphere, also catering for large events.

BOMBAY BASEMENT
Indian

83-85a Haverstock Hill, Camden, NW3 4RL
Nearest Station: Chalk Farm
020 7483 0223
A snug Indian restaurant that is an idyllic place for intimate dining. A beautifully furnished interior ensures guests feel able to relax and unwind as they enjoy exquisite aromas and delicious tastes.

BOMBAY NIGHTS
Indian

90 Fortune Green Road, West Hampstead, NW6 1DS
Nearest Station: West Hampstead
020 7431 4802
Award-winning chef Jude Pinto creates mouth-watering Indian dishes that can be adjusted to each individual palate. Expect nice smiles and warm welcomes as you enter the night.

CAFÉ BUKUSHI
Japanese

245 Watling Street, Radlett, WD7 7AL
Nearest Station:
01923 859 911
A unique fusion of a New York deli and a contemporary sushi bar. Scrumptious sandwiches and salads, burgers and ribs can be enjoyed if the fresh fish sushi and bukushi sauces aren't for you.

CAFÉ MEZZA
Lebanese

144 High Street, Watford, WD17 2EN
Nearest Station: Watford
01923 211 500
A traditional café offering delicious Lebanese food in an amiable environment. Dine on a Friday and Saturday evening and be entertained by authentic belly dancing and Lebanese music.

CAFÉ ROUGE
French

10 High Street, Ruislip, Hillingdon, HA4 7AW
Nearest Station: Ruislip
01895 678 572
An attractive restaurant, a boulevard café or a Parisian-style wine bar; however you see Café Rouge, consistently excellent classic French dishes are always guaranteed.

CAFÉ ROUGE
French

13-13a High Street, Pinner, HA5 5PJ
Nearest Station: Pinner
020 8429 4424
An attractive restaurant, a boulevard café or a Parisian-style wine bar; however you see Café Rouge, consistently excellent classic French dishes are always guaranteed.

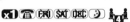

CAFÉ ROUGE
French

38-39 High Street, Hampstead, NW3 1QE
Nearest Station: Hampstead
020 7435 4240
An attractive restaurant, a boulevard café or a Parisian-style wine bar; however you see Café Rouge, consistently excellent classic French dishes are always guaranteed.

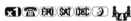

CAFÉ ROUGE
French

120 High Street, St Johns Wood, NW8 7SG
Nearest Station: St. John's Wood
020 7722 8366
An attractive restaurant, a boulevard café or a Parisian-style wine bar; however you see Café Rouge, consistently excellent classic French dishes are always guaranteed.

CASARECCIA
Italian

267 Kilburn High Road, Kilburn, NW6 7JR
Nearest Station: Brondesbury
020 7328 0800
A pleasant and friendly atmosphere in which you'll find infectiously happy staff. Well accomplished recipes make use of the freshest natural ingredients. A perfect place to create special memories.

CELEBRITY RESTAURANT
Indian

714-716 Kenton Road, Harrow, HA3 9QX
Nearest Station: Kingsbury
020 8204 0444
Subtle tones and stylish design make this a really calm, comfortable place to enjoy dinner. The menu is broad and eclectic, while the dishes are done with care and professionalism, and are full of taste.

CLAYE CHEF
Indian/ Bangladeshi

391 High Road, Harrow Weald, HA3 6EL
Nearest Station: Headstone Lane
020 8861 5772
Curry lovers unite at this amiable Indian restaurant. A vast menu presents a wide range of dishes that caters for all tastes, appetites and palates.

When booking restaurants always mention your GS membership

COCO BAMBOO
Brazilian
48 Chalk Farm Road, NW1 8AJ
Nearest Station: Chalk Farm
020 7267 6613
A family-run bar and restaurant serving the finest Brazilian and Caribbean cuisine and a superb selection of exotic cocktails. An authentic South American experience.

D'DEN
African
47 Cricklewood Broadway, Cricklewood, NW2 3JX
Nearest Station: Kilburn
020 8830 5000
A charismatic little restaurant serving distinctive, spicy, fizzing Nigerian-based dishes in an especially vibrant, inviting atmosphere.

DEL'AZIZ
Mediterranean
Swiss Cottage Leisure Centre, Adelaide Road, NW3 3NF
Nearest Station: Swiss Cottage
020 7586 3338
From sun up to sun down, Del'Aziz offers a truly versatile treasure trove of food delights. A delightful family friendly venue serving delicious quiches, tarts, mezze platters and much much more.

FINE BURGER CO.
American
O2 Centre, 255 Finchley Road, Swiss Cottage, NW3 6LU
Nearest Station: Finchley Road
020 7433 0700
This classic, burgeoning burger kitchen sets its stall on fresh, high quality ingredients. Try the quirky milkshakes and crisp, flavourful onion rings.

FREDDYS HARROW
Mediterranean
190 - 194 Station Road, Harrow, HA1 2RH
Nearest Station: Harrow-on-the- Hill
020 8424 8300
Slick and stylish bar and restaurant in Harrow that serves great gourmet burgers and other fulsome, classic dishes; a versatile venue for a great event or evening out.

GRAND UNION
American
102-104 Camden Road, Camden, NW1 9EA
Nearest Station: Camden Town
020 7485 4530
With nostalgic, easygoing style, this restaurant dispatches heartrendingly full plates of wholesome, wide-ranging bar and grill fare at its location in Camden.

Not available Sunday lunch.

GRAND UNION
American
53-79 Highgate Road, Kentish Town, N1 1RA
Nearest Station: Kentish Town
020 7485 1837
Right in Kentish Town, with classic styling, bifurcated into upper bar and basement gig room, this restaurant dispatches hearteningly full plates of wholesome, wide-ranging bar and grill fare.

Not available Sunday lunch.

HATCHETS
European
513 Uxbridge Road, Hatch End, Pinner, HA5 4JS
Nearest Station: Hatch End
020 8428 9973
Mrs Beeton, a former resident of Hatch End, would have approved of this family-friendly neighbourhood restaurant where the emphasis is on good, home-cooked food and welcoming service.

INSPIRAL LOUNGE
Contemporary
250 Camden High Street, Camden, NW1 8QS
Nearest Station: Camden Town
020 7428 5875
A wonderfully innovative dining and entertainment concept. A unique restaurant, bar and music venue that reinforces the importance of personal and planetary health.

KANGANA
Indian
763-765 Harrow Road, Wembley, HA0 2LW
Nearest Station: Sudbury & Harrow Road
020 8904 2636
One of the finest Indian restaurants in North London, delivering a true fine dining experience. Guests can indulge in a range of sumptuous dishes, well-prepared and authentically presented by expert chefs.

KARAHI DUBBA
Indian/Punjabi
51 Surbiton Road, Surbiton, KT1 2HG
Nearest Station: Surbiton
020 8541 3666
Perfect for a pre or post theatre meal, this is an ideal place to ensure stomach rumbling is kept at bay so you can focus on the entertainment. Supreme Punjabi cuisine served in modern surroundings.

LA GAFFE
Italian
107 Heath Street, Hampstead, NW3 6SS
Nearest Station: Hampstead
020 7435 8965
Aiming to maintain high standards of food and service, this highly popular restaurant and wine bar serves great meals and a wide range of beverages at competitive prices. Renowned for fantastic coffee.

LAGAR RESTAURANT-TAPAS BAR
Portuguese
281 Watling Street, Radlett, WD7 7LA
Nearest Station:
01923 855 168
As can be expected from a country famed for its naval exploits, seafood features prominently on this Portuguese menu, positioned next to a perfectly comprised wine list. A dining experience to savour.

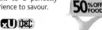

Offer not available on the tapas menu.

LE COCHONNET
Italian
1 Lauderdale Parade, Maida Vale, W9 1LU
Nearest Station: Maida Vale
020 7289 0393
A welcoming, vital and colourful little restaurant specialising particularly in fresh-cooked, tasty and eclectic pizzas, alongside an array of hearty breakfasts, deli dishes, and English and Italian mains.

O'SULLIVAN'S
International

Holiday Inn Elstree, Barnet Bypass, Elstree, WD6 5PU
Nearest Station: Elstree & Borehamwood
0871 942 9071

Receive a warm welcome at this sleek Holiday Inn hotel. O'Sullivan's Restaurant is open for both breakfast and dinner, offering guests a huge selection of delicious food and a range of drinks.

Only one card per table.

PIER 1
Fish and Seafood

30 Hawley Crescent, Camden, NW1 8NP
Nearest Station: Camden Town
020 7267 4495

A true, quality traditional fish and chips experience. Finest cuts of line-caught fish are freshly prepared and filleted by experienced fishmongers. Classic, great tasting food.

PREZZO
Italian

St George's Centre, St Ann's Rd, Harrow, RHA1 1HS
Nearest Station: Harrow-on-the-Hill
020 8427 9588

With a character all of its own, Prezzo oozes contemporary style and enduring charm. Signature pastas, stone-baked pizzas and classic Italian dishes promise a perfect dining choice for the whole family.

PREZZO
Italian

36 High Street, Pinner, HA5 5PW
Nearest Station: Pinner
020 8966 9916

With a character all of its own, Prezzo oozes contemporary style and enduring charm. Signature pastas, stone-baked pizzas and classic Italian dishes promise a perfect dining choice for the whole family.

PREZZO
Italian

29 Green Lane, Northwood, HA6 2PY
Nearest Station: Northwood
01923 829 941

With a character all of its own, Prezzo oozes contemporary style and enduring charm. Signature pastas, stone-baked pizzas and classic Italian dishes promise a perfect dining choice for the whole family.

PREZZO
Italian

82 Watling Street, Radlett, WD7 7AB
Nearest Station:
01923 853 566

With a character all of its own, Prezzo oozes contemporary style and enduring charm. Signature pastas, stone-baked pizzas and classic Italian dishes promise a perfect dining choice for the whole family.

RAM'S RESTAURANT
Indian

203 Kenton Road, Kenton, HA3 0HD
Nearest Station: Kenton
020 8907 2022

Hand-picked chefs bring the finest Punjabi, South Indian and Surti cuisine to their diners. Guests can arrive expecting welcoming, friendly staff who go out of their way to provide an incomparable service.

SHAKA ZULU
Steakhouse/ Seafood

Stables Market, Chalk Farm Road, Camden, NW1 8AH
Nearest Station: Chalk Farm
020 3376 9911

The spirit and culture of the Zulu nation rendered in an awe-inspiring venue. Whether dining in the Seafood & Oyster Bar or the authentic Braai 'Grill' the restaurant comes alive under Executive Chef Barry Vera.

SIMPLY SCRUMPTIOUS
Vegetarian

(Crepes & Shakes) 226 Station Road, Edgware, HA8 7AU
Nearest Station: Edgware
020 8958 6886

A fresh and exciting crêpe and shake bar in Edgware, where you'll find some spectacularly scrumptious treats, be it milkshakes, juices, smoothies or crêpes.

SPICE 6
Indian

22 Station Parade, Willesden Green, NW2 4NH
Nearest Station: Willesden Green
020 8208 2026

Become immersed in rich Indian heritage and enjoy a sophisticated fine dining experience where passion and spice are infused together. Continues a legacy of delicious food and great attention to detail.

SPIRITUAL CAIPIRINHA BAR
Brazilian

4 Ferdinand Street, Camden, NW1 8ER
Nearest Station: Chalk Farm
020 7485 6791

Enjoy a selection of Brazilian delicacies such as exquisite grilled meats and fish, with a drinks list you would expect from a Latin American venue. The world famous Caipirinha cocktail is a must.

THE CUBAN CAMDEN
Cuban

Stables Market, Chalk Farm Road, Camden, NW1 8AH
Nearest Station: Chalk Farm
0333 240 2000

An authentic and unique experience for diners, who can enjoy the Cuban cuisine while admiring the Che Guevara-inspired dining and bar areas. Draws a relaxed informal crowd for a truly chilled evening.

THE DUKE OF YORK
British

2-2a St Anns Terrace, St John's Wood, NW8 6PJ
Nearest Station: St. John's Wood
020 7722 1933

Historic pub situated in beautiful St. John's Wood, where superb food is coupled with good wine and friendly service. Caters for both intimate meals and dinner parties, with food and drink served all day.

THE EDGWAREBURY
British

Barnet Lane, Elstree, WD6 3RE
Nearest Station: Elstree & Borehamwood
0844 736 8602

Fine-dining experience with exquisite dishes and extensive wine list. Intimate and sophisticated venue ideal for parties and dinners. A place to unwind and take advantage of the panoramic views of London.

Gourmet Society discount applies to the à la carte menu

THE FIDDLERS RESTAURANT
Mediterranean
221-227 High Road, Harrow Weald, HA3 5EE
Nearest Station: Harrow & Wealdstone
020 8863 6066
From your fundamentally Italian Rognoncini Trifolati
to the crumbling, sweet lamb of a Greek Kleftiko,
you'll enjoy something very authentic, very warm,
rich and colourful in this charismatic restaurant.

POEM BAR & GRILL
European
94 Boundary Road, St John's Wood, NW8 0RH
Nearest Station: St. Johns Wood
020 7372 3897
A glossy modern Steak House restaurant close to
London's famed Abbey Road Studios and crossing,
Poem Bar and Grill is a popular meeting place for the
St John's Wood gourmet set.

NEW

JAKARTA
Chinese/
7 Shaveshill Pde, Shaveshill Av, Colindale, NW9 6RS
Malaysian/Thai
Nearest Station: Colindale
0208 205 3335
Jakarta is a restaurant full of character with a menu
replete with the tangs and tastes of Indonesian
cuisine. Artefacts and art-work make this place a
welcoming, singular pleasure in which to dine.

NEW

2FOR1
MAIN COURSE

THE PRINCE OF BENGAL
Indian
51 Langley Way, Watford, WD17 3EA
Nearest Station: Watford
01923 253 538
Unfussy, deliciously tasty Indian dishes are to be
found at this versatile Bengali restaurant in Watford.
The dishes are served and prepared with skill,
professionalism and panache.

25%OFF
TOTAL

THE RED TURBAN
Indian
244 Streatfield Road, Harrow, HA3 9BX
Nearest Station: Queensbury
020 8238 9999
Focusing on the regional variety of Indian cuisine, The
Red Turban offers an outstandingly extensive menu
that provides different dishes to diners who may want
to try something new.

2FOR1
3COURSES

THE SPICE ROOM
Indian
12 Kaduna Close, Pinner, HA5 2PZ
Nearest Station: Northwood Hills
020 8868 8835
In a contemporary setting, a unique and innovative
spin has been placed on typically traditional North
Indian dishes at The Spice Room. An ideal location for
any event and any party size.

25%OFF
TOTAL

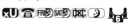

TOPGOLF WATFORD
American
Bushey Mill Lane, Watford, WD24 7AB
Nearest Station: Watford
01923 222 045
What better way to top off your game of golf than
with a fantastic meal or a round of celebratory drinks.
Head to the Bayview café-bar where you can find a
variety of food available all day long.

2FOR1
MAIN COURSE

WALNUT
British
280 West End Lane, West Hampstead, NW6 1LJ
Nearest Station: West Hampstead
020 7794 7772
Walnut's ever-changing, adaptive menu makes full
use of the seasonal produce that is available. This
restaurant channels its energy in seeking out the best
local ingredients for all of their dishes.

2FOR1
3COURSES

WOODLANDS
South Indian
Vegetarian
102 Heath Street, Hampstead, NW3 1DR
Nearest Station: Hampstead
020 7794 3080
South Indian vegetarian cuisine at its very best. The
award-winning kitchen accommodates chefs with at
least 15 years of experience from other Woodlands
restaurants.

25%OFF
TOTAL

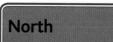
North

36
Italian
36 Queen Parade, Friern Barnet, N11 3DA
Nearest Station: Arnos Grove
020 8361 1411
A contemporary venue delivering fine Italian cuisine
from a menu showcasing an eclectic mix of flavours
and textures with a variety of authentic dishes.
Complement your meal with a pick of choice wines.

2FOR1
MAIN COURSE

AFRICAN TORCH RESTAURANT
African
135-137 High Cross Road, Seven Sisters, N17 9NU
Nearest Station: Tottenham Hale
020 8808 8166
A torch-bearer for West-African cooking, the menu
features many traditional dishes and the akonfem
platter with yam and salad exemplifies the rich
flavours that characterise this cuisine.

50%OFF
FOOD

AFTER OFFICE HOURS
Spanish
70 High Street, Barnet, EN5 5SJ
Nearest Station: High Barnet
020 8449 1142
A stylish, relaxed venue perfect for post-work platters
or pre-party wining and dining. Try the exquisite,
freshly prepared food and tapas, washing it down
with a choice of wine, beer and cocktails.

50%OFF
FOOD

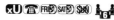

BOUGA
Moroccan
1 Park Road, Crouch End, N8 8TE
Nearest Station: Crouch Hill
020 8348 5609
Beautiful mosaic floors, silk drapes and ornate
handicrafts provide an enchanting atmospheric haven.
The menu draws upon the richness of Moroccan
culture and cuisine, providing exquisite food for all.

25%OFF
TOTAL

CAFÉ ROUGE
French

Leisure Way, West Finchley, N12 0QZ
Nearest Station: West Finchley
020 8446 4777
An attractive restaurant, a boulevard café or a Parisian-style wine bar; however you see Café Rouge, consistently excellent classic French dishes are always guaranteed.

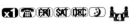

CAFÉ ROUGE
French

45-46 Cannon Hill, Southgate, N14 6LH
Nearest Station: Southgate
020 8886 3336
An attractive restaurant, a boulevard café or a Parisian-style wine bar; however you see Café Rouge, consistently excellent classic French dishes are always guaranteed.

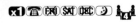

CAFÉ ROUGE
French

6-7 South Grove, Highgate, N6 6BP
Nearest Station: Highgate
020 8342 9797
An attractive restaurant, a boulevard café or a Parisian-style wine bar; however you see Café Rouge, consistently excellent classic French dishes are always guaranteed.

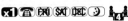

CHEZ TONTON
French

182 East Barnet Road, New Barnet, EN4 8RD
Nearest Station: New Barnet
020 8440 2696
Classic and charming French restaurant in New Barnet with a real air of the bleu blanc rouge. Superbly cooked French fare combines with a choice wine list for a convivial evening or a romantic tête-à-tête.

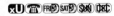

COCK & DRAGON
Thai/British

Chalk Lane, Cockfosters, Barnet, EN4 9HU
Nearest Station: Cockfosters
020 8449 7160
Indulge in authentic Thai cuisine whilst enjoying your favourite beers and fine wines in exemplary Dragon Pub surroundings. Choose from a great variety of well-prepared, exquisitely tasting dishes.

Call beforehand on special event days.

DUDLEY'S PANCAKE HOUSE
European

119 Stroud Green Road, Stroud Green, N4 3PX
Nearest Station: Crouch Hill
020 7281 5437
Using only the freshest and highest quality produce, Dudley's guarantees its reputation for the best Dutch-style pancakes. Alternatively, guests can feast on delicious gourmet bagels, waffles and salads.

EL PANCHO'S RESTAURANT
Mexican

176 Stoke Newington Rd, Stoke New'ton, N16 7UY
Nearest Station: Stoke Newington
020 7923 9588
Classic full-throated Tex-Mex dishes with cool, crisp cocktails and a vital, bright atmosphere.

GREEN DRAGON
Thai/British

889 Green Lanes, Winchmoore Hill, N21 2QP
Nearest Station: Winchmore Hill
020 8360 0005
A real fusion dining experience that deftly succeeds where others have failed. Indulge in traditional Thai cuisine in this unique Dragon pub atmosphere, enjoying authentic beverages and good company.

HENDON HALL HOTEL
European

The Fringe Restaurant, Ashley Ln, Barnet, NW4 1HF
Nearest Station: Hendon Central
020 8203 3341
Passionately crafted British cuisine served with charm in this magnificent country house, of the Hand Picked Hotels group, offering contemporary dining with classic and inventive dishes. 1 AA Rosette.

HONEYMOON RESTAURANT
Chinese

33-35 Park Road, Crouch End, N8 8TE
Nearest Station: Crouch Hill
020 8341 5113
A restaurant with a strong local following that serves an eclectic array of Thai and Chinese dishes. Friendly and accommodating, it's a popular choice.

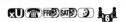

IL BACIO
Italian

61 Stoke Newington Church St, Stoke New'ton, N16 0AR
Nearest Station: Stoke Newington
020 7249 3933
Experience the taste of the entire Italian peninsula all under one roof. The skilful hands of the chefs prepare delectable dishes that emanate Italian culture, with a menu filled with all the classics.

JUNIPER DINING
English and Continental

100 Highbury Park, Highbury, N5 2XE
Nearest Station: Arsenal
020 7288 8716
A family-owned restaurant creating great food, perfectly cooked. Experienced chef-patron Rob Wilkinson delivers a delightful menu that is changed seasonally and supplemented by enticing daily specials.

MISO
Oriental

123 Stroud Green Road, Stroud Green, N4 3PX
Nearest Station: Crouch Hill
020 7272 0900
Testament to its own success, Miso offers stir-fried noodles that arrive steaming, sizzling and sumptuous. Guests enjoy the nutritional values found in each dish, which enhance mind, body and soul.

MUNA'S RESTAURANT
Sudanese/Eritrean

599 Green Lanes, Haringey, N8 0RE
Nearest Station: Harringay Green Lanes
020 8340 8411
Extremely hearty and flavoursome food will tantalise even the most sophisticated of palates. Whether you enjoy your food mild or exceedingly spicy, the kitchen can cater for all tastes and preferences.

When booking restaurants always mention your GS membership

NAMKEEN
Indian

4 Green Lane, Palmers Green, N13 6UT
Nearest Station: Palmers Green
020 8365 7771

A family-run establishment where the chefs are passionate about serving the very best Indian cuisine to their guests. A continually improving menu guarantees diners an excellent dining experience.

OLD ORLEANS
American

202 Southbury Rd, Enfield, EN1 1UY
Nearest Station: Southbury
020 8366 2656

An extraordinarily accurate taste of the Deep South can be found in this unique restaurant. The kitchen deals in classic Louisiana and Cajun recipes such as jambalaya and gumbo to create an exciting menu.

Not available on Bank Holiday weekends. Adult menu only

OUTBACK STEAKHOUSE
Australian

Southbury Road, Enfield, EN1 1YQ
Nearest Station: Southbury
020 8367 7881

Expect big, bold flavours in this laid-back restaurant that is passionate about fresh food. The kitchen prides itself on the soups, sauces and salad dressings which are all made from scratch.

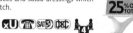

PRADERA TAPAS BAR
Spanish

14 High Street, Crouch End, N8 7PB
Nearest Station: Hornsey
020 8340 9400

With flavours as vibrant as the Spanish sun, this restaurant introduces an authentic setting with a host of dishes to choose from. All food is finely produced and pan-fried to deliver an original taste.

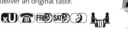

PREZZO
Italian

The Coach House, 26 The Town, Enfield, EN2 6LU
Nearest Station: Enfield Town
020 8366 8817

With a character all of its own, Prezzo oozes contemporary style and enduring charm. Signature pastas, stone-baked pizzas and classic Italian dishes promise a perfect dining choice for the whole family.

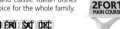

PREZZO
Italian

127-129 Cockfoster Road, Cockfosters, EN4 0DA
Nearest Station: Cockfosters
02084 416917

With a character all of its own, Prezzo oozes contemporary style and enduring charm. Signature pastas, stone-baked pizzas and classic Italian dishes promise a perfect dining choice for the whole family.

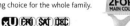

PUBLIC HOUSE
British

54 Islington Park Street, Highbury, N1 1PX
Nearest Station: Highbury &Islington
020 7359 6070

A beautifully designed space for eating and drinking, Public House's innovative style tops off its intriguing, accomplished and adventurous menu. Throw in a heady array of digestifs, and you're set fair.

PUJI PUJI RESTAURANT
Malaysian

122 Balls Pond Road, Dalston, N1 4AE
Nearest Station: Canonbury
020 7923 2112

Traditional Malaysian cuisine created from fresh and fragrant ingredients. With speciality dishes and a 'bring your own alcohol' policy, diners can enjoy a reasonably priced, authentic experience.

RASA TRAVANCORE
Indian

56 Stoke Newington Church St, Stoke New'ton, N16 ONB
Nearest Station: Stoke Newington
020 7249 1340

Inspired by the authentic home cooking of beautiful, spice-rich Kerala, this restaurant's passion is food prepared always with devotion, love, and the finest ingredients. Experience the essence of India.

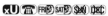

ROYAL INDIA
Indian

47 Stoke Newington Church St, Stoke New'ton, N16 0NX
Nearest Station: Stoke Newington
020 7249 7025

Enjoy the luxurious furnishings that create a warm and inviting ambience at this phenomenal Indian restaurant. The takeaway option means delicious food can be enjoyed in the comfort of your own home.

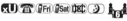

STINGRAY CAFE
Italian

36 Highbury Park, Highbury, N5 2AA
Nearest Station: Canonbury
020 7954 9309

A delightfully charming Italian restaurant that is not only family-friendly, but also a place to share an intimate meal for two. Friendly staff and tasty food ensure a satisfying visit.

STINGRAY CAFE
Italian

135 Fortress Road, NW5 2HR
Nearest Station: Tufnell Park
020 7482 4855

A taste of Europe offering an easily affordable menu which boasts various pizzas and à la carte meals. A delicious and unique alternative is also their own gluten free, organic whole grain pizza and pasta.

SWEET HANDZ RESTAURANT
African

148 Holloway Road, Holloway, N7 8DD
Nearest Station: Holloway Road
020 7700 6427

A wonderful restaurant situated in the heart of London. An extensive menu of traditional and modern Ghanaian cuisine is to be enjoyed with imported African beers, tropical cocktails and fine wine.

TANDOORI NIGHTS
Indian

27 Station Parade, Cockfosters Road, Cockfosters, EN4 0DW
Nearest Station: Cockfosters
020 8441 2131

This venue offer diners a splendid range of curries and Tandoori specialities prepared by master chefs . A rendezvous for all who enjoy the exotic, spicy and healthy dishes of the Indian subcontinent.

TASTE OF NAWAB
Indian

97 Colney Hatch Lane, Muswell Hill, N10 1LR
Nearest Station: Bounds Green
020 8883 6429
Award-winning restaurant with an excellent reputation. Prepare yourself for a gastronomical journey through India and indulge your senses with an extensive menu offering spice-infused authentic dishes.

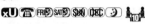

THE LOCK RESTAURANT
British

Heron House, Ferry Lane, Seven Sisters, N17 9NF
Nearest Station: Tottenham Hale
020 8885 2829
A unique blend of casual and fine dining all under the one roof, The Lock has something for everyone. Demonstrates style, elegance and an exemplary gastronomic approach. Awarded 2 AA Rosettes.

THE TRIANGLE
International

1 Ferme Park Road, Haringey, N4 4DS
Nearest Station: Crouch Hill
020 8292 0516
You'll wish you'd found this charming hideaway sooner once you discover its remarkable food and magical atmosphere. The highly original menu will leave you wanting to come back time and time again.

TOKYO JOE'S
Japanese

192-194 High Street, Barnet, EN5 5SZ
Nearest Station: High Barnet

This Japanese restaurant is a new addition to Barnet's bustling restaurant scene, aiming to bring guests a large variety of vibrant, flavoursome dishes and sumptuous regional specialities.

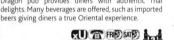
North East

ARDLEIGH & DRAGON
Thai/British

124 Ardleigh Green Road, Hornchurch, RM11 2SH
Nearest Station: Gidea Park
0170 844 2550
Serving divine dishes from the Far East, this charming Dragon pub provides diners with authentic Thai delights. Many beverages are offered, such as imported beers giving diners a true Oriental experience.

AROMA INDIAN RESTAURANT
Indian

55 High Street, Romford, RM1 1JL
Nearest Station: Romford
0170 873 2345
A local favourite having garnered a reputation for a combination of excellent curry and cheerful staff. A familiar and exquisite menu, every dish rich in aromatic Indian flavours and spice.

BHANGRA BEAT
Indian

49 Chigwell Road, South Woodford, E18 1NG
Nearest Station: South Woodford
020 8989 8909
Enjoy superb Indian cuisine as the sounds of Bollywood style music fill the air around you. Meat lovers will fall head over heels for the special balti, which incorporates succulent lamb, chicken and duck.

BHANGRA BEAT
Indian

108 High Road, Chadwell Heath, RM6 6NX
Nearest Station: Chadwell Heath
020 8590 2503
A cosy, family-run establishment serving tasty Indian sub continental cuisine. With an award-winning chef in the kitchen, it is unsurprising that this restaurant increases in popularity by the day.

CAFÉ ROUGE
French

179-181 High Road, Loughton, IG10 4LF
Nearest Station: Loughton
020 8502 2011
An attractive restaurant, a boulevard café or a Parisian-style wine bar; however you see Café Rouge, consistently excellent classic French dishes are always guaranteed.

CINNAMON SPICE
Indian

10 Tadworth Parade, Elm Park, Hornchurch, RM12 5AS
Nearest Station: Elm Park
01708 478 510
Cheerful staff enhance the amiable ambience of this restaurant. Local diners regularly flock to this eatery for its chilled atmosphere and satisfying food. The cinnamon garlic chicken is outstanding.

FOREST TANDOORI
Indian

102 Wood Street, Waltham Forest, E17 3HX
Nearest Station: Walthamstow Central
020 8520 8080
A hidden gem of an Indian restaurant. The food, service and interior are top notch, with the quality of the takeaway being equally excellent.

 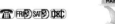

HAWA
Indian

530 High Road, Seven Kings, Ilford, IG3 8EG
Nearest Station: Seven Kings
020 8599 6812
Dine in authentic surroundings while experienced chefs create an exceptional menu showcasing the divine flavours of traditional Indian cuisine. Also delivers an extensive wine list to complement your meal.

JAILHOUSE RESTAURANT
American

44 High Street, Hornchurch, RM12 4UN
Nearest Station: Emerson Park
0170 844 4408
A tempting menu offers mouth-watering culinary delights. The bar prides itself on its vibrant cocktail menu, which offers options for all at inexpensive prices.

Enjoy massive leisure and retail savings with more Gourmet Society

JALALABAD 2 RESTAURANT
Indian

992-994 Eastern Ave, Newbury Park, IG2 7JD
Nearest Station: Newbury Park
020 8478 1366

Whether you choose to eat in or take away, the extensive range of succulent, halal dishes will transport you to India. Authentic tastes created with fine ingredients; a superb culinary experience.

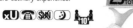

LOCH FYNE
Seafood

280-282 High Road, Loughton, IG10 1RB
Nearest Station: Loughton
020 8532 5140

From the roadside oyster bar that once was, Loch Fyne restaurants now successfully inject energy and passion into great food and wonderful flavours, whilst ensuring their seafood is sustainably sourced.

LONDON DARBAR
Indian

198 Cranbrook Road, Ilford, IG1 4LU
Nearest Station: Ilford
020 8518 3382

Put simply, this is food and drink done like you've never seen it before. Everything on the menu from the mulligatawny soup to the lamb do-paija resonates with the underpinning philosophy 'fresh is best'.

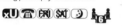

MASALA KING
Indian

8 Chapel Road, Ilford, IG1 2AG
Nearest Station: Ilford
020 8514 2446

Sample a fusion of authentic and Sri Lankan cuisine from the exceptional range on offer, experiencing the divine tastes of different cultures, prepared well to produce a high standard of satisfying cuisine.

MOBY DICK
Carvery

Whalebone Lane North, Chadwell Heath, RM6 6QU
Nearest Station: Chadwell Heath
020 8590 9524

Guests can enjoy the best of British food in this Great British Carvery venue. The well-loved classic is served in an attractive family-friendly pub that offers warm welcomes and friendly smiles.

Call beforehand on special event days.

OLD ORLEANS
American

Wakes Arms Roundabout, High Rd, Epping, CM16 5HW
Nearest Station: Theydon Bois
01992 812 618

An extraordinarily accurate taste of the Deep South can be found in this unique restaurant. The kitchen deals in classic Louisiana and Cajun recipes such as jambalaya and gumbo to create an exciting menu.

Not available on Bank Holiday weekends. Adult menu only.

OUTBACK STEAKHOUSE
Australian

The Brewery, Waterloo Road, Romford, RM1 1AU
Nearest Station: Romford
01708 737 955

Expect big, bold flavours in this laid-back restaurant that is passionate about fresh food. The kitchen prides itself on the soups, sauces and salad dressings which are all made from scratch.

PREZZO
Italian

236 High Street, Epping, CM16 4AP
Nearest Station: Epping
01992 570 056

With a character all of its own, Prezzo oozes contemporary style and enduring charm. Signature pastas, stone-baked pizzas and classic Italian dishes promise a perfect dining choice for the whole family.

PREZZO
Italian

Elmhurst, 98 High Road, South Woodford, E18 2QH
Nearest Station: South Woodford
020 8559 0192

With a character all of its own, Prezzo oozes contemporary style and enduring charm. Signature pastas, stone-baked pizzas and classic Italian dishes promise a perfect dining choice for the whole family.

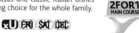

PREZZO
Italian

189 High Street, Hornchurch, RM11 3XT
Nearest Station: Upminster Bridge
01708 455 501

With a character all of its own, Prezzo oozes contemporary style and enduring charm. Signature pastas, stone-baked pizzas and classic Italian dishes promise a perfect dining choice for the whole family.

PREZZO
Italian

8 Johnson Road, Woodford Green, IG8 0XA
Nearest Station: Woodford
020 8505 2400

With a character all of its own, Prezzo oozes contemporary style and enduring charm. Signature pastas, stone-baked pizzas and classic Italian dishes promise a perfect dining choice for the whole family.

QUEEN ELIZABETH
Carvery

95 Forest Side, Chingford, E4 6BA
Nearest Station: Chigwell
020 8529 1160

One of the fabulous Great British Carveries that offers the well-loved classic with a modern twist. A pleasant pub that offers all guests a royal welcome and great service.

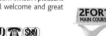

Call beforehand on special event days.

RADHUNI
Indian

206 Main Road, Romford, RM2 5HA
Nearest Station: Gidea Park
01708 739 292

Contemporary Indian cuisine that will completely stimulate your palate. Kind welcoming staff are happy to ensure you have a pleasing dining experience.

ROUGE
International

Redbridge College, Barley Lane, Little Heath, RM6 4XT
Nearest Station: Chadwell Heath
02085 487 400

Support the talented chefs of the future at this on-site restaurant. Wonderful dishes are prepared by chefs-in-training, guaranteeing guests a first-class dining experience.

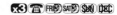

GREATER LONDON

SRI RATHIGA
Indian
312 High Road, Ilford, IG1 1QW
Nearest Station: Ilford
020 8478 7272
Affable staff provide an efficient service and warm friendly smiles in this wonderfully well-maintained restaurant. Ancient traditional recipes are used to create authentic South Indian cuisine.

THEYDON BOIS BALTI HOUSE
Indian
Station Approach, Coppice Row, Theydon Bois, CM16 7EU
Nearest Station: Theydon Bois
01992 814 104
The oldest Tandoori restaurant in the area offering innovative takes on authentic Indian, Persian and Kashmiri dishes. Attentiveness is a key attribute of all the staff at this local friendly restaurant.

TOPGOLF CHIGWELL
British
Abridge Road, Chigwell, IG7 6BX
Nearest Station: Debden
020 8500 2644
What better way to top off your game of golf than with a fantastic meal or a round of celebratory drinks? Head to the Bayview Café/Bar where you can find a variety of food available all day long.

East

62 SPICE
Indian
62 High Street, Wanstead, E11 2RJ
Nearest Station: Wanstead
020 8989 6774
Authentic dishes achieved through the use of the finest ingredients and cooking techniques allow you to savour both the contemporary and familiar tastes of India.

AMURG
Romanian
579 High Road, Leytonstone, E11 4PB
Nearest Station: Leytonstone High Road
020 8556 9602
A Romanian restaurant serving fabulously tasty national cuisine in a charismatic environment. Star-like lights line the ceiling, whilst Friday's live music provides a great start to the weekend.

ANATOLIA
Turkish
277 High Road, Leyton, E10 5QN
Nearest Station: Leyton
020 8558 0401
Great Turkish restaurant, moments from the tube, with a large variety of cuisine prepared by Turkish chefs. The cakes are not to be missed.

BENGAL LANCER
Indian
84 Longbridge Road, Barking, IG11 8SF
Nearest Station: Barking
020 8594 9598
Bengal Lancer is a Tandoori Restaurant featuring classic dishes such as dopiaza, biriyani and house specialities.

BRODIE'S BAR AND RESTAURANT
International
43-44 Fisherman's Walk, Canary Wharf, E14 5HD
Nearest Station: Canary Wharf
020 7719 0202
Bursting with vibrant energy, Brodie's is proud of its character that attracts both small and large parties for all occasions. Main dishes, gourmet sandwiches and delicious desserts are all on offer.

CAFÉ ROUGE
French
29-35 Mackenzie Walk, Canary Wharf, E14 4PH
Nearest Station: Canary Wharf
020 7537 9696
An attractive restaurant, a boulevard café or a Parisian-style wine bar; however you see Café Rouge, consistently excellent classic French dishes are always guaranteed.

 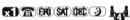

CARIBBEAN SCENE FAMILY
Caribbean
Gerry Raffles Square, Stratford, E15 1BG
Nearest Station: Stratford
020 8522 8660
Celebrates all that is wonderful about Caribbean culture. Stimulate all of your senses with exquisite food, delectable cocktails, aromatic rums and lively music, all in the most vibrant of settings.

CARIBBEAN SCENE ROYALE
Caribbean
17 Western Gateway, Royal Victoria Docks, E16 1AQ
Nearest Station: Royal Victoria
020 7511 2023
Allow the allusive Caribbean theme of the restaurant transport you straight to the islands. From the natural herbs and spices used in the food, to the music and décor, you'll enjoy being in paradise.

CINNAMON SPICE
Indian
10 Tadworth Parade, Elm Park, Hornchurch, RM12 5AS
Nearest Station: Elm Park
01708 478 510
Cheerful staff enhance the amiable ambience of this restaurant. Local diners regularly flock to this eatery for its chilled atmosphere and satisfying food. The cinnamon garlic chicken is outstanding.

CIRRIK RESTAURANT
Mediterranean
1-3 Amhurst Road, Hackney, E8 1LL
Nearest Station: Hackney Central
020 8985 2879
This authentic Turkish restaurant greets you with a mouth-watering aroma of herbs and spices from the grill. Their wide selection of delicious dishes offer something for everyone. Families most welcome.

154

Enjoy massive leisure and retail savings with more Gourmet Society

CLIFTON DOCKLANDS
Indian

32 Westferry Rd, Canary Wharf, E14 8LW
Nearest Station: South Quay
020 7001 2999
The innovative South Asian cuisine is complemented by the refined and sophisticated décor. The friendly and knowledgeable staff ensure that every guest has a relaxing and delicious experience.

CURVE
Seafood

22 Hertsmere Rd, Canary Wharf, E14 4ED
Nearest Station: West India Quay
020 7093 1000
Offering al fresco dining on their terrace or cosy tables inside, the décor and atmosphere are wonderful. The menu tempts with market fresh fish and seafood and a phenomenal selection of wines.

DOCKLANDS BAR AND GRILL
British

Western Gateway, Royal Victoria Docks, E16 1AL
Nearest Station: Royal Victoria
020 7055 2119
The award-winning Docklands Bar and Grill serves exceptional seasonal British and European dishes in a modern and comfortable setting with daily food, wine specials and warm, knowledgeable staff.

DOCKMASTERS HOUSE
Indian

1 Hertsmere Road, Docklands, Tower Hamlets, E14 8JD
Nearest Station: Westferry
020 7345 0345
Classic Indian dishes with an expressive contemporary twist in this charming restaurant and bar. Guests will fall in love with the stunning dining rooms that enhance the building's Georgian character.

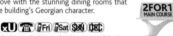

Fri & Sat Strictly bookings on the day only. Closed Sat. daytime/all day Sun.

EL FARO
Spanish

3 Turnberry Quay, Canary Wharf, E14 9RD
Nearest Station: Crossharbour
020 7987 5511
Marvellously set overlooking the river at Turnberry Quay, the enthusiasm of El Faro's owners shines through, not least in the imaginative, fresh flavours of Head Chef Javier Capella.

FORTUNE INN
Chinese

14 London Road, Barking, IG11 8AG
Nearest Station: Barking
020 8594 3311
Spanning the gamut of different flavours from regions of China, the Fortune Inn is lucid in the way it goes about preparing its dishes. Calm and collected, flavourful and piquant, altogether balanced food.

GOURMET PIZZA
Pizza

18-20 Mackenzie Walk, Canary Wharf, E14 4PH
Nearest Station: Canary Wharf
020 7345 9192
Popular with pizza lovers and people watchers alike, this buzzy city restaurant offers lavish pizzas heaped with colour in spacious and comfortable surroundings. A special menu offers alternative treats.

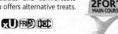

Take-away not included.

INDIANA
Bangladeshi/ Indian

129 Salmon Lane, Tower Hamlets, E14 7PG
Nearest Station: Limehouse
020 7987 2576
A real local institution with chic interior and neon lighting. An interesting menu offers traditional cuisine but also delivers unique creations inspired by the many different flavours of the subcontinent.

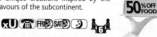

LAHORE ONE RESTAURANT
Indian

218 Commercial Road, E1 2JT
Nearest Station: Shadwell
020 7791 0112
A restaurant that has proudly pioneered a new approach towards traditional Indian cooking. The various flavours of Indian, British, Arabic and Chinese go towards making each dish tasty and delicious.

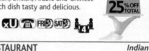

LIME BAR AND RESTAURANT
Indian

1 Manilla St, Regatta Point, Canary Wharf, E14 8JZ
Nearest Station: South Quay
020 7515 4500
Acclaimed Indian restaurant in the curry hotspot of East London. Silky, flavourful vegetable curries and sharper, piquant South Indian-style dishes in a hip, accommodating atmosphere.

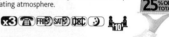

MEZ RESTAURANT
Turkish

571 Manchester Road, Canary Wharf, E14 3NX
Nearest Station: Crossharbour
020 7005 0421
Serving a fabulous range of aromatic, eclectic Turkish cuisine, Mez is a vibrant restaurant for a fulsome dinner and exciting evening out.

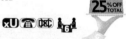

MOBY DICK BAR
British

6 Russell Place, Surrey Quays, Southwark, SE16 7PL
Nearest Station: Surrey Quays
020 7231 6719
Moby Dick Bar is a traditional British pub serving deliciously hearty meals. Offers a wide ranging menu to cater for all ages and tastes, and an exceptional beverage selection of beer, wine and much more.

PASHA RESTAURANT
Turkish

75 Wapping High Street, Wapping, E1W 2YN
Nearest Station: Wapping
020 7702 2040
Classic Turkish dishes that will delight every diner. Moussaka, borek and baklava feature on the menu amongst many other traditional treats. Every guest is guaranteed to be treated like a king.

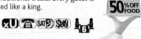

PREZZO
Italian

53 Corbets Tey Road, Upminster, RM14 2AJ
Nearest Station: Upminster
01708 642 096
With a character all of its own, Prezzo oozes contemporary style and enduring charm. Signature pastas, stone-baked pizzas and classic Italian dishes promise a perfect dining choice for the whole family.

155

PREZZO
Italian

37 Westferry Circus, Canary Riverside, E14 8RR
Nearest Station: Canary Wharf
020 7519 1234
With a character all of its own, Prezzo oozes contemporary style and enduring charm. Signature pastas, stone-baked pizzas and classic Italian dishes promise a perfect dining choice for the whole family.

THE TALE OF INDIA
Indian

53 India Dock Road, Isle of Dogs, E14 8HN
Nearest Station: Westferry
020 7537 2546
Classic Indian and Bangladeshi cuisine on the Isle of Dogs; all the array of spices marking out subcontinental cuisine, in a vibrant, buzzy and welcoming setting.

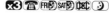

RASA MUDRA
Indian

715 High Rd, Leytonstone, E11 4RD
Nearest Station: Leytonstone High Road
020 8539 1700
Inspired by the authentic home cooking of beautiful, spice-rich Kerala, this restaurant's passion is food prepared always with devotion, love, and the finest ingredients. Experience the essence of India.

URBAN INNS - THE OLD SHIP
British

2 Sylvester Path, Hackney, E8 1EN
Nearest Station: Hackney Central
020 8986 1641
Genial and accommodating urban inn in Hackney where you can enjoy a ranging, seasonal menu that celebrates classic British cuisine while looking to keep it up to date with modern touches.

RIVER SPICE
Indian

83 Wapping Lane, Wapping, E1W 2RW
Nearest Station: Wapping
020 7488 4051
A sleek and stylish venue that creates spicy, flavoursome dishes that reflect original cooking processes and ingredients. Classic and modern Indian cuisine subtly enhanced by Thai and European influences.

South East

RIVER VIEW
Chinese

New Crane Wharf, New Crane Place, Wapping, E1W 3TU
Nearest Station: Wapping
020 7480 6026
Enjoy great river views whilst dining at this well-established venue that delivers quality authentic Chinese cuisine. Offers a vast menu specialising in seafood and other fine dishes.

AMERICAN BAR AND GRILL
American

Millenium Way, O2 Arena, Greenwich, SE10 0AX
Nearest Station: North Greenwich
020 7858 5807
Guests will love the menu that captures every flavour from Maine to Texas. Sip on a cool beer before your all-American feast begins.

Not available on O2 Event Days.

SMOLLENSKY'S
American

1 Reuters Plaza, Canary Wharf, E14 5AJ
Nearest Station: Canary Wharf
020 7719 0101
Cosmopolitan dining in a stylish environment offering diners stunning, modern food. With over 20 years experience, this restaurant continues to offer exceptional dishes perfect for any occasion.

BABUR
Indian

119 Brockley Rise, Forest Hill, SE23 1JP
Nearest Station: Honor Oak Park
020 8291 2400
A committed restaurant skilfully presenting India's many traditional cuisines. The spice-filled menu is complete with favourite dishes, old and new, alongside monthly-changing specials. 2 AA Rosettes.

STAR OF INDIA
Indian

875 High Rd, Leytonstone, E11 1HR
Nearest Station: Leytonstone
020 8989 4028
One of the best Indian restaurants in London boasting two award-winning chefs. Excellent staff provide a friendly atmosphere, serving diners with a huge array of full-flavoured dishes and beverages.

BAR DU MUSÉE
Bistro

17 Nelson Road, Greenwich, SE10 9UB
Nearest Station: Maze Hill
020 8858 4710
A versatile restaurant in Greenwich that has grown from its origins as a tiny neighbourhood bistro but holds firm to the original concept, formulating unpretentious, thoroughly tasty seasonal menus.

THE CLIPPER
British

Rotherhithe Street, Rotherhithe, SE16 5EX
Nearest Station: Canada Water
020 7237 2022
A no-nonsense, traditional pub providing classic food, great beer, and good wine. A popular favourite of the local area and the perfect place to kick back and relax.

BARCELONA TAPAS BAR
Spanish

481 Lordship Lane, Dulwich, SE22 8JY
Nearest Station: Forest Hill
020 8693 5111
An expanding family business offering delicious Spanish food in an authentic atmosphere. Watch the world go by as you relax on the outdoor terrace area, and experience real Spanish flavour.

BENGAL BRASSERIE
Indian

79 Springbank Road, Hither Green, SE13 6SS
Nearest Station: Hither Green
020 8244 2442
Extremely talented chefs work hard in the kitchen to create a variety of tasty dishes originating from all parts of India. A well-established restaurant, popular with both locals and guests from afar.

CAFÉ ROUGE
French

12-13 Market Square, Bromley, BR1 1MA
Nearest Station: Bromley South
020 8460 0470
An attractive restaurant, a boulevard café or a Parisian-style wine bar; however you see Café Rouge, consistently excellent classic French dishes are always guaranteed.

CAFÉ ROUGE
French

9 The High Street, Chislehurst, BR7 5AJ
Nearest Station: Chislehurst
020 8295 5000
An attractive restaurant, a boulevard café or a Parisian-style wine bar; however you see Café Rouge, consistently excellent classic French dishes are always guaranteed.

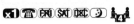

CAFÉ ROUGE
French

Hotel Ibis, 30 Stockwell St, Greenwich, SE10 9JN
Nearest Station: Cutty Sark for Maritime Greenwich
020 8293 6660
An attractive restaurant, a boulevard café or a Parisian-style wine bar; however you see Café Rouge, consistently excellent classic French dishes are always guaranteed.

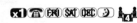

CAFÉ ROUGE
French

96-98 Dulwich Village, Dulwich, SE21 7AQ
Nearest Station: North Dulwich
020 8693 9316
An attractive restaurant, a boulevard café or a Parisian-style wine bar; however you see Café Rouge, consistently excellent classic French dishes are always guaranteed.

CAFÉ ROUGE
French

84 Park Hall Road, Dulwich, SE21 8BW
Nearest Station: West Dulwich
020 8766 0070
An attractive restaurant, a boulevard café or a Parisian-style wine bar; however you see Café Rouge, consistently excellent classic French dishes are always guaranteed.

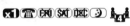

CAFÉ ROUGE
French

16-18 Montpelier Vale, Blackheath, SE3 0TA
Nearest Station: Blackheath
020 8297 2727
An attractive restaurant, a boulevard café or a Parisian-style wine bar; however you see Café Rouge, consistently excellent classic French dishes are always guaranteed.

CUMMIN' UP CARIBBEAN
Caribbean

389 Lewisham High Street, Lewisham, SE13 6NZ
Nearest Station: Lewisham
020 8690 9167
Offering traditional Caribbean cuisine, this vibrant restaurant brings the warm culture and rich flavours of the islands to London. Jamaica's national dish, ackee, saltfish and rice, is a firm winner.

ELEMENTS RESTAURANT & BAR
International

173-185 Greenwich High Road, Greenwich, SE10 8JA
Nearest Station: Greenwich
020 8312 6800
Calm and relaxed hotel-based restaurant that serves hearty, warming international food from an eclectic à la carte menu.

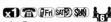

FERRARIS RESTAURANT
Italian

39 East Street, Bromley, BR1 1QQ
Nearest Station: Bromley North
020 8464 8877
Earthy, authentic Italian food in this spruce restaurant in Bromley. A range of dishes from classic staples to more contemporary flavours; menus follow the seasons with a focus on freshness.

Not available with any other offer.

GREENWICH PARK BAR & GRILL
Contemporary

1 King William Walk, Greenwich, SE10 9JF
Nearest Station: Cutty Sark for Maritime Greenwich
020 8853 7860
A leafy indoor oasis delivering a huge range of meals and sublime natural cocktails. Indulge in a Kobe steak burger made from Welsh-raised Japanese cattle, offering a deliciously delicate choice.

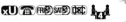

HIMALAYA INDIAN RESTAURANT
Indian

393 Lewisham High Street, Lewisham, SE13 6NZ
Nearest Station: Lewisham
020 8690 2863
Boasting a long-established reputation, this venue provides diners with an affordable yet authentic dining option. Experienced chefs create fine cuisine that is locally recommended.

INC BRASSERIE
English and Continental

Entertainment Ave, O2 Arena, Greenwich, SE10 0DY
Nearest Station: North Greenwich
020 8853 7100
A slice of slick London transported into the O2's entertainment avenue, delivering to diners a fusion of British and French cooking complete with a well-stocked bar both before and after shows or concerts.

Not available on O2 Event Days.

IVORY LOUNGE
Spanish

167 Broadway, Bexleyheath, DA6 7ES
Nearest Station: Bexleyheath
020 8303 9206
Whether it be a lazy lunch, a relaxing dinner, or a cheeky drink; this venue has it all. As day turns to night the candles are lit, the music increases, and this is truly a bar with style.

Offer excludes tapas; they form a separate set menu.

Recommend a friend to the Gourmet Society and receive a free gift.

IVORY LOUNGE
Spanish
2 Ringers Road, Bromley, BR1 1HT
Nearest Station: Bromley South
020 8313 0980
Whether it be a lazy lunch, a relaxing dinner, or a cheeky drink, this venue has it all. As day turns to night the candles are lit and the music increases; this is truly a bar with style.

Offer excludes tapas; they form a separate set menu.

JIMMY MONACO'S LOVE BURGER
American
Entertainment Ave, O2 Arena, Greenwich, SE10 0DY
Nearest Station: North Greenwich
020 8853 7100
Like the O2 Arena where it is sited, this restaurant is all about evolution. Grounded on pure, high quality beef, it serves burgers accompanied by a spectacular smorgasbord of accompaniments.

Not available on O2 Event Days.

JUDAH AND ZULA
Caribbean
135 Trafalgar Road, Greenwich, SE10 9TX
Nearest Station: Maze Hill
020 8305 2500
Take heart from some classic, down-home Caribbean cuisine at this restaurant just down from the Greenwich observatory. A warm, contemporary atmosphere plays host to their fruity and flavourful dishes.

KERALA ZONE
Indian
119 Trafalgar Road, Greenwich, SE10 9TX
Nearest Station: Maze Hill
020 8293 9158
Wholeheartedly abiding by the ancient mantra 'treat your guest like God', the staff are renowned for their excellence in Indian hospitality, while Ayurvedic traditions are maintained in the kitchen.

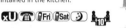

KING WILLIAM RESTAURANT
British
Old Royal Naval College, Greenwich, SE10 9LW
Nearest Station: Cutty Sark for Maritime Greenwich
020 8269 2131
Situated within the Old Royal Navy College, this restaurant is steeped in history. Offering a fine British lunch menu, guests enjoy divine food that is matched by the surroundings.

On Sundays only lunch is served.

LANG SEN
Vietnamese
305 Broadway, Bexleyheath, DA6 8DT
Nearest Station: Bexleyheath
020 8304 6998
A cosmopolitan venue delivering an exciting and innovative Vietnamese menu, with a bar ideal for pre- and post-dinner drinks. Dine in style whilst enjoying a great wine list and a host of live local music.

LE CHARDON
French
65 Lordship Lane, Dulwich, SE22 8EP
Nearest Station: East Dulwich
020 8299 1921
Formerly a grocer's shop, with many of its Victorian features intact, but also decked out for a warmly authentic French feel. Classic French cuisine, from bistro favourites to intriguing specialities.

LOCALE BLACKHEATH
Italian
1 Lawn Terrace, Blackheath, SE3 9LJ
Nearest Station: Blackheath
020 8852 0700
One bella ristorante, this classic Italian neighbourhood joint is full of colour, verve and vitality, as well as offering a warm and chilled out space to bask in the fabulously fresh, homely Italian food.

Not available with any other offer.

LOCALE EAST DULWICH
Italian
58-60 East Dulwich Road, East Dulwich, SE22 9AX
Nearest Station: East Dulwich
020 7732 7575
With an open kitchen and a passion for fine food, Locale is a quintessential Italian neighbourhood restaurant. Scrumptiously tasty pasta, fish and meat dishes can be accompanied by fresh fruit cocktails.

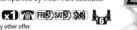
Not available with any other offer.

MISO
Oriental
10 East St, Bromley, BR1 1QX
Nearest Station: Bromley North
020 8460 4678
Testament to its own success, Miso offers stir-fried noodles that arrive steaming, sizzling and sumptuous. A vibrant buzz and happy customers can always be found in this successful eatery.

DETAILED DESCRIPTIONS AVAILABLE ON

www.gourmetsociety.co.uk

MISO
Oriental
132 High Street, Beckenham, BR3 1EB
Nearest Station: Beckenham Junction
020 8658 4498
Testament to its own success, Miso offers stir-fried noodles that arrive steaming, sizzling and sumptuous. Nutritious dishes completely enhance mind, body and soul.

MOGUL RESTAURANT
Indian
10 Greenwich Church Street, Greenwich, SE10 9BJ
Nearest Station: Cutty Sark for Maritime Greenwich
020 8858 1500
Specialising in the distinctive rich flavours of Northern India, the warm and cosy downstairs alcoves are part of this popular restaurant's distinctive atmosphere.

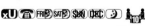

PICKHURST
Carvery
Pickhurst Lane, West Wickham, BR4 0HH
Nearest Station: West Wickham
020 8462 1876
A member of the Great British Carvery group, this architecturally appealing pub serves the best of British food with a modern twist. A popular Tudor-style venue that is a firm local favourite.

Call beforehand on special event days.

PREZZO
Italian

35 Bugsby Way, Greenwich, SE10 0QJ
Nearest Station: Westcombe Park
020 8858 2760
With a character all of its own, Prezzo oozes contemporary style and enduring charm. Signature pastas, stone-baked pizzas and classic Italian dishes promise a perfect dining choice for the whole family.

THE HIDEOUT
Mexican

70 Spital Street, Dartford, DA1 2DT
Nearest Station:
01322 224 691
More-than-generous portions of sumptuous, salty, spicy Tex-Mex dishes come as no surprise in this rewarding little gem of a restaurant. It's worth settling in for a cocktail or two, besides the great food.

PREZZO
Italian

145 - 151 High Street, Beckenham, BR3 1AG
Nearest Station: Beckenham Junction
020 8658 0747
With a character all of its own, Prezzo oozes contemporary style and enduring charm. Signature pastas, stone-baked pizzas and classic Italian dishes promise a perfect dining choice for the whole family.

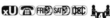

TRAFALGAR TAVERN
Traditional English

Park Row, Greenwich, SE10 9NW
Nearest Station: Maze Hill
020 8858 2909
The setting stunning, the food fantastic; neither the restaurant nor the bar will fail in providing satisfaction. Don't miss the 19th century fish dishes that have been adapted to suit the modern palate.

SPREAD EAGLE
Classic British/ French

1-2 Stockwell Street, Greenwich, SE10 9NW
Nearest Station: Maze Hill
020 8853 2333
High-end dining in a landmark setting, serving luscious French cuisine to diners whilst the décor encapsulates over 300 years of Greenwich history and landscapes in paintings and prints.

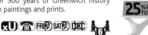

RECOMMEND A FRIEND

see page 18

SWADESH
Indian

120 Lordship Lane, Dulwich, SE22 8HD
Nearest Station: East Dulwich
020 8613 1500
With a modern kitchen and elegant surroundings, Swadesh produce sumptuous Indian cuisine. Simply fine food created by a dedicated chef, with each dish being full of flavour and delicate spice.

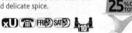

TRATTORIA RAFFAELE
Italian

94 Syndenham Road, Sydenham, SE26 5JX
Nearest Station: Sydenham
020 8778 6262
Fresh, hand-made pizza bases and breads ensure every guest has the tastiest meal. A family-run Italian restaurant where authentic, top-quality dishes are anything but hard to come by.

THE CORIANDER
Indian/ Bangladeshi

1A-3 Station Crescent, Blackheath, SE3 7EQ
Nearest Station: Westcombe Park
020 8858 7878
Stylish and sophisticated Indian restaurant with a focus on superb service and a specialisation in the richness and piquancy of Northern Indian and Bangladeshi cuisine.

UNION SQUARE
Traditional English

Millenium Way, O2 Arena, Greenwich, SE10 0AX
Nearest Station: North Greenwich
020 7858 5815
Allow this hip, flagship restaurant by the iconic O2 Arena to tangle and jangle your taste buds, whether it be pre- show, post-, or simply to drink in the unique location.

Not available on O2 Event Days.

THE CROWN
Modern British

46 Plaistow Lane, Bromley, BR1 3PA
Nearest Station: Sundridge Park
020 8466 1313
Bringing fine food and wine together with a handsome Victorian building that has been extensively and sympathetically restored. Food is produced by a proven team who continue to enjoy culinary success.

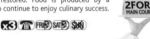

South

THE HERNE TAVERN
British

2 Forest Hill Rd, Dulwich, SE22 0RR
Nearest Station: Honor Oak Park
020 8299 9521
Allow your children to enter the magical landscaped garden as you relax over a glass of wine and feast on a divine lunch or evening meal. Traditionally English dishes make up an admirable menu.

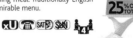

AQUA BRASSERIE
European

33 South End, Croydon, CR0 1BE
Nearest Station: South Croydon
020 8667 0070
First-class dining with a selection of Modern European dishes that combine fresh, simple ingredients with a genuine love for creating exquisite cuisine, perfectly cooked and beautifully presented.

Visit the website regularly to discover the latest restaurants joining the GS

AQUUM
International

68-70 Clapham High Street, Clapham, SW4 7UL
Nearest Station: Clapham North
020 7627 2726
Enjoy an enthralling experience with innovative cocktails, fine food, world class DJ's and a unique party vibe. A cool venue offering guests everything they could wish for.

AUBERGE
French

2153-2156 The Whitgift Center, Croydon, CR0 1LP
Nearest Station: West and East Croydon
020 8680 8337
Auberge adopt a simple approach, using fresh ingredients combined with a little French inspiration to serve classic dishes for all. Ideal for a shopping lunch or an intimate evening out.

BATTERSEA SPICE
Indian

63 Battersea Bridge Road, Battersea, SW11 3AU
Nearest Station: Battersea Park
020 7978 6663
Providing the local neighbourhood and surrounding areas with high quality Indian and Bangladeshi cuisine. A well-regarded restaurant that serves fine food that captures exciting and authentic flavours.

BATTERSEA SPICE ORGANIC
Indian

344 Battersea Park Road, Battersea, SW11 3BY
Nearest Station: Clapham Junction
020 7223 2169
Organic Indian cuisine, covering all the favourites from the subcontinent.

BAYEE VILLAGE CHINESE
Chinese

24 High Street, Wimbledon Village, SW19 5DX
Nearest Station: Wimbledon
020 8947 3533
Spicy Szechuan dishes from the South West to classic Peking cuisine from the North, here you will find a wide range of Chinese meals that will have your mouth watering as soon as you step in the door.

BHARAT BHAVAN
Indian

10 Lower Addiscombe Road, Croydon, CR0 6AA
Nearest Station: East Croydon
020 8688 6239
The Bharat Bhavan is a traditional Indian restaurant that serves authentic South Indian dishes. It also has a wide selection of wines, spirits and beers.

BRASSERIE JAMES
French

47 Balham Hill, Clapham South, SW12 9DR
Nearest Station: Clapham South
020 8772 0057
Guests will love the luxuriousness of this evocative restaurant, which offers French classic dishes and modern European favourites. The raspberry and white chocolate mille-feuille is sensational.

BROADWAY TANDOORI
Indian

250-252 The Broadway, Wimbledon, SW19 1SB
Nearest Station: South Wimbledon
020 8542 7697
Large and small party sizes alike can enjoy the vast array of exquisite Indian dishes on offer in this wonderful restaurant. Daily happy hours and a delivery service are further highlights of this venue.

CAFÉ ROUGE
French

26 High St, Wimbledon Village, SW19 5BY
Nearest Station: Wimbledon
020 8944 5131
An attractive restaurant, a boulevard café or a Parisian-style wine bar; however you see Café Rouge, consistently excellent classic French dishes are always guaranteed.

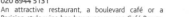

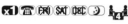

CAFÉ ROUGE
French

40 Abbeville Road, Clapham, SW4 9NG
Nearest Station: Clapham South
020 8673 3399
An attractive restaurant, a boulevard café or a Parisian-style wine bar; however you see Café Rouge, consistently excellent classic French dishes are always guaranteed.

CAFE ZIA
Indian

811-813 Wandsworth Road, Battersea, SW8 3JH
Nearest Station: Wandsworth Road
020 3202 0077
Distinctive dishes are offered with impeccable service. A blend of traditional ingredients are combined with contemporary recipes to create fresh and imaginative dishes.

CHANG THAI
Thai

136 Merton Road, Wimbledon, SW19 1EH
Nearest Station: South Wimbledon
020 8543 6213
Thai main dishes are accompanied by exceptional desserts, wines and beers. Monthly specials provide exciting alternatives to your favourite dishes.

Offer excludes the set menus.

CHILLI CHUTNEY
Indian/Punjabi

20 - 21 The High Parade, Streatham High Rd, SW16 1EX
Nearest Station: Streatham Hill
020 8696 0123
Enticing menus offering the most exciting Lahori dishes that marry authentic ingredients with traditional culinary techniques. Sample the imaginative creations of the Head Chef, such as the lamb saagwala.

Excludes 'King Prawn Sizzler'.

CHINA BOULEVARD ON THE RIVER
Chinese

1 The Boulevard, Smuggler's Way, Wandsworth, SW18 1DE
Nearest Station: Wandsworth Town
020 8874 9878
Sensational panoramic views of the river Thames can be enjoyed as you dine in this superbly spacious restaurant. Here you will be delighted at the wide range of both traditional and exotic dishes.

www.GOURMETSOCIETY.co.uk

CHIPSTEAD TANDOORI
Indian

32-34 Chipstead Station Parade, Chipstead, CR5 3TF
Nearest Station: Chipstead
01737 556 401
Offers tasty tandoori and balti dishes that have been drawing in regular guests for many years. Its convenient location makes it an ideal place to enjoy delicious curry after a busy day.

COAL GRILL + BAR
Mediterranean

5 The Crescent, The Broadway, Wimbledon, SW19 1QD
Nearest Station: Wimbledon
020 8947 8225
Savour fresh, delectable food and sample captivating cocktails, all delivered in a stylish and contemporary space, regularly changed and developed to produce fine culinary results.

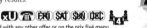

Not to be used with any other offer or on the prix fixé menu.

CRYSTAL PALACE TANDOORI
Indian

24 Weston Hill, Crystal Palace, SE19 1RX
Nearest Station: Crystal Palace
020 8761 1515
Renowned in South London as one of the finest Indian and Bangladeshi restaurants. A wide range of traditional dishes use only the freshest ingredients and free range meat and eggs.

CURRY CENTRE
Bangladeshi

167-169 High Street, Banstead, SM7 2NT
Nearest Station: Banstead
01737 362 648
Situated in a picturesque village on the outskirts of London, this restaurant offers authentic Bangladeshi dishes prepared with passion, experience and fine ingredients.

DALCHINI
Indo - Chinese

1340 London Road, Norbury, SW16 4DG
Nearest Station: Norbury
020 8764 0099
Guests will love the Hakka style of cooking used in the kitchen at Dalchini. Merging Oriental methods with Indian ingredients, the restaurant is proud of the successful, eclectic menu.

DALCHINI
Indo - Chinese

147 Arthur Road, Wimbledon, SW19 8AB
Nearest Station: Wimbledon Park
020 8947 5966
A successful pioneering restaurant offering Hakka cuisine. An exciting marriage of oriental techniques and Indian ingredients characterises the cuisine.

DONNA MARGHERITA
Italian

183 Lavander Hill, Clapham, SW11 5TE
Nearest Station: Clapham Junction
020 7228 2660
Donna Margherita brings Neapolitan cuisine to London with its Southern Italian influence, its menu offers a wide choice of exciting and unusual dishes with a fantastic atmosphere and friendly service.

GAZETTE
French

79 Riverside Plaza, Battersea, SW11 3SE
Nearest Station: Clapham Junction
020 7223 0999
With an extraordinary roster, bearing experience from a Michelin-starred restaurant and a host of other top venues, Gazette produces lucid, supremely accomplished haute cuisine in bright, open surrounds.

GAZETTE
French

1 Ramsden Road, Balham, SW12 8QX
Nearest Station: Balham
020 8772 1232
Classic, full-flavoured French brasserie with all the traditional, fulsome staples. A cordial, open environment that holds to the value of sharing food in company.

GIPSY MOTH
Carvery

The Colonades, Croydon, CR0 4RJ
Nearest Station: Waddon
0208 686 8923
One of the many Great British Carveries that provides the best of British food with a tempting modern twist. This family-friendly pub holds a charm and character all of its own.

Call beforehand on special event days.

GRAND UNION
American

26 Camberwell Grove, Camberwell, SE5 8RE
Nearest Station: Denmark Hill
020 3247 1001
With a classically stylish, welcoming ambience in the character-laden environs of Camberwell Grove, this restaurant dispatches generous plates of wholesome, wide-ranging bar and grill fare.

Not available Sunday lunch.

GRAND UNION
American

123 Acre Lane, Clapham, SW2 5UA
Nearest Station: Clapham North
020 7274 8794
In a coolly stylish ambience, this big restaurant packs out heateningly full plates of wholesome, wide-ranging bar and grill fare. Try the quirky setting of their tree house dining rooms.

Not available Sunday lunch.

HENRY J BEAN'S BAR & GRILL
American

153-161 The Broadway, Wimbledon, SW19 1NE
Nearest Station: Wimbledon
020 8543 5083
A unique brand that can best be described as a typical bar and grill. Simply classic American food complemented by a vast array of beverages, all served with flair in a vibrant and lively atmosphere.

INDIAN ROOM
Indian

59 Bedford Hill, Balham, SW12 1AD
Nearest Station: Balham
07931 132 766
Award-winning Indian restaurant serving delicious, flavoursome food. Feel guilt-free as you savour the scrumptious dishes which are created using a lower fat, lower oil style of cooking.

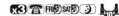

When booking restaurants always mention your GS membership.

ISLAND FUSION
Caribbean

57b Westow Hill, Crystal Palace, SE19 1TS
Nearest Station: Crystal Palace
020 8761 5544
Masterfully blending a mix of cultures, this innovative marriage of West Indian traditional and European modern is fresh, stimulating and sensual. Deliciously unique dining.

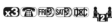

JACKSON'S
Caribbean

62 Clapham High St, Clapham, SW4 7UL
Nearest Station: Clapham North
07539 601 744
A little café with a big heart, this delightfully pleasant venue offers scrumptious Caribbean food for the soul. Try the jerk chicken and you won't be disappointed.

JOANNA'S
European

56 Westow Hill, Crystal Palace, SE19 1RX
Nearest Station: Crystal Palace
020 8670 4052
A well-loved restaurant where diners can enjoy stunning city views as they dine. Guests will love the irresistible treats that can be found on the breakfast, brunch and à la carte menus.

KERALA BHAVAN
Indian

16 London Road, West Croydon, CR0 2TA
Nearest Station: West Croydon
020 8688 6216
Exclusive South Indian restaurant specialising in the deliciously divine Kerala cuisine, which includes a vast array of vegetarian dishes. Home-cooked food is served to an appreciative and loyal clientèle.

KHANA PEENA
Indian

177-179 Brighton Road, Croydon, CR2 6EG
Nearest Station: South Croydon
020 8688 9123
The tastiness of the traditional Indian food has awarded this restaurant its popular reputation. Excellent hospitality guaranteed.

KHYBER
Indian

284 High Street, Croydon, CR0 1NG
Nearest Station: South Croydon
020 8681 6565
With a formidable reputation for high quality food, this restaurant proudly serves Indian cuisine at reasonable prices. The kitchen freshly grinds its own spices to ensure distinct flavour in every dish.

LA PERNELLA
Italian

470 Garratt Lane, Earlsfield, SW18 4HJ
Nearest Station: Earlsfield
07976 824 058
Offers a vast array of delicious pizzas complete with a variety of fresh toppings, alongside an assortment of other authentic dishes. All available to eat in or take away.

LAMBOURNE BAR & GRILL
British

263 The Broadway, Wimbledon, SW19 1SD
Nearest Station: South Wimbledon
020 8545 8661
A captivating vibrancy can be found in this popular bar and restaurant. Offers an impressive menu that strongly focuses on using local ingredients and seasonal produce.

Not available from 7pm on Saturdays.

LE BOUCHON BORDELAIS
French

5-9 Battersea Rise, Clapham, SW11 1HG
Nearest Station: Clapham Junction
020 7738 0307
The loyal following of this desirable French restaurant speaks for its outstanding ability to produce wonderful food in an authentic environment. A firm neighbourhood favourite.

LE CHARDON
French

32 Abbeville Road, Clapham, SW4 9NG
Nearest Station: Clapham South
020 8673 9300
The majestically decorated interior goes hand in hand with magnificent food at this benign French restaurant. Try the classic moules marinières or the tender tuna steak for an unforgettable treat.

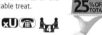

LOCALE BALHAM
Italian

225 Balham High Road, Balham, SW17 7BQ
Nearest Station: Tooting
020 8682 3553
Cool and collected Italian restaurant with all the classic dishes and flavours; hearty and flavourful pasta and risotto, and a line in beautifully seasoned meat and fish with smart accompaniments.

Not available with any other offer.

LOST SOCIETY
European

697 Wandsworth Road, Battersea, SW8 3JF
Nearest Station: Wandsworth Road
020 7652 6526
Innovative and accomplished cuisine combined with stylish, voluptuous deco surroundings in this lush, lively late night bar and restaurant.

MAMMA ROSA
Italian

Watermill Way, Merton Abbey Mills, SW19 2RD
Nearest Station: South Wimbledon
020 8545 0310
Located on the historic site of Merton Abbey Mills, Mamma Rosa is a fabulous Italian restaurant that is well worth the journey. Classic dishes to be enjoyed in a jovial atmosphere.

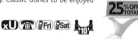

MISO
Oriental

103 - 105 High Street, Croydon, CR0 1QG
Nearest Station: East Croydon
020 8681 7688
Testament to its own success, Miso offers stir-fried noodles that arrive steaming, sizzling and sumptuous. Guests enjoy the nutritional values found in each dish, which enhance mind, body and soul.

MISO
Oriental
11/12 Suffolk House, George Street, Croydon, CR0 1PE
Nearest Station: East Croydon
020 8681 5084
Testament to its own success, Miso offers stir-fried noodles that arrive steaming, sizzling and sumptuous. Guests enjoy the nutritional values found in each dish, which enhance mind, body and soul.

MONTIEN THAI RESTAURANT
Thai
1078-1079 Whitgift Centre, Croydon, CR0 1UX
Nearest Station: East Croydon
020 8681 6601
Montien Thai features the best authentic Thai cuisine all cooked with the freshest ingredients and served by friendly staff in a truly traditional atmosphere.

Accepts large parties.

NINETEEN RESTAURANT AND BAR
Modern British
19 The High Parade, Streatham High Rd, SW16 1EX
Nearest Station: Streatham Hill
020 8835 8289
Welcome to Nineteen where you are treated like family, and where the cosy ambience is complemented by the smell of their delicious modern British cuisine. Superb quality right on your doorstep.

OUT OF THE BLUE
International
140 St Johns Hill, Battersea, SW11 1SL
Nearest Station: Wandsworth Town
020 7207 8548
A fashionable venue to match its trendy location, where an international theme inspires the atmosphere, food and drink on offer. The menu consists of contemporary dishes from six continents.

PASTA HOUSE RISTORANTE
Italian
20 Godstone Road, Caterham, CR3 6RA
Nearest Station: Caterham
01883 330 137
Wonderfully authentic, family-run pasta house with a pleasant clientèle and warm atmosphere. Choose from a variety of modern and traditional dishes all bursting with rich Italian flavour.

PIAF RESTAURANT CAFE BAR
Mediterranean
40 Wimbledon Hill, Wimbledon, SW19 7PA
Nearest Station: Wimbledon
020 8946 3823
Passionately prepared Mediterranean cuisine with an aim to deliver great value and truly appetising food. Offers a menu that blends classic and contemporary dishes with outstanding results.

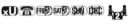

PIZZA METRO PIZZA
Italian
64 Battersea Rise, Battersea, SW11 1EQ
Nearest Station: Clapham Junction
020 7228 3812
A traditional Neapolitan restaurant producing divine pizzas and a wide range of pasta, fish, meat and desserts. 100% Italian ingredients are used, with pizzas made on an authentic wood-burning oven.

Not available Thursday

PLANET SPICE
Indian
88 Selsoon Park Road, Addington, Croydon, CR2 8ST
Nearest Station: Sanderstead
020 8651 3300
Expert chefs, with invaluable previous experience in Madras, delicately prepare dishes cooked in a contemporary style with the added zest of spice. Some of the most authentic cuisine possible.

PREZZO
Italian
26 Station Way, Cheam, SM3 8SQ
Nearest Station: Cheam
020 8643 7490
With a character all of its own, Prezzo oozes contemporary style and enduring charm. Signature pastas, stone-baked pizzas and classic Italian dishes promise a perfect dining choice for the whole family.

PRINCESS OF INDIA
Indian
10 Morden Court Parade, London Road, Merton, SM4 5HJ
Nearest Station: Morden
020 8646 8222
Come and enjoy an authentic restaurant where a selection of traditional Indian dishes are prepared for your pleasure, as well as delicious food for you to take away and dine in your own home.

PUKKA RESTAURANT
Indian
89 Streatham Hill, Streatham, SW2 4UD
Nearest Station: Streatham Hill
020 8671 8254
A warm welcome awaits you at the Pukka Brasserie. Guests will love the fantastically authentic Indian cuisine on offer, which can be fully enjoyed in pleasantly charming surroundings.

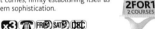

RADHA KRISHNA BHAVAN
Indian
86 Tooting High Street, Tooting, SW17 0RN
Nearest Station: Tooting Broadway
020 8682 0969
Passionate and flavourful food. Specialising in dishes from the north and south of India this restaurant delivers the finest curries, firmly establishing itself as a flagship of Eastern sophistication.

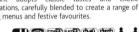

REDS BAR AND GRILL
Mediterranean
86 The Broadway, Wimbledon, SW19 1RQ
Nearest Station: Wimbledon
020 8540 8308
At the heart of a community, this impressive restaurant adopts classic tastes and exotic combinations, carefully blended to create a range of exciting menus and festive favourites.

RIVIERA RESTAURANT
Italian
31-32 Battesrea Square, Battersea, SW11 3RA
Nearest Station: Clapham Junction
020 7978 5395
Captures the flavours and scent of the Mediterranean, offering a wide range of contemporary and traditional dishes which reflect the flavour of Italian cuisine.

Gourmet Society discount applies to the à la carte menu

TABERNERS LOUNGE BAR *International*

28-30 St Georges Walk, Croydon, CR0 1YJ
020 8667 0800   Nearest Station: East Croydon

2FOR1 MAIN COURSE

Breathing new life into a long forgotten bar, the team behind Taberners are enjoying early success with their recently opened lounge bar and restaurant in Croydon.

When it functions as a restaurant, Taberners ensures diners don't go hungry, with hearty, no-nonsense meals using great produce and cooked with care. Sample the cow pie, chunky chips or 28 day-aged steak for an example. There are also a range of Caribbean inspired foods.

Diners can enjoy good value meals from rise and shine to the early hours of the morning – Taberners has a late night licence and transforms into a party venue several nights a week.

RODIZIO BRAZIL *Brazilian*
505 Garratt Lane, Earlsfield, SW18 4SW
Nearest Station: Earlsfield
020 8871 3875
Try the unique Brazilian barbecue way of flaming and serving skewered meats, sausage and poultry. Unlimited amounts of meat are specially marinated and grilled to perfection.

50% OFF FOOD

SD LOUNGE *Caribbean*
7A Station Rise, Tulse Hill, SE27 9BW
Nearest Station: Tulse Hill
020 8674 5501
In a vibrant but chilled-out venue well-known for its live music nights and a great place to enjoy a drink or two, you can eat excellent, down-home Caribbean-style food in a cool, bright interior.

25% OFF TOTAL

ROYAL GARDEN RESTAURANT *Chinese*
Shirley Hills Road, Croydon, CR0 5HQ
Nearest Station: South Croydon
020 8654 6491
A terrific restaurant offering a tranquil retreat in a stunningly unique location. Enjoy an exquisite Chinese feast of all of your favourites dishes in a place that is hard to leave.

25% OFF TOTAL

SPICELAND *Indian British*
212 London Road, Croydon, CR0 2TE
Nearest Station: West Croydon
020 8649 8895
Whether you enjoy your curry meek and mild or hot and spicy, Spiceland can accommodate every palate. Enjoy South Indian cuisine in the relaxed restaurant or in the warmth of your own home.

25% OFF TOTAL

SANTINI'S *Italian*
64 Godstone Road, Kenley, CR8 5AA
Nearest Station: Kenley
020 8668 2159
A slice of Italy. The returning customers indicate the high standards that can be found in both food and atmosphere at this delightful Italian restaurant.

25% OFF TOTAL

SREE KRISHNA *Indian*
192-194 Tooting High Street, Tooting, SW17 0SF
Nearest Station: Tooting Broadway
020 8672 4250
Experience the delights of South Indian cuisine, including vegetarian dishes and varieties such as the tantalising Karaikkudi regional specialities. Unique flavours and spices are infused into every dish.

2FOR1 MAIN COURSE

165

TANDOORI KNIGHTS
Indian

576 Wickham Rd, Croydon, CR0 8DN
Nearest Station: West Wickham
020 8777 0844

Diners faithful to curry dishes flock to this restaurant's doors to indulge in deliciously tasty Indian cuisine. Traditional favourites and rarer North Indian delicacies appear on the menu.

TANDOORI MAHAL
Indian

35 Abbotsbury Road, Morden, SM4 5LJ
Nearest Station: Morden
020 8648 2926

Enjoy many rich and delectable dishes at this well-established and award-winning restaurant that provides patrons with great hospitality and freshly prepared, authentic and wholesome Indian food.

THAI VENUE
Thai

200 Brighton Road, Coulsdon, CR5 2NF
Nearest Station: Smitham
020 8763 9626

A well-regarded, accommodating Thai restaurant that serves excellent food in satisfyingly comprehensive portions at a great price. Simple, sumptuously tasty, and thoroughly effective.

THE BELLE VUE
British

1 Clapham Common Southside, Clapham, SW4 7AA
Nearest Station: Clapham Common
020 7498 9473

Great little low-key pub in Clapham Common where sizeable portions of thoroughgoing, filling fare will leave you sated after one of those lazy, cosy lunches or an evening retreat to the sanctum.

THE BELMONT
Carvery

Brighton Road, Sutton, SM2 5SU
Nearest Station: Belmont
020 8642 9799

One of the many Great British Carveries that offers the much-loved classic with a modern twist. Feast on the best of British food at this beautifully relaxed ivy-covered pub.

Call beforehand on special event days.

THE BES BBQ RESTAURANT
Mediterranean

1064 London Road, Thornton Heath, CR7 7ND
Nearest Station: Norbury
020 8665 1115

Serving a collection of eastern Mediterranean food, this restaurant is a welcoming local place with dishes filled with flavour.

THE BUTCHER AND GRILL
British

39-41 Parkgate Road, Battersea, SW11 4NP
Nearest Station: Battersea Park
020 7924 3999

A unique combination of a modern butcher's shop and informal restaurant. Though there are fish and vegetarian dishes available, steaks are the priority and quality is guaranteed. Awarded 1 AA Rosette.

THE CHILLI ROOM
Indian

24 South End, Croydon, CR0 1DN
Nearest Station: South Croydon
020 8686 4422

Fine Indian chefs create inspirational dishes from all over India. Food is freshly prepared, and caters for all tastes by bringing new and exotic cuisines to the table. An authentic Indian experience.

THE GOOD COMPANIONS
Traditional English Fare

Limpsfield Road, Warlingham, CR6 9RH
Nearest Station: Upper Warlingham
020 8657 6655

Friendly family-run pub with a warm and welcoming atmosphere. The excellent restaurant serves a high standard of traditional pub food from noon each day, which includes an extensive bar menu.

THE LOST ANGEL
Modern British

339 Battersea Park Road, Battersea, SW11 4LS
Nearest Station: Battersea Park
020 7622 2112

A lively and highly enjoyable atmosphere is perfect for any day of the week. Sundays could not be better spent than here, where famous roasts and live music make this an ideal place to end the week.

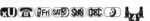

THE MANSION
Modern British

255 Gipsy Road, Tulse Hill, SE27 9QY
Nearest Station: Gipsy Hill
020 8761 9016

A menu perfect for every British food lover, here old favourites and daily specials are available for everyone to enjoy. The kitchen makes excellent use of Barnsley chops, Ruby Red beef and fresh fish.

THE OVAL TANDOORI
Indian

64A - 66 Brixton Road, Oval, SW9 6BP
Nearest Station: Oval
020 7582 1415

Good Food Guide-recommended restaurant serving contemporary Asian cuisine. Renowned for its tailor-made dishes to suit even the most temperamental of palates.

THE STAG INDIAN RESTAURANT
Indian

96 Westbridge Rd, Battersea, SW11 3PH
Nearest Station: Battersea Park
020 7223 7516

A carefully selected menu draws on some of the most popular Indian dishes from the subcontinent. Marvel over the finest assortment of spices and high quality meats that are used in the kitchen.

THE THAI JASMINE
Thai

318 High Street, Sutton, SM1 1PR
Nearest Station: Sutton Common
020 8642 2666

With a highly experienced Thai chef manning the kitchen you will not be disappointed by the range of dishes and variety of tastes available. The North Eastern Thai dishes are spectacular.

When booking restaurants always mention your GS membership

THE THREE BRIDGES
English/Gastro pub

153 Battersea Park Road, Battersea, SW8 4BX
Nearest Station: Battersea Park
020 7720 0204
Stand-out gastro-pub cuisine, served elegantly and with acuity, and prepared such that the flavours of the superb produce are allowed to speak for themselves. A sophisticated jewel of a restaurant.

THE UNION TAVERN
Italian

146 Camberwell New Road, Camberwell, SE5 0RR
Nearest Station: Oval
020 7091 0447
Delicious stone-baked pizzas, tasty salads and wonderful pasta dishes are all available in the midst of Victorian surroundings. Why not sample the lively salsa classes held in the ball room.

THE WATERMILL REST. & GRILL
European

12 Watermill Way, Merton Abbey Mills, SW19 2RD
Nearest Station: South Wimbledon
020 8542 1236
Set against a historical backdrop, this is a perfect place to start the day with breakfast or end it with an evening meal. If perusing over local history has tired you out, relax over a home-made lunch.

TIGER TIGER
International

14 - 16 Croydon High Street, Croydon, CR0 1GT
Nearest Station: East Croydon
020 8662 4949
Situated in the heart of Croydon's high street, Tiger Tiger offers everything all under one roof. Head to one of the five bars for casual drinks, or to the restaurant if you fancy a bite to eat.

TU CHICAS
Mexican

12 Leopold Road, Wimbledon, SW19 7BD
Nearest Station: Wimbledon Park
020 8946 4300
Experience a taste of Mexico at Tu Chicas, where you can find tasty food and fantastically flamboyant cocktails. The closest you can get to Mexico without leaving the country!

VIVA GOA
Indian

24 Westow Hill, Crystal Palace, SE19 1RX
Nearest Station: Crystal Palace
020 8761 1515
Bright and vivacious restaurant that serves the sumptuous amalgam of flavours characterising Goan cuisine; with warm and attentive service and stylish presentation, it's a place to savour.

WILLIE GUNN WINE BAR
European

422 Garrett Lane, Earlsfield, SW18 4NW
Nearest Station: Earlsfield
020 8946 7773
Here the produce is sourced and hand-picked locally to ensure that the European menu is always of highest quality. Customers are invited to sample a variety of different wines.

A TASTE OF MCCLEMENTS
European

8 Station Approach, Kew, TW9 3QB
Nearest Station: Kew Gardens
020 8940 6617
Excellent food prepared to the highest of standards, complete with a popular tasting menu with 18 dishes, all beautifully presented and coupled with by-the-glass matching wine suggestions.

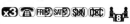

AL FORNO
Italian

1-2-3A Townsend Parade, Kingston upon Thames, KT1 1LY
Nearest Station: Kingston
020 8439 7555
Wholesome Italian cooking in a comfortable and relaxing atmosphere. Whether it's a spot of lunch, a family gathering or a romantic dinner, all diners are treated to a truly perfect experience.

BAR 191
Spanish

191 Worple Road, Raynes Park, SW20 8RE
Nearest Station: Raynes Park
020 8944 5533
A wonderful tapas bar that aspires to authenticity, and achieves it with flair. Both light dishes and hearty meals are on offer so you'll be guaranteed to find something to suit your appetite.

BENGAL CLIPPER
Indian

7 Temple Market, Queens Road, Weybridge, KT13 2DL
Nearest Station:
01932 844 488
Traditional, flavoursome dishes are created by chefs who draw their inspiration from across the subcontinent. The Sunday buffet is a great way to sample many dishes, such as the creamy murgh sagrana.

BLADES
Italian

94 Lower Richmond Road, Putney, SW15 1LL
Nearest Station: Putney
020 8789 0869
An open grill is the centrepiece of this convivial restaurant. Chefs prepare your food to taste as you nibble on delicious antipasti with a refreshing glass of wine.

BROADWAY BAR CAFE
British

43-51 Tolworth Broadway, Tolworth, KT6 7DW
Nearest Station: Tolworth
020 8399 7698
Contemporary and stylish café bar that shows live sporting events and serves straight up, straight down tasty and hearty pub food, along with good and spicy fresh curries.

167

CAFE MASALA — *Indian*
113 Kew Road, Richmond, TW9 2PN
Nearest Station: Richmond
020 8948 0055
A rich variety of Indian dishes are on offer at this wonderful restaurant. Accommodating staff are eager to ensure every guest has a memorable dining experience.

CAFÉ ROUGE — *French*
Portsmouth Rd, Esher, KT10 9AD
Nearest Station:
01372 465 550
An attractive restaurant, a boulevard café or a Parisian-style wine bar; however you see Café Rouge, consistently excellent classic French dishes are always guaranteed.

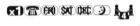

CAFÉ ROUGE — *French*
85 Queens Road, Weybridge, KT13 9UG
Nearest Station:
01932 851 777
An attractive restaurant, a boulevard café or a Parisian-style wine bar; however you see Café Rouge, consistently excellent classic French dishes are always guaranteed.

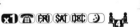

CAFÉ ROUGE — *French*
96-98 High Street, Epsom, KT19 8BR
Nearest Station: Epsom Downs
01372 749 131
An attractive restaurant, a boulevard café or a Parisian-style wine bar; however you see Café Rouge, consistently excellent classic French dishes are always guaranteed.

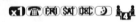

CAFÉ ROUGE — *French*
200 Putney Bridge Road, Putney, SW15 2NA
Nearest Station: Putney
020 8788 4257
An attractive restaurant, a boulevard café or a Parisian-style wine bar; however you see Café Rouge, consistently excellent classic French dishes are always guaranteed.

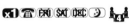

CAFÉ ROUGE — *French*
85 Strand on the Green, Kew, W4 3PU
Nearest Station: Kew Bridge
020 8995 6575
An attractive restaurant, a boulevard café or a Parisian-style wine bar; however you see Café Rouge, consistently excellent classic French dishes are always guaranteed.

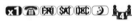

CAFFE PICCOLO — *Italian*
10 High Street, Esher, KT10 9RT
Nearest Station:
01372 465 592
With a warm and welcoming ambience and terrific Italian cuisine, this restaurant offers the perfect venue to enjoy an evening of great food with your favourite company. Children are well catered for.

CAMMASAN ORIENTAL — *Chinese*
Unit 8, Wadbrook St, Charter Quay, Kingston, KT1 1HR
Nearest Station: Kingston
020 8549 3510
Dine in the comfortable Meinton Room, where mouth-watering noodle dishes, curries and salads can be enjoyed. On the banks of the Hogsmill Creek, the outdoor terrace is an idyllic place to soak up the sun.

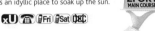

CHEZ LALEE — *Mexican*
6 Griffin Centre, Kingston upon Thames, KT1 1JT
Nearest Station: Kingston
020 8547 3826
Located in Kingston, Chez Lalee serves a wide selection of Mexican dishes including fajitas, burritos and enchiladas. Deliciously prepared and presented food, with choices to suit every palate.

CHINA ROYAL — *Chinese*
110 Canbury Park Road, Kingston upon Thames, KT2 6JZ
Nearest Station: Kingston
020 8541 1988
A charming restaurant serving scrumptiously tasty Chinese cuisine. Guests will enjoy the small cosiness of the interior and the warmly welcoming ambience.

CIRRIK RICHMOND — *Mediterranean*
94 Kew Road, Richmond, TW9 2PQ
Nearest Station: Richmond
020 8940 0033
Turkish cuisine at its finest with authentic recipes and dishes inspired by the great Ottoman Empire, combining fresh aromatic spices and herbs, cooked on an open charcoal grill.

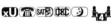

CITIZEN SMITH — *Pizza*
160 Putney High St, Putney, SW15 1RS
Nearest Station: Putney
020 8780 2235
Offering a menu based around its pizza oven, the quirky and tasty cuisine brings a unique feel to Citizen Smith. The fun and friendly service complemented by the delicious food guarantee a great meal.

COCHIN BRASSERIE — *Indian*
193 Lower Richmond Rd, Putney, SW15 1HJ
Nearest Station: Putney
020 8785 6004
Named after a vibrant city in Southwest India, the cuisine is characterised by a blend of spices and coconut. The traditional methods and soft taste of the meat and fish offer a delicious combination.

DEEA — *Bangladeshi*
145-147 Richmond Road, Kingston upon Thames, KT2 5BZ
Nearest Station: Kingston
020 8974 5388
Whilst striving to improve ancient recipes that have been handed down through generations, the kitchen ensures it maintains all of the traditional flavours that make each dish sumptuous and delicious.

Sign up to our newsletter for latest restaurants, offers and more

EVEREST
Indian

14 Ross Parade, Wallington, SM6 8QG
Nearest Station: Wallington
020 8296 6669
Locally renowned for crafting exceptional food at very good prices, using recipes and spices from all over the rich and diverse Indian subcontinent. Truly a jewel in the crown.

FISHWORKS RICHMOND
Seafood

13-19 The Market, The Square, Richmond, TW9 1EA
Nearest Station: Richmond
020 8948 5965
A sleek seafood restaurant with its own fish counter where you can buy fresh from a full cohort; vivid, classic dishes populate the menu and the restaurant is serenely ensconced just off the High Street.

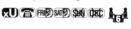

FRANKIE'S EXPRESS
Italian

263 Putney Bridge Road, Putney, SW15 2PU
Nearest Station: Putney
020 8780 3366
Great food at reasonable prices, with unbelievably glamorous yet authentic décor. The sumptuous traditional menu will delight all lovers of Italian cuisine, especially the prosciutto and salumi platters.

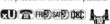

GLISTENING WATERS
Caribbean

5 Ferry Lane, Ferry Quays, Brentford, TW8 0AT
Nearest Station: Brentford
020 8758 1616
Bright and smart in atmosphere, this restaurant serves dishes that draw on the bouncy mix of herbs and spices that characterise Caribbean cuisine, with distinctive and contemporary verve.

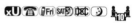
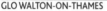

GLO WALTON-ON-THAMES
Pan Asian

Unit 6, The Heart Centre, Walton-On-Thames, KT12 1GH
Nearest Station:
01932 222 004
Contemporary, casual eating. A place for guests to relax in style with good food and great company. Indulge your palate with some fine pan-Asian cuisine and enjoy this fresh dining experience.

GOLDEN CURRY
Indian

19 Hampton Court Parade, East Molesey, KT8 9HB
Nearest Station: Hampton Court
020 8979 4358
Utilising recipes past down from generations, the dishes created here are traditionally cooked and truly authentic. Menu includes specials, with a popular Sunday buffet and a comprehensive drinks list.

GRAND UNION
American

11 London Road, Twickenham, TW1 3SX
Nearest Station: Twickenham
020 8892 2925
With a classically stylish ambience and a buzzing music scene of a Twickenham evening, this restaurant dispatches hearteningly full plates of fulsome, wide-ranging bar and grill fare.

Not available Sunday lunch.

GREEN WATER
Asian Fusion

48 Guildford Street, Chertsey, KT16 9BE
Nearest Station:
01932 569 133
A fusion of Eastern cuisines goes into every dish with the Head Chef crafting sublime food using his wealth of culinary experience, including seafood and vegetarian options. Takeaway service available.

HAMPTONS HOT STONE
Modern European

2-6 Bridge Road, Hampton Court, East Molesey, KT8 9HA
Nearest Station: Hampton Court
020 8979 7676
Sleek and chic, styled in soft contrasting tones, The Hamptons looks across the river at Hampton Court Palace. With its distinctive hot stone cooking technique, it serves fresh-flavoured, healthy cuisine.

HARI KRISHNA
Indian

20 Bridge Road, Hampton Court, East Molesey, KT8 9HA
Nearest Station: Hampton Court
020 8979 1531
A relaxed venue boasting some of the finest and most authentic South Indian cuisine. Serving classical dishes in the originally intended way, ensuring they are light, healthy yet undeniably delicious.

ISLAND
British

Holiday Inn Brentford Lock, High Street, Brentford, TW8 8JZ
Nearest Station: Brentford
020 8232 2000
Relax and unwind as you dine in modern luxury at this fine hotel restaurant. Delightful contemporary cuisine can be enjoyed by the beautiful waterside of the Grand Union Canal.

JAIPUR
Indian

90 The Broadway, Surbiton, KT6 7HT
Nearest Station: Tolworth
020 8399 9165
A classic Indian restaurant serving tasty and authentic Indian food, from traditional favourites to more unknown yet delicious regional specialities. Tantalising cuisine cooked to perfection.

JIMMY SPICES
Multi-Cuisine

1 Derby Square, Epsom, KT19 8AG
Nearest Station: Epsom Downs
01372 748 467
The ultimate destination for food lovers, pioneering multi-cuisine dining with an ambitious and sumptuous menu. Whether you prefer Indian, Thai, Italian or Chinese food, come here and be catered for.

JOY
Indian

37 Brighton Road, Surbiton, KT6 5LR
Nearest Station: Surbiton
020 8390 3988
A gastronomic taste of India's fabulous culinary regions. Using the finest ingredients and authentic recipes, Joy has become the byword for high quality Indian food set in a contemporary environment.

www.gourmetsociety.co.uk

KHYBER PASS
Indian

54 Terrace Road, Walton-On-Thames, KT12 2SA
Nearest Station:
01932 225 670
Feast on classic flavours and be filled with spiced aromas from a menu of favourite dishes and divine chef specialities. Everything you want from an Indian restaurant and takeaway.

KINGSTON LODGE HOTEL
Brasserie

94 Kingston Hill, Kingston upon Thames, KT2 7NP
Nearest Station: Norbiton
020 8541 4481
Experienced chefs give you the special treatment at this fine Brook group hotel restaurant, showcasing a wide choice of expertly prepared dishes with an array of fine wines to complement the divine food.

LA BUVETTE
French

6 Church Walk, Richmond, TW9 1SN
Nearest Station: Richmond
020 8940 6264
A passionate kitchen team that is dedicated to creating well-researched menus and regional French cooking. Enjoy classical dishes such as onglet steaks, scallops and escargots. Awarded 1 AA Rosette.

LA VERANDA RISTORANTE
Italian

19A The Parade, Beynon Road, Carshalton, SM5 3RL
Nearest Station: Carshalton
020 8647 4370
A well-established Italian restaurant founded by two brothers who have worked hard to ensure high quality food and excellent service always emerges at the top of the restaurant's agenda.

RECOMMEND A FRIEND
see page 18

LAYLA RESTAURANT
Lebanese

110 High Street, Esher, KT10 9QL
Nearest Station:
01372 462 333
Taste the exotic flavour of Eastern spice and enjoy its fusion with European sophistication. The evocative décor creates a sensuous atmosphere in which to enjoy multi-course feasts and champagne cocktails.

LE CHIEN QUI FUME
French

107 Walton Road, East Molesey, KT8 0DR
Nearest Station: Hampton Court
020 8979 7150
Influenced by the beauty of a similarly named Parisian restaurant, the owners of this wonderful establishment have a comparable attitude towards high quality food and amiable service.

Closed on Sundays

LE PETIT NANTAIS
French

41 Bridge Road, Hampton Court, East Molesey, KT8 9ER
Nearest Station: Hampton Court
07796 266 006
A well-established traditional bistro that will utterly transport you to the heart of France itself. The beautiful cuisine will blow you away. The fillet steak, in particular, comes highly recommended.

 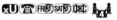

LIME LEAVES FUSION
Malaysian

60-62 Coombe Road, Kingston upon Thames, KT2 7AE
Nearest Station: Norbiton
020 8974 6638
Here you can enjoy the spice and season of classic Southeast Asian food. Building on his own extensive experience, owner Richard Liew puts firm emphasis on eclectic, piquant recipes from across the region.

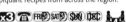 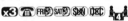

LITTLE BENGAL RESTAURANT
Indian/ Nepalese

45 Fulham High Street, Putney Bridge, SW6 3JJ
Nearest Station: Putney Bridge
020 7371 7839
A fun, friendly Bengali restaurant whose menu isn't all clod-hopping curries but features instead delicately and diversely flavoured, skilfully and imaginatively prepared local specialities.

LITTLE ITALY
Italian

2 Old London Road, Kingston upon Thames, KT2 6SN
Nearest Station: Kingston
020 8547 2133
Little Italy is situated at the end of the high street and is a reliably good Italian restaurant serving up all the classic pasta, pizza and risotto dishes diners love.

LOCH FYNE
Seafood

175 Hampton Road, Twickenham, TW2 5NG
Nearest Station: Fulwell
020 8255 6222
From the roadside oyster bar that once was, Loch Fyne restaurants now successfully inject energy and passion into great food and wonderful flavours, whilst ensuring their seafood is sustainably sourced.

LOCH FYNE
Seafood

17 Portsmouth Street, Cobham, KT11 1JF
Nearest Station:
01932 586 010
From the roadside oyster bar that once was, Loch Fyne restaurants now successfully inject energy and passion into great food and wonderful flavours, whilst ensuring their seafood is sustainably sourced.

MARQUIS OF GRANBY
Carvery

Portsmouth Road, Esher, KT10 9AL
Nearest Station:
020 8398 3815
One of the many Great British Carvery pubs that offers the classic feast for you to enjoy. Situated across the river from Hampton Court, guests can expect to feel comfortable and well looked after.

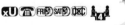   

Call beforehand on special event days.

When booking restaurants always mention your GS membership

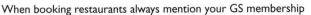

MARZANO
Pizza

53 Northcote Road, Clapham, SW11 1NJ
Nearest Station: Clapham Junction
020 7228 8860
Serving a variety of popular Italian dishes in a warm and welcoming environment, with a menu offering diners a deluxe range of pasta, pizza, and classic meat and fish dishes.

2FOR1
MAIN COURSE

Must mention GS on arrival. Not in conjunction with any other offer.

MISO
Oriental

11/13 Petersham Road, Richmond, TW10 6UH
Nearest Station: Richmond
020 8332 2778
Testament to its own success, Miso offers stir-fried noodles that arrive steaming, sizzling and sumptuous. Guests enjoy the nutritional values found in each dish, which enhance mind, body and soul.

2FOR1
MAIN COURSE

MONGOLIAN GRILL
Mongolian

29 North Street, Old Town, Clapham, SW4 0HJ
Nearest Station: Clapham Common
020 7498 4448
Drawing on the full flavours of traditional Mongolian cuisine, this restaurant offers warm, comforting and filling meals for the winter and a lighter touch in the summer. A unique, welcoming place to eat.

50%OFF
FOOD

À la carte menu only

NEW WORLD
Chinese

1 Wrythe Lane, Carshalton, SM5 1AG
Nearest Station: St. Helier
020 8644 0078
Experience authentic flavour and indulge in finely crafted Chinese cuisine, feasting on an exemplary selection of delicious modern and traditional dishes, each influenced by the country's varying regions.

25%OFF
TOTAL

NORBITON & DRAGON
Thai/British

16 Clifton Road, Kingston upon Thames, KT2 6PW
Nearest Station: Norbiton
020 8546 1951
A classic pub with a delicious Thai menu consisting of authentic dishes and an extensive range of beverages. Hunt down this hidden Dragon pub, as this local favourite is well worth it.

25%OFF
TOTAL

ORGAN & DRAGON
Thai/British

65 London Road, Ewell, KT17 2BL
Nearest Station: Ewell West
020 8393 2242
This charismatic Dragon venue proves that it's possible to serve delicious Thai food in a British pub. Offers guests exquisite traditional dishes that appeal to both the adventurous and the uninitiated.

25%OFF
TOTAL

PALAZZO
Italian

98 Walton Road, East Molesey, KT8 0DL
Nearest Station: Hampton Court
020 8979 5577
Palazzos's family owners showcase their Southern Italian passion for food and hospitality at this friendly restaurant. Their aim is to offer a warm welcome and delicious food, and they duly deliver.

25%OFF
TOTAL

PALLAVI SOUTH INDIAN RESTAURANT
Indian

3 Cross Deep, Heath Rd, Twickenham, TW1 4QJ
Nearest Station: Twickenham
020 8892 2345
South Indian cuisine so superbly tasty it has legions of devoted fans lining up to experience it. Dishes are mainly made up of rice, lentils and semolina, and fish features in many non-vegetarian dishes.

2FOR1
MAIN COURSE

RECOMMEND A FRIEND

see page 18

PIZZA AL ROLLO
Italian

20 Hill Street, Richmond, TW9 1TN
Nearest Station: Richmond
020 8940 8951
Pizza Al Rollo will have pizza lovers in a twist. Famous for its delicious by-the-yard thin-crust authentic pizzas and bonhomie, it is a popular venue that also serves other fine Italian classics.

2FOR1
MAIN COURSE

Must mention GS on arrival. Not in conj. with any other offer.

PREZZO
Italian

The Rotunda, Clarence St, Kingston, KT14 1QJ
Nearest Station: Kingston
020 8549 8687
With a character all of its own, Prezzo oozes contemporary style and enduring charm. Signature pastas, stone-baked pizzas and classic Italian dishes promise a perfect dining choice for the whole family.

2FOR1
MAIN COURSE

PREZZO
Italian

44 Church Street, Weybridge, KT13 8DP
Nearest Station:
01932 844 430
With a character all of its own, Prezzo oozes contemporary style and enduring charm. Signature pastas, stone-baked pizzas and classic Italian dishes promise a perfect dining choice for the whole family.

2FOR1
MAIN COURSE

PREZZO
Italian

109-113 High Street, Shepperton, TW17 9BL
Nearest Station:
01932 269 006
With a character all of its own, Prezzo oozes contemporary style and enduring charm. Signature pastas, stone-baked pizzas and classic Italian dishes promise a perfect dining choice for the whole family.

2FOR1
MAIN COURSE

PREZZO
Italian

Unit 2 Brentford Lock, High Street, Brentford, TW8 8LF
Nearest Station: Brentford
020 8758 0998
With a character all of its own, Prezzo oozes contemporary style and enduring charm. Signature pastas, stone-baked pizzas and classic Italian dishes promise a perfect dining choice for the whole family.

2FOR1
MAIN COURSE

Q VERDE
Mediterranean

291 Sandycombe Road, Kew, TW9 3LU
Nearest Station: Kew Gardens
020 8332 2882
This beautiful family-owned restaurant is one of Kew's best kept secrets, with a rich flavourful menu to suit everyone's taste, complemented by an extensive and well-chosen wine list.

REGATTA
International

Holiday Inn Shepperton, Felix Lane, Shepperton, TW17 8NP
Nearest Station:
01932 899 988
Enjoy a peaceful garden setting close to Heathrow Airport at the Holiday Inn London Shepperton hotel. Relax and dine in the contemporary Regatta Restaurant that showcases dishes from around the world.

1 card per table.

RIVERSIDE VEGETARIA
Vegetarian

64 High Street, Kingston upon Thames, KT1 1HN
Nearest Station: Kingston
020 8546 7992
Experience a culinary trip around the world with a cosmopolitan menu consisting of a wide variety of specialised vegetarian, gluten- and wheat-free dishes. One of Britain's best vegetarian restaurants.

ROCOCO
English/Gastro pub

54 High Street, Kingston upon Thames, KT1 1HN
Nearest Station: Kingston
020 8549 3333
Unique in being one of the few remaining family-run restaurants still alive and cooking, they pride themselves in serving fresh, simple and authentic Italian food to diners alongside full riverside views.

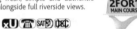

RUPALI
Indian

376 Malden Road, Worcester Park, KT4 7NL
Nearest Station: Worcester Park
0208 330 3046
However you enjoy your curry, this authentic Indian restaurant offers something to suit every palate. Traditional favourite dishes appear alongside house specialities.

SAN MARCO RESTAURANT & BAR
Italian/ Mediterranean

5 Ferry Lane, Brentford, TW8 0AT
Nearest Station: Brentford
020 8758 2777
Come and sample fine Italian food, freshly prepared and beautifully presented. Enjoy authentic, homely tastes in every dish on the ranging menu, but leave space for one of the many mouth-watering desserts.

SATORI SUSHI
Japanese

The Rotunda, Clarence Street, Kingston, KT1 1QJ
Nearest Station: Kingston
020 8546 5533
The dexterous abilities of the chef provide every guest with a memorable dining experience. Watch with anticipation as your sushi is freshly prepared in front of you.

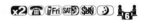

SHAHEE MAHAL
Indian

101 Walton Road, East Molesey, KT8 0DR
Nearest Station: Hampton Court
020 8979 0011
Step into this palace of a restaurant which insists on providing Indian and Bangladeshi dishes to a first-class standard, living up to its royal title.

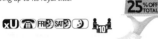

SHANTI TANDOORI
Indian

93 Queen Road, Weybridge, KT13 9UQ
Nearest Station:
01932 821 940
The fine selection of tasty Indian and Bangladeshi dishes have provided this popular restaurant with an admirable local reputation. Balti specialities are not to be missed.

SHEHNAI INDIAN RESTAURANT
Indian

9 Craddocks Parade, Ashtead, KT21 1QL
Nearest Station:
01372 273 818
A menu offering more than the typical Indian restaurant, the large variety of lamb, chicken, duck, mutton and fish dishes provide all guests with an extensive choice. A buffet is available on Sundays.

SRI KRISHNA INN
Indian

332 Kingston Road, Ewel, KT19 0DT
Nearest Station: Stoneleigh
020 8393 0445
A delightful Indian restaurant where unusual South Indian dishes, breads and pancakes are served by amiable staff who will enhance your enjoyment. Try the cashew nut pakoda for a real treat.

SWAGAT
Indian

86 Hill Rise, Richmond, TW10 6UB
Nearest Station: Richmond
020 8940 7557
Fresh, contemporary and traditional Indian cuisine at its best. Experience extravagant flavours and original spices across the menu, while the extensive wine list incorporates a selection of champagnes.

TACUBA
Mexican

10 Bedford Hill, Balham, SW12 9RG
Nearest Station: Balham
020 8673 5394
Feast on delicious beef tacos in this fabulously stylish Mexican restaurant and bar. Sip on a fresh fruit cocktail and indulge in delicious dishes that originate from all over Mexico.

Gourmet Society discount applies to the à la carte menu

THAI DIVINE
Thai
5 Ross Parade, Wallington, SM6 8QG
Nearest Station: Wallington
020 8773 2002
Traditional and authentic Thai cuisine in all its glory; a restaurant that prides itself on its attention to detail and its airy, bright dining space.

2FOR1 3 COURSES

THAI ON THAMES
Thai
48 Old London Road, Kingston upon Thames, KT2 6QF
Nearest Station: Kingston
020 8541 0301
Warmly lit dining space playing home to a range of classic, authentic Thai dishes across three menus: standard, noodle and vegetarian. Fresh, vibrant dishes burst with tang and taste.

2FOR1 2 COURSES

THAI UPON THAMES
Thai
346 Richmond Road, East Twickenham, TW1 2DU
Nearest Station: St. Margarets
020 8892 6808
Classic style to be enjoyed in the most intimately cosy of settings. Outstanding Thai dishes have been replicated and recreated by the Head Chef, such as the amazingly tasty Goong Phu Kao Fai.

50%OFF FOOD

THE GOAT
Carvery
47 Upper Halliford, Shepperton, TW17 8RX
Nearest Station:
01932 782 415
One of the many Great British Carveries that offers classic food with a modern twist. This charming pub has won the heart of many locals with it real ales, great food and friendly service.

2FOR1 MAIN COURSE

Call beforehand on special event days.

THE GRANGE
Pan Asian
Beddington Park, London Rd, Wallington, SM6 7BT
Nearest Station: Hackbridge
020 8773 8195
A menu that accommodates everything from Continental to Indo-Chinese cuisine. Globally inspired dishes make use of the freshest ingredients.

2FOR1 MAIN COURSE

THE ITALIAN TASTE
Italian
44 Victoria Road, Surbiton, KT6 4JL
Nearest Station: Surbiton
020 8241 2105
Authentic Italian food served in a relaxed and pleasant atmosphere. Established for 11 years, the chefs here prepare beautiful fresh dishes including a fantastic fish selection.

25%OFF TOTAL

THE MOGUL
Indian
66 Terrace Road, Walton-On-Thames, KT12 2SA
Nearest Station:
01932 223 319
Popular with the locals, authentic Indian dishes are created with care and delivered efficiently. The relaxed, informal atmosphere makes this a wonderful place to enjoy your favourite Indian cuisine.

2FOR1 MAIN COURSE

THE OLD FIRE STATION
British
55 High Street, Brentford, TW8 0AH
Nearest Station: Brentford
020 8568 5999
Start your night off with one of the famous flamed mojitos that will truly set your evening alight. Tender steaks and scrumptious sticky toffee puddings will have you coming back for more.

2FOR1 MAIN COURSE

THE RAJ INDIAN CUISINE
Indian
163 Ewell Road, Surbiton, KT6 6AW
Nearest Station: Surbiton
020 8390 0251
Along with the wonderfully authentic Indian meals, the restaurant provides you with a special history behind your chosen dish, enriching your knowledge of Indian haute cuisine.

2FOR1 MAIN COURSE

À la carte menu only.

RECOMMEND A FRIEND
see page 18

TOPGOLF SURREY
American
Moated Farm Drive, Addlestone, KT15 2DW
Nearest Station:
01932 858 551
What better way to top off your game of golf than with a fantastic meal or a round of celebratory drinks? Head to the Bayview Café and Bar where you can find a variety of food available all day long.

50%OFF FOOD

VARANASI CHEFS
Indian
142 Battersea High Street, Battersea, SW11 3JR
Nearest Station: Clapham Junction
020 7228 3145
A stylish Battersea restaurant that endeavours to bring the cooking tradition of Baranasi to South London. An exotic, aromatic and flavourful menu offers up subtle and sumptuous, varied dishes.

50%OFF FOOD

VOLARE
Italian
4 Woodthorpe Road, Ashford, TW15 2RY
Nearest Station:
01784 242 769
Charmingly traditional, this award-winning Italian restaurant produces the heartiest family dishes. Specialising in seafood, some of the best dishes are located on the popular à la carte menu.

2FOR1 MAIN COURSE

1 card per table. À la carte menu only.

WOODLANDS PARK HOTEL
British
Oak Room, Woodlands Ln. Cobham, KT11 3QB
Nearest Station:
0845 072 7581
An elegant Hand Picked Hotels restaurant that offering a luxury dining experience. Ornate panelling and dark oak furnishings provide an intimate environment, perfect for a romantic meal. 1 AA Rosette.

25%OFF TOTAL

ZANDER'S
International

23 Cheam Common Road, Worcester Park, KT4 8TL
Nearest Station: Worcester Park
020 8330 3000
Cool and calm, intimate ambience in this neat little restaurant near Worcester Park station; you'll enjoy well-conceived, simply cooked dishes and an accommodating location.

West

AMUSE BOUCHE FULHAM
British

51 Parsons Green Lane, Fulham, SW6 4JA
Nearest Station: Parsons Green
020 7371 8517
Canapés and scrumptious baby bagels make a perfect date with friends, whilst the exceptional range of cocktails and champagnes provide an ideal way to start the night.

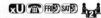

ANARKALI INDIAN CUISINE
Indian

303/305 King Street, Hammersmith, W6 9NH
Nearest Station: Ravenscourt Park
020 8748 1760
Reasonably priced Indian restaurant serving a menu of quintessential Indian food.

ANTONIA'S
Mediterranean

21-22b Hammersmith Broadway Shopping Centre, W6 7AL
Nearest Station: Hammersmith
020 8563 1218
One of Hammersmith's best kept secrets. A daily changing lunch menu of fresh soups, salads, quiches and classic tortillas makes this a firm favourite with the locals for lunch.

AZOU
Moroccan

375 King Street, Hammersmith, W6 9NJ
Nearest Station: Stamford Brook
020 8563 7266
Appeal to your culinary senses and sample the finest in Moroccan, Algerian and Tunisian cuisine. The menu reflects the huge variety of dishes from North Africa and embraces their delicate flavours.

BARBARELLA
Italian

428 Fulham Road, Fulham, W6 1DU
Nearest Station: Fulham Broadway
020 7385 9434
Combining elegant Italian cuisine with late night entertainment, this bar and restaurant has proven an iconic night-life venue in the surrounding area. Devour great food before dancing the night away.

BIANCO NERO
Italian

206-208 Hammersmith Road, Hammersmith, W6 7DP
Nearest Station: Hammersmith
020 8748 0212
Enjoy a fabulous à la carte or set menu in the main restaurant or devour delicious antipasti or pizza in the more casual downstairs bar. Offers sensational wine to match the delightful Italian cuisine.

BLUE STAR
Chinese

51-53 Steyne Road, Acton, W3 9NU
Nearest Station: Acton Central
020 8993 7977
Tasty, accomplished Chinese food in a restaurant characterised by a tranquil, settling ambience.

BRAVO! BRAVO!
European

Park Inn Heathrow, Bath Road, UB7 0DU
Nearest Station: Heathrow Terminals 1, 2, 3
020 8283 2038
Expect all-round entertainment and to be tempted by the buffet or the gourmet à la carte menu, dining in stylish and chic surroundings. As the music volume increases, liven up and dance the night away.

BUKHARA
Indian

764 Great West Road, Isleworth, TW7 5NA
Nearest Station: Syon Lane
020 8758 0011
Using the ancient traditions of tandoori-style cooking as its motivation, the kitchen at Bukhara produces divine North Indian cuisine that guests thoroughly enjoy.

CAFE DE THAI
Thai

20 All Saints Road, Westbourne Park, W11 1HE
Nearest Station: Westbourne Park
020 7243 3001
Exquisite and unique Thai restaurant showcasing an array of intense and flavourful dishes, with fresh ingredients being their essential secret. A venue that ensures diners a memorable experience.

CAFE PASTA
Italian

229-231 Kensington High St, Kensington, W8 6SA
Nearest Station: High Street Kensington
020 7938 1461
Traditional Italian dishes freshly prepared and served to your table by affable staff. Expect tasty cuisine in a comfortable and welcoming environment.

CAFÉ ROUGE
French

227-229 Chiswick High Road, Chiswick, W4 2DW
Nearest Station: Turnham Green
020 8742 7447
An attractive restaurant, a boulevard café or a Parisian-style wine bar; however you see Café Rouge, consistently excellent classic French dishes are always guaranteed.

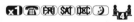

GREATER LONDON

174

Discounted hotel rates for GS members on our website

CAFÉ ROUGE
French

17 The Green, Ealing, W5 5DA
Nearest Station: Ealing Broadway
020 8579 2788
An attractive restaurant, a boulevard café or a Parisian-style wine bar; however you see Café Rouge, consistently excellent classic French dishes are always guaranteed.

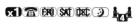

CAFÉ ROUGE
French

98-100 Shepherds Bush Road, Hammersmith, W6 7PD
Nearest Station: Goldhawk Road
020 7602 7732
An attractive restaurant, a boulevard café or a Parisian-style wine bar; however you see Café Rouge, consistently excellent classic French dishes are always guaranteed.

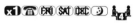

CAFÉ ROUGE
French

2 Lancer Sq, Kensington Church St, Kensington, W8 4EH
Nearest Station: High Street Kensington
020 7938 4200
An attractive restaurant, a boulevard café or a Parisian-style wine bar; however you see Café Rouge, consistently excellent classic French dishes are always guaranteed.

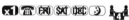

CAFFE PICCOLO
Italian

26 Chiswick High Road, Chiswick, W4 1TE
Nearest Station: Stamford Brook
020 8747 9989
A characterful Italian restaurant that oozes a personality all of its own. Generous portions of delicious food are served by terrific waiting staff who will brighten even the dullest of days.

CHEZ KRISTOF
French

111 Hammersmith Grove, Hammersmith, W6 0NQ
Nearest Station: Hammersmith
020 8741 1177
A vibrant, lively bar and restaurant that offers stylish cocktails and dreamy French cuisine. The adventurous will enjoy the roast pigeon, whilst guests cannot go wrong with the crab and mayonnaise.

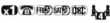

DEL'AZIZ
Mediterranean

24 - 32 Vanston Place, Fulham, SW6 1AX
Nearest Station: Fulham Broadway
020 7386 0086
From sun up to sun down, Del'Aziz offers a truly versatile treasure trove of food delights. Diners enjoy the elegant and stylish atmosphere in which they can sample the pleasures of exotic cuisine.

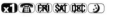

DEL'AZIZ
Mediterranean

Upper Southern Terrace, Westfield Ctr, Shepherd's Bush, W12 7GB
Nearest Station: White City
020 8740 0666
From sun up to sun down, Del'Aziz offers a truly versatile treasure trove of food delights. A perfect combination of a stylish deli and elegant restaurant, stunningly located on the upper southern terrace.

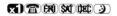

DELHI 6
Indian

Blenheim Ctr, Prince Regent Road, Hounslow, TW3 1NE
Nearest Station: Hounslow East
020 8572 7100
A contemporary blend of light textures and subtle spices make flavoursome food that you won't forget. The chef's exceptional commitment to his skills in the kitchen creates a colourful experience.

DONBOIS THAI RESTAURANT
Thai

311 New Kings Road, Fulham, SW6 4RF
Nearest Station: Parsons Green
020 7736 8833
Lovers of tasty Thai cuisine will be extremely pleased with the flavourful dishes on offer here. Dishes overflow with deliciousness and are served in generous portions.

EL METRO
Spanish

10 Effie Road, Fulham, SW6 1TB
Nearest Station: Fulham Broadway
020 7384 1264
With a keen sense of place and an ambition to be its own little 'Castle in Spain', El Metro serves vital, zesty Spanish classics along with juicy gourmet burgers and other dishes for breadth.

EL PASO MEXICANA
Mexican

24 Fulham Palace Road, Hammersmith, W6 9PH
Nearest Station: Hammersmith
020 8741 9913
Experience varied flavours, colourful decoration, and a variety of spices and ingredients, all at this authentic Mexican restaurant that delivers an exemplary list of expertly prepared dishes.

FEZ RESTAURANT
Moroccan

32 Fulham Palace Road, Hammersmith, W6 9PH
Nearest Station: Hammersmith
020 8563 7176
Well-regarded Moroccan and Lebanese restaurant serving superb quality traditional cuisine and boasting an especial line in outstanding couscous. A charismatic, charming place to eat.

FIRST FLOOR RESTAURANT
Modern European

186 Portobello Road, Notting Hill, W11 1LA
Nearest Station: Ladbroke Grove
020 7243 0072
Marvellously elegant, charismatic restaurant on the Portobello Road; well-conceived and -proportioned dishes can be found on the à la carte menu of this popular local spot.

GREATER LONDON

175

FLAMINGO
African

31 Goldhawk Road, Shepherd's Bush, W12 8QQ
Nearest Station: Shepherd's Bush
020 8740 7865
A kitchen dedicated to the exotic flavours of North Africa can be found at this charming Shepherd's Bush restaurant. Of note is the door ingudai.

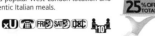

FRANKIE'S BRAGANZA
Italian

68 Chiswick High Road, Chiswick, W4 1SY
Nearest Station: Stamford Brook
020 8987 9988
An addition to the Marco Pierre White-Frankie Dettori chain of friendly, family restaurants, Frankie's Braganza sits in a popular West London location and serves rich, authentic Italian meals.

FRANKIE'S SPORTS BAR & GRILL
Italian

Stamford Bridge, Fulham Road, Fulham, SW6 1HS
Nearest Station: Fulham Broadway
020 7957 8298
Sleek and hip sports bar from the Marco Pierre White-Frankie Dettori stable, home to a range of rich, tasty Italian fare.

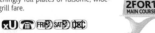

GRAND UNION
American

243 Goldhawk Road, Shepherd's Bush, W12 8EU
Nearest Station: Ravenscourt Park
020 8741 2312
With a classically stylish ambience, open kitchen, and a buzzing music scene of an evening, this restaurant dispatches hearteningly full plates of fulsome, wide-ranging bar and grill fare.

Not available Sunday lunch.

GREEN CHILLI
Indian

220 King Street, Hammersmith, W6 0RA
Nearest Station: Ravenscourt Park
020 8748 0111
A simple philosophy towards food, inspired from traditional recipes and created using classical methods. No compromise on décor or produce ensures maximum quality with minimum fuss.

INDIAN ZEST
Indian

Thames Street, Sunbury-on-Thames, TW16 5QF
Nearest Station:
01932 765 000
Elegance and fine cooking are key features of this venue, with an eclectic menu managed by highly experienced personnel. Good food and fair pricing all captured in an understated yet refined ambience.

INDIAN ZING
Indian

236 King Street, Hammersmith, W6 0RF
Nearest Station: Ravenscourt Park
020 8748 5959
Elegantly simple Indian restaurant launched by chef-proprietor Manoj Vasaikar, who is experienced and renowned within this field. Creative and exciting Indian cooking where quality is guaranteed.

JAIME'S SPANISH TAPAS
Spanish

28 Fulham Palace Road, Hammersmith, W6 9PH
Nearest Station: Hammersmith
020 8563 0869
While away the time eating delicious tapas from an extensive array of traditional and modern choices, and drinking choice wines, all at reasonable prices.

JONGLEURS HAMMERSMITH
International

Rutland Grove, Hammersmith, W6 9DJ
Nearest Station: Hammersmith
0870 011 1960
Great entertainment and food is delivered at all of these premier comedy clubs. An excellent selection of sharing platters, gourmet burgers and freshly made pizzas to enjoy while you watch the show.

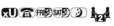

KARAAM LEBANESE
Lebanese

71 New Broadway, Ealing, W5 5AL
Nearest Station: Ealing Broadway
020 8566 4433
Deriving its influences from the ethos of Lebanese culture, the kitchen at Karaam takes generosity as its care value in achieving great food, service, and quality of presentation.

KENSINGTON TANDOORI
Indian

1 Abingdon Road, Kensington, W8 6AH
Nearest Station: High Street Kensington
020 7937 6182
It will be tempting to fill up on the deliciously tasty starters, which are freshly prepared and cooked to perfection. However, the speciality North Indian dishes are worth saving room for.

KISHMISH
Indian

448-450 Fulham Road, Fulham, SW6 1DL
Nearest Station: Fulham Broadway
020 7385 6953
Passionately dedicated to providing classic and contemporary Indian cuisine, this restaurant serves beautiful dishes that capture the essence of real authentic subcontinental flavour.

KLEFTIKO
Greek

186 Holland Park Avenue, Holland Park, W11 4UJ
Nearest Station: Shepherd's Bush
020 7603 0807
A classic Greek eatery boasting a fine assortment of dishes including succulent meats with fragrant juices, served within comfortable surroundings, all delicious and modestly priced.

KONKAN
Indian

107 Station Road, West Drayton, UB7 7LT
Nearest Station: West Drayton
01895 420 973
Drawing on the delicious tastes found in the Konkan area, the owners of this fantastic restaurant invite you to enjoy an exotic celebration of fabulously tasty Indian and Goan cuisine.

Sign up to our newsletter for latest restaurants, offers and more

LA LANTERNA
Italian

135 Kensington Church St, Kensington, W8 7LP
Nearest Station: Notting Hill Gate
020 7221 7348
An authentic Italian dining experience delivering an array of divine dishes and fine wines to all of its guests, all served by knowledgeable, attentive staff. A warm favourite of locals and visitors alike.

LA PICCOLA PIZZERIA
Italian

243 King Street, Hammersmith, W6 9LP
Nearest Station: Ravenscourt Park
020 8563 7360
Wonderfully homely atmosphere that enhances the terrifically tasty dishes on offer. A main menu bursting full of deliciously tempting pizzas, pastas and meat dishes accompanies a daily specials board.

LAGUNA RESTAURANT
Indian

1-4 Culmington Parade, 123 Uxbridge Rd, Ealing, W13 9BD
Nearest Station: West Ealing
020 8579 9992
Holding a desire to exceed guest expectations, the staff at this Indian restaurant go out of their way to ensure every diner has an unforgettable experience. A popular choice for many occasions.

LAM'S
Chinese

216 King Street, Hammersmith, W6 0RA
Nearest Station: Ravenscourt Park
020 8748 6982
Striving for perfection with every dish, the chefs at Lam's produce superb Chinese cuisine which maintains the restaurant's excellent reputation. Affable staff provide a genial service.

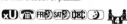

LARA RESTAURANT
Mediterranean

3-4 Bedford Park Corner, Turnham Green, W4 1LS
Nearest Station: Turnham Green
020 8995 3779
Take full advantage of the exciting and varied menu on offer in this fantastically wonderful Mediterranean restaurant. An attractive restaurant serving enjoyable mezze in a suitably relaxed setting.

LUNA NUOVA
Italian

773 Fulham Road, Fulham, SW6 5HA
Nearest Station: Parsons Green
020 7371 9774
Bang in the heart of Fulham, Luna Nuova is no twilight of the idols; rather, it's a superbly fun, buzzy place with a friendly feel that serves fresh and imaginative Italian cuisine with a touch of pizzazz.

LUNA ROSSA
Italian

190-192 Kensington Park Road, Notting Hill, W11 2ES
Nearest Station: Ladbroke Grove
020 7229 0482
Book to avoid disappointment at this wonderfully located restaurant, which runs parallel to the famous Portobello Road. Luna Rossa brings the unforgettable aromas of Italy to the streets of London.

MANDALOUN
Lebanese

496 Fulham Road, Fulham, SW6 5NH
Nearest Station: Parsons Green
020 7835 8687
Keenly aware of its family roots, the Mandaloun restaurant is rich with the characteristically fulsome, mellow and earthy flavours of Lebanese cuisine.

MANGO & SILK
Indian

199 Upper Richmond Road West, Mortlake, SW14 8QT
Nearest Station: Mortlake
020 8876 6220
Awarded a Michelin Bib Gourmand in 2010, this cracking restaurant has a fresh, calm environment and serves a stunning range of eclectic, classical dishes with roots in India's multiple culinary cultures.

MANZARA
Turkish

24 Penbridge Road, Notting Hill, W11 3HL
Nearest Station: Notting Hill Gate
020 7727 3062
With a diverse menu that expands beyond its Turkish staple dishes, this characterful café has a bright, lively setting and an emphasis on organic produce; it offers full, flavoursome Mediterranean tastes.

MARCO BY MARCO PIERRE WHITE
Classic British/ French

Stamford Bridge, Fulham Road, Fulham, SW6 1HS
Nearest Station: Fulham Broadway
020 7915 2929
Culinary delights from both sides of the Channel are fused to create divine French cuisine with some modern British flair. Another Marco Pierre White success. Awarded 2 AA Rosettes.

MIMINO GEORGIAN RESTAURANT
Georgian

197C Kensington High Street, Kensington, W8 6BA
Nearest Station: High Street Kensington
020 7937 1551
Zauri Goreli's passion for Georgian food translates into a distinctive experience of this little-known cuisine and culture. His knowledge and enthusiasm are infectious; the dishes are hearty and delicious.

MISSION
Oriental

116 Wandsworth Bridge Road, Parsons Green, SW6 2TF
Nearest Station: Parsons Green
020 7736 3322
A globally inspired cuisine delivered in a modern environment, offering a huge breadth of tastes and textures. Quality food, well-prepared and cooked to perfection, with a great outside terraced area.

MOOMBA BAR & KITCHEN
English and Continental

5 Lacy Road, Putney, SW15 1NH
Nearest Station: Putney
020 8785 9151
With its ranging menu and characterful vibe, Moomba's dishes are to savour, from a delicate but filling eggs Benedict breakfast to a perfectly cooked loin of lamb with lentils and tzatziki for dinner.

GREATER LONDON

NAKED NOSH
English and Continental

606 Fulham Road, Fulham, SW6 5RP
Nearest Station: Parsons Green
020 7736 7007
The Naked Nosh philosophy is simple: good, fresh, locally sourced produce and deliciously authentic recipes delivered to your door. Special fixed price menus are perfect if you are catering for friends.

NAPA
British

Moran Hotel, 626 Chiswick High Rd, Chiswick, W4 5RN
Nearest Station: Gunnersbury
020 8996 5200
Quality seasonal produce is the driving force behind the modern British menu at this fantastic Chiswick restaurant. Breakfast and dinner is served on a daily basis.

NAPULE
Italian

585 Fulham Broadway, Fulham, SW6 5VA
Nearest Station: Parsons Green
020 7381 1122
A welcome retreat from city life, indulging guests in the finest Italian cuisine. Fantastic, authentic pizza is the highlight of this vibrant local restaurant, along with many other traditional dishes.

NAYAAB
Indian

309 New Kings Road, Fulham, SW6 4RF
Nearest Station: Parsons Green
020 7731 6993
A menu that fully achieves the kitchen's goal to maintain traditional Indian favourites whilst leaving room for the culinary adventurous, who desire to explore new styles of cuisine.

NEPALESE TANDOORI RESTAURANT
Nepalese

121 Uxbridge Road, Shepherd's Bush, W12 8NL
Nearest Station: Shepherd's bush Market
020 8740 7551
An outstanding restaurant that is committed to preserving the Nepalese culture and tradition. The kitchen passionately recreates daal, bhaat and tarkari dishes for diners to devour.

NOTTINGDALE CAFE
European

Nicholas Road, Notting Hill, W11 4AN
Nearest Station: Holland Park
020 7221 2223
An exceptional guest-oriented service, specialising in provincial Italian and French dishes with a healthy respect for the best British produce, complete with a beautifully matching wine list.

PALMYRA
Lebanese

Stamford Bridge, Fulham Road, Fulham, SW6 1HS
Nearest Station: Kew Gardens
020 8948 7019
A fabulous Lebanese restaurant well known for its mouth-watering vegetarian and Mediterranean dishes. Enjoy your meal in the cosy interior of the restaurant or under the stars in the extended garden.

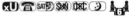

PLANEAT WORLD FOOD
International

1 Roslin Square, Roslin Road, Acton, W3 8DH
Nearest Station: South Acton
020 8992 4040
A dedicated and authentic venue where every dish is prepared by a specialist chef, using traditional methods. The world on a plate direct to your door. Takeaway only.

Takeaway only.

PREZZO
Italian

35A Kensington High St, Kensington, W8 5BA
Nearest Station: High Street Kensington
020 7930 4288
With a character all of its own, Prezzo oozes contemporary style and enduring charm. Signature pastas, stone-baked pizzas and classic Italian dishes promise a perfect dining choice for the whole family.

RISTORANTE BELVEDERE
Italian

11-12 Abbey Parade, Ealing, W5 1EE
Nearest Station: Hanger Lane
020 8998 9786
A fine family-run Italian restaurant situated in a most distinctive part of the city. The Neapolitan menu includes fabulous home-made pastas, traditional salads and amazing meat and fish dishes.

RUBY & SEQUOIA
Modern European

6-8 All Saints Road, Westbourne Park, W11 1HH
Nearest Station: Westbourne Park
020 7243 6363
A bright and lively restaurant in a glamorous venue, offering a mixture of tables and booths alongside a divine menu making this restaurant great for a meal, drinks or any occasion.

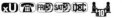

RUBY GRAND
Modern British

227 King Street, Hammersmith, W6 9JT
Nearest Station: Ravenscourt Park
020 8748 3391
The lounge, conservatory and walled garden make this an idyllic spot to enjoy afternoon or evening dining. Fresh food is paramount and the effort that goes into every dish can be seen in the open kitchen.

RUMI LOUNGE
Lebanese

531 Kings Road, Fulham, SW10 0TZ
Nearest Station: Fulham Broadway
020 7349 0810
A cool urban hangout where a mellow atmosphere and deliciously chilled cocktails will completely relax you. The Lebanese and Middle Eastern menu offers an abundance of mezze-style dishes for you to enjoy.

SEASONING RESTAURANT
Indian

84d-86 Lillie Road, Fulham, SW6 1TL
Nearest Station: West Brompton
020 7386 0303
Asian-fusion dishes express the kitchen's culinary prowess and a passion for cultural transfusion. The menu also plays home to exotic Mughlai recipes and traditional northern Indian dishes.

Enjoy massive leisure and retail savings with more Gourmet Society

SEASONS DINING ROOM
British
323 King Street, Hammersmith, W6 7PU
Nearest Station: Goldhawk Road
020 8748 2002
Enticing dishes make the most of seasonal British and European produce and the very best natural flavours. Try the tasty cheeses and even a fine British wine to round off your main meal.

SHILPA INDIAN RESTAURANT
Indian
206 King Street, Hammersmith, W6 0RA
Nearest Station: Ravenscourt Park
020 8741 3127
A delightful menu accommodating the very best Indian dishes. Specialists in South Indian and Kerala recipes in particular, the food here is honest, tasty and exceedingly satisfying.

SITAR TANDOORI
Indian
104 South Ealing Road, Ealing, W5 4QJ
Nearest Station: South Ealing
020 8567 9146
It is easy to understand how this attractive restaurant has gained a loyal local following. Guests love the authentic Indian cuisine that the kitchen has to offer.

STICKY FINGERS
American
1 Phillimore Gardens, Kensington, W8 7QG
Nearest Station: High Street Kensington
020 7937 8690
Award-winning burgers, tender steaks, succulent ribs and fresh fish dishes make memorable dining occasions. Lively, reliable, and family-friendly, this remains one of London's favourite restaurants.

TABERNACLE CENTRE
International
Powis Square, Notting Hill, W11 2AY
Nearest Station: Westbourne Park
0870 011 1960
Be entertained whilst revelling in a mouth-watering selection of sharing platters, gourmet burgers and freshly made pizzas. Amazing entertainment and great food provide the makings of a fantastic evening.

TATRA RESTAURANT
Modern Polish
24 Goldhawk Road, Shepherd's Bush, W12 8DH
Nearest Station: Goldhawk Road
020 8749 8193
Modern and stylish interior to match the outstandingly well-prepared Polish and East European cuisine. With a vast selection of vodkas including home-made flavoured varieties, this venue is truly unique.

THAI RIVER
Thai
308 Latimer Road, W10 6QW
Nearest Station: Latimer Road
020 8960 5988
Feel at home in the luxurious spaciousness of this restaurant's interior. Bring along your own alcohol to add the finishing touch to a superbly cooked Thai meal.

THE CLARENDON
European
123a Clarendon Road, Notting Hill, W11 4JG
Nearest Station: Latimer Road
020 7229 1500
All-in-one pub, cocktail lounge bar and restaurant providing a welcome oasis of calm. Offers an exciting menu that changes seasonally with different exquisite dishes on offer to satisfy all guests.

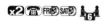

THE DURELL ARMS
British
704 Fulham Road, Fulham, SW6 5SB
Nearest Station: Parsons Green
020 7736 3014
Quality menu with daily specials, produced using the freshest ingredients, including their renowned Sunday roast where diners get a true taste of home-cooking. Historical setting with contemporary touch.

THE FAT BADGER
Modern Pub
310 Portobello Road, Notting Hill, W10 5TA
Nearest Station: Westbourne Park
020 8969 4500
In the airy upstairs dining rooms you'll enjoy a smart and superbly done meal. Try the musky pheasant and bacon salad followed by the great flavour contrast of baked squash stuffed with cheese and spinach.

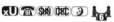

THE FEST
German
678-680 Fulham Road, Fulham, SW6 5SA
Nearest Station: Parsons Green
020 7736 5293
An authentic Oktoberfest experience outside of Munich. Enjoy a sample of the world's biggest party all year round, with imports from beer to pork knuckles. Caters for all events.

THE GATE
Pan Asian
87 Notting Hill Gate, Notting Hill, W11 3JZ
Nearest Station: Notting Hill Gate
020 7727 9007
A place for the chic, gorgeous, cosmopolitan party crowd, offering a night of fine dining, chilled lounge atmosphere and all-night dancing. Enjoy delicious Asian cuisine and a formidable cocktail bar.

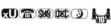

THE GREEDY BUDDHA
Indian/ Nepalese
144 Wandsworth Bridge Road, Parsons Green, SW6 2UH
Nearest Station: Parsons Green
020 7751 3311
A sleek, smart, contemporary corner restaurant, and rare purveyor of real Nepalese food. All dishes are authentic and freshly prepared. They also have live music nights here - Great food, great music.

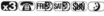

THE IDLE HOUR
Contemporary
62 Railway Side, Barnes, SW13 0PQ
Nearest Station: Barnes
020 8878 5555
Food to warm your soul in the winter and vitalise your senses in the summer. The warmly lit interior is perfectly cosy on a dark December night, whilst the secluded sun trap is lovely on a balmy evening.

Telephone booking essential

THE IDLE HOUR
European

171 Greyhound Road, Barons Court, W6 8NL
Nearest Station: Barons Court
020 7386 9007
Exceptionally acclaimed London pub where you'll enjoy a winning atmosphere and a choice menu focused on fresh, simple dishes; one of its best features is that it never forgets that it is, at heart, a pub.

2FOR1 MAIN COURSE

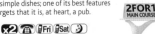

Telephone booking essential

THE MEAT & WINE CO
International

Unit 1026, Westfield Centre, Shepherd's Bush, W12 7GA
Nearest Station: White City
020 8749 5914
Providing steaks worth leaving home for, this steakhouse is famous for perfectly aged superior-quality beef, grilled to perfection. The 10.5 metre towering wall of wine will leave you awestruck.

2FOR1 MAIN COURSE

THE NAKED TURTLE
European

505 - 507 Upper Richmond Road West, Mortlake, SW14 7DE
Nearest Station: Mortlake
020 8878 1995
Embark on a food-lover's adventure as you explore the culinary imaginations that have created the most fabulous of menus. The restaurant is famously adorned with singing staff and live music.

50%OFF FOOD

THE SOUTHERN BELLE
American

175-177, Fulham Palace Road, Hammersmith, W6 8QT
Nearest Station: Hammersmith
020 7381 8682
Classic down-home diner fare near Roehampton University at this vibrant and buzz-filled restaurant. Dig into succulent chicken wings, a quirky pizza or a cracking rack of ribs.

50%OFF FOOD

TUSCANY RISTORANTE
Italian

Heathrow Marriott Hotel, Bath Road, UB3 5AN
Nearest Station: Heathrow Terminals 1, 2, 3
020 8990 1100
Step into the theatre of a live open kitchen where this great food is accompanied by the very best Italian hospitality. Enjoy the intimacy of the restaurant and swim in the vast selection of fine wines.

25%OFF TOTAL

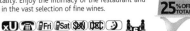

TWENTY NINE RESTAURANT
European

29-31 Lampton Road, Hounslow, TW3 4BN
Nearest Station: Osterley
020 8572 3131
Twentynine is a modern and sophisticated hotel-based restaurant and bar offering modern British and European cuisine - fresh food made with quality ingredients.

50%OFF FOOD

UNCLES CAFE
European

305 Portobello Road, Notting Hill, W10 5TD
Nearest Station: Ladbroke Grove
020 8962 0090
The perfect cosy setting for a good and proper breakfast, as well as rendezvous with friends or simply people-watching through the day, this café is low-key and comfortable like a favourite shoe.

25%OFF TOTAL

URBAN KARAHI
Indian

47 Greenford Avenue, Hanwell, W7 1LP
Nearest Station: Hanwell
020 8579 4474
An emphasis on refined yet creative Indian cuisine leads to a menu which incorporates both traditional classic favourites and original new dishes that apply eastern flavours with a western twist. Delicious.

50%OFF FOOD

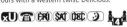

VICINO
Italian

189 New Kings Road, Fulham, SW6 4SW
Nearest Station: Parsons Green
020 7736 1145
Lucid, bright and pretty neighbourhood restaurant with a friendly buzz and a line in fluid, fresh, mellow and authentically Italian flavours through all its dishes.

25%OFF TOTAL

Sundays offer only available for lunch service.

VINE INN
Modern British

121 Hillingdon Road, Hillingdon, UB10 0JQ
Nearest Station: Uxbridge
01895 259 596
Part of the Best of British group, the Vine Inn is a welcoming haven for a cosmopolitan clientèle that nevertheless stays true to its sense of tradition - to substantial recognition.

2FOR1 2 COURSES

Min. 2 courses must be purchased.

WALMER CASTLE
Thai/British

58 Ledbury Road, Notting Hill, W11 2AJ
Nearest Station: Westbourne Park
020 7229 4620
Great Thai food and good vibes all round here at this outstanding Dragon venue. Feast on classic Thai favourites and discover outstanding flavours whilst taking advantage of the extensive drinks selection.

25%OFF TOTAL

Call beforehand on special event days.

WINGS RESTAURANT
International

Holiday Inn Heathrow, Bath Road-Sipson Way, UB7 0DP
Nearest Station: Heathrow Terminals 1, 2, 3
020 8990 0000
Take care not to be distracted into missing your flight by the sophisticated, surprising contemporary dining on offer at the Heathrow Holiday Inn's Wings restaurant: it's a more-than-fleeting possibility.

50%OFF FOOD

WOK AROUND THE WORLD
Asian/European

4 Portal Way, Acton, W3 6RT
Nearest Station: North Acton
020 8753 0800
An informal venue serving a fusion of quality Asian and European cuisine. The theatre of the open kitchen makes this an exciting experience as you watch your meal being prepared before your eyes.

50%OFF FOOD

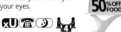

ZAYKA INDIAN CUISINE
Indian

8 South Ealing Road, Ealing, W5 4QA
Nearest Station: South Ealing
020 8579 7278
Bright and welcoming Nepalese and Indian restaurant that serves delicious, fresh-flavoured and finely spiced dishes. They also focus on healthy choices for ingredients, without sacrificing flavour.

2FOR1 MAIN COURSE

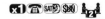

GREATER LONDON

180

Gourmet Society discount applies to the à la carte menu

Want _even_ _more_ restaurants?

Gourmet Society keeps on growing....

To discover the latest additions to our partner restaurants, check the website regularly.

www.gourmetsociety.co.uk

- More nationwide chains than ever before

- Unforgettable hotel restaurants

- Michelin-starred, AA rosette winners and 'local heroes'

- And every cuisine imaginable.....

www.gourmetsociety.co.uk
is the place to find the most recent restaurants that are looking forward to welcoming you with great dining discounts.

Simply log in and begin your restaurant search.

East Anglia

Two physical features underpin East Anglia's distinctive produce and local cuisines: on the one hand, the expansive arable flatlands; on the other, the long, sweeping coastline. From the latter, you might try the special delicacy of a Cromer crab, or enjoy the distinctive deep colour of the Stiffkey Blue cockle. Among the distinctive produce that grows in the region is the salty, tangy Marsh Samphire plants which naturally pairs excellently with the fish with which it shares the seas. Add into the mix the sweet, stout flavour of Suffolk ham, traditionally produced from pigs bred in the county and you'll find East Anglia's local specialities are multiple and eclectic.

You'll find a part of England, then, inestimably rich in fresh and local produce; its restaurants, perhaps to a unique extent, often reflect this. It is an area full of market towns and villages, and much less to do with the big cities that serve as hubs for dining elsewhere. As a result, this is a region in which you can really get to know the distinctive, local feel of a welcoming village pub or seaside restaurant.

This year we are considering all areas inside the M25 to be part of Greater London. Diners in this region should also check the Greater London section to be sure not to overlook any great restaurants.

Cambridgeshire

EAST ANGLIA

BAR ROOM RESTAURANT
European

Holiday Inn P'borough West, Thorpe Wood, P'borough, PE3 6SG
01733 289 988
Stoke yourself with a full-bodied breakfast or ease back after a long day with a delicious dinner in this airy, stylish contemporary restaurant at the Peterborough West Holiday Inn.

Only one card can be used per table.

CHANCELLOR'S, GONVILLE HOTEL
British

Best Western Hotel, Gonville Place, Cambridge, CB1 1LY
01223 221 109
An ideally located hotel with spectacular views of a 25 acre open park. Explore the historical city by foot, before retreating for a well-cooked, accomplished dinner in the restaurant.

CAFÉ NAZ
Indian/ Bangladeshi

45/47 Castle Street, Cambridge, CB3 0AH
01223 363 666
A well-loved, stylish restaurant offering outstanding food and affable service. Both local curry lovers and Cambridge tourists enjoy the superb Indian cuisine on offer in this neatly situated venue.

CAFÉ ROUGE
French

24-26 Bridge St, Cambridge, CB2 1UJ
01223 364 961
An attractive restaurant, a boulevard café or a Parisian-style wine bar; however you see Café Rouge, consistently excellent classic French dishes are always guaranteed.

CANTONESE KITCHEN
Cantonese

22 Norwood Road, March, PE15 8QF
01354 657 777
Decades of culinary experience are reflected in the Head Chef's delicious masterpiece dishes. Cantonese cuisine is at its very best, with satay skewers and beef in black bean sauce coming in as favourites.

CASTLE LODGE HOTEL
British

50 New Barns Road, Ely, CB7 4PW
01353 662 276
Enter the snug, comfortable bar at this Ely guest house before settling in for one of their delicious home-made dinners. Not just a place for a great breakfast, the Sunday carvery comes highly recommended.

CROWN INN
British

Bridge Road, Broughton, Huntingdon, PE28 3AY
01487 824 428
Drop down into this pretty Cambridgeshire hamlet, home to the distinctive, characterful Crown Inn. With attention set on simplicity and quality, it has received recognition for its full, flavoursome food.

184

DE LUCA CUCINA
Italian

83 Regent Street, Cambridge, CB2 1AW
01223 356 666
Sip on a vodka martini or relax over a cappuccino at the bar before being shown through to the skylight restaurant, complete with open plan kitchen. Quality and value are high on the agenda.

FIDDLESTICKS
British

26 London Rd, Wansford-In-England, Peterborough, PE8 6JE
01780 784 111
A restaurant with a great local reputation for abundant, flavour-laden dishes in a charming, accommodating space.

FITZBILLIES
English and Continental

52 Trumpington Street, Cambridge, CB2 1RG
01223 352 500
A renowned Cambridge restaurant that serves fabulous cakes and coffee in the daytime and fine, classical English dishes in the evening. A superb location and a warm, inviting atmosphere.

GOLDEN INN CHINESE RESTAURANT
Chinese

64 High Street, Ramsey, Huntingdon, PE26 1AA
01487 710 057
In the pretty Fenland town of Ramsey, this restaurant specialises in the gamut of tastes true to Cantonese cuisine, focusing on fresh flavours and lush, juicy seafood.

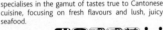

DETAILED DESCRIPTIONS AVAILABLE ON

www.gourmetsociety.co.uk

HOTEL DU VIN
European

Trumpington Street, Cambridge, CB2 1QA
01223 227 330
The finest, fresh local produce, simple European recipes, a stunning choice of wines; these are the elements of the trademark Hotel du Vin bistro. A quirky, stylish converted town building. 1 AA Rosette.

KOHINOOR TANDOORI
Indian

74 Mill Road, Cambridge, CB1 2AS
01223 323 639
One of the best curry houses in Cambridge and the surrounding areas, the staff are attentive and accommodating while the cuisine is delicious, particularly the traditional specials.

LAHORE TANDOORI
Indian

539 Lincoln Road, Peterborough, PE1 2PB
01733 555 399
A great Indian restaurant delivering fine cuisine, well-prepared and -presented, offering diners dishes filled with spice and rich, authentic aromas.

Gourmet Society discount applies to the à la carte menu

LINTON TANDOORI
Indian
6-8 Bartlow Road, Linton, CB21 4LY
01223 890 030
Warm welcomes and amiable smiles will greet you at the door in this local restaurant. The staff provide excellent service whatever the party size, while the delightful menu will tickle your taste buds.

ORCHARDS AT THE HAYCOCK HOTEL
British
London Rd, Wansford, Peterborough, PE8 6JA
01780 782 223
Enjoy splendid views of the award-winning hotel gardens as you dine in this charming conservatory. A traditional British menu offers guests table d'hôte-style lunches and à la carte evening meals.

LOCH FYNE
Seafood
The Old Dairy, Elton, Peterborough, PE8 6SH
01832 280 298
From the roadside oyster bar that once was, Loch Fyne restaurants now successfully inject energy and passion into great food and wonderful flavours, whilst ensuring their seafood is sustainably sourced.

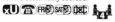

PREZZO
Italian
12-14 High Street, Ely, CB7 4JZ
01353 659 832
With a character all of its own, Prezzo oozes contemporary style and enduring charm. Signature pastas, stone-baked pizzas and classic Italian dishes promise a perfect dining choice for the whole family.

LOCH FYNE
Seafood
The Little Rose, 37 Trumpington St, Cambridge, CB2 1QY
01223 362 433
From the roadside oyster bar that once was, Loch Fyne restaurants now successfully inject energy and passion into great food and wonderful flavours, whilst ensuring their seafood is sustainably sourced.

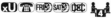

PREZZO
Italian
2 Cowgate, Peterborough, PE1 1NA
01733 349 832
With a character all of its own, Prezzo oozes contemporary style and enduring charm. Signature pastas, stone-baked pizzas and classic Italian dishes promise a perfect dining choice for the whole family.

MAI THAI
Thai
Hobbs Pavilion, Park Terrace, Cambridge, CB1 1JH
01223 367 480
A calm minimalist design creates a soothing ambience that will completely relax you. Warm weather encourages diners to eat outside, where you can enjoy views of Cambridge's most famous park.

RAINBOW CAFE
Vegetarian
9A Kings Parade, Cambridge, CB2 1SJ
01223 321 551
Delicious selections of vegetarian food at this acclaimed café. The restaurant serves exceptional dishes with great care over the provenance of the produce, with a variety of international flavours.

Rainbow café does not take bookings.

MASA RESTAURANT
Mediterranean
76-78 High Street, Sawston, CB2 4HJ
01223 711 711
Masa serves food conscious of the range of influences that can be traced through Turkish cuisine. Delicate spices, slow-cooked crumbling meats and warming vegetable stews characterise this restaurant.

RAJMAHAL
Indian
7 Barnwell Road, Cambridge, CB5 8RG
01223 244 955
Be greeted with a smile and get lost in the truly divine Indian menu on offer. Indulge your senses with a variety of delectable dishes, including various specialities and a range classic Indian beverages.

MONTAZ BAR AND RESTAURANT
Indian/ Bangladeshi
39-41 Market Street, Ely, CB7 4LZ
01353 669 910
Delicious Indian and Bangladeshi cuisine garners a marvellous reputation for this popular restaurant. An ideal place to socialise or enjoy an intimate meal in stylish surroundings.

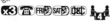

SHIRAZ RESTAURANT
Persian
84 Regent Street, Cambridge, CB2 1DP
01223 307 581
A delectable selection of Persian dishes occupies the menu at this wondrous restaurant. Watch as your food is vibrantly prepared over the charcoal grill before feasting by candlelight.

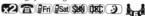

NEEDHAMS RESTAURANT
International
186 Main Street, Witchford, Ely, CB6 2HT
01353 661 405
Nestled away in the village of Witchford, this beautifully converted farmhouse is home to a well-established restaurant with an impressive reputation. Dishes draw upon influences from around the world.

SITAR
Indian
43 High Street, Cherry Hinton, Cambridge, CB1 9HX
01223 249 955
A wonderful restaurant offering dine-in and takeaway options. Whether you choose to enjoy the ambience of the restaurant or the comfort of your own home, you'll be impressed by the high-quality dishes.

OLIVERS LODGE HOTEL
International
50 Needingworth Road, St Ives, PE27 5JP
01480 463 252
An extensive menu offers fresh fish and seasonal game amongst many other tasty dishes. Enjoy à la carte dining in an affable atmosphere, or opt for the bar menu for a lighter meal.

SLEPE HALL HOTEL
Fine Dining
Ramsey Road, St Ives, PE27 5RB
01480 463 122
This venue offers a wide choice of light meals and main dishes to suit every taste, with their chefs using only the finest ingredients. Open and friendly fine dining, where booking is essential.

EAST ANGLIA

185

www.gourmetsociety.co.uk

SULTAN TANDOORI RESTAURANT
Indian

16 London Road, St Ives, PE27 5ES
01480 464 650
Home-style Bangladeshi and Indian fine dining, that specialises in fish dishes. High quality and consistency is a key feature, producing mouth-watering flavours with unique herbs and spices every time.

2FOR1 3 COURSES

DETAILED DESCRIPTIONS AVAILABLE ON

www.gourmetsociety.co.uk

SWEET OLIVES
Mediterranean

5 Fletton Ave, Peterborough, PE2 8AX
01733 562 572
Sophisticated eating with fine food at good value. A tantalising Mediterranean menu, crafted by creative chefs, offering huge choice. Fresh and delicious dishes that appeal to all.

2FOR1 MAIN COURSE

THE VINE BAR & KITCHEN
Contemporary

170 East Road, Cambridge, CB2 1RG
01223 367 888
Unusual dishes and seasonally appropriate meals are served in this fresh, laid-back restaurant and bar. Soothing jazz melodies will ensure that enjoying your meal is your only concern.

2FOR1 MAIN COURSE

THE BANYAN TREE
Indian

9 Church Street, Werrington, Peterborough, PE4 6QA
01733 570 111
With a menu that predominantly consists of Moghlai cuisine, this restaurant provides Indian food like you've never tasted before. An impressive selection of dishes are provided for the vegetarian diner.

25%OFF TOTAL

Essex

THE BASKERVILLES HOTEL
International

Main Street, Baston, Peterborough, PE6 9PB
01778 560 010
A Sunday carvery and a fine à la carte menu will have you wanting to return time and time again. Enjoy the comfort of the lounge-bar area or the well-maintained child friendly garden.

25%OFF TOTAL

BACCHUS
European

43 Alexandra Street, Southend-on-Sea, SS1 1BW
01702 348 088
A promise of fine dining and indulgence, whether you visit for the elegance of high tea, the seasonal main menus or a bespoke set menu created in collaboration with the Head Chef.

2FOR1 3 COURSES

THE BRIDGE HOUSE
British

Market Square, St Neots, PE19 2AP
01480 472 044
Gorgeous riverside location and a cosy, accommodating interior; a place to enjoy superbly cooked, wholesome and delicious pub food: rich stews, juicy meats and tenderly cooked veg.

2FOR1 MAIN COURSE

BARDA RESTAURANT
European

30 Broomfield Road, Chelmsford, CM1 1SW
01245 357 799
Fine dining from chefs of the highest calibre. Barda is recognised in the Good Food Guide 2010 and the Michelin Guide 2010, and lives up to this acclaim with fresh, flavourful dishes right across the menu.

2FOR1 3 COURSES

THE CHEQUERED SKIPPER
British

Ashton, Oundle, Peterborough, PE8 5LD
01832 273 494
A country pub delivering a menu of fresh country themes with a modern take on many traditional dishes. A stylish and modern environment for diners to enjoy an informal taste of the countryside.

25%OFF TOTAL

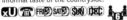

CAFÉ ELITE
British

5 The Rows, Harlow, CM20 1BX
0127 942 5518
A cracking place for light to hearty breakfasts and home-made lunches and dinners. Stop and refuel after a morning of shopping, or chat amongst friends for that well needed catch up.

25%OFF TOTAL

THE PACKHORSE
Modern Pub

4 Lincoln Rd, Northborough, Peterborough, PE6 9BL
01733 252 300
An idyllic venue that is perfect for both cosy drinks with friends or a meal with the family. Situated in a 13th century inn, enjoy seasonal, fresh food and the character of the historic original features.

25%OFF TOTAL

CAFÉ ROUGE
French

84-84a High Street, Brentwood, CM14 4AP
01277 262 466
An attractive restaurant, a boulevard café or a Parisian-style wine bar; however you see Café Rouge, consistently excellent classic French dishes are always guaranteed.

50%OFF FOOD

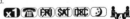

THE RUDDY DUCK
European

12 St Pegas Road, Peakirk, Peterborough, PE6 7NF
01733 252 426
Be wholly satisfied by the fresh and tasty food available. Priding itself as a traditional hearty pub, the owner focus on the quality of food and his wealth of experience makes this pub a winner.

2FOR1 2 COURSES

CAFÉ ROUGE
French

219 Moulsham St, Chelmsford, CM2 0LR
01245 250 588
An attractive restaurant, a boulevard café or a Parisian-style wine bar; however you see Café Rouge, consistently excellent classic French dishes are always guaranteed.

50%OFF FOOD

Sign up to our newsletter for latest restaurants, offers and more

CAFÉ ROUGE
French

59 High Street, Colchester, CO1 1DH
01206 541 839

An attractive restaurant, a boulevard café or a Parisian-style wine bar; however you see Café Rouge, consistently excellent classic French dishes are always guaranteed.

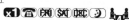

CAFÉ ROUGE
French

The Broadwalk, Lakeside Centre, Thurrock, RM20 2ZN
01708 890 857

An attractive restaurant, a boulevard café or a Parisian-style wine bar; however you see Café Rouge, consistently excellent classic French dishes are always guaranteed.

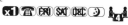

DISH RESTAURANT
European

13A King Street, Saffron Walden, CB10 1HE
01799 513 300

Dish Restaurant is housed in the beautiful former 'mint' in the heart of Saffron Walden. They pride themselves on using great locally produce to create delicious and uncomplicated dishes.

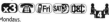

Offer unavailable on Mondays.

DUNMOW'S CHINA GARDEN
Chinese

1st Floor 27 High Street, Great Dunmow, CM6 1AB
01371 872 845

This elegant and family-run restaurant specialise in Peking, Szechuan and Cantonese cuisine. It's renowned for its delicious seafood dishes, excellent service and traditional style.

HALFWAY HOUSE
Carvery

213 Eastern Esplanade, Southend-on-Sea, SS1 3AD
01702 588 645

One of the many Great British Carvery pubs that offers the best of British food with a wonderful modern twist. This 19th century Coach House is now captivating and stylish and a local popular favourite.

Call beforehand for special event days.

INDIAN RUCHI
Indian

9 High Street, Billericay, CM12 9BE
01277 630 933

With an enviable central location, this Indian restaurant really does have everything going for it. Superbly fresh and tasty dishes can be enjoyed in a warm and friendly atmosphere.

JONGLEURS CLACTON
European

The Boardwalk, Pier Gap, Clacton-On-Sea, CO15 1QX
0870 011 1960

Great food and entertainment is delivered at all of these premier comedy clubs. An excellent selection of sharing platters, gourmet burgers and freshly made pizzas to enjoy while you watch the show.

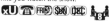

KINGS BRASSERIE
British

King Street, High Ongar, CM5 9NS
01277 822 220

A regularly changing menu offering seasonally influenced modern British cuisine. A highly popular restaurant providing both indoor and outdoor seating and catering facilities for the larger occasion.

Formerly Wheatsheaf Brasserie

LA TOSCANA
Italian

Old Barn Court, High Street, Billericay, CM12 9BY
01277 630 120

Beautifully presented food that tastes even better than it looks. The finest ingredients go into every dish, while the chef takes every care to ensure each meal is prepared to the highest standard.

LA VISTA
Italian

23-25 Church Street, Gt Baddow, Chelmsford, CM2 7HX
01245 478 884

Both those in need of superb Italian food and guests who want to enjoy a drink with friends flock to this marvellously stylish restaurant. Guests enjoy the champagne cocktails and fine array of wines.

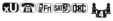

LATINO'S RESTAURANT
Spanish

205 London Road, Hadleigh, Benfleet, SS7 2RD
0170 255 5010

Great food and outstanding wines offered in a friendly and authentic atmosphere. An extensive menu offers diners everything from fresh tapas and paella to mouth-watering steaks.

LE RAJ
Indian

5-7 Broadway, Tilbury, RM18 7BP
01375 843 384

Fine Indian dishes to savour and enjoy, whether you want an intimate meal or an easy takeaway. Exceptional standards and high-quality ingredients sets them apart from the competition.

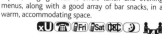

LOCH FYNE
Seafood

109-111 Bond Street, Chelmsford, CM1 1GS
01245 293 620

From the roadside oyster bar that once was, Loch Fyne restaurants now successfully inject energy and passion into great food and wonderful flavours, whilst ensuring their seafood is sustainably sourced.

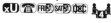

MARCO'S BAR
Spanish

30 Eastwood Road, Rayleigh, SS6 7JQ
01268 773 311

Marco's tapas has all the right zing and zest for a superb, ranging meal. It offers lunch and evening menus, along with a good array of bar snacks, in a warm, accommodating space.

MASONS RESTAURANT AND BAR
Contemporary

155 Ingrave Road, Brentwood, CM13 2AA
01277 261 331

An ideal place to eat with business clients over lunch, or wine and dine with family and friends in the evening. A wonderfully warm décor creates an intimate dining experience.

MASONS TOO
Contemporary

London Road, Widford, Chelmsford, CM2 8TE
01245 346 877

In a smooth and suave setting, Masons Too serves uncluttered, classic dishes with rich and seasoned flavours.

EAST ANGLIA

MUMBAI-SE
Indian
12 Hamlet Court Road, Westcliff-on-Sea, SS0 7LX
01702 330 575
Mirroring Mumbai's love affair with home-made food, simplicity produces the best results at this fabulous Indian restaurant. Minimal oil levels create great food that's good for you.

NIP-PON
Japanese
2 Middleborough, Colchester, CO1 1QS
01206 366 666
A Japanese fusion restaurant specialising in the finest, freshest Japanese cuisine, with a menu of well-prepared, contemporary dishes. Great variety in both taste and texture.

OLD ORLEANS
American
Unit 900, Lakeside Centre, Grays, RM20 2ZS
01708 868 454
An extraordinarily accurate taste of the Deep South can be found In this unique restaurant. The kitchen deals in classic Louisiana and Cajun recipes such as jambalaya and gumbo to create an exciting menu.

Not available on Bank Holiday weekends. Adult menu only.

OUTBACK STEAKHOUSE
Australian
Yardley Bus. Pk., Miles Gray Road, Basildon, S14 3GN
01268 534 663
Expect big, bold flavours in this laid-back restaurant that is passionate about fresh food. The kitchen prides itself on the soups, sauces and salad dressings which are all made from scratch.

PREZZO
Italian
5 Market Hill, Halstead, CO9 2AR
01787 474 271
With a character all of its own, Prezzo oozes contemporary style and enduring charm. Signature pastas, stone-baked pizzas and classic Italian dishes promise a perfect dining choice for the whole family.

PREZZO
Italian
113-115 Bond Street, Chelmsford, CM1 1GD
01245 264 335
With a character all of its own, Prezzo oozes contemporary style and enduring charm. Signature pastas, stone-baked pizzas and classic Italian dishes promise a perfect dining choice for the whole family.

PREZZO
Italian
4 Marine Parade West, Clacton-On-Sea, CO15 1QZ
01255 223 894
With a character all of its own, Prezzo oozes contemporary style and enduring charm. Signature pastas, stone-baked pizzas and classic Italian dishes promise a perfect dining choice for the whole family.

PREZZO
Italian
69 High Street, Maldon, CM9 5EP
01621 842 544
With a character all of its own, Prezzo oozes contemporary style and enduring charm. Signature pastas, stone-baked pizzas and classic Italian dishes promise a perfect dining choice for the whole family.

PREZZO
Italian
129-129A High Street, Brentwood, CM14 4RZ
01277 216 641
With a character all of its own, Prezzo oozes contemporary style and enduring charm. Signature pastas, stone-baked pizzas and classic Italian dishes promise a perfect dining choice for the whole family.

PREZZO
Italian
1 Cross Street, Saffron Walden, CB10 1EX
01799 521 260
With a character all of its own, Prezzo oozes contemporary style and enduring charm. Signature pastas, stone-baked pizzas and classic Italian dishes promise a perfect dining choice for the whole family.

PREZZO
Italian
6 High Street, Billericay, CM12 9BQ
01277 658 273
With a character all of its own, Prezzo oozes contemporary style and enduring charm. Signature pastas, stone-baked pizzas and classic Italian dishes promise a perfect dining choice for the whole family.

PREZZO
Italian
1 Culver Street East, Colchester, CO1 1LD
01206 573 388
With a character all of its own, Prezzo oozes contemporary style and enduring charm. Signature pastas, stone-baked pizzas and classic Italian dishes promise a perfect dining choice for the whole family.

PREZZO
Italian
Unit 2 Freeport Village, Charter Way, Braintree, CM7 8YH
01376 569 022
With a character all of its own, Prezzo oozes contemporary style and enduring charm. Signature pastas, stone-baked pizzas and classic Italian dishes promise a perfect dining choice for the whole family.

PREZZO
Italian
8 Baddow Road, Chelmsford, CM2 0DG
01245 358 533
With a character all of its own, Prezzo oozes contemporary style and enduring charm. Signature pastas, stone-baked pizzas and classic Italian dishes promise a perfect dining choice for the whole family.

RAYLEIGH LODGE
Carvery
70 The Chase, Rayleigh, SS6 8RW
01268 742 149
One of the many Great British Carvery pubs that places a modern twist on the well-loved classic. British food lovers can enjoy their meal in this old hunting lodge that once belonged to Henry VIII.

RBG @ PARK INN HARLOW
British
Park Inn by Radisson, Harlow, CM18 7BA
01279 829 988
A grill bar that boasts tasty succulent steaks, fresh from the grill, and serves classic New York-style cocktails. Relax in the lavish surroundings and enjoy exceptional food and service.

188

Visit the website regularly to discover the latest restaurants joining the GS

RBG @ PARK INN THURROCK
British

High Road, North Stifford, Thurrock, RM16 5UE
01708 719 988
Decked out in the Regency style, this hotel-based restaurant provides a calming and charming environment in which to enjoy their range of gourmet burgers, chargrilled dishes and homely classic desserts.

ROSE INN
Modern British

Wakering Rd, Grt. Wakering, Southend-on-Sea SS3 0PY
01702 588 008
A 19th century pub in Essex that is part of the Best of British group, the Rose Inn is classic in its welcome, its low-beamed cosiness, and the thorough, full flavours of its English fare.

Minimum of two courses must be purchased.

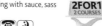
RECOMMEND A FRIEND
see page 18

SAND BAR & SEAFOOD COMPANY
Contemporary

71 Broadway, Leigh-On-Sea, SS9 1PE
01702 480 067
With a fast-growing reputation for fantastic food spreading far and wide, this restaurant offers a relaxed venue in which guests can enjoy a wonderful meal. A charming retreat from the bustling Broadway.

SHANTI INDIAN CUISINE
Indian

24-26 Coggeshall Rd, Braintree, CM7 9BY
01376 331 900
A unique dining experience in the heart of Braintree. A constantly evolving menu plays host to a wide range of delicious Indian dishes, which are carefully matched against the extensive wine list.

SOUTHCHURCH TANDOORI
Indian

565 Southchurch Road, Southend-on-Sea, SS1 2PN
01702 615 666
Classic local Indian restaurant serving a brilliant array of the old favourite dishes, from baltis to tandoori recipes. Enjoy a meal that's brimming with sauce, sass and spice.

SQUARE 1 RESTAURANT
Mediterranean

15 High Street, Great Dunmow, CM6 1AB
01371 859 922
Dishes of sublime quality crafted by the highly experienced Head Chef. Enjoy top-quality wines and champagne, along with fantastic service and a pleasant atmosphere. Entered in the Michelin Guide 2009.

THAI HOUSE
Thai

21B High Street (1st Floor), Billericay, CM12 9BA
01277 632 424
Tucked away in Billericay this restaurant does a good line in the balanced flavours that you'll find in all the best Thai cuisine. Without frills, you'll enjoy simple rich flavours and a warm welcome.

THAI ORCHID
Thai

1 South Street, Brentwood, CM14 4BJ
01277 263 791
A warmly accommodating meal awaits in this good local restaurant where you can count on all the range of complex but clean flavours that characterise the best in Thai cuisine.

THE BRASSERIE AT MARKS TEY
Modern British

BW Marks Tey Hotel, London Rd, Colchester, CO6 1DU
01206 210 001
Offering sophisticated brassiere-style food with a modern twist, guests can enjoy a relaxed three course meal right down to informal light snacks. An ideal choice for business and leisure travellers.

THE COMPASSES AT PATTISWICK
British

Compasses Road, Pattiswick, CM77 8BG
01376 561 322
Perfect retreat for those seeking good food and company in stunning surroundings. A country pub that strives to deliver simple, rural dishes that allow the quality of the ingredients to shine through.

THE CONTENTED SOLE
Mediterranean

80 High Street, Burnham-On-Crouch, CM0 8AA
01621 786 900
With Michelin-starred kitchen experience, the chefs here source quality ingredients to produce a simple, confident menu. Must-try dishes include the sole, naturally; enjoy their choice wine list to boot.

THE CORNER LOUNGE
Italian

1 Exchange Way, Chelmsford, CM1 1XB
01245 505 880
Using ingredients sourced direct from Italy to create a menu of traditional and modern dishes, this family-run restaurant offers diners a truly authentic experience.

COUNTY KITCHEN
European

Rainsford Road, Chelmsford, CM1 2PZ
01245 455700
Head Chef Wayne Browning, is passionate about food, where it comes from and here quality is never compromised. Only the best ingredients from local farmers are used to create the delicious dishes offered.

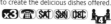

THE SHEPHERD & DOG
British

Gore Rd, Stambridge, Rochford, SS4 2DA
01702 258279
The Shepherd & Dog prides itself on food that is locally sourced and freshly prepared, the best quality ingredients and delicious seasonal menus. Make yourself at home in this traditional country pub.

THE HARBOURSIDE AT THE PIER
Seafood

The Quay, Harwich, CO12 3HH
01255 241 212
This delightful restaurant offers not only views of the harbour but also its landed catch. Fresh seafood is the kitchen's speciality, which can be enjoyed with champagne at the bar or in the restaurant.

189

THE LABWORTH
British

Western Esplanade, Furthurwick Rd, Canvey Island, SS8 7DW
01268 683 209
Great prices for outstanding food made from prime ingredients. Whilst maintaining the innate English Heritage of the building, both the atmosphere and the interior décor are modern and contemporary.

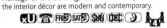

THE LEMON TREE
Modern British

48 St Johns Street, Colchester, CO2 7AD
01206 767 337
Cooking the finest modern European cuisine, this restaurant focuses on warm welcomes and great food. The kitchen draws on the influences of guests' preferences to create amazingly satisfying dishes.

THE OLIVE TREE
Mediterranean

66-68 Rosemary Road, Clacton-On-Sea, CO15 1TE
01255 473 931
Indulge in divine Mediterranean cuisine at this popular and stylish restaurant. Prides itself on quality and value, also hosting superb entertainment nights with live music and traditional dancing.

THE POLASH RESTAURANT
Indian

169 Station Road, Burnham on Crouch, CM0 8HJ
01621 782 233
A highly recommended restaurant that serves delightful food with a friendly smile. Curry lovers will enjoy the thought and effort that goes into every tasty dish.

THE RED HERRING
Fine Dining

Colchester Road, West Bergholt, Colchester, CO6 3JQ
01206 242 046
Friendly and welcoming seafood bistro in West Bergholt; clean and clear flavours mark out its array of dishes that can be enjoyed in this bright, light building in delicious surrounds.

THE RED LION HOTEL
Traditional English Fare

High Street, Colchester, CO1 1DJ
01206 577 986
In a restaurant set under the old timber beams of the Red Lion Hotel's former banqueting hall, diners can feast on suitably classic dishes with a modern twist. A Brook Hotel.

THE RESTAURANT ON CHURCH ST
European

2 Church Street, Saffron Walden, CB10 1JW
01799 526 444
Beautifully presented modern European cuisine with a contemporary North African influence. A perfect haven to create a memorable experience, this restaurant is warm and personable enough for any occasion.

THE SWAN AT FELSTED
European

Station Road, Felsted, CM6 3DG
01371 820 245
Epitomising the beauty of its picturesque surroundings, The Swan has enjoyed its pride-of-place position for centuries. The award-winning restaurant focuses on a menu designed to stimulate the senses.

THE WHITE HART
Fine Dining

Poole Street, Great Yeldham, CO9 4HJ
01787 237 250
This pub's rural location is brilliantly reflected by its traditional style inside. The large timber-framed house is home to wood-beamed ceilings and open fireplaces, as well as tasty, classic pub food.

THE WHITE HORSE
European

The Street, Pleshey, Chelmsford, CM3 1HA
01245 237 281
Good old-fashioned pub food, home cooked and scrumptious. Once you've experienced the kind welcome that greets all guests at this pub-restaurant you'll want to come back over and over again.

WHITEHALL HOTEL
Modern British

Church End, Broxted, Dunmow, CM6 2BZ
01279 850 603
A famous restaurant serving some of the finest dishes in the country. Delivering a fantastic selection of fresh, mouth-watering cuisine in the magnificent surroundings of a luxurious Brook hotel.

THE KINGS OAK HOTEL
Modern British

Pauls Nursery Rd, High Beach, Loughton, IG10 4AE
020 5085000
In amongst the dappled shade of the Great Monk Wood near Loughton sits this distinctive hotel-pub-restaurant, whose dining room menu is as striking as the venue itself. Of note, is the breast of goose.

NEW

Norfolk

BELLA ITALIA
Italian

3 Red Lion Street, Norwich, NR1 3QF
01603 614 676
Inspiring Italian cuisine can be found in this wonderful restaurant chain. Enjoy an aromatic cappuccino, a delicious panini or a mouth-watering evening meal, and allow yourself to live 'la dolce vita'.

BELLA ITALIA
Italian

8 Exchange Street, Norwich, NR2 1AT
01603 767 171
Inspiring Italian cuisine can be found in this wonderful restaurant chain. Enjoy an aromatic cappuccino, a delicious panini or a mouth-watering evening meal, and allow yourself to live 'la dolce vita'.

BELLA ITALIA
Italian

4AA Leisure Scheme, Riverside, Norwich, NR1 1EE
01603 615 584
Inspiring Italian cuisine can be found in this wonderful restaurant chain. Enjoy an aromatic cappuccino, a delicious panini or a mouth-watering evening meal, and allow yourself to live 'la dolce vita'.

When booking restaurants always mention your GS membership

BELUGA BAR & EATERIE
Fine Dining
2 Upper King St, Norwich, NR3 1HA
07545 697 395
Enjoy decadence and luxury without the guilt in this phenomenal bar and restaurant. Try the pork loin with a champagne and honey glaze as a sumptuous sample of this warm, eclectic menu.

BRADLEY'S RESTAURANT
British
10 South Quay, King's Lynn, PE30 5DT
01553 819 888
Priding itself on its success in offering fine cuisine and an unrivalled wine list, this restaurant is a friendly place to dine. Watch the sunset over the river as you enjoy an evening drink.

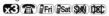

BRUMMELLS
Seafood
7 Magdalen Street, Norwich, NR3 1LE
01603 625 555
This double AA Rosette-rated restaurant serves exceptional seafood. It has been justly acclaimed for its attention to superlative produce and excellent cooking; the dining room is quirky and full of charm.

CAFÉ ROUGE
French
29 Exchange Street, Norwich, NR2 1DP
01603 624 230
An attractive restaurant, a boulevard café or a Parisian-style wine bar; however you see Café Rouge, consistently excellent classic French dishes are always guaranteed.

CANTON
Chinese
Market Place, Market Street, Norwich, NR16 2AD
01953 717 110
Indulge your senses and sample the sumptuous delights of renowned food and outstanding service. Set in a fantastic riverside location, this restaurant offers an excellent array of authentic Chinese fare.

DUNSTON HALL HOTEL
Contemporary
Brasserie Bar & Grill, Ipswich Rd, Norwich, NR14 8PQ
01508 470 444
Located in a Victorian manor house surrounded by tranquil wooded parkland, the Brasserie offers the finest seasonal dishes with an excellent choice of wines. Perfect for any event; reservations advised.

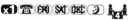

ELM FARM COUNTRY HOUSE
British
Norwich Road, Horsham, NR10 3HH
01603 898 366
A beautiful country house that offers guests and visitors use of a pleasant restaurant. Take advantage of hot and cold buffets served all day, boasting a large selection of quality food and drinks.

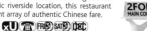

FLINTS RESTAURANT
Fine Dining
Barnham Broom Hotel, Honingham Rd, Norwich, NR9 4DD
01603 759 393
Flints Restaurant at the Barnham Broom Hotel has been recognised with 2 AA Rosettes and serves an imaginative and accomplished array of dishes. Fine dining in a stylish, calm ambience.

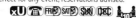

FRAZER'S RESTAURANT
Fine Dining
Sea Marge Hotel, 16 High St, Overstrand, NR27 0AB
01263 579 579
Fresh, elegantly conceived seasonal menus in this AA Rosette-recognised beachfront restaurant, set in a stunning building in Overstrand on the Norfolk coast.

HARRY RAMSDEN'S
British
11, Marine Parade, Great Yarmouth, NR30 3AH
01493 330 444
Enjoy classic seaside food from crisp batter to golden chips at this famous British restaurant. Doing what they do best, Harry Ramsden's truly delivers.

Not available during August or in takeaway.

HENRY'S CAFE BAR
European
Haymarket, Norwich, NR2 1QD
01603 625 365
The perfect escape from the bustle of the city shops with an exquisite menu of diverse and sophisticated options for everyone to enjoy, in an atmosphere to suit any mood in this refined and friendly space.

DETAILED DESCRIPTIONS AVAILABLE ON

www.gourmetsociety.co.uk

IVORY'S RESTAURANT & CAFE BAR
International
Theatre Street, Norwich, NR2 1RQ
01603 627 526
Boasting one of the finest Georgian rooms in Norwich, both traditional and contemporary dishes are available with a firm emphasis on quality. The ideal place to relax and enjoy lunch and dinner.

KINGS ARMS CHINESE & THAI
Chinese/Thai
1 Panxworth Road, South Walsham, Norwich, NR13 6DY
01603 270 039
Offers scrumptious Chinese and Thai dishes at reasonable prices. Carefully prepared and well-presented tasty food will have you coming back time and time again.

KING'S HEAD HOTEL
Carvery
Station Road, Norwich, NR12 8UR
01603 782 429
One of the many Great British Carveries offering the best of British food for guests to enjoy. Offering food fit for a king, diners love the high-quality meals and great service at this old coaching inn.

Call beforehand on special event days.

LABONE INDIAN CUISINE
Indian
40 Cromer Road, Sheringham, NR26 8RR
01263 821 120
Traditional South Indian cuisine guaranteed to excite and delight. A wide range of dishes are on offer in an authentic atmosphere.

LABONE INDIAN CUISINE *Indian*
13A Mundesley Road, North Walsham, Norwich, NR28 0AD
01692 500 119
A local well-established restaurant serving traditional South Indian food. A variety of tasty dishes are on offer for you to enjoy.

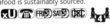

LOCH FYNE *Seafood*
30-32 St Giles Street, Norwich, NR2 1LL
01603 723 450
From the roadside oyster bar that once was, Loch Fyne restaurants now successfully inject energy and passion into great food and wonderful flavours, whilst ensuring their seafood is sustainably sourced.

MARKET BISTRO *Modern British*
11 Saturday Market Place, Kings Lynn, PE30 5DQ
0155 377 1483
This personal, close-knit bistro in King's Lynn serves food that is anything but impersonal: full, savoury flavours drawn out by chef Richard Golding who runs the restaurant with wife Lucy.

NIMMI *Indian*
17-19 Whitehart Street, Thetford, IP24 1AA
01842 761 260
Sumptuous Indian dishes to be found on an extensive menu. Holding an astounding reputation for excellent food, meat lovers, vegetarians and sensitive palates are all successfully catered for.

NUMBER 12 *Modern British*
12 Farmers Avenue, Norwich, NR1 3JX
01603 611 135
A restaurant overflowing with charm and character. Well-maintained wooden floorboards and beamed ceilings are complemented by the neutral colour scheme. Enjoy a menu that offers flavoursome food.

PREZZO *Italian*
2-6 Thorpe Road, Norwich, NR1 1RY
01603 660 404
With a character all of its own, Prezzo oozes contemporary style and enduring charm. Signature pastas, stone-baked pizzas and classic Italian dishes promise a perfect dining choice for the whole family.

PREZZO *Italian*
22 Tuesday Market Place, King's Lynn, PE30 1JJ
01553 777 616
With a character all of its own, Prezzo oozes contemporary style and enduring charm. Signature pastas, stone-baked pizzas and classic Italian dishes promise a perfect dining choice for the whole family.

PRINCE OF INDIA *Indian*
19 Prince of Wales Road, Norwich, NR1 1BD
01603 616 937
A highly recommended traditional-style restaurant. Simply good food with reasonable prices and attentive staff. Serves up some of the hottest curries in Norwich for all those who love their heat and spice.

Q'S COFFEE SHOP AND BISTRO *British*
2 Quaker Lane, Fakenham, NR21 9BQ
0132 885 1003
Only a stone's throw away from the Norfolk coast, this quaint coffee shop and bistro is beautifully located in the town of Fakenham. Guests love the variety of snacks, lunches and dinners on offer.

RAMADA HOTEL *Fine Dining*
Beveridge Way, King's Lynn, PE30 4NB
01553 771 707
The restaurant offers a wide-ranging menu enough to excite any diner, from rib eye steaks to Asian stir-fries. All food is fresh and flavoursome, delivered by professional and diligent staff.

RARE GRILL & STEAKHOUSE *British*
30-34 Unthank Road, Norwich, NR2 2RB
01603 615 655
Unwind with a relaxed dining experience in this opulent but elegant restaurant, whose food is exceptionally tailored, unusually uncomplicated and extraordinarily delicious.

RED PEPPER THAI RESTAURANT *Thai*
2A Magdalen Street, Thetford, IP24 2BN
01842 764 000
Aiming to please, the staff at this authentic Thai takeaway provide excellent food with fantastic service. Enjoy the delicious kiaw krob in the comfort of your own home.

10% off total bill after first visit.

RELISH *European*
Old Street, Newton Flotman, Norwich. NR15 1PD
01508 470 548
Here at Relish, the kitchen uses only the freshest seasonal produce from personally vetted suppliers. All dishes are served with unmatchable bread baked in Woodbridge.

SAKURA *Japanese*
5 White Lion Street, Norwich, NR2 1QA
01603 663 838
Enjoy the innovative dining concept you'll find at this authentic Japanese restaurant. Grill your own meal on the built in barbecue roaster whilst you sip a cold Japanese beer.

ST BENEDICTS RESTAURANT *French*
No 9 St Benedicts Street, Norwich, NR2 4PE
01603 765 377
A French bistro with a beautifully prepared and presented menu. Exquisite, fresh flavours underpin the owner's passionate style, perfectly complemented by a choice wine list. Awarded 1 AA Rosette.

SURREY TAVERN *British*
44-46 Surrey Street, Norwich, NR1 3NY
01603 630 478
A stylish and comfortable pub offering good ale, great food, and cheerful service. Tuck into British dishes made with flair, which can be accompanied by a thirst-quenching beer or a stunning glass of wine.

Enjoy massive leisure and retail savings with more Gourmet Society

SWALLOWTAILS
British

Broom Hall Country Hotel, Saham Toney, Watton, IP25 7EX
01953 882 125
Small and neatly conceived restaurant in Saham Toney with its focus firmly on a range of tasty, fulsome home-cooked food prepared with local produce; a warm welcome and a delicious, leisurely meal await.

THE INDIA GATE
Indian

41 St James Street, King's Lynn, PE30 5BZ
01553 776 489
Offering a perfect ambience in which diners can savour Eastern cuisine cooked with delicate herbs and spices in a traditional clay oven. Takes pride in its high standards of cooking and attentive service.

THAI DRAGON
Thai

20 Princess of Wales Road, Norwich, NR1 1LB
01603 627 775
A menu that epitomises the creativity and authenticity of Thai cuisine. The Thai green curry made with aubergines and coconut milk is just one example of the fantastic dishes on offer.

THE KESWICK HOTEL
English and Continental

The Keswick Hotel, Walcott Road, Bacton, NR12 0LS
01692 650 468
Peruse a menu that you can be sure was designed with only the best produce in mind. Priding itself on home-made quality, the kitchen is especially committed to the outstanding meat they use in many dishes.

THAI ON THE RIVER NORWICH
Thai

Floating Restaurant, Riverside, Norwich, NR1 1EE
01603 767 800
Award-winning Thai restaurant where the warm atmosphere is inviting and the beautifully prepared dishes are plentiful. The à la carte menu provides an abundant supply of first-class appetisers.

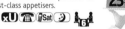

THE LANGTRY
Brasserie

79 Unthank Road, Norwich, NR2 2PE
01603 469 347
Cool and calm pub in Norwich which serves superb quality Italian-style gourmet pizzas. With their perfectly done bases and vivid array of toppings, you're sure to savour these crisp, melting specialities.

THE BUCK INN
British

55 Yarmouth Rd, Thorpe St Anthony, Norwich, NR7 0EW
01603 434 682
Charming pub in a serene part of Norfolk where you'll enjoy imaginative takes on pub favourites, cooked and presented with verve; stylishly done but losing none of the satisfying simplicity.

THE LODGE BAR & RESTAURANT
British

Main Road, North Tuddenham, NR20 3DJ
01362 638 466
An eclectic mix of old and new defines the nature and environment of The Lodge. The 19th century building is now home to a delightful restaurant that serves first-class food and real ales.

THE DALES COUNTRY HOUSE HOTEL
British

Upcher's, Lodge Hill, U. Sheringham, NR26 8TJ
01263 824 555
Enjoy refined flavours as clear as the sweeping stretch of Norfolk coastline from which this restaurant sits just a little inland. The quality and presentation are fit for its stately country house setting

CONGHAM HALL HOTEL RESTAURANT
Fine Dining

Grimston, King's Lynn PE32 1AH
01485 600250
Offering divine menus of imaginative dishes, with the finest seasonal produce. Indeed the garden of this Georgian manor produces 700 different herbs, salads and baby vegetables, picked daily for the chef.

NEW

THE GREYHOUND INN
Locally Sourced

The Green, Hickling, Norwich, NR12 0YA
01692 598 306
A great range of full-flavoured dishes on offer at this friendly, traditional village inn; recognised for its ale, food and hospitality, you can count on a great atmosphere and a thoroughgoing, fresh meal.

THE MERCHANTS OF COLEGATE
Contemporary

30-32 Colegate, Norwich, NR3 1BG
01603 611 711
An elegantly furnished restaurant hosting a wide variety of succulent dishes that will have you spoilt for choice. Famous for its superb take on monkfish, as well as some supremely decadent desserts.

THE HAMILTON
British

23-24 North Drive, Great Yarmouth, NR30 4EW
01493 844 662
Traditional, locally sourced, and home-made cooking that ranges from light snacks up to their 'gut-busting' Hamilton mixed grill. Their menu is constantly updated so there is no shortage of variety.

THE OLD CROWN PUB AND RESTAURANT
Traditional English

The Old Crown, Crown Road, Buxton, NR10 5EN
01603 279 958
A traditional, homely inn in Buxton that serves superbly cooked, full-flavoured meals using great fresh ingredients; it specialises in tender, striated and sumptuous steaks, simply and beautifully done.

THE HERB GARDEN
Fine Dining

9 Garden Street, Cromer, NR27 0HF
01263 511 559
Exceptional food made with the best local ingredients helps provide a memorable meal. A bright and friendly atmosphere where the sultry wine and scintillating food are a perfect match.

THE OLD VICARAGE RESTAURANT
Fine Dining

The Old Vicarage, The Street, Hemsby, NR29 4EU
01493 731 557
Vibrant and flavoursome dishes created in a simple yet effective manner. The chef-proprietor brooks no complacency about customer satisfaction, and you'll enjoy the passionate style of this restaurant.

EAST ANGLIA

193

THE PARK HOTEL
British

29 Denmark Street, Diss, IP22 4LE
01379 642 244
Innovative and superb value food at this hotel restaurant in Diss. Menus are constantly evolving not only with the season's produce but also customer requests. Enjoy thoughtful, superb-quality dining.

The offer excludes Sunday lunchtime.

THE REFECTORY RESTAURANT AND COFFEE SHOP
English and Continental

Norwich Cathedral, 12 The Close, Norwich, NR1 4DH
01603 218 322
Support local suppliers and contribute to the upkeep of Norwich Cathedral by feasting on freshly prepared meals. Enjoy your lunch in the knowledge that all profits made here go towards a good cause.

THE RIVERGARDEN
British

36 Yarmouth Road, Thorpe St Andrew, Norwich, NR7 0EQ
01603 703 900
Absorb the intimate and relaxing vibes of this small, candlelit restaurant where you will be delighted with the phenomenal cuisine on offer. The riverside location is perfect for a summer's day.

WINEPRESS@WENSUM AT MAID'S HEAD HOTEL
European

Tombland, Norwich, NR3 1LB
01603 209 955
With a menu overseen by outstanding Executive Chef Daniel Galmiche, with his Michelin-starred experience, this exceptional hotel-based restaurant is unfussy in manner and deliciously precise in execution.

KINGS HEAD
British

90 High Street, Hadleigh, IP7 5EF
01473 828 855
Feast on classic favourites or indulge in the more modern dish in this wonderfully situated pub. A wood-burning stove and inglenook fire enhance the warm welcome that greets you at the door.

LEMON TREE BISTRO
Modern European

3 Church St, Framlingham, Woodbridge, IP13 9BE
01728 621 232
A sensibly priced bistro that delivers a relaxing atmosphere for guests to enjoy amazing food, all day long. Perfectly placed just off the market square, this venue really has something for everyone.

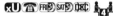

LOCH FYNE
Seafood

Old Sub Station, 1 Duke St, Ipswich, IP3 0AE
01473 269 810
From the roadside oyster bar that once was, Loch Fyne restaurants now successfully inject energy and passion into great food and wonderful flavours, whilst ensuring their seafood is sustainably sourced.

MAHARANI
Indian

46 Norwich Road, Ipswich, IP1 2NJ
01473 213 388
Classic Bangladeshi recipes underpin this acclaimed restaurant, supplemented by an ongoing openness to new tastes; it specialises in flavourful fish dishes and rich bhunas.

OLD ORLEANS
American

Cardinal Park, 27 Grafton Way, Ipswich, IP1 1AX
01473 215 581
An extraordinarily accurate taste of the Deep South can be found in this unique restaurant. The kitchen deals in classic Louisiana and Cajun recipes such as jambalaya and gumbo to create an exciting menu.

Not available on Bank Holiday weekends. Adult menu only.

Suffolk

AQUA EIGHT
Pan Asian

8 Lion Street, Ipswich, IP1 1DQ
01473 218 989
Delicious pan-Asian cuisine served in an intimate setting, with a truly divine menu offering specials such as the delectable wasabi sirloin steak, complemented by a range of carefully selected fine wines.

CAFÉ ROUGE
French

59 Abbeygate St, Bury St Edmunds, IP33 1LB
01284 764 477
An attractive restaurant, a boulevard café or a Parisian-style wine bar; however you see Café Rouge, consistently excellent classic French dishes are always guaranteed.

DARK HORSE RESTAURANT
European

Kiln Lane, Stowlangtoft, Bury St Edmunds, IP31 3JY
01359 232 223
An ideal place to spend your evening. With an evocative French bistro feel to it, the restaurant walls are lined with the work of local artists that can be admired and even purchased.

PIATTO
Italian

23 Small Gate, Beccles, NR34 9AD
01502 711 711
A brightly rustic Italian restaurant that prides itself on its well-decorated interior and fabulous cuisine. Deep-pan pizzas and divine pasta dishes will have you emerging satisfied.

PIZZA AND PANCAKE
Italian

18-32 Station Square, Lowestoft, NR32 1BA
01502 501 880
Pizza and Pancake is a contemporary, modern restaurant with friendly and efficient staff. All their food is fresh, delicious, and cooked to order, with pizza made from fresh dough every day.

PREZZO
Italian

54-55 Gainsborough Street, Sudbury, CO10 2ET
01787 880 852
With a character all of its own, Prezzo oozes contemporary style and enduring charm. Signature pastas, stone-baked pizzas and classic Italian dishes promise a perfect dining choice for the whole family.

194

Recommend a friend to the Gourmet Society and receive a free gift.

PREZZO
Italian
1 Church Street, Woodbridge, IP12 1DS
01394 610 401
With a character all of its own, Prezzo oozes contemporary style and enduring charm. Signature pastas, stone-baked pizzas and classic Italian dishes promise a perfect dining choice for the whole family.

SPICE FUSION INDIAN & THAI RESTAURANT
Thai/Indian
39 Upper Orwell Street, Ipswich, IP4 1HP
01473 212 414
A bright, modern restaurant delivering a fusion of Indian and Thai flavours. Offering an extensive range of dishes, all diners can delight in experiencing some of the greatest cuisines in the world.

PREZZO
Italian
2 Exeter Road, Newmarket, CB8 8LT
01638 669 676
With a character all of its own, Prezzo oozes contemporary style and enduring charm. Signature pastas, stone-baked pizzas and classic Italian dishes promise a perfect dining choice for the whole family.

THAI PAVILION
Thai
3 Friars Street, Sudbury, CO10 2AA
01787 315 656
Accommodating Thai restaurant on the pretty Friars Street in Sudbury, where you can enjoy a warming meal of the fresh, eclectic and clean flavours that distinguish Thai cooking.

PREZZO
Italian
Unit 2, Ehringshausen Way, Haverhill, CB9 0BB
01440 767 878
With a character all of its own, Prezzo oozes contemporary style and enduring charm. Signature pastas, stone-baked pizzas and classic Italian dishes promise a perfect dining choice for the whole family.

PREZZO
Italian
35-36 Abbeygate Street, Bury St Edmunds, IP33 1LW
01284 756260
With a character all of its own, Prezzo oozes contemporary style and enduring charm. Signature pastas, stone-baked pizzas and classic Italian dishes promise a perfect dining choice for the whole family.

NEW

PREZZO
Italian
146 High Street, Aldeburgh, IP15 5AQ
01728 454 452
With a character all of its own, Prezzo oozes contemporary style and enduring charm. Signature pastas, stone-baked pizzas and classic Italian dishes promise a perfect dining choice for the whole family.

FREDERICK'S RESTAURANT
Fine Dining
Ickworth Hotel, Horringer, Bury St Edmunds, IP29 5QE
01284 735350
Frederick's Restaurant has been awarded two AA rosettes and is situated in the original dining rooms frequented by the family who owned this Suffolk Estate.

NEW

PREZZO
Italian
9 Saltgate, Beccles, NR34 9AN
01502 715 036
With a character all of its own, Prezzo oozes contemporary style and enduring charm. Signature pastas, stone-baked pizzas and classic Italian dishes promise a perfect dining choice for the whole family.

THE OLD SCOTCH INDIAN RESTAURANT
Indian
4 The Avenue, Newmarket, CB8 9AA
01638 663 400
Fine Indian dining in Newmarket; classic flavours spruced up with contemporary flashes and served smartly and elegantly in these lovely old tea rooms.

QUEENS HEAD
British
The Street, Bramfield, IP19 9HT
01986 784 214
Award-winning dining pub close to the stunning Suffolk coast, providing hearty home-cooked meals produced from quality local and organic produce.

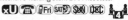

THE STAR
European
The Street, Lidgate, Newmarket, CB8 9PP
01638 500 275
A quintessential English pub made complete by its log fires, oak beams and draught bitters. The food however is typically Mediterranean, and the menu is embodied by many impressive and exciting dishes.

SCUTCHERS OF LONG MELFORD
British
Westgate Street, Long Melford, CO10 9DP
01787 310 200
Featured in many major restaurant guides, this family-run restaurant combines tradition with contemporary chic. Expect the friendliest service and admirably attentive waiting staff. 2 AA Rosettes.

THE SWAN HOTEL
Fine Dining
Market Square, Southwold, IP18 6EG
01502 722 186
This is a wonderful retreat that exudes timeless style while maintaining every modern comfort. Both à la carte and lighter meals are available, making the menu suitable for all pockets and appetites.

SHEPHERD & DOG
Carvery
Felixstowe Road, Ipswich, IP10 0DF
01473 659 210
A well-loved member of the Great British Carvery group offering the best of British food with a modern twist. A firm family-friendly favourite with both locals and visitors.

Call beforehand on special event days.

WICKED @ ST PETER'S
British
St Peter's Hall, South Elmham, Bungay, NR35 1NQ
01986 782 288
A visual as well as culinary delight; dine like a Tudor in this stunning restaurant. Locally sourced produce underwrites their dishes, all cooked from scratch. Enjoy the award-winning ale brewed on-site.

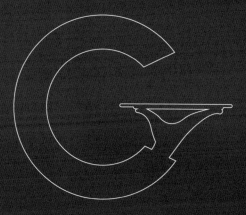

Wales

Though small, Wales has a diverse terrain. Coupled with its rivers and long coastline, this country has always yielded a wealth of fresh foods, in particular wild animals and seafood. Sheep farming is extensive here as even a cursory glance at the rolling hillsides will testify. Lamb, formerly eaten on only special occasions has gained popularity and the excellent grazing pastures have encouraged the making of fine ewes' milk cheeses.

The fishing culture is also strong. Fisheries are common, whilst shallower waters yield plenty of cockles and laver (seaweed), which is deliciously rolled with cornmeal to produce a true Welsh delicacy.

Welsh cuisine reflects the country's Celtic roots with popular ingredients following old traditions and being widely used. Welsh cakes made on traditional bakestones are as ubiquitous as ever, whilst oats, the staple food of the ancient Welsh, remain a firm favourite in cooking. Naturally, so too is the leek, national symbol of Wales for centuries - its likeness worn by soldiers as a badge of identity - and today, as before times, used to craft delicious soups and stews, pies and sauces.

Wales is today home to some of the finest dining in the world, and the best restaurants will tempt with culinary delights; roast spring lamb teamed with fresh mint sauce, the cheesy Welsh rarebit, the hearty Shepherd's pie. All are synonymous with Wales and best enjoyed within her boundaries, amongst the magnificent landscapes which produced them.

Clwyd

Dyfed

GREENBANK
Steakhouse

Hill Street, Llangollen, LL20 EU
01978 861 835
An impressive Victorian town house hotel that boasts a delicious steakhouse restaurant. Combining friendly service and a cosy atmosphere, they deliver wholesome food with a fine choice of beers and wine.

HURST HOUSE ON THE MARSH
Modern British

East Marsh, Laugharne, SA33 4RS
01944 427 417
Enjoy a warming, hearty dish, or choose to indulge in a more refined supper from the house and tasting menus. This charming hotel successfully mixes old and new to create a unique dining experience.

LEGENDS BAR & RESTAURANT
Bistro

Caeau Farm, Gresford Road, Hope, LL12 9SD
01978 769 172
Tasty and hearty home-cooked food in a cosy, cool space with a Hollywood Legends theme.

2FOR1
MAIN COURSE

LANGOSTINOS
British

1-6 Castle Buildings, Murray St., Llanelli, SA15 1AQ
01554 773 711
A bright, relaxed and elegant brasserie-style steakhouse in Llanelli; contemporary cooking full of taste and complemented by the genial ambience and friendly service. Fresh and seasonal flavours.

2FOR1
3 COURSES

TAMARIND THAI
Thai

Lyndale Hotel, 410 Abergele Road, Colwyn Bay, LL29 9AB
01492 515 429
Combining locally sourced produce with the spice and bite of classic Thai cuisine, this hotel-based restaurant sits close to the seafront in Colwyn Bay and promises excellent service in a serene setting.

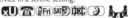

RESTAURANT 7TEEN & DELI
British

17 Queen Street, Carmarthen, SA31 1JT
01267 229 599
A fresh, innovative restaurant in Carmarthen with a focus on thorough, accomplished simplicity in its cooking, borne out by the clean, distinct and exceptionally full flavours that congregate in each dish.

ORCHARD RESTAURANT
Modern British

Beaufort Park Hotel, New Brighton, Mold, CH7 6RQ
01352 758 646
Unwind and relax as you peruse the wonderful menu and sip on a glass of fine wine. Speciality seasonal dishes make the most of the fine Welsh produce and local ingredients that are on offer.

2FOR1
MAIN COURSE

DETAILED DESCRIPTIONS AVAILABLE ON
www.gourmetsociety.co.uk

THE CHEQUERS RESTAURANT & BAR
Fine Dining

Northrop Hall, Chester Road, Mold, CH7 6HJ
01244 816 181
With an air of opulence and style, delight in the contemporary cuisine on offer; from an imaginative and sweetly tender 'Celebration of Welsh Lamb' to a warm and musky guinea fowl breast, you're set fair.

2FOR1
MAIN COURSE

Offer only applies to table d'hôte menu.

TRAETH
Modern British

South John Street, New Quay, SA45 9NP
01545 561 844
Choose a light or hearty breakfast, bistro lunch, or choose from the daily changing dinner menu featuring wonderfully cooked, amazingly fresh and honest food. Enjoy the stylish yet simple approach.

THE GOLDEN LION
European

Chester Road, Rossett, LL12 0HN
01244 571 020
A traditionally adorned pub that has a phenomenal reputation for fantastic food. Feel completely at home in this cosy, warming establishment, where genial staff provide exceptional service.

2FOR1
MAIN COURSE

TRUBSHAWS RESTAURANT
Modern European

Diplomat Hotel, Felinfoel, Llanelli, SA15 3PJ
01554 756 156
Highly regarded locally, Trubshaws Restaurant in the Diplomat Hotel serves fresh and seasonal dishes in a bright and elegant dining room. No need to be diplomatic: enjoy and let your guard down.

THE WEST ARMS
Welsh

LLanarmon DC, Llangollen, LL20 7LD
01691 600 665
Sit by the open log fire in winter and reflect on the day's activities while enjoying an array of fruity and fulsome dishes. Simple and clean but eclectic and imaginative flavours. 2 AA Rosettes.

VALLEY RESTAURANT & THE FALCONDALE
British

Falcondale Drive, Lampeter, SA48 7RX
01570 422 910
Enveloped by sublime valleys and breathtaking scenery, this mansion boasts a homely ambience and a warm, welcoming service. Complete your dining experience with one of the many fine wines.

2FOR1
MAIN COURSE

Gourmet Society discount applies to the à la carte menu

Glamorgan

BA ORIENT
Japanese

Unit 27, Mermaid Quay, Cardiff, CF10 5BZ
02920 463 939
Elegant Japanese cuisine in sophisticated surroundings, where expert mixologists are on hand to craft and serve the finest cocktails, along with an array of wines and champagnes.

BOSPHORUS RESTAURANT
Turkish

31 Mermaid Quay, Cardiff, CF10 5BZ
02920 487 477
Turkish cuisine with an enthusiastic flair that is guaranteed to excite and delight you. This characterful restaurant has charmed many guests with its use of fresh local ingredients.

2FOR1
MAIN COURSE

CAFE DI NAPOLI
Italian

28 Windsor Road, Neath, West Glamorgan, SA11 1LU
01639 643 741
Highly experienced chefs craft perfectly superb, authentic Italian cuisine, complemented by a fine array of carefully selected choice wines. Come and experience true Italian dining.

50%OFF
FOOD

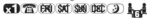

CAFE JAZZ
European

21 St Mary Street, Cardiff, CF10 1PL
02929 387 026
Get your weekly fix of jazz, blues and food at Café Jazz. Old, new, local and international sounds will soothe the soul as delicious food is devoured. Fine live performances to be expected.

25%OFF
TOTAL

CAFÉ ROUGE
French

Mermaid Quay, Cardiff, CF10 5BZ
02920 497 638
An attractive restaurant, a boulevard café or a Parisian-style wine bar; however you see Café Rouge, consistently excellent classic French dishes are always guaranteed.

50%OFF
FOOD

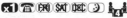

CAFÉ ROUGE
French

Unit UG03, St Davids II, Cardiff, CF10 1EW
02920 236 574
An attractive restaurant, a boulevard café or a Parisian-style wine bar; however you see Café Rouge, consistently excellent classic French dishes are always guaranteed.

50%OFF
FOOD

CARDAMOM INDIAN
Indian

442C Cowbridge Road, E Victoria Park, Cardiff, CF5 1JN
02920 233 506
Expect fine food and wonderfully friendly service in a hospitable environment. Warm welcomes and delicious Indian dishes make this a winning place to dine.

2FOR1
MAIN COURSE

DIZZY LLAMA,
International

24 Churchill Way, Cardiff, CF10 2DY
02920 343 424
Imaginative and diverse menu of well-cooked dishes, from tapas to beef fillets, in a vibrant and buzzy basement location in the centre of Cardiff. With a widespread following, it's worth a spin.

25%OFF
TOTAL

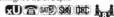

ELAICHI THE SULLY INN
Indian/ Bangladeshi

4 Cog Road, Sully, Penarth, CF64 5TD
02920 530 176
A great Indian restaurant showcasing an exceptional menu filled with exquisite dishes, all complemented by a fine wine list. Quality food whether you choose to dine in or take away.

2FOR1
MAIN COURSE

EVEREST TANDOORI
Indian

34 Taff Vale Shopping Centre, Pontypridd, CF37 4TH
01443 406 640
This classic curry house will sit you down and fill you up with not only the well-known staples of Indian restaurants, but also some hidden regional gems, like the Gurkha Massala.

2FOR1
MAIN COURSE

FFRESH
Welsh

Wales Millennium Centre, Cardiff, CF10 5AL
02920 636 465
Friendly staff efficiently deliver fresh and delicious lunches and dinners, along with an exceptional range of drinks. The home of great food at the heart of Cardiff Bay.

2FOR1
3 COURSES

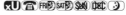

PREZZO
Italian

14 Bridge Street, St Davids Dewi Sant, Cardiff, CF10 2EF
02920 397 512
With a character all of its own, Prezzo oozes contemporary style and enduring charm. Signature pastas, stone-baked pizzas and classic Italian dishes promise a perfect dining choice for the whole family.

NEW

2FOR1
MAIN COURSE

RECOMMEND A FRIEND

see page 18

HARRY RAMSDEN'S
British

Landsea House, Stuart Place, Cardiff Bay, Cardiff, CF10 5BU
02920 463 334
Delicious fish and chips, served with a dash of salt and vinegar, from a British institution. Indulge in the taste of the seaside any time at this long running, ever-popular restaurant.

25%OFF
TOTAL

Not available during August or in takeaway.

HAVELI
Pan Asian

157 City Road, Cardiff, CF24 3BQ
02920 482 882
Using seductive spices, experienced chefs create innovative and contemporary pan-Asian cuisine. Fragrant, flavourful dishes are produced from fine ingredients and delivered in this stylish setting.

25%OFF
TOTAL

WALES

199

HENRYS CAFE BAR
European

Park Chambers, Park Place, Cardiff, CF10 3DN
02920 224 672
An oasis for every type of person with a delicious, well-prepared menu ideal for lunch, dinner or a light snack. Henrys also boasts extensive wine and champagne lists and a choice of cocktails to die for.

LOCH FYNE
Seafood

Stalling Down, Cowbridge, CF71 7DT
01446 776 070
From the roadside oyster bar that once was, Loch Fyne restaurants now successfully inject energy and passion into great food and wonderful flavours, whilst ensuring their seafood is sustainably sourced.

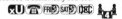

ICHIBAN JAPANESE
Japanese

167 Albany Rd, Roath, Cardiff, CF24 3NT
02920 463 333
The freshest ingredients go into every dish at this outstanding restaurant. Superbly healthy sushi and noodle dishes can be fully enjoyed without breaking the diet.

LORENZA'S RISTORANTE ITALIANO
Italian

153-155 Cryws Road, Cardiff, CF24 4NH
02920 232 261
A classic and highly satisfying Italian dining experience, providing every customer with a warm welcome and delectable, authentic cuisine, with choices that will appeal to all appetites.

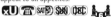

ICHIBAN JAPANESE
Japanese

201 Cowbridge Road East, Cardiff, CF11 9AJ
02920 668 833
Get some welcome relief from stodgy takeaway fare and try some healthy, fresh Japanese cuisine at this eat-in restaurant. Ichiban is Japanese for 'number one', and sums up their top-notch food and service.

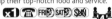

MANGO HOUSE
Indian

Grand Hotel, Westgate Street, Cardiff, CF10 1DD
02920 232 266
Indian food lovers will be delighted with the freshly prepared recipes here, offering diners a wonderful array of dishes created from the flavours and spices of the subcontinent.

LAS HAVANAS
Tapas

17/19 City Road, Roath, Cardiff, CF24 3BJ
02920 493 337
An exciting, innovative and refreshing approach to Latin cooking, crafted with passion and flair. Traditional recipes, adapted into contemporary dishes that still retain their superbly authentic quality.

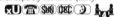

MEDITERRANEO AT BOATHOUSE
Italian

10 The Esplanade, Penarth, CF64 3AU
02920 703 428
Inflected by the maritime history of its setting, this restaurant specialises in seafood prepared alla italiano; warm, mellow flavours in a beautiful, characterful seafront setting.

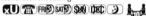

W A L E S

MIMOSA KITCHEN & BAR

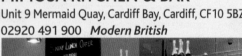

Unit 9 Mermaid Quay, Cardiff Bay, Cardiff, CF10 5BZ
02920 491 900 *Modern British*

In the heart of Cardiff Bay, Mimosa Kitchen & Bar is a bustling meeting point for the cities' cosmopolitan drinkers and diners.

Mimosa Kitchen & Bar proposes a contemporary menu, all freshly prepared to order by expert chefs. Where possible all ingredients are locally sourced, free-range and fair-trade with 100% traceability. The menu features traditional Welsh favourites such as cawl, Welsh black beef, cockles & laverbread as well as a wide selection of vegetarian dishes and a cracking breakfast selection.

Mimosa takes its name from the Mimosa tea clipper which set sail in 1865 carrying 159 Welsh folk intent on creating a new Wales in Patagonia, Argentina. The success of that long-ago journey is today evidenced by a 20,000 strong population of descendents, about a quarter of whom speak Welsh. As befits its forward-thinking forbearers, Mimosa boasts a striking contemporary design enhanced and nuanced by the use of natural textures such as Welsh slate, wenge wood, and leather seating, on which to soak up the bustling yet relaxed atmosphere.

Sign up to our newsletter for latest restaurants, offers and more

NEALE'S HOLM HOUSE
British
Holm House, Marine Parade, Penarth, CF64 3BG
02920 701 572
Situated within a hotel that oozes splendour and magnificence, this haven of a restaurant is not only idyllically located but also offers the most terrific food, providing a true taste of Wales.

OLD ORLEANS
American
Fairfax House, 17-19 Church St, Cardiff, CF10 1BG
02920 222 078
An extraordinarily accurate taste of the Deep South can be found in this unique restaurant. The kitchen deals in classic Louisiana and Cajun recipes such as jambalaya and gumbo to create an exciting menu.

Not available on Bank Holiday weekends. Adult menu only.

PEARL OF THE ORIENT
Oriental
First Floor, Mermaid Quay, Cardiff Bay, CF10 5BZ
02920 498 080
A formal fine dining experience is on offer at this delightful oriental restaurant. Live piano music enhances the characterful atmosphere, making this an ideal place to enjoy an array of dishes.

POSITANO RESTAURANT
Italian
9-10 Church Street, Cardiff, CF10 1BG
02920 235 810
A fine à la carte menu accommodates delicious Italian cuisine. For guests who feel spoilt for choice, the set menu offers carefully selected combinations that are guaranteed to excite, delight and satisfy.

PREZZO
Italian
106 St Mary Street, Cardiff, CF10 9NQ
02920 227 785
With a character all of its own, Prezzo oozes contemporary style and enduring charm. Signature pastas, stone-baked pizzas and classic Italian dishes promise a perfect dining choice for the whole family.

PUCCINI
Mediterranean
120 Albany Rd, Cardiff, CF24 3RU
02920 493 031
Come dine at this calming oasis where an extensive tapas menu and a real assortment of Mediterranean dishes are on offer. A dining area reminiscent of Italy is the ideal setting for an intimate meal.

RAGLANS AT COPTHORNE HOTEL
International
Copthorne Way, Culverhouse Cross, Cardiff, CF5 6DH
02920 599 100
It's easy to see how this quietly stylish restaurant has won its 2 AA Rosettes. Great food and fine wine make an outstanding combination, whilst the lakeside setting is perfect for intimate dining.

RBG @ PARK INN CARDIFF NORTH
Contemporary
Park Inn Cardiff North, Cardiff, CF23 9XF
02920 589 988
Known for serving some of the best gourmet burgers in town, RBG at the Park Inn Hotel in Cardiff's city centre is a stylish and modern restaurant and grill. Delicious, convenient and affordable food.

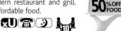

SPICE QUARTER
Indian
Unit 8b, The Old Brewery Quarter, Cardiff, CF10 1FG
02920 220 075
A rare, authentic Indian dining experience. An exquisite selection of meals, from traditional old favourites to exiting specials, are created by original chefs recruited from Delhi and Bombay.

 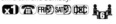

THAI EDGE CARDIFF
Thai
Unit 8, The Old Brewery Quarter, Cardiff, CF10 1FG
02920 235 665
Each dish combines the most amazing array of herbs, roots and spices such as galangal and krachai to create a subtle blend of flavours. Authentic Thai cuisine that will have you coming back for more.

THE BUTCHERS @ ALLTWEN
Fresh Fish/Pub Classics
Alltwen Hill, Pontardawe, SA8 3BP
01792 863 100
This warm, welcoming pub-restaurant provides a bright, fresh menu and is becoming known for a stock in trade of fresh, simply prepared, perfectly seasoned fish. Enjoy, with the pub's spectacular views.

THE OLD POST OFFICE
European
Reenwood Lane, St Fagans, Cardiff, CF5 6EL
02920 565 400
Set in an old village Post Office, this listed building holds many a story. Guests can indulge in contemporary dining with traditional dishes boasting modern European influences. Awarded 1 AA Rosette.

DETAILED DESCRIPTIONS AVAILABLE ON

www.gourmetsociety.co.uk

THE STAR INN
Welsh
Ewenny Road, Wick, Cowbridge, CF71 7QA
01656 890 519
In beautiful Welsh surroundings, this friendly and committed inn will charm you with its locally sourced, freshly cooked dishes from the classic Welsh and British pub food canon.

 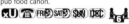

TIGER TIGER
International
Greyfriars Road, Cardiff, CF10 3QB
02920 391 944
Experience a new casual style of drinking and dining any day of the week. Whether you fancy a traditional favourite or a taste of the East, Tiger offers a large array of dishes.

ZUSHI
Japanese
The Aspect, 140 Queen Street, Cardiff, CF10 2GP
02920 669 911
Vivid and lively conveyor-belt sushi and noodle bar in the centre of Cardiff. Enjoy the beautifully prepared, seasoned sushi in an environment that is perfect for the buzz of urban work and play.

WALES

201

Gwent

BELLA MAMMA'S
Italian

108 Lower Dock Street, Newport, NP20 2AG
01633 244 226
Art Deco-influenced Italian ristorante in Newport with colourful, flavour-filled canonical dishes; worth going beyond your standard repertoire to try the outstanding traditional specialities.

1861

1861 Cross Ash, Abergavenny, NP7 8PB
0845 388 1861 *Locally Sourced*

2FOR1
MAIN COURSE

The picturesque hamlet of Cross Ash, just outside Abergavenny, is home to a truly gourmet cuisine experience. Simon King, co-owner and head chef, has worked in some of the country's top restaurants. Fine dining is very much his forte along with a deep understanding of the importance of food provenance. This sensitivity to produce, led him to Monmouthshire, a part of Wales that he and wife Kate, believe to be a genuine food destination.

With an abundance of local ingredients now at their disposal Simon and Kate create exquisite seasonal menus that visitors can enjoy at a fair price and in a comfortable atmosphere.

Simon's French techniques and Scandinavian search for perfection in the kitchen, coupled with Kate's warm and welcoming front of house service, have already won 1861, two AA rosettes.

BISTRO PREGO
Modern European

7 Church Street, Monmouth, NP25 3BX
01600 712 600
Swiftly gaining a reputation for excellence due to their outstanding range of fine food and wine, with a menu offering modern European dishes that are a real delight to the senses.

25%OFF TOTAL

BLADES RESTAURANT
British

Beaufort Hotel, Beaufort Square, Chepstow, NP16 5EP
01291 622 497
A family-run restaurant where the staff pride themselves on their efficient and friendly service and great value for money. The modern à la carte menu has won the restaurant its award-winning status.

25%OFF TOTAL

INDIAN SUMMER
Indian

Unit 5 Oldway Centre, Monmouth, NP25 3PS
01600 719 519
Fashionable yet affordable. Highly experienced chefs create delectable cuisine with great Indian flamboyance, so expect high quality food and a warm and traditional welcome.

25%OFF TOTAL

MANGO HOUSE
Indian

The Mango House, Glenroy House, Caldicot, NP26 3HY
01633 882 655
Sample the flavour and spice of the Indian subcontinent through various well-prepared and sumptuous dishes. Traditional ingredients and recipes are used to create fine, high-quality cuisine.

2FOR1
MAIN COURSE

MORGAN'S AT MARIOTT ST PIERRE PARK
International

St Pierre Park, Hayesgate, Chepstow, NP16 6YA
01291 635 265
This restaurant's contemporary menu is inflected by the tender, hearty style of traditional Welsh cuisine. Enjoy the savoury, fresh flavours in the serene, rolling green of South Wales's countryside.

25%OFF TOTAL

RAFTERS AT THE CELTIC MANOR
British

The Twenty Ten Clubhouse, Coldra Woods, NP18 1HQ
01633 410 262
Occupied with modern elegance, this outstanding restaurant oozes a charming character that will be enjoyed by all guests. Be blown away by exquisite Welsh beef and fresh seafood. 1 AA Rosette.

25%OFF TOTAL

Visit the website regularly to discover the latest restaurants joining the GS

THE BELL AT SKENFRITH
British

Skenfrith, Nr Monmouth, NP7 8UH
01600 750 235
With two AA Rosettes to its name, this restaurant is known for its ranging, fresh menu and superbly accomplished cooking; with a focus on sourcing locally and seasonal classics.

Sunday lunch excluded.

THE CLYTHA ARMS
International

Clytha, Old Raglan Road, Abergavenny, NP7 9BW
01873 840 206
Friendly and homely food-led pub between Raglan and Abergavenny; enjoy the finely cooked, eclectic dishes, from musky wild boar in rioja to a zippy Caribbean fruit curry with crayfish.

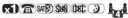

THE FARMER'S DAUGHTER
Welsh

Croescarneinion Farm, Bassaleg, NP10 8RR
01633 892 800
Fantastically personable and relaxed restaurant tucked away on the land of a working farm. With great care, attention to detail, and flexibility to diners' tastes, the restaurant is a distinctive treat.

THE HALL INN
British

Old Raglan Road, Gwehelog, NP15 1RB
01291 672 381
Enjoy a friendly atmosphere, superb, flavoursome and savoury dishes of great pub fare, and a pleasingly diverse array of real ales, draughts, wines and spirits at the bar.

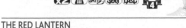

THE LODGE AT CELTIC MANOR
British

The Lodge, Coldra Woods, The Usk Valley, NP18 1HQ
01633 410 262
In this restaurant at Celtic Manor, home of the 2010 Ryder Cup, you'll find luxury and comfort along with superb views. An accomplished, rustic British menu features succulent steaks and fresh seafood.

THE RED LANTERN
Chinese

Bank Street, Chepstow, NP16 5EL
01291 627 726
A fabulous restaurant that has introduced the great nuances of Chinese cuisine to the local area. Their Peking, Szechuan and Guangdong dishes are all delicious, whilst the fried Dover sole is incredible.

THE RIVERSIDE HOTEL
British

Riverside Hotel, Cinderhill St, Monmouth, NP25 5EY
01600 715 577
A warm and lovely inn, where the restaurant is smart and accommodating and serves good, accomplished fare. You'll enjoy trying out the array of beers and ciders behind the bar to wash it all down.

THREE BLACKBIRDS INN
Modern British

Llantarnam, Cwnbran, NP44 3AY
01633 483 130
A fine place for that pint and a dinner after a yomp in the mountains; just as much to enjoy the hearty, home-cooked fare while absorbing the sublime scenery from afar. Part of the Best of British group.

ZEST RESTAURANT
English and Continental

Marriott St.Pierre Hotel, Chepstow, NP16 6YA
01291 625 261
The second of two restaurants at the Marriott St Pierre offering contemporary dining in a relaxed environment. Start your day with a morning coffee and pastry, or join them for lunch and dinner.

ANN'S PANTRY
Bistro

Arfryn, Moelfre, LL72 8HL
01248 410 386
Indulge in tantalising bistro food from mouth-watering braised lamb to fresh, succulent crab and lobster. With an emphasis on fresh produce and perfect cooking, this restaurant will not disappoint.

SEIONT MANOR HOTEL
British

The Llwyn y Brain Restaurant, Llanrug, LL55 2AQ
0845 072 7550
Mouth-watering, decadent, double-AA Rosette dining in this magnificent country house, part of the Hand Picked Hotels group. Feast in a dining hall full of remarkable character and charm.

THE DRIVEN GOOSE
International

Yr Hafod, Trefriw, Nr Betwys-y-Coed, LL27 0RQ
01492 640 029
International dishes created with fresh, local ingredients deliver a unique tasting cuisine. With a daily changing menu and an emphasis on satisfying the customer, all are catered for at this bistro.

RECOMMEND A FRIEND
see page 18

BRADFORD ARMS HOTEL
British

North Road, Llanymynech, SY22 6EJ
01691 830 582
This restaurant is beautifully set in the stunning landscape touching on the Welsh-English border, and has a diverse menu that serves hearty, high quality food.

WALES

West Midlands

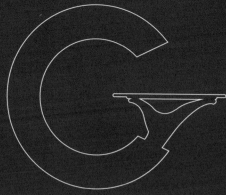

The West Midlands is an area that truly captures the heart of England not only in its centrality but also its culture, beauty and food. It also plays host to miles upon miles of beautiful countryside and farmland. This in turn results in fresh home-grown foods that guarantee classic English dishes a firm position on menus.

Local produce is anything but hard to come by and meat, poultry, vegetable and dairy produce is of the highest quality. Herefordshire apples make some of the world's best cider, whilst Warwickshire ale is a pub staple here, served with a hearty Warwickshire stew. Even those unfamiliar with the West Midlands will not be strangers to the infamous Staffordshire oatcakes.

A delightful national character can be found in the West Midlands, amidst its country pubs and quaint, village tea-houses. Yet the area is also host to a wide variety of International cuisine, which has resulted in delectable dishes from around the world being brought to the core of England. Locals have a healthy appetite for Indian, Bangladeshi and Pakistani restaurants in particular, which has fuelled the evolution of some of the very best curry houses in Britain and given rise to Balti cuisine, born in Birmingham in the 1970s.

Whether desirous of the quintessential afternoon tea, or owner of a curry-loving belly, you'll find yourself well catered for here, where the essence of old Englishness is met by modern-day British multiculturalism.

Shropshire

BADA BING
International

New Row, Town Centre, Telford, TF3 4BX
07723 092 226
Immerse yourself in sumptuous, stylish surroundings as you browse the extensive food and drink menus. English, Italian and Mexican dishes can be accompanied by delicious thirst-quenching cocktails.

BARON OF BEEF
British

Chapel Lawn Road, Bucknell, SY7 0AH
01547 530 549
Idyllically located in the pretty village of Bucknell, the stunning views of the rolling hills add to the character and charm of this country inn. Expect welcomes as warm as the crackling log fire inside.

BROOKS AROUND THE CORNER
British

69 Church Street, Oswestry, SY11 2SZ
01691 654 742
A fantastic selection of meat, fish and vegetarian dishes await you at this splendid restaurant. The vegetarian sausages are a firm favourite, whilst the daily changing fish board reflects its freshness.

BUTLER'S BAR & RESTAURANT
European

Park House Hotel, Park St, Shifnal TF11 9BA
01952 460 128
A relaxing atmosphere to be enjoyed in complete comfort. Take advantage of the bar's array of inside amenities, or enjoy your food and drink in the pleasurable garden. Awarded 1 AA Rosette.

CROMWELLS INN
European

11 Dogpole, Shrewsbury, SY1 1EN
01743 361 440
Set in the medieval streets of Shrewsbury, Cromwells offers an atmospheric setting with friendly staff. The fine seasonal cuisine is produced from the best local ingredients and prepared with passion.

CROSS KEYS INN
British

Kinnerley, Oswestry, SY10 8DB
01691 682 861
The cuisine is simple, honest and cooked with a minimum of fuss so the qualities of the food shine through. The homely and delicious dishes are everything pub food ought to be.

DA VINCI
Italian

26 High Street, Ironbridge, Telford, TF8 7AD
01952 432 250
Offering delicious contemporary and traditional Italian dishes with a passion for quality rustic ingredients. With a wine list to complement each regional dish, the attention to detail is superb.

FEATHERS HOTEL
Fine Dining

Bull Ring, Ludlow, SY8 1AA
01584 875 261
Creative and imaginative menus drawn up from quality local ingredients. This popular and well-regarded restaurant is in a beautiful setting and serves flavourful, textured food. Awarded 1 AA Rosette.

GARTELLS AT THE SUN INN
British

Marton, Welshpool, SY21 8JP
01938 561 211
Modern and stylish family-run restaurant that ranges eclectically through modern English and Mediterranean flavours, with a firm emphasis on fresh, local produce.

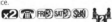

HAUGHTON HALL
European

Haughton Lane, Shifnal, TF11 8HG
01952 468 300
Decorated with timeless style and situated in 35 acres of gardens, the restaurant at Haughton Hall provides diners with a range of contemporary dishes, with a taste to suit everyone.

HOT ROCK RESTAURANT
Indian

14 Bridgnorth Road, Worfield, Bridgnorth, WV15 5NR
01746 716 666
Experience the finest Indian and Bangladeshi cuisine on offer, with all food being expertly produced to form unique-tasting dishes. All dishes can be tailored to your taste and dietary requirements.

LA ROSA
Italian

19 Church St, Wellington, TF1 2DL
01952 254 666
An enchanting restaurant suitably catering for every occasion, be it a romantic evening out or a business lunch. Guests will find a magical blend of Italian cuisine and amiable service.

LOCH FYNE
Seafood

Talbot House, Market Street, Shrewsbury, SY1 1LG
01743 277 140
From the roadside oyster bar that once was, Loch Fyne restaurants now successfully inject energy and passion into great food and wonderful flavours, whilst ensuring their seafood is sustainably sourced.

PEPPERS
Indian

A41-A49 Prees Heath, Whitchurch, SY13 3JT
01948 666 338
Curry fans will be in their element at this Indian restaurant. A vast array of delicious delights occupy the menu, whilst the staff offer friendly smiles and efficient service.

PIZZA TWO FOUR
Italian

24 Leg Street, Oswestry, SY11 2NN
01691 654 693
The place to go for finely prepared and presented pizzas, delivered in a welcoming environment. A cosy family-friendly pizzeria and pasta restaurant proving to be a firm favourite with customers.

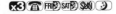

Gourmet Society discount applies to the à la carte menu

PEN-Y-DYFFRYN HALL

Rhydycroesau, Oswestry, SY10 7JD
01691 653 700 *Fine Dining*

The Pen Y Dyffryn hotel sits on a hillside yards from the Welsh border. The restaurant, with its huge, south-facing sash windows, overlooking the rolling hills all around is central to the experience awaiting visitors to this rural retreat. Their food is healthy, locally sourced, and tends to make good use of organic produce. Game features regularly on the menu along with other traditional delights.

Head Chef David Morris has been at Pen-y-Dyffryn for many years, and makes it his business to change the menu every single day of the year, specifically varying in accordance to the seasons. Every night is surprise night but there is always a choice of four dishes at each course, including a vegetarian dish, along with canapés and a surprise appetiser.

Holding the longest-established double AA Rosette award in Shropshire and a Michelin listing, Pen Y Dyffryn regularly makes the pages of esteemed hotel and restaurant guides.

PREZZO
Italian

30 Church Street, Oswestry, SY11 2SP
01691 650 932

With a character all of its own, Prezzo oozes contemporary style and enduring charm. Signature pastas, stone-baked pizzas and classic Italian dishes promise a perfect dining choice for the whole family.

SHAPLA RESTAURANT
Indian

58 Broad Street, Ludlow, SY8 1NH
01584 875 153

A great Indian restaurant that presents an appealing menu. Tasty traditional dishes can be enjoyed in attractive surroundings.

RENAISSANCE RESTAURANT
British

29a Princess Street, Shrewsbury, SY1 1LW
01743 354 289

A combination of fine food and a subtly elegant ambience. The chefs expertly demonstrate traditional English culinary skills, producing outstanding dishes bursting with flavour and heavenly aromas.

THE ASTON
Fresh Fish/Pub Classics

Wellington Road, Newport, TF10 9EJ
01952 820 469

A local haunt for those looking for good food and a friendly atmosphere. The menu features classic pub dishes cooked to perfection, and is sure to please even the most discerning gourmet.

SARACENS AT HADNALL
International

Shrewsbury Road, Hadnall, SY4 4AG
01939 210 877

A charming, listed 18th century coaching inn now plays host to an outstanding restaurant offering the most beautifully prepared and presented British and International cuisine. Awarded 1 AA Rosette.

THE BOYNE ARMS
British

Burwarton, Bridgnorth, WV16 6QH
01746 787 214

Traditional family hospitality in a fresh environment, using local ingredients to create a range of versatile menus. Also boasts a relaxing bar area offering a wide selection of real ales and wines.

SAROS RESTAURANT
Indian

12 Moat Street, Bridgnorth, WV16 4EP
01746 762 848

A menu to be thoroughly savoured. Indian and Bangladeshi cuisine is created with a twist that makes your favourite dishes even tastier. Combines excellent food with great prices.

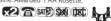

THE BROOKLANDS
European

Mill Road, Shrewsbury, SY3 9JT
01743 344 270

Both inspired cooking and fine flavours feature on the menu, offering both traditional and contemporary dishes, using only the finest local produce. A tranquil ambience fills this top-quality venue.

207

THE CROWN COUNTRY INN
European

Munslow, Craven Arms, SY7 9ET
01584 841 205
Historical inn producing a variety of traditional and exotic fare, including an ever-changing selection of daily specials. Dishes make use of fine ingredients that satisfy all guests. 2 AA Rosettes.

THE CURRY HOUSE
Indian

29 Mardol, Shrewsbury, SY1 1PU
01743 356 035
Longstanding and genial Indian restaurant in Shrewsbury with a well-developed menu that combines classic dishes with a suppleness toward new flavours, priding itself on freshness and local sourcing.

THE PARK INN
International

Forgegate, Telford Centre, Telford, TF3 4NA
01952 429 988
Situated in a wonderfully picturesque county, this hotel and restaurant is a great place to dine and rest after exploring all that Telford has to offer.

THE QUEENS HEAD
British

Queens Head, Oswestry, SY11 4EB
01691 610 255
Classic country inn-style dining with a contemporary and continental twist. Wholesome dishes are made with the finest local ingredients making the meals here outstanding in quality.

THE RAJ MAHAL
Indian

26 Leg Street, Oswestry, SY11 2NN
01691 652 566
Modern Indian restaurant and takeaway with a classic feel, serving dishes from traditional favourites to distinctive specialities; full of verve, flavour and warm welcomes.

THE SUN AT NORBURY
European

Norbury, Bishops Castle, SY9 5DX
01588 650 680
A renowned 'restaurant with rooms', this Inn is the perfect place to both eat and stay. Focusing on the quality of good food, dishes are tenderly prepared and carefully presented for your enjoyment.

THE WALLS
British

Welsh Walls, Oswestry, SY11 1AW
01691 670 970
With its vaulting, high-beamed dining space and crisp, colourful produce, the fundamentals of The Walls are very fine indeed. Superbly accomplished cooking and imaginative flavours top it off.

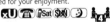

THE WATERSIDE AT THE MILL HOTEL
British

Allum Bridge, Alveley, Bridgnorth, WV15 6HL
01746 780 437
The food here will ignite your taste-buds like never before. The flambé dishes come to life both in the kitchen and in the mouth, where fantastic flavours set fire to all of your senses.

TIN TIN
Cantonese

Wellington Road, Donnington, Telford, TF2 8AJ
01952 608 688
Mr. Wing Lui brings to your table dishes cooked by Chinese and Malaysian chefs. Although the cuisine is mainly Cantonese you can expect to taste both Japanese and Thai notes in many of the delicious dishes.

TRAITORS GATE BRASSERIE
Mediterranean

Castle Street, Shrewsbury, SY1 2BX
01743 249 152
Hidden away from the hustle and bustle of the high street, quality is never amiss at this friendly brasserie. The ambience of the restaurant and the delicious food will inevitably help you unwind.

WHITE HOUSE
European

Affcot, Church Stretton, SY6 6RL
01694 781 202
Formerly a 17th century blacksmith's shop, this restaurant makes extensive use of fresh seasonal produce and the owners appreciate the value and importance of good local suppliers.

Staffordshire

99 STATION STREET
Modern British

99 Station Street, Burton Upon Trent, DE14 1BT
01283 516 859
AA Rosette winning Head Chef Daniel Pilkington crafts delicious, hearty food, and having been trained as a pastry chef delivers stunning desserts. All available with fine cheese and a compact wine list.

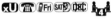

ARTHURS AT GAIL COURT HOTEL
Traditional English Fare

Station St, Burton Upon Trent, DE14 1BN
01283 741 155
Excellent food made with the freshest ingredients, whilst providing a high standard of service combined with comfortable surroundings. A sumptuous menu offering traditional English fare.

BANK HOUSE HOTEL
European

Church Street, Uttoxeter, ST14 8AG
01889 566 922
Fantastically situated in the heart of the town centre, this restaurant has maintained all the characteristic features of the original bank that it once was. A wonderful à la carte menu is on offer.

BEST WESTERN MOAT HOUSE
European

Etruria Hall, Festival Way, Stoke-On-Trent, ST1 5BQ
0870 225 4601
Ideally located near Stoke, this hotel restaurant is modern and comfortable and offers a diverse range of breakfast, lunch and dinner options, inspired by modern international cuisines, for all the family.

Only one card per table.

Sign up to our newsletter for latest restaurants, offers and more

BOUJAN BILASH
Bangladeshi/Indian
39B Tamworth Street, Lichfield, W13 6JW
01543 262 520
This restaurant has friendly staff and serves a wide repertoire of subcontinental dishes to choose from. The naan breads are fine examples of the genre and definitely worth a try.

BRAMSHALL'S LITTLE SECRET
British
Robin Hood, Leigh Lane, Bramshall, Uttoxeter, ST14 5BH
01889 566 032
Great quality, classic English pub fare at this lovely little restaurant ensconced in the Staffordshire countryside.

BULL AND SPECTACLES
European
Uttoxeter Road, Blithbury, WS15 3HY
01889 504 201
Great old-fashioned English pub with classic, hearty food to match. With its characterful timber floors, the Bull and Spectacles is known for fulsome food at great value.

CAFÉ INDIA
Indian
Ivetsey Bank, Wheaton Aston, Stafford, ST19 9QT
01785 841 144
A comfortable setting in which romantic meals, special occasions and business dinners can be catered for. Offering a wide range of freshly cooked Indian and Bangladeshi dishes in pleasant surroundings.

CHANDLERS RESTAURANT
English and Continental
Corn Exchange, Conduit Street, Lichfield, WS13 6JU
01543 416 688
Featured in the Michelin Good Food Guide, this restaurant is renowned for using the finest fresh ingredients for a menu that boasts a great range of daily changing fresh fish, among other treats.

CHAUTARI
Nepalese
8 Lombard Street, Lichfield, WS13 6DR
01543 253 415
'Chautari's' are found on the famous paths to Nepal. Embark on your own trail to culinary pleasure as you enter this tremendous restaurant. The spiced fresh salmon brochette is mouth-wateringly good.

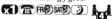

CHINA GARDEN
Chinese
12 High Green Court, Newhall St, Cannock, WS11 1GR
01543 570 888
The kitchen here holds an impressively strong passion for providing food that creates strong sensory impact. Expect both delicious tastes and exciting textures in each and every dish.

DILSHAD
Indian
1 Ashworth House, Cannock Rd, Chadsmoor, Cannock, WS11 5DZ
01543 570 264
Dig some fantastic curries at this Indian restaurant in Cannock; it's not just the warm welcome, but the superlative richness of the flavours in their dishes. Treat yourself to an unfussy, delicious meal.

ENRICO'S
Italian
New Street, Burton Upon Trent, DE14 3QN
01283 533 230
Sumptuous and authentic Italian food, ideal for a fine intimate meal or a family gathering. See what real Italian dishes should taste like at prices to suit all pockets.

FOX & HOUNDS
English and Continental
44 Main Street, Shenstone, WS14 0NB
01543 480 257
With many awards and a loyal following, this attractive restaurant has a real appeal about it. A varied menu offers delightful dishes that can be enjoyed in modern, comfortable surroundings.

GRILL ROOM AT THREE QUEENS HOTEL
Fine Dining
1 Bridge Street, Burton Upon Trent, DE14 1SY
01283 523 800
Capturing the essence and the ambience of an era long gone, this restaurant also offers superb dishes made from local produce. The Leicestershire-reared beef is sensational.

KASHMIR GARDEN
Indian
257 High Street, Tunstall, Stoke On Trent, ST6 5EG
01782 839 366
Traditionally prepared and presented, this restaurant delivers quality Indian cuisine filled with rich flavours and delicate textures; a diverse menu of classic and speciality dishes.

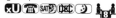

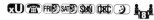

DETAILED DESCRIPTIONS AVAILABLE ON
www.gourmetsociety.co.uk

KUDOS
Indian
9 Coleshill Street, Fazeley, Tamworth, B78 3RB
01827 254 777
This fine Indian restaurant delivers a menu of classic and fusion dishes alongside a wide range of drinks. Friendly staff endeavour to satisfy every diner, however discerning their palate.

LA BELLA NAPOLI
Italian
6-14 Cheapside Hanley, Stoke On Trent, ST1 1HE
01782 283 318
Popular, buzzy Italian restaurant whose superbly cooked, deeply flavourful cuisine attracts diners first time around and then, more often than not, for repeat performances.

LE JARDIN PUNJABI
Indian
26 Bird Street, Lichfield, WS13 6PR
01543 416 748
Punjabi dishes bursting with flavour. The restaurant's consistency in good food and wonderfully friendly service guarantees its popularity. The saag paneer comes highly recommended.

MALABAR
Indian

1-2 Water Street, Stafford, ST16 2AG
01785 227 500

Exotic spices and rich ingredients go into every dish on the menu at this fantastic Indian restaurant. Friendly staff are more than happy to advise you should you feel spoilt for choice.

NAJMOON
Indian

17a Market Place, Uttoxeter, ST14 8HY
01889 564 946

Outstanding levels of thought and care go into each and every dish, where authentic Indian and Bangladeshi cuisine occupies a regularly updated menu.

OSTLER
Fine Dining

BW Manor House Hotel, Audley Road, Alsager, ST7 2QQ
01270 884 000

Recognised with an AA Rosette, the Ostler combines hearty British fare with touches of Mediterranean influence; mouth-wateringly cooked meats and fish are combined with sharp, sassy accompanying flavours.

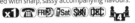

PADMA LOUNGE BAR & RESTAURANT
Indian

8 High Green Court, Newhall St, Cannock, WS11 1GR
01543 502 101

With quality spices direct from India, the food here clearly benefits as the chefs use them skilfully to delicately flavour the cuisine, giving diners an authentic culinary experience.

PASCAL AT THE OLD VICARAGE
Classic British/ French

2 Main Street, Branston, Burton Upon Trent, DE14 3EX
01283 533 222

A monthly changing menu allows regular diners to consistently try new and exciting dishes. Drawing on French influences, the English cuisine demonstrates the owner's passion for delicious food.

PLAZA RESTAURANT
Indian

4 Mill Street, Cannock, WS11 0DL
01543 506 016

Everything you would expect from a fine Indian restaurant. Exceptional food, pleasant surroundings and friendly service. Includes an extensive menu filled with Indian classics created in a proven style.

PORTOBELLO
Italian

12 Silver Street, Tamworth, B79 7NH
01827 54474

Musky and refreshing wines are available from a menu laden with Old and New World bottles for you to try. An extensive à la carte menu offers exciting Italian dishes, from pizzas to steaks.

PORTOBELLO RISTORANTE
Italian

17-19 High Street, Aldridge, WS9 8LX
01922 744 777

Watch excellent chefs expertly prepare your food from the finest ingredients available in an open-plan kitchen. Ideal for lunch or a quiet evening meal, this Italian restaurant delivers fine, deluxe food.

QUEEN'S HEAD
British

Main Road, Newton Regis, Tamworth, B79 0NF
01827 830 271

A pub in Tamworth offering a warm and friendly atmosphere with good quality food served daily. The service is outstanding, and prices thoroughly reasonable. Locally renowned for their Sunday lunches.

RARE LOUNGEBAR & STEAKHOUSE
Steakhouse

39 Ironmarket, Newcastle-Under-Lyme, ST5 1PB
01782 740 750

Whatever the occasion, Rare can cater for you. The smell of succulent steaks will have your mouth watering in no time, whilst the lounge area is an ideal place to sip a thirst-quenching cocktail or two.

RESTAURANT GILMORE
European

Strine's Farm, Beamhurst, Uttoxeter, ST14 5DZ
01889 507 100

An exceptional farmhouse restaurant opened by a couple who have both spent over 25 years in the catering trade. The food dazzles, with an innovative approach to classical dishes. Awarded 2 AA Rosettes.

RUCHI
Indian

Bagot Street, Abbots Bromley, WS15 3DB
01283 840 008

For a superbly authentic Indian meal in wonderful surroundings, The Ruchi delivers every time. The restaurant has an admirable reputation that draws in diners from the whole of Staffordshire.

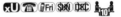

SAKI SPICE TANDOORI
Indian

32 Waterloo Road, Burslem, Stoke On Trent, ST6 3ES
01584 875 153

The Head Chef provides exciting new and traditional dishes that never disappoint. The divine king prawn moranjon is a traditional Bangladeshi dish and is exquisitely gratifying.

Formerly Gram Bangla.

SIMON'S CANTONESE & SEAFOOD
Chinese

520 Chester Road, Little Aston, WS9 0PU
0121 580 9293

Take it easy at the bar and enjoy a drink or two before taking your seat and enjoying fabulous Cantonese cuisine in a cosy and elegant environment. Also popular for its astoundingly good seafood dishes.

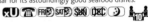

SO TAPAS BAR & BISTRO
European

1 Offa House, Orchard Street, Tamworth, B79 7RE
01827 54175

Chilled-out boutique bar with a line in simple, savoury tapas and a great ambience for a glass of something with friends. You'll also find rich and silky flavours on their broad, bistro-style menu.

SYMPHONY RESTAURANT BAR & GRILL
European

70-72 Crewe Road, Alsager, ST7 2HA
01270 876 999

Classic dishes with a modern twist. Roasted butternut squash, coriander and feta Wellington, for example, is a divine delight for the palate. Every dish is rich in flavour at this renowned restaurant.

Visit the website regularly to discover the latest restaurants joining the GS

TAJ MAHAL
Indian

29 Liverpool Road, Stoke On Trent, ST4 1AN
01782 412 121
A great quality, down-the-line Indian restaurant that serves a broad range of colourful, spicy and flavourful dishes with excellent service and a warm, accommodating ambience.

TEMPTATIONS
Indian

127 New Street, Burton Upon Trent, DE14 3QW
01283 562 106
Both locals and visitors from afar enjoy the exquisite flavours of Rajasthan and Bangladesh that find their way into each meal. The fish dishes and the Rongila Khama are deservedly popular.

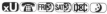

THE BARN AT SWINFEN
British

Heart of the Country Homefarm, London Road, Swinfen, WS14 9QR
01543 480 307
A welcoming AA Rosette-recognised restaurant serving deep, complex taste combinations found in its sublime dishes. A lovely retreat for an excellent quality meal.

THE BLYTHE INN
European

Stowe by Chartley, Stafford, ST18 0LT
01889 500 487
A beautifully restored inn that is snuggled cosily away in a wonderful Staffordshire valley. A very comfortable and enjoyable place to have lunch or evening dinner.

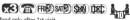

25% offer on food only after 1st visit.

THE BRADFORD ARMS
British

Ivetsey Bank, Wheaton Aston, Stafford, ST19 9QT
01785 840 297
Popular, traditional pub food served in a beautiful Grade II building. Offers a wide selection of home-made British cuisine and traditional ales.

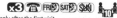

Avaialable on food only after the first visit.

RECOMMEND A FRIEND
see page 18

THE MALT HOUSE
British

Tamworth Road, Tamworth, B78 2DL
01827 872 152
Enjoy superb home-cooked dishes that bring a piece of culinary theatre to your table, as heated volcanic rocks cook your food while you watch. A fresh, vibrant dining experience.

THE PEPPER TREE
European

9-10 Union Street, Burton Upon Trent, DE14 1AA
01283 500 602
The rich, European cuisine never fails to please at this inviting restaurant. With an impressive wine cellar, friendly staff and an outstanding menu, this town centre venue has everything going for it.

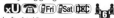

25% offer on food only after 1st visit.

THE PLOUGH INN
British

2 Ravens Lane, Stoke On Trent, ST7 8PS
01782 720 469
A great little pub serving delicious food from a ranging menu, whilst a wide selection of drinks are also available. Friendly, efficient staff ensure all diners are catered for.

THE PLOUGH INN
British

Huddlesford Lane, Huddlesford, Lichfield, WS13 8PY
01543 432 369
Offering the finest locally sourced food, this real ale-serving pub provides superbly mastered meals in the friendliest of atmospheres. Open fires and al fresco seating make this perfect in all weather.

THE RED LION VILLAGE INN
European

Duffield Lane, Newborough, DE13 8SH
01283 575 785
A cosy country pub offering guests a fresh, home-cooked menu filled with hearty, delicious, and exceptionally priced dishes. A family-friendly venue perfect for great food and drink alike.

THE SHOULDER OF MUTTON
European

16 Main Street, Barton Under Needwood, DE13 8AA
01283 712 568
The centrepiece of this village, the pub is the epitome of the classic green scene. In a building dating back to 1640, here you can revel in the terrific atmosphere and indulge in fine food and real ale.

THE THREE HORSESHOES
British

2 Station Road, Burton Upon Trent, DE13 8DR
01283 716 268
A delightful, home-made menu, including a delicious range of deserts and where possible ingredients are sourced locally making great use of seasonally available fish and game.

TUMBLEDOWN FARM
Carvery

4 Crosses Lane, Cannock, WS11 1RU
01543 500 891
Enjoy a classic British roast dinner at this magnificent member of the Great British Carvery group. A charmingly modern pub that boasts a stylish interior and inviting country hospitality.

Call before special event days.

VERVE GRILL AND OVEN
European

Village Hotel, Tempus Drive, Walsall, WS2 8TJ
01922 633 661
Here, options are aplenty. Grab a bite to eat in the grill or chill out after work in the café. Enjoy the imaginative dishes that are seasoned with a fresh smile and attentive service.

VICTORIA HOTEL
Carvery

Brampton Road, Newcastle-under-Lyme, ST5 0SJ
01782 615 170
One of the many Great British Carveries serving the best of British food with a modern twist. Victorious in that ambition, this great pub hosts highly experienced staff and has a warm, charming interior.

211

Warwickshire

1450 CAFE BAR
European

21 Spon Street, Coventry, CV1 3BA
02476 229 274
1450 Café Bar in the heart of Coventry has a touch of the Medieval about it. A varied menu that is sure to please the palate, with the 'vittels' ranging from pasta dishes to traditional English fare.

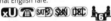

AGRA PALACE
Indian

12 Abbey Green, Nuneaton, CV11 5DR
02476 350 515
Dine In beautiful and comfortable private seating areas, taking advantage of perfectly crafted Indian dishes whilst sampling a selection of drinks, including globally selected wines.

AQUA FOOD & MOOD
Lebanese

12-14 Jury St, Warwick, CV34 4EW
01926 495 491
If you're unfamiliar with the warming, sumptuous and distinct flavours of Lebanese cooking, this is the place to draw you in. In an elegant setting, with superbly done dishes, you'll be hooked and crooked.

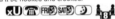

ARROW MILL
European

Arrow, Alcester, B49 5NL
01789 762 419
Traditionally prepared, simple fare that has clearly taken advantage of the amazing local produce the area has to offer. Hearty and flavoursome dishes prepared and presented to the highest standards.

BALTI COTTAGE
Bangladeshi/Indian

107 High Street, Coleshill, B46 3BP
01675 464 122
Bangladeshi cuisine has a world famous reputation for being rich and diverse. This warm, welcoming restaurant provides some of the very best dishes from across the South East Asian subcontinent.

BEECHWOOD HOTEL
British

Sandpits Lane, Coventry, CV6 2FR
02475 338 662
Enjoy the respite in this rurally located hotel and restaurant. Delicious food will provide you with a memorable dining experience, whilst the exhaustive wine list can be broken down by the sommelier.

BEEN BAR & RESTAURANT
Oriental

29 Chandos Street, Leamington Spa, CV32 4RN
01926 431 935
Showcasing a wide variety of authentic Oriental dishes including Chinese, Malaysian and Singaporean cuisine classics and specials, owner Kate Wong prides herself on quality food and exemplary service.

À la carte only. Not 'all you can eat' menu

BENGAL SPICE RESTAURANT
Indian

318 Hillmorton Road, Hillmorton, Rugby, CV22 5BP
01788 540 222
Good, unfussy restaurant specialising in North Indian food. Settle in to enjoy a simple, flavoursome meal at a good price. Through the rather retro frontage, you'll find a great welcome and a tasty dinner.

BENTLEY'S RESTAURANT
British

The Brittania Coventry, Cathedral Square, Coventry, CV1 5RP
02476 633 733
Adjoining the famous landmark of Coventry Cathedral, The Britannia is ideally located for rest, respite, dinner and drinks, whilst the restaurant has a well-deserved reputation for its irresistible food.

BEST WESTERN FALSTAFF
European

16 Warwick New Road, Leamington Spa, CV32 5JQ
01926 312 044
Maintaining all of the original grace and character of the three Victorian mansions from which it was created, this hotel boasts a restaurant and bar where you can enjoy a relaxing vibe and a quality meal.

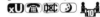

BLUE MANGO
Indian

76 Albany Road, Earlsdon, Coventry,CV5 6JU
02476 672 653
Expect familiar dishes cooked superbly and with a distinctive twist. Knowledgeable staff add to the welcoming vibrancy of the restaurant, whilst the stylish décor makes it an attractive place to dine.

BLUE ORCHID
Thai/Indian

14 The Butts, Earlsdon, CV1 3GR
02476 231 799
The popularity of this restaurant testifies to the talent in the kitchen and the exquisite Thai and Indian food it serves. Among other favourite signature dishes, the meen mappas tetal is highly rated.

BOMBAY TANDOORI
Indian

38-40 Regent Street, Leamington Spa, CV32 5EG
01926 420 521
Having established an excellent reputation, The Bombay continues to provide quality food at reasonable prices. Karai and thali dishes are superb, although the chef will cater for all individual tastes.

CAFÉ PASTA
Italian

10-11 Sheep Street, Stratford-Upon-Avon, CV37 6EF
01789 262 910
Delicious Italian cuisine, perfect for all occasions. Ideally situated for theatregoers, this well-located restaurant offers high-quality food at great prices. The ravioli rustica is a star.

CAFÉ ROUGE
French

95-99 Regent Street, Leamington Spa, CV32 4NT
01926 330 565
An attractive restaurant, a boulevard café or a Parisian-style wine bar; however you see Café Rouge, consistently excellent classic French dishes are always guaranteed.

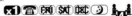

When booking restaurants always mention your GS membership

CAFÉ ROUGE
French
18 Sheep Street, Stratford-Upon-Avon, CV37 6EF
01789 263 526
An attractive restaurant, a boulevard café or a Parisian-style wine bar; however you see Café Rouge, consistently excellent classic French dishes are always guaranteed.

 50%OFF FOOD

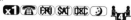

CHAPEL HOUSE HOTEL
Fine Dining
Friars Gate, Atherstone, CV9 1EY
01827 718 949
Enjoy a range of tender and flavoursome dishes: melt-in-the-mouth meats and some fabulous sweetbreads. The restaurant also has an especial line in imaginative desserts. Awarded 1 AA Rosette.

 2FOR1 MAIN COURSE

COCONUT LAGOON
Indian
149 Warwick Road, Kenilworth, CV8 1HY
01926 864 500
This acclaimed restaurant combines cuisine from several South Indian states, presenting a gastronomic journey through the delicious legacy left by the diverse European influences on the region.

 2FOR1 3 COURSES

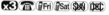

COCONUT LAGOON
Indian
21 Sheep Street, Stratford-Upon-Avon, CV37 6EF
01789 293 546
This acclaimed restaurant combines cuisine from several South Indian states, presenting a gastronomic journey through the delicious legacy left by the diverse European influences on the region.

 2FOR1 2 COURSES

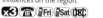

CROSSED KHUKRIS GURKHA
Nepalese
115 Abbey Street, Nuneaton, CV11 5BX
02476 344 488
The eclectic mix of flavours that comprise Nepalese cuisine is derived from the diverse make up of the country. Balancing flavour, texture and style in each dish, the chefs create culinary masterpieces.

 2FOR1 MAIN COURSE

DELHI PALACE
Indian
51 High St, Leamington Spa, CV31 1LN
01926 420 944
Delicious, traditional and reasonably priced; the dishes at this terrific Indian restaurant are really something to write home about. Food fit for a king.

 25%OFF TOTAL

DOGMA BAR AND RESTAURANT
International
Priory Place, Fairfax Street, Coventry, CV1 5RZ
02476 230 088
Kick back in this comfortable space, and enjoy great food served by exceptional staff. Make sure not to forget the fantastic array of drinks, ranging from beers and spirits to champagne and cocktails.

2FOR1 3 COURSES

ELEVEN
French
11 Regent Place, Old Town, Leamington Spa, CV31 1EH
01926 424 723
In the beautiful town of Leamington Spa, this sparkling little bistro serves superbly realised, fine French cuisine in an intimate, congenial setting.

 25%OFF TOTAL

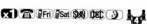

EPISODE
British
64 Upper Holly Walk, Leamington Spa, CV32 4JL
01926 883 777
Episode's philosophy on your plate, with the promise of serving only what they would want to eat themselves. Fresh, delicious produce sourced from the best possible places used to create fine dishes.

 2FOR1 MAIN COURSE

ETTINGTON PARK HOTEL
Fine Dining
Oak Room, Stratford-Upon-Avon, CV37 8BU
0845 027 2454
Under Head Chef Gary Lissemore's creative direction, this Hand Picked Hotels restaurant delivers full-flavoured fine dining in the luxurious surroundings of this country house setting. 2 AA Rosettes.

 25%OFF TOTAL

EXOTICA BENGAL CUISINE
Bangladeshi
68 Lower Street, Hillmorton, Rugby, CV21 4NU
01788 551 584
Setting the standard high in this area, Exotica Bengal Cuisine offer a sensational menu combining classical and modern Bangladeshi dishes as well as European choices to cater for all tastes.

 25%OFF TOTAL

FAIRWAYS RESTAURANT
European
Windmill Village Hotel, Birmingham Rd, Coventry, CV5 9AL
02476 404 040
Hosting a highly experienced, well-travelled chef is just one of the many great things about this restaurant. Both the gratifying atmosphere and the outstanding food make this a spectacular place to dine.

 2FOR1 MAIN COURSE

FELLINIS AT THE RAMADA
Mediterranean
The Butts, Earlsdon, Coventry, CV1 3GG
02476 238 110
Relaxing, friendly atmosphere; the restaurant offers children the chance to make their own pizza. The food is warming and Mediterranean, focused on the quality of ingredients.

 25%OFF TOTAL

FIVE RIVERS
Indian
20-22 Victoria Terrace, Leamington Spa, CV31 3AB
01926 431 999
Ambitious, imaginative Indian restaurant that combines the classic flavours with a flash of theatre; cool, bright dining and an inviting bar.

 25%OFF TOTAL

GEORGETOWN
Malaysian
23 Sheep Street, Stratford-Upon-Avon, CV37 6EF
01789 204 445
Delightfully spicy combinations at this intriguing restaurant. Malay, Mandarin and Tamil traditions are all accessed for piquancy and flavour. A regular live pianist and relaxed ambience round things off.

 2FOR1 2 COURSES

GILBERT SCOTT AT BROWNSOVER HALL
British
Brownsover Lane, Old Brownsover, Rugby, CV21 1HU
01788 546 100
Dramatically striking in appearance, the hotel takes full advantage of its situation within a Victorian mansion. Decadent dishes in the restaurant provide a suitable match for the magnificent surroundings.

 25%OFF TOTAL

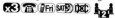

GROSVENOR HOTEL
Indian

Clifton Road, Rugby, CV21 3QQ
01788 535 686
Indulge in a chic, stylish bar and brasserie restaurant of striking sophistication within this fine hotel. Boasts a delectable contemporary menu with extensive options of fine food and drink.

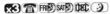

HABIBI
Arabic

142 Far Gosford Street, Coventry, CV1 5DY
02476 220 669
An original Arabic restaurant that welcomes all to experience the sounds and tastes of the East. Offers an extensive halal menu that is freshly prepared using a diverse range of herbs and spices.

HARRINGTONS ON THE HILL
British

42 Castle Hill, Kenilworth, CV8 1NB
01926 852 074
There is nothing pretentious about this delightful venue, which offers a warm welcome and an uncomplicated, high-quality menu. Experience exceptional culinary skills in a small, almost rustic environment.

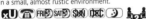

HELP OUT MILL RESTAURANT
British

Heather Lane, Shackerstone, CV13 0BT
01530 260 666
A hidden restaurant that is truly unique. Feel at home here, with the venue putting emphasis on ensuring their guests are completely relaxed. Enjoy their hugely popular carvery.

HOAR PARK FARM RESTAURANT
English and Continental

Hoar Park Village, Nuneaton Rd, Nuneaton, CV10 0QU
02476 394 433
Enjoy picturesque views of the countryside whilst feasting on hearty, home-cooked food, from light lunches to Sunday dinners. Great food with a superb variety of wines available.

HONILEY COURT HOTEL
Modern British

Meer End Road, Honiley, Kenilworth, CV8 1NP
01926 484 234
This Brook hotel restaurant is popular with locals and guests alike, as the venue offers an extensive list of fine food, ideally complemented by a selection of wines from around the world.

KAKOOTI
European

16 Spon Street, Coventry, CV1 3BA
02476 221 392
Charmingly candlelit and oozing with character, this charismatic restaurant is beautifully situated within a 16th century building. The mussels with white wine and the fillet of beef are simply divine.

KAVI
Indian

Ramada Hotel, Chesford Bridge, Kenilworth, CV8 2LN
01926 858 331
Luxury Indian dining in a well-placed location. Panoramic floor-to-ceiling windows provide outstanding views of the river Avon and the surrounding meadows.

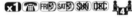

KINGS HEAD
British

Old Watling Street, Atherstone, CV9 2PA
01827 717 945
A delightful pub serving real ales and hearty wholesome food. Its excellent service and pleasant location make this a popular place to eat and drink, as guests enjoy watching the narrow boats on the canal.

LOCH FYNE
Seafood

Clarendon House Hotel, High St, Kenilworth CV8 1LZ
01926 515 450
From the roadside oyster bar that once was, Loch Fyne restaurants now successfully inject energy and passion into great food and wonderful flavours, whilst ensuring their seafood is sustainably sourced.

MACDONALD ANSTY HALL HOTEL
European

Main Road, Ansty, CV7 9HZ
02476 612 222
From the finest Scottish beef to corn-fed chicken and fresh wild fish, the produce is excellently sourced and creatively used, so that every dish is as outstanding as the next.

MASALA CLUB RESTAURANT
Indian

235 Station Rd, Balsall Common, Coventry, CV7 7EG
01676 533 210
Try this lively, classy Indian restaurant and its superbly wide-ranging menu of aromatic starters and clear, distinctive main-course flavours.

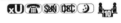

NICOLINIS RISTORANTE
Italian

14 The Parade, Leamington Spa, CV32 4DW
01926 421 620
Guests will be blown away by the subtle modern twists on traditional Italian dishes. Start the day with a delicious breakfast or take advantage of the extensive à la carte menus for dinner.

NO.1 SHAKESPEARE STREET
European

1 Shakespeare Street, Stratford-Upon-Avon, CV37 6RN
01789 264 787
A wonderfully bright and spacious restaurant that focuses on producing delicious cuisine. The award-winning Head Chef cooks up divine dishes such as braised chicken with dumplings and tender lamb shanks.

OLD BLACK HORSE INN
European

17 Market Place, Market Bosworth, CV13 0LF
01455 290 278
A traditional 'pub on the square' and now a top dining destination and first class gastronomic experience; owner Sam Matson cooks European cuisine from seasonal and local ingredients. Booking essential.

Mention GS when you advance book.

OLD ORLEANS
American

The Sky Dome, Croft Rd, Coventry, CV1 3AZ
02476 631 760
An extraordinarily accurate taste of the Deep South can be found in this unique restaurant. The kitchen deals in classic Louisiana and Cajun recipes such as jambalaya and gumbo to create an exciting menu.

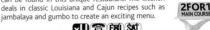

Not available on Bank Holiday weekends. Adult menu only.

Gourmet Society discount applies to the à la carte menu

OTHELLO'S AT THE MERCURE
European

Chapel St, Stratford-Upon-Avon, CV37 6ER
01789 294 997
A well-loved aspect of the Shakespeare Hotel, which has maintained its original distinctive features while managing to appeal to the modern diner. A vibrant atmosphere and great food await you.

PETIT GOURMAND
French

101 Warwick Road, Kenilworth, CV8 1HL
01926 864 567
An AA Rosette French restaurant renowned for gourmet dining. Exquisite dishes are crafted using local, ethical produce, delivered in a truly unique setting with perfect ambience.

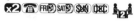

PLAYWRIGHTS
International

4-6 Hay Lane, Cathedral Quarter, Coventry, CV1 5RF
02476 231 441
Playwrights is a café, bistro and bar rolled into one. The menu offers an extensive selection of tasty bites which can be added to more substantial and delicious dishes.

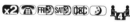

PORRIDGE POT
Carvery

Longbridge Manor, Longbridge, Warwick, CV34 6RA
01926 401 697
A fantastic member of the Great British Carvery group where guests can expect the best of British food with a delightfully modern twist. A perfectly located pub for visitors of the nearby Warwick Castle.

Call beforehand on special event days.

PREZZO
Italian

25 Regent Grove, Leamington Spa, CV32 4NN
01926 431 833
With a character all of its own, Prezzo oozes contemporary style and enduring charm. Signature pastas, stone-baked pizzas and classic Italian dishes promise a perfect dining choice for the whole family.

PREZZO
Italian

1-3 High Street, Warwick, CV34 4AP
01926 475 867
With a character all of its own, Prezzo oozes contemporary style and enduring charm. Signature pastas, stone-baked pizzas and classic Italian dishes promise a perfect dining choice for the whole family.

QUEANS
Fine Dining

15 Dormer Place, Leamington Spa, CV32 5AA
01926 315 522
Refreshingly congenial service, a uniquely warm atmosphere and unsurpassed cuisine. Truly a fine dining experience for any guest, with an astonishing sixteen home-made indulgent ice creams also on offer.

QUICKEN TREE
Fine Dining

Heart of England Centre, Meriden Rd, Fillongley, CV7 8DX
01676 543 300
The privacy, peace and sanctuary of the Quicken Tree affords a warm welcome to all guests, allowing you to dine in modern elegance. Select from a menu of traditional, home-cooked, hearty dishes.

RAFFLES
Malaysian

57 Warwick Road, Kenilworth, CV8 1HN
01926 864 300
Britain's first colonial Malaysian restaurant brings a diverse range of exquisite cuisines together, all served in their own regal house style and ballroom setting. Delicious options available for all.

RAJDHANI
Indian

1 Cambourne Dr, Horeston Grange, Nuneaton, CV11 6GU
02476 352 254
Mouth-watering balti tandoori cuisine expertly prepared and cooked ensuring excellent flavours and spice. A friendly family restaurant where a warm welcome and high standards are guaranteed.

REGENCY BAR & RESTAURANT
Fine Dining

Manor Hotel, Main Road, Meriden, CV7 7NH
01676 522 735
Offering a variety of dishes suitable for all palates and individual tastes, the owners proudly welcome you to enjoy their well-regarded, first-class food and service.

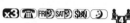

ROBBIE'S OF WARWICK
International

74 Smith Street, Warwick, CV34 4HU
01926 400 470
Feast in this 15th century timber-framed building, situated in the heart of the oldest part of town. Superlative international cuisine is created using the best of local produce by the talented Head Chef.

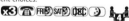

SAFFRON GOLD
Indian

Westage House, Market St, Warwick, CV34 4DE
01926 402 061
A hugely popular Indian restaurant with an impressive, varied menu, offering traditional dishes whilst also providing the adventurous diner with many different choices.

SEASONS
Modern British

115 Warwick Street, Leamington Spa, CV32 4QZ
01926 424 340
An affordable price tag is attached to high-quality local food that is prepared to an excellent standard. Friendly staff enhance the warm atmosphere which will envelop you as soon as you enter.

ROZANA TANDOORI
Indian

28 Augusta Place, Leamington Spa, CV32 5EL
01926 428620
This busy, family-run Indian restaurant in Leamington Spa shows up well in its attention to detail. Generous portions, value-for-money and rich taste are also the order of the day.

NEW

SOFTLEY'S
European

2 Market Place, Market Bosworth, CV13 0LE
01455 290 464
An intimate restaurant providing a comfortable atmosphere, where diners can enjoy high quality dishes whilst overlooking the historical market place. Food is prepared using the best local ingredients.

WEST MIDLANDS

215

SORRENTO....A TASTE OF ITALY
Italian

7-8 Ely Street, Stratford-Upon-Avon, CV37 6LW
01789 297 999
Take great delight in the warm atmosphere and tasty Italian food at this wonderful family-run restaurant. An ideal place to enjoy à la carte dining before heading to the nearby theatre.

2FOR1 MAIN COURSE

À La carte only; not any set or special value menus.

SPA'S RESTAURANT
European

Olympus Avenue, Tachbrook Park, Warwick, CV34 6RJ
01926 425 522
Relaxed dining where guests can choose from a tasty menu offering a variety of European and international dishes. Ideal for visitors travelling to see the historical sights this area has to offer.

25%OFF TOTAL

10% off accommodation, subject to availability.

STRADA
Italian

90A Livery Street, Leamington Spa, CV32 4AT
01926 420 094
A dedicated menu offering traditional Italian dishes in a stylish and contemporary setting. The chefs use only the finest ingredients such as Parma ham and buffalo mozzarella imported directly from Italy.

25%OFF TOTAL

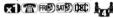

STUDLEY SPICE
Indian

75-77 Alcester Road, Studley, B80 7NJ
01527 850 077
Guests will love the authentic Indian cuisine on offer in this relaxed restaurant. The mouth-watering dishes are guaranteed to satisfy every palate.

2FOR1 MAIN COURSE

THE BELL INN
European

Banbury Road, Ladbroke, Southam, CV47 2BY
01926 813 562
This restaurant serves a gastro-style menu of fulsome, flavourful fare in a cool, bright, bijou traditional pub setting; try their lounge for a chance to unwind, or an al fresco dining experience outside.

2FOR1 2 COURSES

THE BLUE BOAR INN
English and Continental

Temple Grafton, Stratford-upon-Avon, B49 6NR
01789 750 010
Feast on traditional favourites as well as new tastes and experiences at this increasingly popular pub. Make sure you leave room for the deliciously divine home-made desserts which you won't want to miss.

2FOR1 MAIN COURSE

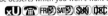

THE BRASSERIE
Fine Dining

Brooklands Grange Hotel, Holyhead Rd, Coventry, CV5 8HX
02476 601 601
Relax over a drink and browse this AA Rosette-winning restaurant's menu as you relax in its 16th century Jacobean bar, which successfully captures the style and charm of the location.

25%OFF TOTAL

THE BRASSERIE
International

Holiday Inn, London Rd, Coventry, CV8 3DY
0870 400 7216
A modern and friendly environment serving quality food from a menu that boasts a wide choice of international dishes for guests to choose from. Lounge bar also available for a full selection of beverages.

25%OFF TOTAL

THE BRIDGE RESTAURANT
European

Somers Road, Stonebridge, CV7 7PL
01676 522 442
Calm, relaxing ambience to this smartly styled restaurant at Stonebridge Golf Club, where you can enjoy a delicious, sophisticated meal with views over the course and its gentle rolling green.

2FOR1 MAIN COURSE

THE FALCON
British

Birmingham Road, Hatton, CV35 7HA
01926 484 281
This venue invites both diners and drinkers to enjoy new, relaxed surroundings, priding themselves in high-quality food, sourcing local produce to create their fresh in-season menu.

25%OFF TOTAL

THE GARDEN ROOM
Modern British

The Grosvenor, Warwick Rd, Stratford-Upon-Avon, CV37 6YT
01789 269 213
An exquisite Georgian building, steeped in its own history, now plays home to this treasured hotel. Fantastically located, guests can take advantage of local attractions before dining and reclining.

2FOR1 MAIN COURSE

THE GEORGE
British

Watling Street, Kilsby, Rugby, CV23 8YE
01788 822 229
When done with this kind of skill and care, there's little to rival no-nonsense, classic pub fare. The short crust steak & ale pie is a real treat; the Devon crab a smart and delicious addition.

2FOR1 3 COURSES

THE GEORGE HOTEL
British

High Street, Shipston on Stour, CV36 4AJ
01608 661 453
This popular hotel-restaurant has created an exciting British menu, with temptations such as the real-ale battered fish and chips and chargrilled Hereford cross sirloin steak, all cooked to perfection.

25%OFF TOTAL

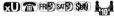

THE GOLDEN CROSS
British

Wixford Road, Ardens Grafton, Alcester, B50 4LG
01789 772 420
With several areas to dine in, and a completely fresh home-cooked menu, with something for all tastes, customers will be truly satisfied. Only the very best produce is used, with fish coming in daily.

2FOR1 MAIN COURSE

THE GRAND UNION
Fine Dining

66-68 Clemens Street, Leamington Spa, CV31 2DN
01926 888 278
Delightful canal-side bar and fine-dining restaurant. Customers are able to select food from a weekly changing menu, while the creative chefs use fresh seasonal ingredients and endeavour to cater for all.

2FOR1 MAIN COURSE

THE HERCULES COUNTRY INN
British

Main Street, Sutton Cheney, CV13 0AG
01455 292 591
An old coaching inn tucked away in picturesque surroundings where visitors can enjoy the beer garden in summer and real fires in winter, regular live entertainment and real ale.

25%OFF TOTAL

Recommend a friend to the Gourmet Society and receive a free gift.

SEETAR TANDOORI
Indian
55 Warwick Road, Kenilworth, CV8 1HN
01926 851585
Since opening its doors in 1989 Seetar Tandoori has become a cornerstone of Kenilworth's food map. With a dedication to authentic Indian cuisine and fantastic, friendly service, join the loyal following.

THE MINT
Indian
13 Queens Rd, The Butts, Earlsdon, Coventry, CV1 3GJ
02476 226 111
A unique menu of modernised Indian Cuisine that still retains authentic flavour, yet combines with different accents from around the world, with a design and décor that embodies this creative style.

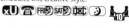

THE MOORINGS BAR & GRILL
British
Myton Road, Leamington Spa, CV31 3NY
01926 425 043
Holding an enviable reputation for its exceptional food and attractive location, this outstanding waterside pub and restaurant is a great place to spend your afternoon or evening.

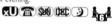

THE OAK ROOM
Fine Dining
Nailcote Hall Hotel, Nailcote Lane, Berkswell, CV7 7DE
02476 466 174
Renowned as one of Britain's most romantic hotels, the restaurant situated here acts as the perfect place for those special occasions. Make memories as you indulge in outstanding international cuisine.

THE OLD THATCHED COTTAGE
International
Southam Road, Dunchurch, CV22 6NG
01788 810 417
A selection of wines from around the globe are available in a variety of dining experiences. Sample the bar snacks in the lounge or opt for the à la carte menu which offers skilfully prepared dishes.

THE PLOUGH INN
International
Plough Hill Rd, Galley Common, Nuneaton, CV10 9NY
02476 392 425
Well-lit and oozing with character, this attractive inn maintains all the right aspects of tradition. Expect great pub food prepared and served to a high standard.

THE REDGATE STEAK & ALEHOUSE
Steakhouse
Watling Street, Fenny Drayton, Nuneaton, CV10 0RY
02476 383 384
Relax in style in this modern eatery, where emphasis is placed wholly on quality. Don't miss the 21 day-aged beef menu which provides you with a choice of 5 steaks in a variety of sizes.

THE SHAKESPEARE
British
56 Tavistock Street, Leamington Spa, CV32 5PW
01926 421 212
Smart, lively pub-restaurant in Leamington Spa, where you can count on some great-quality, homely and fulsome dishes; the place buzzes, and is involved in local food festivals, so booking is a good idea.

UPTON BARN RESTAURANT
English and Continental
Manor Farm, Upton, CV13 6JX
01455 212 374
Nestled in the countryside, this restaurant draws on the produce of local butchers to bring you great country cooking. The à la carte menu provides a wonderful variety of dishes at a good price.

USHA
Indian
28 Meer Street, Stratford-Upon-Avon, CV37 6QB
01789 297 348
Usha has an outstanding collection of accolades can only be an encouragement to dine in this highly commended restaurant. Some of the finest aromatic Indian cuisine, produced in their unique clay oven.

VERMILLION RESTAURANT
European
7a Eastfield Place, Rugby, CV21 3AT
01788 550 222
An open kitchen allows you to see the skill with which each dish is created, while the al fresco garden and the soothing jazz sounds allow you to relax and enjoy the sensational seasonal cuisine.

WARWICK SPICE
Indian/Bangladeshi
24 Smith Street, Warwick, CV34 4HS
01926 491 736
This restaurant revels in its reputation for high-quality, delicious food and unstinting consistency. The talents of the award-winning chef have casual diners soon becoming regulars.

WASHFORD MILL
Carvery
Icknield Street Drive, Studley, B80 7BD
01527 523 068
One of the many Great British Carveries where guests can enjoy the best of British food. A modern twist has been placed on both the food and the pub's décor, making this a popular place to drink and dine.

Call before special event days.

West Midlands

24 CARAT BISTRO
British
27 Warstone Lane, Hockley, Birmingham, B18 6JQ
0121 236 0519
In the heart of Birmingham's Jewellery Quarter, this venue's aim is to provide good, home-cooked food at a modest price. A hidden gem serving everything from hearty breakfasts to traditional bread pudding.

AKBARS RESTAURANT
Indian
184 Hagley Road, Edgbaston, Birmingham, B16 9NY
0121 452 1862
A well-known Indian restaurant offering outstanding traditional cuisine. A busy buzz characterises the venue, meaning guests can enjoy high-quality food in an amiable atmosphere.

One card per party. Only Akbars in Birmingham.

AMBIANCE AT THE PEPPER MILL
Mediterranean

11 Coventry Road, Coleshill, B46 3BB
01675 462 172
A warm ambience characterises this lovely restaurant in Coleshill. Among their sumptuous culinary treats are juicy, flavourful flat-field mushrooms in garlic and a clear, simple avocado with shrimp.

2FOR1
MAIN COURSE

AROUND THE WORLD IN 80 DISHES
International

9 Brindleyplace, Birmingham, B1 2HJ
0121 643 5577
Take a trip around the world with a mouth-watering buffet that features authentic Chinese, Indian, Thai, Mexican and Italian cuisines. A family-friendly venue that really does cater for all tastes.

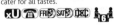

25%OFF
TOTAL

ASHA'S RESTAURANT
Indian

12-22 Newhall Street, Birmingham, B3 3LX
0121 200 2767
Bollywood legend Asha Bhosle's first UK restaurant, delivering an impressive menu of Northwest Indian cuisine. The dishes on offer match the authentic venue, full of genuine colour, flavour and spice.

2FOR1
MAIN COURSE

ASIAN GRILL RESTAURANT
Indian

91 Park Road, Sutton Coldfield, B73 6BT
0121 354 7491
A delightful culinary experience where the passionate chefs have created an outstanding menu that fuses traditional and modern flavours and techniques. Thrill your palate with a taste of South Asia.

2FOR1
2 COURSES

ATHENS
Mediterranean

31 Paradise Circus, Birmingham, B1 2BJ
0121 643 5526
Revive your holiday memories with a visit to Athens, where you can enjoy typically Greek food and Mediterranean fare. Traditional food, drink, and dance are the ingredients for a truly authentic evening.

25%OFF
TOTAL

BARAJEE
Indian

265 Broad Street, Birmingham, B1 2DS
0121 643 6700
A superb restaurant that offers creative menus in a modern, slightly retro venue. Indian and Bangladeshi cuisine is lovingly prepared to ensure it tastes its very best.

25%OFF
TOTAL

BARTONS ARMS
Thai

144 High Street, Aston, B6 4UP
0121 333 5988
At this welcoming pub-restaurant you will find an unusual but winning combination of real ale with Thai cuisine, served in a classical Victorian building. Try the duck noodle soup for a real treat.

25%OFF
TOTAL

BEECHES BAR & GRILL
International

Marsh Lane, Hampton in Arden, Solihull, B92 0AH
01675 442 277
An impressive steak menu along with an array of grilled fish makes this a great place to dine. Try the unique 'wine flight' option, which allows guests to sample three distinct wines from around the world.

2FOR1
MAIN COURSE

BLUE MANGO
Indian

Gas Street Basin, Birmingham, B1 2DS
0121 633 4422
Fine Indian cuisine can be enjoyed alongside a delicious cocktail or an exclusive bottle of wine. Perfect for those in need of a great quality, good old fashioned curry fix.

25%OFF
TOTAL

Max. £50 discount. Limited covers on Fri/Sat nights. One card per table.

BLUU
European

Islington Gates, Fleet Street, Birmingham, B3 1JH
0121 236 9013
Bluu is an atmospheric restaurant and bar, the restaurant offering a wide choice of formal or relaxed dining. The brasserie's open market-style kitchen serves great food all day.

25%OFF
TOTAL

BOHEMIA
Contemporary

23 Oak Tree Lane, Selly Oak, Birmingham, B29 6JE
0121 471 2713
Bohemia's aim is purely and simply to provide modern and imaginative food at a fair price. The kitchen prides itself on its use of fresh local produce, from which it creates the most divine dishes.

2FOR1
MAIN COURSE

BROOKES AT HOLIDAY INN SOLIHULL
International

61 Homer Road, Solihull, B91 3QD
0121 623 9988
In this red-brick hotel centred around a pretty lake and fountains, find a vibrant modern restaurant and bar offering an array of food and drink to cater for tastes from around the world.

Only one card per table.

CAFÉ RICKSHAW
Indian

20 Chapel Ash, Wolverhampton, WV3 0TN
01902 425 353
Sumptuous Indian cuisine to be enjoyed in elegant and tasteful surroundings. While all of the dishes here are unique in taste and flavour, they're equal in quality and proportion.

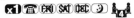

25%OFF
TOTAL

CAFÉ ROUGE
French

The Mailbox, Wharfside St, Birmingham, B1 1XL
0121 665 6437
An attractive restaurant, a boulevard café or a Parisian-style wine bar; however you see Café Rouge, consistently excellent classic French dishes are always guaranteed.

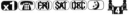

50%OFF
FOOD

CAFÉ ROUGE
French

The Water's Edge, Brindleyplace, Birmingham, B1 2HL
0121 643 6556
An attractive restaurant, a boulevard café or a Parisian-style wine bar; however you see Café Rouge, consistently excellent classic French dishes are always guaranteed.

50%OFF
FOOD

CAFÉ ROUGE
French

42-44 High Street, Harborne, Brimingham, B17 9NE
0121 426 4197
An attractive restaurant, a boulevard café or a Parisian-style wine bar; however you see Café Rouge, consistently excellent classic French dishes are always guaranteed.

50%OFF
FOOD

Discounted hotel rates for GS members on our website

CAFÉ ROUGE
French

98 New Street, Birmingham, B2 4NS
0121 633 8125
An attractive restaurant, a boulevard café or a Parisian-style wine bar; however you see Café Rouge, consistently excellent classic French dishes are always guaranteed.

50% OFF FOOD

CAFÉ ROUGE
French

The Bullring, Birmingham, B5 4BG
0121 616 1463
An attractive restaurant, a boulevard café or a Parisian-style wine bar; however you see Café Rouge, consistently excellent classic French dishes are always guaranteed.

50% OFF FOOD

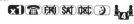

CAFÉ ROUGE
French

134 High Street, Solihull, B91 3SX
0121 711 8881
An attractive restaurant, a boulevard café or a Parisian-style wine bar; however you see Café Rouge, consistently excellent classic French dishes are always guaranteed.

50% OFF FOOD

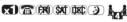

CELEBRITY INDIAN RESTAURANT
Indian

44 Broad Street, Brindley Place, Birmingham, B1 2HP
0121 643 8969
An appealing commingling of traditional and contemporary Indian cuisines, the food at Celebrity Indian Restaurant is the real star, even if the elegant, distinctive dining space vies for that crown.

2FOR1 MAIN COURSE

CLUB ROOM @ RAMADA JARVIS
Contemporary

Penns Lane, Walmley, Sutton Coldfield, B76 1LH
0844 815 9022
Offering contemporary bistro-style food whilst overlooking a picturesque lake, perfect for a relaxing break. The delicious menu offers temptations from starters through to desserts. Be sure to leave room.

25% OFF TOTAL

CRYSTAL RIVERS
Mediterranean

The Mailbox, Wharfside St, Birmingham, B1 1XL
0121 643 7979
Formerly known as Café Lazeez, this refurbished restaurant offers a sumptuous and decadent dining experience. With their Punjab-inspired menu they use traditional cooking methods to create exquisite meal.

2FOR1 2 COURSES

DA SANTINO RESTAURANT
Italian

12 Forest Court, Dorridge, Solihull, B93 8HN
01564 772 547
Classic Italian cuisine with a seafood-rich menu. Service is exceptional and the loyal clientèle are testament to the restaurant's success in serving up a memorable, delicious experience.

25% OFF TOTAL

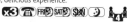

DEOLALI BAR AND RESTAURANT
Indian

23A St Mary's Row, Moseley, Birmingham, B13 8HW
0121 442 2222
Offering dishes that perfectly represent the deliciousness of South Indian cuisine. Relax and unwind in a warm and comfortable environment as you enjoy a high-class dining experience.

25% OFF TOTAL

After the first visit, the 25% off only applies to food.

DRAGON VALE
Chinese

83 High Street, Coleshill, B46 3AG
01675 462 463
This popular and lively Chinese restaurant serves classic dishes with traditional service in a beautiful surrounding. The extensive wine list and well-crafted menu offer something for everyone.

25% OFF TOTAL

FILINI AT THE RADISSON
Italian

12 Holloway Circus, Queensway, Birmingham, B1 1BT
0121 654 6000
Proclaiming a culinary philosophy of 'filini', this hotel-based restaurant produces uncluttered, clear flavours based on modern Italian cuisine.

25% OFF TOTAL

FOX & DOGS
British

Little Sutton Road, Sutton Coldfield, B75 6QB
0121 308 7560
One of the many Great British Carvery pubs where the well-loved classic feast is met by modern desires. The warm, charming nature of this pub offers a welcome to all who come through the door.

2FOR1 MAIN COURSE

Call beforehand on special event days.

GRESWOLDE BRASSERIE & HOTEL
Contemporary

High Street, Knowle, Solihull, B93 0LL
01564 772 711
High level of service and a skilled kitchen team led by Head Chef Richard Bowers set the tone for this venue, sited in a lovely little village but only a short distance from Birmingham's vibrant bustle.

25% OFF TOTAL

HANDMADE BURGER CO.
American

The Water's Edge, Brindleyplace, Birmingham, B1 2JB
0121 665 6542
Truly passionate about fresh food, the handmade burger Co. hand-make everything, from their delicious burgers and chips, to their delectable vegetables and coleslaws. Over 40 different burgers offered.

25% OFF TOTAL

HANDMADE BURGER CO.
American

17 Mill Lane Arc, Solihull, B91 3GS
0121 711 3004
Be spoilt for choice with over 40 fresh and delicious beef, chicken, lamb, fish and veggie burgers to choose from. Everything is handmade to perfection ensuring the quality of the food is superb.

25% OFF TOTAL

HENLEY PALACE
Indian British

Birmingham Road, Henley In Arden, B95 5QR
01564 792 689
A unique dining experience offering guests a combination of authentic and traditional Indian and Bengali dishes, as well as pizza and various other English dishes, in a friendly and relaxed atmosphere.

25% OFF TOTAL

HOGARTH'S HOTEL
European

Four Ashes Road, Dorridge, Solihull, B93 8QE
01564 779 988
In a secluded venue set in acres of beautiful woodland, chefs passionately create exceptional food that appeals to all palates, delivering it into a hospitable and peaceful atmosphere.

25% OFF TOTAL

Sunday offer only after 6pm.

219

HOTEL DU VIN

European

Church Street, Birmingham, B3 2NR
0121 200 0600
The finest, fresh local produce, simple European recipes, a stunning choice of wines; these are the trademark of a Hotel du Vin bistro. A distinctive venue with an ornate courtyard feature. 1 AA Rosette.

ISABELLAS RESTAURANT

Italian

856 Bristol Road, Selley Oak, Birmingham, B29 6HW
0121 247 2010
Nothing but fine, authentic Italian cuisine here, with an extensive menu offering guests a variety of dishes firmly rooted in Italy's rich culinary culture. Expect divine flavours and choice wines.

ITIHAAS

Indian

18 Fleet Street, Birmingham, B3 1JL
0121 212 3383
A small and sophisticated venue delivering mouth-watering dishes following the traditions of Mogul and Maharaja India, where food was perceived as a pleasure rather than a necessity.

JAFRANY BALTI RESTAURANT

Indian

36 The Mill Walk, Northfield, Birmingham, B31 4HH
0121 475 6233
This restaurant is a quiet oasis in the rustic surroundings of Northfield, delivering exotic Indian cuisine rich in aroma and spices. Perfect dining whatever the occasion.

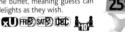

JIMMY SPICES

International

Regency Wharf, Broad Street, Birmingham, B1 2DS
0121 643 2111
Diners who have an eclectic palate should head to Jimmy Spices. Indian, Thai, Italian and Chinese dishes make up a multi-cuisine buffet, meaning guests can try as many different delights as they wish.

JIMMY SPICES

International

101 The Parade, Sutton Coldfield, B72 1PL
0121 355 1912
The ultimate destination for food lovers, pioneering multi-cuisine dining with an ambitious and sumptuous menu. Whether you prefer Indian, Thai, Italian or Chinese food, come here and be catered for.

JIMMY SPICES

International

64-66 Station Road, Solihull, B91 3RX
0121 709 2111
The ultimate destination for food lovers, pioneering multi-cuisine dining with an ambitious and sumptuous menu. Whether you prefer Indian, Thai, Italian or Chinese food, come here and be catered for.

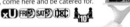

JOJOLAPA NEPALESE & INDIAN

Nepalese

55 New Hall Street, Birmingham, B3 8RB
0121 212 2511
An elegant venue delivering distinctive and ambrosial dishes from Nepal's unique cuisine. Enjoy quality food that will truly delight your taste buds, served in a truly authentic setting.

JOLOKIA RESTAURANT

Pan-Asian

2571a Stratford Road, Solihull, B91 6NL
01564 784 800
Extraordinary, vibrant pan-Asian cuisine; taking its name from the worlds hottest chilli, some of the dishes here are devilishly spicy. High-quality food by experienced chefs, who aim to please all tastes.

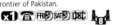

KABABISH RESTAURANT

Indian

29 Woodbridge Road, Moseley, B13 8EH
0121 449 5556
Relax and unwind in this tastefully decorated and elegantly lit restaurant. Exotic herbs and spices are distinctly blended using the traditional methods of the North West frontier of Pakistan.

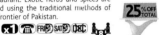

KABABISH RESTAURANT

Indian

266 Jockey Road, Sutton Coldfield, B73 5XP
0121 355 5062
Relax and unwind in this tastefully decorated and elegantly lit restaurant. Exotic herbs and spices are distinctly blended using the traditional methods of the North West frontier of Pakistan.

KINNAREE THAI RESTAURANT

Thai

22 Waterfront Walk, Birmingham, B1 1SN
0121 665 6568
Enter an exotic, mystical atmosphere where the focus is placed on divine food in traditionally magical surroundings. The chicken and noodles in red curry soup is out of this world.

KNOWLE INDIAN BRASSERIE

Indian

1690 High Street, Knowle, Solihull, B93 0LY
01564 776 453
A small intimate Indian restaurant that offers a large number of completely unique speciality dishes. Affable staff will cater to your every need.

LA CAVERNA HOTEL

Italian

2327 Coventry Road, Sheldon, B26 3PG
0121 743 7917
Renowned for its fabulous Italian cuisine served in a warm inviting environment. Fine seafood dishes, such as the lobster soup and the scallops in bacon, are especially popular.

LA TASCA

Spanish

Regency Wharf 2, Broad Street, Birmingham, B1 2DS
0121 643 9888
La Tasca is all about terrific tapas. The 30 plus dishes that are on offer are perfect for sharing with friends and loved ones. Sip on a glass of the ever-popular sangria in wonderfully warm surroundings.

Excludes 'Menu Rapido'

LA TASCA

Spanish

44 Mill Lane Arcade, Touchwood, Solihull, B91 3GS
0121 709 1846
La Tasca is all about terrific tapas. The 30 plus dishes that are on offer are perfect for sharing with friends and loved ones. Sip on a glass of the ever-popular sangria in wonderfully warm surroundings.

Gourmet Society discount applies to the à la carte menu

LOCANTA PICCALILLI
Italian

31 Ludgate Hill, Birmingham, B3 1EH
0121 236 7227
Locanta Piccalilli is an Italian restaurant of the first order. Erkan, the proprietor, buys fresh fish, meats and vegetables each morning, and offers up some spectacularly tasty, silken and savoury dishes.

Maximum of 2 cards in a party.

LOCH FYNE
Seafood

The Bank House, High Street, Knowle, B93 0JU
01564 732 750
From the roadside oyster bar that once was, Loch Fyne restaurants now successfully inject energy and passion into great food and wonderful flavours, whilst ensuring their seafood is sustainably sourced.

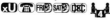

LONGFELLOWS
British

255 Hampton Ln, Catherine-de-Barnes, Solihull, B91 2TJ
0121 705 0547
This versatile, welcoming restaurant specialises in imaginative and flavourful takes on English staples. Its line in succulent, seasonal game marks it out, along with its tender, tasty seafood dishes.

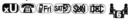

MALMAISON
European

The Mailbox, 1 Wharfside St, Birmingham, B1 1RD
0121 246 5000
This stylish and characterful Mal brasserie focuses on fresh local produce for its inviting and diverse menus; hearty, delicious game sourced from nearby on the Welsh border is a particular specialty.

2FOR1
MAIN COURSE

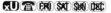

MACHAN EXPRESS CAFÉ
Modern British

101 Brindley House, Newhall St, Birmingham, B3 1LL
0121 236 6166
A great café serving a variety of delicious food, catering for all of its guests. A stylish little escape from the hustle and bustle; the perfect spot for a quiet lunch or an after-work meal.

25%OFF
TOTAL

MANGO SPICE
Indian

6a Hill Village Rd, Mere Green, Sutton Coldfield, B75 5BA
0121 308 0022
This Indian restaurant testifies to the multiplicity of the continent's culinary and cultural traditions. You can count on a variety of vivid, fulsome and tasty dishes along with an accommodating ambience.

2FOR1
MAIN COURSE

MARSTON FARM HOTEL
Traditional English Fare

Bodymoor Heath, Sutton Coldfield, B76 9JD
01827 872 133
Set in beautiful countryside, this Brook hotel's Courtyard Restaurant allows diners to sample a variety of mouth-watering meals coupled with warm, friendly service of the highest order.

25%OFF
TOTAL

MASH HOUSE
English/Gastro pub

The Water's Edge, Brindleyplace, Birmingham, B1 2HL
0121 643 2707
An excellent array of more than 30 classic British dishes served in a cool and contemporary environment, perfect for brunch, lunch or dinner. The best mash in town, so why not try all 5 varieties on offer.

2FOR1
MAIN COURSE

MECHU GRILL
Contemporary

59 Summer Row, Birmingham, B3 1SS
0121 710 4222
Mechu's sleek, stylish setting combines with a real emphasis on clear, uncluttered flavours, with splashes of informality for a cool, comfortable evening out.

25%OFF
TOTAL

METRO BAR & GRILL
International

73 Cornwall Street, Birmingham, B3 2DF
0121 200 1911
Cool and contemporary, Metro is a bar and grill that focuses on the importance of simplicity and variety in its menus. Clean, distinct flavours populate their dishes, with delicate seasoning and spices.

25%OFF
TOTAL

METRO BAR & GRILL
International

680-684 Warwick Road, Solihull, B91 3DX
0121 705 9495
Cool and contemporary, Metro is a bar and grill that focuses on the importance of simplicity and variety in its menus. Clean, distinct flavours populate their dishes, with delicate seasoning and spices.

25%OFF
TOTAL

MILAN INDIAN CUISINE
Indian

93 Newhall Street, Birmingham, B3 1LH
0121 236 0671
This restaurant juxtaposes its basis in North Indian cooking with an openness to other flavours; it is known for its great array of vegetarian dishes and serves light, tasty food in a cosy ambience.

2FOR1
2 COURSES

MINT
Bangladeshi/ Indian

Unit 3 Yew Tree Retail Park, Yardley, B25 8YP
0121 789 8908
Innovative, acclaimed Indian and Bangladeshi restaurant that supplements all the classics with distinctive house specialities; a real range from delicately spiced to bold and flavoursome dishes.

2FOR1
MAIN COURSE

MIYAKO TEPPANYAKI
Japanese

Arcadian Centre, Ladywell Walk, Birmingham, B5 4ST
0121 622 5183
This restaurant showcases the full flavourful range of Japanese cuisine. Try the succulent fillet steak, cooked on the traditional Hibarchi; not to be outdone are its fresh, vibrant vegetarian dishes.

25%OFF
TOTAL

MUST DIM SUM & RESTAURANT
Chinese

11 Newhall Street, Birmingham, B3 3NY
0121 212 2266
A Chinese tapas experience with an extensive variety of food on offer, from pork, beef and fish dishes to countless vegetarian options. The essence of traditional Eastern cooking with an innovative twist.

25%OFF
TOTAL

NATHANIELS
British

13 St Mary's Row, Moseley, B13 8HW
0121 449 9618
A seasonally changing à la carte menu and a deservedly popular lunch menu make this a perfect place to dine. Delicious steaks are to be devoured before moving on to the mind-blowing desserts.

2FOR1
2 COURSES

NEW HALL HOTEL (TERRACE)
Brasserie

Walmley Road, Sutton Coldfield, B76 1QX
0121 378 2442
A superb restaurant offering home-cooked treats inside a moated manor, and is a renowned member of the Hand Picked Hotels group, where each talented chef offers their own signature dish. 2 AA Rosettes.

NEW HALL HOTEL (THE BRIDGE)
Fine Dining

Walmley Rd, Sutton Coldfield, B76 1QX
0121 378 2442
An architecturally stunning building is home to an impressive Hand Picked Hotels group restaurant that produces exquisite cuisine. High standards have gained them a prestigious reputation.

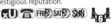

NEEL AKASH
Indian

31 School Street, Wolverhampton, WV1 4LR
01902 424 511
A well-regarded establishment with a spice-filled and fragrant menu, rich in Indian classics, catering for all tastes and preferences. Delicious, authentic food delivered at a very high standard.

NUTHURST GRANGE HOTEL
Fine Dining

Nuthurst Grange Lane, Hockley Heath, Solihull, B94 5NL
01564 783 972
Enjoy the range of dining possibilities at this intimate and relaxed restaurant, from canapés with your pre-meal drinks, to petit fours with your coffee; find everything you require. Awarded 2 AA Rosettes.

OLD ORLEANS
American

80 Broad Street, Birmingham, B15 1AU
0121 633 0144
An extraordinarily accurate taste of the Deep South can be found in this unique restaurant. The kitchen deals in classic Louisiana and Cajun recipes such as jambalaya and gumbo to create an exciting menu.

Not available on Bank Holiday weekends. Adult menu only.

OLD ORLEANS
American

Unit 13, Star City, Watson Rd, Nechells, B7 5SA
0121 327 8275
An extraordinarily accurate taste of the Deep South can be found in this unique restaurant. The kitchen deals in classic Louisiana and Cajun recipes such as jambalaya and gumbo to create an exciting menu.

Not available on Bank Holiday weekends. Adult menu only.

PAD THAI
Thai

86 Holloway Head, Birmingham, B1 1NB
01216 666 669
Taking this name from the classic street-stall noodle dish, this wonderful Thai restaurant offers all the tastiness of the food and all the friendliness of Thai culture.

PINOCCHIO
Italian

8 Chad Square, Edgbaston, Brimingham, B15 3TQ
0121 454 8672
An unmistakeable Mediterranean flair can be tasted in every dish at Pinocchio's. A wide variety of pasta dishes feature alongside exquisite veal and tasty beef dishes.

POLASH
Indian

85 High Street, Coleshill, B46 3AG
01675 462 868
Quality Indian food cooked to perfection using fresh ingredients, ensuring every dish on their extensive menu is full of natural flavour and spice.

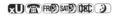

POPPYRED
British

The Arcadian Centre, Hurst St, Birmingham B5 4TD
0121 687 1200
A stylish venue underpinned by a fashionable ethos. The food is just as impressive with a sumptuous new range of special dishes each week complemented by an impressive wine and drink selection.

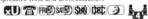

PUNJABI HAVELI
Indian

1558 Stratford Road, Hall Green, Brimingham, B28 9HA
0121 745 3636
A wonderful restaurant serving deliciously fresh Punjabi cuisine. Guests can taste authenticity and quality in every dish created by Head Chef Sukhdey Singh who originates from the region of Punjab.

PURBANI TANDOORI RESTAURANT
Indian

41-43 Birch Street, Wolverhampton, WV1 4JW
01902 424 030
Good quality, simple and traditional Indian cuisine populates a menu showcasing all the classic Indian dishes. Made with quality ingredients, they provide rich and fragrant flavours.

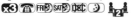

RAJ INDIAN CUISINE
Indian

30 Birmingham Road, Great Barr, Birmingham, B43 6NR
0121 357 8368
Conveniently located, this classical Indian restaurant delivers sumptuous-tasting food from a greatly varied menu, with recommended dishes including the prawn Jhinga Mossalla.

RBG @ PARK INN B'HAM WEST
English and Continental

Birmingham Road, West Bromwich, B70 6RS
0121 609 9988
A versatile hotel-based restaurant whose accomplishment in everything from a full English breakfast, to a big, bold working lunch, to a Mothers' Day treat, marks it out. Contemporary, stylish and sassy.

RED BAR & LOUNGE
International

Temple Street, Birmingham, B2 5BN
0121 643 0194
An underground oasis providing slick table service, gourmet sandwiches, fantastic cocktails, an eclectic spirit selection and extensive champagne and wine lists. Unwind in a intimate and relaxing venue.

REGARDS
Indian

27 Chad Square, Edgbaston, Birmingham, B15 3TQ
0121 455 6697
Quality Indian cooking from a restaurant which prides itself on exceeding customers' expectations every time. Complete with private dining area, this venue is an excellent choice whatever occasion.

Sign up to our newsletter for latest restaurants, offers and more

ROYAL SPICE
Bangladeshi/ Indian
953-955 Bristol Rd South, Northfield, Brimingham, B31 2QT
0121 477 5223
Renowned for its fabulously flavoured balti dishes, this fine restaurant offers superbly authentic Indian and Bangladeshi dishes for all to enjoy. The popular five course meal comes highly recommended.

RUBY CANTONESE RESTAURANT
Cantonese
2A Barnsley Road, Edgbaston, Brimingham, B17 8ED
0121 429 8805
Delivering delicious Cantonese cuisine that successfully satisfies every time. Boasting a highly experienced chef, the kitchen produces favourite dishes from satay skewers to beef in black bean sauce.

2FOR1 MAIN COURSE

SAFARI
African
256 Great Lister Street, Birmingham, B7 4DA
0121 333 3208
A unique takeaway and delivery outlet specialising in African snacks. Try the 'Rolex' - a popular street dish from the Wandegeya district of Kampala, which the kitchen has down to perfection.

25% OFF TOTAL

SAFFRON
Indian
909 Wolverhampton Road, Oldbury, B69 4RR
0121 552 1752
Vintage aromas and delicious flavours are exquisitely balanced in each and every dish. Valuing traditional methods of Indian cooking, the menu succeeds in serving extraordinarily appetising meals.

2FOR1 MAIN COURSE

SHADES OF RAJ
Indian
52 Station Road, Solihull, B91 3RX
0121 704 0353
Presenting delicious dishes that focus on both taste and texture whilst maintaining an eye on healthy eating. The fine wine list will satisfy the desires of all budding wine connoisseurs.

SHAHI MASALA
Multi-Cuisine
8 Burney Lane, Birmingham, B8 2AH
0121 783 4121
A delicious, eclectic variety of dishes that will satisfy every palate and appetite. Indian, Chinese and Italian buffet menus are changed daily, meaning diners can enjoy something different every time.

25% OFF TOTAL

SHANGHAIYE
Chinese
G/F 86 Holloway Head, Birmingham, B1 1NB
0121 666 6669
Passionately produces timeless dishes that will forever evoke a taste of the Orient. Before feasting on your favourite Chinese dish, why not sing for your supper on the karaoke.

25% OFF TOTAL

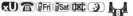

SHERWOODS INDIAN RESTAURANT
Indian
1492 Stratford Road, Hall Green, Brimingham, B28 9ET
0121 733 7363
Satisfy your senses and sample a true taste of India. The kitchen focuses its energy on producing high-quality food at great prices. The sizzling lamb balti is particularly popular.

2FOR1 3 COURSES

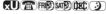

SHAH'S RESTAURANT
1160 Warwick Road, Acocks Green, B27 6BP
0121 707 8297 *Bangladeshi / Indian*

2FOR1 MAIN COURSE

Visit Shah's Restaurant Birmingham. Immerse yourself in the authentic flavours of the wonderful food. Devour a traditional biryani and travel backwards through time on the rich flavours of the era of the Moghuls. Close your eyes and be transported to the languid banks of the River Sylhet as you feast on 'Banglar Prem' a carefully executed speciality comprising succulent pieces of lamb, chicken and prawns.

Every night, the chefs at Shah's demonstrate their expertise serving guests the finest cuisine from Bangladesh and India. Their passion for the dishes of these venerable regions is evident in every mouth-watering bite of the aromatic menus offered.

Shah's offers decidedly traditional and adventurous contemporary dishes and there are an outstanding number of fish and seafood specialities including the superb 'Shahan Shah Seabass'.

A pleasing number of vegetarian and side dishes round out the menu and guests are invited to bring their own alcohol into the restaurant should they wish.

The service is as fresh and subtle as the décor: at once informative, helpful and then discreet, allowing guests to savour their delicious and eagerly anticipated meals at leisure.

SHIMLA PINKS — *Indian*
Fiveways Leisure Centre, Broad St, Birmingham, B15 1AY
0121 633 0366
Incorporates new and exciting dishes amongst a menu of traditional Indian cuisine. The visually pleasing interior ensures you enjoy your meal in an outstanding setting. A beacon to curry lovers.

Maximum discount £50.

SHIMLA PINKS — *Indian*
44 Station Road, Solihull, B91 3RX
0121 633 0366
Incorporates new and exciting dishes amongst a menu of traditional Indian cuisine. The visually pleasing interior ensures you enjoy your meal in an outstanding setting. A beacon to curry lovers.

Maximum discount £50.

STRADA — *Italian*
The Mailbox, Wharfside St, Birmingham, B1 1XL
0121 643 7279
A dedicated menu offering traditional Italian dishes in a stylish and contemporary setting. The chefs use only the finest ingredients such as Parma ham and buffalo mozzarella imported directly from Italy.

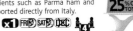

SWEET CHILLIES CUISINE — *Indian*
836 Yardleywood Road, Moseley, Birmingham, B13 0JE
0121 443 2737
Excite your palate with delicious food from Bengal, the eastern region of India. Highly recommended for lovers of spice, yet chefs here also endeavour to cater for other guests and dietary requirements.

THE ATRIUM RESTAURANT — *European*
The Belfry Hotel, Wishaw, Sutton Coldfield, B76 9PR
01675 470 301
Escape to the country and enter a wonderful realm of pleasure. Take a break from that round of golf and enjoy a well-deserved meal, offered to you in an appealingly relaxed atmosphere.

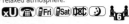

THE BLACK EAGLE — *British*
16 Factory Road, Hockley, Brimingham, B18 5JU
0121 523 4008
An award-winning pub providing great value food and an excellent range of permanent and guest ales. A great menu which offers traditional favourites and daily specials in a warm atmosphere.

THE COWSHED — *European*
Clive Farm, Clive Road, Pattingham, WV6 7EN
01902 701 888
Imaginative, contemporary British cuisine to be found in this characterful restaurant with oak beams and galleried balcony, all set on a working farm. Locally sourced and freshly cooked dishes.

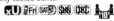

THE CROSS CAFE BAR — *International*
145-147 Alcester Road, Moseley, Birmingham, B13 8JP
0121 449 6300
One of Moseley's most popular venues, a perfect ambience completely unpretentious. Diligent and caring staff deliver clever but simple food. Also offering a variety of vegan and vegetarian dishes.

THE DOG INN — *British*
Dog Lane, Nether Whitacre, Coleshill, B46 2DU
01675 481 318
Superbly kept beers, fine food and a traditional atmosphere, all provided by a knowledgeable and welcoming landlady and her staff. Great value dishes, with guest ales added every week.

THE EDGBASTON PALACE HOTEL — *European*
198-200 Hagley Road, Edgbaston, Brimingham, B16 9PQ
0121 452 1577
What better place to dine than in this magnificent Victorian building situated in the leafy suburb of Edgbaston. Enjoy dining in the most beautiful surroundings.

THE FRENCH RESTAURANT — *French*
The Belfry Hotel, Wishaw, Sutton Coldfield, B76 9PR
01675 470 301
A dining experience to suit every occasion and taste, with award-winning cuisine featuring contemporary meat and fish dishes, to speciality desserts. Has its own cocktail bar for patrons to use if desired.

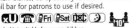

Smart dress code. Not suitable for young children.

THE GEORGE — *Bistro*
Ramada, The Square, Solihull, B91 3RF
0844 815 9011
A phenomenal hotel restaurant that offers internationally inspired cuisine for breakfast lunch and dinner. Enjoy magnificent views of the bowling green and admire the oil paintings that line the walls.

THE GRILL ROOM — *International*
Holiday Inn Birmingham Airport, Coventry Rd, B26 3QW
0800 400 9007
The Grill Room doors open up to a world of devoted hospitality, fine cuisine and vibrant atmosphere. Meticulous preparation goes into every single order submitted to the kitchen.

THE LEA MARSTON HOTEL — *Fine Dining*
Adderley Restaurant, Haunch Lane, B76 0BY
01675 470 468
Experience fine dining at its very best with the dinner or à la carte menu. Elegantly prepared dishes are served in the most stylish of settings. Relax over a drink or two in the Atrium lounge and bar.

THE LLOYDS INDIAN RESTAURANT — *Indian*
7 Station Road, Knowle, Solihull, B93 0HL
01564 775 777
Culinary pleasures need not be guilty ones when dining at this delightful Indian restaurant. The quality of the produce can be tasted in every divine dish, all exceptionally reasonable in price.

THE PAVILLION AT QUALITY HOTEL — *International*
166 Hagley Rd, Edgbaston, Birmingham, B16 9NZ
0121 454 6621
Browse the à la carte menu or head straight for the carvery at this wonderful hotel restaurant. Admire the garden views that are visible from the Pavilion and the Terrace Bar.

WEST MIDLANDS

224

Visit the website regularly to discover the latest restaurants joining the GS

THE PLOUGH & HARROW HOTEL
English and Continental

135 Hagley Road, Edgbaston, Brimingham, B16 8LS
0121 454 4111

Just a stone's throw away from the city centre, this 18th century building is now home to an ideally situated hotel and restaurant. Unwind over a fabulous cocktail or indulge in delicious food.

THE PLOUGH HARBORNE
Modern Pub

21 High St, Harborne, Birmingham, B17 9NT
0121 427 3678

One fine gastro-pub on the outskirts of Birmingham. A hip local vibe and quirky, incisive dishes make this the sort of place that can easily become a favourite haunt.

THE PORTLAND HOTEL
English and Continental

313 Hagley Road, Edgbaston, B16 9LQ
0121 455 0535

A restaurant that is equally as popular with non-residents as it is with hotel guests. Inexpensive meals are served in the most elegant of settings.

THE PUNCHBOWL
British

Mill Lane, Lapworth, Solihull, B94 6HR
01564 784 564

Pop in for an impromptu lunch with friends, or relax over romantic candlelight with loved ones. The pub encompasses all the right traditional features, whilst creating a modern style and atmosphere.

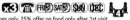
Sunday, evenings only. 25% offer on food only after 1st visit.

THE PURPLE ROOMS
Indian

1076 Stratford Road, Hall Green, Birmingham, B28 8AD
0121 702 2193

The award-winning status of this restaurant reflects its culinary excellence, with a vast menu providing mouth-watering dishes in abundance. The superb fish curries are highly recommended.

THE RAINBOW
British

Brewood Road, Coven, Wolverhampton, WV9 5DH
01902 798 182

Diverse menu at this cosy and accommodating country pub, where you can settle in for a drink or enjoy their fresh and hearty home-style food.

THE SPORTS CAFE
International

240 Broad Street, Birmingham, B1 2HG
0121 633 4000

Vivid spot in Birmingham where you can catch a match, shoot some pool or dance your heart out and enjoy their meaty, classic diner-style fare in the meantime.

THE STANDARD
Indian

27 Cleveland Street, Wolverhampton, WV1 3HT
0871 717 9132

Attention to detail and a highly personable service can be expected at this well-established Indian restaurant. Spirits and wines from around the world will provide the perfect accompanying drink.

THE SYLHET SPICE CUISINE
Indian

27-29 York Road, Kingsheath, Solihull, B14 7SA
0121 444 6644

Drawing on all the old favourites as well as a distinctive array of signature dishes, this Indian restaurant is firmly focused on authenticity and quality in its tastes from Bangladesh, India and Pakistan.

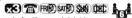
Bookings taken only after 10pm on excluded nights.

THE TOWNHOUSE
European

727 Warwick Road, Solihull, B91 3DA
0121 704 1567

Cosmopolitan diners will love the modernity and stylishness of this restaurant and bar. The impressive European dishes and the care that is taken over each order make this a highly recommended place.

THE WAREHOUSE CAFE
Vegetarian

54-57 Allison Street, Digbeth, Birmingham, B5 5TH
0121 633 0261

Outstanding vegetarian and vegan food at this restaurant in Birmingham, whose commitment to ethical practices stands apart but doesn't overshadow the fresh and sumptuous flavours of its diverse recipes.

THE VINE INN
Fine Dining

Vine Lane, Clent, Stourbridge, DY9 9PH
01562 882 491

A new menu offers some traditional favourites – steamed steak and kidney pudding and slow cooked glazed pork belly as well as more unusual specialities such as wild boar, other game dishes and fish.

TIN TIN CHINESE RESTAURANT
Chinese

9F The Water's Edge, Brindleyplace, Brimingham, B1 2HL
0121 633 0888

Unique both in style and experience, Tin Tin maintains its status as the best for elegant Cantonese cuisine. The restaurant presents you with superb dishes cooked by a revolutionary team of chefs.

ULYSSES GREEK RESTAURANT
Greek

42a Bristol Street, Birmingham, B5 7AA
0121 622 3159

Established in 1986, this family-owned restaurant maintains its authentic and traditional Greek menu. In the heart of the city you can fully enjoy fine Greek and organic wines from Tripoli.

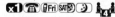

VALENTINO'S RESTAURANT
Italian

73 High Street, Harborne, Birmingham, B17 9NS
0121 427 2560

Deliciously simple yet delectably sophisticated, Valentino's offers a varied menu for all to enjoy, which is matched by the extensive wine list. The daily specials prove to be exceedingly popular.

VITO'S ITALIAN RESTAURANT
Italian

5 St Johns Way, Knowle, Solihull, B93 0LE
01564 739 395

Offering an explosion of culinary tastes which reflect the flavours and aromas of the Mediterranean. The quality of the food is of the same high standard as you could find in any Italian city.

WEST 12 RESTAURANT
European

12 Hagley Road, Edgbaston, Birmingham, B16 8SJ
0121 452 7007
Fine dining awaits you in the stylish West 12 restaurant and bar, which specialises in contemporary British cuisine such as Scottish beef and Welsh Lamb. A great chance to relax and eat well.

BANK HOUSE HOTEL
Traditional English Fare

Bransford, Worcester, WR6 5JD
01886 833 551
Another Brook hotel restaurant that truly delivers, showcasing a wide variety of traditional cuisine with a contemporary twist, coupled with panoramic views and exemplary service.

WINE REPUBLIC
European

Centenary Square, Broad Street, Birmingham, B1 2EP
0121 644 6464
Just moments away from the hub of the city, eat al fresco and watch Centenary Square go by as the sun goes down and the city comes to life. Open for morning coffee, light lunches and fabulous dinners.

BANTS
British

Worcester Road, Upton Snodsbury, WR7 4NN
01905 381 282
Enjoy great food in stylish surroundings. Making use of fresh local produce, the menu reflects the seasons to ensure the very best and most appropriate English dishes are on offer all year round.

YE OLDE TOLL HOUSE
British

40 Walsall Street, Willenhall, WV13 2ER
01902 605 575
An unforgettable eating experience, here you will find imaginative dishes at affordable prices. The Old World interior encourages the maintenance of the restaurant's traditional splendour and atmosphere.

2FOR1
MAIN COURSE

BENGAL FUSION
Indian

174 High Street, Lye, Stourbridge, Dudley, DY9 8LN
01384 891 111
Deliciously warming Bengali cuisine is served in a comfortable, contemporary setting. Tantalise your taste buds with an exceptional selection of starters, main dishes, and after-dinner delights.

CADMORE LODGE
British

Berrington Green, St Michaels, Tenbury Wells, WR15 8TQ
01584 810 044
Enjoy spectacular lake views as you dine in this beautiful restaurant, located in idyllic countryside. The baked supreme of corn-fed chicken with crisp chorizo is highly recommended. 1 AA Rosette.

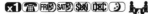

Worcestershire/ Herefordshire

BROCKENCOTE HALL

Chaddesley Corbett, Kidderminster, DY10 4PY
01562 777 876   *Fine Dining*

Brockencote Hall is a magnificent country house hotel and restaurant in a pastoral setting just outside the small Worcestershire village of Chaddesley Corbett. Set in 70 acres of landscaped grounds complete with dovecote, gatehouse, lake and many fine specimen trees, the estate dates back over 300 years to a more elegant, peaceful age.

Brockencote Hall's elegant dining room, with its glorious views out across the grounds, is well known for its fine table offering traditional French cuisine, with occasional regional and seasonal specialities, complemented by an excellent wine cellar and discreet yet friendly service.

Recognised by the AA with two rosettes and by other respected bodies, the restaurant owes its success to a menu of traditional French cuisine, a tempting choice of lighter dishes and the gentle guidance of experienced service staff.

When booking restaurants always mention your GS membership

CAFÉ ROUGE
French

5 Friar Street, Worcester, WR1 2LZ
01905 613 055
An attractive restaurant, a boulevard café or a Parisian-style wine bar; however you see Café Rouge, consistently excellent classic French dishes are always guaranteed.

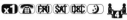

COLWALL PARK HOTEL
Fine Dining

Seasons Restaurant, Colwall, Malvern, WR13 6QG
01684 540 000
Award-winning Head Chef James Garth produces modern British dishes with the finest local and seasonal ingredients. The restaurant has a contemporary and modern feel for a wonderful evening meal. 2 AA rosettes.

'DINE' INDIAN & BANGLADESHI
Indian

44 High Street, Brierley Hill, Dudley, DY5 3AE
01384 482 444
A restaurant whose priorities simply lie in quality, flavour, and service. With high-standard dishes created by an expert chef with 18 years experience, diners will not be disappointed.

FOWNES HOTEL
European

City Walls Road, Worcester, WR1 2AP
01905 613 151
The restaurant of the Fownes hotel provides outstanding service and comfort for guests as well as appetising, flavourful meals. The perfect venue for conferences, business, or simply for pleasure.

Enquire for room discounts for GS members.

FRENCH CONNECTION
French

3 Coventry Street, Stourbridge, Dudley, DY8 1EP
01384 390 940
Highly regarded bistro that serves rounded, classic French dishes with a great emphasis on technique and precision; unstinting on French culinary tradition and keen to foreground its history and culture.

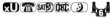

FUSION BRASSERIE
Brasserie

Hawbridge, Stoulton, Worcester, WR7 4RJ
01905 840 647
A promise of good service, fresh food, fine wines, and friendly smiles in a relaxing atmosphere. This exciting restaurant is set in a unique 1960s 'retro pub', but the food is anything but old-fashioned.

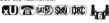

GAINSBOROUGH HOUSE HOTEL
Contemporary

Bewdley Hill, Kidderminster, DY11 6BS
01562 820 041
Well-regarded, luxurious restaurant in the Gainsborough House Hotel; its sweet, succulent carvery is a Sunday speciality.

GREENS RESTAURANT
British

Wharton Park Golf Club, Long Bank, Bewdley, DY12 2QW
01299 405 222
A warm dining experience offered within the realms of a beautifully situated golf club. A weekly changing menu delivers fresh, high standard food coupled with a real emphasis on good hospitality.

HALFWAY HOUSE INN
European

Bastonford, Powick, Malvern, Worcester, WR2 4SL
01905 831 098
Expect perfect hospitality coupled with traditional, home-cooked food, with specialities in seafood, steaks and unmissable Sunday roasts. Simple, fine food to be enjoyed with quality ales and wine.

HARRY RAMSDEN'S
British

The Merry Hill Centre, Dudley, DY5 1SY
01384 486 888
Visit this national treasure and enjoy some of the finest fish and chips in the country. Harry Ramsden's continues to deliver quality food, as it has done throughout its illustrious history.

Not available during August or in takeaway.

HARRY'S
British

The Chase Hotel, Gloucester Rd, Ross on Wye, HR9 5LH
01989 763 161
While retaining its historic Georgian features, this venue presents modern, fresh dining. The subtle décor complements the traditional cuisine, with delectable food worthy of its AA rosette.

INN & BRASSERIE
British

Broadway Road, Broadway, WR12 7HP
01386 852 461
Combining the contemporary with the classic in an idyllic village setting, this inn delivers a unique blend of style and informality. A modern brasserie that retains traditional country elegance.

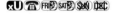

JIMMY PICKLES
Indian

76 High Street, Pershore, WR10 1DU
01386 555 900
Set in the tranquil surroundings of the countryside, this exquisite Indian restaurant offers a heavenly selection of delicious dishes, rich in flavour and enhanced with selected spices.

KABEN
Bangladeshi

The Blue Ball, Old High St, Dudley, DY5 1SE
01384 484 827
Popular with the customers, this restaurant boasts a comprehensive menu of specialist dishes and traditional curries, alongside essential sundries and tasty desserts.

RILYS EVESHAM
Indian

2/3 Waterside, Evesham, WR11 1BS
01386 45289
The reopened Rilys offers guests a unique insight into real Indian cuisine, prepared and cooked by award winning chefs using only the freshest and highest quality ingredients.

PASHA
Indian

56 St John's, Worcester, WR2 5AJ
01905 426 327
Outstanding Indian and Bengali dishes served in a modern interior boasting innovative artworks. Ensuring customer satisfaction at all times, the staff are amiable and will cater for your every need.

PENGETHLEY MANOR
Fine Dining

Pengethley Park, Ross on Wye, HR9 6LL
01989 730 211

A luxurious venue where the warmth and grandeur of the restaurant is only exceeded by an astonishingly high standard of freshly sourced, elegant cuisine, for which they have won many accolades.

THE ANCHOR INN
European

Drake Street, Welland, Malvern, WR13 6LN
01684 592 317

A wonderful inn situated in a beautiful 17th century building within award-winning gardens. Whether you want to dine and drink or rest and relax, you'll be pleasantly satisfied at The Anchor Inn.

PIOS RESTAURANT
Italian

White Horse Hotel, Churches Row, Pershore, WR10 1BH
01386 554 038

In a combined pub-hotel, proprietor Pio creates and serves divinely authentic Italian dishes coupled with traditional background music. An eloquent and incredibly tasty dining experience.

THE BLUE LAGOON
Indian

8 Waterside, Evesham, R11 1BS
01386 429 383

Melting and piquantly marinated slow-cooked meats populate the dishes of this Bangladeshi restaurant; the classics are there too, but it's dishes like, say, the Boal Shatkora that stand out from the crowd.

PREZZO
Italian

22-24 High Street, Bromsgrove, B61 8HQ
01527 874 614

With a character all of its own, Prezzo oozes contemporary style and enduring charm. Signature pastas, stone-baked pizzas and classic Italian dishes promise a perfect dining choice for the whole family.

THE BOMBAY PALACE
Indian

38 The Tything, Worcester, WR1 1JL
01905 613 969

Enjoy a tryst with this accommodating Indian restaurant in Worcester, where you'll find the gamut of classic curries, cooked well and drawing out all the fulsome and tasty aromas to savour.

REDOLENCE SPICE
Indian

17-21 Unicorn Hill, Redditch, B97 4QR
01527 65970

Experience Indian luxury at its finest. Delivers passionate food from an extensive menu offering a vast array of vegetarian and meat dishes to suit every palate, using an intriguing blend of ingredients.

THE BRAMBLINGS AT THE ABBEY
English and Continental

Hither Green Lane, Dagnell End Road, Redditch, B98 9BE
01527 406 600

Elegant dining with a focus on great service and innovative menus. A stylish atmosphere and a warm welcome is provided for all guests. The Sunday lunch carvery is very popular and pre-booking is a must.

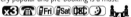

RILYS REDDITCH
Indian

1B The Quadrant, Alcester Street, Redditch, B98 8AE
01527 60544

A new and fresh approach to distinctive food, fine wine and excellent customer service. Each dish combines rich and fragrant Indian flavours with a western approach, serving up a menu full of variety.

THE BRIDGE AT WILTON
Modern British

Wilton, Ross on Wye, HR9 6AA
01989 562 655

This Michelin-recommended and 2 AA Rosette-rated restaurant attracts gourmet food hunters from around the country. The Head Chef creates unique, and truly imaginative dishes of the highest standards.

SPARROWGRASS
British

BW Salford Hall Hotel, Abbots Salford, Evesham, WR11 8UT
01386 871 300

A traditional venue offering delicious food in a warm and welcoming atmosphere. Professional, friendly staff serve quality dishes from an innovative menu created using fresh local produce.

THE DEWDROP INN
Contemporary

Bell Lane, Lower Broadheath, WR2 6RR
01905 640 012

Whether you fancy a night's stay in a beautiful bed and breakfast guest house or simply a scrumptious bite to eat, this cosy inn will meet your requirements. Seasonal bar and à la carte menus available.

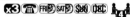

STONE MANOR HOTEL
European

Field's Restaurant, Stone, Kidderminster, DY10 4PJ
01562 777 555

With an imaginative menu and freshly delivered produce, the food created here is of the highest standard. Teamed with an extensive wine list, this venue serves up a pleasurable dining experience.

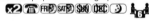

THE GRANARY HOTEL
International

Heath Lane, Shenstone, Kidderminster, DY10 4BS
01562 777 535

A contemporary hotel with a restaurant at its heart. The chef and his team use only the finest, freshest ingredients, sourced locally wherever possible, to produce the exquisite dishes on offer.

TALBOT HOTEL
British

New Street, Ledbury, HR8 2DX
01531 632 963

Combining the very best hospitality and atmosphere, this lovely hotel and pub extends a warm welcome to every visitor, whilst delivering a menu filled with fine, home-made British cuisine.

Offer excludes Sunday lunch and Christmas menus

THE INN AT STONEHALL
European

Stonehall Common, Kempsey, WR5 3QG
01905 820 462

A gastro-pub offering diners delightfully simple, modern British cuisine with a touch of French influence. This restored Victorian venue offers historical ambience coupled with excellent food and service

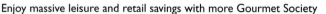

Enjoy massive leisure and retail savings with more Gourmet Society

THE OLD RECTORY
International

Ipsley Lane, Ipsley, Redditch, B98 0AP
0152 752 3000
A beautiful hotel and restaurant steeped in history. Having stood for over 500 years, The Old Rectory offers a beautiful blend of traditional features with modern décor.

2FOR1 MAIN COURSE

THE RAJPUT
Indian

41 Load Street, Bewdley, DY12 2AS
01299 409 409
A splendid place to enjoy fine dining in the midst of a pretty and peaceful Georgian town. Sophisticated use of Indian herbs and spices make every dish delectable and flavoursome.

25%OFF TOTAL

THE ROYAL FORESTER INN
British

Callow Hill, Bewdley, Kidderminster, DY14 9XW
01299 266 286
Allow the soothing tones of the live pianist to enhance your dining experience at this wonderful restaurant, whilst you enjoy a wonderful British menu accompanied by premium wines and local guest ales.

2FOR1 MAIN COURSE

Offer applies to à la carte menu only. Not special menus.

THE SPRING
International

Mt. Pleasant Hotel, 50 Belle Vue Terrace, Malvern, WR14 4PZ
01684 561 837
Fresh, locally sourced classic dishes go with the gorgeous setting of this Malvern hotel restaurant. Try the thoroughgoing bar menu, or a refined Gressingham duck breast in the main restaurant.

2FOR1 2 COURSES

THE WELLINGTON
Modern British

Wellington, Hereford, HR4 8AT
01432 830 367
Owner Ross Williams has been passionate about good food well before he embarked on his adventure with The Wellington. One of the county's finest dining pubs.

2FOR1 MAIN COURSE

TRUMPET INN
British

Trumpet, Ledbury, HR8 2RA
01531 670 277
A traditional country pub and restaurant offering locally produced, home-cooked food and superb cask ales including the famous Wadworth 6X. Enjoy wholesome food and drink alongside fine company.

25%OFF TOTAL

Offer excludes Sunday lunch and Christmas menus.

TWICE THE SPICE
Indian

97-98 High Street, Dudley, DY1 1QP
01384 232 425
Good quality local Indian restaurant in Dudley. Enjoy a mouth-watering curry with fluffy naan and all the trimmings.

2FOR1 3 COURSES

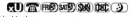

Must book in advance.

WALL HEATH TANDOORI
Indian

4 High Street, Kingswinford, Dudley, DY6 0HA
01384 287 402
Situated in Wall Heath's adjacent village Kingswinford, this restaurant offers pleasing Indian cuisine at affordable prices. Extremely popular with the local community, booking is recommended.

2FOR1 MAIN COURSE

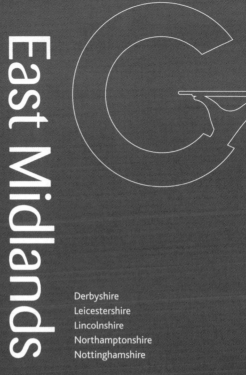

East Midlands

The East Midlands is an area rich with distinctive, innovative producers. You don't need to be a pub quiz expert to know that Melton Mowbray is to pork pies as Champagne is to champagne: the only place that does the real deal. Less known, perhaps, is Melton's status as a hub for exquisite stilton and preparations of local game. Bakewell originates the tart of tarts, while there are few sager choices than a coarse-cut Lincolnshire sausage. East Midlands cheeses are indeed renowned: Hartington in Derbyshire is also known for its stiltons, while Leicester put its name to the classic red.

With so much in the way of fresh produce and innovative traditional recipes, the East Midlands is unsurprisingly flush in restaurants that have a line in this kind of classic fare; add to this the prevalence of the classic country pub throughout these big, central counties and you have one of the ingredients of a characteristic food dialect. But only one: Leicester's large Asian population, for example, means the city boasts a commensurate quality of Indian restaurants; the region is open and cosmopolitan and this is reflected in the range of different cuisines to be found in it. Where the two meet – the history of excellence in produce and the contemporary eclecticism – you'll find a region rich in culinary character, and as apt for a food tour through the villages and towns as it is for a simple and superb meal out in one of its great cities

Derbyshire

EAST MIDLANDS

ALISON HOUSE — *European*
Intake Lane, Cromford, Matlock, DE4 3RH
01629 822 211
A tranquil, renovated 18th century country house with exquisite dining facilities. A high-quality and varied menu of home-cooked meals crafted with imagination and flair, including vegetarian dishes.

BARCELO BUXTON PALACE — *International*
Palace Road, Buxton, SK17 6AG
01298 22001
Dine in elegance and timeless style in the restaurant of the magnificent Palace Hotel. The focal point of Buxton's hospitality scene since 1868.

BAY TREE — *International*
4 Potter Street, Melbourne, DE73 8HW
01332 863 358
A multi award-winning restaurant, well-regarded in surrounding areas. Serving the best of New World cuisine and boasting an outstanding wine list, choose from snacks to à la carte and table d'hôte.

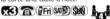

BLENHEIM HOUSE — *Modern British*
56-58 Main Street, Etwall, DE65 6LP
01283 732 254
A home from home for weary travellers and regulars alike. Chef Martin Rose demonstrates not only a great sympathy for his produce but also a genuine flare for presentation.

BUCKINGHAM'S — *British*
85 Newbold Road, Newbold, Chesterfield, S41 7PU
01246 201 041
Ridding itself of traditional restaurant expectations, this restaurant offers a 'surprise menu' that is created based on your own requirements, likes and dislikes. The food will exceed satisfaction.

2FOR1 3COURSES

CRICKETTS INN — *British*
Burton Road, Acresford, Swadlincote, DE12 8AP
01283 760 359
Friendly, local, rooted inn. With a real attention to local sourcing, and an investment in proper traditional home-cooking, the inn serves up some great pub fare and additional treats from local game.

DOVECOTE RESTAURANT — *Fine Dining*
Morley Hayes Hotel, Main Road, Morley, DE7 6DG
01332 780 480
The award-winning Dovecote offers beautiful views of the Derbyshire countryside whilst serving fantastic British and European dishes. Sample the well-stocked wine cellar and the popular Sunday lunch.

2FOR1 MAIN COURSE

EDEN GARDENS — *Asian Fusion*
1 Queen Street, Derby, DE1 3DJ
01332 418 800
Indian, Thai and Chinese dining, showcasing the distinctive flavours of Eastern cuisine. In stylish surrounds, try such treats as horin tikka - succulent venison marinated in aromatic herbs and spices.

2FOR1 MAIN COURSE

EL TORO — *Spanish*
147 London Road, Derby, DE1 2QN
01332 360 850
El Toro's Spanish owner and Head Chef bring with them a wealth of experience and training; the restaurant serves eclectic and flavourful tapas dishes that have a strong sense of authenticity.

2FOR1 3COURSES

FARAAZ RESTAURANT — *Indian*
129 Dale Road, Matlock, DE24 3LU
01629 57400
Loved by locals and tourists alike, this venue is a stylish and contemporary eatery renowned for its authentic Indian, Pakistani and Bangladeshi fare, with a variety of Asian dishes and flavours on offer.

GALLERY CAFE — *European*
50 St John Street, Ashbourne, DE6 1GH
01335 347 425
Award-winning café in Ashbourne that serves home-cooked food of the highest quality. Sumptuous patés go along with luxurious cakes in this characterful location, part of a contemporary art gallery.

Minimum of 2 courses must be purchased.

ISTANBUL — *Turkish*
37 Corn Market, Derby, DE1 2DG
01332 380 082
Experience the Mediterranean taste at this restaurant with its distinguished menu that provides varied and delectable dishes, encompassing traditional and unique cooking dating back to the Ottomans.

LE MISTRAL — *French*
23 Market Place, Wirksworth, DE4 4ET
01629 824 840
Winner of 'Best International Restaurant in Derbyshire' 2009. A French-style café, bar and bistro serving top-quality, fresh food accompanied by a vast selection of wines, beers and espresso.

2FOR1 3COURSES

LE MISTRAL — *French*
Bridge Street, Bakewell, DE45 1DS
01629 810 077
A French-style café, bar and bistro serving top-quality, fresh food accompanied by a vast selection of wines, beers and espresso. For a slice of French charm, Le Mistral is the perfect place to dine.

2FOR1 3COURSES

MASA RESTAURANT — *Contemporary*
The Old Chapel, Brook Street, Derby, DE1 3PF
01332 203 345
In charismatic surroundings, Masa's 2 AA Rosette-recognised food is elegant and classic; on the Sunday set menu, try a sharp, delicious gravadlax followed by the hale rump of beef with Yorkshire pudding.

2FOR1 2COURSES

Gourmet Society discount applies to the à la carte menu

232

MEXICO
Mexican

34-35 Sadler Gate, Derby, DE1 3NR
01332 342 090
Though you can immerse yourself in an exceptional burrito, steak quesadilla or chicken fajita at this Mexican joint, it pays off to go off the beaten track for one of their truly fabulous 'especiales'.

MILEBURNE RESTAURANT
European

2 Blanch Croft, Melbourne, DE73 8GG
01332 864 170
A restaurant that does a superb job with its simple aim: good British food made with quality, locally sourced ingredients, all served in a laid-back and welcoming environment. A local treasure.

MR GRUNDY'S TAVERN
European

Georgian House Hotel, Ashbourne Rd, Derby, DE22 3AD
01332 349 806
Whatever the weather, here you will find the perfect place to drink and dine. Curl up on the sofa in front of open fires or soak up the sun in a lively atmospheric beer garden. A wonderful place to unwind.

2FOR1
MAIN COURSE
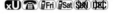

MUSHROOM HALL
International

Main Street, Albert Village, Swadlincote, DE11 8EN
01283 217 464
Little Hanoi is a quality restaurant that has established an excellent reputation for good Vietnamese food. Offers a wide variety of sumptuous dishes at affordable prices, served in an authentic setting.

2FOR1
3 COURSES

NEW BATH HOTEL
Traditional English Fare

New Bath Road, Matlock Bath, DE4 3PX
01629 583 454
Contemporary and classic in equal measure, this restaurant serves finely cooked, cultured dishes in the elegant surroundings of the Brook New Bath Hotel and its magnificent dining rooms.

NONNAS
Italian

131 Chatsworth Road, Chesterfield, S40 2AP
01246 380 035
Passionately ambitious and incredibly dedicated to bringing the delights of Italian food and wine to the British public. With a bakery and an upstairs Milanese bar, Nonna's is more than just a restaurant.

2FOR1
MAIN COURSE

OLD ORLEANS
American

Pride Park Way, Pride Park, Derby, DE24 8SQ
01332 386 439
An extraordinarily accurate taste of the Deep South can be found in this unique restaurant. The kitchen uses classic Louisiana and Cajun recipes such as jambalaya and gumbo to create an exciting menu.

2FOR1
MAIN COURSE

Not available on Bank Holiday weekends. Adult menu only.

OPULENCE @ CATHEDRAL QUARTER HOTEL
Contemporary

16 St Marys Gate, Derby, DE1 3JR
01332 546 080
Admirably located in a beautiful Victorian ballroom where stunning décor complements its traditional character. Wonderfully presented dishes make use of the freshest seasonal ingredients.

PEVERIL OF THE PEAK
European

Thorpe, Ashbourne, DE6 2AW
01335 350 396
A luxurious environment famed for award winning food, creating an array of succulent dishes that have been prepared with the finest ingredients and cooked to perfection. A meal for every occasion.

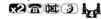

PRIEST HOUSE HOTEL (THE BRASSERIE)
European

Kings Mill, Castle Donington, DE74 2RR
01332 810 649
Positioned in the heart of the country, enjoy a relaxed, informal style of dining at this Hand Picked Hotels group venue, with The Brasserie especially popular for escaping life's hustle and bustle.

PRIEST HOUSE HOTEL (FINE DINING)
European

Kings Mill, Castle Donington, DE74 2RR
01332 810 649
Travel through woodlands to dine in this delightful Hand Picked Hotels restaurant. Discover the magnificence of its food and atmosphere; you'll understand how it earned its fine reputation and 2 AA Rosettes.

RAINBOW BISTRO AND CAFE
Bistro

14a High Street East, Glossop, SK13 8DA
01457 865 990
An intimate, cosy and stylish restaurant, serving exceptional food. The finest and freshest of local produce is used wherever possible, and dishes are prepared with imagination and flair.

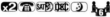

REUBEN'S RESTAURANT
Contemporary

The Ramada Hotel, Appleby Magna, DE12 7BQ
01530 279 500
Contemporary bistro food delivered in stylish surroundings, with a menu offering a variety of hearty and healthy meals alongside traditional favourites including steaks, pasta and salads.

SAFFRON RESTAURANT
Indian

7 Curzon Street, Derby, DE1 1LH
01332 344 786
A well-established restaurant specialising in heavenly Indian and Bangladeshi cuisine. Tender meats and gratifying sauces will have you wishing you'd dined here before.

SAGE AT DONINGTON MANOR
European

High Street, Castle Donington, DE74 2PP
01332 810 253
An AA Rosette-winning restaurant maintaining many of its original period features. Chef Jeff Cadden has created a sophisticated menu of dishes complemented by an extensive wine list.

2FOR1
3 COURSES

SANTO'S HIGHAM FARM HOTEL
Italian

Main Road, Higham, DE55 6EH
01773 833 812
Exquisite dishes to be found on carefully designed à la carte and table d'hôte menus. Choose from the fine selection of seafood on offer or enjoy a delicate light lunch in the sports bar.

2FOR1
MAIN COURSE

Table d'hôte menu only.

SHERWOOD RESTAURANT
European

Beverley Rd, Castle Donington, DE74 2SH
01332 850 700
A superb hotel-restaurant offering a relaxing environment in which British and continental cuisine can be enjoyed. Medieval style furnishings recall local legend Robin Hood.

THE DOVECOTE RESTAURANT
British

The Melbourne View, Station Rd, Melbourne, DE7 8BR
01332 865 353
With seasonal menus paired with an extensive wine list, diners can relax in the warm ambience of the restaurant as food is prepared to the highest standard. Free bottle of wine for members booking a room.

Members booking a room receive a bottle of house wine. Lunchtime service only for bookings of 8+.

STONES RESTAURANT
British

1c Dale Road, Matlock, DE4 3LT
01629 56061
Intimate dining in a relaxed setting; enjoy lunch, dinner, or a glass of wine from the extensive wine list. Fresh, appetising food made using local produce, with indulgent desserts. 2 AA Rosettes.

THE GEORGE HOTEL
Modern Pub

34 Norfolk Street, Glossop, SK13 7QU
01457 855 449
Situated in the centre of Glossop, The George Hotel offers excellent pub grub combined with an extensive bar menu and specials board. All food is home made and from locally sourced produce.

THE BRIDGE INN
European

3 Mansfield Road, Chestergreen, Derby, DE1 3QY
01332 371 360
An excellent sports pub that offers a relaxed ambience and high-quality cuisine. A popular place to meet friends and begin the evening with a bang.

THE HOLLY BUSH
European

Main Street, Oakthorpe, Swadlincote, DE12 7RB
01530 270 943
Lovely village pub that is genial, warm, and proud of the freshness of their food. Besides being a great spot for a drink, you'll enjoy high-quality, unfussy and beautifully cooked dishes.

THE BULLS HEAD
British

Denby Common, Denby, DE5 8PW
01773 513 000
Boasts an extensive menu offering over 70 main course dishes including succulent, locally reared, farm-assured steaks and chicken specialities. Sophisticated décor creates a serene atmosphere.

Offer excludes Sunday lunches, but is available after 4pm.

THE HOLLY BUSH
British

Main Street, Church Broughton, DE65 5AS
01283 585 345
Peak District pub serving an extensive menu of home-made food created with high-quality local and seasonal produce. Includes a traditional bar, award-winning cask ales, and a spacious beer garden.

THE DINING ROOM

33 St John Street, Ashbourne, DE6 1GP

01335 300 666 *European*

Offer is for one free main course with the purchase of one other from the 8 course tasting menu

A serious approach to fine dining is found at this small destination restaurant in Ashbourne. Chef and proprietor Peter Dale produces tasting menus of exceptional quality, which showcase local produce and both classic and modern cookery methods.

All food is produced in the kitchens, from breads to ice-creams and raw ingredients are sourced - as far as possible - from within a 30 mile radius.

With dishes which mix flavours, textures and ingredients in surprising ways, with incredible presentation and panache, the Dining Room is an essential culinary stopping point for all those with a serious appreciation of modern British cooking.

Sign up to our newsletter for latest restaurants, offers and more

THE HOLLY BUSH INN
Fine Dining
1 Melbourne Lane, Breedon on the Hill, DE73 8AT
01332 862 359
Discover this local treasure and you won't look back. Serving some of the finest cuisine in the area, guests will adore the cordial service provided by the congenial staff.

Always phone and book in advance.

THE KEGWORTH WHITEHOUSE HOTEL
European
Packington Hill, Kegworth, DE74 2DF
01509 672 427
The monthly changing menu here means that you're always able to try something new. Browse the extensive wine list which will undoubtedly provide you with an excellent drink to partner your meal.

Offer available at lunch in Lounge 24, evenings in Sullivans Brasserie.

THE MOGUL RESTAURANT
Indian/ Bangladeshi
41-43 Green Lane, Derby, DE1 1RS
01332 203 343
A traditional curry house with its own modest character. A menu full of moreish specialities and more popular subcontinental dishes; favourites include the paneer tikka and the achari lamb.

THE NEW WATER MARGIN
Cantonese
72-74 Burton Road, Derby, DE1 1TG
01332 364 754
Step inside this authentic Chinese restaurant where you can enjoy Peking and Cantonese cuisines in a pleasant atmosphere. An extensive buffet offers favourite Chinese dishes for you to sample.

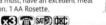

THE OLD POST
European
43 Holywell Street, Chesterfield, S41 7SH
01246 279 479
The Old Post crafts British and European dishes with skill and panache. This restaurant's particular line in full-flavoured game is a must; have an excellent meal in a charismatic location. 1 AA Rosette.

THE PADDOCK HOTEL
European
222 Station Road, Melbourne, DE73 8BQ
01332 864 716
Dine al fresco or by the open kitchen in the restaurant of this warm and attractive hotel. Menus using locally sourced produce are presented.

THE PLOUGH INN
British
33 Hallgate, Diseworth, DE74 2QJ
01332 810 333
By maintaining the herringbone masonry and the weathered beams, this delightful inn successfully radiates a warm and welcoming atmosphere. Tables and seating are spread across three main areas.

THE RAJ RESTAURANT
Indian
432 Kedleston Road, Allestree, Derby, DE22 2TF
01332 553 554
Provides a warm welcome to all. The lavish bar area and the warm and cosy reception, complete with widescreen plasma TV, both ensure that the tone is set; subsequently, enjoy some classic Indian food.

THE RISLEY PARK
British
Derby Road, Risley, DE72 3SS
0115 939 2313
With its magnificent décor and equally splendid menu, Risley Park fully deserves its award-winning status and admirable reputation. The à la carte menu offers over 70 fabulous main courses to choose from.

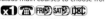

Offer excludes Sunday lunches, but is available after 4pm.

THE SHAKESPEARE
British
117 London Road, Shardlow, DE72 2GP
01332 792 728
A bluff but refined country pub that offers a properly warm welcome and some superbly cooked, flavourful and seasoned dishes.

After first visit, offer applies to food only.

THE SPOTTED COW INN
International
12 Town Street, Holbrook, DE56 0TA
01332 881 200
The highest standards of quality and presentation at this pub ensure that your drinking and dining experience is entirely pleasurable. The vast menu has something for all appetites and every budget.

THE SQUARE RESTAURANT
European
The Rutland Arms Hotel, The Square, Bakewell, DE45 1BT
01629 812 812
Beautifully located hotel whose dishes offer superb levels of taste right across the menu. Attesting to its culinary excellence are an array of awards; after a walk in the Peaks, this is a great base camp.

Offer only for table d'hôte only, on meals up to £18.

THE SWAN INN
European
Lichfield Rd, Draycott in the Clay, DE6 5GZ
01283 820 031
A family-friendly village pub set in extensive grounds. Traditional British favourites are served and the specials menu changes regularly.

THE THREE HORSESHOES
British
44-46 Main Street, Breedon on the Hill, DE73 8AN
01332 695 129
A blend of classic furnishings and contemporary ambience; enjoy a modern, delectable menu in ultimate comfort. Local produce, from game to fine English cheeses, underpin an imaginative, accomplished menu.

DETAILED DESCRIPTIONS AVAILABLE ON
www.gourmetsociety.co.uk

THE TUDOR HOTEL
British
101 Bondgate, Castle Donington, DE74 2NR
01332 810 875
Daily specials and home-made desserts make the restaurant here an attractive choice when choosing where to dine. The two public bars also serve great quality meals cooked to order.

EAST MIDLANDS

235

THE VERNON ARMS
European

Main Road, Sudbury, DE6 5HS
01283 585 329
A cracking pub in Sudbury where you'll enjoy a good pint and some full-bodied traditional food, from a top notch local bangers and mash to some thick, tasty pub sandwiches.

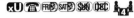

THE WATTS RUSSELL ARMS
Modern Pub

Hopedale, Alstonefield, DE6 2GD
01335 310 126
A picture-perfect pub situated in the idyllic surroundings of the Peak District National Park. Fine real ales are always on offer, whilst the selection of malt whiskies will warm you on cold winter nights.

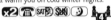

HAUS
British

33 Wardwick, Cathedral Quarter, Derby, DE1 1HA
01332 347 288
Jacobean House is one of Derby's most impressive buildings. When the cooking and presentation are excellent too, haus becomes the perfect choice for a relaxed but refined meal in elegant surroundings.

NEW
2FOR1 3 COURSES

THE YEAVELEY ARMS
Fine Dining

Rodsley Lane, Yeaveley, Ashbourne, DE6 2DT
01335 330 771
A friendly and cheerful atmosphere that will draw you in and set you up for a superb meal of filling food. In a fine dining ambience, enjoy the locally sourced produce cooked with skill and accomplishment.

2FOR1 MAIN COURSE

THYME AT THE INTERNATIONAL
European

International Hotel, 288 Burton Road, Derby, DE23 6AD
01332 369 321
Clear-minded hotel-based restaurant that serves some superb, thoughtful and imaginative dishes; worth a visit for the sumptuous swordfish alone. Also caters for larger events.

TREBLE BOB
Carvery

Chesterfield Road, Tally's End, Barlborough, S43 4TX
01246 813 005
One of the wonderful Great British Carveries offering the well-loved classic with a modern twist. Welcoming staff and mouth-watering food make this a popular local favourite.

2FOR1 MAIN COURSE

Call beforehand on special events.

TWENTY FOUR AT THE LION HOTEL
Contemporary

Bridge Street, Belper, DE56 1AX
01773 824 033
This intimately furnished pub has everything you need for a comfortable, sophisticated dining experience, where the contemporary setting is matched by the menu of wholesome food and fine beverages.

YEW LODGE HOTEL
British

33 Packington Hill, Kegworth, DE74 2DF
01509 672 518
A double AA Rosette-winning hotel restaurant in beautiful countryside surroundings. Drawing on locally sourced ingredients, the food here is flavourful, accomplished and worthy of your time.

ZEST

2FOR1 MAIN COURSE

16d George Street, Derby, DE1 1EH
01332 381 101 *European*

Since opening in 1998 Zest has become something of a cultural institution in the Derby area and is generally considered to be one of Derby's most stylish restaurants - a testament to the designers, as it was originally a stable building.

The original concept for Zest as a restaurant is one that provides the community with fine dining in a relaxed friendly environment. The menu certainly hits the mark

and is best described as contemporary European/British cuisine. The food is excellent with plenty of choice for everyone, and it is always of the highest quality. Zest is a fine example of a restaurant that does not have fancy or formal pretensions but where the professionalism of all those involved shines through. Members should also check out sister restaurant Amarone, which recently opened in Nottingham.

Visit the website regularly to discover the latest restaurants joining the GS

Leicestershire

ASHOKA
Indian
257 Melton Road, Leicester, LE4 7AN
0116 266 2185
At Ashoka a completely new experience in Indian cuisine awaits, providing traditionally popular dishes and new recipes, superbly crafted using the finest produce, herbs and spices.

ASPECTS AT THE PLOUGH
Indian
7 Mill Hill, Enderby, Leicester, LE19 4AL
0116 286 3307
Enjoy an English lunch with Indian specials, or celebrate the rich diversity of Indian cuisine in the evening with experienced and acclaimed chefs creating delicately spiced and authentic-tasting dishes.

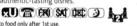

Offer applies to food only after 1st use.

BANGLA LOUNGE
Bangladeshi
91 Trinity Lane, Hinckley, LE10 0BJ
01455 615 111
Modernised Indian cuisine that retains authentic flavours yet is crafted with a contemporary fusion approach. Executive chef Abdul Haque uses expert knowledge to create incredible Indian dishes.

BARCELONETA
Mediterranean
54 Queens Road, Leicester, LE2 1TU
0116 270 8408
Authentic, lively restaurant serving fresh tapas and larger dishes complemented by a varied wine list. The proprietor sources many of the bottles directly from Spain.

Not to be used with any other offers or promotions.

BENGAL SPICE
Indian
77 Market Street, Ashby De La Zouch, LE65 1AH
01530 413 799
Placing emphasis on the importance of refined yet creative Indian cuisine, the kitchen at Bengal Spice aims to offer a menu that incorporates traditional classic favourites and unique new dishes.

BLACK BULL
British
2 Teigh Road, Market Overton, LE15 7PW
01572 767 677
Overlooking views of fields and the church in the picturesque village of Market Overton, this charming rural pub is the ideal spot for a pint of local beer and some delicious home-cooked food.

CAFÉ ROUGE
French
Unit R4, Highcross, Leicester, LE1 4SD
0116 251 8067
An attractive restaurant, a boulevard café or a Parisian-style wine bar; however you see Café Rouge, consistently excellent classic French dishes are always guaranteed.

COLOURWORKS
European
2 Westbridge Close, Leicester, LE3 5LW
0116 262 4170
This modern restaurant boasts a vibrant yet intimate atmosphere, gorgeous riverside views, and simply sublime food, offering diners a simple and unpretentious experience.

CUISINE OF INDIA
Indian
Kelmarsh Avenue, Wigston, LE18 3QW
0116 281 1926
The modern and spacious dining area provides stylish and comfortable surroundings. The exciting, authentic Asian cuisine and high standards are popular both locally and further afield.

DINE INDIA
Indian
62 Main Street, Countesthorpe, LE8 5QX
0116 277 8777
Experience a warm welcome from the friendly staff of this highly popular restaurant, consistently voted among the best in the local area. The menu combines the traditional and the modern.

ENTROPY
European
42 Hinckley Road, Leicester, LE3 0RB
0116 225 9650
Steeped in local history this characterful restaurant is renowned as a landmark in the local area, serving great bistro-pub dishes and priding themselves in quality food, drink and high standards of care.

Offer not available at any time at the weekend.

GOLDEN AKASH TANDOORI
Indian
159 London Road, Leicester, LE2 1EG
0116 255 9030
Close to Leicester's main concert hall and prominently placed, this Indian restaurant succeeds in its clear-minded aims: high-quality, flavourful Indian food in a congenial, welcoming environment.

HANDMADE BURGER CO.
American
14 Highcross Lane, Leicester, LE1 4SD
0116 242 5875
Fresh food made with real passion. Delivers an extensive range of gourmet burgers served with a choice of gorgeous chips, crisp vegetables, creamy coleslaw and many others. Real quality, handmade cooking.

HERITAGE
Indian
58 Leicester Road, Narborough, Leicester, LE19 2DG
0116 286 1919
Some of the best Indian food in the area, offering diners a wide variety of choice with a menu boasting options that go beyond ordinary venues. Relax and enjoy your food in a warm, authentic setting.

HERMITAGE PARK HOTEL
European
The Lamphouse, Whitwick Road, Coalville, LE67 3FA
01530 814 814
Dine in the fully glazed atrium of this lovely hotel, with a menu of delectable dishes rooted in a range of European cuisines. Enjoy lunch or dinner with quality food and a selection of beverages.

After first visit, offer applies only to food.

INDIAN OCEAN
Indian

11 Swan Street, Loughborough, LE11 5BJ
01509 266 934
Delight your senses with a taste of India as chefs create a menu filled with fragrant and flavoursome dishes. Food is prepared and presented with passion and care, making this venue truly worth a visit.

LA ZOUCH
British

2 Kilwardby Street, Ashby De La Zouch, LE65 2FQ
01530 412 536
A beautiful listed building offers the local area an outstanding place to dine. A monthly changing table d'hôte menu appears alongside the pleasing à la carte. A loyal following indicates its excellence.

À la carte & table d'hôte only. Must present the card on arrival.

LAUGHING BUDDHA
Chinese

3 Woodgate, Loughborough, LE11 2TY
01509 236 868
A pleasing local restaurant serving traditional Cantonese and Peking-style cuisine in a lavishly spacious setting. Staff are passionate about serving first-rate food with outstanding hospitality.

LEEJA PALACE
Indian

13 The Parade, Oadby, Leicester, LE2 5BB
0116 271 0482
Classically comfortable, modern and warm Indian restaurant that serves the gamut of Indian cuisine, juxtaposing traditional flavours with a modern twist.

LITTLE INDIA
Indian

St Peter's Road, Arnesby, LE8 5WJ
0116 247 8251
Regionally renowned Indian restaurant that goes beyond the staples with imaginative, eccentric and extremely tasty new recipes.

LITTLE ITALY
Italian

326 Welford Road, Knighton, Leicester, LE2 6EH
0116 270 8695
Family-run restaurant with full, rich tomato-based dishes along with a silky marinara as its speciality.

MANNERS ARMS - BEATERS BAR
British

6 Croxton Road, Knipton, NG32 1RH
01476 879 222
Chef Austin Charlton offers local, fresh produce, simply cooked and beautifully presented in this charmingly restored, country pursuit-themed hotel. Awarded 1 AA Rosette.

Offer available on bar snack menu.

MR CHAN'S
Chinese

14 Bedford Square, Loughborough, LE11 2TP
01509 216 216
An exceedingly popular restaurant serving outstanding Cantonese and Peking cuisine. Pay Mr Chan a visit if you like to be met by an impressive selection of dishes at affordable prices.

Sunday offer excludes buffet.

POPPADOMS
Indian

330 Welford Road, Leicester, LE2 6EH
0116 244 8888
Being spoilt for choice will be the only problem you encounter at this wonderful Indian restaurant. An extensive menu offers sumptuous curries that will suit every palate.

PREZZO
Italian

22 Silver Street, Leicester, LE1 5ET
0116 251 3343
With a character all of its own, Prezzo oozes contemporary style and enduring charm. Signature pastas, stone-baked pizzas and classic Italian dishes promise a perfect dining choice for the whole family.

QUORN EXCHANGE
European

10-12 High Street, Quorn, LE12 8DT
01509 621 444
Light and airy dining space in which to enjoy a panoply of contemporary and cosmopolitan cuisine. A focus on fine produce, rich flavours, and just the right wine to accompany.

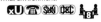

Only one card allowed per table.

QUORN GRANGE
Fine Dining

88 Wood Lane, Quorn, LE12 8DB
01509 412 167
The Buddon within the Quorn Grange hotel is a haven of tranquillity, offering exceptional food in an eclectic style designed to delight the most discerning palate. Fine dining in an informal environment.

RED HOUSE
British

23 Main Street, Nether Broughton, LE14 3HB
01664 822 429
Enjoy monthly live jazz suppers, Sunday lunches, real ales, and an innovative menu all set within a charming village. Hearty British food served with a smile, and an emphasis on fresh, local produce.

RED LION INN
Carvery

933 Loughborough Road, Rothley, LE7 7NJ
0116 230 2488
Enjoy the best of British food in this wonderful Great British Carvery venue. A popular place to eat and drink, this charming, characterful pub offers high-quality meals and a great selection of drinks.

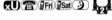

Call beforehand for special event days.

RED VEIL EXCLUSIVE INDIAN
Indian

45 Nottingham Road, Loughborough, LE11 1ER
01509 265 165
Tantalise your senses with a trip to this exclusive venue, filled with sensual music, lush surroundings, and most importantly extraordinary food exceeding all your culinary expectations.

ROYAL HOTEL
English and Continental

Station Road, Ashby De La Zouch, LE65 2GP
01530 412 833
Traditional English and Continental cuisine is served in this wonderfully situated restaurant. Daily blackboard specials and delicious desserts are the talking point of regular diners.

When booking restaurants always mention your GS membership

RUTLAND & DERBY
European

Millstone Lane, Leicester, LE15JN
0116 262 3299
'Tradition with ambition' is the ethos of this genteel pub. Wonderfully traditional food and award-winning ales can be enjoyed in light contemporary surroundings.

SAYONARA THALI RESTAURANT
Vegetarian

49 Belgrave Road, Leicester, LE4 6AR
0116 266 5888
Thalis is a vegetarian cuisine that combines dhal, curry, bread and pickles, served on a steel plate. Guests dine here because of its reliably good food, never lacking in fine, authentic taste.

SHEARSBY BATH
European

Bruntingthorpe Road, Shearsby, LE17 6PP
0116 247 8202
This elegantly decorated family-run establishment offering sublime dishes from the à la carte menu. Try the crab and mango millefeuille or deconstructed black forest gâteau: any choice is unforgettable.

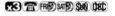

SHIMLA PINKS
Indian

65-69 London Road, Leicester, LE2 0PE
0116 247 1471
Incorporates new and exciting dishes amongst a menu of traditional Indian cuisine. The visually pleasing interior ensures you enjoy your meal in an outstanding setting. A beacon to curry lovers.

NICK'S RESTAURANT
European

11 Market Place, Oakham, LE15 6HT
01572 723 199
Nick's is a smart, elegant restaurant in the Lord Nelson's House Hotel. Traditional in style, with a beautiful open fireplace, cosy chairs and warm lighting, it offers a great atmosphere in which to dine.

NEW

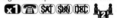

STANTON LAKES
International

Broughton Road, Stoney Stanton, LE9 4JA
01455 283 043
In idyllic surroundings guests can enjoy an array of excellently cooked dishes that reflect great quality and value for money. A unique venue suitable for individuals and all varieties of celebrations.

STEAM TRUMPET
International

286 Main Street, Thornton, Leicester, LE67 1AJ
01530 231 258
Enjoy hearty home-cooked food while sampling one of the eight hand-pulled real ales, or the fine selection of continental lagers. A firm favourite with walkers and locals looking for something special.

TAJ MAHAL RESTAURANT
Indian

12-14 Highfield Street, Leicester, LE2 1AB
0116 254 0328
Friendly and accommodating local Indian restaurant in Leicester with a line in flavoursome, deliciously spicy dishes. Generous portions, plenty of atmosphere and a comfortable dining space.

TARAJ PALACE
Indian

1183 Melton Road, Syston, LE7 2JT
0116 260 7777
A restaurant synonymous with quality food, attentive service and good prices. Boasts a menu reflecting authentic Indian tastes with a modern touch coupled with stylish and contemporary décor to match.

THAI SABAI
Thai

24 Burton Street, Melton Mowbray, LE13 1AF
01664 850 036
One of the first truly authentic Thai restaurants in the area. Provides Siam favourites with a unique twist, to ensure every guest enjoys an exceptionally well-prepared meal.

THE BELPER ARMS
European

Main Street, Newton Burgoland, LE67 2SE
01530 270 530
A little Leicestershire pub with plenty of character that serves strong and hearty pub fare alongside its excellent selection of ales, all in an accommodating and history-laden atmosphere.

Need to call for evening bookings only.

THE BRANT INN
British

Leicester Road, Groby, Leicester, LE6 0DU
0116 287 2703
Bring your family along to this warmly welcoming pub, where home-cooked food is available in abundance. The chef offers daily specials alongside the everyday menu.

THE BULL AND LION INN
British

48 High Street, Packington, Ashby De La Zouch, LE65 1WH
01530 413 882
Great village pub where you'll enjoy a pint of the finest and some warming, filling food. A classic feel, rooted and down to earth, with a brilliant pie night. Booking, we should add, is essential.

THE BUTLER'S HOUSE
British

34 Windsor Street, Burbage, LE10 2EF
01455 234 342
A restaurant around which there subsists a buzz. On recommendation of the Gourmet Society's members, The Butler's House serves richly flavoured, sophisticated food in a deliciously homely dining space.

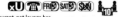

THE CROWDED HOUSE
Contemporary

12 Bath Street, Ashby De La Zouch, LE65 2FH
01530 411 116
Relaxed surroundings that offer a wide range of wines, cocktails and menus to suit a range of palates, available from bar, lounge or restaurant. The Crowded House has something to offer everyone.

Offer only for restaurant, not lounge bar.

THE CROWN
Bistro

The Crown, Main Street, Tur Langton, LE8 0PJ
01858 545 264
One of the oldest pubs in Leicestershire, classically warm and friendly. Serves both modern and traditional British food ideal for lunch and in the evening. Complete with open fires and quality real ale.

THE FORGE INN
Modern British

Main Street, Glenfields, Leicester, LE3 8DG
0116 287 1702
Smart and stylish dining pub where you can enjoy an eclectic range of well-cooked dishes at a sound price; try the classic old-fashioned bangers and mash, or a herby plate of delicious bass.

THE ROBIN HOOD
International

2 Spring Lane, Swannington, Coalville, LE67 8QQ
01530 831 137
Serves lunch and evening bar meals with a sumptuous traditional roast on a Sunday. For superb home-cooked food, traditional ales and special food evenings, this is a wonderful choice.

THE GREY LADY
International

Sharpley Hill, Newtown Linford, LE6 0AH
01530 243 558
Both sophistication and vivacity are to be found in this superb restaurant, for an exclusive but affordable dining experience. Dine formally or enjoy an intimate, relaxed meal; both are catered for here.

THE ROYAL ARMS
British

Main Street, Sutton Cheney, CV13 0AG
01455 290 263
A warm and friendly welcome awaits guests of this beautifully situated village hotel and restaurant. Sample home-reared beef amongst other seasonal offerings from the à la carte or informal bar menu.

THE GREYHOUND COACHING INN
British

Market Street, Lutterworth, LE17 4EJ
01455 553 307
Full of history, this renovated coaching inn offers a comprehensive menu featuring creative English and international cuisine. A well-chosen wine list that you can enjoy in the 18th century courtyard.

THE VILLAGE RESTAURANT
European

544 Bradgate Road, Newtown Linford, LE6 0HB
01530 245 801
In a fresh, chic environment, you'll be struck by the quality of the dishes. Adding modern European influences to supplement classic British recipes, the chefs make full use of the finest local produce.

Available evenings only.

THE HUNTING LODGE
British

38 South Street, Barrow Upon Soar, LE12 8LZ
01509 412 337
Charismatic setting for this restaurant that delivers a huge range of popular British food. With several accompanying wines and beers to choose from, this is a contemporary venue for all to enjoy.

Offer excludes Sunday lunches, but is available after 4pm.

THE WHIPPER-IN HOTEL
Modern European

The Market Place, Oakham, LE15 6DT
01572 756 971
Savour a delicious meal at this renowned restaurant in the lovely and comfortable surroundings of this Brook hotel, boasting a cuisine that combines innovation with traditional use of methods and produce.

THE LIME KILNS
International

Watling Street, Burbage, LE10 3ED
01455 631 158
Sip on a glass of wine and dine on delicious bar food whilst watching the waterway wildlife and colourful narrowboats. This old coaching house is a wonderful place to enjoy real ales and tasty treats.

THE WHITE HORSE
British

White Horse Lane, Birstall, Leicester, LE4 4EF
0116 267 1038
Local pub with a keen sense of its history on the Grand Union Canal. Serves warming, hearty and fulsome food; with awards for food and drink under its belt, The White Horse is worth taking for a hack.

THE MANOR HOUSE AT QUORN
Contemporary

The Manor House, Woodhouse Road, Quorn, LE12 8AL
01509 413 416
A wonderful, modern country pub where great beers and first-rate meals are served with a smile. The à la carte menu offers fine meats, poultry and game, guaranteeing its irresistibility.

THE WILLOW
British

215 Humbstone Lane, Thurmaston, LE4 9JR
0116 269 3549
Quality family dining pub, close to Abbey Park's boating lake. Stylishly decorated, with a warm contemporary ambience, you'll enjoy some hearty, thoroughgoing food along with a pint of the finest.

THE PLOUGH INN
British

Main Street, Normanton On Soar, Loughborough, LE12 5HB
01509 842 228
If you're looking for a cosy place to drink and eat hearty, classic pub food, this country inn is just what you need. Free moorings in the riverside garden make this a perfect stop for a boatman's lunch.

Offer excludes Sunday lunches, but is available after 4pm.

WESTFIELD HOUSE HOTEL
International

Enderby Road, Blaby, Leicester, LE8 4GD
0116 278 7898
The critically acclaimed Hunters Restaurant at this luxurious Brook Hotel serves modern English cuisine with a Mediterranean influence, whilst global specials regularly feature on the exquisite menu.

THE QUEEN'S HEAD
Fine Dining

2 Long Street, Belton, LE12 9TP
01530 222 359
Recognised with two AA Rosettes, this smart, sassy eatery serves sumptuous and skilfully conceived dishes, like their pot roast partridge or the calves tongue salad. A superb location and a special meal.

One card per table.

WINDMILL & BRASCOTE
British

Brascote, Newbold Verdon, LE9 9LE
01455 824 433
Tasty meals, classic favourites and Mediterranean fish dishes are served in a beautiful rural setting. Widely appreciated in the area for excellent value, a good selection of wines and a relaxed ambience.

240

ZAMANIS
Italian
11 Rushton Yard, Market St, Ashby De La Zouch, LE65 1AL
01530 560 719
A favourite with the locals, Zamanis serves the finest quality Italian food. Situated in the centre of town, the unique courtyard location offers you the chance to make good use of its adjacent wine bar.

ZUCCHERO WORLD BUFFET
International
126 Charles Street, Leicester, LE1 1LB
0116 251 1558
Travel the world on the tip of your taste buds as Zucchero offers you over 90 dishes from six different cuisines. This revolutionary world buffet serves up quality food at excellent value for money.

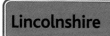
Lincolnshire
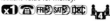

BIZZARRO
Italian
23 Wormgate, Boston, PE21 6NR
01205 353 007
Occupying two floors and four dining rooms of a Georgian town-house, Bizzarro combines its situational magnificence with an admirably relaxed ambiance. Outstanding Italian cuisine that will blow you away.

BLUE BELL INN
European
Main Road, Belchford, Horncastle, LN9 6LQ
01507 533 602
Quality traditional fare mixed with some adventurous dishes for the more curious palates. The wine list is extensive and features guest wines each month, a treat for the sommelier in you.

CINNAMON BAY
Indian
Odeon Multiplex, Brayford Wharf N., Lincoln, LN1 1YX
01522 511 511
The patrons of this restaurant pride themselves on offering Indian cooking just as it would be in their own homes. With eyes firmly on authenticity of flavour, they serve up a mean array of great dishes.

DOGMA BAR AND RESTAURANT
European
272 High Street, Lincoln, LN2 1JG
01522 522 533
Dogma's award-winning team serve business lunches as well as simply prepared, fresh evening meals. They also do fantastic drinks in this sexy, laid-back bar and restaurant.

GORKHA SQUARE RESTAURANT
Indian
1 Wharf Road, Grantham, NG31 6BA
01476 574 477
Whilst the authentic recipes are transported from thousands of miles, the ingredients most certainly are not. The kitchen prides itself on its use of fresh local produce and Nepalese influences.

HAVEN AT SUPREME INNS
Classic British/ French
Bicker Bar, Swineshaead, Boston, PE20 3AN
01205 822 804
Superb home-cooked food, freshly prepared by experienced chefs using locally sourced produce. Its spacious, beautifully refurbished dining space is a perfect venue whether for business or pleasure.

HES
Turkish
12 Wharf Road, Grantham, NG31 6BA
01476 566 900
An award-winning Turkish restaurant that evokes a wonderful, warm Mediterranean atmosphere coupled with excellent customer service. Mouth-watering dishes make this venue a real Turkish delight.

 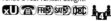

MACH RESTAURANT
Indian
Wragby Road East, North Greetwell, Lincoln, LN2 4RA
01522 754 488
Tranquilly situated on the edges of Lincoln, here you can enjoy a flavoursome array of classical and contemporary Indian recipes with knowledgeable and attentive staff to guide you.

PERKINS PANTRY
British
7 Mercer Row, Louth, LN11 9JG
01507 609 709
Welcome to the farm kitchen. Critically acclaimed cuisine with wholesome, fresh, local food prepared in the traditional way. Offers à la carte and several special menus every day.

PREZZO
Italian
Unit A1 The Glass Mill, Brayford Wharf N, Lincoln, LN1 1YX
01522 528 595
With a character all of its own, Prezzo oozes contemporary style and enduring charm. Signature pastas, stone-baked pizzas and classic Italian dishes promise a perfect dining choice for the whole family.

PREZZO
Italian
Elsom House, 1 Broad Street, Spalding, PE11 1TB
01775 769 948
With a character all of its own, Prezzo oozes contemporary style and enduring charm. Signature pastas, stone-baked pizzas and classic Italian dishes promise a perfect dining choice for the whole family.

PREZZO
Italian
20 Wide Bargate, Boston, PE21 6RF
01205 356 003
With a character all of its own, Prezzo oozes contemporary style and enduring charm. Signature pastas, stone-baked pizzas and classic Italian dishes promise a perfect dining choice for the whole family.

PREZZO
Italian
11 All Saints Place, Stamford, PE9 2AR
01780 766 772
With a character all of its own, Prezzo oozes contemporary style and enduring charm. Signature pastas, stone-baked pizzas and classic Italian dishes promise a perfect dining choice for the whole family.

241

SORRENTO'S
Italian

11 Market Place, Grantham, NG31 6LJ
01476 571 200
Traditional Italian restaurant delivering fine food in an architecturally sublime building, offering diners a high level of comfort and service. A family-run business providing a quality eating experience.

STAMFORD BALTI HUT
Indian

16 All Saints Place, Stamford, PE9 2AD
01780 762 013
With a fine line in slow cooking, for the fullest of flavours and melting texture throughout its dishes, this well-regarded Indian restaurant is classic and accomplished; a sumptuous experience.

THAI ONE ON
Thai

Wigford Way, Brayford Wharf N, Lincoln, LN1 1YX
01522 512 473
Feast on authentic cuisine in a traditional Thai manner. Specialist 'banquets' provide a large array of dishes to fill your table, so you can sample a little of everything.

RECOMMEND A FRIEND
see page 18

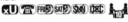

THE GEORGE AND DRAGON
Traditional English Fare

High Street, Hagworthingham, PE23 4NA
01507 588 255
Eclectic and classic cuisine, from a 'gravy' steak and ale pie to a tasty tiger prawn balti, in this idyll of a Lincolnshire country pub. If hunger be the dragon, it's laid to rest here.

THE THATCHED COTTAGE
British

Pools Lane, Sutterton, Boston, PE20 2EZ
01205 460 870
In a characteristically charming and nostalgic setting, with its beams, columns and trusses, you'll enjoy fresh produce cooked simply and to a high quality with excellent presentation.

2FOR1 3 COURSES

THREE TUNS
English / Gastro Pub

Thurlby Road, Bilsby, Alford, LN13 9PU
01507 462 297
A small food-led pub situated in the lovely village of Bilsby. Try the varied menu and sample a delicious steak or choose from a range of traditional pub fare with a modern twist.

2FOR1 3 COURSES

VILLAGE LIMITS
British

Stixwould Road, Woodhall Spa, LN10 6UJ
01526 353 312
Award-winning and fabulous, this restaurant serves up the most enjoyable traditional dishes at brilliant prices. An ever-changing specials board is available as well as their wonderful à la carte.

2FOR1 MAIN COURSE

WASHINGBOROUGH HALL
European

Church Hill, Washingborough, Lincoln, LN4 1BE
01522 790 340
Located in a magnificent listed Georgian manor house, the grand setting has been maintained. The food is traditional British, cooked up with verve and accomplishment from quality, seasonal local produce.

WINTERINGHAM FIELDS
British

1 Silver Street, Winteringham, DN15 9ND
01724 733 096
Situated in a 16th century manor house, this is one of the most intimate and secretive places you could ever wish to stumble across. Its award-winning reputation is enough to challenge Europe's finest.

Northamptonshire

ALI'S RESTAURANT
Indian

9 Pytchley Court, Corby, NN17 2QD
01536 402 953
A restaurant that serves the highest standards of authentic Indian cuisine. The relaxed, friendly atmosphere of the restaurant together with excellent service makes this a lovely dining experience.

2FOR1 3 COURSES

BLUE MOON
Indian

1 Talbot Road, Northampton, NN1 4HZ
01604 627 861
The excellent service is a perfect match for the superb food on offer at this Indian restaurant. The khaas roast comes highly recommended, as do the exceptional mouth-watering kebabs.

2FOR1 3 COURSES

BOMBAY PALACE
Indian

9-11 Welford Road, Kingsthorpe, NN2 8AE
01604 713 899
An amiable, friendly local restaurant that has a loyal following of diners from the surrounding area. Courteous staff provide you with fine, tasty and rich Indian food.

2FOR1 MAIN COURSE

DELHI COTTAGE
Indian

25 St Leonard's Rd, Far Cotton, Northampton, NN4 8DL
01604 766 144
A well-established restaurant serving fine Indian cuisine. The shatkora chicken, a dish made with Bangladeshi citrus fruits and blended spices, comes highly recommended.

DUNKLEY'S
British

Castle Ashby Station, Grendon Road, Whiston, NN7 1NP
01604 810 546
Set in the scenic Northamptonshire countryside around the old goods sheds and carriages of Castle Ashby Station. This venue offers a delicious menu amongst the restored railway artefacts.

Offer not available on Mondays.

Recommend a friend to the Gourmet Society and receive a free gift.

EASTERN SPICE
Indian
56-60 High Street, Irthlingborough, NN9 5TN
01933 650 044
A popular Indian restaurant with a convenient central location. Guests enjoy the week-night banquets that offer a fine selection of delicious meals. Mild to spicy dishes are on offer.

EDWARDS RESTAURANT
British
West Haddon Road, Crick, NN6 7SQ
01788 822 517
Accommodating restaurant by the canal in Crick with a line in characterful, rich flavours; from a smoky, mellow tripartite terrine for starters, to superb, fulsome pork belly with black pudding mash.

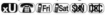

FORT KOCHI
Indian
28-34 Wellington Street, Northampton, NN1 3AS
01604 628 080
Begin a mouth-watering journey to a mesmerising world of spices by entering this restaurant, where each dish is being served with a distinctive style. The expert chefs prepare perfectly authentic cuisine.

FUEL
International
Barcelo Hotel, Sedgemoor Way, Daventry, NN11 0SG
01327 307 000
With a keen investment in its extensive, well-conceived wine list, this hotel-based restaurant offers a tasty, diverse menu.

GREENS
Contemporary
Windingbrook Lane, Collingtree, NN4 0XN
01604 663 963
Within the prestigious Collingtree Park Golf Club guests can take advantage of relaxing cuisine, a suave cocktail bar and fantastic wine list. Captivating surroundings with exceptional food.

Open only Thursday-Sunday

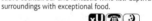

INDIAN BRASSERIE
Indian
95 Weedon Road, St James, Northampton, NN5 5BG
01604 581 312
Be tempted by an unrivalled range of authentic and imaginative fusion dishes, cooked to the highest standards, using only the best quality and freshest ingredients.

KHUSHBOO
Indian
73 High Street, Brackley, NN13 7BW
01280 701 555
A comfortable and affable restaurant specialising in traditional Indian and Bangladeshi cuisine. Inviting staff warmly welcome you into this pleasant dining venue.

LANGBERRYS
British
Kettering Park Hotel & Spa, Kettering, NN15 6XT
01536 416 666
The restaurant of this beautifully luxurious hotel certainly showcases the region's excellent produce by delivering creative daily menus. Boasts an enviable reputation along with an AA Rosette.

QUEENS HEAD INN
British
Station Rd, Nassington, Peterborough, PE8 6QB
01780 784 006
A lovely looking, beautifully located, even idyllic little hotel and pub. The Inn offers high-quality British cuisine in bright dining rooms - there is something of the gastro-pub about the menu too.

NEW

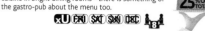

MAHARAJA
Indian
146-152 Wellingborough Road, Northampton, NN1 4DT
01604 437 049
A fine Indian restaurant that uses only the finest produce, ingredients and fresh seasonal, native vegetables. Coupled with over 32 years experience this results in a meal prepared to the highest standard.

PALASH BARI
Indian
1 Watling Street, Fosters Booth, Towcester, NN12 8LB
01327 830 500
In the sleepy village of Fosters Booth sits this delightful Indian restaurant, offering food that will truly wake up your senses. The 'Wine, Dine and Fly' package is certainly a special treat.

PREZZO
Italian
Unit B, 3 Wood Hill, Northampton, NN1 2DA
01604 632 733
With a character all of its own, Prezzo oozes contemporary style and enduring charm. Signature pastas, stone-baked pizzas and classic Italian dishes promise a perfect dining choice for the whole family.

SAFFRON
Indian
21 Castilian St, Northampton, NN1 1JS
01604 630 800
A nouvelle-tandoori restaurant with a magnificent unique twist. Whilst you can still enjoy your favourite Indian and tandoori dishes, the menu also contains an exquisite range of venison and duck dishes.

SPICE LOUNGE
Indian
3-5 Newland Street, Kettering, NN16 8JH
01536 411 176
Authentic Indian restaurant that captures the spice and flavours of a culture. Combines a passion for quality and flavour with outstanding customer service to deliver a memorable dining experience.

TASTE OF SPICE
Indian
38a Main Road, Duston, Northampton, NN5 6JF
01604 754 999
Family-run business providing quality food and service. Spice up your evenings with a wide range of curries to suit all tastes, vegetarian and seafood varieties, and a selection of delicious desserts.

THE WHEATSHEAF
Traditional English
15 Main Road,Crick, NN6 7TU
01788 823 824
An old coaching inn dating back to 1770, the pub has retained much of the atmosphere of the past yet will surprise you with its extensive menu and traditional range of beers.

NEW

243

THE COCK INN AT DENFORD
British

High Street, Denford, Kettering, NN14 4EQ
01832 732 565
An inviting inn with a quiet charm. All dishes are freshly prepared and cooked to order, with regularly updated menus and fresh fish delivered daily. A quality, informal, real country pub.

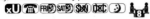

THE DYNASTY
Chinese

12 High Street, Long Buckby, NN6 7RD
01327 842 007
Situated within a picturesque village, this venue provides a relaxing atmosphere where both food and staff are excellent. Offers an extensive Chinese menu, along with additional Thai and Malaysian dishes.

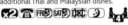

THE GURKHAS RESTAURANT
Indian/Nepalese

Harborough Road, Desborough, Kettering, NN14 2UG
01536 764 518
Providing customers with fantastic Indian and Nepalese cuisine in authentic surroundings. I lighly experienced owners deliver the ultimate in Indian restaurant dining, with full range of drinks available.

2FOR1 2COURSES

THE RAJ RESTAURANT
Indian

46-50 Rockingham Road, Kettering, NN16 8JT
01536 513 606
If you are looking for delicious Indian cuisine served in modern and stylish settings, then this is the place for you. Friendly service and smiles are brought to your table along with the flavoursome food.

2FOR1 2COURSES

WOODWARDS AT THE BOAT INN
British

The Boat Inn, Stoke Bruerne, Towcester, NN12 7SB
01604 862 428
An unexpectedly refined menu includes sublime duck breast, marvellous beef fillet, and gourmet steaks to provide a treat for any diner. Benefit from the experience and tradition at the core of this inn.

2FOR1 MAIN COURSE

Nottinghamshire

PRETTY ORCHID
Malaysian

12 Pepper St, Bridlesmith Gate, Nottingham, NG1 2GH
0115 958 8344
One of the city's most popular Malaysian restaurants. With an accomplished menu of exotic delicacies and a friendly, inviting team this beguiling restaurant has got foodies buzzing.

NEW
25%OFF TOTAL

ALLEY CAFE BAR
Vegetarian

1a Cannon Court, Long Row West, Nottingham, NG1 6JE
0115 955 1013
Inventive & traditional vegetarian cuisine showcasing innovation, quality and choice is served at this relaxed eco-conscious café. At night, world music DJs transform Alley into a hip, stylish bar.

25%OFF TOTAL
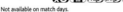

ANDWHYNOT
International

62 Leeming Street, Mansfield, NG18 1NG
01623 633 330
Combine a European café bar with all the elegance of a restaurant and the result will be AndWhyNot. The globally influenced menu offers everything from light bites to main meals.

BALTI HOUSE
Indian

35 Heathcote Street, Hockley, Nottingham, NG1 3AG
0115 945 2177
An accommodating Indian restaurant that has fed the Bangladeshi cricket team and thrives on doing things a bit differently. Serves up all the classic sauces but also lighter, subcontinental summer dishes.

2FOR1 2COURSES

BISTRO LIVE
Bistro

2 Barker Gate, The Lace Market, Nottingham, NG1 1JS
0115 947 3666
Best described as a 'live music restaurant', Bistro offers a complete night out of eating, drinking and dancing, culminating in live bands every evening. The good value menu offers snacks and full meals.

15% off Friday & Saturday, 25% off Thursday.

BODRUM RESTAURANT
Turkish

133 - 135 Mansfield Road, Nottingham, NG1 3FQ
0115 947 0439
Taste the rich vibrancy of Turkish cuisine in the impressive Bodrum Restaurant. Popular with regular customers, the chefs ensure that every care is taken during the preparation of each dish.

25%OFF TOTAL

BOMBAY BRASSERIE
Indian

39 Plains Road, Mapperley, Nottingham, NG3 5JU
0115 955 5177
Contemporary eatery with traditional values; an Indian restaurant focused on simplicity, plenty of flavour and superb service.

25%OFF TOTAL

Opening hours: Weekdays 17.30 - 11.30pm

BOMBAY BRASSERIE
Indian

124 High Road, Beeston, NG9 2LN
0115 922 2228
Wonderful Indian restaurant offering fantastic cuisine at reasonable prices.

25%OFF TOTAL

BOMBAY BRIDGFORD
Indian

1a Radcliffe Rd, West Bridgford, Nottingham, NG2 5FF
0115 981 7565
Near to Trent Bridge cricket ground, enjoy an exceptional Indian meal, from regional specialities to traditional family recipes: delicate spices and aromas, the essence of culinary India.

2FOR1 2COURSES

Not available on match days.

CAFÉ ROUGE
French

31 Bridlesmith Gate, Nottingham, NG1 2GR
0115 958 2230
An attractive restaurant, a boulevard café or a Parisian-style wine bar; however you see Café Rouge, consistently excellent classic French dishes are always guaranteed.

50%OFF FOOD

Discounted hotel rates for GS members on our website

CAPOCCI
International

57-58 Upper Parliament Street, Nottingham, NG1 2AG
0115 947 3622
Specialising in pre-theatre meals, business lunches and relaxed Saturday dining, all served in tasteful surroundings. Choose from a staggering array of Mediterranean and Italian country dishes and wines.

 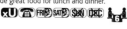

CAST RESTAURANT
European

Wellington Circus, Nottingham, NG1 5AF
0115 852 3898
Placing a British take on world cuisine, a contemporary twist adding unique flavours to carefully sourced produce. An exceptional variety of dishes are available, guaranteeing something for everyone.

Offer available Monday - Thursday from 8pm. Sunday 12.30 - 5pm

CHATTERLEY HOUSE HOTEL
Contemporary

Coronation Road, Cossall, NG16 2RU
0115 930 4519
Wonderfully located on the edge of Cossall village, this is a restaurant that can be easily accessed from surrounding areas. Both the bar and the à la carte menu provide great food for lunch and dinner.

 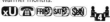

CHESTERFIELD AT BINGHAM
Contemporary

Church Street, Bingham, NG13 8AL
01949 837 342
Located in an attractive listed building where many of the original features have been maintained to create a characteristic, classic charm. Enjoy al fresco wining and dining in the warmer months.

CHINO LATINO
Pan Asian

41 Maid Marian Way, Nottingham, NG1 6GD
0115 947 7444
Multi award-winning restaurant offering delicious modern Pan-Asian cuisine and glamorous cocktails. Every appetite, big or small, will find something tempting and sumptuous on the constantly evolving menu.

25% discount is not applied to cocktails.

CHUTNEY
Indian

41 Friar Lane, Nottingham, NG1 6DD
0115 924 1743
Chutney is a happy mix of local Indian and a fine dining Indian restaurant. The menu offers traditional favourites and many chef's specialities. Locally acknowledged as a fantastic, buzzing venue.

CITY SPICE
Indian

7-9 Thurland Street, West Bridgford, Nottingham, NG2 7AD
0115 941 7374
A firm favourite with the curry-loving population of Nottingham. Spice levels vary from mild and delicate to hot and fiery, meaning all palates are carefully catered for.

CLUMBER PARK HOTEL
British

Normanton Bar & Grill, Blyth Rd, Clumber Pk, S80 3PA
01623 835 333
This bar and grill on the edge of Sherwood Forest offers a varied menu using local ingredients. The traditional Sunday carvery makes it ideal whether you're just passing through or in for a longer stay.

 **2FOR1** 2 COURSES

COLWICK HALL
Malaysian

Racecourse Road, West Bridgford, Nottingham, NG2 4BH
0115 950 0566
The magnificent Colwick Hall is a Georgian country house nestled in acres of parkland and host to this unique colonial Malaysian restaurant, where the exquisite cuisine is honoured with regal service.

After first visit, offer applies to food only.

CROWNE PLAZA NOTTINGHAM

Wollaton Street, Nottingham, NG1 5RH
0871 942 9161
From the informal, lively Swatch Bar & Lounge, to the more serene Lace Maker Restaurant, you're sure to enjoy a finely cooked, deliciously flavoursome meal at this hotel in Nottingham.

EAST MIDLANDS

CURRY LOUNGE
2FOR1 MAIN COURSE

110 Upper Parliament Street, Nottingham, NG1 6LN
0115 9418844 *Indian*

Essential to book in advance and mention you are a GS member.

A consistently award-winning restaurant in Nottingham's city centre, the Curry Lounge has risen to nationwide acclaim, all the while earning the praise of regular customers. This accomplished but characterful restaurant continues to go from strength to strength.

Curry Lounge sets its stall on innovation and evolution, whilst serving traditional Indian and Punjabi cuisine which is always freshly prepared and cooked to order. Quality is a given: the meat is free range, the cooking oils are light, and the greens are fresh.

Recognising the increasing importance of eating well, Curry Lounge has also conducted a recent drive to reduce calories across the menu. This has proven that their fabulous dishes can offer a wholesome, balanced meal while compromising not an inch on taste - nor on the value they ascribe to traditional cooking methods.

The Gourmet Society is proud to give its members the opportunity to enjoy this stand-out, flagship restaurant with their exclusive offer.

245

www.gourmetsociety.co.uk

CUTLERS RESTAURANT @ THE GRANGE HOTEL
European

The Grange Hotel, 73 London Road, Newark, NG24 1RZ
01636 703 399
The Grange is a cosy hotel that houses the AA Rosette-rated restaurant 'Cutlers', providing an extensive à la carte menu combining traditional British cuisine with other exciting European flavours.

DAKOTA GRILL
British

Lake View Drive, Annesley, Nottingham, NG15 0EA
01623 727 670
With their belief in fantastic food from local suppliers, cooked by exceptional emerging chefs, it's no surprise Dakota is a popular retreat. At root, it always stays focused on the origins of the produce.

DOGMA BAR AND RESTAURANT
European

9 Byard Lane, Nottingham, NG1 2GJ
0115 988 6830
Probably the most famous bar in Nottingham for showcasing top musical talent yet also home to a wonderful modern restaurant offering a distinct, serene space to enjoy fine food in sumptuous surroundings.

Must mention GS card when booking.

FIRE & ICE
Modern European

40 Bridgford Road, West Bridgford, Nottingham, NG2 6AP
0115 981 9000
Rich in European cuisine, this family-run establishment creates tantalising, freshly prepared dishes cooked to perfection, with an impressive selection of wines, cocktails, beers and champagne to enjoy.

FIVE RIVERS
Indian

40 Gordon Road, West Bridgford, NG2 5LN
0115 982 6449
A refreshing concept in fusion Indian cuisine, bringing together the very best recipes from Eastern and Western cultures to provide an outstanding food experience.

HEMLOCK STONE & DRAGON
Thai/British

Bramcote Lane, Nottingham, NG8 2QQ
0115 928 4463
A blend of traditional pub hospitality with the best the Orient has to offer. Boasting a menu comprising of many Thai delicacies, this exemplary Dragon pub will certainly not disappoint.

INDIGO
Indian

884 Woodborough Road, Mapperley, Nottingham, NG3 5QR
0115 962 3333
Enjoy high-quality restaurant food in the comfort of your own home. Sensational traditional and contemporary Indian cuisine delivered to your door.

JONGLEURS
International

10 Thurland Street, Nottingham, NG1 3DR
0870 011 1960
Great entertainment and food is delivered at all of these premier comedy clubs. An excellent selection of sharing platters, gourmet burgers and freshly made pizzas to enjoy while you watch the show.

LA PARISIENNE
French

12 King Street, Southwell, NG25 0EN
01636 816 573
A little bit of France nestles cosily in the picturesque surroundings of Southwell. A wonderful restaurant that offer the classically rich flavours of French cuisine as well as Moroccan-influenced dishes.

LA TASCA
Spanish

9 Weekday Cross, The Lace Market, Nottingham, NG1 2GB
0115 959 9456
La Tasca is all about terrific tapas. The 30 plus dishes that are on offer are perfect for sharing with friends and loved ones. Sip on a glass of the ever-popular sangria in wonderfully warm surroundings.

Excludes 'Menu Rapido'.

LAGUNA TANDOORI
Indian

43 Mount Street, Nottingham, NG1 6HE
0115 941 1632
The restaurant's tandoori clay oven is its signature tool, religiously used to provide authentic, flavoursome dishes. Delicious Indian cuisine served by a charming, friendly team of staff.

108 GRILL @ ALEA CASINO
British

108 Upper Parliament Street, Nottingham, NG1 6LF
0115 8720601
With hearty British fare on offer, 108 Grill go to great lengths to ensure the quality of their food such as the 28 day aged steaks from Derbyshire. Go all in and you'll find that 108 Grill is a sure bet.

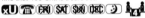

LANTONG THAI RESTAURANT
Thai

32 Lower Parliament Street, Nottingham, NG1 3DA
0115 924 3011
Both city dwellers and guests from afar enjoy the centrality of this favourable Thai restaurant. Both meat lovers and vegetarians can enjoy the extensive menu that offers deliciously fresh, authentic food.

LE MISTRAL
French

2-3 Eldon Chambers, Nottingham, NG1 2GJ
0115 941 0401
A French-style café, bar and bistro serving top-quality, fresh food accompanied by a vast selection of wines, beers and a unique house-blend espresso. Try the recommended cheese and charcuterie platters.

LE MISTRAL
French

575 Mansfield Road, Sherwood, Nottingham, NG5 2JN
0115 9116 116
A French-style café, bar and bistro serving top-quality, fresh food accompanied by a vast selection of wines, beers and a unique house-blend espresso. Try the recommended cheese and charcuterie platters.

LOCH FYNE
Seafood

17 King Street, Nottingham, NG1 2AY
0115 988 6849
From the roadside oyster bar that once was, Loch Fyne restaurants now successfully inject energy and passion into great food and wonderful flavours, whilst ensuring their seafood is sustainably sourced.

Gourmet Society discount applies to the à la carte menu

LOCKS RESTAURANT
Fine Dining
Trent Lock Golf Centre, Lock Lane, Long Eaton, NG10 2FY
0115 946 1184
With an exceptional location, Locks restaurant boasts elegant, creative specials to go with its hearty, succulent grill and carvery menus in a classic and refined setting.

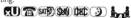

MOGAL-E-AZAM
Indian
7-9 Goldsmith Street, Nottingham, NG1 5JS
0115 947 3820
This acclaimed Indian restaurant, one of the largest in the Midlands, specialises in the rich flavours of the tandoor, while also offering the range of classic Indian dishes, cooked to perfection.

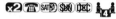

LUIGI'S RISTORANTE ITALIANO
Italian
98-100 Nottingham Road, Arnold, NG5 6LF
0115 920 6404
This warm, accommodating Italian restaurant just north of Nottingham combines its superb feeling for atmosphere and service with classic, homely, fulsome Italian flavours.

NO 4 WOOD STREET
Fine Dining
4 Wood Street, Mansfield, NG18 1QA
01623 424 824
Local chef Michael Sindall returned to Mansfield to offer a gourmet dining experience, after successful tenures under the Roux Brothers and Marco Pierre White. Now leading a local renaissance of good food.

MARC & DAINA'S
French
589a Mansfield Road, Sherwood, Nottingham, NG5 2FW
0115 960 3720
Relax and enjoy sensational French food, warm service and an unpretentious air. Marc and Daina use herbs and tomatoes from the restaurant's garden, where guests can also enjoy their meal.

Excludes lobster.

PAPPAS RESTAURANT
Greek
25 radcliffe road, West Bridgford, NG2 5FF
0115 981 9091
A well-established restaurant that is a result of a family's passion for good food, wine, music and dancing. A traditional Greek-Cypriot taverna that oozes character and spirit.

THE FOX AT KIRTON
English and Continental
Main Street, Kirton, NG22 9LP
01623 835 748
The Fox is a classic country pub that serves a strong array of well-prepared, relentlessly satisfying pub dishes. Favourites have to include the wedge-like traditional sandwiches (perfect pub food).

PARK BAR AT HART'S HOTEL
British
Standard Hill, Park Row, Nottingham, NG1 6FN
0115 988 1900
In the contemporary luxury of the Hart Hotel, enjoy exquisite service, striking food and a considered wine list featuring small producers. Chef and proprietor devote much time to sourcing quality produce.

Offer for Park Bar, Hart's Hotel, not Hart's Restaurant.

MERCHANTS
Fine Dining
Lace Market Hotel, 29-31 High Pavement, Nottingham, NG1 1HE
0115 852 3232
Double AA Rosette-rated restaurant that serves inventive and thrilling dishes using the best local and seasonal produce. The setting is lush and opulent, with a boudoir feel for a touch of satin and lace.

PICCOLO
Mediterranean
Unit 2, Farleys Lane, Hucknall, NG15 6EF
0115 968 1001
Enjoy Piccolo's impressive range of Mediterranean dishes, including a sumptuous range of pasta and pizza, whilst watching the chefs at work in the large open-plan kitchen.

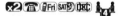

LAMBS AT THE MARKET
Cattle Market House, Nottingham Rd, Mansfield, NG18 1BJ
01623 424880 *British*

Lambs at the Market is a family run restaurant housed in a wonderful grade 2 listed building. Designed by local architect Watson Fothergill in 1877 the building was used as the tavern joined to the cattle market in the late 19th into 20th century. Now fully renovated with the help of local tradesmen it lends the perfect ambience for a laid back dining experience. Head chef and joint owner Troy Lamb is a big advocate of local produce and endeavours to use as many local ingredients and suppliers as possible. Local ingredients means seasonality and freshness is guaranteed. The menu changes daily depending on the availability of ingredients, offering varied traditional and modern British food. Everything is prepared in house including the much admired freshly made bread and desserts.

EAST MIDLANDS

247

PREZZO
Italian

21-23 Forman Street, Nottingham, NG1 4AA
0115 941 4798
With a character all of its own, Prezzo oozes contemporary style and enduring charm. Signature pastas, stone-baked pizzas and classic Italian dishes promise a perfect dining choice for the whole family.

STRADA
Italian

The Cornerhouse, Burton St, Nottingham, NG1 4DB
0115 947 5009
A dedicated menu offering traditional Italian dishes in a stylish and contemporary setting. The chefs use only the finest ingredients such as Parma ham and buffalo mozzarella, imported directly from Italy.

RESTAURANT 1877
Modern British

128 Derby Rd, Canning Circus, Nottingham, NG1 5FB
0115 958 8008
Contemporary restaurant complete with innovative menu, where wholesome dishes are produced to the highest standards. Affordable fine dining; guests are provided with a memorable experience.

TAMATANGA
Indian

The Cornerhouse, Burton St, Nottingham, NG1 4DB
0115 958 4848
A unique experience of eating Indian food complete with funky communal tables and electronic hand-held service. A simple but varied menu offers a range of distinctive tastes coupled with value for money.

ROYAL THAI RESTAURANT
Thai

189 Mansfield Road, Nottingham, NG1 3FS
0115 948 3001
Situated in the city's most cosmopolitan area, this restaurant prides itself on serving spectacular Thai food in a soothing atmosphere. Diners will be impressed by the incredibly friendly waiting staff.

THE APPROACH
Modern Pub

12-18 Friar Lane, Nottingham, NG1 6DQ
0115 950 6149
Vibrant venue in Nottingham that covers your day and night: stylish interior in which to settle for a drink at the end of the day; an atmospheric air in the evenings for live entertainment and tasty food.

SALTWATER
British

The Cornerhouse, Burton St, Nottingham, NG1 4DB
0115 924 2664
An inventive and ever-changing British menu is offered in this stunning restaurant; delight in panoramic views of the city and drinks from award-winning bartenders in the rooftop cocktail lounge.

THE CARNARVON
British

Fackley Road, Teversal, Sutton In Ashfield, NG17 3JA
01623 559 676
Superb British pub with contrasting décor producing an airy modern ambience. Guests can take advantage of the extensive menu, as well as the wide range of beverages on offer.

Offer excludes Sunday Lunches, but is available after 4pm

SARACENS HEAD
Fine Dining

Market Place, Southwell, NG25 0HE
01636 812 701
Owner Jonny Bingham has a rich welcome for those dining in the historic Saracens Head, a coaching inn established in 1460. Featured in all major guides, the food, like Jonny, is charming and delightful.

THE ELWES ARMS
Fresh Fish/Pub Classics

303 Oakdale Road, Carlton, Nottingham, NG4 1DH
0115 987 1280
A lively pub and restaurant with a great atmosphere. Coupling friendly, attentive staff with quality, wholesome food and value for money, this venue is sure to appeal to all.

SAVERA TANDOORI RESTAURANT
Indian

365 Derby Road, Lenton Hillside, NG7 2EB
0115 978 1904
Exotic fragrant Indian spices are used to create traditional dishes originating from Northern India. Enjoy each dish's distinctive flavour and aroma.

THE HEMSLEY
Contemporary

Nottingham University, Library Road, Nottingham, NG7 2RD
0115 846 6336
Nestled in glorious grounds, this restaurant offers imaginable and delectable food combined with attentive service. Freshly prepared food with carefully chosen wine to complement the available dishes.

SIMLA INDIAN RESTAURANT
Indian

5 James Street, Kimberley, NG16 2LP
0115 945 9350
Simla enjoys a fantastic reputation, attracting visitors from far and wide who come for the top-quality Indian dishes. Old favourites to new flavour combinations, all offered at great value.

Offer not available Mondays.

THE KING'S HEAD
Fine Dining

6 High Street, Collingham, Newark, NG23 7LA
01636 892 341
Highly regarded pub-restaurant in Newark whose skilled cooking and commitment to excellence in presentation and service sets it apart. They also serve full breakfasts or a Danish with coffee from 9.30am.

SPICE
Indian

459 Westdale Lane, Mapperley, Nottingham, NG3 6DH
0115 962 3555
Quality Indian takeaway that serves a wide range of vibrant, flavourful, smooth and spicy dishes at good value.

THE LARDER ON GOOSEGATE
British

16-22 Goosegate, Nottingham, NG1 1FE
0115 950 0111
A commitment to understanding the provenance of the food served to customers is matched with unwavering support for nearby farmers, growers and producers. The result is a varied, delicious menu.

Gourmet Society discount applies to the à la carte menu

TONIC
Chapel Quarter, Nottingham, NG1 6JS
0115 941 4770 *International*

From early morning coffee and lunch 'on-the-go', to an informal bar meal or full à la carte, Tonic is uniquely equipped to cater for the discerning customer whatever the occasion or budget. The common thread is fresh local produce, delivered daily and cooked to order with the emphasis on natural flavours and colours.

The first floor restaurant is framed by theatre, from the exclusive cocktail bar and video art installation, to dramatic booth seating and the open plan kitchen which provides a window into the art of their modern take on world cuisine.

Tonic pulls off that trickiest of tricks - 'comfortable cool' with great food and drink at sensible prices and friendly, attentive service.

Awarded two AA Rosettes in 2010 for culinary excellence, Tonic will exceed your expectations.

THE LIVING ROOM *British*
7 High Pavement, Lace Market, Nottingham, NG1 1HF
0115 988 6870
Step into The Living Room and you can count on the savvy, distinctive neighbourhood vibe that plays home to eclectically drawn, supremely tasty cuisine. Settle back in this spacious Nottingham venue.

Must purchase minimum 3 courses/person inc mains.

THE OLD VOLUNTEER *English / Gastro Pub*
61 Caythorpe Road, Caythorpe, Nottingham, NG14 7EB
0115 966 5967
A lively, open-armed atmosphere and a thoroughly classic range of pub standards. This pub-restaurant has a great deal of charm, is extremely welcoming and forthcoming, and serves up a mean dinner.

THE OLIVE TREE *Spanish*
9-14 St James' Terrace, Nottingham, NG1 6FW
0115 941 1997
A great place for an informal lunch or a feisty evening meal. Be sure not to miss out on the delicious tapas on Friday and Saturday nights, offered alongside an array of traditional Spanish dishes.

THE PEACOCK INN *European*
The Peacock Inn, Main Street, Redmile, NG13 0GA
01949 842 554
A shining example of traditional English hospitality. The restaurant serves well-conceived and superbly executed dishes along with tantalising desserts and a great selection of wines.

THEATRE ROYAL *European*
Theatre Royal, Theatre Square, Nottingham, NG1 5ND
0115 989 5569
Open for both matinée and evening performances, offering silver service and table d'hôte. Non-theatregoers are just as welcome to enjoy the delicious menu, highlighting some of the best European dishes.

WELBECK HOTEL *European*
Talbot Street, Nottingham, NG1 5GS
0115 841 1000
The relaxing Mediterranean feel is enhanced by the informal bar which overlooks the city, whilst night time sees the space intimately transformed as the tables are elegantly clothed and candlelit.

WOODBOROUGH HALL *Fine Dining*
Bank Hill, Woodborough, NG14 6EF
0115 965 4466
Elegant and vibrant fine cuisine from a kitchen led by acclaimed chef Des Sweeney; the Hall is a sparkling setting, built around the time of the Restoration and maintaining an air of uncluttered splendour.

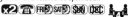

YIANNI'S *Greek*
67 Haydn Road, Sherwood, Nottingham, NG5 2LA
0115 985 6648
Enjoy a night of authentic Greek cuisine and hospitality at this restaurant. Dazzling platters for sharing, or some meltingly tasty meat and fish dishes, all earthy and fruity and full of flavour.

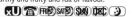

On monthly live music night GS cards will not be accepted all day.

249

North West

A long tradition of growing some of the most flavourful produce and using it to cook speciality dishes and local delicacies has produced great foods proud to call the North West home. Foods so good, most carry their birthplace as their name. Take the oldest and arguably the most popular of British cheeses, Cheshire; or the delicious, curved Cumberland sausage (placed on nothing finer than a flour-topped barm cake); or the melting Lancashire hotpot, silky and wholesome, the result of a long cooking time and great ingredients.

Sweets maintain this proud trend. The custard and jam filled Manchester tart is ever-popular as too is its Lancashire counterpart, the Eccles cake, tasty testimony of the area's sweet pastry making heritage.

In the optimistic thrust of its iconic cities and the idyllic surroundings of the picturesque countryside, dining out in the North West is always an enjoyable affair. The atmosphere and cuisine nicely capture the various tones of this most animated and charismatic of regions. Delivering cuisine with a strong northern imprint, multicultural flavours are also unsurprisingly integrated into the local offerings, as befits the former home of the world's largest docks. Global influences which were long ago imported into the kitchens, culinary styles and palates of locals continue to thrive today on the same outward looking appetites. So whatever your preference, you'll find it here.

Cheshire

1851 AT PECKFORTON CASTLE
British

Peck'n Castle, Stonehouse Lane, Tarporley, CW6 9TN
01829 260 930
An opulent location to enjoy finely cooked, imaginatively combined flavours making use of the strength of Cheshire's produce. Refined and elegant; awarded 2 AA rosettes.

ASIA FUSION
Asian Fusion

104 Foregate Street, Chester, CH1 1HB
01244 322 597
A contemporary restaurant that retains its Asian identity and cultural roots. Delicious fusion of cuisines offering guests variety in an array of flavours and spices, providing tremendous value for money.

BISTRO BLU
Bistro

23 The Groves, Chester, CH1 1SD
01244 322 481
While you can't go wrong with the moules marinières or the rich coq au vin, the more adventurous diner may opt for the deep braised wood-pigeon or sumptuous country game casserole. Great food guaranteed.

BODDINGTON & DRAGON
Thai/British

Racecourse Road, Wilmslow, SK9 5LR
01625 525 849
Delight your senses at this accomplished Dragon pub that serves divine Thai food. Choose your dream dish and complement it with a fine selection of beers and choice wine.

BRISCOLA
Italian

88-90 Palmerston Street, Bollington, Macc., SK10 5PW
01625 573 898
An Italian-style café serving pizzas and pastas alongside its à la carte and special menus. Families, couples and groups of friends will feel at home in this warm and inviting restaurant.

Call for availability Fri / Sat early evening.

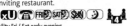

CAFÉ ROUGE
French

Kinsey Road, Cheshire Oaks, Ellesmere Port, CH65 9JJ
0151 357 1201
An attractive restaurant, a boulevard café or a Parisian-style wine bar; however you see Café Rouge, consistently excellent classic French dishes are always guaranteed.

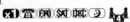

CAPRI RESTAURANT
British

Knutsford Old Road, Warrington, WA4 2LD
0192 526 7471
This bijou restaurant really showcases the excellence of British produce and cuisine. It serves up classic dishes from quality ingredients with a great deal of skill and imaginative verve.

CARDAMON CUISINE
Indian British

109A London Rd, Warrington, WA4 6LG
01925 212 552
Fresh, vibrant flavours characterise the dishes at Cardamon. The talented chefs are dedicated to producing good quality curry, serving up both old favourites and less well known delicacies.

CHETWODE ARMS
Traditional English Fare

Street Lane, Lower Whitley, WA4 4EN
01925 730 203
A warm and cosy country pub with all the familiarities and comforts of home. Idyllically located in the heart of the countryside, local dishes like the Cheshire rabbit prove exceedingly popular.

CHIMNEY HOUSE HOTEL
Modern British

Congleton Road, Sandbach, CW11 4ST
01270 764 141
A warm and welcoming in-house restaurant at the Brook Chimney House Hotel, presenting a modern brassiere-style dining experience. Open for lunch and dinner, including hearty traditional Sunday lunch.

CIRO'S BRASSERIE
Modern European

Grosvenor Pulford, Wrexham Rd, Pulford, CH4 9DG
01244 570 560
This Mediterranean-style restaurant offers modern European cuisine with an emphasis on using fresh local ingredients. The unique décor and al fresco coffee bar offer a delightful and elegant experience.

COCK & PHEASANT
Modern British

15 Bollington Rd, Bollington, Macclesfield, SK10 5EJ
01625 573 289
This locally acclaimed, picturesque pub in Bollington, part of the Best of British group, is a treat in summer with its superb floral displays, and throughout the year with its eclectic food and top beers.

Must purchase min 2 courses.

CRABWALL MANOR HOTEL
Modern British

Parkgate Road, Mollington, Chester, CH1 6NE
01244 851 666
Set in a conservatory with views over the beautiful gardens, this Brook hotel in-house restaurant serves deliciously modern, interesting and varied English cuisine in a unpretentious atmosphere.

CROWNE PLAZA CHESTER
International

Trinity Way, Chester, CH1 2BD
01244 899 988
With a passionate chef and able team, this hotel-restaurant serves up a wide variety of dishes. Settle back in the stylish restaurant with its relaxed ambience and stunning views across the Welsh hills.

Only one card can be used per table.

FRANCS RESTAURANT
French

14 Cuppin Street, Chester, CH1 2BN
01244 317 952
An original French bistro with a buzzing atmosphere, that keeps the very best of rustic ideas and throws in a few of their own. Although the French Franc is dead, Chester's Franc is most certainly alive.

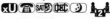

Gourmet Society discount applies to the à la carte menu

FRESH
English and Continental
Fresh, Wood Street, Macclesfield, SK11 6JQ
01625 500 999
The best of fresh, local produce coupled with an affordable pizza and platter section. Enjoy sumptuous food with a selection of drinks including fresh cocktails, something of a speciality here.

LOCH FYNE
Seafood
The Royal George, King Street, Knutsford, WA16 6GR
01565 622 980
From the roadside oyster bar that once was, Loch Fyne restaurants now successfully inject energy and passion into great food and wonderful flavours, whilst ensuring their seafood is sustainably sourced.

FROGG MANOR
British
Nantwich Road, Chester, CH3 9JH
01829 782 629
Owned and run by the self-confessed eccentric John Sykes, aiming to treat guests to a veritable wonderland of fine food and good company. An evening at Frogg Manor is guaranteed to be magical.

Must purchase 3 courses

MD'S RESTAURANT
European
38 Watergate Street, Chester, CH1 2LA
01244 400 322
In this ambient 14th century listed building, take in some fulsome food from a range of cultures: from duck leg with noodles for a starter, to a phlegmatic pan-fried halibut steak.

Not open on Sunday, Monday, Tuesday evenings.

GAINSBOROUGH RESTAURANT
European
Willington Hall, Tarporley, Willington, CW6 0NB
01829 752 321
Dine in the Gainsborough Restaurant with full delicious à la carte and table d'hôte menus. Local produce is freshly prepared by excellent chefs and complemented by an extensive wine list.

MEMPHIS BELLE
Carvery
Gemini Retail Park, Warrington, WA5 8WF
01925 712 173
One of the many Great British Carveries that Gourmet Society members can enjoy. Indulge in the best of British food at this classic and comfortable pub, where you will feel completely relaxed.

Call before on special event days.

HILLTOPS RESTAURANT
International
Overton Hill, Bellemonte Road, Frodsham, WA6 6HH
01928 735 255
Indulge yourself in stunning panoramic views and delightful seasonal food, with the fish menu locally recommended. Offers guests a range of experiences, from fine champagne dining to 70s and 80s nights.

MITCHELLS BAR & BRASSERIE
Mediterranean
Lynedale House, High Street, Tattenhall, CH3 9PX
01829 771 477
At Mitchells you will enjoy hearty, homely Mediterranean food from a menu that is kept as fresh as the locally-sourced produce, changing each month to follow the seasons.

IL POMODORO
Italian
60-66 Park Lane, Poynton, SK12 1RE
01625 878 989
Enjoy superb, authentic Italian food at this cosy restaurant in Poynton. Using ingredients of the highest quality and with the skill and technique to bring out the best in it, this is a place to savour.

MOJO BAR AND TAPAS
Spanish
15 Cairo Street, Warrington, WA1 1EE
01925 576 576
Immerse yourself in authentic Spanish ambience, and sample the extensive menus and wine lists on offer at this fine tapas bar and restaurant. Exceptional food and service to match.

LA BOCA
Mexican
Groves Bistro, 1 Souters Lane, Chester, CH1 1SD
01244 311 518
Marrying the food and the culture of Latin America, the exciting menu is sure to please whether you are there for dining or dancing. Focuses on producing a pleasurable atmosphere for all to enjoy.

MOLLINGTON BANASTRE HOTEL
Traditional English Fare
Parkgate Road, Mollington, Chester, CH1 6NN
01244 851 471
In a stately building and a beautiful locale, this Brook Hotel restaurant offers accomplished, contemporary dining in formal but relaxed surroundings. Popular with locals and visitors alike.

LEGH ARMS
Carvery
London Road, Macclesfield, SK10 4NA
01625 829 211
One of the many Great British Carvery pubs Gourmet Society members can enjoy. Offering the best of British food in a charming old farmhouse, guests will love the warm welcomes and real ales.

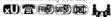

Call before on special event days.

MUGHLI
Indian
44-46 King Street, Knutsford, WA1 6DT
01565 631 010
A true taste of the Indian subcontinent, this restaurant offers freshly prepared traditional and contemporary Mughlai dishes that are scrumptiously tasty. Genteel staff cater to your every need.

LOCH FYNE
Seafood
Brook Lane, Alderley Edge, SK9 7RU
01625 587 670
From the roadside oyster bar that once was, Loch Fyne restaurants now successfully inject energy and passion into great food and wonderful flavours, whilst ensuring their seafood is sustainably sourced.

ODDFELLOWS
Classic British/ French
20 Lower Bridge Street, Chester, CH1 1RS
01244 400 001
Celebrated chef Richard Phillips leads a team in producing some of the finest food in the North West, with award-winning menus that showcase unique dishes full of flavours and textures. 1 AA Rosette.

253

OSTERIA MAURO
Italian

Wimslow Road, Mottram St Andrew, Macc. SK10 4QH
01625 828 111

This rustic Italian restaurant makes use of the former pub in which you'll find it to give a cosy, down-home vibe, while the food has just the right earthiness and warmth for an authentically Italian meal.

OSWALDS @ HELTERSKELTER
British

31 Church Street, Frodsham, WA6 6PN
01928 733 361

Ale lovers will wish they'd discovered this fantastic pub long ago. Serving over 20 different cask ales a week, guests will be spoilt for choice when it comes to choosing a drink to accompany their food.

2FOR1
2 COURSES

RING O' BELLS
English/Gastro pub

Village Road, Christleton, Chester, CH3 7AS
01244 335 422

At the heart of a pretty village, contemporary meets traditional at this high-quality pub. A classic gastro-pub menu delivered alongside new delectable signature dishes is sure to delight all guests.

2FOR1
3 COURSES

ROOKERY HALL HOTEL
British

Main Rd, Nantwich, NCW5 6DQ
08450 727 533

A beautifully located Hand Picked Hotels restaurant satisfying the most discerning palates. The Head Chef creates masterpiece dishes in a charming and well-preserved Georgian mansion. 2 AA Rosettes.

25%OFF
TOTAL

SHILLONG
Indian

111 Boughton, Chester, CH3 5BH
01244 311 112

Named after a hillside town in North East India, whose beauty and wonder is reflected in this amiable restaurant. The climate of Shillong is mirrored by a warm and welcoming atmosphere.

25%OFF
TOTAL

SPIRIT
British

Park Manor, Knutsford Rd, Warrington, WA4 1DQ
01925 232 527

A stunning listed building that oozes 19th century Georgian beauty sets a great first impression at this English bistro. Each dish is crafted with scrupulous attention to detail which cannot go unnoticed.

25%OFF
TOTAL

STUART'S TABLE @ FARMERS ARMS
Modern British

Huxley Lane, Chester, CH3 9BG
01829 781 342

Enjoy the loveliness of the Cheshire countryside as you dine in a warm and welcoming environment. Whilst succulent British steaks are a speciality, a well-balanced menu is on offer.

25%OFF
TOTAL

SYLK WINE BAR & RESTAURANT
Modern British

3-7 Samuel Street, Macclesfield, SK11 6UW
01625 420 333

Deliciously tender lamb, succulent fillets of beef and monkfish cheeks appear on the distinctive menu at Sylk. Award-winning chefs and friendly staff make for a winning combination.

25%OFF
TOTAL

SYMPHONY BAR & GRILL
European

48 Congleton Road, Sandbach CW11 1HG
01270 763 664

Sister restaurant to the Staffordshire Symphony Bar and Grill, this Sandbach venue is renowned across Cheshire for its fine wines and exquisite food. Charming, attentive staff cater to your every need.

25%OFF
TOTAL

THE BARN
British

Sandfield Farm, Chester Rd, Bridge Trafford CH2 4JR
01244 300 100

Stylish converted dairy farm where you can enjoy a superb line in fresh, up-to-date and seasonally tailored cuisine, drawing on eclectic culinary traditions but always well-conceived, tender and tasty.

25%OFF
TOTAL

THE BEAR'S PAW
English/Gastro pub

School Lane, Warmingham, Sandbach, CW11 3QN
01270 526 317

This characterful inn in picturesque Warmingham is a nexus for ales from local micro-breweries. Serves hearty, home-cooked meals, and boasts a warm, classic feel touched with a little contemporary style.

2FOR1
MAIN COURSE

THE CALVELEY ARMS
English and Continental

Whitchurch Road, Handley, Chester, CH3 9DT
01829 770 619

Popular food-led pub that produces an array of interesting, mouth-watering and fresh-flavoured dishes; try their superb lobster, or ease back with a steamy plate of moules marinière.

25%OFF
TOTAL

THE COTTAGE
English and Continental

Cottage Hotel, London Road, Allostock, WA16 9LU
01565 722 470

Bright and delightful dining rooms play host to a delicious array of eclectic foods, from a surprising and delicious nut roast to a simple, classic rack of lamb with mint vinaigrette. Enjoy, in style.

2FOR1
2 COURSES

THE EGERTON ARMS
Fresh Fish/Pub Classics

The Egerton Arms, Knutsford Road, Chelford, SK11 9BB
01625 861 366

Traditional family-run country pub with a close focus on fulsome, tasty classics. On Wednesdays you can enjoy a taste of Brussels with frites and mussels: an imaginative and delicious theme night.

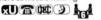
2FOR1
MAIN COURSE

THE FARNDON
British

High Street, Farndon, CH3 6PU
01829 270 570

A delightful 16th century building plays home to this wonderful village pub. Guests fall in love with the countryside location, while the Farndon burgers and home-made crumbles have all mouths watering.

25%OFF
TOTAL

THE FAULKNER BAR & KITCHEN
Bistro

48 Faulkner Street, Hoole, Chester, CH2 3BE
01244 328 195

An informal, urban bar and bistro situated in Chester's happening suburb, Hoole. Friendly staff serve classic dishes with a modern twist, including home-made tapas, brunch, and pizza menus.

2FOR1
3 COURSES

Sign up to our newsletter for latest restaurants, offers and more

THE FOOLS NOOK
Modern Pub

Leek Road, Macclesfield, SK11 0JF
01260 253 662
Named after a jester, this charming 17th century pub has a menu ranging from traditional British fare such as steak suet puddings to Thai fish cakes, ever rotating with the seasons.

THE GOSHAWK
British

Station Road, Mouldsworth, CH3 8AJ
01928 740 900
Back in the day, the Goshawk Inn was renowned for late-night dances and an easygoing manner. Now blends premium elements of food, drink, and hospitality; it's a little gem in the heart of the country.

THE LIVING ROOM
British

13 St Werburgh Street, Chester, CH1 2DY
01244 405 910
Step into The Living Room and you can count on the savvy, distinctive neighbourhood vibe that plays home to eclectically drawn, supremely tasty cuisine. Ensconce yourself in this lovely Chester venue.

Must purchase min 3 courses pp, inc. main.

THE PELICAN
Brasserie

10 Commonhall Street, Chester, CH1 2BJ
01244 313 258
Atmospheric restaurant in Chester with fantastic terrace gardens to enjoy your meal al fresco; eclectic and playful menu leads to simple and exceptionally cooked dishes.

THE PHEASANT INN
English/Gastro pub

Higher Burwardsley, Tattenhall CH3 9PF
01829 770 434
Spectacular views and great attention to detail in this popular and buzzing village pub where you can enjoy hearty and wholesome dishes while taking a step back and warming to the atmospheric location.

THE RECTORY
British

18A St Oswalds House, Chester, CH1 2DY
01244 315 528
From pork belly cassoulet to a mille-feuille of roasted vegetables, or a quirky pie of the day, you'll enjoy the rich and accomplished flavours of The Rectory without needing to cast up a prayer.

THE STAMFORD BRIDGE INN
British

Tarvin Road, Chester, CH3 7HN
01829 740 229
Famous for its friendly hospitality and delicious home-cooked food, the lavish lounge area and the fabulous garden make this a wonderful place to drink and dine at any time of the year.

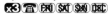

THE TERRACE RESTAURANT
Indian

Macon Way, Crewe, CW1 6DR
01270 504 050
With a range of intriguing Indian dishes, from dry gin-fried chicken to mutton rogan josh, along with a succulent grill menu, this hotel restaurant is smart, contemporary and accomplished in its touches.

THE WHITE APRON
Mediterranean

27 Church Street, Warrington, WA1 2SS
01925 444 894
Memories of holidays gone by will come flooding back to you once you taste the fantastic flavours of the Mediterranean at this restaurant. Taste the effort that is put into every single dish.

Must order starter and main per person.

TRADERS AT HOLIDAY INN RUNCORN
English and Continental

Beechwood, Runcorn, WA7 3HA
0871 942 9070
In a relaxed and informal atmosphere diners can choose from a number of menus, whether it be à la carte dining or tasty bar snacks. Food can be adapted for dietary requirements, catering for all guests.

WALTON ARMS
Carvery

148 Old Chester Road, Warrington, WA4 6TG
01925 262 659
One member of the Great British Carvery group of pubs that Gourmet Society members can enjoy. The well-loved classic is served in this characterful 19th century venue, where guests always emerge delighted.

Call before special event days.

WATERGATE GRILL
International

43 Watergate Row, Chester, CH1 2LE
01244 347 207
Bringing the Anglo-American culinary style to Britain. The menu takes its inspiration from the border towns of Texas as well as the stylish New York, with a small measure of England thrown into the mix.

Cumbria

BANKFIELD HOUSE COUNTRY HOTEL
European

Kiksanton, Millom, LA18 5LL
01229 772 276
Fantastic wholesome food served in a beautifully located hotel-restaurant. The traditional Sunday lunch is a particular speciality and has many regulars returning week after week.

BARBON INN
British

Barbon Main Street, Barbon, Carnforth, LA6 2LJ
01524 276 233
A characterful pub bearing the marks of history; the food, on the other hand, is thoroughly contemporary. Fresh, delicious British dishes, to be enjoyed with a choice glass of something excellent.

BERESFORD'S RESTAURANT
Modern European

Beresford Road, Windermere, LA23 2JG
01539 488 488
Situated in some of England's finest scenery, this fabulous, forward-thinking restaurant serves a superbly crafted and great-tasting array of cuisine, the fresh fish being a particular highlight.

NORTH WEST

255

CASA ROMANA
Italian

44 Warwick Road, Carlisle, CA1 1DN
01228 591 969
A firmly established Italian restaurant serving classic, renowned dishes, from pasta specialities to gourmet pizzas. Sublime desserts will round off any main meal.

GS offer cannot be used with Happy Hour offer (5.30-6.30pm).

CASA ROMANA
Italian

132 Queen Street, Whitehaven, CA28 7QF
01946 591 901
The second child of the Casa Romana family, this award-winning restaurant maintains the excellent standards set by its sister. Italian food at its very best, served in smart but unpretentious surroundings.

GS offer cannot be used with Happy Hour offer (5.30-6.30pm).

DAMSON DENE
Modern British

Crosthwaite, Kendal, LA8 8JE
01539 568 676
New culinary delights are brought to the menu on a daily basis by the restaurant's talented chefs. The kitchen has its own Victorian garden, which allows each dish to be made from the freshest produce.

THE GLOBE INN
English/Gastro pub

8 Market Place, Kendal, LA9 4TN
01539 733 589
Freshly cooked food that can be enjoyed over a refreshing pint of real cask ale sums up the experience of this centrally located Kendal pub. A non-branded pub experience which is fast disappearing.

NEW

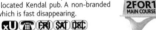

GRAYTHWAITE MANOR HOTEL
British

Fernhill Road, Grange over Sands, LA11 7JE
01539 532 001
A beautiful country manor hotel with idyllic surroundings whose restaurant caters for every palate, whether it be for an informal meeting or an exquisite banquet. A comfortable fine dining experience.

HOLME BISTRO
European

56-58 Denton Street, Denton Holme, Carlisle, CA2 5EH
01228 534 343
A lovely bistro that produces simple, quality food and strives to ensure every customer has a memorable experience. A dedicated kitchen team have created a wonderful, fresh menu that changes regularly.

INDIGO
Indian

92 Denton Street, Denton Holme, Carlisle, CA2 5EN
01228 527 527
This venue offers a dining experience that stems from a truly creative and authentic menu of Indian food. Well-trained chefs create mouth-watering dishes filled with zest and spice.

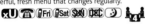

LINTHWAITE HOUSE HOTEL
Modern British

Crook Road, Windermere, LA23 3JA
01539 488 600
Talented young chef Richard Kearsley leads this Windermere kitchen, producing imaginative, technically superb dishes in this elegant and serene restaurant.

NEWBY BRIDGE HOTEL
Modern British

Newby Bridge, Ulverston, LA12 8NA
0153 953 1222
Directly overlooking Lake Windermere in five acres of beautiful land, dining and resting at the Newby Bridge will be a real pleasure. A daily changing menu in the restaurant accommodates local produce.

RIVERSIDE HOTEL
Modern British

Beezon Road, Kendal, LA9 6EQ
0153 973 4861
Enjoy river views in a luxury en-suite bedroom, or dine in the Riverside restaurant for ultimate pleasure. The kitchen makes use of its own produce garden to ensure every dish is fresh and tasty.

SPICE OF BENGAL
Indian

3 Kelsick Road, Ambleside, LA22 0BZ
0153 943 1250
Both meat lovers and vegetarians can satisfy their curry cravings at this wonderful Indian restaurant. Affable waiting staff provide a friendly service and wide smiles.

TEZA
Indian

4a-b English Gate Pl., Botchergate, Carlisle, CA1 1RP
01228 525 111
This restaurant prides itself on taking a distinctive approach to Indian cuisine through the vision of its Head Chef; you'll find here a real range of flavours that move beyond the staple classics.

THE GLOBE INN
Traditional English Fare

Calthwaite, Penrith, CA11 9QT
0176 888 5238
Classic and hearty home-made food at this well-rooted but exceptionally welcoming local inn. With a great big meal and a pint, you can take the world off your shoulders at The Globe.

THE RESTAURANT @ LOVELADY SHIELD
British

Lovelady Lane, Alston, CA9 3LX
01434 381 203
Quaintly nestled in the foothills, this elegant country house hosts a menu that is brimming with an imaginative variety of scrumptious dishes that are British at heart with a continental edge.

THE TEMPLE THAI
Thai

1 Cavendish Street, Ulverston, LA12 7AD
01229 580 566
Traditionally cooked Thai cuisine that will enliven your senses. Maintaining their ethos of providing delicious, non-westernised dishes, this is a fabulous place to enjoy bona fide Thai food.

TRAVELLERS REST INN
British

Keswick Road, Ambleside, LA22 9RR
01539 435 604
The Travellers Rest epitomises the traditional Lakeland inn. Immerse yourself into the picturesque village of Grasmere, whilst feasting on local dishes and ales. Full of character and tradition.

Visit the website regularly to discover the latest restaurants joining the GS

Gtr Manchester

110 RESTAURANT
European

Circus Casino, 110 Portland St, Manchester, M1 4RL
0161 228 0077
Being based within a casino, this venue delivers fine dining and gaming, for a throw of the dice beyond the typical. All dishes are a simple delight, created using fresh and fine ingredients.

888 RESTAURANT
English and Continental

888 Oldham Road, Newton Heath, M40 2BS
0161 277 6910
Classic English cuisine with touches of flavour from other culinary cultures; a restaurant with a softly elegant ambience where you can enjoy the fulsome menu and an array of good wines and beers.

AL BILAL
Indian

87 Wilmslow Road, Rusholme, Manchester, M14 5SU
0161 257 0006
A sophisticated and tranquil environment for diners to enjoy the culinary delights of well-prepared Indian cuisine, where the staff pride themselves in providing quality dishes and exemplary service.

AL NAWAZ
Indian/Punjabi

74-84 Wilmslow Road, Rusholme, Manchester, M14 5AL
0161 249 0044
Serving a home style of cooking that incorporates Indian, Punjabi, and vegetarian cuisine, this restaurant delivers a variety of food with the chefs happy to vary any dish according to individual taste.

AMBIENTE
Spanish

4B Worsley Road, Worsley, M28 2NL
0161 793 6003
Serving up a sumptuous array of Spanish and Mediterranean dishes, Ambiente's style is laid-back and calm, while the food is prepared freshly, consistently and with superb quality produce.

ANTELOPE
Indian

13 Manchester Road West, Walkden, M38 9EG
0161 790 7008
The Antelope employs 'East meets West' culinary expertise to create sophisticated and unique dishes. Offers a wide range of vegetarian and seafood options, each intertwined with a fusion of flavours.

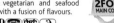

B LOUNGE @ BRIDGE
British

58 Bridge St, Manchester, M3 3BW
0161 834 0242
Whether you arrive in need of a cuddle from one of the giant leather sofas or a simply scrumptious lunch, this lounge and restaurant offers it all. Surf and turf combines the best of land and sea.

B LOUNGE PICCADILLY
British

97 Piccadilly, Manchester, M1 2DB
0161 236 4161
A stylish place to dine and drink. Guests can find a place of relaxation within the lively vibrant heart of the city centre. A traditional mouth-watering menu and an excellent range of drinks are on offer.

BACCHANALIA
Modern European

15-17 Chapel Walks, Manchester, M2 1HN
0161 819 1997
Simple, honest food, cooked fresh to order. Popular favourites make an appearance on the comprehensive menu, as well as a selection of special dishes, all cooked by passionate and creative chefs.

BAR ON 3 / ARTS BRASSERIE
International

Ramada, Portland Street, Manchester, M1 4PH
0161 236 8414
Take in the lively buzz of the city as you dine in the spacious and relaxing brasserie and bar. Phenomenal dishes such as Thai-spiced chicken salad and pan-fried sea bass are cooked to perfection.

BARBIROLLI
British

31 Lower Mosley St, Manchester, M2 3WS
0161 236 3060
A smart, sophisticated live music venue, set on a stunning waterfront location. As well as two bars and a performance stage, diners can delight in the sumptuous cocktail lounge with booth dining.

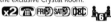

BARCA RESTAURANT
Italian

Catalan Square, Castlefield, Manchester, M3 4RU
0161 839 7099
An ideally located restaurant and bar, beautifully stylish and sparklingly atmospheric. Soak up the sun on the canal side terrace, or indulge in the luxuriousness of the exclusive Crystal Room.

BELUGA
European

2 Mount Street, Manchester, M2 5WQ
0161 833 3339
Renowned for its lively, bustling atmosphere, Beluga provides a perfect setting for unwinding after work or for an intimate dinner. Their amiable staff are obliging and attentive.

BLUE PARROT BAR AND GRILLE
Steakhouse

Westminster House, 11 Portland St, Manchester M1 3DY
0161 236 8359
Succulent steaks and juicy burgers occupy much of the menu at this great restaurant. Quickly establishing itself as a fantastic place to dine, Blue Parrot offers great food and tremendous service.

BLUU
British

85 High Street, Manchester, M4 1BD
0161 839 7195
Bluu is an atmospheric restaurant and bar with regular live music nights and a large street-side terrace perfect for summer evenings. A distinctive place set in a trendy and understated part of the city.

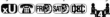

CAFÉ MEF
Italian

Unit 7 Chill Factor, Manchester, M41 7JA
0161 748 2255
A fresh and vibrant place to dine, providing guests with a true taste of Italy with a wide mix of modern and classic dishes. A little piece of 'la dolce vita' in Manchester.

CAFÉ ROUGE
French

137 The Orient, Trafford Centre, Manchester M17 8EQ
01617 471 927
An attractive restaurant, a boulevard café or a Parisian-style wine bar; however you see Café Rouge, consistently excellent classic French dishes are always guaranteed.

CAFÉ ROUGE
French

651-653 Wilmslow Rd, Didsbury, Manchester, M20 6QZ
0161 438 0444
An attractive restaurant, a boulevard café or a Parisian-style wine bar; however you see Café Rouge, consistently excellent classic French dishes are always guaranteed.

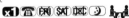

CAFÉ ROUGE
French

82-84 Deansgate, Manchester, M3 2ER
0161 839 0414
An attractive restaurant, a boulevard café or a Parisian-style wine bar; however you see Café Rouge, consistently excellent classic French dishes are always guaranteed.

CAFÉ ROUGE
French

Spinningfields, Manchester, M3 3AN
01618 390456
An attractive restaurant, a boulevard café or a Parisian-style wine bar; however you see Café Rouge, consistently excellent classic French dishes are always guaranteed.

 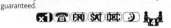

CAFÉ ROUGE
French

The Printworks, Manchester, M4 2BS
0161 832 7749
An attractive restaurant, a boulevard café or a Parisian-style wine bar; however you see Café Rouge, consistently excellent classic French dishes are always guaranteed.

 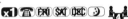

CAFÉ ROUGE
French

The Lowry Outlet Mall, Salford Quays, Manchester, M50 3AZ
0161 877 3971
An attractive restaurant, a boulevard café or a Parisian-style wine bar; however you see Café Rouge, consistently excellent classic French dishes are always guaranteed.

CHEADLE GRILL
Modern European

7A Wilmslow Rd, Heald Green, Stockport, SK8 1DW
0161 491 2915
A highly modern and stylish brasserie, truly worthy of any diner's custom, with an extensive menu that caters for all tastes. A place for quality food and drink delivered with attentive service.

CHOICE BAR & RESTAURANT
2FOR1
3 COURSES

Castle Quay, Castlefield, Manchester, M15 4NT
0161 833 3400 *Modern British*

Choice Bar & Restaurant is an independent multi award-winning modern British restaurant in the historic Castlefield area. Stunningly located inside a former spice merchant and besides the canal, Choice features a large outside seating area taking full advantage of its buzzy situation.

Choice Bar & Restaurant specialises in regional cooking, working with the North West's finest bespoke suppliers to bring a taste of the region to Manchester plates and in the process winning a place in the heart of Mancunians and those from further afield.

The menu reads like a roll call of regionally renowned produce: Lancashire black pudding, Cheshire air dried ham, Cumbrian bred beef, Lancashire beef, Lancashire cheese, Eccles cakes and Manchester breads, all make seasonal if not perennial appearances on the à la carte menus.

When booking restaurants always mention your GS membership

CHILLI CHILLI
Indian
20 Wellington Road South, Stockport, SK4 1AA
0161 476 0786
A popular restaurant serving traditional and authentic Indian cuisine that covers a range of classic dishes along with chef's specialities; serves big, filling portions and maintains great value for money.

CHILLI GRILL
Portuguese
5a Wilbraham Road, Fallowfield, M14 6JS
0161 249 3999
Popular, prized local restaurant that serves supremely tasty chargrilled meats, sizzlingly seasoned and marinated with spicy, flavour-laden sauces. Great variety, value and ambience.

CIAO BELLA
Italian
42 Portland Street, Manchester, M1 4GS
07876 260 690
Brilliant, distinctive Italian restaurant in Manchester. Chef Donato Loi serves up great dishes from family recipes; the pollo saltimbocca, for example, is wholesome, full-flavoured, rich and vibrant.

COCOTOO
Italian
57 Whitworth Street West, Manchester, M1 5WW
0161 237 5458
Stylish Italian restaurant, part of the Cabrelli group, which stands out for its superbly extensive menu and cracking quality of service. In a distinctive, striking space, enjoy the wholesome classic fare.

DESTINO'S
Italian
50 Pall Mall, Manchester, M2 1AQ
0161 832 4600
Sip on a well-deserved glass of champagne or relax and unwind over a delicious coffee in this artistically inclined restaurant. Enjoy lovingly prepared Italian cuisine al fresco in the warmer months.

DILLI
Indian
60 Stamford New Rd, Altrincham, WA14 1EE
0161 929 7484
Dilli's diners love their award-winning food that faithfully reconstitutes traditional Indian specialities. Adventurous culinary explorers will love the dishes from the regions of Chettinad and Mangalore.

 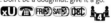 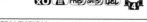 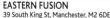

DOUGH PIZZA KITCHEN
Italian
75-77 High Street, Manchester, M4 1FS
0161 834 9411
A stylish urban pizza parlour known for being exceptionally family-friendly but also for its exceptional array of toppings, characterful ambience and cool location. Don't be a doughnut: give it a go.

EASTERN FUSION
Indian
39 South King St, Manchester, M2 6DE
0161 834 0287
A welcoming, contemporary-style Indian restaurant that balances traditional classics with newer, fusion-style dishes.

EFES RESTAURANT
Turkish
46 Princess Street, Manchester, M1 6HR
0161 236 1824
Relive your summer holidays as the home-cooked, healthy dishes are unique and as authentic as it gets. Enjoy food, live music, and belly dancers at Manchester's original Turkish and Mediterranean taverna.

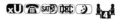

ETROP GRANGE
European
Thorley Lane, Manchester Airport, M90 4EG
0161 445 0500
In an elegant Georgian mansion, this AA Rosette-recognised restaurant serves superbly realised, fine cuisine delivered by its team of acclaimed chefs.

EVUNA
Spanish
277-279 Deansgate, Manchester, M3 4EW
0161 819 2752
Central, stylishly conceived little restaurant that serves vivid, fulsome Spanish cuisine; it has a close, cosy vibe for an intimate dinner, while also catering for large events.

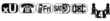

GO PIZZA
Italian
Unit 17 The Arndale, Manchester, M4 3AQ
0161 425 8225
For those with a busy lifestyle, Go delivers fast fresh food from divine pizzas to delicious baguettes, all prepared to quality standards, providing excellent value for money.

GREEN TEA RESTAURANT
Chinese
222 Burton Road, Manchester, M20 2LW
0161 445 5395
A warm and friendly Chinese eatery with genuine décor and quality authentic cuisine. The tea menu is well populated as you would imagine, with options such as goji berry and the classic green tea.

GURKHA GRILL
Nepalese
194-198 Burton Road, West Didsbury, Manchester, M20 1LH
0161 445 5444
One of Manchester's best kept secrets, where divine Nepalese and Indian cuisine can be devoured in supreme surroundings. Home-made spices are added to traditional dishes, locking in unique flavours.

HARAPPA
Indian
106 Higher Hill Gate, Stockport, SK1 3QH
0161 4776 757
Specialist chefs combine tasty and exotic dishes from across the Asian subcontinent with healthy eating in mind. Maintaining original recipes, they create delicious and nutritious dishes full of flavour.

HARDIES AT HOLIDAY INN BOLTON
International
1 Higher Bridge Street, Bolton, BL1 2EW
01204 879 988
A perfectly situated, friendly Holiday Inn. Delicious food is served all day in the sunny and airy Hardies Restaurant, from a wide-ranging buffet breakfast to succulent steak and pasta dishes.

1 card per table.

HARRY RAMSDEN'S
British

Castlemore Retail Pk, Chester Rd, M'chester, M16 0SN
0161 848 0973
Visit this national treasure and enjoy some of the finest fish and chips in the country. Harry Ramsden's continues to deliver quality food as it has always done throughout its long-running history.

Not available during August or in takeaway.

HENRY J BEANS
North American

The Printworks, Manchester, M4 2BS
0161 827 7820
A unique brand that can best be described as a typical bar and grill. Simply classic American food complemented by a vast array of beverages, all served with flair in a vibrant and lively atmosphere.

KANTIPUR
Nepalese

238 Wellington Road South, Stockport, SK2 6NW
0161 476 2688
Nepalese cuisine is growing in popularity for its distinctive flavours; this restaurant is ahead of the curve with its authentic, beautifully realised dishes that ought to tempt you into something fresh.

2FOR1
3 COURSES

KHANDOKER BRAMHALL
Indian

10 Fir Road, Stockport, SK7 2NP
0161 439 1050
Serving delicious authentic cuisine from the subcontinent to the curry faithful with a potent combination of locally sourced produce and sumptuous Indian delicacies.

2FOR1
MAIN COURSE

KHANDOKER RESTAURANT
Indian

812 Kingsway, Manchester, M20 5WY
07951 820 811
Enjoy a collection of authentic mouth-watering dishes from the Indian subcontinent, including divine, traditional delicacies. Quality food, service, and more than reasonable prices.

KITCHEN @ THE CIRCLE
British

13 Barton Arcade, Barton Square, Manchester, M3 2BB
0161 817 4921
Understated British style blends with modern luxuriousness in this attractively fashionable venue. Rustic dishes created with a contemporary edge are on offer from breakfast through to dinner.

2FOR1
MAIN COURSE

LA TASCA
Spanish

10-12 Warburton St, Didsbury, Manchester M20 6WA
0161 438 0044
La Tasca is all about terrific tapas. The 30 plus dishes that are on offer are perfect for sharing with friends and loved ones. Sip on a glass of the ever-popular sangria in wonderfully warm surroundings.

50%OFF FOOD

LAL HAWELI
Indian

68-72 Wilmslow Road, Rusholme, Manchester, M14 5AL
0161 248 9700
Situated in the heart of Manchester's famous Curry Mile, this well-established Indian restaurant serves some of the best curry around. Local and visiting curry lovers are wise to dine here.

2FOR1
MAIN COURSE

LAL QILA
Indian

123 - 127 Wilmslow Rd, Rusholme, Manchester, M14 5AN
0161 224 9999
With a profound consciousness of tradition and hospitality, Lal Qila combines a languid atmosphere with fresh, vibrant ingredients for an authentic and exciting dining experience.

2FOR1
MAIN COURSE

LAL QILA
Indian

310 Deansgate, Manchester M3 4HE
0161 839 6730
With a profound consciousness of tradition and hospitality, Lal Qila combines a languid atmosphere with fresh, vibrant ingredients for an authentic and exciting dining experience.

2FOR1
MAIN COURSE

LAMMARS
Contemporary

Fourways House, 57 Hilton St, Manchester, M1 2EJ
0161 237 9058
Brilliantly located in the city's trendy Northern Quarter, this award-winning bar and restaurant is chic, stylish, and guarantees a fun night out. The tapas is extremely popular with regular diners.

2FOR1
MAIN COURSE

LAST MONSOON
Indian

54 King Street West, Stockport, SK3 0DT
0161 476 4266
A unique fusion of Eastern cuisine from Bangladesh, India and Nepal along with some select European dishes for the less adventurous, prepared with new recipes and traditional cooking techniques.

2FOR1
2 COURSES

LEONIS LATIN CELLAR
Italian

Bow Lane, Manchester, M2 4FW
0161 835 1254
Classic, earthy Italian flavours combine with the vibrancy and zest of contemporary Latin American food in a bright, lively and welcoming environment.

2FOR1
3 COURSES

LEZZET RESTAURANT
Turkish

37 St Petersgate, Stockport, SK1 1DH
0161 480 7013
A taste experience from the diverse cuisine of Turkey. Fresh, locally sourced produce meets with Middle Eastern flair, creating exquisite dishes that evoke the exoticism of this captivating culture.

2FOR1
3 COURSES

LIME
European

The Lowry Plaza, Salford Quays, Manchester, M50 3AG
0161 869 0440
A stunning bar-restaurant renowned for its buzzing atmosphere. Sited opposite the Lowry Theatre, the large outdoor space is popular in summer, whilst the irresistible menu attracts diners all year round.

25%OFF TOTAL

LOCH FYNE
Seafood

848 Wilmslow Rd, Didsbury, Manchester, M20 2RN
0161 446 4190
From the roadside oyster bar that once was, Loch Fyne restaurants now successfully inject energy and passion into great food and wonderful flavours, whilst ensuring their seafood is sustainably sourced.

25%OFF TOTAL

Enjoy massive leisure and retail savings with more Gourmet Society

LOUNGE TEN — *French*
10 Tib Lane, Manchester, M2 4JB
0161 834 1331
Glamorous decadence too good to feel guilty about. Reminiscent of the late 19th century Parisian nightclubs, Lounge 10 offers luxurious furnishings and delicious French cuisine.

LUSO — *Portuguese*
63 Bridge St, Manchester, M3 3BQ
0161 839 5550
Luso's menu keeps pace with the seasons and comprises a range of flavourful dishes that reflect the global reach and variations of Portuguese-influenced cuisine. A bright, unfussy and stylish ambience.

MALMAISON — *European*
Piccadilly, Manchester, M1 1LZ
0161 278 1000
Sensational décor evokes memories of the 19th century Parisian Moulin Rouge. Step inside expecting to find luxurious furnishings, a mouth-watering menu and unforgettable charm. 1 AA rosette.

MANGO'S CAFE BAR — *Caribbean*
642 Oldham Rd, Failsworth, Manchester, M35 9DU
0161 684 9958
A new restaurant in Failsworth where you can settle in for some good old-fashioned jerk chicken, or a top rice and peas. The place has an open, welcoming vibe and the food is tasty, filling and no-nonsense.

NEW

MOËT RESTAURANT & BAR — *Modern European*
Selfridges, Exchange Square, Manchester, M3 1BD
0161 838 0540
Super-stylish, chic, city-centre champagne bar where you can enjoy that splash of sophistication and simply to watch the world go by.

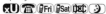

MOSS NOOK RESTAURANT — *Modern British*
Ringway Rd, Moss Nook, Manchester, M22 5NA
0161 437 4778
Divine British classic dishes make up an award-winning menu at The Moss Nook. Friendly staff ensure every guest is well accommodated for at this AA Rosette venue, upholding their outstanding reputation.

2FOR1 2 COURSES

MUGHLI — *Indian*
28-32 Wilmslow Road, Rusholme, Manchester, M15 5TQ
0161 248 0900
At the heart of Manchester's famous Curry Mile has an outstanding reputation for mouth-watering dishes, signature karahi sauce and family management that upholds true quality and service.

25%OFF TOTAL

NEW HONG KONG — *Chinese*
47 Faulkner St, Manchester, M1 4EE
0161 236 0565
One of the original Chinese restaurants around which Manchester's popular hotspot Chinatown has grown. Situated next to the Chinese arch, this restaurant values its admirable location and reputation.

2FOR1 MAIN COURSE

NEW SAMSI — *Japanese*
38 Whitworth St, Manchester, M1 3NR
0161 279 0022
A well-established Japanese restaurant widely recognised for its outstanding cuisine. The menu successfully encompasses dishes from every region of Japan at affordable prices.

O BAR AND GRILL — *British*
The Printworks, Manchester, M4 2BS
0161 834 2414
Situated within an exciting entertainment venue in the heart of the city and focusing on delivering outstanding food, the kitchen here offers great quality burgers, salads, and everything in between.

2FOR1 3 COURSES

OCA RESTAURANT — *Pizza*
Waterside Plaza, Sale, M33 7BS
0161 962 6666
Desirable gourmet pizza to be devoured in contemporary surroundings. Diners can enjoy the waterside location whatever the weather, due to the lovely covered and uncovered al fresco areas.

2FOR1 MAIN COURSE

OKRA AT HOLIDAY INN MCR. WEST — *Pan Asian*
Liverpool St, Salford, Manchester, M5 4LT
0161 743 0080
Situated in the pleasant Holiday Inn, guests will enjoy the contemporary feel of the restaurant and the fine food on offer. European and pan-Asian cuisine is complemented by a fantastic selection of wines.

25%OFF TOTAL

OLD ORLEANS — *American*
The Printworks, Manchester, M4 2BS
0161 839 4430
An extraordinarily accurate taste of the Deep South can be found in this unique restaurant. The kitchen deals in classic Louisiana and Cajun recipes such as jambalaya and gumbo to create an exciting menu.

2FOR1 MAIN COURSE
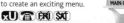

Not available on Bank Holiday weekends. Adult menu only.

OLIVERS RESTAURANT — *Modern British*
547 Chester Road, Woodford, Stockport, SK7 1PR
0161 440 8715
Locally sourced ingredients are beautifully cooked and presented in this phenomenal independent restaurant. High levels of passion and talent go into every order.

25%OFF TOTAL

PACIFICA-CANTONESE — *Chinese*
5-7 Church Road, Eccles, M30 0DL
0161 707 8828
A well-regarded Cantonese restaurant serving eclectic, authentic dishes that range farther afield than usually seen in England; stylish, sassy and with flavours to savour.

PASSAGE TO INDIA — *Indian*
168 Monton Road, Monton, M30 9GA
0161 787 7546
Whether you want the comfort of your favourite Indian dish or you want to try something a little bit different, this superbly luxurious restaurant will cater for you.

2FOR1 2 COURSES

NORTH WEST

261

PERUGA AT WOODHEYS
European

Glossop Road, Marple Bridge, Stockport, SK6 5RX
01457 852 704
Tasty, wholesome, honest food, from beer-battered fish with hand cut chips to pan-fried English fillet steak. An extensive menu with options to suit all tastes and preferences.

2FOR1
MAIN COURSE

PROHIBITION
British

2 -10 St.Mary's Street, Manchester, M3 2LB
0161 831 9326
Offering everything you'll need for a great evening. The finest cuts of seasoned beef make the finest burgers, while the impressive cocktail list will have you wanting to sample them all.

2FOR1
2 COURSES

SANGAM CHEADLE
Indian

202 Wilmslow Rd, Heald Green, Stockport, SK8 3BH
0161 436 8809
One of the two successful Sangam restaurants situated in Manchester. Popular for its delicious Indian cuisine and courteous service, guests will undoubtedly leave with an eye on their return.

2FOR1
MAIN COURSE

POTTERS
British

114 The Orient, Trafford Centre, Manchester, M17 8EH
0161 746 8629
Take a break and enjoy a dish from a menu of timeless British food. Something for the whole family, including a fantastic kids menu. Great food in relaxed and comfortable surroundings.

50%OFF
FOOD

SANGAM DIDSBURY
Indian

762 Wilmslow Rd, Didsbury, Manchester, M20 2DR
0161 446 1155
Sangam Didsbury is every bit as attractive as its sister restaurant. Popular for its delicious Indian cuisine and courteous service, guests will undoubtedly leave desiring to return.

2FOR1
MAIN COURSE

PRIDE OF BENGAL
Indian

2 George Lane, Bredbury, Stockport, SK6 1AS
0161 406 6451
Loyal customers travel far and wide to taste the famous pepsilla, or the tasty chicken simla. Indian cuisine is served by a friendly team of staff, who are happy to help you choose from the menu.

2FOR1
MAIN COURSE

SHAHI MASALA
Indian

16-18 Wilmslow Road, Rusholme, Manchester, M14 5TQ
0161 248 8344
Situated in the heart of Manchester's famous Curry Mile, this Indian restaurant has quickly earned its reputation for being spectacular. Mild or spicy, sweet or savoury, here you'll find it all.

25%OFF
TOTAL

STOCK

50%OFF
FOOD

The Stock Exchange, 4 Norfolk St, Manchester, M2 1DW
0161 839 6644 *Italian*

Housed within the Edwardian splendour of Manchester's former Stock Exchange, Stock has rapidly become renowned as the city's premier Italian Restaurant.

Presiding over the kitchen is executive chef and founder Enzo Mauro. Insisting on using only the finest and freshest ingredients, Enzo delivers his own inimitable style of Italian cuisine to the appreciative diners.

From classic anti pasta and home-made gnocchi to the now legendary steak Fiorentina and mixed seafood platter, this is food at its best. The menu at Stock is complemented by an abundance of market fresh specials and vegetarian delights, ensuring that all comers are well catered for.

On regular evenings, the sounds of jazz mix with the lively atmosphere to conjure up an ebullient atmosphere and deliver not just a memorable meal but a complete night out.

Combined with the award winning wines and warm and friendly service, the Stock experience is quite simply outstanding.

SIAM ORCHID
Thai

54 Portland Street, Manchester, M1 4QU
01612 361 388
One of Manchester's first Thai restaurants. Cosy and intimate, here you can enjoy scrumptious cuisine in calm and relaxed settings. Alternatively head to the bar which boasts full karaoke facilities.

STRESA
Italian

Ramada Salford Quays, Trafford Rd, M'chester, M5 3AW
0161 941 5305
The ideal location for business lunches, match-day meals and pre-theatre dinners. Chefs create rustic Italian favourites and innovative dishes from a huge selection meat, fish and vegetarian choices.

MORE RESTAURANTS ONLINE
www.gourmetsociety.co.uk

SWADESH BOWDON
Indian

3 Richmond Rd, Bowdon, Altrincham, WA14 2TT
0161 941 5311
Sister restaurant to the Swadesh Manchester, this exclusive Indian restaurant offers vibrant cuisine in a stunningly furnished interior. Treasured ancient recipes provide deliciously authentic dishes.

SWADESH MANCHESTER
Indian

98 Portland St, Manchester, M1 4GY
0161 236 1313
Sister restaurant to Swadesh Bowden, this exclusive Indian restaurant offers vibrant cuisine in the very heart of the city. Treasured ancient recipes provide deliciously authentic dishes.

TAPS BAR AND RESTAURANT
Flemish

1 Gt Northern Tower, Watson St., Manchester, M3 4EE
0161 819 5167
Serve draught beer with your very own table-pump system. Accompanied by hearty Flemish cuisine, Taps is a unique drinking and dining experience.

TERRACE AT HOLIDAY INN MCR AIRPORT
International

Altrincham Road, Manchester, SK9 4LR
01625 889 988
Choose the smart Holiday Inn Manchester Airport hotel in a country setting, minutes from Manchester Airport, with a restaurant that delivers a variety of dining options to suit all tastes and budgets.

1 card per table.

THE DINING ROOMS
British

Worsley Park Hotel, Walkden Road, Worsley, M28 7DY
0161 975 2000
Enter The Dining Rooms to find a lavish, lively and well-lit setting where you can enjoy well-prepared food. Relax over pre and post dinner drinks in the chic and stylish Chimney Bar.

THE FAIRFIELD ARMS
Modern British

92 Manchester Road, Audenshaw, M34 5GB
0161 371 1331
Part of the Best of British group, the impressive red-brick façade of this pub restaurant opens up to a welcoming, yet elegant, Victorian dining space. Its fulsome, hearty pub food is a treat.

THE FAT LOAF
British

844-846 Wilmslow Rd, Didsbury, Manchester, M20 2RN
0161 438 0319
In a building of great character and style, this venue delivers a menu of huge variety produced by well-established chefs. Also houses an impressive bar with several draught beer and ales available.

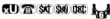

THE FAT LOAF
Modern British

62 Green Lane, Sale, M33 5PG
0161 972 0397
A little gem loved by the local community for its modest pricing and rigorous attention to locally-sourced, seasonal produce. The Fat Loaf has been long been seen as a fantastic restaurant to dine at.

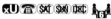

THE FAT LOAF
Modern British

28 - 32 Greenwood Street, Altrincham, WA14 1RZ
0161 929 6700
Growing in reputation for, good honest, seasonal food at a reasonable price, this second Fat Loaf Restaurant delivers a strong traditional British flavour with old favourites next to more modern dishes.

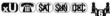

RECOMMEND A FRIEND
see page 18

THE HALE KITCHEN
British

149 Ashley Road, Altrincham, WA14 2UW
0161 926 4670
A charming, traditional menu of the best seasonal and local produce. With a relaxing atmosphere and a touch of glamour you can enjoy a meal or simply relax, sampling the eclectic range of drinks.

THE LIVING ROOM
British

80 Deansgate, Manchester, M3 2ER
0161 832 0083
Step into The Living Room and you can count on the savvy, distinctive neighbourhood vibe that plays home to eclectically drawn, supremely tasty cuisine. A chic and lofty, laid-back feel here in Manchester.

Must purchase min 3 courses pp, inc. main.

THE MARKET RESTAURANT
Modern British

104 High Street, Manchester, M4 1HQ
0161 834 3743
Situated in a trendy and cosmopolitan part of the city, the inside of this well-established restaurant is homely and welcoming. Local speciality dishes and scrumptious desserts make it a must.

263

THE ROEBUCK
Traditional English

Church Road, Flixton, Manchester, M41 6HD
0161 748 4046
The Roebuck is a classic British pub in Flixton, recently refurbished but maintaining its traditional character, and a great place to settle in for a drink or a bite to eat from the broad menu of old favourites.

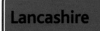
Lancashire

NORTHERN QUARTER RESTAURANT
Modern British

108 High Street, Manchester, M4 1HQ
0161 832 7115
Dine in the heart of Manchester's famous Northern Quarter. Characteristic of the area itself, this fabulous restaurant offers fulsome, fresh food and boasts an attractively vibrant atmosphere.

1725
Spanish

28 Market Street, Lancaster, LA1 1HT
01524 66898
Deliciously fresh, home-made tapas to be enjoyed with cask ales, choice wine, and continental lagers, all in one of Lancaster's oldest buildings. Open all week with a lunch, evening and tapas menu.

THE OLD RECTORY HOTEL
British

Meadow Lane, Haughton Green, Denton, M34 7GD
0161 336 7516
Outstanding classic English cuisine served at a well-regarded restaurant which holds a continually flourishing reputation. Relax and dine in the most refined style.

AJ'S BISTRO
British

65 Topping Street, Blackpool, FY1 3AF
01253 626 111
A step aside from typical seaside fare, AJ's bistro serves filling dishes of full-throated flavour, from its fresh and refulgent seafood assiette to its lustrous, succulent steaks of various cuts.

TIGER TIGER
British

The Printworks, Manchester, M4 2BS
0161 385 8080
A great place to drink and dine from lunch until late. Choose from one of the many differently themed bars, or dine in the stylish contemporary restaurant where the menu ranges from steaks to salads

ASHFIELD BISTRO
Bistro

Bispham Campus, Ashfield Rd, Blackpool, FY2 0HP
01253 356 127
Stylish bistro food prepared by talented chefs-in-training and served to you in a cool, lovely dining space overlooking Morecambe bay. Quality coffees, melt-in-the-mouth pastries and a top light lunch.

YABA AFRICAN RESTAURANT
African

110 Hulme High Street, Manchester, M15 5JP
0161 226 6998
You're due a cracking experience in this imaginative, thoughtful restaurant that serves brilliant authentic Caribbean and African cuisine; a truly welcoming, unique place to eat.

BANGLA FUSION
Asian Fusion

Edenfield Road, Nordon, Rochdale, OL12 7TY
01706 345 345
Countless delights fill the menu at this comfortable restaurant and wine bar. Sea bass, red snapper, and the incredibly popular 'fusion duck' are all highly recommended.

DETAILED DESCRIPTIONS AVAILABLE ON
www.gourmetsociety.co.uk

BANGLA FUSION
Bangladeshi/ Indian

Liverpool Old Road, Preston, PR4 5JQ
01772 610 800
A plush dining space opens up invitingly at this fusion restaurant near Preston, whose array of dishes draw on an innovative and eclectic range of flavours from across the Eastern and Western canons.

ZAIKA
Indian

2 Gt Northern Tower, Watson St, Manchester, M3 4EE
0161 839 5111
Sensational cuisine that will have your mouth watering as soon as you enter. A thoroughly extensive menu, offering food from the homes of regional gourmet families and Maharaja's areas.

BLACK LANE ENDS TAVERN
British

Skipton Old Road, Colne, BB8 7EP
01282 863 070
A true country pub with a strong following of locals and frequent visitors. Experience a warm welcome, home-cooked food, real ales and much more at this traditional and friendly venue.

ZOUK
Indian

Unit 5 Quadrangle, Chester St, Manchester, M1 5QS
0161 233 1090
A popular restaurant in the heart of the city. Boasting an extensive menu, Zouk brings to the table excellent meat dishes cooked in an authentic manner, as well as traditional dishes from Balochistan.

BURLINGTON DINING ROOMS
Bistro

502 Garstang Rd, Broughton, Preston, PR6 8NA
01772 863 424
Cosy and elegant, smart and relaxed, Burlingtons serves classic, seasoned and savoury dishes from a menu that Head Chef Stuart Kennedy keeps on its toes with great selections from fresh, local produce.

Discounted hotel rates for GS members on our website

BURLINGTONS CAFE
Bistro
9-10 Cheapside, Preston, PR1 2AP
01772 563 350
Cosy and elegant, smart and relaxed, Burlingtons serves classic, seasoned and savoury dishes from a menu that Head Chef Stuart Kennedy keeps on its toes with great selections from fresh, local produce.

CINNAMON
Indian
487 Preston Road, Standish, WN6 0QD
01257 426 661
The fine, fresh ingredients on which Cinnamon prides itself can be discerned in the restaurant's range of distinctive, flavourful dishes.

CASCADES
English and Continental
80 Dickson Road, Blackpool, FY1 2BU
01253 624 947
Cascades' meals are something quite special. Imaginatively conceived, skilfully prepared and beautifully presented, they raise a smile even before your first bite.

COURTFIELD RESTAURANT
Fine Dining
Bispham Campus, Ashfield Rd, Blackpool, FY2 OHP
01253 356 127
Fine dining prepared by chefs-in-training. Support these talented young chefs while savouring the exceptional quality and fresh ideas that go into their menus here. A relaxed feel and a superb price.

FIVEWAYS
Carvery
County Road, Ormskirk, L39 1NN
01695 579 755
One of the many Great British Carveries where a modern twist is placed on the well-loved classic dish. Enjoy the best of British food in this charmingly modern pub that is a winner with the locals.

Call before special event days.

FRESCA ITALIAN RESTAURANT
Italian
Gatehead Buss Pk, Delph New Rd, Oldham, OL3 5DE
01457 870 797
For a sophisticated dining experience, head to Fresca. A vibrant, fun-filled atmosphere is enhanced by the theatrical pleasure of the open kitchen. Children and special occasions are well catered for.

FRESCO FRESCO
Italian
29-31 Town Road, Croston, PR26 9RA
01772 601 100
Fresh by name, fresh by... By focusing on the quality of its produce, grown to order by a market gardener family friend, this Italian restaurant charms and delights with exuberantly tasty dishes.

FUSION ROOM
British
80 Friargate, Preston, PR1 2ED
01772 880 180
An exceptional selection of modern British food with an Eastern twist created by a young, energetic team with passion, experience and the skills needed to produce a fantastic dining experience.

GER-HANA
Mongolian
411 Blackburn Road, Oswaldtwistle, Accrington, BB5 4NA
01254 396 777
Insuperable flavours from the lamentably neglected Mongolian culinary tradition. Down-to-earth, juicy meats and vegetables, spiced and flavoured with incense while you watch.

HARE & HOUNDS
Modern British
400 Bolton Road West, Holcombe, BL0 9RY
01706 822 107
A stand-out pub in a picturesque village, where beers are as flavourful, deep and rich as its excellent pub grub. Part of the Best of British group, this highly individual pub comes strongly recommended.

Must purchase min 2 courses.

HARRY RAMSDEN'S
British
60-63 Promenade, Blackpool, FY1 4QU
01253 294 386
World-famous fish and chips from a British institution. Revel in classic seaside food: from crisp batter to golden chips, nobody does it quite like Harry Ramsden's.

Not available during August or in takeaway.

INDIAN OCEAN
Indian
Stamford Street East, Ashton Under Lyne, OL6 6QH
01613 433 343
This dining experience extends beyond a simple meal. Enjoy drinks in their spacious bar before or after your delicious food, that includes a blend of traditional recipes and British classics.

INSIDEOUT
British
100 Higher Walton Road, Preston, PR5 4HR
0177 225 1366
Award-winning chef Mark Wilkinson cooks and prepares divine dishes from a menu that is liberally sprinkled with variety, changing daily and embracing different national and cultural influences.

JALI FINE INDIAN DINING
Indian
286 North Promenade, Blackpool, FY1 2EZ
01253 622 223
Awarded an AA Rosette for its excellence, this fantastic Indian restaurant is dedicated to providing authentic cuisine from across the subcontinent. Rarely seen Indian delicacies are on offer.

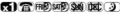

JOLLY CROFTERS
Modern British
Chorley Old Road, Horwich, BL6 6RE
01204 696 885
On the cusp of the striding Pennine moors, this pub is just the place for a post-yomp pint and replenishing dinner. Part of the Best of British group, the food includes a popular, finely done daily roast.

KING KARAI
Indian
28-30 Watery Lane, Preston, PR2 2NN
0177 273 6838
Experience an authentic North Indian meal in a venue with a great reputation, safe in the knowledge that the food will be flavoursome and made to perfection.

MADISONS RESTAURANT
British

St Mary's Gate, Rochdale, OL16 1DZ
01706 346 990
Ideally situated in the centre of Rochdale, Madisons offers an intimate, atmospheric environment, perfect for smaller parties, as well as private dining areas for the larger occasion.

 25%OFF TOTAL

MAMMA MIA AT CROSSWAYS
Italian

Whalley Road, Burnley, BB12 8JR
01282 772 170
A top-quality restaurant serving fine Italian cuisine, complete with an on-site take away so guests can enjoy fresh culinary delights in their own home. Enjoy the beautiful terrace for al fresco dining.

 2FOR1 MAIN COURSE

MANGIAMO
Italian

108 Bolton Road, Darwen, BB3 1BZ
01254 760 770
A cosy, charismatic ambience to this Italian ristorante provides a fit setting for its ranging menu of earthy, flavourful traditional recipes. Look out for the specials nights.

2FOR1 3COURSES

PIPERS RESTAURANT
British

46-47 High Street, Garstang, Preston, PR3 1EA
01995 606 665
A beautiful restaurant with a warm, cottage feel, serving devilishly tasty food. Boasts delicious dishes made from local produce with a variety of ingredients being of Fair Trade origin.

2FOR1 3COURSES

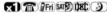

PROSECCO RISTORANTE
Italian

63 Bradshawgate, Bolton, BL1 1QD
01204 363 636
For a true Italian experience in England, visit Prosecco. A popular local restaurant where the very best dishes can be found, such as the vitello al marsala, which offers tender veal in a sumptuous sauce.

25%OFF TOTAL

QUITE SIMPLY FRENCH
French

27a St George's Quay, Lancaster, LA1 1RD
01524 843 199
Committing itself to its name, this restaurant has an ever-changing menu bursting with magnificent French dishes for you to devour. Lobster fans can take their pick from the live in-house tank.

2FOR1 MAIN COURSE

Offer excludes Monday special offer.

RBG @ PARK INN LEIGH
Modern European

Park Inn, Sale Way, Leigh Sports Village, WN7 4JY
01942 366 334
Step inside the comfortable and well-located Park Inn to find an outstanding bar and grill, where great food can be enjoyed. A delicious menu offers classic steaks and gourmet burgers.

25%OFF TOTAL

RELISH TAPAS @ THE GROTTON
Spanish

Oldham Rd, Grotton, Oldham, OL4 5SE
0161 624 2376
A delightful restaurant serving high-quality dishes at outstanding prices. Guests will find an impressive menu that offers everything from hot braised beef sandwiches to wild boar and real ale sausages.

25%OFF TOTAL

RETREAT RESTAURANT
British

319-321 Chorley New Road, Bolton, BL1 5BP
01204 849 313
Delicate fish that will melt in your mouth and hearty chargrilled steaks make this a perfect place to dine. A calming atmosphere ensures every guest has a relaxing dining experience.

 2FOR1 3COURSES

RUFFORD ARMS HOTEL
British

380 Liverpool Road, Rufford, L40 1SQ
01704 822 040
Placing its emphasis on contemporary English-style cuisine, served smartly and creatively for a fulsome, savoury and delicious meal, this restaurant is beautifully set, with a welcoming ambience.

 25%OFF TOTAL

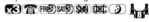

SPICE LOUNGE
Indian

Wilpshire Road, Blackburn, BB1 4AD
01254 247 583
The rich vibrancy of India is captured as chefs produce refined and creative Indian food. The menu incorporates classic favourites and new dishes that apply eastern flavours with a Western touch.

2FOR1 3COURSES

SUHAG SPICE LOUNGE
Indian

185 Yorkshire Street, Rochdale, OL12 0DR
01706 643 187
Distinctive Indian restaurant in Rochdale that serves fresh and extremely flavourful dishes - deep, aromatic sauces; sweet, smoky or spice-laden marinades - with exceptional, attentive service.

2FOR1 2COURSES

SYKESIDE COUNTRY HOUSE HOTEL
British

Rawtenstall Road End, Haslingden, BB4 6QE
01706 831 163
Charming traditional hotel-based restaurant which serves a ranging menu of warming, delicious dishes; combined with the cosy and genial atmosphere, it's a place really to savour.

2FOR1 3COURSES

THE ASSHETON ARMS
European

Downham, Clitheroe, BB7 4BJ
01200 441 227
Situated in a beautiful village in the Ribble Valley, this pub offers an exceptional selection of mouth-watering food to suit all tastes. Seafood lovers will adore the wide range of fish on offer.

 25%OFF TOTAL

THE BEACON AT DALTON
English and Continental

Beacon Lane, Dalton, Wigan, WN8 7RR
01695 622 771
Acclaimed Lancashire pub restaurant whose dining room is light and breezy and whose food, ranging from pub grub to the contemporary à la carte menu, is smart, bright and fulsome in its flavours.

2FOR1 3COURSES

THE BLACK BULL COUNTRY INN
French

Rimington Lane, Rimington, BB7 4DS
01200 415 960
In a countryside inn at the foot of Pendle Hill, you'll enjoy the delicious juxtaposition of a menu that isn't all English pub fare, but instead serves rich, tasty and beautifully executed French cuisine.

 2FOR1 MAIN COURSE

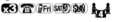

Gourmet Society discount applies to the à la carte menu

THE CARTLAND AT BEDFORD HOTEL
English and Continental
307-313 Clifton Drive Sth, Lytham St Annes, FY8 1HN
01253 724 636
This hotel restaurant is designed to serve the needs of The Bedford's guests; as a result, its superb, homely food is also exceptionally appealing for visiting diners. Absolutely worth a try.

MORTIMER'S
Modern Pub
34-45 King Street, Wigan, WN1 1BT
01942 824 180
Mortimers is a cracking pub in the heart of Wigan which is great for a night out, to watch a match, and also to get some good old fashioned, satisfying pub food at a great price.

(NEW)

THE FENWICK
Modern Pub
The Fenwick, Lancaster Road, Claughton, LA2 9LA
01524 222 298
With a kitchen headed by highly regarded chef Michael Weston-Cole, this retreat of a pub restaurant serves a broad range of classics: burgers, steaks, and imaginative, resoundingly good sharing platters.

THE FOX INN BISTRO
Bistro
Roby Mill Village, Upholland, Wigan, WN8 0QF
01695 622 449
Proudly independent country inn with a sense of fun to go with their high standards of preparation and presentation. The food is fresh, wholesome and unpretentious, the ambience open and inviting.

THE GOLDEN FLEECE
British
41 Oldham Road, Denshaw, Saddleworth, OL3 5SS
01457 874 910
Warm and welcoming pub providing customers with traditional British cuisine. Relaxed atmosphere, with menu and bar facilities to cater for all.

2FOR1 2 COURSES

THE GREYHOUND
British
Sporting Lodge Inns, Warrington Road, Leigh, WN7 3XQ
01942 671 256
Diverse and eclectic dishes in this hotel-restaurant in Leigh. Priding themselves on warmth of welcome and classic, hearty fare. If you're after a good evening you can be sure to find it at The Greyhound.

2FOR1 MAIN COURSE

THE PLOUGH
Modern Pub
Plough Inn, Main Road, Galgate, LA2 0LQ
01524 751 337
From a steak and stout pie to a Chinese chicken salad, The Plough serves smart, eclectic dishes in a warm and accommodating ambience, aiming for the feel of a local for locals and non-locals alike.

THE PUNCHBOWL
Modern Pub
5-9 Church Street, Churchtown, Preston, PR3 0HT
01995 603 360
From a Fylde sausage to a Thai-spiced monkfish fillet, The Punchbowl serves smart, eclectic dishes in a warm and accommodating ambience, aiming for the feel of a local for locals and non-locals alike.

THE ROEBUCK INN
European
Brighton Road, Strinesdale, Oldham, OL4 3RB
0161 624 7819
In this charming West Yorkshire inn just near Strinesdale reservoir you'll enjoy a superb array of menus filled with classic pub-style fare, of an especial sophistication and quality.

THE WATERSIDE RESTAURANT
Mediterranean
1 Inghams lane, Littleborough, Rochdale, OL15 0AY
01706 376 250
The chef's passion for food can be fully tasted in the deliciousness of all the dishes on offer. Drawing produce from each Mediterranean country, the food here captures the intense flavour of the region.

2FOR1 2 COURSES
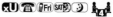

THE WHITEHALL HOTEL
British
MJs Restaurant, Ross Street, Darwen, BB3 2JU
01254 704 986
A majestic Victorian manor house lovingly transformed into a traditional country house hotel. Sit back and relax in the beautifully adorned interior, or explore the exquisitely landscaped gardens.

THE WOODMAN INN
British
129 Todmorden Road, Burnley, BB11 3EX
01282 422 715
Charismatic, historical Lancashire pub with a great local reputation for its food, cosy atmosphere, and all the trimmings. A local pub run with a personal touch that's certainly not just for local people.

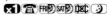

THYME AT THE SIRLOIN INN
British
Station Road, Houghton, Preston, PR5 0DD
01254 852 293
Award-winning restaurant serving traditional Lancashire dishes; here you will find an ever-changing menu as the kitchen consciously maintains best use of fine local produce.

2FOR1 2 COURSES

TOAST CAFE BAR & GRILL
Mediterranean
28 Corporation Street, Blackpool, FY1 1EJ
05603 111 758
Beautifully presented food, created fresh from high-quality ingredients. A perfect place for relaxing, dining and drinking in the heart of Blackpool.

2FOR1 MAIN COURSE

TRADERS BRASSERIE
Brasserie
Traders, The Globe Centre, Accrington, BB5 0RE
01254 602 022
Support the talented chefs of the future at this elegant contemporary restaurant. Wonderful dishes are prepared by chefs-in-training, guaranteeing guests a first-class dining experience.

2FOR1 MAIN COURSE

VARDONS AT SHAW HILL HOTEL
Fine Dining
Whittle le Woods, Preston Road, PR6 7PP
01257 269 221
Situated in a splendid Georgian mansion, Vardon's offers you award-winning dishes in the most delightful of settings. Look out over the golf course as your culinary delight is prepared.

VIVA ESPANA
Tapas
12 Winter Hey Road, Horwich, BL6 7AA
01204 438 235
A brilliantly welcoming little slice of Spain in Horwich. For a cosy, intimate setting, look no further than Viva Espana, where freshly prepared, Murcia-inspired tapas dishes are readily available.

VOUJON
Indian
688-692 Manchester Road, Oldham, OL9 7ST
0161 682 4600
Experience a little piece of India in Lancashire, with a combination of classic Indian dishes and less well-known specialities guaranteed to enthral your taste buds. A must-visit restaurant.

Merseyside

ACADEMY RESTAURANT
Modern European
Tradewind Square, Duke Street, Liverpool, L1 5BG
0151 252 4512
Support the talented chefs of the future at this terrific college restaurant. Wonderful dishes are prepared by chefs-in-training, guaranteeing guests a first-class dining experience.

Closed during the summer break.

AGRA FORT
Indian
Agra House, Cambridge Rd, Ellesmere Port, CH65 4AE
01513 551 516
The first stop for genuine Indian cuisine with a range of aromatic and spice-infused food to suit every palate. Every dish is created with quality, classic ingredients for that truly authentic taste.

ANDERSONS BAR
International
26 Exchange Street East, Liverpool, L2 3PH
01512 431 330
A contemporary bar serving fresh food made to order. Mediterranean delights range from scrumptious pasta to a wide selection of tapas dishes, whilst smaller appetites are also catered for.

BELLA ITALIA
Italian
39 Ranelagh Street, Liverpool, L1 1JP
0151 707 2121
Inspiring Italian cuisine available for breakfast through until dinner. Enjoy an aromatic cappuccino, a delicious panini or a mouth-watering evening meal and allow yourself to live 'la dolce vita'.

BRITANNIA SPICE
Indian
18-19 The Parade, Parkgate, Neston, CH64 6SA
0151 336 1774
Boasting dishes from across the subcontinent, Britannia Spice is a classic Indian restaurant serving good quality, spice-laden and taste-drenched dishes.

BURNING KITCHEN
Modern British
The Ship & Mitre, 133 Dale Street, Liverpool, L2 2JH
07794 287 549
Open, imaginative restaurant that cultivates both its dishes and its ambience with pleasure and care. Its array of gourmet burgers are a quiet concert; its menus are versatile, fresh and full of flavour.

CAFÉ ROUGE
French
Upper Floor, The Met Quarter, Liverpool, L1 6AU
0151 258 1879
An attractive restaurant, a boulevard café or a Parisian-style wine bar; however you see Café Rouge, consistently excellent classic French dishes are always guaranteed.

CAFÉ ROUGE
French
14 Paradise Street, Liverpool, L1 8JF
01517 098 657
An attractive restaurant, a boulevard café or a Parisian-style wine bar; however you see Café Rouge, consistently excellent classic French dishes are always guaranteed.

CAFE SEKANDER
Indian
156 Allerton Road, Liverpool, L18 6HG
0151 724 4300
If you're hungry for curry then head to Café Sekander for exciting culinary delights. Efficient and friendly staff are more than happy to cater to your every need.

CAFE SPORTS ENGLAND
Modern British
42-46 Stanley Street, Liverpool, L1 6AL
0151 239 5070
Family friendly café offering wholesome food for all to enjoy. Casual and informal style dining that is perfect for a family evening meal out out.

Offer not available on Liverpool game nights.

CASA MIA
Italian
1 Grange Road, West Kirby, CH48 4DY
0151 625 1503
A glowing restaurant specialising in lavish Italian cuisine. A brilliantly friendly atmosphere in which great food and wonderful wines can be enjoyed.

CHINA RESTAURANT
Chinese
85 Eastbank Street, Southport, PR8 1DG
01704 548 972
Classic, accomplished local Chinese restaurant generating dishes with a depth of flavour, and an atmosphere that is calm, collected and accommodating.

CHINESE DELIGHT
Chinese
98 South Road, Waterloo, Liverpool, L22 0LY
0151 920 8887
Scrumptious traditional Chinese dishes can be enjoyed in stylish, relaxed surroundings. Reasonably priced meals make this an excellent place to dine with family and friends.

Sign up to our newsletter for latest restaurants, offers and more

CHIQUITO
Mexican
11 Coliseum Way, Cheshire Oaks, Ellesmere Port, CH65 9JJ
0151 348 8510
Straight-up and -down, hearty and flavourful Mexican food in a vibrant, buzzy environment; bright and vivacious Latin American music completes the effect.

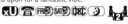

CHRISTAKIS GREEK TAVERNA
Greek
7 York Street , Liverpool, L1 5BN
0151 708 7377
Buzzing, informal taverna in Liverpool. This popular haunt serves some sumptuous, tender, herby Greek classics, features some great live entertainment, and can be relied upon for a fantastic vibe.

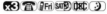

CINNAMON BAR & LOUNGE
Modern British
13-17 Scarisbrick Avenue, Southport, PR8 INN
01704 536 926
This friendly and relaxed bar and lounge offer the perfect place meet, eat, dine and relax. The contemporary cuisine and town centre location offers diners a wonderful experience without exception.

2FOR1
MAIN COURSE

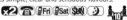

DA CAPO
Mediterranean
Lombard Chambers, Bixteth Street, Liverpool, L3 9NG
0151 236 1881
Enjoy the warmth of Mediterranean cuisine on offer at Da Capo. Perfectly situated, stylishly adorned and with a profound investment in freshness and the quality of its simple, clear and sensuous flavours.

RECOMMEND A FRIEND
see page 18

EL NINO
Spanish
117-119 South Road, Liverpool, L22 0LT
0151 928 4630
El Nino pride themselves on the quality of their food and wines, but most of all on the diligent service and value for money provided to customers. A Spanish experience to be remembered.

ELUDE
European
13-15 Porter St, Docklands, Liverpool, L3 7BL
0151 227 3882
With rich roots in Liverpool's monumental legacy of popular music, this characterful restaurant serves contemporary European dishes prepared from a careful choice of quality produce.

2FOR1
3 COURSES

GALA LEO CASINO
Modern British
44 Chaloner Street, Liverpool, L3 4BF
0151 709 8878
Next to the world famous Albert Dock within the Gala Leo Casino, this restaurant offers a delectable and modern menu for diners to enjoy as well as the panoramic river views.

2FOR1
MAIN COURSE

GO PIZZA
Italian
John Lennon Liverpool Airport, Liverpool, M3 5NF
0151 486 5744
For those with a busy lifestyle, Go delivers fast fresh food from divine pizzas to delicious baguettes, all prepared to quality standards, providing excellent value for money.

2FOR1
MAIN COURSE

GOLDEN CASTLE
Chinese
318 Stanley Road, Bootle, L20 3ET
0151 944 2393
A relaxed and convivial Chinese restaurant serving tasty, authentic and piquant dishes. Aromatic and classic, you'll enjoy your savoury Chinese meal.

2FOR1
MAIN COURSE

JADE GARDEN
Chinese
75 Market Street, Hoylake, CH47 2BH
0151 632 2421
A firmly established family-run business offering deliciously tasty Chinese cuisine.

2FOR1
MAIN COURSE

KING WAH RESTAURANT
Chinese
914 New Chester Road, Bromborough, CH62 6AU
0151 327 2039
Guests love the wide range of dishes in this traditional Chinese restaurant. The staff at King Wah's value every customer and offer attentive friendly service.

LADY JADE
Cantonese
19 St Oswalds Street, Old Swan, Liverpool, L13 5SA
0151 228 6888
An enchantingly exotic ambience awaits you at Lady Jade. Out-of-this-world Peking and Cantonese dishes are devoured by both regulars and guests from afar. The Hors d'oeuvres are incredible.

2FOR1
MAIN COURSE

LITTLE PIZZA KITCHEN
Italian
44 St John Road, Waterloo, Liverpool, L22 9QG
0151 286 1299
The kitchen has a simple aim, and achieves it successfully: to produce high-quality food based on Italian cooking traditions. Open for coffee and breakfast calzones to evening pizzas and pasta dishes.

2FOR1
MAIN COURSE

LOCH FYNE
Seafood
Ring O Bells, Village Road, West Kirby, CH48 7HE
0151 929 6750
From the roadside oyster bar that once was, Loch Fyne restaurants now successfully inject energy and passion into great food and wonderful flavours, whilst ensuring their seafood is sustainably sourced.

WAREHOUSE KITCHEN & BAR
International
30 West Street, Southport, PR8 1QN
01704 544662
An international menu with some eclectic and imaginative flavour combinations, be it the venison burger with beetroot and red onion relish, the blackened cod with sweet miso, or the great grilled halibut.

NEW

2FOR1
MAIN COURSE

Members must call or email, stating their Gourmet Society membership before using.

NORTH WEST

MALMAISON
European

William Jessop Way, Princes Dock, Liverpool, L3 1QZ
0151 229 5000
Epitomising modern elegance, Malmaison Liverpool follows an inspired New York Gothic theme, ideally located by the riverside. A chic menu showcases local produce and delicious flavours. 1 AA Rosette.

RADISSON BLU HOTEL LIVERPOOL
Italian

107 Old Hall Street, Liverpool, L3 9BD
0151 966 1500
Widely regarded as one of the top Liverpool restaurants, Filini offers modern Italian food. The restaurant merges the best local and Italian produce to create mouth-watering dishes.

MANDARIN RESTAURANT
Chinese

73-79 Victoria Street, Liverpool, L1 6DE
0151 227 9011
Incredible Peking and Cantonese cuisine, an enchanting ambience and affable staff make this a desirable place to dine, conveniently located in the heart of the city.

PREZZO
Italian

U2 Coliseum Way, Cheshire Oaks, Ellesmere Port, CH65 9HD
0151 357 1394
With a character all of its own, Prezzo oozes contemporary style and enduring charm. Signature pastas, stone-baked pizzas and classic Italian dishes promise a perfect dining choice for the whole family.

MASALA WOK
Asian Fusion

47 Ranelagh Street, Liverpool, L1 1JR
0151 709 0443
Imaginative and ambitious restaurant fusing Indian and Chinese cuisines for a unique experience full of vim and verve, and a mean tarka daal.

REVOLUTION
Modern European

2 Temple Court, Liverpool, L2 6PY
0151 236 0905
Whatever the occasion, this popular bar and restaurant is passionate about food and drink, delivering sumptuous dishes and the very best in vodka, cocktails and wine.

MAYUR
Indian

130 Duke Street, Liverpool, L1 5AG
0151 709 9955
A pleasant Indian dining experience can be expected at Mayur. The plush interior oozes opulence and sophistication, wilst every dish is bursting with intense rich flavour.

RONNIES BISTRO
International

14a Houghton Street, Southport, PR9 0NS
01704 537 301
A fabulous bistro presenting a mouth-watering menu combining a delicious mix of pizzas, pasta dishes and chargrilled meats. A great place to enjoy tasty Bistro meals at affordable prices.

MELLO WINE BAR & BISTRO
Bistro

167-169 Allerton Road, Liverpool, L18 6HG
0151 724 6655
Dine in stylish, relaxed surroundings at this elegant wine bar and bistro. Warm and welcoming staff serve guests with exquisite food that invites a repeated performance.

SABAI
Thai

26 North John Street, Liverpool, L2 9RU
0151 236 7655
Contemporary and stylish space to complement the fresh-flavoured, piquant and scrumptious Thai food. Superb service and a relaxing, convivial atmosphere complete the experience.

MERCHANTS BAR & RESTAURANT
British

56-62 Castle Street, Liverpool, L2 7LQ
0151 702 7897
A sleek and modern restaurant, bar and cocktail lounge on Castle Street in Liverpool, Merchants makes best use of its stunning setting – high windows, marble columns – with a contemporary baroque style.

SAVINA RESTAURANT
Mexican

138 Duke Street, Liverpool, L1 5AG
0151 708 9095
Honest, modern cuisine is created from ingredients sourced from all over Mexico. Experience an abundance of varying tastes, flavours and spices as you enjoy a great evening out.

MILLON
Indian

187 Allerton Road, Liverpool, L18 6HG
0151 729 0220
Specialising in flavourful tandoori dishes, this modern-styled restaurant serves tasty dishes with flavours from a range of Indian traditions. Try the chef's recommendations for their imaginative twists.

SHELDRAKES
Mediterranean

Banks Road, Wirral, CH60 9JS
0151 342 1556
Boasting some of the best views of Merseyside, this restaurant offers diners a gourmet menu comprising of delicious, well-prepared dishes such as the truly delectable Cheshire fillet steak with Parma ham.

NEIGHBOURHOOD
Modern European

261 Woolton Road, Childwall, Liverpool, L16 8NA
0151 737 2266
Eating at Neighbourhood combines the warmth of a Parisian bistro with the familiarity of dining at the house of an old friend. Rustic food available for breakfast through to dinner.

SHIP INN
Modern British

804 Warrington Road, Liverpool, L35 6PE
0151 426 4165
Part of the Best of British group, this pub-restaurant promises thoroughgoing and hearty favourites: meaty, fruity and tender, just like the cask ales you can enjoy to wash the whole thing down.

Visit the website regularly to discover the latest restaurants joining the GS

SIGNALS
International

Holiday Inn Liverpool, Lime St, Liverpool, L1 1NQ
0151 709 7090
The Head Chef here has successfully built up a great reputation for creating superb classic and international dishes for guests. Seasonal table d'hôte menus are supported by an extensive wine list.

SURMA TANDOORI
Indian

271-273 Hoylake Road, Moreton, Wirral, CH46 0RL
0151 677 1331
A classic, popular Tandoori restaurant without unnecessary fripperies that serves a great range of fresh and flavourful Indian dishes with excellent service, in a comfortable, easygoing atmosphere.

TAJ MAHAL
Indian

35/37 Bath Street, Southport, PR9 0DP
01704 545 070
Specialising in balti and tandoori dishes, this restaurant delivers a fragrant and delicately spiced menu with wide-ranging choice. Expertly prepared food served in a contemporary, comfortable setting.

THE BOAT HOUSE
European

1 The Parade, Parkgate, Neston, CH64 6RN
0151 336 4187
Wonderfully prepared food to be enjoyed in superb surroundings. Sample signature dishes such as the tender lamb shank or the delectable woodland mushroom crostini.

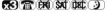

THE DINING ROOMS
European

38 The Promenade, Southport, PR8 1QU
01704 548 549
Enjoy delicious, freshly prepared meals in this warm and welcoming hotel restaurant. Dine in the bright and airy conservatory, where amiable staff are more than happy to cater to your every need.

THE JAMES MONRO
Modern British

69 Tithebarn Street, Liverpool, L2 2EN
0151 236 9700
With firm emphasis on the flavours of Little Italy, the Latin Quarter and the great American plains, this is an authentic dining experience. Sensibly priced food served in an unpretentious environment.

THE LIVING ROOM
British

15 Victoria Street, Liverpool, L2 5QS
0151 236 1999
Step into The Living Room and you can count on the savvy, distinctive neighbourhood vibe that plays home to eclectically drawn, supremely tasty cuisine. A welcoming shift of gears in this Liverpool haunt.

Must purchase min 3 courses pp, inc. main.

THE MONRO
Modern British

92 Duke Street, Liverpool, L1 5AG
0151 707 9933
A dining experience you won't be forgetting in a hurry. Exceptional contemporary surroundings provide the perfect setting to enjoy the accolade-winning cuisine that will blow you away.

THE PORTRAIT HOUSE
International

5/6 The Quadrant, Hoylake, CH47 2EE
0151 632 4444
Named after the photographic studio it once was, this building is now home to talented chefs and happy customers. Enjoy the exquisite fusion of contemporary and classic cuisine.

THE RENSHAW GRILL
American

13-15 Renshaw Street, Liverpool, L1 2SA
0151 708 4008
Effortlessly hip bar and grill with fine cuts of meat and fish cooked to a perfect fifth, resolving in warm harmony with the high-class, stylish and contemporary cocktail menu.

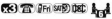

TRATTORIA O'SOLE MIO
Italian

1 Avondale Road, Southport, PR9 0EP
01704 501 120
Pleasingly old-country feel to this trattoria off Southport's Lord Street. Its dishes are flavour-laden authentic Italian classics; l'aria fresca pare gia na festa in this homely and vibrant little place.

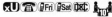

TREE TOPS
Fine Dining

Southport Old Road, Formby, L37 0AB
01704 572 430
Whatever your choice this restaurant has a selection of menus to whet the appetite. The à la carte menu takes in a range of cosmopolitan influences, often adding an individual twist.

TSO'S
Chinese

4 Queens Square, Liverpool, L1 1HF
0151 709 2811
If you often find yourself spoilt for choice, TSO's is the place for you. Here you can sample an array of Chinese dishes, the buffet providing over 70 for you to choose from.

WHAT'S COOKING
International

154-158 Telegraph Road, Heswall, CH48 1PE
0151 342 1966
Take a break from cooking and pay a visit to the family-friendly diner that serves piled-high plates and where smiles are easy to come by. Enjoyable for all ages.

ZELIGS
Italian

8 Thomas Steers Way, Liverpool, L1 8LW
0151 709 7097
Thoroughly vibrant and buzzy restaurant and bar whose features and contemporary style plays host to flavourful, modern Italian cuisine for a meal and an evening full of panache.

271

North East

The North East is an attractive, all-encompassing region, with an eclectic fusion of everything from cosmopolitan cities, marinas, seaside towns and windswept countryside studded with stone-walled market villages. All of which utterly encapsulates British charm.

Those working up an appetite from a day's rambling the windswept moors are well catered for with comforting and delicious local ingredients transformed into hearty dishes; the region is home to the finest Northumberland and Cheviot heather-fed lamb as well as a magnanimous array of beef and game. Seafood lovers are regularly satisfied with salmon from the rivers of Tweed and Tyne and anyone partying the night away in Leeds or Tyneside can expect a delicious start to the day with a serving of smoky, wonderful, Craster kippers.

The region's eateries very much focus on classic dishes and local produce; you won't have to trawl pub after pub to find a hearty stew or a good old meat and potato pie, followed by some delicious Wensleydale cheese. The warm tearooms of Yorkshire are the perfect place to pop in for a brew, with traditional tea loaf, parkin and Yorkshire spice cake all making the perfect sweet treat. In fishing villages, visitors can have their fill of pot fishing, be it by taking part or devouring the daily catch at a local seafood restaurant. And in the seaside towns the familiar smell of fish and chips will call forth nostalgic memories of childhood seaside holidays, every time.

Cleveland

J'S @ 636, PARKMORE HOTEL — *European*
636 Yarm Rd, Eaglescliffe, Middlesborough, TS16 0DH
01642 786 815
The restaurant of this tastefully converted Victorian house serves classic dishes made with the finest local produce from the nearby village of Yarm and the surrounding areas.

AL FORNO — *Italian*
2 Southfield Road, Middlesbrough, TS1 3BZ
01642 242 191
The busy bistro buzz makes this a fantastic place to meet and eat. Diners can tuck into a big Tuscan breakfast, grab a sandwich or sit down to a hearty, home-cooked Italian dinner.

2FOR1 2 COURSES

KAMINAKI — *Greek*
92 Church Road, Stockton On Tees, TS18 1TW
01642 607 949
An impressive restaurant closely modelled on a Greek taverna. Fantastically authentic atmosphere and food make this a comfortable place to enjoy great food and good times.

 2FOR1 MAIN COURSE

CAFÉ INDIA — *Indian*
21-23 Whitby Street, Hartlepool, TS24 7AB
01429 275 252
Original Indian cuisine at its very best. Elegant surroundings transfer you to a stylish haven in which diners enjoy divine dishes that are served and devoured.

2FOR1 MAIN COURSE

L'ALLEGRIA — *Italian*
27-31 Bridge Road, Stockton On Tees, TS18 3AE
01642 670 880
Tuscan breakfasts and hearty home-cooked evening Italian meals are on offer in this relaxed restaurant. An informal setting where you can relax over a cappuccino or glass of wine.

2FOR1 2 COURSES

CAFÉ INDIGO — *Indian*
Lockwood Beck Road, Lingdale, Saltburn-by-the-Sea, TS12 3LF
01287 650 114
Stunning surroundings, sensational views and sumptuous food make this an ideal place for lunch and dinner. Relying on the subtlety of fragrant herbs and spices, each dish has an abundance of flavour.

2FOR1 MAIN COURSE

LEVEN RESTAURANT — *Fine Dining*
Crathorne Hall Hotel, Crathorne, Yarm, TS15 0AR
0845 072 7440
Enjoy double AA Rosette dining in the elegant surroundings of this Hand Picked Hotels group, grand country house. The beautiful dining room creates a special ambience, ideal to mark any special occasion.

 25%OFF TOTAL

CAFÉ INDIGO — *Indian*
Castlegate Mill, 5 Castlegate Quay, Stockton on Tees, TS18 1BZ
01642 677 144
Stunning surroundings, sensational views and sumptuous food make this an ideal place for lunch and dinner. Relying on the subtlety of fragrant herbs and spices, each dish has an abundance of flavour.

2FOR1 MAIN COURSE

MASSALA — *Indian*
118 Borough Road, Middlesbrough, TS1 2ES
01642 250 145
Massala offers a diverse, mouth-watering range of curries in a classy, cosy dining room, with quick, friendly and attentive service.

2FOR1 2 COURSES

CAFÉ INDIGO — *Indian*
Picture House Buildings, Mill Lane, Billingham, TS23 1HE
01642 550 044
Stunning surroundings and sumptuous food make this an ideal place for lunch and dinner. Relying on the subtlety of fragrant herbs and spices, each dish has an abundance of flavour.

2FOR1 MAIN COURSE

MAXIMO'S — *Italian*
The Old Brewery, Castle Eden, Hartlepool, TS27 4SU
01429 839 299
A gorgeous restaurant complete with attentive, extremely helpful staff, and a great choice of authentic and traditional dishes. Highly recommended in the area; simply first-class food.

25%OFF TOTAL

EASTERN PARADISE — *Chinese*
8 Amber Street, Saltburn-by-the-Sea, TS12 1DT
01287 622 698
An excellent independently owned restaurant that has become an established part of the town's 21st century landscape. A wide selection of classic dishes served with a list of drinks and a personal touch.

 25%OFF TOTAL

MOHUJOS — *Mexican*
113 Station Road, Billingham, TS23 2RL
01642 881 478
Mohujos distinguishes itself with its range of lively Mexican dishes. Particularly prized are their chilli con carne, home-made piri piri sauce, and rich, Mexican-inflected take on chicken parmesan.

2FOR1 2 COURSES

ELIANO'S BRASSERIE — *Italian*
20 Fairbridge Street, Middlesbrough, TS1 5DJ
01642 868 566
Bringing a wealth of experience from restaurants across Europe, owner Rosa leads this exciting Italian restaurant serving homely, flavoursome food in a classic setting.

2FOR1 MAIN COURSE

OODLES NOODLES BAR AND CAFÉ — *Pan Asian*
136 Linthorpe Road, Middlesbrough, TS1 3RA
01642 243 809
A wide range of deliciously tempting hot dishes are on offer in this New York-style noodle bar. Super sandwiches are also on offer, with the 'Hot Provencette' proving to be an exceedingly popular choice.

 25%OFF TOTAL

Gourmet Society discount applies to the à la carte menu

RAUDIN'S RESTAURANT
French

The York Hotel, 185 York Road, Hartlepool, TS26 9EE
01429 867 373

Excels in a diversity of cuisine, from fried crocodile tail to succulent steaks, all prepared by highly experienced French chef Daniel Raudin. Fine delicacies without an eye-watering price-tag.

THE ITALIA RESTAURANT
Italian

BW Grand Hotel, Swainson St, Hartlepool, TS24 8AA
01429 266 345

Delicious food in a magical location, as diners are treated to excellent service and an enticing menu. A renowned brand maintaining a great reputation. **2FOR1** 3 COURSES

Maximum 1 card per party.

THE TAVISTOCK ITALIA
Italian

335a Marton Road, Middlesbrough, TS4 2PA
01642 817 638

A Parisian-themed restaurant boasting a cosmopolitan-style menu and instantly appealing atmosphere. With an AA Rosette for outstanding quality, first class food and great hospitality are guaranteed. **2FOR1** 3 COURSES

Maximum 1 card per party.

County Durham

AUSTIN'S BAR & BISTRO
Fine Dining

DCCC The County Ground, Chester-Le-Street, DH3 3QR
0191 388 3335

A leading light in culinary excellence, as attested to by their AA Rosette. In an idyllic and unique setting this restaurant allows diners to experience first-class fine dining at an affordable price. **25%OFF TOTAL**

BISTRO 21
French

Aykley Heads House, Aykley Heads, Durham, DH1 5TS
0191 384 4354

This AA Rosette-awarded bistro serves high-quality dishes in comfortable surroundings. The refreshing atmosphere ensures guests feel relaxed and at ease as they enjoy French-inspired meals. **2FOR1** 2 COURSES

Booking on the day essential throughout December.

CAFÉ INDIGO
Indian

36 Bondgate, Darlington, DL3 7JJ
01325 287 927

Stunning surroundings, sensational views and sumptuous food make this an ideal place for lunch and dinner. Relying on the subtlety of fragrant herbs and spices, each dish has an abundance of flavour. **2FOR1** MAIN COURSE

CAFÉ ROUGE
French

21 Silver Street, Durham, DH1 3RB
0191 384 3429

An attractive restaurant, a boulevard café or a Parisian-style wine bar; however you see Café Rouge, consistently excellent classic French dishes are always guaranteed. **50%OFF FOOD**

CHANG THAI
Thai

7 Market Place, Bishop Auckland, DL14 7NJ
01388 605 011

Culinary delights will please all in this delightful Thai restaurant. Attentive staff proudly welcome you into this warm and inviting environment in which to savour the fine dishes. **2FOR1** 3 COURSES

FILINI AT RADISSION SAS HOTEL
Italian

Framwelgate Waterside, Durham, DH1 5TL
0191 372 7200

Uncluttered, clear flavours grounded in modern Italian cuisine at this hotel-based restaurant. **25%OFF TOTAL**

FOFFANO'S
Italian/ Mediterranean

3-5 Bakhouse Hill, Darlington, DL1 5QA
01325 242 086

A wonderfully authentic Mediterranean atmosphere showcasing a menu filled with classic Italian food and other sumptuous dishes. Everything is fresh and home made, in respect of the best Italian traditions. **2FOR1** 3 COURSES

GOURMET SPOT
European

The Avenue, Durham, DH1 4DX
0191 384 6655

This exciting, ambitious restaurant in Durham offers high-level, contemporary fine dining. Its imaginative dishes and techniques have received national acclaim, and the restaurant continues to push itself. **2FOR1** MAIN COURSE

Not available Monday. À la carte menu only. Two 3 course meals MUST be ordered to claim the offer

HALL GARTH HOTEL
European

Coatham Mundeville, Darlington, DL1 3LU
01325 300 400

You needn't be staying at the Hall Garth to enjoy their fantastic restaurants. Food and drink have always been essential pleasures for guests at a country estate, and the dining here does not disappoint. **25%OFF TOTAL**

HELME PARK
Italian

Helme Park, Firtree, Bishop Auckland, DL13 4NW
01388 730 970

Fine dining coupled with great prices, where guests can decide from a wide selection of well prepared, flavourful dishes, with every item on the menu bearing a hallmark of quality. **25%OFF TOTAL**

HIGHLAND LADDIE
British

88 Haughton Green, Darlington, DL1 2DF
01325 363 816

A truly traditional pub serving hearty, home-cooked food and an array of delightfully unusual real ales. Food is served in cosy, welcoming surroundings where all are catered for. **2FOR1** 3 COURSES

OCHIS RESTAURANT
Caribbean

30-32 Bondgate, Darlington, DL3 7JJ
01325 282 675

Perfectly located in the heart of town, this is a popular place for both special occasions and spontaneous evenings out. Enjoy Caribbean and Mediterranean fine cuisine, with wines from around the world. **2FOR1** MAIN COURSE

OLDFIELDS
International

18 Claypath, Durham, DH1 1RH
0191 370 9595

Superb food at great value for money, in a stylish and welcoming environment. Expect your every requirement to be dealt with efficiently and with exceptional hospitality. A wonderful place to relax.

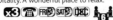

Excludes 6-7pm twilight fixed menu.

PAN DIN THAI RESTAURANT
Thai

4 South Crescent, Seaham, SR7 7HD
0191 581 2348

Offering dishes that are melting pots of succulent flavours, enhanced by a unique blend of herbs and spices. Thai beer and wine will further enrich your experience of truly tasty Thai cuisine.

RIVERSIDE RESTAURANT
British

Bridge End, Barnard Castle, DL12 9BE
01833 637 576

A warm and cosy place to come and enjoy a special dinner or a hearty Sunday lunch. Riverside has built a reputation for delivering wholesome food, properly prepared and filled with flavour.

ROYAL THAI RESTAURANT
Thai

94-96 Parkgate, Darlington, DL1 1RS
01325 361 717

Creating both an atmosphere and a menu that strongly reflects the real Thai experience, this restaurant deservedly boasts a Four-Star Gold Master Chef award for its superb cuisine.

SEAHAM HALL
British

Lord Byron's Walk, Seaham, SR7 7AG
0191 516 1400

A simply outstanding restaurant that expertly caters for guests whatever the party size. Its award-winning status is well deserved for the stunning food and excellent hospitality. Awarded 3 AA Rosettes.

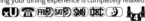

SEVEN STARS INN
British

High Street North, Shincliffe, Durham, DH1 2NU
0191 384 8454

A traditionally decorated restaurant; magical candlelight and divine tasting food make any evening spent here equal to perfection. The staff focus on ensuring your dining experience is completely relaxed.

SPICE ISLAND
Indian

9 Market Place, Barnard Castle, DL12 8NF
01833 630 575

Passionately crafted fine Indian food filled with spice and flavour. Head Chef Babul Miah takes great care, pride and satisfaction in creating the finest cuisine available in a tranquil, stylish setting.

SPICE ISLAND
Indian

100 Main Street, Shildon, DL4 1AQ
01388 777 775

Visitors return time and time again to experience the pleasures of the food on offer here. Believing food to be one of life's exquisite pleasures, the Head Chef ensures every dish is made to perfection.

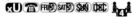

SPICE VENUE
Indian

23 Newmarket Street, Consett, DH8 5LQ
01207 583 765

A modern-style Indian restaurant held in high regard, offering a remarking array of flavoursome dishes to its guests. Fresh ingredients are used to create high-quality food every time.

THE ANCIENT UNICORN
British

Main Street, Bowes, Barnard Castle, DL12 9HL
01833 628 321

A welcoming retreat of a pub-restaurant whose array of crafted, palate-whetting regional specialities are worth the hike. Fine cuisine with dishes inspired by culinary nuances from around the world.

THE BRIDGE
European

Whorlton Village, Barnard Castle, DL12 8XD
01833 627 341

The excitement of the city fused with quality local produce, by well-known North East chef Paul O'Hara. Extensive dish choice and a wine list assembled to complement the depth of flavour in the menu.

THE CARLBURY ARMS
British

Piercebridge, Darlington, DL2 3SJ
01325 374 286

Classic pub setting for a traditional pub meal, in a historic and picturesque setting. Focusing on the quality of its produce, the pub-restaurant serves seasoned and succulent English fare.

THE MANOR HOUSE
European

The Green, West Auckland, DL14 9HW
01388 834 834

The two restaurants here mean that you can choose between fine dining and formality, or wonderful food in a more relaxed environment. Exquisite meals can be found wherever you decide to dine.

2 cards per party only.

THE MINER'S ARMS
English/Gastro pub

41 Manor Road, Medomsley, Consett, DH8 6QN
01207 560 428

Succulent rib-eye steaks can be devoured in this gastro-style pub which offers lunch and evening meals of tremendous quality. A weekly changing specials menu offers delicious alternatives.

THE RED LION
British

North Bitchburn Terrace, North Bitchburn, DL15 8AL
01388 763 561

The owners specialise in serving up superb food in this warm and inviting pub. Serving four real ales, this is a popular place with locals who enjoy the good beer, great grub, and efficient service.

THE STONEBRIDGE INN
British

Nevilles Cross, Durham, DH1 4PJ
0191 386 9591

Ideally located, the whole family can enjoy a wonderful meal in this quaint village pub. Real ale lovers will be especially happy here, with three cask ales available.

Sign up to our newsletter for latest restaurants, offers and more

TIA'S
Tex-Mex
84 Claypath, Durham, DH1 1RG
0191 383 9001
Saddle up for a Tex-Mex feast at this buzzy restaurant in Durham that serves all the classics with a bit of flair, and a good deal of value for money. The cocktail range is an extra treat.

Offer does not apply during happy hour (5pm-7.15pm).

BISTRO EN GLAZE
French
Laburnum House, Wylam, NE41 8AJ
01661 852 185
An impressive restaurant that attracts diners from near and far. Its regular clientèle from the surrounding areas testifies to the outstanding quality of the French-influenced food on offer.

BLUE BELL RESTAURANT
British
1 Market Place, Belford, NE70 7NE
01668 213 543
Award-winning dishes prepared by highly trained chefs. Dining in the garden restaurant or the hotel bar offer two very unique dining experiences, although scrumptious food can be found in both.

Northumberland

ARAMEE II
Indian
59 Front Street, Prudhoe, NE42 5AA
01661 833 355
A totally unique Indian restaurant, not just in location but in quality of food and service. A simply delicious Indian experience from beginning to end.

CORBRIDGE TANDOORI
Indian
8 The Market Place, Corbridge, NE45 5AW
01434 633 676
This local favourite offers a delicious combination of traditional and modern Indian and Bangladeshi dishes. The friendly and knowledgeable team provide great service in a warm, welcoming atmosphere.

BATTLESTEADS
British
Wark, Hexham, NE48 3LS
01434 230 209
Seasonal game, Cumbrian beef and Northumbrian lamb are just some examples of the fine produce used in the kitchen at Battlesteads. Cooked superbly, these local ingredients underpin some excellent dishes.

DALCHINI
Indian
15 Narrowgate, Alnwick, NE66 1JH
01665 606 336
Succumb to the temptations of Dalchini's mouth-watering cuisine and you won't regret it. Classic Indian dishes are on offer alongside more surprising treats, such as the tasty stuffed pepper starter.

BEWICKES AT CLOSE HOUSE
Close House, Heddon on the Wall, NE15 0HT
01661 852 255 *French*

Close House is an elegant and beautifully restored 18th Century Mansion situated in the beautiful surroundings of the Tyne Valley. Set in its own lush parkland the House and its fine dining restaurant, Bewickes, is a wonderful and welcome escape from city streets, yet only a convenient 15 minutes from Newcastle itself.

Charming Bewickes restaurant is maintained under the supreme talents and unimpeachable standards of Head Chef Chris Delany. His unflinching credo drives him to source seasonal, local and top quality ingredients wherever possible. These are prepared with the utmost care and respect to deliver unforgettable dishes orchestrated into a seamless meal.

Dining at Close House is an experience to be savoured; guests should allow time to appreciate not only the talents of the kitchen but also the stirring surroundings of this beautiful corner of England.

NORTH EAST

277

DE VERE SLALEY HALL HOTEL

2FOR1
3 COURSES

Slaley Hall Hotel, Hexham, NE47 OBX

01434 673 350 *British*

An Edwardian mansion set in 1000 acres of Northumberland moorland and forest, De Vere Slaley Hall is an elegant luxury hotel. Its unique location, with fabulous interiors and a team of passionate staff, will ensure any visit to De Vere Slaley Hall is an unforgettable one.

Offering a choice of three restaurants - Duke's Grill, Hadrian's Brasserie and The Claret Jug - the food is classic British with a local, contemporary twist. Their food philosophy is simple: Legendary local ingredients ideally sourced within 15 miles of the hotel, prepared to perfection.

Duke's Grill

Duke's Grill in the classic Edwardian drawing room captures the essence of Northumberland's harvest, from land, river and the sea. Prepared lovingly by our Chefs the exquisite meals and wide selection of wines and cheeses will linger long in the memory.

Hadrian's Brasserie

This restaurant has stunning views and a menu to match! It's ideal for an evening of exciting food and perfectly selected wine and is an exquisitely designed restaurant, serving the freshest Northumberland produce with locally inspired must-try dishes and seasonal specials – truly wonderful.

The Claret Jug

The Claret Jug looks out over the golf course and specialises in classic dishes and legendary breakfasts. Guests can enjoy a light meal during the day, then in the evening it transforms into a deluxe bistro, with a fabulous menu and well chosen wine list as well as a large selection of local and national ales.

Visitors won't find a 19th hole quite like The Claret Jug – clubhouse extraordinaire - home to local must-try dishes, where a relaxed and friendly atmosphere and an extensive selection of fresh ales and wines await.

DIWAN-E-AM *Indian*
4-5 County Mills, 23 Priestpopple, Hexham, NE46 1PN
01434 606 575
Diwan-E-Am takes pride in delighting all food lovers with its use of fresh herbs and spices and traditional cooking methods. The varied and tempting menu pays homage to vegetarian cooking.

2FOR1 2 COURSES

ITALIA PLUS *Italian*
Coquetvale Hotel, Station Road, Rothbury, NE65 7QH
01669 622 900
True Italian style is on offer at this wonderful hotel, providing guests with everything they need. Deliciously fresh dishes cooked to order by professional chefs. Great all-round dining.

25%OFF TOTAL

DOBSON RESTAURANT *European*
Macdonald Linden Hall Hotel, Morpeth, NE65 8XF
01670 500 000
Inside a beautiful Georgian hotel surrounded by a golf course, this restaurant offers golfers and guests alike delectable and inspiring continental cuisine, teamed with impeccable service. 2 AA Rosettes.

25%OFF TOTAL

LA BODEGA *Spanish*
Newgate Sreet, Morpeth, NE61 1BU
01670 516 055
Within walking distance of local attractions, this popular restaurant serves Mediterranean-style dishes that are complemented by a great range of wines. The tapas menu is perfect for a late evening treat.

25%OFF TOTAL

EASTERN SPICE *Indian*
55A Front Street, Prudhoe, NE42 5AA
01661 834 355
An Indian fusion menu combining curry house classics with innovative dishes, topped off with chef's specialities. A cosy restaurant that delivers quality food with authentic, spiced flavours.

25%OFF TOTAL

MULINOS *Italian/ Mediterranean*
79 Waterloo Road, Blyth, NE24 1BU
01670 353 311
An enjoyable atmosphere in which excellent food can be relished. Pizzas, pastas and steaks are all available, as well as a wide range of wonderful tapas dishes that are incredibly popular.

2FOR1 MAIN COURSE

GENERAL HAVELOCK INN *British*
9 Ratcliffe Road, Haydon Bridge, NE47 6ER
01434 684 376
Full-blooded, hearty and fresh pub-style fare in a warm Northumberland inn. Backing onto the river, it's a lovely setting for a distinctive, delicious pub meal.

25%OFF TOTAL

RIVERDALE HALL HOTEL *International*
Bellingham, Hexham, NE48 2JT
01434 220 254
Recipient of the Les Routiers Gold Plate Award, this restaurant has an enviable reputation for high-quality, refined cuisine, complemented with locally produced sorbets, ice creams and regional cheese.

2FOR1 MAIN COURSE

Visit the website regularly to discover the latest restaurants joining the GS

SAN LORENZO
Italian
Old Church, Cramlington, NE23 1DN
01670 735 222
A perfect Italian haunt whatever the occasion.
Wholesome, honest Italian dishes are designed to
tickle your taste buds and have your mouth watering.
An equally great children's menu is also available.

25% OFF TOTAL

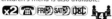

Tyne & Wear

THE BARN AT BEAL
British
Beal Farm, Beal, Berwick Upon Tweed, TD15 2PB
01289 381 477
A restaurant that serves excellent, fresh and locally
sourced produce as part of a project aimed at drawing
attention to the importance of agriculture to the
national landscape. Good values and great food.

2FOR1 MAIN COURSE

On Saturdays offer is only available in the evening.

A TASTE OF PERSIA
Persian
14 Marlborough Crescent, Newcastle, NE1 4EE
0191 221 0088
A dining room with beautiful décor matched by its
unique cuisine, with the origins of many of the dishes
steeped in history. A distinctive menu offering a
selection of unusual yet delectable dishes.

25% OFF TOTAL

THE BOYSON RESTAURANT
Fine Dining
Longhirst Hall, Morpeth, NE61 3LL
01670 795 000
Set in beautiful woodland and gardens, The Boyson
uses locally sourced or organically produced
ingredients in creating their real honest food. Fresh
and healthy, and without compromising on quality.

25% OFF TOTAL

ACROPOLIS
Greek
3 St Hilda Street, South Shields, NE33 1QD
0191 456 3333
Open the lid on this treasure chest of Greek culinary
delights. Guests will be impressed by the warm
Mediterranean welcomes and the tasty Greek
delicacies.

2FOR1 2 COURSES

Maximum of 3 cards per party.

THE COUNTY RESTAURANT
Contemporary
Priestpopple, Hexham, NE46 1PS
01434 603 601
Relax and unwind in this rural family-run restaurant.
Friendly service offered in a calm yet formal setting.
The individually tailored menu can cater for intimate
meals for two or for larger occasions.

2FOR1 3 COURSES

Sunday Lunch excluded. No food served on Sunday evening.

AMORE
Italian
11 Tavistock Place, Sunderland, SR1 1PB
0191 565 0077
An incredibly popular restaurant that serves Italian
cuisine with a fiery modern edge. The smooth sounds
of jazz on Tuesday evenings provide an evocative
ambience.

25% OFF TOTAL

THE MASONS ARMS
British
Rennington, Alnwick, NE66 3RX
01665 577 275
Explore the local coast and countryside before
heading to this award-winning inn and restaurant
for fresh food and real ales. Substantial home-cooked
meals will satisfy your well-earned appetite.

25% OFF TOTAL

AROMA TANDOORI
Indian
215 High St, Gosforth, Newcastle, NE3 1HQ
0191 284 1117
A great restaurant in Gosworth offering delightful
Indian cuisine. While away an evening as you enjoy
the many starters and curries that make up the menu.

2FOR1 MAIN COURSE

AS YOU LIKE IT
European
Archbold Terrace, Jesmond, Newcastle, NE2 1DB
0191 281 2277
Whether you sample the renowned British comfort
food or the more adventurous global offerings, the
food on offer is simply exquisite, with four bars and
live music to complete your night out in style.

2FOR1 2 COURSES

DETAILED DESCRIPTIONS AVAILABLE ON

www.gourmetsociety.co.uk

THE WANSBECK RESTAURANT
British
Northumberland College, Ashington, NE63 9RG
01670 841 210
Support the talented chefs of the future at this on-
site restaurant. Wonderful dishes are prepared by
chefs-in-training, guaranteeing guests a first-class
dining experience.

25% OFF TOTAL

BAR BLANC
International
38-42 Osbourne Rd, Jesmond, Newcastle, NE22 2AL
0191 2815126
Bar Blanc is the in-house restaurant of Whites Hotel
in Jesmond, Newcastle. It serves a great range of
delicious Indian cuisine throughout the day, and a fine
selection of English and Continental dishes.

NEW

25% OFF TOTAL

VALLEY CONNECTION 301
Indian
Market Place, Hexham, NE46 3NX
01434 601 234
Maybe you have a usual Indian dish that you cannot
move away from, or perhaps you want to try an
unusual speciality. Either way, this restaurant will suit
all of your needs.

2FOR1 MAIN COURSE

BEWICKES AT CLOSE HOUSE
French
Close House, Heddon on the Wall, NE15 0HT
01661 852 255
Escape to the country and enjoy the magnificent
beauty of the Tyne valley. Situated in a mansion that
maintains all its historic grandeur, here you will find
superb dishes with strong French influences.

25% OFF TOTAL

NORTH EAST

279

NORTH EAST

BLACKFRIARS *European*
Friar Street, Newcastle, NE1 4XN
0191 261 5945
The culinary focus is on interesting flavour and contemporary presentation, while the oak beams and reclaimed furniture ensure this restored 13th century building oozes with Medieval charm. 1 AA Rosette.

BIG MUSSEL *Seafood*
15, The Side, Quayside, Newcastle, NE1 3JE
0191 232 1057
Revel in seafood galore at this fabulous fish restaurant, from traditional fish and chips to the more elaborate sea bass with braised cabbage and bacon. The kitchen also offers meat and vegetarian dishes.

BILLABONG AT THE CALEDONIAN HOTEL *European*
Osborne Road, Jesmond, Newcastle, NE2 2AT
0191 281 7881
Relax and unwind in chic surroundings as you feast on delectable European cuisine. Weekly special dishes are offered alongside a wonderful à la carte menu. Old and New World wines available.

BLUE COYOTE *Contemporary*
56 Pilgrim Street, Newcastle, NE1 6SF
0191 222 0130
Expect a large selection of dishes and sizeable portions in this fun and friendly restaurant and bar. The desserts have a well-deserved reputation for being scrumptiously good.

BRASSERIE @ THE SAGE GATESHEAD *Fine Dining*
The Sage, St Marys Square, Gateshead, NE8 2JR
0191 443 4670
Fantastic food at phenomenal prices; the monthly changing menu is unbeatable. The combination of iconic surroundings and outstanding meals makes this a fine place to eat and drink.

Only available after 8pm on show nights.

BRICKLANE *Indian*
4 Denton Road, Gateshead, NE11 7BD
0191 275 3492
Another addition to Newcastle's restaurant scene, although this one is a little gem. Authentic Indian cuisine delicately crafted with a range of traditional herbs and spices, along with fine ingredients.

CAFÉ BANGLA *Indian*
2 St Bede's, Station Road, East Boldon, NE36 0LE
0191 519 0929
Popular and high-quality tandoori restaurant with a broad, bold range of curries and other sub continental dishes.
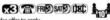
Minimum of 4 diners for offer to apply.

CAFE NEON *Mediterranean*
8 Bigg Market, Newcastle, NE1 1UW
0191 260 2577
Enjoy a quick and easy bite to eat or an authentic Mediterranean meal in this lively-by-day, relaxed-by-night café. Fabulous food and drink in a venue that well represents the city's café culture.

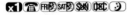

CAFÉ ROUGE *French*
MetroCentre, Gateshead, NE11 9XR
01914 605 502
An attractive restaurant, a boulevard café or a Parisian-style wine bar; however you see Café Rouge, consistently excellent classic French dishes are always guaranteed.

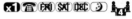

CHARLIES CHAMPAGNE BAR & RESTAURANT *Fine Dining*
57-60 Sandhill, Watergate Buildings, Newcastle, NE1 3RJ
0191 222 0164
With unrivaled views across the Tyne, Charlie's offers many culinary delights and incredible drinks; as befits its moniker, over 50 Champagnes are available.

Formerly Tavistock Italia

CONVIVIUM AT HOLIDAY INN NEWCASTLE *International*
Great North Road, Newcastle, NE13 6BP
0871 423 4818
Relax and dine in the spacious and peaceful Holiday Inn Newcastle-upon-Tyne. Choose from a classic English or continental breakfast, and try the evening menu that blends modern and traditional cuisine.

1 card per table

CRAWCROOK TANDOORI *Indian*
17-19 Main Street, Crawcrook, Ryton, NE40 4TX
0191 413 3373
A family restaurant with a cosmopolitan edge, serving modern yet authentic Indian food in a chic, contemporary setting. Expect a warm welcome and fine food.

D'ACQUA *Mediterranean*
26-28 John Street, Basement, Sunderland, SR1 1JG
0191 565 1988
James Shadforth is a local chef with big ambitions and passion for the industry. He has worked his way up in kitchens from the age of 15 and now, only nine years later, presents the excellent D'ACQUA.

DARAZ *Bangladeshi*
4 Holly Avenue West, Jesmond, Newcastle, NE2 2AR
0191 281 8431
Only the freshest herbs and spices are used in the preparation of the wide selection of dishes here, with Bangladeshi cuisine being the house speciality. A family-run restaurant with a great reputation.

Only 1 card per table.

DAYS OF THE RAJ *Indian*
49 Great North Road, Newcastle, NE3 2HH
0191 284 9555
Combining the best of Eastern and Western cultures, this Indian cuisine is a subtle mixture of exotic flavours achieved by the blending of authentic spices. Flavoursome dishes to suit all tastes.

EL CASTANO *Mediterranean*
44 Osborne Road, Jesmond, Newcastle, NE2 2AL
0191 281 9111
Authentic, popular tapas bar in Jesmond, offering a range of zesty dishes and a bright, open vibe.

280

When booking restaurants always mention your GS membership

ESSY'S
Italian

Pier Block Yard, South Pier, South Shields, NE33 2JX
0191 455 4477
Essy's is located on the Pier in a beautiful small building with a wonderful view. Enjoy delectable Italian food served alongside chef's specials such as the 'black pudding tower'.

 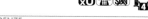

FIRENZE
Italian

7 Osbourne Road, Jesmond, Newcastle, NE2 2AE
0191 281 2136
Proudly independent Italian restaurant serving fresh, fulsome food: thick, firm gnocchi and prime meat cuts with savoury sauces. Authentic, inviting Italian cuisine.

FISHERMAN'S LODGE
Modern British

Deep Dene House, Jesmond, Newcastle, NE7 7BQ
0191 281 3281
This serene, stylish restaurant is known for its fresh, flavourful seafood, as well as for a pleasantly surprising sideline in succulent, locally-sourced meat and game.

FRANCO'S
Italian

1 Brentwood Mews, Jesmond, Newcastle, NE2 3DH
0191 281 3434
This restaurant has it all: style, atmosphere, quality food and excellent service. Owned by an Italian couple who combine their passion for food and hospitality to provide a venue fit for any occasion.

FREGATE RESTAURANT
British

Sea Hotel, Sea Road, South Shields, NE33 2LD
0191 427 0999
Light, bright dining area with stunning sea views for a calm, relaxed meal; classic, clean and sophisticated flavours throughout the well-conceived menu.

FREYA'S RESTAURANT AT ASPERS
International

Aspers at The Gate, Newgate St, Newcastle, NE1 5TG
0191 255 0400
A casual eating environment throughout the day. Late breakfast, lunch and dinner are all covered with delicious menus offering dishes ranging from tempting steaks to delectable grilled fish.

Aspers is open to those aged 18+. Photo ID required.

GREEN'S BRASSERIE
European

Gosforth, Parkway, Newcastle, NE12 8ET
0191 213 0070
A brasserie situated within a health club boasting a full menu of excellent, balanced light and main meals. First-rate food complete with a wide range of alcoholic and soft drinks.

HARRY RAMSDEN'S
British

Metro Park West, Gibside Way, Gateshead, NE11 9XS
0191 460 2625
Established in 1928, Harry Ramsden's is as much of an institution as fish and chips themselves. Treat yourself to some traditional comfort food with the unmistakeable taste of the seaside.

Not available during August or in takeaway.

HIMALAYA
Indian

33 Esplanade, Whitley Bay, NE26 2AL
0191 251 3629
A locally popular venue offering quality Indian cuisine, good value and ocean views. Time and time again this restaurant delivers quality food, with classic dishes from tikka to tandoori.

HO CHINESE BUFFET
Chinese

41 Gallowgate, Newcastle, NE1 4SG
0191 221 2270
Immerse yourself in a culture with seventy-five varieties of oriental dishes at this buffet-style restaurant. All food is freshly prepared and of great quality, offered at remarkably low prices.

HORTON GRANGE
International

Berwick Hill, Newcastle, NE13 6BU
01661 860 686
Appreciate the beautiful scenery and enjoy excellent dishes created with quality produce. Imaginative menus provide for every type of diner and includes seasonal specialities such as the grilled halibut.

HOTEL DU VIN
Bistro

Allan House, City Road, Newcastle, NE1 2BE
0191 229 2215
The finest, freshest local produce, simple European recipes, a stunning choice of wines; these are the elements of the trademark Hotel du Vin bistro.

IMPERIAL DRAGON
Chinese

86 High Street East, Wallsend, NE28 7RH
0191 262 8788
The vastness and diversity of China's geography is reflected in the eclectic cuisine showcased here, with a cooking style that produces delicious results.

JASHN
Indian

Whickham Bank, Newcastle, NE16 3BP
0191 488 8505
A blend of classic and contemporary cuisine lines the menu here, with every dish delicately spiced and flavoured.

KESAR
Indian

76-78 Church Way, North Shields, NE29 0AA
0191 259 5976
Brings elegant Indian cuisine to the city. Well-recognised for its award-winning status and delicious dishes.

KILLINGWORTH ARMS
British

Killingworth Village, Killingworth, Newcastle, NE12 6BL
0191 268 1423
A family-friendly pub offering great food and guaranteeing good times. Wonderfully located in the historical village of Killingworth, this is a great place to rest, relax and enjoy a delicious meal.

À la carte menu only. Offer not available on carvery.

NORTH EAST

KISII
Indian
Whitley Bay Metro Stn, Station Rd, Whitley Bay, NE26 2QY
0191 253 7077
An established, family-run restaurant that attracts regular diners from the surrounding areas. Offers tasty Indian cuisine that can be suited to any palate.

KOH-I-NOOR
Indian
26 Cloth Market, Newcastle, NE1 1EE
0191 232 5379
A late night, family-run restaurant with an owner boasting 18 years experience. Heavenly rich and fragrant dishes that cater for all tastes: the ideal spot for celebrations before a night on the town.

KOMAL
Indian
14 Brentwood Av, Jesmond, Newcastle, NE2 3DH
0191 281 4878
Don't miss the speciality balti dishes in this fine Indian restaurant, where the primary focus remains on producing honest, home-style cooking. Offers a perfect respite from the busy streets of the city.

Only 1 card per party.

LA GABBIA
Italian
1 Boyd St, Shieldfield, Newcastle, NE2 1AP
0191 232 6666
A menu that goes beyond pasta and pizza with an extensive and impressive range of interesting meat and fish dishes. For the pasta fanatic, the ricotta and spinach tortellini is phenomenal.

LA VITA
Italian
210 Heaton Road, Heaton, Newcastle, NE6 5HP
0191 265 0044
An impressive restaurant offering a menu bursting with tremendously good, classic Italian dishes. A specials board offers delightful variations, such as a corking lamb shank in red wine sauce.

LIBRARY AND PRINT ROOM
British
Matfen Hall, Matfen, Newcastle, NE20 0RH
01661 886 500
This acclaimed restaurant has 2 AA Rosettes attesting to the quality of its food. Overlooking the 18th green of Matfen Hall's golf course, the Keepers Lodge serves fabulous food in an idyllic setting.

LIGHT OF INDIA
Indian
120-122 High Street East, Wallsend, NE28 7RH
0191 234 5556
Highly recommended by locals, Light of India uses fresh ingredients and traditional recipes to create a diverse range of Indian culinary delights for down-to-earth prices.

LITTLE SAIGON
Vietnamese
6 Bigg Market, Newcastle NE1 1UW
0191 233 0766
Vietnam's long history and vibrant culture has left a legacy of truly inspirational cuisine, showcased here among the eclectic array of beautiful, healthy dishes concocted out of exotic ingredients.

282

LOCH FYNE
Seafood
West Avenue, Gosforth, Newcastle-Upon-Tyne, NE3 4ES
0191 559 320
From the roadside oyster bar that once was, Loch Fyne restaurants now successfully inject energy and passion into great food and wonderful flavours, whilst ensuring their seafood is sustainably sourced.

MALMAISON
European
Quayside, Newcastle, NE1 3DX
0191 245 5000
Striking and charismatic décor in a brasserie whose focus is on fresh, locally sourced produce and a contemporary, stylish ambience. Enjoy this sassy Newcastle Mal and its distinctive style. 1 AA Rosette.

MANDARIN
Chinese
14 Stowell Street, Newcastle, NE1 4XQ
0191 261 7960
Set in Newcastle's Chinatown, the Mandarin draws on piquant flavours from the many traditions and techniques of Chinese cuisine; it provides the classics, while adding innovative original tastes.

MING DYNASTY
Chinese
7 High Street West, Sunderland, SR1 3EX
0191 514 2578
A lively, central Chinese restaurant that draws especially on the clear, fresh flavours of Cantonese cuisine, along with a full range of bright, classic Chinese dishes.

MODERN TANDOORI
Indian
174 High Street West, Wallsend, NE28 8HZ
0191 234 2749
This place is a must for lovers of Bangladeshi and Indian cuisine, with the rich, vibrant, and flavoursome cuisine always being perfectly cooked and beautifully presented.

MRS ALI
Indian
11-17 Archbold Terrace, Jesmond, Newcastle, NE2 1DB
0191 281 9988
This contemporary pan-Asian restaurant revels in its attention to detail with an observance of classic Indian tradition and an onus on hospitality to go with their use of natural, fresh herbs and spices.

NAZ RESTAURANT
Indian
4-7 St Thomas Street, Sunderland, SR1 1NW
0191 510 2060
The opulent décor enhances the vivaciousness of this vibrant restaurant. Both curry-loving locals and guests from afar highly recommend the house speciality shahi raan, which will blow you away.

NEW BENGAL
Indian
232 High Street, Gosforth, Newcastle, NE3 1HH
0191 284 1295
Cosy, accommodating Indian restaurant in Gosforth where you'll find the air rich with the scent of fresh spices and the menu filled with everything from old favourites to house specialities.

Enjoy massive leisure and retail savings with more Gourmet Society

NO.1 ORIENTAL BUFFET
Chinese
41 Stowell Street, Newcastle, NE1 4YB
0191 261 5787
Families and small parties will appreciate the relaxed atmosphere that can be enjoyed here. A buffet boasting over 70 Chinese dishes guarantees something tasty for everyone.

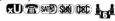

NOOSH RESTAURANT
International
St Nicholas Street, Newcastle, NE1 1PE
0191 232 4663
Contemporary European meets classical Middle Eastern cuisine at this savvy restaurant. There are some scintillating dishes to be found here, all based on strong local knowledge and supplier relationships.

OLD ORLEANS
American
Timber Beach Rd, Wessington Way, Sunderland, SR5 3XG
0191 516 9009
An extraordinarily accurate taste of the Deep South can be found in this unique restaurant. The kitchen deals in classic Louisiana and Cajun recipes such as jambalaya and gumbo to create an exciting menu.

2FOR1
MAIN COURSE

Not available on Bank Holiday weekends. Adult menu only.

OLIVIANA'S
Italian
5-7 The Side, Quayside, Newcastle, TNE1 3JE
0191 232 5537
Reasonably priced Italian cuisine can be expected at Oliviana's. While away the evening over your favourite dish and a bottle of fine wine.

ORCHID
Chinese
Old Bonded Warehouse, The Close, Newcastle, NE1 3RF
0191 221 1388
Using the modern style of international fusion cooking to complement the restaurant's cosmopolitan location, this wonderful restaurant hosts an innovative Chinese menu that caters for all taste buds.

2FOR1
MAIN COURSE

PAPRIKA CAFÉ
European
46 Frederick Street, Sunderland, SR1 1NF
0191 564 0606
Delivering a great dining experience throughout the day and into the evening, this award-winning restaurant offers high-quality food at great value for money, in a charismatic, friendly atmosphere.

Closed on Mondays

PARADISO
Mediterranean
1 Market Lane, Newcastle, NE1 6QQ
0191 221 1240
Discreetly hidden down a quaint cobbled street, this restaurant epitomises Italian stylishness. Lamb shank with mustard and leek mash and Moroccan monkfish are just two of the tasty treats you can try.

2FOR1
2 COURSES

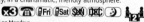

PEPPY'S
Italian
16 Addycombe Terrace, Heaton, Newcastle, NE6 5DP
0191 240 0300
A traditional Italian restaurant offering an authentic taste to its diners, with well-prepared and -presented dishes and a high-class specials board. A local favourite for both couples and families alike.

2FOR1
2 COURSES

PITCHER & PIANO
British
108 Quayside, Newcastle, NE1 3DX
0191 232 4110
Passion for the best service, premium drinks and great food, and a commitment to creating a contemporary, cool ambience define the character of life at this modern bar.

PLAZA TANDOORI
Indian
4 Palace Building, Grand Parade, Tynemouth, NE30 4JS
0191 257 4344
Besides an adherence to its name - that is, a specialisation in tandoori - this Bangladeshi restaurant walks a mile in the eclectic's shoes: trout and duck dishes supplement the staple chicken and lamb.

2FOR1
MAIN COURSE

RASA NEWCASTLE
Indian
27 Queen street, Newcastle, NE1 3UG
0191 232 7799
Inspired by the authentic home cooking of beautiful, spice-rich Kerala, this restaurant's passion is food prepared always with devotion, love, and the finest ingredients.

2FOR1
MAIN COURSE

ROMNA TANDOORI
Indian
43 Esplanade, Whitley Bay, NE26 2AE
0191 251 3583
Offering first-rate authentic Indian cuisine, this restaurant is one of the best value in Whitley bay. A varied menu delivers classic dishes that are cooked to perfection time and time again.

2FOR1
3 COURSES

RUPALI RESTAURANT
Indian
6 Bigg Market, Newcastle, NE1 1UW
0191 232 8629
Providing a range of mild to extremely spicy Indian dishes. For the brave only, the infamous 'curry hell' is free for those who succeed in eating every mouthful of the world's hottest curry.

2FOR1
2 COURSES

SAGAWA
Japanese
2-10 Cross Street, Newcastle, NE1 4XE
0191 261 8323
Serves delicious culinary pleasures to be enjoyed without the guilty conscience. Healthy, flavoursome Japanese dishes are offered in this welcoming venue, where a lively buzz will keep you coming back.

SALSA TAPAS BAR
Spanish
89 Westgate Road, Newcastle upon Tyne, NE1 4AE
0191 221 1022
Sample enticing tapas dishes such as minted lamb meatballs, tempura battered brie and tiger prawns in garlic. Meet with friends over a jug of Sangria and enjoy informal social grazing in a chilled out style.

50%OFF
FOOD

Open, Mon - Sat 11am - midnight; Sun noon - 11pm

SAMPAN
Indian
3 Brewery Lane, Ponteland, NE20 9NZ
01661 820 869
Classic Indian dishes in a relaxed, cosy environment. Pop into Sampan in Ponteland for a good, simple and enjoyable local Indian meal.

2FOR1
MAIN COURSE

SAN CARLOS
Italian
54 South Parade, Whitley Bay, NE26 2RQ
0191 251 7800
Italian fare and rustic contemporary dishes make for an exciting menu that is full of satisfyingly tasty dishes for you to enjoy. Swordfish and lemon sole find their way in amongst pizzas and steaks.

SHEARER'S
International
St James' Park, Strawberry Place, Newcastle, NE1 4ST
0191 201 8688
Fantastically tasty food is cooked by award-winning chefs who form part of the respected banqueting team at Newcastle United. A tremendous menu accompanied by a superb range of drinks.

Offer is only available to diners.

SAN LORENZO
Italian
123 High Street, Gosforth, Newcastle, NE3 1HA
0191 213 0399
The quality of the food at this rustic Italian restaurant set it a notch above, while remaining relatively inexpensive. Those fond of fish will love the trio de pesce from the specials board.

SILK ROOM RESTAURANT
Contemporary
Trinity Gardens, Newcastle, E1 2HF
0191 260 3506
This popular bar and restaurant is a breath of fresh air to the dining scene on Newcastle Quayside. Mouth-watering cuisine is served in intimate boutique surroundings.

Certain delicacies not included in GS discount. Check website for information.

SAROO
Indian
32 West Road, Newcastle, NE4 9HB
0191 298 3688
Holding firm to a passion for authentic Indian and Kashmiri cuisine, this restaurant impressively provides wonderfully tasty dishes in a bright and welcoming setting. The dahi baigon is fabulous

2FOR1
3 COURSES

SIMPLY GREEK TAVERN
Greek
2/4 Bigg Market, Newcastle, NE1 1UW
0191 222 0035
Step inside this classic taverna and you're transported as if to Greece. From the whitewash walls to the delectable, herby delicacies on the menu, the owners ensure you have a truly Greek experience.

2FOR1
2 COURSES

Maximum 1 card per party.

SHAHE
Indian
30 Wansbeck Road, Gosforth, Newcastle, NE3 3HQ
0191 285 1801
'Shahe' means 'royal': the wide variety of dishes and delicate flavours of India ensure this restaurant lives up to its name. Richly decadent food is served in lavish, royal palace-style surroundings.

2FOR1
MAIN COURSE

SIX AT THE BALTIC
British
BALTIC Centre, Gateshead Quays, Gateshead, NE8 3BA
0191 440 4948
Iconic location for this restaurant with a line in striking but simply cooked dishes; you'll enjoy the visual and olfactory qualities of their contemporary British cuisine and its imaginative flavours.

2FOR1
2 COURSES

SECCO
2FOR1
MAIN COURSE
86 Pilgrim Street, Newcastle, NE1 6SG
0191 230 0444 *Italian*

It is essential to book in advance mentioning Gourmet Society. Like all GS restaurants the offer applies to the a la carte menu

Elegant and opulent, Secco is a two storey venue in the heart of Newcastle which specialises in good quality Italian drinking and dining inspired, by the Salento region of Southern Italy - sometimes recognised as the 'heel' of the Italian 'boot'.

After managing Secco for four years, Hamed Fardoust took over in July 2009 determined to build on the art works of the creators of Secco; the interior of Secco is designed to induce a sense of supreme well-being. It glows with rich colour, striking patterns and textured materials full of subtle detail.

Hamed has also continued the award winning Secco approach to dining, in that he continues to champion the very best in local, seasonal produce from the northeast of England and southern tip of Italy. Located on the second floor, the restaurant specialises in a superb interpretation of authentic, yet simple Italian food, using the finest, seasonal ingredients from Northumberland and the best of Southern Italian staples which is complemented by a wine list befitting the finest Italian enoteca.

Recommend a friend to the Gourmet Society and receive a free gift.

SONNY'S ITALIA
Italian

Front Street, North Shields, NE30 4DX
0191 296 0755
Widely travelled and experienced chef Ken leads the kitchen of this Riviera-style restaurant, serving classical, homely Mediterranean food and drink in a vibrant and welcoming atmosphere.

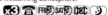

SONNY'S LOCALE
Italian

Front Street, Whickham, NE16 4DT
0191 496 0066
Bright, accommodating and buzzy little independent Italian restaurant in the lovely town of Whickham. Charming and atmospheric, it serves simple, mouth-watering, richly flavoured Italian dishes.

SPICE BOLLYWOOD
Indian

Unit 16-17, The Studio, Gateshead, NE11 9YG
0191 460 9449
Offers patrons all the classic Indian dishes, like onion bhajis and lamb curry. Immersed in a Bollywood setting diners can enjoy sumptuous food in an authentic atmosphere.

Offer not available in November.

SPICE CUBE
Indian

The Gate, Newgate St, Newcastle, NE1 5TG
0191 222 1181
Slick and stylish contemporary design in this restaurant whose cuisine meets all the classic expectations of a great Indian meal. Colourful, rich and spicy, you'll be swept away.

STARTERS AND PUDS
European

2-6 Shakespeare St, Newcastle, NE1 6AQ
0191 233 2515
Exciting new concept in leisurely eating, taking the best of savoury and sweet cuisine and combining it with attentive service and a warm atmosphere. No mains necessary.

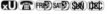

Main courses not on menu. The offer is therefore: One free starter, side & pudding.

STRADA
Italian

Blackett Street, Old Eldon Square, Newcastle, NE1 7JG
0191 261 6070
A dedicated menu offering traditional Italian dishes in a stylish and contemporary setting. The chefs use only the finest ingredients such as Parma ham and buffalo mozzarella imported directly from Italy.

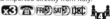

SWAN
Carvery

Heddon on the Wall, Newcastle, NE15 0DR
01661 853 161
One of the many Great British Carveries serving the well-loved classic with a modern twist. Drink and dine in Heddon's oldest building, where 18th century features add to the charming interior.

Call beforehand for special events.

TAKDIR
Indian

11 East Parade, Whitley Bay, NE26 1AP
0191 253 0236
Classic and reliable Indian menu, spiced up with chef specialities such as the delectable chicken tikka achari, which is a spiced pickle dish. An inviting atmosphere providing well-cooked flavoursome food.

TANDOORI INTERNATIONAL
Indian

97 Ocean Road, South Shields, NE33 2JL
0191 456 2000
Family-run for two generations hailing from the Sylhet region of Bangladesh; the chefs here are particular masters of Sylheti cuisine and masala dishes.

TAVISTOCK ITALIA
Italian

BW Roker Hotel, Roker Terrace, Sunderland, SR6 9ND
0191 567 1786
This stunning Victorian building is home to an impressive hotel and restaurant. Dine in style at either the Tavistock Italia.

Maximum 1 card per party.

TAVISTOCK THAI CHINA
Chinese/ Malaysian/Thai

BW Roker Hotel, Roker Terrace, Sunderland, SR6 9ND
0191 567 1786
Whatever your favourite oriental dish, here you'll find it made with an extra touch of authenticity. The kitchen hosts a team of talented chefs all originating from Thailand and across the Orient.

Maximum 1 card per party.

THAI SIAM
Thai

16 Stowell Street, Newcastle, NE1 4XQ
0191 232 0261
For those who already have a firm favourite, the à la carte menu offer a large variety of Thai dishes for your satisfaction; alternatively, the set banquets are a great way to sample a bit of everything.

THE CORNERHOUSE HOTEL
British

Heaton Road, Heaton, Newcastle, NE6 5RP
0191 265 9602
It's great to enjoy beautifully cooked, straight-down-the-line pub food at great value for money; the Corner House Hotel's restaurant, in friendly and genial surroundings, does just that.

THE GODFATHER
Italian

3 Market Street, Newcastle, NE1 6JE
0191 232 6171
This venue caters for couples as well as larger parties, providing an authentic atmosphere. The menu contains many traditional and contemporary dishes, along with the chef's delicious specialities.

THE GRAINGER ROOMS
British

7 Higham Place, Newcastle, NE1 8AF
0191 232 4949
Great food created using local produce, fish from sustainable sources, and seasonal wild foods. Awarded a Michelin Bib Gourmand for 2010. Extensive wine choices.

THE GREENHOUSE BRASSERIE
British

Quarryfield Road, Gateshead, NE8 3BE
0191 490 2414
Ideal place to enjoy top-quality, modern British food. Dishes are reasonably priced and made from the very best local and seasonal ingredients, served in a relaxed environment. A local favourite.

NORTH EAST

THE IVY RYTON
Italian/Mediterranean

Parsons Drive, Ryton, NE40 3RA
0191 413 6444
A fresh venue that boasts a classic pizzeria menu and many other classic options to choose from. Wonderful, friendly staff serve quality food in a relaxed and casual atmosphere, catering for all tastes.

2FOR1 MAIN COURSE

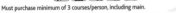

THE LAST DAYS OF THE RAJ
Indian

168 Kells Lane, Low Fell, Gateshead, NE9 5HY
0191 482 6494
A winning establishment with the locals, this quality Indian restaurant provides traditional cuisine amidst luxurious surroundings. Their balti, thali and vegetarian dishes are all wonderfully delicious.

2FOR1 MAIN COURSE

THE LIVING ROOM
International

12 Grey Street, Newcastle, NE1 6AE
0191 255 4450
Step into The Living Room and you can count on the savvy, distinctive neighbourhood vibe that plays home to eclectically drawn, supremely tasty cuisine. Cosy up in this snug, stylish Newcastle haunt.

2FOR1 3COURSES

Must purchase minimum of 3 courses/person, including main.

THE MAGPIE ROOM
British

St James' Park, Newcastle, NE1 4ST
0844 372 1892
This restaurant serves food in the function room at St James Park, home of the renowned institution, Newcastle United FC. On Sundays GS Members can enjoy a thoroughgoing four course Sunday lunch before a tour of the stadium.

25%OFF TOTAL

Restaurant only open Sundays. 25% discount on food only.

THE MOGUL RAJ
Indian

15 - 17 Merton Way, Ponteland, NE20 9PY
01661 821 550
The fantastic Indian dishes served here are worth travelling that extra mile for. Once you discover its satisfying tastiness, you will be reluctant to share your chosen dish.

2FOR1 MAIN COURSE

THE OLIVE GARDEN
Italian

22 Vine Place, Sunderland, SR1 3NA
0191 510 9444
Allow the warm ambience and laid-back atmosphere transfer you to a rustic Italy where the food is perfectly prepared and presented. An admirably intimate and romantic setting.

2FOR1 MAIN COURSE

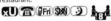

THE PLATE RESTAURANT
International

Marriott Hotel, High Gosforth Park, Newcastle, NE3 5HN
0191 236 4111
Boasting 12 acres of parkland and an enviable location, the Marriott at Gosworth Park offers guests everything. Fine dining can be found in the 1 AA Rosette winning restaurant.

25%OFF TOTAL

O DE V DELUXE BRASSERIE
European

Pipewellgate House, Quayside, Gateshead, NE8 2BJ
0191 341 0031
O de V's simple, stylish design gives it an extremely homely feel as a restaurant. A deluxe brasserie, fusion steakhouse and margarita bar, this is a casual yet elegant restaurant.

NEW

2FOR1 3COURSES

THE VILLAGE HOTEL
International

Cobalt Business Park, West Allotment, Newcastle, NE27 0BY
0191 270 1414
Whether dining for business or pleasure, the restaurant here is ideally located close to the city and the coast. Imaginatively transformed seasonal classics can be found on this well designed menu.

2FOR1 MAIN COURSE

The GS offer is valid in the restaurant only.

THROWING STONES
British

Glass Centre, Liberty Way, Sunderland, SR6 0GL
0191 565 3939
Characterful café and restaurant at the National Glass Centre; acclaimed in its own right as a leading restaurant in the North East, it serves a diversity of dishes with verve and élan.

25%OFF TOTAL

TIGER TIGER
British

The Gate, Newgate Street, Newcastle, NE1 5RE
0191 235 7065
A great place to dine and drink, from lunch until late. Choose from one of the many differently themed bars, or dine in the stylish contemporary restaurant where the menu ranges from steaks to salads.

50%OFF FOOD

VARANDA
Indian

Rectory Lodge, Rectory Lane, Whickham, NE16 4PD
0191 488 0040
A bright gem of a restaurant, this place offers not only great food but an atmosphere to match. Expect an artistic menu that is eager to transform stock dishes into new taste sensations.

2FOR1 MAIN COURSE

WHITLEY BAY TANDOORI
Indian

40 Esplanade, Whitley Bay, NE26 2AE
0191 252 9483
Whitley Bay Tandoori does just as it says on the tin, with a bright and hospitable ambience playing host to the full gamut of classic Indian dishes, and an especial line in tandoori recipes.

2FOR1 MAIN COURSE

Yorkshire

23 BAR AND RESTAURANT
British

3 West One Plaza, Fitzwilliam St, Sheffield, S1 4JB
0114 272 2323
An unprecedented dining and drinking environment that delivers a committed service and fine British cuisine. An award-winning venue that takes pride in every aspect of guests' dining experience.

2FOR1 MAIN COURSE

701 AT HOLIDAY INN HARROGATE
International

Kings Road, Harrogate, HG1 1XX
0871 942 9261
This contemporary Holiday Inn is situated perfectly for either business or pleasure. Both stylish restaurants delivers quality, freshly cooked food, catering for guests in every situation.

25%OFF TOTAL

1 card per table.

286

Discounted hotel rates for GS members on our website

BED RESTAURANT
British
20 Kings Road, Harrogate, HG1 5JW
01423 568 600
Stay in Bed and dine in style. Whatever the attire or occasion, receive a warm welcome and leave fully satisfied. The only problem is deciding who to take with you.

BENGAL SPICE
Indian
21 Cheltenham Cresent, Harrogate, HG1 1DH
01423 502 610
Offering Indian and Bangladeshi cuisine that will exceed all of your expectations. Whether you enjoy delicate flavours or fiery spices, the authenticity of each dish will really set your night on fire.

BEVERLEY ARMS HOTEL
Traditional English Fare
North Bar, Beverley East, Beverley, HU17 8DD
01482 869 241
Dine in the classically decorated restaurant of this wonderful Brook hotel, a former coach house dating to 1794. Guests and in-the-know locals are invited to feast on a wide range of traditional dishes.

BLACKWELL OX INN
Modern British
Huby Road, Sutton on the Forest, York, YO61 1DT
01347 810 328
Chef Steven Holding delivers simple, classic food in this gorgeous North Yorkshire inn; local produce is a key focus, and you can wash the lot down with a robust pint of the finest. Awarded 1 AA Rosette.

BOMBAY SPICE
Indian/Bangladeshi
58 Goodram Gate, York, YO1 7LF
01904 613 298
A warm, charming Indian restaurant in York whose menu delivers all the traditional favourites along with some esoteric delights; the knowledgeable staff will have you up to speed on these in no time.

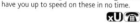

BRETTS FISH RESTAURANT
Fish and Seafood
12/14 North Lane, Headingley, Leeds, LS6 3HE
0113 232 3344
Step inside this beautiful ivy-covered Victorian house and expect to be blown away by the fish and chips. Icelandic haddock and chips made from Lincolnshire potatoes make up the signature dish.

BROOKLANDS AT HOLDIAY INN BARNSLEY
European
Barnsley Rd, Dodworth, Barnsley, S75 3JT
01226 299 571
Tempting English and continental cuisine can be enjoyed in pristine surroundings. Guests will love the famous Barnsley chops and fabulous wine list which have earned the restaurant a great reputation.

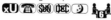

BROWN COW & DRAGON
Thai/British
Selby Road, Leeds, LS15 7AY
0113 264 6112
A Thai cuisine and British pub combination done properly. This renowned Dragon pub showcases an impressive array of authentic dishes and imported beverages, with something to tempt everyone's taste buds.

BURLINGTONS RESTAURANT
Contemporary
91 High Street, Bridlington, YO16 4PN
01262 400 383
A restaurant run by husband and wife offering food that incorporates influences from all over the world. Co-owner and chef David injects Thai twists and Italian freshness into some very English dishes.

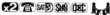

CAFE NO.8 BISTRO
European
8 Gillygate, York, YO31 7EQ
01904 653 074
Classic timelessness meets contemporary chic in this small café bistro. Situated in the beautiful city of York, the tranquil ambience of its location is transferred to the interior of the venue.

CAFÉ ROUGE
French
21-29 Beulah Street, Harrogate, HG1 1JZ
01423 500 043
An attractive restaurant, a boulevard café or a Parisian-style wine bar; however you see Café Rouge, consistently excellent classic French dishes are always guaranteed.

CAFÉ ROUGE
French
The Light, 64 The Headrow, Leeds, LS1 8EH
0113 246 1620
An attractive restaurant, a boulevard café or a Parisian-style wine bar; however you see Café Rouge, consistently excellent classic French dishes are always guaranteed.

CAFÉ ROUGE
French
Sheffield Centre, St Paul's Place, Sheffield, S1 2JL
0114 275 3815
An attractive restaurant, a boulevard café or a Parisian-style wine bar; however you see Café Rouge, consistently excellent classic French dishes are always guaranteed.

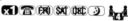

CAFÉ ROUGE
French
383-385 Ecclesall Raod, Sheffield, S11 8PG
0114 268 2232
An attractive restaurant, a boulevard café or a Parisian-style wine bar; however you see Café Rouge, consistently excellent classic French dishes are always guaranteed.

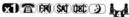

CAFÉ ROUGE
French
The Adams House, 52 Lower Petergate, York, YO1 7HZ
01904 673 293
An attractive restaurant, a boulevard café or a Parisian-style wine bar; however you see Café Rouge, consistently excellent classic French dishes are always guaranteed.

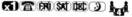

CANTEEN
Locally Sourced
32-44 Sandygate Rd, Crosspool, Sheffield, S10 5RY
0114 266 6096
Multi award-winning chef Richard Smith provides outstanding quality dishes in this terrific restaurant. A fast-paced menu offers tasty treats that are cooked in the lively, vibrant open kitchen.

CARAMBA TAPAS AND BAR
Spanish
34a Oxford Street, Harrogate, HG1 1PP
01423 505 300
A stylish bar that focuses on the original traits of tapas dining. Enjoy crispy calamari or slow-cooked pork as you chat with friends and indulge in wine that will suitably complement your selections.

CARLTON BORE
British
Main Street, Carlton Husthwaite, Thirsk, YO7 2BW
01845 501 265
A refreshing blend of country house décor and country inn informality, where the best local and seasonal produce is engaged. Each dish is well-supported by a wine list packed with award winners.

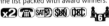

CASA MIA GRANDE
Italian
33 Harrogate Rd, Chapel Allerton, Leeds, LS7 3PD
0113 239 2555
Fresh fish cooked before your eyes and delicious home-made pasta are just two of the restaurant's unbeatable specialities. The award-winning leccabaffi with scampi and mango will guarantee satisfaction.

CASA MIA MILLENNIUM
Italian
Millennium Square, Great George St, Leeds, LS2 3AD
0113 245 4121
Perfect for lunch, dinner, or even a snack, dine inside or al fresco and enjoy the hustle and bustle of the vibrant city centre at this restaurant, situated in the exclusive Millennium Square.

CHAMPS SPORTS BAR AND RESTAURANT
American
315-319 Ecclesall Road, Sheffield, S11 8NX
0114 266 6333
Mouth-watering burgers, succulent steaks and scrumptious Mexican dishes are all on offer at this popular bar and restaurant. Leave room for the delicious ice cream sundaes which are too good to miss.

CLOCKTOWER
British
Rudding Park, Follifoot, Harrogate, HG3 1JH
01423 871 350
If food is your passion look no further than Clocktower. Yorkshire produce cooked to perfection and a monthly Food Heroes menu whose principal ingredients are sourced within 75 miles. Awarded 2 AA Rosettes.

COAL GRILL + BAR
Mediterranean
The Oasis, Meadowhall Centre, Sheffield, S9 1EP
0114 251 6706
Known for fresh, delectable food and captivating cocktails, this restaurant offers many fine dishes including their fiery 'flame-grilled fire-sticks'. Delivers a developed and enhanced menu.

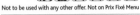
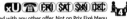
Not to be used with any other offer. Not on Prix Fixé Menu

COURTYARD AT OX PASTURE HALL
Modern British
Lady Edith's Drive, Raincliffe Woods, Scarborough, YO12 5TD
01723 365 293
Relax, unwind and enjoy award-winning food in the most elegant of surroundings. Fine summer days can be idyllically spent in the garden terrace. The Whitby crab and roasted scallops are superb.

DA-CLAUDIO
Italian
4 Harcourt Place, Scarborough, YO11 2EP
01723 354 648
A blend of innovative and traditional Italian cuisine is served with a wine choice to complement every dish. The friendly service, pleasant atmosphere and novel menu complete the dining experience.

DARCY'S BRASSERIE
British
Mosborough Hall Hotel, High St, Mosborough, S20 5EA
0114 248 4353
A calm oasis of a restaurant which offers contemporary dining in opulent surroundings. The excellence of the food and atmosphere at Darcy's ensures a regular crowd of fans.

DESIGN HOUSE
British
Dean Clough Mills, Halifax, HX3 5AX
01422 383 242
Ultra-modern restaurant where superb, award-winning cuisine is matched by an extensive wine list. Enjoy the refreshing, informal ambience, whilst taking advantage of great food at fantastic prices.

DISTRIKT
Mediterranean
7 Duncan Street, Leeds, LS1 6DQ
0113 243 3674
Distrikt, renowned for its tapas, combines a love for underground electronic music with an eclectic mix of Middle Eastern, Mediterranean and British influences in its fresh, locally sourced food.

DROVERS REST @ THE FLEECE
British
9-11 Westgate, Rillington, Malton, YO17 8LN
01944 758 464
Boasting high-class, seasonally varied dining, this conveniently located pub is an ideal place to bring the family. Places exciting English cuisine at the heart of the menu.

DUKE OF YORK
British
West Street, Shelf, Halifax, HX3 7LN
01422 203 925
A characterful inn housing a dining area that offers both formal and informal dining. Delivers British food complemented by cask ales and an interesting selection of wines and liqueurs.

GEORGE & DRAGON
Modern Pub
Doncaster Road, Whitley, Goole, DN14 0HY
01977 661 319
Traditional, hearty pub food for when any other meal just won't do, delivered by a committed team who relish the opportunity of extending a warm welcome and offering quality service to every guest.

GEORGE HOTEL
Traditional English Fare
St George's Square, Huddersfield, HD1 1JA
01484 515 444
Undoubtedly one of Huddersfield's most prestigious settings, the in-house restaurant of this splendid Brook hotel delivers traditional English and Yorkshire delicacies in an elegant and refined atmosphere.

Gourmet Society discount applies to the à la carte menu

GRANGEMOOR RESTAURANT
Modern European
The Old Golf House, New Hey Rd, Hudd'field, HD3 3YP
0844 736 8609
Restaurant with breathtaking views, perfect for an enjoyable family dinner or intimate meal. Excellent modern cuisine complemented by a well-stocked bar, and al fresco dining.

HANDMADE BURGER CO.
American
The Oasis, Meadowhall Centre, Sheffield, S9 1EP
0114 256 8945
Real quality, handmade cooking, crafted with passion and excellence. Enjoy the finest burgers from an exhaustive selection, all made fresh with many divine side orders to choose from.

HARROGATE BRASSERIE
British
26-30 Cheltenham Parade, Harrogate, HG1 1DB
01423 505 041
Come dine at this exceptional brasserie that proposes a menu filled with seasonal dishes bursting with flavour and flair. All served in a intimate dining area soothed by the velvet sounds of jazz.

Booking ahead and mentioning GS is essential.

HARRY RAMSDEN'S
British
White Cross, Guiseley, Leeds, LS20 8LZ
01943 874 641
Harry himself used to serve fish and chips from this very spot. Today we can all continue to enjoy his legacy of delicious seaside food, best served with a sprinkle of salt, and a dash of vinegar.

Not available during August or in takeaway.

HARRY RAMSDEN'S
British
23, Foreshore Road, Scarborough, YO11 1PB
01723 376 727
The classic fish and chips combo, perfected. Britain's best loved 'chippy' renowned for their famous seaside food, serving guests quality dishes time and time again.

Not available during August or in takeaway.

HENRY J BEANS
American
1 Tower Street, York, YO1 9WD
01904 648 111
A fun and friendly American grill delivering diners exactly what they want. A great selection of mouth-watering dishes, all traditionally American, from hot dogs to delicious steaks and ribs.

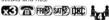

HENRY'S CAFE BAR
European
10 Greek Street, Leeds, LS1 5RU
0113 245 9424
An oasis for every guest with a delicious, well-prepared menu ideal for lunch, dinner or a light snack. Henrys also boasts an extensive wine and champagne list and a choice of cocktails to die for.

HOTEL DU VIN
European
Prospect Place, Harrogate, HG1 1LB
01423 856 800
The finest, freshest local produce, simple European recipes, a stunning choice of wines; these are the elements of the trademark Hotel du Vin bistro. Enjoy amazing views with glass in hand. 2 AA Rosettes.

HOTEL DU VIN
European
89 The Mount, York, YO24 1AX
01904 557 350
The finest, freshest local produce, simple European recipes, a stunning choice of wines; these are the elements of the trademark Hotel du Vin bistro. A beautiful grade II listed York venue. 1 AA Rosette.

HQ AT THE GRAND
Modern British
The Grand Hotel and Spa, Station Rise, York, YO1 6HT
01904 380 038
A pristine, well-decorated interior provides a dining haven in which you can enjoy wholesome British dishes. Classic favourites appear alongside more adventurous gastronomic delights.

JAKES
Italian
47 Oxford Street, Harrogate, HG1 1PW
01423 536 606
A varied menu accommodates both the Yorkshire and Italian food lover from beautiful breakfasts to divine dinners, whilst the home-made cakes offer every guest a slice of heaven.

KASHMIRI AROMA ILKLEY
Indian
Coutances Way, Ilkley, LS29 7HQ
01943 865 554
An aromatic, fragrant and spice-filled menu that reflects the cultural diversities of India. Choose to dine à la carte or sample the tantalising buffet selections. Fine Indian dining and hospitality.

KASHMIRI AROMA WOODSEATS
Indian
798 Chesterfield Road, Woodseats, Sheffield, S8 0SF
01142 587 780
Authentic and exquisite cuisine showcasing the diverse culture of Indian and its culinary delights. The menu is extensive, offering vegetarian and non-vegetarian food that is all halal.

KENNEDY'S
Contemporary
1 Little Stonegate, York, YO1 8AX
01904 620 222
A lively cosmopolitan area is home to this unique bar and restaurant. The stylish contemporary atmosphere attracts an eclectic clientèle.

KHANS BEVERLEY
Indian
4 North Bar Without, Beverley, HU17 7AA
01482 868 300
A constant inflow of diners indicates this restaurant's excellence. Guests will enjoy speciality dishes such as the tandoori fish massala, whilst the brave can try the garlic chilli roof-lifter.

LA CANTINA 44
Mediterranean
1a Austhorpe Road, Cross Gates, Leeds, LS15 8QR
0113 368 0066
La Cantina 44's vast selection of dishes ensures a comprehensively satisfied palate. The restaurant offers superb Mediterranean cuisine made from the freshest ingredients.

LA VECCHIA SCUOLA
Italian
62 Low Petergate, York, YO1 7HZ
01904 644 600
Authentic, adventurous, and creative Italian cuisine in the heart of the city, where the level of attentive service matches the exquisite standard of the food. This is fine dining without the formalities.

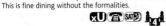

LAZY LOUNGE
English and Continental
29 Wellington Street, Leeds, LS1 4JY
0113 244 6055
An exclusive wine bar in the heart of the city's financial district. Sample a wonderful, unknown wine, or choose a comforting glass of your favourite. An exclusive menu offers great food.

LE JARDIN
French / European
7 Montpellier Parade, Harrogate, HG1 2TJ
01423 507 323
Family-run restaurant, whose dining area overlooks Montpellier Gardens in Harrogate. Its homely ambience ideally sets off the restaurant's traditional, locally sourced food.

 2FOR1 3COURSES

LEEDS SEVENTEEN
Modern British
Nursery Lane, Alwoodley, Leeds LS17 7HW
0113 266 2594
Suitably proud of their Yorkshire heritage, the kitchen team of this local gem pride themselves on sourcing local produce whenever possible to create contemporary British dishes with a Continental flare.

LIVE LOUNGE
Contemporary
75 Lidget Street, Lindley, Huddersfield, HD3 3JP
01484 646 416
Pleasurable dining guaranteed. The Head Chef here makes full use of his talents by producing exceptionally tasty contemporary dishes that can be complemented by one of the many fine wines on offer.

LOCH FYNE
Seafood
The Old Post Office, 2 City Square, Leeds, LS1 3ES
0113 391 7550
From the roadside oyster bar that once was, Loch Fyne restaurants now successfully inject energy and passion into great food and wonderful flavours, whilst ensuring their seafood is sustainably sourced.

LOCH FYNE
Seafood
Glossop Road, Sheffield, S10 2HQ
0114 270 3940
From the roadside oyster bar that once was, Loch Fyne restaurants now successfully inject energy and passion into great food and wonderful flavours, whilst ensuring their seafood is sustainably sourced.

LOCH FYNE
Seafood
Foss Bridge Street, Walmgate, York, YO1 9TJ
01904 650 910
From the roadside oyster bar that once was, Loch Fyne restaurants now successfully inject energy and passion into great food and wonderful flavours, whilst ensuring their seafood is sustainably sourced.

MALMAISON
European
1 Swinegate, Leeds, LS1 4AG
0113 398 1000
Striking and charismatic décor in this brasserie whose focus is on fresh, locally sourced produce and a contemporary, stylish ambience. Enjoy this stylish Leeds Mal and its distinctive style. 1 AA Rosette.

 2FOR1 MAIN COURSE

MARKET BRASSERIE AT HOLIDAY INN
International
High Road, Warmsworth, Doncaster, DN4 9UX
0871 942 9061
Fill your plate from the full English or continental breakfast buffets in the sunny Market Brasserie. In the evening, international dishes like the Thai red chicken curry are served.

Only one card can be used per table.

MEDUSA BAR
Modern European
8-10 Town Street, Horsforth, Leeds, LS18 4RJ
0113 259 0110
Medusa's hip styling provides a home to silky, savoury starters, beautifully cooked hearty mains, and smoothly wanton desserts.

 2FOR1 MAIN COURSE

MORENOS
Moroccan
54-56 Temple Newsam Rd, Leeds, LS15 0DR
0113 260 4844
Guests love the earthy tastes and terrific textures of the Moroccan cuisine on offer at Moreno's. The warm interior ensures diners relax, all the better to enjoy the famous, slow-cooked lamb tagine.

MUCKLES
English/Gastro pub
11 West Park, Harrogate, HG1 1BL
01423 858 153
Take time out for some classically hearty, well-cooked English pub food at this characterful inn in Harrogate. Welcoming, accommodating and well-located, it promises a treat of an evening.

MUJIB
Indian
32 Devonshire Place, Harrogate, HG1 4AD
01423 875 522
Modernised Indian cuisine that takes the most enjoyable accents from dishes found across the world. Flavoursome meals and attentive waiting staff guarantee your visit will make a lasting impression.

 2FOR1 MAIN COURSE

NAG'S HEAD
Carvery
New Hey Road, Huddersfield, HD2 2EA
01422 373 758
One of over 30 Great British Carvery pubs offering Gourmet Society members the best of British food. Enjoy well-loved classic dishes in this characterful, family-friendly pub with a popular reputation.

 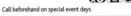 **2FOR1** MAIN COURSE

Call beforehand on special event days.

NORTH BAR
Traditional English Fare
Beverley Arms Hotel, Beverley, HU17 8BB
01482 869 241
Freshly prepared and wholly traditional cuisine is on offer at this classically decorated Brook Hotel restaurant, making it an ideal place in which to dine, relax and unwind.

Sign up to our newsletter for latest restaurants, offers and more

NONNA'S

535- 41 Ecclesall Road, Sheffield, S11 8PR

0114 268 6166 *Italian*

When the doors of Nonna's opened in 1996 the team nurtured the ambition to share their passion for authentic Italian foods and wines with the British public. There was no great business plan, just a desire to bring the true taste of Italian life to this part of the world, and a dream to open British eyes to creamy cappuccinos, strong dark espressos and the delights of traditional mortadella, formaggi and pastas of all shapes and sizes.

To this day the passion still burns as brightly and diners feast on traditional Italian cuisine made with the best produce both Yorkshire and Italy have to offer. The wine list betrays the deep respect the owners have for diverse and fabulous national offerings.

All menus are seasonal and all dietary requirements can be catered for. This popular restaurant has brought a little piece of Italy to Yorkshire for some time, simultaneously attracting the attention of world famous chefs and the admiration of the local crowd.

1 AA rosette.

NOSH BRASSERIE @ 25
European

25 Newmarket Street, Skipton, BD23 2JE
01756 793 676

Stylish minimalism underpins this restaurant's distinctive ambience, with three individually designed dining areas offering variety. Its award-winning success is underpinned by exceptional food.

PREZZO
Italian

631-633 Ecclesall Road, Sheffield, S11 8PT
01142 670 565

With a character all of its own, Prezzo oozes contemporary style and enduring charm. Signature pastas, stone-baked pizzas and classic Italian dishes promise a perfect dining choice for the whole family.

NEW

POPOLO
European

5a Leopold Square, Sheffield, S1 2JG
0114 275 8405

Enjoy a mouth-watering mix of modern Italian food, carefully designed to cater for the more adventurous Italian food lover. A vast array of menu options caters for all; crisp pizzas and tempting desserts.

POTTERS SHEFFIELD
British

54a The Oasis, Sheffield, S9 1EE
0114 256 8867

Take a break and enjoy a dish from a menu of timeless British food. Something for the whole family, including a fantastic kids menu. Great food in relaxed and comfortable surroundings.

PREZZO
Italian

Unit 26 Marshalls Yard, Beaumont St, Gainsborough, DN21 2NA
01427 611 934

With a character all of its own, Prezzo oozes contemporary style and enduring charm. Signature pastas, stone-baked pizzas and classic Italian dishes promise a perfect dining choice for the whole family.

PREZZO
Italian

Unit 41, St Stephens Ferensway, Hull, HU2 8LN
01482 223 277

With a character all of its own, Prezzo oozes contemporary style and enduring charm. Signature pastas, stone-baked pizzas and classic Italian dishes promise a perfect dining choice for the whole family.

PREZZO
Italian

Valley Centertainment, Broughton Lane, Sheffield, S9 2EP
0114 244 7477

With a character all of its own, Prezzo oozes contemporary style and enduring charm. Signature pastas, stone-baked pizzas and classic Italian dishes promise a perfect dining choice for the whole family.

PREZZO
Italian

2-4 Albert Street, Harrogate, HG1 1JG
01423 520 447

With a character all of its own, Prezzo oozes contemporary style and enduring charm. Signature pastas, stone-baked pizzas and classic Italian dishes promise a perfect dining choice for the whole family.

PROHIBITION
British
Yorkshire House, Greek Street, Leeds, LS1 5SH
0113 224 0005
From top class burgers made from the finest cuts of properly aged and lightly seasoned beef to sharing platters of succulent seafood, Prohibition is a versatile bar-restaurant that does things with flair.

RESTAURANT 55
British
49-55 Eastborough, Scarborough, YO11 1NH
01723 365 921
Hugely popular seafood establishment offering diners amazingly fresh food and spectacular views of the south bay. There are numerous delectable fish, salad, and shellfish dishes on the menu.

SAGE BISTRO
European
11 Mount Parade, Harrogate, HG1 1BX
01423 500 089
Enjoy a relaxed evening meal after a hard day of shopping, or indulge in delicious cuisine before heading to the nearby theatre. The Head Chef's passion for good food can be tasted in every dish.

SAM'S CHOP HOUSE
British
8 South Parade, Leeds, LS1 5QX
01132 042 490
A charming British restaurant serving delicious food to an ever-increasing legion of fans. Expertly cooked treats such as the Swaledale sausages are continually popular.

SAN PIETRO
International
11 High Street East, Scunthorpe, DN15 6UH
01724 277 774
A phenomenally exquisite place to drink, dine and catch up with friends. Opt for the elegant dining room for luxury surroundings, before heading to the mellow mill room for an after dinner cocktail.

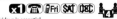
Calling ahead on Fridays is essential.

SANTINI'S ITALIAN RESTAURANT
Italian/ Mediterranean
8C Netherhall Road, Doncaster, DN1 1PW
01302 768 878
Owners Dario and Claire have over 15 years experience and carry on a family tradition that began in Sicily many years ago. Enjoy authentic Italian classics with something traditional to suit every palate.

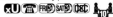

SHANGTHAI
Chinese
32 King Street, Huddersfield, HD1 2QT
01484 531 999
Traditional and tasty, here you'll find fine Cantonese cuisine to be enjoyed in a contemporary and relaxed atmosphere, where all dishes are served with a smile.

SHIRAZ
Persian
759 - 761 Abbeydale Road, Sheffield, S7 2BG
0114 255 1888
An exceptional Persian restaurant that offers everything curious guests may have anticipated. Unquestionably authentic dishes are served in generous portions and can be completed with a cup of Persian tea.

SHOOTERS SPORTS CAFE
International
123 The Headrow, Leeds, LS1 5RD
0113 243 2300
A sociable venue delivering food and entertainment on a grand scale with bars, big screens, pool tables and a dining area. Enjoy a selection of appetising meals whilst soaking up the lively atmosphere.

SPICE 4U
Indian
41 Hungate, Pickering, YO18 7DG
01751 473 334
A family-owned restaurant bringing authentic Indian cuisine to both the people of Wetherby and visitors from afar. Regular guests enjoy the genuine taste of the East in their classic and speciality dishes.

SPICE MARKET CAFE
Pan Asian
371-373 Ecclesall Road, Sheffield, S11 8PF
0114 266 5541
East-meets-West experience offering everything from Sri Lankan and Japanese to Indian and Thai dishes. A minimalist look and diverse menu, always with quality cooking, hearty portions and value for money.

STALLINGBOROUGH GRANGE
British
Riby Road, Stallingborough, DN41 8BU
01469 561 302
A picturesque country house steeped in history. From delicious bar meals to signature dishes, accompanied by fine wines and traditional ales, this bar and restaurant is the perfect venue for all occasions.

STORM BAR & RESTAURANT
British
Swan Road, Harrogate, HG1 2SS
01423 560 666
Specialises in fish and seafood, but also has some fine meat and game on its menu. Sumptuous dishes crafted with passion from quality produce, all at great prices. A relaxed vibe and a surpassing meal.

TANDOORI NIGHT
Indian
3 Castle Hill, Richmond, DL10 4QP
01748 826 677
Classic Indian cuisine served in a picturesque village. Renowned for its helpful staff and atmospheric surroundings, this venue offers quality, authentic dishes created to delight your taste buds.

TEMUJIN RESTAURANT
Mongolian
Bridge Croft Mills, Tanyard Rd, Milnsbridge, HD3 4NN
01484 461 111
Take your stir-fry request directly to the chef in this creatively laid out restaurant. The buffet plays host to everything from chicken to crocodile, mussels to Tofu and quorn.

TEMUJIN RESTAURANT
Mongolian
1st Flr, No. 1 Warehouse, Canal Basin, Halifax, HX6 2AG
01422 835 500
Take your stir-fry request directly to the chef in this creatively laid out restaurant. The buffet plays host to everything from chicken to crocodile, mussels to tofu and quorn.

Visit the website regularly to discover the latest restaurants joining the GS

THAI EDGE
Thai
7 Calverley Street, Leeds, LS1 3DY
0113 243 6333
Thai Edge encapsulates contemporary Oriental design and exotic Thai cuisine. All palates are catered for, whether you prefer subtle sophisticated flavours or hot and spicy tastes.

One card per party. Cheapest main meal free.

THAI ELEPHANT
Thai
13-15 Cheltenham Parade, Harrogate, HG1 1DD
01423 530 099
Charming, forthcoming Thai restaurant whose range of dishes is as popular as its warm welcome to diners. Thai cuisine's vivid, vibrant colours are brought out to the full.

THAI FEVER
Thai
3-7 Saltaire Road, Shipley, BD18 3HH
01274 580 033
Feast on deliciously tasty dishes that incorporate notes of Thai and Singaporean flavours, without breaking your diet. Using reduced calorie levels, this is a perfect choice for the health-conscious.

THAI SABAI RESTAURANT
Thai
2 The Parade, North Lane, Headingley, Leeds, LS6 3HP
0113 275 8613
Knowledgeable, attentive staff are happy to help you choose from the extensive array of dishes on the menu at Thai Sabai. Mouth-watering dishes, such as the gung op woon sen, are unforgettable.

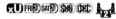

THE BEEHIVE
British
Main Street, Thorner, Leeds, LS14 3DE
0113 2017171
Operating on the principle of 'real value for money' this cosy village restaurant offers a casual and relaxed dining experience. Without fuss; but absolutely with quality food and wine.

THE BILTMORE BAR & GRILL
European
29 Swinegate, York, YO1 9AZ
01904 610 075
Opulent dining in sumptuous surroundings. Luxurious sofas, booths and dining areas make a relaxing space in which guests can devour the delicious English and French dishes that are on offer.

THE BLUE BELL INN
Modern British
Weaverthorpe, Malton, YO17 8EX
01944 738 204
A popular restaurant, well known for its excellent food and cosy ambience. Modern English cuisine guarantees a delicious dining experience.

THE BOHEMIAN
International
53 Chesterfield Road, Sheffield, S8 0RL
0114 255 7796
One of Sheffield's first veggie, vegan and fish establishments, offering a pleasant dining experience by serving healthy, enjoyable food. Revel in rich British bohemian culture and great company.

Offer not available on corkage or juices.

THE BRIDGE
British
Walshford, Wetherby, Leeds, LS22 5HS
01937 580 115
Steeped in history, offering a truly unique experience. Diners are given a choice of various appealing dishes, freshly prepared, and served in a dining room complete with fascinating historical features.

THE CHILLI LODGE
Indian
Knabbs Lane, Silkstone Common, Barnsley, S75 4RD
01226 792 300
Chic and contemporary, this Indian restaurant in Silkstone Common takes great care with the taste of its classic favourites while also taking seriously its aim to produce innovative and tasty new dishes.

THE DOG AND GUN INN
Modern Pub
Denholme Road, Oxenhope, Keighley, BD22 9SN
01535 643 159
Good home-cooked food and excellent award-winning beer; part of the Best of British group. The menu provides guests with a superb choice of pub food coupled with an wine list to complement the meal.

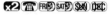

THE GASCOIGNE ARMS
English/Gastro pub
2 Main Street, Barwick in Elmet, Leeds, LS15 4JQ
0113 281 2265
A great place for a piled-high plate of some classic, unpretentious but completely satisfying pub grub. Settle in for a Sunday lunch or make an evening of it with a pint to wash down your dinner.

THE GARDEN ROOM AT BURN HALL
Fine Dining
Burn Hall Hotel, Tollerton Road, Huby, YO61 1JB
01347 825 400
Taking its name from the sensational hotel gardens that are beautifully overlooked by this restaurant, The Garden Room offers appealing dishes that make extensive use of local and own-grown produce.

THE GEORGE
European
20 High Street, Kirton In Lindsey, DN21 4LX
01652 640 600
This venue combines a friendly service and a fantastic menu, from fillet steaks to sea bass. All the food is freshly prepared and is coupled with a specially selected wine list to complement each dish.

THE INN AT TROWAY
Modern Pub
Snowdon Lane, Troway, Sheffield, S21 5RU
01246 417 666
Hearty pub classics prepared by chefs who are passionate about local produce. Rustic originality is maintained at the core of this fantastic award-winning pub.

THE LIME HOUSE RESTAURANT
International
55 Goodramgate, York, YO1 7LS
01904 632 734
It is easy to see how this award-winning restaurant gained its popular reputation. The owners identify culinary variety as being vital for a successfully satisfying menu.

NORTH EAST

THE LIVING ROOM
British
7 Greek Street, Leeds, LS1 5RW
0113 380 0930
Step into The Living Room and you can count on the savvy, distinctive neighbourhood vibe that plays home to eclectically drawn, supremely tasty cuisine. Clean, classic lines characterise this Leeds venue.

Must purchase minimum of 3 courses/person, including main.

THE LIVING ROOM
British
Merchant Exchange, 1 Bridge Street, York, YO1 6DD
01904 461 000
Step into The Living Room and you can count on the savvy, distinctive neighbourhood vibe that plays home to eclectically drawn, supremely tasty cuisine. Plush, snug and with superb views across the Ouse.

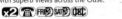
Must purchase minimum of 3 courses/person, including main.

THE MALT
English and Continental
Main Street, Burley in Wharfedale, Ilkley, LS29 7DN
01943 862 207
A highly experienced award-winning chef produces outstanding traditional food. An attractive restaurant to both locals and visitors from afar, who enjoy the good use of fresh local produce.

THE MANSION
British
Mansion Lane, Roundhay, Leeds, LS8 2HH
0113 269 1000
Enjoy delightful views of the 700 acres in which this classical building is situated in. Guests will be overwhelmed by the interior magnificence and grandeur of this listed venue.

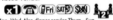
Lunch service only Mon- Wed. Also dinner service Thurs - Sun.

THE MERRION HOTEL
Traditional English Fare
The Merrion Centre, Wade Lane, Leeds, LS2 8NH
0113 243 9191
This restaurant from the Brook group, formulates a range of accomplished, fulsome dishes with both contemporary and traditional inflections, stylishly set in elegant dining rooms.

THE NEEDLESS INN
English and Continental
Scotchman Lane, Morley, LS27 0NZ
01924 472 986
Situated between two busy town centres, this ideally located inn is a great place for a rest away from the hustle and bustle of everyday life. Enjoy views of country fields as you feast on daily specials.

THE OLD BORE
British
Oldham Road, Rishworth, Sowerby Bridge, HX6 4QU
01422 822 291
Fantastic produce, such as rare-breed pork, fantastic wild fish and Cornish crab, is used extensively in the kitchen. Enjoy vibrant, tasty dishes in a 19th century converted coaching inn. 1 AA Rosette.

THE OLD DEANERY
Fine Dining
Minster Road, Ripon, HG4 1QS
01765 600 003
The bright sparkle of this treasured Yorkshire jewel is not to be missed. Its award-winning status is just one reason to dine in this unforgettable restaurant. Priceless cuisine in heavenly surroundings.

294

THE OLD WHITE BEARE
British
Village Street, Norwood Green, HX3 8QG
01274 675 545
An impressive reputation belongs to this ideally located pub. Quality beers and imaginatively created food are on offer and guarantee all guests a great time.

THE OLD TRAMSHED
English/Gastro Pub
199 Bingley Road, Saltaire, BD18 4DH
01274 582 111
A pub-restaurant that prides itself on using fresh, local produce and offering up superb cask ales, this is a great place to sit back, relax, drink and eat whether you're from nearby or visiting Saltaire.

THE OLIVE TREE GREEK
Greek
55 Rodley Lane, Rodley, LS13 1NG
0113 256 9283
Weekend Bouzouki performances bring this place to life. Put on your dancing shoes if you are a willing participant, or sit back and be jovially entertained as you feast on traditional Greek dishes.

THE ORIGINAL DILRAJ TANDOORI
Indian
8-12 High Street, Barnsley, S75 3RF
01226 202 606
One of Barnsley's finest Indian restaurants, with a great reputation for the very best hospitality and authentic cuisine. A unique dining experience for locals and visitors alike.

THE PARK ROW BAR & BRASSIERE
European
23 The Headrow, Leeds, LS1 5RD
0113 243 2300
Indulge in a menu of pub classics and enjoy quality food at this stylish venue. With a relaxing ambience, this is a perfect chance for a well-deserved break from hectic city living.

RECOMMEND A FRIEND
see page 18

THE ROYAL HOTEL
British
Saint Nichola's Street, Scarborough, YO11 2HE
01723 364 333
The sensational view of Scarborough's South Bay is not the only thing that should encourage you to dine here. Traditional Yorkshire fare makes this a fabulous place to eat, any time of the day.

THE STAR INN
Modern Pub
Main Street, Weaverthorpe, Malton, YO17 8EY
01944 738 273
A gem of a North Yorks inn whose philosophy is for freshness and home-making; the crisp beer-battered fish is great against the distinctive twang of their own ketchup. Something a bit special.

When booking restaurants always mention your GS membership

THE WOODMAN INN
British

Burneston, Bedale, DL8 2HX
01677 422 066
This pleasant pub has built a reputation for good food and warm company, and has many local fans. Visit The Woodman Inn for a lesson in English hospitality.

THE WOODSIDE
Carvery

299 Bow Lane, Leeds, LS18 4DD
0113 258 2341
A Great British Carvery pub that serves the best of British food with a modern twist. Charming and friendly, the staff warmly welcome guests so that each and every diner leaves with a smile of their own.

Call beforehand on special event days.

THE WORSLEY ARMS HOTEL
British

High Street, Hovingham, YO62 4LA
01653 628 234
Maintaining its historical purpose of providing comfort for travellers from both near and far, this is a pleasing place to both rest and dine. Old World charm exudes from all aspects of this hotel.

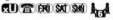

THE YELLOW LION
British

Worksop Road, Aston, Sheffield, S26 2EB
0114 287 2283
Tasty and down-to-earth pub food is offered in this family-orientated inn in Aston, just outside Sheffield. At a great price and with a lot of homely character, it serves up a cracking meal.

TIGER TIGER
International

The Light, 117 Albion Street, Leeds, LS2 8DY
0113 236 6999
Whatever your requirements, Tiger Tiger will undoubtedly suit your needs. Offering relaxed dining, chilled-out drinking and all-night partying, both the venue and the menu offers something for everyone.

TRADERS @ HOLIDAY INN WAKEFIELD
British

M1 Junction 40, Queens Drive, Ossett, Wakefield, WF5 9BE
01924 230 600
Comfortable restaurant at the Holiday Inn at Wakefield. You'll enjoy a range of traditional and contemporary dishes cooked confidently for a breadth of occasions, whether formal or relaxed.

WEAVERS IN HAWORTH
British

13-17 West Lane, Keighley, BD22 8DW
01535 643 822
Charismatic and intimate dining rooms are the setting for Weavers' distinctive, acclaimed British cooking: a commingling of the traditional and modern. Awarded 1 AA Rosette.

WEETWOOD HALL'S BRASSERIE
Brasserie

Otley Road, Leeds, LS16 5PS
0113 230 6000
Enjoy a refreshing glass of wine, a frothy cappuccino or a delicious light meal in an environment that is perfect during the day for one-to-one meetings. Free wi-fi is available for a working lunch.

WELLINGTON HEIFER INN
Traditional English

Ainderby Steeple, Northallerton, DL7 9PU
01609 775 542
Landlord Kenny and his wife Pauline welcome you with open arms to their traditional village pub in the heart of Yorkshire. Friendly locals and classic English food await here at this little country gem.

WOOD HALL HOTEL
British

Trip Lane, Wetherby, LS22 4JA
08450 727 564
The Georgian Restaurant at this Hand Picked Hotels venue offers classic dishes with a touch of flair. The wine list includes Old World classics and intriguing New World arrivals. 2 AA Rosettes.

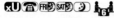

WREA HEAD
European

Off Barmour Lane, Scalby, Scarborough, YO13 0PB
01723 378 211
Its outstanding reputation makes Wrea Head the perfect place to eat. Choose to dine in the traditional and beautiful setting of the restaurant, or in the less formal Cocktail Lounge and Bar.

WRYGARTH INN
Traditional English

Station Road, Great Hatfield, HU11 4UY
01964 533 300
With depictions of bygone eras lining the walls, it is easy to see how this wonderfully cosy inn is steeped in history. Staying close to its roots, it offers fine food and the best of British hospitality.

DETAILED DESCRIPTIONS AVAILABLE ON

www.gourmetsociety.co.uk

YOYO BAR & RESTAURANT
Japanese/ Malaysian/Thai

Rosse Street, Off Saltaire Road, Shipley, BD18 3SW
01274 599 880
Offering Oriental cuisine, as well as catering for children and alternate dietary needs, this restaurant ensures everyone is satisfied. Cocktails and light bites available.

YOYO CAFE BAR
European

29 Chapel Street, Little Germany, Bradford, BD1 5DT
01274 727 287
From macro (a global agglomeration of flavours) to micro (focusing on locally sourced ingredients) this fusion café bar in Bradford does everything with panache; bright, convivial and vibrant.

ZOUK
Indian

1312 Leeds Road, Bradford, BD3 8LF
01274 258 025
A family-run business, the kitchen here is dedicated to good food made with passion. Fuses authentic Lahore cuisine with healthy eating within a stylish setting. Open for breakfast through to supper.

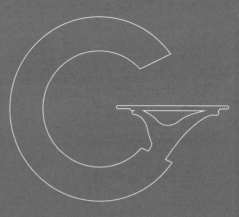

Scotland

There is nowhere more bountiful than the natural larders of Scotland, where the finest and freshest produce is readily available from the rugged and mountainous Highlands, the fertile valleys of the Lowlands, the vast moors of the Southern Uplands and the sparkling lochs and the seas surrounding the mainland and her many Isles.

Consider: Angus beef is the winning ingredient in many a burger. Succulent venison, plump pheasant and grouse are amongst the best, most widely sought of their kind. River-fresh Scottish salmon which lends itself perfectly to a thousand delicious treatments is shipped far and wide accompanied by its aqueous neighbours, mussel, scallops and some of the world's finest crab and lobster.

Amidst such abundance, Scottish cuisine has developed distinctive recipes, with every day cooking still referencing traditional dishes made with locally grown ingredients. Haggis, the iconic Scottish delicacy, rich and intense, often shares a plate with neeps and tatties on tables across the country and not just on Burns' night!

As a result of foreign and local influences through time, traditional Scottish produce and techniques today mingle with international counterparts. This constant exchange has heralded a renaissance in Scottish cuisine with more Scottish restaurants receiving international acclaim at the same time as international restaurants have set up shop across the region, to the delight of Scots and diners alike.

For ease of reference we've included restaurants in Edinburgh amongst the Midlothian listings, and Glasgow restaurants in the Lanarkshire listings, despite the independent status of these two great cities.

Aberdeenshire

210 BISTRO
Bistro

210 South Market Street, Aberdeen, AB11 5PQ
01224 211 857
A unique venue that meets the exacting standards of the business community and casual diners. The perfect place to enjoy both traditional and contemporary recipes, or simply relax with friends.

BLAIRS RESTAURANT @ MERCURE ARDOE
British

South Deeside Road, Blairs, Aberdeen, AB12 5YP
01224 860 624
Inspired by the royal residence of the nearby Balmoral castle, this four star 19th century mansion houses a hotel and restaurant fit for a king. Award-winning chefs create superb dishes time after time.

CARMELITE BAR AND GRILL
Scottish

Stirling Street, Merchant Quarter, Aberdenn, AB11 6JU
01224 589 101
Making use of the best Scottish suppliers of local produce, the Head Chef passionately creates fantastic dishes for your enjoyment. The succulent Aberdeen beef and tasty Shetland lamb are both heavenly.

CONGO BAR AND DINER
American

Codona's Aberdeen, Sunset Blvd, Aberdeen, AB24 5ED
01224 595 910
This family restaurant offers a choice of favourites such as steaks, salads, pizzas and pasta dishes. Overlooking the fun indoor Congo adventure golf course you can grab a bite to eat with your family.

FRANCO'S RESTAURANT
Italian

40 High Street, Banchory, AB31 5SR
01330 826 093
A different kind of experience for lunch and dinner with a menu that focuses on local food in conjunction with some of the most traditional Italian dishes. A taste of Italy delivered to perfection.

HANDMADE BURGER CO.
American

9 First Level Mall, Guild Square, Aberdeen, AB11 5RG
01224 580 400
Each day the chefs at Handmade Burger Co. make over 40 delicious burgers, handmade and pressed to the highest standards. The same care is applied to the chips, coleslaw, veg and onion rings; Try them all.

LA STELLA RESTAURANT
Scottish

28 Adelphi, Aberdeen, AB11 5BL
01224 211 414
Scottish fare with a modern twist. Making use of outstanding local produce, the kitchen aims to ensure that every diner has a truly unique experience.

MOONLIGHT TANDOORI
Indian

34 Balmellie Street, Turriff, AB53 4DU
01888 562 636
Perfect for the curry faithful and everyone else, with a wide ranging menu. A pairing of authentic Indian cuisine and friendly service, this pleasant restaurant is quickly becoming a local favourite.

OGILVIES RESTAURANT
British

Fraserburgh Rd, Peterhead, AB42 3BN
01779 471 121
Set within its own extensive gardens, this purpose-built hotel is the owner of 105 beautiful bedrooms, a luxurious spa and and award-winning kitchen. The restaurant offers fine meals you'll want to savour.

SOURCE GRILL @ ABERDEEN MARRIOT
International

Overton Circle, Aberdeen, AB21 7JY
01224 770 011
Within the Marriott hotel, this restaurant offers wonderful Scottish and International cuisines, providing diners an extensive variety of delectable dishes to suit all tastes.

SPICEMILL
Indian

Grandholm Cres., Bridge of Don, Aberdeen, AB22 8AA
01224 821 700
Innovative venue serving the best dishes from across the Indian subcontinent. Huge variety to cater for all tastes and preferences, providing diners with a tantalising experience of Indian culture.

SUNSET BAR AND DINER
American

Codona's Aberdeen, Sunset Boulevard, AB24 5ED
01224 595 910
Retro American family diner offering huge party platters, old favourites, world famous chicken wings and fantastic desserts. Something for everyone, with great options for adults and kids alike.

THE ATHENAEUM
Contemporary

5-9 Union Street, Aberdeen, AB11 5BU
01224 595 585
The grandeur of the building's interior is transferred to the design within this beautifully adorned restaurant. Admire the local artwork that decorates the venue whilst sampling tasty, creative dishes.

THE COCK AND BULL RESTAURANT
International

Ellon Road, Balmedien, Aberdeen, AB23 8XY
01358 743 249
An intimate inn where food is made from fresh local ingredients. The menu also benefits from seasonal changes and is complemented by the chef's daily specials. Honest and affordable food.

THE STAGE DOOR RESTAURANT
European

26 North Silver Street, Aberdeen, AB10 1RL
01224 642 111
Scottish cuisine with a continental influence, here the steaks are a divine speciality. Ideally situated in the heart of Aberdeen's cultural centre, this a fabulous choice for pre-performance dining.

SCOTLAND

298

Gourmet Society discount applies to the à la carte menu

TIGER TIGER
International
1-2 Shiprow, Aberdeen, AB39 2JD
01224 252 434
Open from lunch until late, the restaurant, lively club and five bars will satisfy you at any time of the day. With so much happening all under one roof, it really is your one-stop for entertainment.

YATAI
Japanese
73-75 Skene Street, Aberdeen, AB10 1QD
01224 658 521
Taking its name from the small food stalls found across Japan, Yatai attempts to mirror the ethos of such stall proprietors. Combines the finest local produce with imported Japanese ingredients.

THE GARDEN ROOM AT THE LANDMARK
Scottish
The Landmark Hotel, Kingsway West, Dundee, DD2 5JT
01382 641 122
Recently refurbished site where there is a distinct emphasis on flavour and freshness, with ingredients sourced from local markets and regions. Both the service and wine list complement the food on offer.

THE PLAYWRIGHT
Locally Sourced
11 Tay Square, Dundee, DD1 1PB
01382 223113
With everything from freshly baked bread to the chef's signature ice cream made on the premises, this restaurant has a distinctive flair about it. The tiramisu pannacotta is a spectacular dessert.

NEW

Angus

Ayrshire

ASHOKA SHAK DUNDEE
Indian
7 Dayton Drive, Dundee, DD2 3SQ
01382 858 169
This fantastic eatery is extremely popular with local curry lovers, serving up a superb selection of quality Indian dishes. Eat in or take away at this authentic Ahoka Shak restaurant.

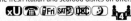

BETTOLINI TRATTORIA
Italian
Camperdown Street, City Quay, Dundee, DD1 3JA
01382 224 420
A perfect place to end the day and begin your evening, where the relaxed and friendly atmosphere will enhance your overall dining experience. Guests will love the fresh Italian and seafood dishes on offer.

THE GRILL ROOM & STEAKHOUSE
Steakhouse
33 Castle Street, Dundee, DD1 3AD
01382 200 999
The very best steaks offered in a wonderfully popular restaurant. Renowned for its superb hospitality and flexibility to suit all appetites.

THE BLUE MARLIN
Seafood
9 Reform Street, Dundee, DD5 4BA
01382 534 001
A kitchen that plays home to a chef who appreciates good quality food made from excellent ingredients. The menu makes full use of the prime catch of the local coastal waters and the finest Scottish beef.

THE CRAIGTON COACH INN
British
Craigton of Monikie, Dundee, DD5 3QN
01382 370 223
A reputable and rural restaurant with an emphasis on local, fresh produce and attentive, polite staff. The steak pie is just one of the dishes renowned for its excellent taste and fulsome portions.

AYR INDIA @ ALLOWAY PLACE
Indian
1A Alloway Place, Ayr, KA7 2AA
01292 261 026
While the original restaurant focusses on traditional food, the emphasis here is firmly placed on contemporary dishes, while still providing quality and authentic flavours.

AYR INDIA TANDOORI RESTAURANT
Indian
10 Seafield Road, Ayr Seafront, Ayr, KA7 4AD
01292 263 731
A menu showcasing everything delicious about traditional Indian cuisine, complete with attentive staff and the right beverages. For a true taste of the subcontinent in Scotland, this is the place to go.

THE PINEWOOD RESTAURANT
Scottish
180 Main Street, Prestwick, KA9 1PG
01292 478 966
Both local and international produce go into creating the most flavoursome of dishes. Scottish beef and west coast fish are just two examples of the fantastic supplies used in the kitchen.

THE SORN INN
Modern British
35 Main Street, Sorn, East Ayrshire, KA5 6HU
01290 551 305
With 2 AA Rosettes for its excellent food, this pub is an absolute must for all food lovers. Diners will be impressed by the attention to detail in presentation and the sensational tastes of all dishes.

THE WILD BLOSSOM
Cantonese
17 Riccarton Road, Hurlford, Kilmarnock, KA1 5AH
01563 521 234
Deep Chinese flavours at this restaurant in Hurlford with its eclectic menu, warm welcome to anyone and everyone, and its richly aromatic dishes. Give these culinary delights a whirl.

299

Berwickshire

Dunbartonshire

SIAMESE KITCHEN
Thai

12 Murray Street, Duns, TD11 3DE
01361 883 470

An exciting marriage of eastern and western gastronomic influences, creating a cuisine that is uniquely alternative. Eye-wateringly hot to mild and refined dishes also available.

2FOR1 3 COURSES

CUCINA
Italian

Unit 3, The Galleries, Balloch Rd, Balloch, G83 8SS
01389 755 455

This friendly and contemporary Italian restaurant offers attentive service, fantastic imported ingredients and a great atmosphere. Their varied menu offers delicious steaks, pizzas, fish and pasta dishes.

25% OFF TOTAL

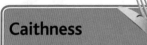

Caithness

DETAILED DESCRIPTIONS AVAILABLE ON

www.gourmetsociety.co.uk

THE SCHOOLHOUSE RESTAURANT
Scottish

John O'Groats, Wick, Caithness, KW1 4YS
01955 611 714

Making the most of the outstanding ingredients readily available in Caithness, the menu regularly changes so that new and unusual delights can be sampled along with all the old favourites.

25% OFF TOTAL

GOLDEN STAR TANDOORI
Indian

100 Balloch Road, Balloch, G83 8SR
01389 721 077

Acclaimed Indian restaurant just by the shore of Loch Lomond which specialises in the clarified, spicy flavours of Punjabi cooking, while also drawing in influences from other Indian regional cuisines.

2FOR1 MAIN COURSE

DE VERE CAMERON HOUSE HOTEL

25% OFF TOTAL

Cameron House on Loch Lomond, Dunbartonshire, G83 8QZ

01389 755 565 *International*

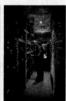

A multi million pound refurbishment, a baronial mansion, a Championship golf course, a penthouse overlooking Loch Lomond and some of the most supreme dining imaginable, all bundled up and served with the heartiest of Scottish hospitality. De Vere Cameron House on Loch Lomond is every part the five star Scottish experience.

Guests and Gourmet Society members have a choice of restaurants; the unequalled Cameron Grill, the relaxed New England style Boat House or the inviting Claret Jug, the best 19th hole in Scotland!

Cameron Grill

A stunning restaurant, the Cameron Grill has taken hotel dining to another level and serves the finest steaks and grill style dining in the Highlands. Its contemporary interior is influenced by the very roots of Scotland's history. The menu has been created using delights from Scotland's larder, expertly prepared and served

in an unpretentious manner. The choice of ingredients is so vital to the restaurant that they are even part of the decor with a fully functional butchery as a key feature as well as a walk-in cellar which can be explored by diners.

The Claret Jug

This is the perfect 19th hole for golfers and also serves a choice of delightful dishes from light bites to classic favourites and all with breathtaking views over the golf course. The Claret Jug has a great atmosphere and hearty fare, open for breakfast, lunch and dinner, daily.

The Boat House

After a short wander from the main hotel you enter the New England style Boathouse restaurant on the lochside marina. Enjoy fresh pizzas straight from the wood-burning oven, excellent seafood, alfresco seating and a friendly, relaxed atmosphere.

Sign up to our newsletter for latest restaurants, offers and more

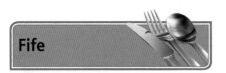

Fife

DURBAR
Indian

282-284 High Street, Kirkcaldy, KY1 1LB
01592 265 795
Acclaimed Chef Jamuna Datt Tewari brings his blend of traditional classic dishes and contemporary house specialities to delight every diner. The open kitchen offers a glimpse of the chefs hard at work.

HOTEL DU VIN
European

40 The Scores, St Andrews, KY16 9AS
01334 472 611
The finest, freshest local produce, simple European recipes, a stunning choice of wines; these are the elements of the trademark Hotel du Vin bistro. Refurbished this year, be wined and dined in style.

QUEENSFERRY HOTEL
International

St Margarets Head, North Queensferry, KY11 1HP
01383 410 000
In this Brook Hotel, the in-house restaurant offers a unique dining experience with both traditional and international cuisine enhanced by the spectacular setting, ideal for all dining occasions.

SPRINGFIELD TAVERN
British

The Cross, Springfield, Cupar, KY15 5SJ
01334 653 305
A wonderful local pub offering both locals and guests from afar great food and a vast selection of beverages.

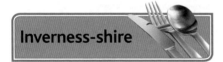

Inverness-shire

ADAM'S DINING ROOM
Fine Dining

The Culloden House Hotel, Inverness, IV2 7BZ
01463 790 461
Highly rated and regarded restaurant at the stately Culloden House that serves outstanding, double AA rosette-winning cuisine including fine, musky game and superbly flavourful local produce.

ASH
Scottish

18 Academy Street, Inverness, IV1 1LG
01463 231 926
A venue providing diners ample opportunity to sample glorious Scottish highland and internationally renowned cuisine. Courteous service perfectly complements the superb range of delicious food on offer.

AULD ALLIANCE RESTAURANT
French

East Terrace, Kingussie, PH21 1JS
01540 661 506
At the heart of a beautiful national park this is one of the best places to dine in the Highlands. Enjoy the welcoming log fire and fine dining at this special gourmet destination.

BEN NEVIS
Scottish

103 High St, Fort William, PH33 6DG
01397 702 295
This traditional and hugely popular venue in the famous Highland town is part of the Best of British group. The menu consists of local fare: haggis, neeps and tatties for a perfect taste of bonny Scotland.

Min. 2 courses must be purchased.

CRANNAG BISTRO
Scottish

Dornoch Road, Ardgay, IV24 3EB
01863 766 111
The simple, unpretentious cuisine offers a novel experience to any diner. Uses local beef, venison, pork and seafood to create traditional dishes in a warm, friendly and beautiful setting.

HARRY RAMSDEN'S
Fish and Seafood

Inshes Retail Park, Inverness, IV2 3TW
01463 713 345
Experience the national classic dish of fish and chips in all its glory. Perfectly cooked and seasoned, food here gives diners a true taste of the seaside, all delivered by this fine British institution.

Not available during August or in takeaway.

LA TORTILLA ASESINA
Spanish

99 Castle Street, Inverness, IV2 3EA
01463 709 809
With a menu boasting over 40 tapas dishes it is no wonder that this authentic Spanish restaurant has a wonderful reputation. Affable, knowledgeable staff are happy to help if you are spoilt for choice.

LOCH NESS LODGE
Fine Dining

Brachla, Loch Ness, Inverness, IV3 8LA
01456 459 469
This fine dining establishment utilises its wonderful seasonal range of produce to create creative, contemporary dishes, happily tailoring the menu to please each guest. Awarded 2 AA Rosettes.

RIVER HOUSE RESTAURANT
Scottish

1 Greig Street, Inverness, IV3 5PT
01463 222 033
An incredible restaurant serving the finest Scottish cuisine. Exquisite dishes not only sound phenomenal on the menu, but also look and taste even better than expected. Divine food not to be missed out on.

ROYAL TANDOORI
Indian

43 Grampian Road, Aviemore, PH22 1RH
01479 811 199
Holding an excellent reputation with both locals and tourists, this Indian restaurant offers outstanding cuisine for all to enjoy. Spicy curry fans will love the challenge of the 'roof-lifter' dish.

THE CORNER GRILL *Steakhouse*
50 Union Street, Inverness, IV1 1PX
01463 226 767
The Corner Grill is a modern Scottish steakhouse which uses only local produce.

Lanarkshire

1 BISTRO @ DOWNSTAIRS *Mediterranean*
Downstairs@192 Pitt Street, Glasgow, G2 4DY
0141 332 5300
Variegated Mediterranean cuisine at this downstairs bistro in the heart of Glasgow. Drawing together the variety of warming tastes from the region, it will leave you sated and smiling.

AISHAHS INDIAN TAPAS *Indian*
10 Hillington Rd South, Cardonald, Glasgow, G52 2AA
0141 810 3914
A cracking addition to Glasgow's Indian restaurant scene whose capacity to go beyond the staples without undue bells and whistles helps to distinguish it.

ALLA TURCA GRILL AND MEZZE BAR *Turkish*
192 Pitt Street, Glasgow, G2 4DY
0141 332 5300
Authentic food made fresh: the hallmark of real Turkish cuisine. Enjoy fine cooking in a powerfully atmospheric setting, with beautiful sounds of the traditional lute of Turkey and Iran filling the room.

ASHOKA ASHTON LANE *Indian*
19 Ashton Lane, Glasgow, G12 8SJ
0141 337 1115
Take a saunter down the cobbled stones of Ashton Lane and be enticed by the intoxicating aromas and spice-filled dishes of the amazing Ashoka restaurant. Authentic and most certainly irresistible.

ASHOKA AT THE MILL *Indian*
500 Corselet Road, Darnley, Glasgow, G53 7RN
0141 876 0458
A stunning Ashoka restaurant that combines a historic medieval farmhouse setting with a classy contemporary twist in its vast interior; the heavenly food bursts with flavour and freshness.

ASHOKA AT THE QUAY *Indian*
Unit D2 The Quay Leisure Park, Glasgow, G5 8NP
0141 429 4492
Another addition to the superb Ashoka restaurants, taking diners on a culinary adventure with a delicious range of authentic Indian dishes to choose from on their mouth-watering menu.

ASHOKA BEARSDEN *Indian*
9 Kirk Road, Bearsden, Glasgow, G61 3RG
0141 570 0075
Simplistic yet stylish interior coupled with the finest Indian food, this Ashoka restaurant demonstrates continued quality and exceptional service, sending ripples of delight throughout the community.

ASHOKA SHAK *Indian*
Linwood Road, Pheonix Retail Park, Glasgow, PA1 2AB
0800 195 3195
'Thali' means plate in Hindi and Ashoka proudly offers regional thalis from the length and breadth of India, as well as flavoursome curry favourites. The first of the wildly successful Ashoka group.

ASHOKA SHAK COATBRIDGE *Indian*
Showcase Leisure Park, Coatbridge, SG69 7TS
01236 437 181
With a legendary reputation for quality and service, Ashoka Shak truly delivers authentic Indian delights and invites diners to set out on an exciting journey of culinary discovery.

ASHOKA SOUTH SIDE *Indian*
268 Clarkston Road, Glasgow, G44 3EA
0141 637 0711
Another Ashoka restaurant bursting with Eastern promise, perfect for curry lovers and even the uninitiated. A range of authentically crafted dishes with tastes and spices to suit every preference.

ASHOKA WEST END *Indian*
1284 Argyle Street, Glasgow, G3 8AB
0141 339 3371
Immortalised as a famous culinary landmark, the Ashoka West End restaurant acts like a magnet to Glasgow's colossal curry eating fraternity, showcasing a vast array of freshly made, authentic dishes.

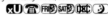

BELLINI *Italian*
67-69 Kilmarnock Road, Glasgow, G41 3YR
0141 649 6096
A casual yet sophisticated atmosphere with a menu delivering a contemporary take on classic Italian tastes. An ideal destination all day whether it be for fresh coffee, a light lunch, or exquisite dinner.

BARBAROSSA RESTAURANT *Scottish*
Cartside House, 1-7 Clarkston Road, Glasgow, G44 4EF
0141 560 3898
Acclaimed Glasgow restaurant with a diverse menu rooted in stonking local Scottish produce and uncluttered combinations of flavours to accompany it. A warm and stylish ambience for a relaxed meal.

BELLA NAPOLI *Italian*
85 Kilmarnock Road, Glasgow, G41 3YR
0141 632 4222
A well-established family-run restaurant offering fine Italian cuisine. The chef Domenico has Italian roots and uses his origin to provide guests with magnificently authentic Italian food.

Visit the website regularly to discover the latest restaurants joining the GS

SCOTLAND

BLUE RUPEE
Indian

163 Eastkilbride Road, Burnside, Glasgow, G73 5EA
0141 634 0019
Guests will love the rich Indian dishes that make up the vastly diverse menu at this great restaurant. Attentive and accommodating service is guaranteed.

BO'VINE
Steakhouse

385 Byres Road, Glasgow, G12 8AU
0141 341 6540
Making the most of Scotland's superb cattle, Bo'Vine is rooted in local produce. There are influences from French cooking here too; as they put it, "a little flair and influence from the Auld Alliance."

NEW

CAFE SPICE
Indian

76 Stirling Street, Airdrie, ML6 0AS
01236 755 123
Classic mouth-watering Indian recipes are used to create both new and traditional dishes at this fantastically authentic restaurant. The outstanding food and service will ensure you leave with a smile.

CHARCOALS
Indian

26A Renfield Street, Glasgow, G2 1LU
0141 221 9251
The vibrancy of this restaurant initiates a perfect ambience for guests to enjoy Indian cuisine. The delivery service is ideal if you are in need of a cosy night in without the hassle of cooking.

COLLAGE RESTAURANT
European

Radisson Blu Hotel, 301 Argyle St, Glasgow, G2 8DL
0141 225 2046
Sir Peter Blake and Roy Ackerman join together to deliver a combination of art and food. A blend of Mediterranean and Scottish cuisine with a modern twist will delight the most experienced diner.

CROWNE PLAZA GLASGOW
International

Congress Road, Glasgow, G3 8QT
0871 942 9091
Guests at this hotel have a choice of two dining options, with cuisine from around the world. Views over the Clyde can be enjoyed in One Restaurant; snacks and drinks are served in the Quarterdeck Bar.

Only one card can be used per table.

CRYUS' ASHOKA
Indian

108 Elderslie Street, Glasgow, G3 7AR
0141 221 1761
Bright and brassy Indian restaurant with keen and attentive staff serving a range of Indian dishes that go beyond curry house staples. Enjoy the warming marinades with slow-cooked, tender meats and fish.

DI MAGGIO'S
Italian

21 Royal Exchange Square, Glasgow, G1 3AJ
0141 248 2111
Proud of its motto 'our family serving your family', Di Maggio's believes that the essence of the Italian family is paramount to the restaurant's success. Enjoy the vibrant location of this restaurant.

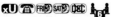

DI MAGGIO'S
Italian

1038 Pollokshaws Road, Glasgow, G41 3EB
0141 632 7924
Proud of its motto 'our family serving your family', Di Maggio's believes that the essence of the Italian family is paramount to the restaurant's success. All occasions are delightfully catered for.

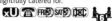

DI MAGGIO'S
Italian

163 West Nile Street, Glasgow, G1 3RL
0141 333 4999
Proud of its motto 'our family serving your family', Di Maggio's believes that the essence of the Italian family is paramount to the restaurant's success. The wood-burning oven makes the tastiest food.

DI MAGGIO'S
Italian

61 Ruthven Lane, Glasgow, G12 9BG
0141 357 0874
Proud of its motto 'our family serving your family', Di Maggio's believes that the essence of the Italian family is paramount to the restaurant's success. A real slice of Glasgow's culinary heritage.

DI MAGGIO'S
Italian

42 Gateside Street, Hamilton, ML3 7JQ
01698 891 828
Ideally located in the historic town of Hamilton. Proud of its motto 'our family serving your family', Di Maggio's believes that the essence of the Italian family is paramount to the restaurant's success.

DI MAGGIO'S
Italian

1 Rochsolloch Road, Airdrie, ML6 9BG
01236 766 561
Proud of its motto 'our family serving your family', Di Maggio's believes that the essence of the Italian family is paramount to the restaurant's success. Guests adore the hearty home-cooked Italian food.

DI MAGGIO'S
Italian

Stroud Road, East Kilbride, G75 0YA
01355 242 222
Proud of its motto 'our family serving your family', Di Maggio's believes that the essence of the Italian family is paramount to the restaurant's success. The cabaret and karaoke nights are highly popular.

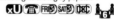

DINE
European

205 Fenwick Road, Giffnock, Glasgow, G46 6JD
0141 621 1903
A delightful love story formed the grounding of this delightful restaurant. The owners Phil and Gio blend their restaurant experience and passion for catering to create the most excellent eatery.

FOUR SEASONS
Chinese

87 Cambridge Street, Glasgow, G3 6RU
0141 332 2666
The finest fresh ingredients are used with authentic oriental spices, to create traditional Chinese meals with a modern twist. Perfect for business lunches, pre-theatre appetisers or romantic dinners.

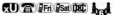

SCOTLAND

303

GUY'S RESTAURANT & BAR
Modern British
24 Candleriggs, Merchant City, Glasgow, G1 1LD
0141 552 1114
Held in high regard, this venue offers a great ambience and friendly staff that really enhance the dining experience, not forgetting the simply delicious food that is superb value for money.

2FOR1
3 COURSES

MISTER SINGH'S INDIA
Indian
149 Elderlie St, Glasgow, G3 7JR
0141 204 0186
A popular restaurant that often caters for business and executive lunches. An eclectic blend of clientèle fills the restaurant each evening, where scrumptious curries and crispy naan breads are devoured.

2FOR1
MAIN COURSE

HARRY RAMSDEN'S
British
251 Paisley Road, Glasgow, G5 8RA
0141 429 3700
World famous fish and chips from a British institution. Enjoy classic seaside food, from crisp batter to golden chips; nobody does it quite like Harry Ramsden's.

25%OFF
TOTAL

Not available during August or in takeaway.

ML ONE @ MOTHERWELL COLLEGE
Modern European
1 Enterprise Way, Motherwell, ML1 2TX
01698 232 323
Support the talented chefs of the future at this terrific on-site restaurant. Wonderful dishes are prepared by chefs-in-training, guaranteeing guests a first-class dining experience.

2FOR1
MAIN COURSE

THE RESTAURANT AT PARK INN
Scottish
Park Inn, 2 Port Dundas Street, Glasgow, G2 3LD
0141 333 1500
This stylish city centre hotel restaurant offers a mouth watering menu with a unique Scottish flair. Head Chef also offers two daily specials, always including a vegetarian selection.

25%OFF
TOTAL

Formerly Oshi

INDIAN GALLERY
Indian
450 Sauchiehall Street, Glasgow, G2 3JD
0141 332 3355
Indian dining at its finest. Lunch, evening and à la carte menus include traditional and modern Indian and Asian dishes for you to enjoy.

2FOR1
MAIN COURSE

PANDA CHINESE CUISINE
Chinese
Springfield Quay, Paisley Road, Glasgow, G5 8NP
0141 429 0988
One of the most beautiful Chinese restaurants in Glasgow, with a stylish dining room expected of a first-class venue. Talented chefs craft sublime cuisine, creating a perfect blend of authentic flavours.

2FOR1
3 COURSES

Also 20% off on buffet (not with any other offer).

KAMA SUTRA
Indian
331 Sauchiehall Street, Glasgow, G2 3HW
0141 332 0055
A fantastic eatery extremely popular with local curry lovers, serving up a superb selection of quality Indian dishes that are rich in flavour and authentic aroma. All available to eat in or takeaway.

2FOR1
2 COURSES

PAPERINOS WEST END
Italian
283 Byres Road, Glasgow, G12 8UD
0141 334 3811
The sister restaurant to the original Paperino's in the city centre, this West End eatery maintains the exceptional standards that had already been set. Delicious home-made desserts must be made room for.

2FOR1
3 COURSES

PREZZO
Italian
35 St Vincent Place, Glasgow, G1 2ER
01412 489815
With a character all of its own, Prezzo oozes contemporary style and enduring charm. Signature pastas, stone-baked pizzas and classic Italian dishes promise a prefect dining choice for the whole family.

NEW

2FOR1
MAIN COURSE

PAPERINOS@78
Italian
78 St Vincent Street, Glasgow, G2 5UB
0141 248 7878
The latest addition to this family of restaurants, Paperinos@78 maintains the high standards that have been previously set by its sisters. Delicious pasta, pizza, fish and meat dishes await you.

2FOR1
3 COURSES

L'ARIOSTO
Italian
92-94 Mitchell Street, Glasgow, G1 3NQ
0141 221 0971
A perfectly situated Italian restaurant where business lunches, post-shopping respites and pre-theatre dinners can be enjoyed. High quality food whatever the occasion.

25%OFF
TOTAL

PAPERINO'S
Italian
283 Sauchiehall Street, Glasgow, G2 3HQ
0141 332 3800
Diners will be instantaneously pleased by the cosy and relaxed atmosphere that can be found at Paperino's. Mozzarella sticks are perfect for a starter whilst the home-made cheesecake must not be missed.

2FOR1
3 COURSES

MALMAISON
European
278 West George St, Glasgow, G2 4LL
0141 572 1000
This former Church has become one of Glasgow's most heavenly dining and resting venues. With great food and service, it's easy to see how Malmaison has gained such a faithful congregation. 1 AA Rosette.

2FOR1
MAIN COURSE

PEEL PARK
Carvery
Eaglasham Road, Glasgow, G75 8LW
01355 222 747
Another of the Great British Carvery pubs that offers the best of British food with a modern twist. This charming venue has an attractive reputation as being one of the best family eateries in town.

2FOR1
MAIN COURSE

Call beforehand on special event days.

When booking restaurants always mention your GS membership

PIAZZA ITALIA RESTAURANT
Italian
15 John Street, The Italian Centre, Glasgow, G1 1HP
0141 552 4433
One of Glasgow's premier Italian restaurants. Prepare yourself for authentic dining that guarantees a true taste of Italy, served by staff that are knowledgeable in the range of classic wine on offer.

RAWALPINDI TANDOORI
Indian
321 Sauchiehall Street, Glasgow, G2 3HW
0141 332 4180
This traditional family-run restaurant offers divinely tasty Indian cuisine in an authentic interior, delivering a dining experience attractive to families, couples, and late-night socialites.

PJ'S INDIA
Indian
15 Kent Road, Charring Cross, Glasgow, G3 7EH
0141 248 8333
Culinary genius is provided here as an experienced team deliver rich, fragrant Indian cuisine. Diners are offered an à la carte menu or gastronomic buffet, both excellently crafted with passion and spice.

 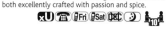

REDCHILLIES INDIAN TAPAS
Indian
57 Union Street, Glasgow, G1 3RB
0141 222 2128
Indian tapas, allowing guests to choose from a range of sumptuous scaled-down classic dishes to share with friends and family. Experience Indian cuisine in delicious bite-sized dishes.

PINK TURBAN
Indian
157 Wishaw Rd, Waterloo, Wishaw, ML2 8EN
01698 375 835
Alongside the old favourites, the restaurant has some excellent specialities, not least the majestic 'Turban special', with chicken and lamb tikka, mince and prawns in a fantastically rich bhoona sauce.

NEW

SANNINO ELMBANK STREET
Italian
61a Elmbank Street, Glasgow, G2 4PQ
0141 332 3565
A characterful chequerboard dining space plays host to this popular, established and recognised pizzeria. Simple and classic, meltingly homely pizzas along with rich and colourful pasta dishes.

PREZZO
Italian
Unit F1, Silverburn Centre, 763 Barrhead Rd, G53 6QR
01418 811 467
With a character all of its own, Prezzo oozes contemporary style and enduring charm. Signature pastas, stone-baked pizzas and classic Italian dishes promise a perfect dining choice for the whole family.

SHEZAN TANDOORI
Indian
1096 Cathcart Road, Glasgow, G42 9XW
0141 649 4776
Dine in contemporary surroundings at the Shezan Tandoori. Guests enjoy the excellent quality of the Indian cuisine, whilst the affable waiting staff provide smiles and efficient service.

SAPPORO TEPPANYAKI
2-6 Ingram Street, Merchant City, Glasgow, G1 1HA
0141 553 4060   *Japanese*

Teppanyaki cooking is the scene-stealing showman of culinary theatrics. Sapporo Teppanyaki has its act nailed and offers one of the most entertaining meals out in Glasgow. Not only are its charismatic show chefs past masters at their art, the whole restaurant, with its bold primary colours and close-knit feel, is geared towards providing a vibrant and thoroughly unique dining experience.

Diners are seated at one of the large Teppanyaki tables; there, they are witness to some of the best culinary juggling around. Choosing from steaks and grilled fish to noodles and rice, they are then witness to the chefs' exceptional skills preparing the dishes. Similarly, a wide selection of cocktails is available from the accomplished bar staff who sling drinks with almost as much flair as their show chef colleagues.

Sapporo Teppanyaki is a stand-out restaurant. With its cheerful staff, and a participatory atmosphere that other restaurants look at through envious eyes, it's an experience not to be missed.

SHIMLA COTTAGE — *Indian*
109 Sunnyside Road, Ayr, ML5 3HR
01236 436 030
Fresh and ambitious Indian restaurant in Ayr that serves spicy and hearty food with attentive and friendly service in a welcoming environment.

SUTHERLANDS — *Scottish*
973 Sauchiehall Street, Glasgow, G3 7TQ
0141 357 4711
Great value for money and a wonderful experience whatever the occasion. Taking advantage of Scotland's extensive larder, dishes are made fresh using carefully sourced ingredients by an experienced team.

TAPAS INTERNATIONAL — *Spanish*
1293, Argyle street, Glasgow, G3 8TL
0141 569 6378
Tapas forms a vital part of Spanish culture and daily traditions. An ideal way to socialise and catch up with friends, a vast array of tapas dishes can be shared and enjoyed, making a perfect evening out.

TASTE GOOD INN — *Chinese*
7 Burn Place, Cambuslang, Glasgow, G72 7DS
0141 569 1101
Enjoy Cantonese and Peking favourites whilst basking in smooth décor with a touch of luxury.   Regular karaoke nights on Friday and Saturdays.

THE BOATHOUSE — *European*
Auchinstarry Marina, Kilsyth, G65 9SG
01236 829 201
An admirably located pub and restaurant that overlooks the beautiful marina and the Campsie Fells. Rest and relax in one of the luxurious bedrooms or simply come and dine on divine lunches and dinners.

THE LIVING ROOM — *British*
150 St Vincent Street, Glasgow, G2 5NE
0141 229 0607
Step into The Living Room and you can count on the savvy, distinctive neighbourhood vibe that plays home to eclectically drawn, supremely tasty cuisine. Settle into the gentle warmth of this Glasgow venue.

Must purchase min 3 courses/person inc main.

THE SPORTS CAFÉ — *Modern Pub*
292-332 Sauchiehall Street, Glasgow, G2 3JA
0161 9 720 397
Legendary atmosphere with a menu made up of favourites such as burgers, which are their speciality, along with delicious deep-filled pies. Perfect food for enjoying the big game.

THE VICEROY — *Indian*
480 Paisley Road, Glasgow, G5 8RE
0141 429 2222
Retreat for a good quality curry at this Indian restaurant in Glasgow. Warm and welcoming service provides dishes with classic flavours; at root it's a good, honest local curry house.

TIGER TIGER GLASGOW — *International*
The Glasshouse, 20 Glassford Street, Glasgow, LG1 1UL
0141 553 4888
Dine and relax, drink and chill, or dance and party at Tiger Tiger. With a delightful restaurant, a laid-back lounge and a contemporary bar, the venue offers a range of environments.

URBAN BAR AND BRASSERIE — *European*
23-25 St. Vincent Place, Glasgow, G1 2DT
0141 248 5636
Presenting classic dishes in the chef's own inimitable contemporary style, the fine menu is matched by this award-winning restaurant's stunning setting and elegant ambience. Awarded 1 AA Rosette.

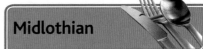

Midlothian

AL DENTE RESTAURANT — *Italian*
139 Easter Road, Edinburgh, EH7 5QA
0131 652 1932
Pure Italian food, unadulterated by cream or pre-cooked pasta, always fresh and delicious. Both the food and surroundings are authentic, everything one would expect in a traditional Italian restaurant.

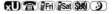

AMICUS APPLE — *Contemporary*
17 Frederick Street, Edinburgh, EH2 2EY
0131 226 6055
One of Edinburgh's most popular bars with its combination of chic interior, friendly staff and a delightful menu perfect for lunch or light bites. Amicus Apple is anything but forbidden fruit.

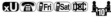

ANN PURNA — *Indian*
44-45 St. Patricks Square, Edinburgh, EH8 9ET
0131 662 1807
A popular feature on the Edinburgh scene since the early 1990s, this restaurant serves delicious Gujarati-influenced vegetarian cooking in an unfussy dining space that is both homely and comfortable.

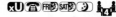

ATRIUM — *British*
10 Cambridge Street, Edinburgh, EH1 2ED
0131 228 8882
This restaurant's philosophy is simple; quality produce handled lightly, cooked precisely and presented with minimum fuss. Hearty, wholesome food for everyone to enjoy. Awarded 2 AA Rosettes.

BLUE — *British*
10 Cambridge Street, Edinburgh, EH1 2ED
0131 221 1222
A bustling city centre restaurant that offers fantastic food in an elegantly decorated interior. Blue fully lives up to the exceptional standards set by its award-winning sister restaurant, The Atrium.

Enjoy massive leisure and retail savings with more Gourmet Society

BOND NO 9
European

84 Commercial St, The Shore, Leith, Edinburgh, EH6 6LX
0131 555 5578

Its situation in one of the oldest parts of the city provides this delightful restaurant and bar with a charismatic character and personality. A charming environment that offers luscious comfort.

CAFÉ ROUGE
French

43 Frederick Street, Edinburgh, EH2 1EP
0131 225 4515

An attractive restaurant, a boulevard café or a Parisian-style wine bar; however you see Café Rouge, consistently excellent classic French dishes are always guaranteed.

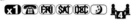

CAFE ST HONORE
French

34 North West Thistle St. Lane, Edinburgh, EH2 1EA
0131 226 2211

Neatly snuggled down a cobbled lane in the heart of the city's New Town, this restaurant is a dream for food lovers. Lavish French décor reflects the longstanding friendship between Scotland and France.

CHANNINGS RESTAURANT
European

12-16 South Learmonth Gardens, Edinburgh EH4 1EZ
0131 315 2225

A first-class neighbourhood bistro offering superb taste combinations in its many dishes. Fresh, seasonal and organic ingredients ensure each meal is exquisite in taste and flavour. 1 AA Rosette.

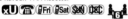

CHINA TOWN RESTAURANT
Cantonese

3 Atholl Place, Edinburgh, EH3 8HP
0131 228 3333

An outstanding Cantonese restaurant which comes second to none with its chic décor and contemporary cuisine. Speciality seafood dishes such as the sea bass and halibut will blow you away.

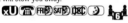

CRAIGIEBIELD
Scottish

50 Bog Road, Penicuik, EH26 9BZ
0196 867 2557

Offering the best of Scottish cuisine using fresh local ingredients, its reputation for fine dining is deserved. The beautiful surroundings just outside Edinburgh allow for a relaxing and cosy experience.

DANIEL'S BISTRO
Bistro

88 Commercial Street, Leith, EH6 6LX
0131 553 5933

A stylish and contemporary bistro in a lovely Edinburgh harbour setting. Serving vibrant and flavour-filled French-influenced cuisine, Daniel's is a great space and a great eat.

Offer available to 18.30, Friday and Saturdays.

ELBOW BAR & KITCHEN
European

133-135 East Claremont Street, Edinburgh, EH7 4JA
0131 556 5662

Elbow aim simply to deliver good value, top quality food in a comfortable atmosphere. Boasting an imaginative menu, this is the place to enjoy a casual eating experience throughout the day.

HENRY J. BEANS
American

Princes Street, Edinburgh, EH1 2AB
0131 222 8883

Simple and classic American food, consistently created to perfection by the Henry J. Bean's brand with great imagination and flair. A relaxed and friendly place to meet and eat.

HOTEL DU VIN
European

11 Bistro Place, Edinburgh, EH1 1EZ
0131 247 4900

The finest, freshest local produce, simple European recipes, a stunning choice of wines; these are the elements of the trademark Hotel du Vin bistro. Awarded 2 AA Rosettes.

INDIAN MELA
Indian/ Bangladeshi

63 Clerk Street, Edinburgh, EH8 9JQ
0131 667 1035

Take a journey through the subcontinent of India and sample the delicious array of food, ranging from the rich and lavish to the more savoury dishes, all complemented with fresh, handmade wheat breads.

INDIGO YARD
International

7 Charlotte Street, Edinburgh, EH2 4QZ
0131 220 5603

One of the city's most highly acclaimed venues with a reputation for outstanding service, fine food, and an atmosphere that is second to none. Great for daytime eating and drinking, and evening relaxation.

IVORY LOUNGE
Spanish

126 George Street, Edinburgh, EH2 4JN
0131 220 6180

Whether it be a lazy lunch, a relaxing dinner, or a cheeky drink, this venue has it all. As day turns to night the candles are lit, the music rises, and this shows itself truly to be a bar with style.

JUSTINLEES INN
Modern British

1-5 Dalhouse Road, Eskbank, EH22 3AT
0131 663 2166

This fresh and bright inn serves a gamut of tasty food that matches the location. Part of the Best of British group, it is distinctive and welcoming with a fantastic array of great ales.

Min. 2 courses must be purchased.

KINGS BALTI
Indian

79 Buccleuch Street, Edinburgh, EH8 9LS
0131 662 9212

Wonderfully located restaurant serving real authentic balti dishes. Guests enjoy the traditional cooking methods that are used to ensure the tastiest meals are produced.

LA BAGATELLE
French

22A Brougham Place, Tollcross, Edinburgh, EH3 9JU
0131 229 0869

Combining the finest quality produce of both Scotland and France, this wonderful French restaurant is a haven for fine food lovers. An outstandingly experienced chef prepares each dish with time and care.

SCOTLAND

307

LA CANTINA
Mexican

72 Commercial Quay, Leith, Edinburgh, EH6 6LX
0131 538 0022
Demonstrating the eclecticism of Mexican cuisine, the menu here boasts a range of popular, classic dishes as well as divine traditional delicacies. Enjoy quality food and sample exquisite cocktails.

MONTPELIERS BAR AND BRASSERIE
Brasserie

159-161 Bruntsfield Place, Edinburgh, EH10 4DG
0131 229 3115
Having quietly perfected a welcoming formula of comfortable, stylish surroundings, classic drinks and good quality dining at a reasonable price, this is the perfect venue.

LA GARRIGUE
French

31 Jeffrey Street, Edinburgh, EH1 1DH
0131 557 3032
A cross between an up-market restaurant and a French bistro, the ambience at La Garrigue is charming and relaxed, while the food is well-accomplished and exceptionally tasty. Awarded 2 AA Rosettes.

MYA
Thai

92 Commercial Street, Leith, Edinburgh, EH6 6LX
0131 554 4000
Presenting its guests with exemplary service and an imaginative cuisine, situated on a fashionable commercial quay, this restaurant delights in delivering a range of delicious and aromatic Thai dishes.

LA STAZIONE
Italian

Ryries Bar, 1 Haymarket Terrace, Edinburgh, EH12 5EY
0131 337 7582
A little piece of Italy has been preserved for the upper floor of the traditional Haymarket pub, Ryries. The Head Chef cooks up many Italian delights from penne arrabiata to tagliatelle salmone.

THE BRASSERIE
British

Norton House Hotel, Ingliston, Edinburgh, EH28 8LX
0131 333 1275
Enjoy classically traditional British cuisine in a beautiful Hand Picked Hotel. Passion and care goes into every dish to accompany the outstanding ingredients. Awarded 3 AA Rosettes.

LOCH FYNE
Seafood

25 Pier Place, Leith, Edinburgh, EH6 4LP
0131 559 3900
From the roadside oyster bar that once was, Loch Fyne restaurants now successfully inject energy and passion into great food and wonderful flavours, whilst ensuring their seafood is sustainably sourced.

PASSAGE TO INDIA
Indian

20 Union Place, Edinburgh, EH1 3NQ
0131 556 4547
A cracking Indian restaurant just across from the Edinburgh Playhouse Theatre. Serves finely flavoured, subtly spiced dishes, specialising in particular in Punjabi cuisine.

L'ARTICHAUT
Vegetarian

14 Eyre Place, Edinburgh, EH3 5EP
0131 558 1608
Eat fresh, eat well at this enjoyable vegetarian restaurant. The kitchen aims to delight and excite the vegetarian diner, whilst offering the meat-loving guest an impressive alternative experience.

POTTERS EDINBURGH
British

Ocean Terminal, Leith, Edinburgh, EH6 7DZ
0131 555 6700
Take a break and enjoy a dish from a menu of timeless British food; something for the whole family, including a fantastic kids selection. Great food in relaxed and comfortable surroundings.

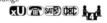

MALMAISON
European

1 Tower Place, Leith, Edinburgh EH6 7DB
0131 468 5000
Edinburgh Mal is a gorgeous riverside property, inviting you to feast from a well-constructed menu. Favouring local produce with dazzling choice wines, meals here are to be lingered over. 2 AA Rosettes.

Subject to availability during Edinburgh Festival.

PREZZO
Italian

25 Pier Place, Edinburgh, Leith, EH6 4LP
0131 552 4356
With a character all of its own, Prezzo oozes contemporary style and enduring charm. Signature pastas, stone-baked pizzas and classic Italian dishes promise a perfect dining choice for the whole family.

MANNA MAHAL RESTAURANT
Indian

113 Buccleuch St, Edinburgh, EH8 9NG
0131 662 9111
In the heart of the city sits this delightful restaurant where tasty South Indian cuisine is guaranteed to satisfy all appetites and palates. Expect amiable staff who offer attentive service.

PRINCE BALTI HOUSE
Indian

11 Seafield Road East, Edinburgh, EH15 1EB
0131 657 1155
A highly skilled team of chefs put their talents to use in The Prince Balti House kitchen. A mouth-watering range of delicacies from Bangladesh, Nepal and India are all on offer.

MONTEITHS
Scottish

61 High Street, The Royal Mile, Edinburgh, EH1 1SR
0131 557 0330
Escape city living and indulge in delectable food coupled with gorgeous cocktails and an assortment of other beverages. Whether it be lunch or dinner, enter this enchanting atmosphere, kick back and enjoy.

RESTAURANT AT THE BONHAM
European

35 Drumsheugh Gardens, Edinburgh, EH3 7RN
0131 274 7444
A sophisticated venue rooted in French tradition and given zest with expertly sourced, seasonal Scottish produce. Minimalist décor ensures the coveted two AA rosette food is the definite focus.

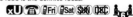

Enjoy massive leisure and retail savings with more Gourmet Society

RICK'S
International
55a Frederick Street, Edinburgh, EH2 1HL
0131 622 7800
A stunning Edinburgh city centre hotel with a chic and stylish restaurant to match. Delivers a Scottish-themed contemporary menu that uses only the best ingredients with a firm emphasis on local produce.

RYAN'S CELLAR BAR
Scottish
2 Hope Street, Edinburgh, EH2 4DB
0131 226 7005
A modern Scottish à la carte menu is on offer at this characterful bar. The venison with port and juniper berry jus is phenomenal, while the regular jazz nights provide popular entertainment.

SAFFRANI
Indian
11 South College Street, Edinburgh, EH8 9AA
0131 667 1597
A varied crowd constantly flows through the doors of this unique Indian restaurant. With a menu that focuses on seafood dishes and a wide selection of wines, this restaurant has everything going for it.

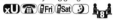

SOURCE GRILL RESTAURANT
European
Edinburgh Marriott, Glasgow Rd, Edinburgh, EH12 8NF
0131 334 9191
Renowned for fine hospitality and food, with a menu featuring fresh regional produce and signature steak dishes, this restaurant offers a modern and stylish dining environment.

SURUCHI
Indian
14a Nicolson Street, Edinburgh, EH8 9DH
0131 556 6583
Suruchi offers a truly celebratory Indian atmosphere for diners to enjoy fabulous flavours from the length and breadth of the subcontinent.

SURUCHI TOO
Indian
121 Constitution Street, Leith, Edinburgh, EH6 7AE
0131 554 3268
Wholesome dishes from every corner of India with spices, herbs, and flavours to lure any diner into a true Indian atmosphere. A comprehensive wine list is also offered to enhance your dining experience.

SYGN BAR AND RESTAURANT
Modern British
15 Charlotte Lane, Edinburgh, EH2 4QZ
0131 225 6060
Sample visually stunning, fresh and appetising dishes created using Scotland's bountiful larder. Receive excellent service whilst enjoying a classic, original cocktail. Modern dining for any occasion.

THE ATHOLL AT THE HOWARD
Scottish
34 Great King Street, Edinburgh, EH3 6QH
0131 557 3500
An expertly composed Scottish menu serves the ambrosial beauty of this Georgian setting extremely well. The Atholl has gradually evolved into a greatly sought-after restaurant. Awarded 1 AA Rosette.

THE LIVING ROOM
European
113-115 George Street, Edinburgh, EH2 4JN
0131 226 0880
Step into The Living Room and you can count on the savvy, distinctive neighbourhood vibe that plays home to eclectically drawn, supremely tasty cuisine. Take some time at this stylish Edinburgh restaurant.

Must purchase min 3 courses/person inc main.

THE NEW BELL RESTAURANT
Scottish
233 Causewayside, Edinburgh, EH9 1PH
0131 668 2868
Here you will find a frequently changing menu providing well-balanced modern Scottish cuisine. Fresh flavours and new tastes are presented with style and flair.

THE OLIVE BRANCH BISTRO
Mediterranean
19 Colinton Road, Edinburgh, EH10 5DP
0131 452 8453
An amazing selection of tasty treats and decadent dishes available for breakfast, brunch, lunch and dinner. The private function room is a matchless place for private dining or corporate entertainment.

THE OLIVE BRANCH BISTRO
Mediterranean
91 Broughton Street, Edinburgh, EH1 3RX
0131 557 8589
An amazing selection of tasty treats and decadent dishes available for breakfast, brunch, lunch and dinner. A splendid place to watch the world go by.

THE VERANDAH
Indian/ Bangladeshi
17 Dalry Road, Edinburgh, EH11 2BQ
0131 337 5828
Rejecting conventional expectations of Indian restaurants, this award-winning place has well earned its status as 'Best Indian Restaurant' by the Scottish Good Food Guide.

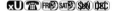

THE VINTNERS ROOMS
French
87a Giles Street, Edinburgh, EH6 6BZ
0131 554 6767
Step across into the elegant space of this Edinburgh restaurant to enjoy its charismatic ambience and rich, accomplished French à la carte menu, complemented with a superb wine list. 2 AA Rosettes.

THE WEE WINDAES
Scottish
144 High Street, Royal Mile, Edinburgh, EH1 1QS
0131 225 5144
Set on the Royal Mile, these distinctive, refined Edinburgh dining rooms play host to a gamut of fine, elegant dishes, from the musky deer terrine to a rambunctious haunch of highland venison.

This offer is not available in August.

THE WESTROOM
European
3 Melville Place, Edinburgh, EH3 7PR
0131 629 9868
An outstanding array of options available for breakfast and lunch, ranging from scrumptious scones to more elaborately crafted meals. Open the drinks menu to find the perfect evening cocktail.

SCOTLAND

309

www.gourmetsociety.co.uk

TIGERLILY
International

125 George Street, Edinburgh, EH2 4JN
0131 225 5005
Whether planning a business lunch or a romantic dinner for two, Tigerlily impresses with its dazzling, classically chic menu and flexible, sophisticated dining space.

ZUCCA
Italian

15-17 Grindlay Street, Edinburgh, EH3 9AX
0131 221 9323
A restaurant that sets its stall out to serve homely, high quality Italian cuisine cooked with the freshness, simplicity and earthiness that characterise the best food from out of Italy.

Morayshire

THE LOFT BISTRO & VENUE
Scottish

East Grange Farm, Kinloss, IV36 2UD
01343 850 111
Superb Scottish farmhouse food is on offer in this cosy bistro. The original cart shed and stables has been transformed into a unique dining space where bottled ales and speciality beers are available.

RECOMMEND A FRIEND

see page 18

XORIATIKI
Greek

87/91 High Street, Mold, Elgin, IV30 1EA
0134 354 6868
Keep your marbles by visiting this Greek restaurant in Elgin. Sharing a name with the fresh-flavoured salad stocked with herbs and feta, Xoriatiki is true to form with its bright and colourful flavours.

Peebleshire

THE HORSESHOE INN
Fine Dining

The Horseshoe Inn, Eddleston, EH45 8QP
01721 730 225
Fine dining at its French best in this thoroughly superb, roundly acclaimed restaurant. Recognised with 3 AA Rosettes, you'll enjoy crafted, accomplished dishes running the gamut of defined, rich flavours.

Perthshire

63 TAY STREET RESTAURANT
Modern European

63 Tay Street, Perth, PH2 8NN
01738 441 451
In the heart of historic Perth, culinary delights await with a menu strongly emphasising seasonality, complemented by new world wines and a fair amount of older classics. Awarded 2 AA Rosettes.

CAFE CIRCA
Scottish

The Scottish Antiques Centre, Doune, FK16 6HG
01786 841 683
Hot bustling bistro where you can find a cool calm moment with an array of gorgeously cooked, well-prepared and -presented dishes derived from high quality local Scottish produce.

DARJEELING
Indian

3-5 Atholl Street, Dunkeld, PH8 0AR
01350 727 427
Highly skilled chefs prepare mouth-watering treats from Bangladesh and India. Using great quality produce and the finest ingredients, the kitchen captures the delicious flavours of the Indian subcontinent.

KERACHERS RESTAURANT
Scottish

168 South Street, Perth, PH2 8NY
01738 449 777
Whether a craving for a bowl of mussels brings you here or an appetite for a full à la carte meal, you won't be disappointed. The restaurant may specialise in seafood, but the menu caters for all.

MAZA INDIAN BUFFET RESTAURANT
Indian

222-224 High Street, Perth, PH1 5PA
01738 447 980
A popular, classic Indian restaurant in Perth whose specialities include a nentara full of spice and flavour; all the gamut of dishes you would expect is also here in this friendly, well-served restaurant.

NURJAHAN INDIAN RESTAURANT
Indian

70 Tay Street, Perth, PH2 8NN
0173 863 5030
Yours will be yet another heart that Nurjahan restaurant wins over. Indulge in original authentic Indian cuisine in beautiful surroundings. Diners can expect to be warmly welcomed and well looked after.

THE ANTIQUARY RESTAURANT
Scottish

Lower Mill Street, Blairgowrie, PH10 6AQ
01250 873 232
With its experienced chef-patron duo, this restaurant brings with it a ranging menu of superbly executed dishes - try the wild boar chop with butternut squash purée - and a commitment to ethical practice.

Discounted hotel rates for GS members on our website

Renfrewshire

POTTERS BRAEHEAD
British

Unit 14b Xscape, Braehead, Renfrew, PA4 8XU
0141 886 6320
Take a break and enjoy a dish from a menu of timeless British food. Something for the whole family, including a fantastic kids selection. Great food in relaxed and comfortable surroundings.

50% FOOD OFF

Scottish Islands

BRECHIN'S BRASSERIE
Scottish

2 Bridgend Street, Rothesay, PA20 0HU
01700 502 922
Excellent dishes made from outstanding produce. Taste the freshness of the freshly baked rolls, ciabattas and Danish pastries, whilst the Belgian coffee beans make a cup full of bliss.

2FOR1 2 COURSES

Ross-shire / Isle of Skye

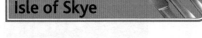

CARRON RESTAURANT
Scottish

Cam-allt, Strathcarron, IV54 8YX
01520 722 488
Indulge in picturesque views over the loch as your meal is prepared in front of you on a chargrill. Steak and local seafood are heavenly choices, whilst the dessert trolley must not be missed.

2FOR1 MAIN COURSE

JJS BISTRO
Bistro

Struan, Braccadale, Isle of Skye, IV56 8FB
01470 572 782
A glowing guestbook reveals this restaurant's fantastic reputation for fine food and excellent service. Guests can expect to be warmly welcomed and exceptionally pleased with what this bistro has to offer.

25% TOTAL OFF

Roxburghshire

THE MELGUND
International

11 Melgund Place, Hawick, TD9 9HY
01450 374 148
An impressively furnished bar and restaurant providing tempting meals and a pleasing drinks selection. Expect genial service and a lovely warm welcome on arrival.

2FOR1 3 COURSES

THE SUNRISE
Indian

51 High Street, Jedburgh, TD8 6DQ
01835 863 503
An accommodating Indian restaurant in Jedburgh where you're sure to enjoy the great range of classic, flavourful curries and leftfield specialities.

25% TOTAL OFF

Stirlingshire

PIERRES RESTAURANT
Scottish

140 Grahams Road, Falkirk, FK2 7BZ
01324 635 843
Traditional Scottish food created with the best of Scottish produce and the principles of French cuisine. Offering a widely varying menu specialising in seafood, this restaurant produces gratifying dishes.

25% TOTAL OFF

TAIYUAN
Chinese

4 Weir Street, Falkirk, FK1 1RA
01324 629 223
Offers first-class service and high-quality food. The staff at Taiyuan are happy to help you decide on a dish should the extensive Chinese menu leave you feeling spoilt for choice.

25% TOTAL OFF

THE WHEELHOUSE
European

Millennium Wheel Drive, Falkirk, FK1 4AD
01324 673 490
The panoramic windows allow you to take in the world outside whilst being warmly and comfortably seated in the restaurant's pleasant interior. The kitchen makes use of some of the finest fresh food.

2FOR1 MAIN COURSE

West Lothian

ASHOKA SHAK
Indian

26 Mcarthur Glen Outlet, Livingston, EH54 6QX
01506 416 622
Spicing up the lives of curry lovers in Livingston and visitors alike, the Ashoka Shak - complete with a grand design - delivers authentic Indian dishes cooked to perfection.

2FOR1 3 COURSES

311

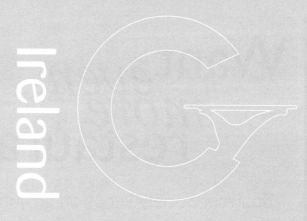

Ireland

Gourmet Society has travelled the length and breadth of Northern Ireland and Eire to offer you discount dining in hundreds of outstanding places.

- Widely recognised as Ireland's best restaurant, you can feast in elegance at the two Michelin starred Restaurant Patrick Guilbaud.
- Enjoy the incredible locally-reared meats on offer at the Enigma restaurant.
- Sample the two AA Rosette winning cuisine on offer at The Tea Rooms in the boutique Clarence Hotel.

And enjoy a warm welcome at many more pubs, cafés, delis, pizzerias and local favourites waiting to serve you great dining promotions.

Where will your appetite take you?
Whether in a traditional pub or contemporary urban kitchen, you will find some of the freshest, finest food available in the world. Excellent seafood, beef, lamb and pork are transformed into scrumptious dishes thanks to the combination of skilful local producers, inspired chefs and a rich culinary heritage.

Planning a trip to Ireland?
Every journey will be memorable, whether you enjoy breathtaking costal drives, vibrant city breaks or the tranquillity of the lush interior.

Ireland enjoys a well-earned reputation as a place where great hospitality meets good times. Given this, it's only natural that the number of Gourmet Society partner restaurants here keeps on growing.

Discover them all on our website **www.gourmetsociety.co.uk** and while you're online, secure great prices on accommodation using the discount hotel booking service.

Want *even more* restaurants?

Gourmet Society keeps on growing....

To discover the latest additions to our partner restaurants, check the website regularly.
www.gourmetsociety.co.uk

- More nationwide chains than ever before

- Unforgettable hotel restaurants

- Michelin-starred, AA rosette winners and 'local heroes'

- And every cuisine imaginable.....

www.gourmetsociety.co.uk
is the place to find the most recent restaurants that are looking forward to welcoming you with great dining discounts.

Simply log in and begin your restaurant search.

NOTES
Use this space for recording new restaurants joining the Gourmet Society.

NOTES

Use this space for recording new restaurants joining the Gourmet Society.

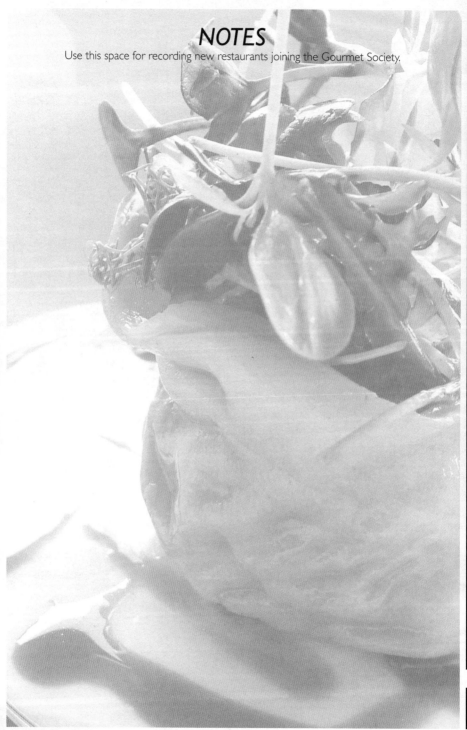

NOTES
Use this space for recording new restaurants joining the Gourmet Society.

Recommend
a Friend

Share the pleasures and benefits of Gourmet Society membership with a friend. When they join, both of you will receive a little something from us.

Make sure your friend quotes your Gourmet Society membership number when they join and we will send you a complimentary bottle of wine; to say 'thank you'.

We will give your friend a special concessionary rate on membership; to say 'thanks for joining the country's best dining club'.

To recommend a friend visit our website at **www.gourmetsociety.co.uk/join** and use your membership number as the promotional code on the 'join now' page.

Or call the Customer Services Team on **0845 257 4477**
(calls are charged at a local rate from a BT landline).

You can also complete the form at the back of this guide and send to us in the post

In order to receive complimentary bottle of wine, your friend must become a member of the Gourmet Society and quote your membership number at the time of joining. This offer is not valid in conjunction with any other promotional joining offer. We reserve the right to substitute wine for a gift of similar value.

Recommend a Friend

Recommend a friend, and not only will they get a special discount off Gourmet Society membership, but we'll give you a complimentary bottle of wine (see page 18 for more details).

Your friends can apply now and take advantage of a 25% discount. Only £39.95 for a full 12 month membership (RRP £53.50).

Save more by purchasing three memberships for the special price of just £79.90.

existing member's details

Name:

Membership No: Tel:

new member's details

Name:

Address:

Postcode: Tel:

Email:

If you are taking advantage of of the three membership offer:

2nd Name:

3rd Name:

Payment methods:

By post: Complete the form and send to "FREEPOST THE GOURMET BUSINESS". Either fill in your credit/debit card details below or send a cheque made payable to The Gourmet Business.

By phone: 0800 043 1978

credit / debit card instructions

Card No:

Expiry: Valid: CVN No: (last three digits on the reverse)

Issue No (if applicable):   Amount: £39.95   £79.90

Signature: Date: -   -